Lonely Planet Publications
land | London

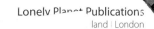

D1149925

Andrea Schulte-Peevers &
Tom Parkinson

Berlin

The Top Five

1 Museumsinsel
Feast on art and sculpture from around the world (p79)

2 Unter den Linden
View the architecture on this journey through history (p73)

3 Scheunenviertel
Take the city's pulse in the streets of this vibrant quarter (p95)

4 Schloss Charlottenburg
Revel in royal pomposity and the fabulous gardens (p110)

5 Reichstag
Stand in awe of the weight of its history (p102)

Contents

Published by Lonely Planet Publications Pty Ltd
ABN 36 005 607 983

Australia Head Office, Locked Bag 1, Footscray,
Victoria 3011, ☎ 03 8379 8000, fax 03 8379 8111,
talk2us@lonelyplanet.com.au

USA 150 Linden St, Oakland, CA 94607,
☎ 510 893 8555, toll free 800 275 8555,
fax 510 893 8572, info@lonelyplanet.com

UK 72–82 Rosebery Ave, Clerkenwell, London,
EC1R 4RW, ☎ 020 7841 9000, fax 020 7841 9001,
go@lonelyplanet.co.uk

© Lonely Planet Publications Pty Ltd 2006
Photographs © Richard Nebesky and as listed
(p308) 2006

The Authors

Andrea Schulte-Peevers

Andrea has logged countless miles in almost 60 countries and carries her dog-eared passport like a badge of honour. Raised in Germany and educated in London and at UCLA, she's built a career on writing about her native country. She's contributed to about 30 Lonely Planet titles, including all five editions of this book. Andrea considers Berlin among the truly great cities. She's been back time and again revisiting old friends and favourite places – and discovering new ones. She's seen Berlin shed its Cold War–era brooding and blossom into a confident metropolis, celebrating its edginess and verve. Los Angeles is now Andrea's home, but if she were to move back to Germany, you'd find her name in the Berlin phone book. She wrote the Architecture, History, Sights, Walking Berlin, Eating, Shopping, Sleeping and Directory chapters.

Tom Parkinson

Tom wrote the City Life, Arts, Entertainment and Excursions chapters. He first visited Berlin after leaving school, and only really began to appreciate everything that makes it special when he lived there for a year as part of his German degree. Since then the city has kept hold of its position as Tom's favourite modern metropolis, and immersing himself in Europe's most exciting entertainment scene continues to be a joy as well as a job. In the course of researching this edition he acquired several hundred flyers, raced through three neighbouring states and clocked up a personal record of 17 clubs in one night, figures he describes simply as 'beatable'.

PHOTOGRAPHER
Richard Nebesky

Richard was not born with a camera in his hand; however, it wasn't long before his father, an avid photo enthusiast, gave him his first happy-snap unit. Ever since then, the camera has been by his side. Richard has written and photographed for numerous Lonely Planet guides as well as for various magazines and other travel guide book publishers. Being Prague based, Richard has a close affinity with all central European cities – Berlin included.

ANDREA'S TOP BERLIN DAY

Much of Berlin doesn't wake up until mid-morning and, if possible, neither do I. I get the day going with a leisurely breakfast at Tim's Canadian Deli (p180) in Schöneberg. It's Saturday and the city's best farmers market on Winterfeldtplatz (p241) is on. As I stock up my mobile beeps with a message from Christiane: 'Care 2 join me at Alte Nationalgalerie (p79)?'; sounds good. After our culture fix, we catch up on gossip while sauntering around the Tiergarten (p99) then take in the sunset from the dome atop the Reichstag (p102). Time for dinner. We decide to go exotic and head over to Kasbah (p169) to feast on our favourite Middle Eastern dish, *tajiine,* a fragrant stew of veggies, meat and a secret melange of spices. Later we hook up with friends at Heinz Minki (p195) for drinks. From there we're off to nearby Watergate (p202), still one of Berlin's most sizzling clubs. Ears ringing, we quietly watch the sun rise over the river. Time to go home.

Introducing Berlin

The bear is a fitting symbol of Berlin – gruff, endlessly adaptable, forceful, fiercely protective of its young, able to endure times that would spell doom to a lesser species and, at once, loveable and frightening in some of its aspects.

With a history that has disproportionately shaped Europe's destiny – for both good and ill – Berlin today is a galvanic force in German, European and world affairs, wielding great influence in the realms of science, technology, commerce, architecture and the arts. The 'new world order' – however you may wish to define it – has a well-tuned, roaring outpost here.

Brassy, bold and beautiful in its austerity, Berlin is a sexy temptress that will ensnare you with her infinite riches; she's a creative genius that will amaze you with ideas and trends uniquely her own; she's a hotbed of hedonism, feasting passionately on the bountiful buffet of life; and, above all, she's a clever chameleon, endlessly adaptable and thriving on change, almost pursuing it like a drug. Berlin is all that and then some to the people who live here and those ready to make the journey to the depths of her past, present and future.

Berlin functions on a welcoming and exquisitely human scale. It's a city in which you can embrace and be embraced, relish and revel in its abundant charms and variety with total abandon, and feel energised in ways that you'll feel in few other world-class cities. A simple *'Wie geht's?'* (how are you?) uttered in any pub or street-side café may well unleash a torrent of opinions and perceptions in perfect English. And, boy, do Berliners have their opinions! It's no exaggeration to say that your average cabbie can hold forth respectably on any subject from the best sausage in the city, through the meanderings of Nietzsche, to the likely outcome of elections anywhere in the world – Berliners are that broadly learned and curious about the world and its people.

Since reunification, Berlin has undergone a massive evolution in how it presents and regards itself. Gone is its self-perception as a beleaguered and schizoid city existing beneath the ominous presence of the Wall. What Berlin is now becoming is surprising, innovative and stunning – even by its own standards. The last vestiges of communism have been detonated, rebuilt, or at least received cheerier paint. All that's worth salvaging has been lovingly and expensively restored while some of the world's greatest new architecture jostles for position with the classical splendour of old Berlin.

LOWDOWN

Population 3.39 million

Time zone Western European (GMT+1hr)

3-star double room from €100

Latte macchiato €2.50–3

Glass of beer €2.50

U-Bahn ticket €2.20

Currywurst €1.50–2

Doner kebab €2–2.50

Pack of 18 cigarettes €4

Your own 'movie' of time spent in Berlin – whether you're indulging your appetites, drinking in culture by the bucketful, or exploring pathways, parks and forests within the city – will most likely star a huge international cast, thronging with gusto into the streets. And if you don't party hearty, you just don't belong in Berlin! The sheer exuberance of the city sweeps you along with its throbbing beat and hurls you – via one of the best transport systems in the world – into its pulsing club life, vibrant neighbourhoods, dining and arts scenes and close encounters with some of the greatest historical sights in all of Europe.

Your time in the city will be spent rubbing shoulders with influence peddlers and politicos from every corner of the planet, from government courtiers to fashion couturiers and the cultural illuminati. Berlin is one of their primary playgrounds and you'll find them – bedecked in their Armani and Versace – roaming the lobbies of corporate temples, the sumptuous halls of baroque opera houses and at tables in the city's exquisite gourmet shrines. 'Gourmet shrines,' you say, incredulously? Yup, it's true. Dining in Berlin is reaching previously unscaled heights. Sure, you can still grab a quick curbside *Currywurst* (curried sausage), but you'll also be increasingly snared by the tempting aromas of the Far and Middle East, the Americas and the dining dynasties of France and Italy.

Whatever memories remain in the Berlin psyche from days of the 'Wall' are losing their biting edge and fading into forgettable pastels. Yesterday's dour correspondent for Pravda now runs an ad agency with major contracts from Sony and Disney. A browbeaten teacher of the official communist line is now a real estate tycoon with a mobile phone screwed to her ear and a lovely villa in Capri, thank you very much! The teenage daughters of immigrant Anatolian shepherds have shirked their headscarves, now opting to sheathe their legs in French silk. The headlong creative rush of this new Berlin wastes scant time in dwelling on the past.

And if there's a single earmark of the Berlin mentality – past and present – it would have to be that of tolerance. Some may not like what you do, how you look or what you eat, but most Berliners follow the motto of Frederick the Great: *Jeder nach seiner Façon,* which loosely translates as 'live and let live'. It's no coincidence that one in every 7.5 Berlin residents is an immigrant, or that one of Europe's liveliest gay and lesbian scenes flourishes here.

All these factors make Berlin a most 'un-German' city; one largely free of the rigid social structure so entrenched elsewhere in the country. A trendsetter by nature and necessity, Berlin feeds on fledgling moods, trends and appetites, and processes them into the new *Zeitgeist,* which is then exported to the rest of the country and beyond. The world has always looked to Berlin – sometimes in fascination, sometimes in horror and sometimes even in deep sympathy. At once repellent and seductive, light-hearted and brooding, Berlin continues to be a city of exhilarating extremes.

Travelling to Berlin *demands* that you abandon yourself to its pleasures and forget about how you might behave at home. This is a larger-than-life city with a past, a present and a future, and a creative and youthful vibe that will have you shouting *Ich bin ein Berliner!* So join in and unleash your inner omnivore. Berlin is indeed a bear, but it's one that's learned how to dance and sing, and, above all else, *roar!*

ESSENTIAL BERLIN

Bar-hopping (p192) Just pick a neighbourhood

Altes Museum (p80) Nefertiti and other stunners from antiquity

Unter den Linden (p73) A phalanx of blockbuster sights

Reichstag dome (p102) Berlin from above

Scheunenviertel (p95) Boutique, bar and gallery hopping

City Life

City Life

BERLIN TODAY

Variety is not just the spice of life in Berlin – it's the main ingredient, the heart of everything that drives and defines one of Europe's most unpredictable capitals. The city is very much a product of its time, scarred but never destroyed by its traumatic history, and much of the unique atmosphere here stems from constantly having to adapt to new circumstances and upheavals.

From division to reunification, multiculturalism to internationalism, Berlin has been at the forefront of everything big in Germany ever since it was first made the capital, and everyone living here knows that they're part of something special. Where else can you find Islamic gardens alongside Holocaust memorials, World Cup football alongside elephant races, or rooftop cabaret alongside basement sex clubs? And where else could a gay mayor hint at a taste for leather just weeks before an election? Nothing here is average, and even the norms are twisted as far as they'll go.

In recent years Berlin has weathered social problems, corruption and bankruptcy,

HOT CONVERSATION TOPICS

- World Cup football! Who won, who lost, and was it rigged?
- Angela Merkel. Enough said.
- Yorckstrasse 59 – the squat saga continues.
- Multiculturalism and the pros or cons of integration.
- Hot spots – where's in, where's out, where's closed.
- What the Senate should be spending Berlin's money on.
- Are roof terraces the new black?
- World Cup football! At last it's over!

and now finds itself somewhat reluctantly in the hands of centre-right conservative and first-ever female chancellor Angela Merkel. Throughout it all, though, the bright young things of the city's overwhelmingly work-age population throw themselves wholeheartedly into all the activities that make up its cultural kaleidoscope, and while they may have plenty to say on all the issues, nothing gets in the way of the crucial pursuit of lifestyle in all its forms.

It's not just the people here that make Berlin so infinitely variable. Physically, too, the city is constantly evolving, throwing up new architecture so fast that there's always something new to discover. And, any building that isn't being built, renovated or reconstructed, could still be repurposed to feed the rapacious inventiveness of the arts and nightlife scenes.

Above all, Berlin's restless dynamism is founded on a code of insistent individuality, where the mix defines the whole in every walk of life. Even today you'll feel the overriding sense of a city permanently in flux, reinventing itself on a daily basis. Whatever you're into, it's an exciting place to watch past, present and future trends meld, develop and explode out to the rest of the continent.

CITY CALENDAR

Berlin is very much a party town, and almost every weekend sees some form of event, anniversary or celebration; the arts scene is particularly active, and the **ICC Messe centre** (Map pp328–9; ☎ 30 380; www.icc-berlin.de; Messedamm 22, Charlottenburg) holds a wide-ranging programme of trade fairs throughout the year, many of which are open to the public.

While winter can be very cold, especially compared to recent hot European summers, visitors come to Berlin at all times of year, often for specific events. High points are the Berlinale, Germany's high-profile February film festival, and the Day of German Unity on 3 October, when Berliners do their best to re-create the fall of the Wall. See the Directory (p296) for a full list of public holidays.

JANUARY

BERLINER SECHSTAGERENNEN
☎ 4430 4430; www.sechstagerennen-berlin.de
Almost 100 years old, this is Berlin's premier international cycling event (see p216).

INTERNATIONALE GRÜNE WOCHE
☎ 30 380; ICC Messe
International Green Week, officially a week-long consumer fair for food, agriculture and gardening, is a great excuse for gorging on exotic morsels from around the world.

LANGE NACHT DER MUSEEN
☎ 283 973; www.lange-nacht-der-museen.de
On the last Saturday of January, 150,000 visitors take the opportunity to wander round Berlin's museums at night, with most doors staying open until at least midnight. It can be surprisingly sociable, and the whole thing is repeated in August on the last Saturday of the month.

SPIRIT OF FASHION
☎ 040-3571 6548; www.spirit-of-fashion.com
This alternative fashion fair moved to Berlin from Hamburg in 2004, bringing goth, punk, glam and all kinds of offbeat styles to a captive audience of chic freaks.

FEBRUARY

BERLINALE
☎ 259 200; www.berlinale.de
The Internationale Filmfestspiele Berlin (Berlin International Film Festival), better known as the Berlinale, is Germany's answer to the Cannes and Venice film festivals, and is no less prestigious. Stars, starlets, directors, critics and the world's A-to-Z-list celebrities faithfully turn out to catch the two-week event, with about 750 films screened at various theatres around town. Many screenings are quickly sold out, so check the schedule early and call the cinema for ticket availability. As well as awarding the Golden and Silver Bears, the festival also sees the award ceremony for the Teddy, a gay and lesbian film prize.

MARCH

INTERNATIONALE TOURISMUS BÖRSE
☎ 30 380; www.itb-berlin.de; ICC Messe
Reportedly the world's largest travel show with over 10,000 exhibitors, the ITB

(International Tourism Fair) brings together travel professionals from all over the world. It's open to the public at the weekend.

MAERZMUSIK
☎ 2548 9128; www.maerzmusik.de
Founded in 1967 under the GDR regime as the biannual Muzik-Biennale, Berlin's principal forum for new and experimental music has been held yearly under the new name 'March Music' since 2002.

APRIL

FESTTAGE
☎ 2035 4555; www.staatsoper-berlin.org; Philharmonie/Staatsoper Unter den Linden
'Festival Days' is an annual 10-day festival of high-profile gala concerts and operas, bringing renowned conductors, soloists and orchestras to Berlin.

MAY

MAIFEIERTAG
Not for those of a nervous disposition, May Day (1 May) sees Berlin's central districts become the venue for large-scale anti-capitalist demonstrations. Traditionally, right-wing groups schedule their marches for the same day, the police turn out in force and within a couple of hours there'll be chaos. That means violence, vandalism and burning vehicles – we only mention it at all so you can stay out of the way.

BRITSPOTTING
☎ 4404 0494; www.britspotting.de
It's hard to imagine the Brits returning the compliment, but this small festival of British films that never made it into the multiplexes is a surprising hit with Berlin arthouse buffs. Participating screens include the Acud (p204), Central (see Babylon p214) and fsk (p215).

GAY & LESBIAN RUN
☎ 445 7561; glrinfo@gmx.de
Formerly held exclusively in Berlin, this highly unorthodox fun run has become nomadic and only returns to the capital every couple of years (most recently in 2005). It's worth catching when it does; after all, what better way to show solidarity than by pounding the streets with your queer peers?

KARNEVAL DER KULTUREN
☎ 622 2024; www.karneval-berlin.de
This is a lively street festival with a parade of flamboyantly costumed people dancing and playing music on floats.

LADIES' GERMAN OPEN
The only German stop on the international tennis circuit, this is always a big event (see p217 for more).

SEHSÜCHTE
☎ 0331-620 2780; www.sehsuechte.de
Berlin's International Student Film Festival, now based in Potsdam, provides six days of the most random, experimental, alternative and occasionally pretentious cinematic efforts around. Non-student amateur filmmakers can also submit entries, so get that DV cam out!

THEATERTREFFEN BERLIN
☎ 2548 9269; www.theatertreffen-berlin.de
The Berlin Theatre Meeting stages three weeks of new productions by emerging and established German-language ensembles from Germany, Austria and Switzerland.

JUNE
ALL NATIONS FESTIVAL
☎ 863 9160; www.allnationsfestival.de
For one day in June or July, Berlin's foreign embassies open their doors to promote their respective countries, with food, drink, music and talks. A shuttle bus ferries visitors around.

CHRISTOPHER STREET DAY
☎ 0177-277 3176; www.csd-berlin.de
Commemorating the anniversary of the 1969 Stonewall riots in New York, this is Berlin's biggest gay parade, with over 400,000 people coming out to play on the city streets. Outrageous costumes, rainbow flags, techno music and naked torsos are guaranteed.

Christopher Street Day Parade (this page)

FÊTE DE LA MUSIQUE
☎ 0190-581 058; www.lafetedelamusique.com
This unique festival of free concerts, held worldwide on 21 June, is the brainchild of former French culture minister Jack Lang, who first managed to persuade international musicians to play without pay in 1982. Up to 500 bands now turn up for the Berlin event alone.

JULY
BREAD & BUTTER
☎ 400 440; www.breadandbutter.com
The trade fair that aims to put Berlin at the heart of European fashion (see p17) is going from strength to strength, and now has a twin event in Barcelona as well as a winter fixture around the end of January.

CLASSIC OPEN AIR GENDARMENMARKT
☎ 843 7350; www.classic-openair.ch
A prestigious series of alfresco classical concerts held on the Gendarmenmarkt in early July.

FOTOMARATHON
☎ 4434 2254; www.fotomarathon.de
Putting art photography firmly in the public domain, this inspired event calls on keen snappers to take 24 pictures in 12 hours on 24 separate themes.

LOVE PARADE
☎ 284 620; www.loveparade.de
2006 saw the resurrection of the world's biggest techno street party, in part thanks to the World Cup, which helped persuade previously reluctant sponsors to put up the necessary cash. The format's the same as ever but the floats are now provided free and participants are decided by a panel of judges and by online votes – visit the website to nominate your favourite DJ talent! The purists will no doubt grumble, but after several years' absence the LP might just have a whole new lease of life.

AUGUST
BERLINER GAUKLERFEST
☎ 03375-295 148; www.gauklerfest.de
In the first week of August this lively circus festival, now in its 16th year, occupies the eastern end of Unter den Linden with a colourful array of performers.

FUCKPARADE
☎ 069-9435 9090; www.fuckparade.org
Several thousand hardcore anti-capitalist, anti-globalisation and antifascist protesters turn out every year for this political street party, originally conceived to bemoan the commercialisation of the Love Parade.

HANFPARADE
www.hanfparade.de
Germany's contribution to the ongoing debate on the legalisation of the hemp plant – you'll hear a lot about its industrial applications (like that's why 10,000 slightly dazed people take to the streets every year).

INTERNATIONALE FUNKAUSSTELLUNG
☎ 30 338; ICC Messe
The huge International Consumer Electronics Fair is open to the public, demonstrating the gadgets everyone will be wanting for Christmas.

INTERNATIONALES TANZFEST BERLIN
☎ 2590 0427; www.tanzfest.de; Hebbel Am Ufer
The top date on the Berlin dance calendar, attracting loose-limbed talent and highly experimental choreography from around the globe.

SEPTEMBER
ART FORUM BERLIN
☎ 30 380; www.art-forum-berlin.com
An international contemporary art fair hosted by Berlin's leading galleries, running from the very end of September into October.

BERLIN MARATHON
www.berlin-marathon.com
The best street race in the country, with a route that takes it past a lot of people's front doors (see p216).

BERLIN PHOTOGRAPHY FESTIVAL
☎ 2007 4990; www.berlin-photography-festival.de
With the core exhibition supplemented by events and displays in galleries around town, this feast of images runs for up to six weeks.

BERLINER LISTE
☎ 2809 6115; www.berliner-liste.org
Held around the same time as the Art Forum, the Berliner Liste brings together local and international galleries in shared stands, encouraging cooperation and creating some interesting juxtapositions.

FOLSOM EUROPE
www.folsom-europe.com
In 2005 this massive fetish festival was opened by none other than Berlin's beloved gay mayor, Klaus Wowereit, raising quite a few eyebrows under those rubber masks. Consolidating the city's anything-goes reputation, it's a cavalcade of latex, leather, straps, whips and chains, covering every facet of sexuality imaginable.

INTERNATIONALES LITERATURFESTIVAL
☎ 2787 8620; www.literaturfestival.com
Founded in 2001, this rapidly growing international literature festival puts on readings and events under a different country theme each year.

POPKOMM
☎ 3038 3009; www.popkomm.de
The country's biggest independent music trade fair, showcasing new bands and record labels, moved to Berlin from Cologne in 2004. The fair is accompanied by a week of concerts, workshops and events, combining big names and unknown talent, and also incorporates the annual *Clubnacht* (Club Night), where €11 gets you entry to 30 different clubs.

OCTOBER
JAZZ IN DEN MINISTERGÄRTEN
www.jazzland.de; In den Ministergärten 1-10
Once a year, five state representative buildings around the ministerial gardens near Potsdamer Platz open their doors to the public for this night of jazz concerts.

LESBIAN FILM FESTIVAL
☎ 7871 8109; www.lesbenfilmfestival.de
One of the longest-running events of its kind, Berlin's LFF celebrated its 20th anniversary in 2004 with a week of women's movies at the Acud cinema (p204) and SO36 club (p202).

PREVIEW BERLIN
☎ 7262 67522; www.previewberlin.de
This emerging art fair runs in tandem with the Art Forum (p11), displaying new works from young artists trying to breakthrough.

TAG DER DEUTSCHEN EINHEIT
The 3 October has been declared the national 'Day of German Unity', and Berlin takes it particularly seriously, with street parties from the Brandenburg Gate to the Roten Rathaus and all kinds of other celebrations around town. Luckily David Hasselhoff hasn't been invited back.

NOVEMBER
JAZZFEST BERLIN
☎ 2548 9279; www.jazzfest-berlin.de
A top-rated jazz festival, with performances held at venues throughout the city.

SPIELZEITEUROPA
☎ 254 890; www.spielzeiteuropa.de
Under the 'Playtime Europe' banner, the Berliner Festspiele stage up to 15 plays

based on a national theme (eg the Netherlands, the Balkans) between November and January.

VERZAUBERT INTERNATIONAL QUEER FILM FESTIVAL
www.verzaubertfilmfest.com
The Berlin leg of the 'Enchanted' festival takes over the Kino International (p215) from late November, at the end of a tour taking in Munich, Frankfurt and Cologne. The scope and range of the films included is generally huge.

DECEMBER
BERLIN BIENNALE
☎ 2434 5970; www.berlinbiennale.de
Presenting new art at unusual sites around town, this biennial exhibition of contemporary art (last held in 2005) was founded by the Kunst-Werke centre (p96).

NIKOLAUS
St Nicholas' Day, on 6 December, is traditionally when children leave their shoes out to receive sweets if they've been good, and a stone if they've been bad. Eventually this custom developed into Father Christmas' more international yearly rounds, but in Germany they seem pretty attached to the original – all kinds of clubs hold Nikolaus parties, complete with footwear-invading St Nicks.

WEIHNACHTSMÄRKTE
Christmas markets of all shapes and sizes are held from late November to around 21 December at locations around Berlin, including Breitscheidplatz, Winterfeldtplatz, Unter den Linden, Alexanderplatz and the Marktplatz in Spandau.

SILVESTER
This is the German name for New Year's Eve celebrations. For first-timers the only place to be at midnight is out with the crowds on Unter den Linden, cooing at the fireworks, trying to ignore the dismal chart music from the stages all along the road, quaffing cheap *Sekt* (sparkling wine) from street stalls, hugging strangers and generally enjoying the sociable atmosphere. Pros and purists may prefer to investigate some of the many, many other events on offer.

CULTURE

IDENTITY

With just under 3.4 million inhabitants, Berlin is Germany's largest city. Statistically its average denizen is politically liberal, nominally Protestant (though probably not practising) and educated to degree level with an excellent grasp of English. They drink, smoke, recycle and use public transport, though those without bicycles may have a car in town. Chances are they're also young, professional and well travelled. Very few of the standard 'humourless German' stereotypes apply to Berliners – city dwellers here are as cosmopolitan and broad-minded as they come, and they're unlikely to thank you for dredging up the same tired old clichés in conversation!

One particular feature of the local character, known throughout the country, is *Berliner Schnauze,* the slightly abrasive in-your-face attitude that distinguishes the Berlin sense of humour. It can take some getting used to, but once you recognise the essential wit behind it, you'll quickly get used to trading pithy remarks and go that one step closer to appreciating the heart behind the city's rough exterior.

Within Berlin, identity is predominantly defined by district, and every *Bezirk* has its own unique character, reflecting the nature of its 'typical' inhabitants. Charlottenburg, Wilmersdorf and Tiergarten are reliably affluent areas, attracting bourgeois bachelors, suited business types and local celebrities; Schöneberg, too, is relatively upscale, but is most noted for its prominent gay population. Kreuzberg is divided into the smarter bohemian western section along Bergmannstrasse, and the old alternative patch around Kottbusser Tor – now home to much of Berlin's Turkish population. A similar split characterises Mitte, separating the very wealthy Friedrichstrasse/Unter den Linden area from the more studenty area to the north. Friedrichshain is known for its nonconformist punk and squatter communities, while Prenzlauer Berg is more on the arty side of experimental, with large gay and student contingents. Of the outer districts, Wedding and Lichtenberg have the worst reputations, known for their right-wing undercurrents and an unhappy mix of immigrants and working class families. East–West divisions, too, are still an issue for some people, though with demographics shifting, incomes gradually balancing out and rivalries fading, few of the old *Ossi/Wessi* (Easterner/Westerner) stereotypes still apply.

As the country's most multicultural city, Berlin is also heavily influenced by its minorities, with an amazing patchwork of people from 185 foreign nations making up almost 14% of the total population. The largest groups are those of Turkish descent and eastern Europeans from Poland, the former states of Yugoslavia and the old Soviet republics. The steady growth

---

A MATTER OF HONOUR

The latest issue to hit the headlines in Berlin has been a wave of so-called *Ehrenmorde* (honour killings) among the Turkish population. Attributed largely to families with hardline Muslim beliefs, these murders all involve young women who have attempted to break away from their marriages or families, killed by their own husbands, brothers or cousins for 'shaming' themselves by rejecting the traditional Islamic lifestyle.

The shooting of Hatin Sürücü in Tempelhof in February 2005 was a particularly high-profile case, coming as the sixth such killing in the space of just four months. Even more worrying is the reaction to it in certain sections of the community. Several male Turkish students are said to have supported the murder in a school discussion, citing Sürücü's Westernised lifestyle as a justification, and some pressure groups have suggested that the police are reluctant to take action in these incidents due to potential accusations of racism. Knee-jerk calls for forced assimilation and anti-Islamic legislation have added to the tension and threatened to alienate borderline traditional families still further.

Of course, the whole scenario is very much against the grain in the wider context of multicultural Berlin, and groups from all sides of society have rushed to suggest solutions to the problem, from ethics classes to public media discussions. The Islamic Federation (www.if-berlin.de) runs a number of initiatives to foster a better understanding of the Muslim religion and its central tenets, including an open day when non-Muslims can tour some of the city's mosques. With the integration debate still raging, however, it will take more than these good intentions to bring Berlin's diverse communities truly together.

in foreign nationals since reunification has, however, been offset by a decline in the indigenous population, due in part to the exodus of young families from the capital to the surrounding countryside, and the overall population of the city has actually fallen since 1993.

Despite the city's legendary tolerance, few groups mix on a day-to-day basis. The Senate even has a member for integration and migration matters, responsible for keeping track of developments and trying to encourage better relationships between communities. Racial tensions are rare but increasing, particularly in the outer eastern districts. Neo-Nazi and other right-wing groups are still vastly outnumbered by antifascist activists, but there has been an increase in violent incidents involving young Muslims. A recent spate of 'honour killings' (see the boxed text p13) has reignited the debate on immigration and cultural differences.

Berlin is also an extremely youthful city; 57% of residents are under the age of 44 and, by contrast, only 17% are over 65. The student population amounts to a sizeable presence of 150,000, with three major universities – the Freie Universität (FU), Technische Universität (TU) and Humboldt Universität (HU) – attracting academic talent from all over the country. In 2003, protests over proposed funding cuts demonstrated the impact the student body can have on city life, and their inventive nonviolent actions provided a good illustration of the creative buzz of the capital.

However, the number of actual children residing in the city is declining, and birth rates are going down – the immigrant birth rate has even halved since 1991, suggesting that many people are now coming to Berlin to work and returning home to raise their families.

LIFESTYLE

Lifestyle here is defined by activity above all else, and Berliners are invariably busy people; with an average 40-hour working week, they're always on their way to the office, the gym, the shops, the pub, the cinema, the theatre or all of the above. Many average-earning people have cleaners, and when Berliners are not eating out, dinner will be something quick and easy (if the microwave didn't exist, Berlin would have paid someone to invent it). Staying in and watching TV is a last resort for locals here, and even if they specifically want to watch a programme they'll probably be doing something else at the same time.

Professional salaries in Berlin range from around €2000 to €5000 a month before tax, allowing for some very reasonable disposable income. Full-time work is the norm for both sexes and, in general, male and female employees earn roughly the same – but as ever there are far fewer women than men at the very top of the wage scale. With average debts of €16,500 per capita, Berliners clearly aren't credit-card shy either!

Perhaps because of their frantic schedules, family is less of a priority for many Berlin-dwellers, and in the central districts the vast majority of households are single-occupancy. There is also an increasing trend towards single parenthood, and as many first-born children now live with one parent as with two.

Berliners tend to be very opinionated, and conversations may well touch on many subjects, from international politics to local curiosities. It is OK to mention 'the War', if done with tact and relevance; after all, history is still current affairs here (just look for the 'Living Past' section in Berlin bookshops), and a lot of people you meet will have grown up demanding explanations for all the events of the last 60 years. What will cause offence is a 'victor' mentality, which

ZERO INTOLERANCE

Berlin's diversity extends further than its ethnic mix. It's estimated that 500,000 gays and lesbians currently call the city home, and they're by no means a silent minority. With an active scene and a real sense of community, it's widely considered second only to Amsterdam as Europe's gay capital. Just to reinforce the point, popular SPD minister Klaus Wowereit (affectionately dubbed 'Wowi') was elected as governing mayor, making Berlin the second European city ever to be led by an openly gay politician.

And the famously accepting atmosphere doesn't stop there. Sex and sexuality are entirely everyday matters to the unshockable city folk, and there are very few itches that can't be quite openly and legally scratched here – the brand-new Olympiastadion mega-brothel (built for the 2006 World Cup) and the active sex club scene (p204) are the very tip of the iceberg. To crown off this reputation, Berlin was voted Most Fetish-Friendly City in the international World's Sexiest Cities poll 2005 – quite an accolade!

BERLIN LIVING

The typical Berlin dwelling is a spacious rented 1½-bedroom apartment on at least the first floor of a large postwar house (no-one wants to live at street level), probably facing onto a *Hinterhof* (courtyard) full of coloured bins. The apartment itself has very high ceilings, large windows and, as often as not, stripped wood floors; the kitchen will almost invariably be the smallest room in the house, used mainly for stacking crates of beer and mineral water. Many homes still have the traditional tiled heating stoves in place, though no-one actually uses them. A roof terrace is currently the must-have feature for aspirational city-dwellers.

Berlin flats are usually nicely turned-out, whatever the style favoured by the occupant, and a lot of attention is paid to design, though comfort is also considered. At least one item of furniture will come from Ikea; depending on income, the rest may come from the Stilwerk centre, Polish craftsmen, a flea market or eBay – as long as it fits the look of the room.

Rent is calculated according to space, starting at around €400 a month for 50 sq metres (depending on the district). Any conversation about costs with a Berlin tenant will inevitably lead to them asking you how many square metres your place is – do some sums before you leave home!

For a sneak peek into some of the city's more stylish flats, look for the *Berlin Apartments* book (teNeues, 2000) edited by Paco Asensio.

is perceived as self-righteous and gloating, or the suggestion that fascist ideas are intrinsically German, which is downright bigoted.

Overall, locals are accommodating and fairly helpful towards visitors, and many will volunteer assistance if you look lost. This politeness does not necessarily extend to friendliness, however, and in public, people usually maintain a degree of reserve towards strangers – you won't find many conversations striking up on the U-Bahn, buskers and beggars are often frowned at, and Berlin bus drivers have a reputation for being the rudest in Europe.

On the other hand, in younger company it's easy to talk to just about anyone, particularly around the many student hangouts (remember German students are generally older than elsewhere, often graduating at 28 rather than 21), and if you start frequenting a place you'll quickly get to know staff and regulars. You'll also probably find people very open after a relatively short time, discussing sex, relationships and life with equal candour.

Another key feature of Berlin's lifestyle is the concept of the *Szene,* the indefinable 'scene' that determines where the fashionable young set go out, and what they wear, drink or talk about. As an outsider it can be pretty tricky keeping track of what's in, and of course as soon as anything becomes too popular the real scene people go elsewhere.

Obviously, much of the above applies mainly to *Neu-Berliner* (New Berliners) or *Wahl-Berliner* (Berliners by choice), people who have moved here rather than being born in the city. Some of the most 'authentic' denizens are the working-class mullet-sporting *Ossis* you'll see in the dingiest *Kneipen* (pubs) in districts like Wedding and Lichtenberg, and unlike the newbies they tend not to welcome visitors.

FOOD & DRINK

As in any cosmopolitan city, sophisticated Berliners will often opt for Thai or another of the many international options on offer, but traditional Berlin cuisine still exists and forms the basis of the menu at most ordinary *Kneipen*. Overall, it tends to be high-calorie, hearty and heavy on the meat; pork is a staple, prepared in umpteen ways, including *Kasseler Rippen* (smoked pork chops) and *Eisbein* (knuckle). Minced meat often comes in the form of a *Boulette,* a cross between a meatball and a hamburger. Other regulars are roast chicken, schnitzel and *Sauerbraten* (beef marinated in vinegar and spices), usually with sauerkraut and potatoes on the side.

The true Berlin classic, however, is *Currywurst* – a spicy sausage in tangy curried ketchup, typically served with chips (fries) – and stalls all over town sell them in the millions (see the boxed text on p179). Thanks to the large Turkish population, doner (or döner) kebabs are also a fast-food highlight here, served in thick crusty bread and far superior to limp imitations elsewhere.

Grocery on Bergmanstrasse, Kreuzberg

Eating is predominantly a communal activity, and most people eat out with colleagues at lunchtime or with friends in the evening; mid-afternoon coffee and cake is *de rigueur* at weekends, as is a cheeky döner on your way home after a night out. Cooking, on the whole, is something you only do in emergencies or on very special occasions.

Sunday brunch is a social institution in its own right, lasting a couple of hours and providing the ideal excuse to meet up with friends and discuss the weekend's events over a leisurely bite. Almost every café, bistro, restaurant, bar and lounge that opens before dinner time will have some kind of buffet on offer from morning until the afternoon, and they're always popular affairs, especially in student areas.

This being Germany, beer is the drink of choice for both sexes, and you'll find a variety of local, national and import brews on offer. *Fassbier* (draught beer) is generally limited to one or two brands of local lager or Pils, usually served in 300mL glasses. Berlin's particular speciality is *Berliner Weisse,* a light, sour beer served with a shot of raspberry (red) or woodruff (green) syrup – be warned though, by drinking this stuff you're advertising yourself as a tourist.

All places stock at least one variety of *Weizenbier* (wheat beer), which comes in 500mL bottles with a choice of *Hefe* (yeasty) and *Kristall* (filtered); this is most Berliners' preference for afternoon or early evening drinking. Other options may include *Schwarzbier* (black beer, like porter), *Dunkelbier* (dark ale), *Bock* (strong, seasonal beer) and *Kölsch* (Cologne Pils). Non-alcoholic Clausthaler and Becks are common, and you can also drink your lager as an *Alster/Radler* (with lemonade or orangeade) or a *Diesel* (with coke). One brave reader recommends the delightful-sounding *Affenkotze* ('monkey puke' – coke and banana juice)!

Wine is mainly popular in restaurants, with widely varying German and international selections available. The best German bottles are dry Riesling, Müller-Thurgau and Silvaner whites. Champagne, too, has lost none of its exalted status in Berlin's swisher bars; for less special occasions, local *Sekt* and Italian *prosecco* (sometimes served on ice) are well-tried and often excellent alternatives.

Cocktails have undergone a major renaissance over the last few years, and the majority of new pubs opening in Berlin are cocktail bars; as a result you can now get fruity mixed drinks at just about any hostelry in town. For the best taste sensations sample the house creations at one of the serious specialist places.

For daytime stimulation most people go for coffee, often in huge cups with lots of milk. There's nothing wrong with the tap water, but you'd never catch anyone drinking it – sparkling mineral water is the norm. Fruit juices, shakes and smoothies have all caught on in a big way, and the ubiquitous *Apfelschorle* (apple juice with sparkling water) remains a refreshing favourite.

FASHION

In clothes, as in all things, Berlin is a very casual city. Except for formal gourmet restaurants, there's no need to dress up for most occasions (unless you particularly want to). Some of the more exclusive nightclubs do have dress codes, but it's generally originality they're looking for rather than expense. On a day-to-day basis most people aren't overly concerned about what they wear, and with the ongoing retro craze you're just as likely to see Berlin's bright young things blowing their cash in second-hand stores, which abound in Kreuzberg, as in designer outlets. The humble T-shirt is perhaps the single best-selling item in the city, tailored for all tastes.

Of course, designer fashion is hardly neglected, and the moneyed shoppers who patronise the big houses have no shortage of choice in the flash boutiques around the Ku'damm and along Friedrichstrasse. However, individuality ranks above all else, and Europe's most tolerant city has no time for clones – different scenes have their own looks, but there's never a single 'uniform' to follow. It's quite possible to be fashionable without spending a fortune, but personal style is essential whether you're a glamour girl or a grunge boy.

Accessories are equally important, and just about anything can be used to put the finishing touches on a Berlin outfit: glasses from IC!Berlin, hats from Fiona Bennett, jewellery and bags from such local labels as IchIchIch. Hair and make-up are more a matter of personal taste, though a certain amount of styling can be expected from both sexes on a night out. While many women favour shorter crops and bob cuts, men tend to grow their hair out a bit; thankfully mullets and rats' tails are now largely restricted to the very young and the terminally '80s! Piercings and tattoos are very common among younger people, especially women, and the more alternative the scene the more extreme the decoration.

For the latest tips on what's hot and what's horrible, consult www.fashionunited.de or www.modesearch.de.

BERLIN EN VOGUE

Mayor Klaus Wowereit got some strange looks on a visit to London back in 2003, when he proclaimed Berlin to be a 'fashion capital' – the city has shown a remarkably lackadaisical attitude towards international fashion in the past. But, as in the arts, experimentation is the order of the day here, and with the latest streetwear boom, Berlin has come to be a fertile spot for innovative young talent, finally showing its potential to return to the forefront of global fashion.

Wowereit's boast was inspired by the success of Bread & Butter (p10) – the fashion industry trade fair inaugurated in 2000, where over 400 brands congregate to exhibit their products to retailers and the press. The event has put the Berlin scene firmly on the fashion map, providing an ideal forum for city's 350 designers and seven fashion schools. Following the fair, summer is the time when eagerly awaited new ranges from independent labels such as Hafenstadt, Hartbo & L'wig, FIRMA, Irie Daily, Hasipop, Butterfly Soulfire and Urban Speed should hit the market.

SPORT

Sport is no exception to the Berlin rule of variety in all things – there are teams representing just about every recognised sport you can think of, from beach volleyball and water polo to handball, American football and chess boxing.

Of course the dominant sport here is and always will be football. The beautiful game came to Germany with a vengeance for the FIFA World Cup in 2006, with the freshly renovated Olympic Stadium proudly hosting the climactic final. Back in 2005, however, revelations of a huge match-fixing scandal threatened to cast a pall over the whole event, when German referee Robert Hoyzer was sentenced to 2½ years in prison. Expect fans and cynics alike to keep a close eye on all proceedings for quite some time to come.

On a national level, Hertha BSC (p217), Berlin's *Bundesliga* (premier league) soccer team, is famed for the dramatic ups and downs of its fortunes, and seems to have spent a lot of time in recent seasons hovering agonisingly close to the top of the table. The season runs from September until May or June, with a winter break.

Lower-league football is also popular. In the *Bundesliga's* second division, the Zweite Liga, FC Union Berlin (p217) is the former team from East Berlin, currently showing drastic improvement from the miserable slump they've endured in previous years. Another 15 local leagues pit teams from the various districts against each other and against sides from other national cities, playing on tiny pitches around town, with lively support often based on an entirely impenetrable mesh of rivalries and old scores.

Ice hockey is another Berlin obsession. There used to be two teams here, but the western Capitals went bankrupt a few years ago, leaving the eastern Eisbären (p217) alone in the national league. Like American football, many of the star players (such as Eisbären darling Sven Felski) are enlisted from professional clubs in the USA and Canada, but supporters adopt them wholeheartedly, and a foreign player who 'defects' to a rival side will receive just as hostile a reception as any local star who does the same. The hockey season is September to April.

Other well-supported games include basketball (played October to April), with Alba Berlin (p216) putting in recent solid wins against European opposition, and American football (season running May to October), where Berlin Thunder (p216) is one of the leading teams. Athletics, tennis and horse racing are the most popular individual competitions. See the Entertainment chapter (p216) for full details on clubs, events and other sports facilities.

MEDIA

Media coverage in liberal, politicised Berlin is typically broad for a European capital, but the newspaper with the largest circulation is the *BZ,* which is borderline sensationalist and practically devoid of meaningful content. Even this is a step up from identikit rival, the *Berliner Kurier,* and national über-rag *Bild,* the pride of media tycoon Axel Springer's publishing empire (see the boxed text, opposite). The *BZ* is also responsible for news content on the infoscreens now found in U-Bahn trains, tightening its grip on populist media coverage in the city. It should not be confused with the respected *Berliner Zeitung,* a left-leaning daily newspaper that is most widely read in the eastern districts and was recently controversially acquired, along with the *Kurier,* by a former chief executive of the Mirror Group of tabloids in the UK.

Of the other broadsheets, the *Berliner Morgenpost* is especially noted for its vast classified section, while *Der Tagesspiegel* has a centre-right political orientation, a solid news and foreign section, and decent cultural coverage. At the left end of the spectrum is the *tageszeitung* or *taz,* which appeals to an intellectual crowd with its news analysis and thorough reporting. Early editions of many dailies are available after 9pm.

Die Zeit is a highbrow national weekly newspaper, with in-depth reporting on everything from politics to fashion. Germany's most widely read weekly news magazines are *Der Spiegel* and the much lighter *Focus* – both offer hard-hitting investigative journalism and a certain degree of government criticism. *Stern* bites harder on the popular nerve, and *Neon* pushes for the youth market. *Zitty* and *Tip* are Berlin's best what's-on magazines (see p191 for more). You'll also inevitably encounter people selling *Motz* and *Der Strassenfeger,* the city's two homeless self-help publications.

English-language newspapers and magazines, mostly from the UK and the USA, are readily available in bookstores and at international newsagents. The *Ex-Berliner*

TOP FIVE BERLIN WEBSITES

- www.berlin.de – official city site
- www.berlin-online.de (in German) – more city info
- www.berlin.gay-web.de – gay information and listings
- www.tip-berlin.de (in German) – entertainment listings, ads etc
- berlin.blogplan.de (in German) – interactive map of city blogs

KING OF THE SPRINGERS

Hamburg-born publisher Axel Springer (1912–85) was essentially the German answer to Rupert Murdoch, a colourful and often controversial figure who did much to shape the current state of the German media. Having taken over the family firm from his father after WWII, Springer created *Bild* in 1952, based on the model of British tabloid newspapers, and went on to build a huge portfolio of magazines and papers including *Die Welt*, the *Berliner Morgenpost* and pioneering teen mag *Bravo*.

The first wave of controversy came in 1967, when students and the Gruppe 47 forum of liberal authors protested that Springer's virtual monopoly was a threat to press freedom. *Bild*, too, became notorious for its vocal criticism of student demonstrations and for supposedly aggressive investigative tactics on the part of reporters. In 1977 journalist Günter Wallraff went undercover at the *Bild* offices and later published a book alleging serious breaches of ethics among its staff (tapping subjects' phones, for example). The following year the paper was sued for erroneously labelling student Eleonore Poensgen a terrorist.

Amid all this attention, Springer maintained a dual existence, often reviled in public, but highly respected for his commitment to German-Jewish reconciliation, a personal project that he pursued for most of his life. By the time he died in 1985 he had received countless awards, citations and honorary doctorates from Jewish institutions in Germany and Israel, as well as the American Friendship Medal.

Springer also considered himself a German patriot and was a staunch proponent of reunification – in 1958 he even visited Moscow to outline his plans to Khrushchev in person. When this somehow failed to work, he made support for reunification editorial policy in all his titles and refused to recognise the legitimacy of the East German state; to hammer home the point, any mention of the GDR was put in inverted commas. Sadly for Springer, he died just four years before his vision was realised, missing out on what would doubtless have been publishing's biggest ever 'I told you so'.

Even after his death, Springer managed to make his presence felt: his will left Axel Springer Ltd to his fifth wife and his two children, stipulating that they couldn't sell any of it for 30 years. In 2005 the firm even managed to stir up controversy again by bidding to acquire the ProSieben and Sat1 TV channels, a move currently under the scrutiny of the monopolies watchdog. The man may have gone, but his name clearly lives on – at least until 2015.

is aimed primarily at the anglophone ex-pat community, providing a very readable perspective on the city.

Germany has two national public TV channels, the ARD (Allgemeiner Rundfunk Deutschlands) and the ZDF (Zweites Deutsches Fernsehen). RBB (Rundfunk Berlin Brandenburg) is the regional public station; local cable stations include TVB, FAB and the non-commercial Offener Kanal Berlin. Generally, programming is relatively highbrow, featuring political coverage, discussion forums, foreign films and restricted advertising.

Private cable TV provides a familiar array of sitcoms, soap operas, chat shows, feature films and drama, overwhelmingly dominated by dubbed US imports. ProSieben, Sat1 and Vox generally have the best selection; Kabel 1 shows some real archive sitcoms, and RTL and RTL II have many of the latest US offerings, though they're often mocked for gratuitous nudity in factual programming (something both private and public channels are frequently guilty of). Arte, the French/German shared arts channel, provides more serious fare.

German news station n-tv is a recent addition to the airwaves. DSF and EuroSport are dedicated sports channels, while MTV (in German) and its local equivalent VIVA can also be received. Several Turkish-language channels cater for Germany's large population with roots in Turkey. Commercial breaks are frequent on all these stations. After 11pm, roughly twice a week, a handful of the private cable channels switch entirely to erotic content. English-language stations available on cable or satellite include CNN, BBC World, CNBC and MSNBC.

With so many studios and production companies around, Berlin is not short of homegrown TV shows and personalities. Cult teen soap *Gute Zeiten, Schlechte Zeiten* (GZSZ; 'Good Times, Bad Times') is filmed in nearby Potsdam (p268). One particularly beloved broadcaster, entertainer and gameshow host, Harald Juhnke, died in 2005, and was honoured with a monument in his native Berlin district of Wedding within weeks!

Berlin has a bewildering choice of radio stations, many modelled on the US format of chart pop and oldies interspersed with inane banter and adverts. Among the more sophisticated stations are Radio Eins (95.8), which has high-quality topical programming, and

SFB4 (106.8) – also known as Radio Multikulti – an excellent multicultural station. Jazz fiends should check out Jazzradio at 101.9, while classical music rules Klassik-Radio at 101.3. InfoRadio at 93.1 has an all-news format, including live interviews, and Radio 100.6 focuses on local news. The BBC broadcasts at 90.2.

As you'd expect from a city with such a strong alternative scene, independent media has a considerable presence here, and all kinds of small-scale publications hit the streets and the web every week, covering themes from the political to the cultural via the very marginal. Internet blogging has also taken off as a logical continuation of this trend; check out berlin. metblogs.com for English-language commentary, or consult de.indymedia.org for links to a range of German sites.

LANGUAGE

Only a small number of Berliners speak the pure Berlinisch dialect, but the strong regional accent is also very distinctive. Listen out for *ge* pronounced as a soft *je,* the soft *ch* as a hard *ck,* or *das* as *det;* reading the phonetic spelling in Berlin cartoons will give you an idea of how it works. Slang words abound for just about anything (*Olle* is a woman, *Molle* or *Pulle* a beer, *Stampe* a pub) and almost all the public buildings in the city have nicknames – only a true Berliner would think to call the Haus der Kulturen der Welt the 'Pregnant Oyster', for example.

In 1998 Berlin, along with the rest of Germany, had to adapt to a thorough spelling reform, standardising some of the quirks and inconsistencies in the German language. Surprisingly for such an opinionated bunch, most Berliners took the changes in their stride, but many other states organised citizens' petitions in protest. In the end, though, the reform prevailed, and from 2005 the new orthography became the official standard, with barely a peep of complaint to be heard. For more information about the spelling changes visit www .neue-rechtschreibung.de.

See the Language chapter (p303) for useful phrases in German, or check out Deutsche Welle's dialect guide (www.dw-world.de/dialektatlas) for a few localised pointers.

ECONOMY & COSTS

Germany is the world's third largest economic power (behind the USA and Japan), is a committed member of the EU, and has been a member of the G8 (formerly G7) group of industrial nations since 1974. In recent years, however, the German economy has weakened, in part due to foreign competition, antiquated machinery, technophobia, high wages and social-security overheads. Berlin has been hit along with the rest of the country, with its own spending crisis to boot.

Economic restructuring has had a major impact on the city's employment base, and more than half the workforce is now in the service sector, including state and federal government agencies. In fact, Berlin has more than twice as many civil servants as any other big city in Germany – one in 10 people holds a government job in eastern Berlin.

Reunification was initially responsible for a growth spurt, but it didn't take long to fizzle. Unemployment figures are at record highs, with around 300,000 (18%) people out of work in 2005, and training opportunities for young people are in short supply, with just 336 places against 5800 applicants in Berlin and Brandenburg. The statistics would likely be worse if entrepreneurship

HOW MUCH?

Caipirinha €5

Currywurst €1.50-2

Doner kebab €2-2.50

Glass of beer €2.50

Latte macchiato €2.50-3

Midweek cinema ticket €5.90

Nightclub entry €8

Public transport day pass €5.80

Tabloid newspaper €0.50

Taxi home €15 (eg from Alexanderplatz to Charlottenburg)

hadn't picked up some of the slack. Around 158,000 people in the Berlin area are now self-employed, especially in the fields of finance, corporate services, construction, commerce and tourism.

Tourism is perhaps the key growth sector right now, boosted by high-profile events such as the football World Cup. In 2005 over six million visitors came to Berlin, up a massive one million since 2003, with a 17% increase in foreign visitors since 2004. Another driving force is information and communication technology, serving an increasingly computer-literate population; growth areas also include software development, marketing, advertising, law and financial services.

In terms of costs, Berlin is on a par with many European capitals and is still considerably cheaper than London or Paris, with the cost of living rising roughly 1% every year. Hotel accommodation is comparatively low-priced as well, and plenty of

Potsdamer Platz (p103)

excellent hostels cater for less demanding travellers. Snackers and self-caterers will find food reassuringly affordable, and while top-flight restaurants charge exactly what you'd expect, there's no shortage of smaller cafés and bistros where a meal needn't be an investment.

There are also plenty of opportunities to save a few euros on various activities during your stay; many museums are free on one particular day every week or month, cinemas are almost half price before 5pm Monday to Wednesday, and most restaurants offer a range of set menus and special meals for children, seniors and theatregoers. Families are also well catered for, with many attractions offering good-value *Familienkarten,* which usually cover two adults and two (or more) children.

On average you can reckon on spending around €90 to €160 a day for a short stay in three-star accommodation with three ample meals a day; luxury-lovers could easily double or treble that figure to get the finest the city has to offer, and budget travellers could probably subsist on as little as €40 a day if they're really easy-going.

GOVERNMENT & POLITICS

Along with Hamburg and Bremen, Berlin is a German city-state. Its government consists of the *Abgeordnetenhaus* (parliament, or legislative body) and the *Senat* (Senate, or executive body). Members of parliament are voted in directly by the electorate for a five-year term. Their primary function is to pass legislation and to elect and supervise the Senate.

The Senate consists of the *Regierender Bürgermeister* (governing mayor) and eight senators. The mayor sets policy and represents Berlin internationally and nationally; senators have similar roles to cabinet ministers, with each in charge of a particular department. The seat of government for the mayor and the Senate is the Rotes Rathaus (Red Town Hall; p94), while parliament meets in the Abgeordnetenhaus (p122) on Niederkirchnerstrasse, opposite the Martin-Gropius-Bau.

After reunification, Berlin also became the official seat of the national government once again – parliament returned to Sir Norman Foster's Reichstag in 1999, and the *Bundesrat* (upper house) moved into the restored Preussisches Herrenhaus building in 2000. Some ministries, such as Defence and Education, still maintain headquarters in Bonn, partly to stop the former West German capital from sinking into political oblivion, but also partly to placate a school of thought which felt that, given its history, Berlin should not be handed too much power for symbolic reasons. To all extents and purposes, however, Berlin has

BERLIN DISTRICTS

In 2001, Berlin's 23 *Bezirke* (districts) were reduced to 12 in an effort to curb bureaucracy. Most of the 'new' districts were created by merging existing ones, and each now has a population of roughly 300,000. The divisions are: Mitte, Friedrichshain-Kreuzberg, Pankow (incorporating Prenzlauer Berg), Charlottenburg-Wilmersdorf, Spandau, Steglitz-Zehlendorf, Tempelhof-Schöneberg, Neukölln, Treptow-Köpenick, Marzahn-Hellersdorf, Lichtenberg and Reinickendorf.

As the old district names are still used, the move hasn't made much difference to visitors, but locals in some areas complained bitterly at being lumped together with their neighbours. The merging of Kreuzberg and Friedrichshain must have particularly rankled – 'activists' organised mass district-wide water fights to protest!

resumed its rightful role as capital of the united Germany, and few people now give Bonn a second thought.

From 1984 the dominant party in Berlin, as in Germany, was the centre-right Christliche Demokratische Union (CDU; Christian Democratic Union). In elections held in 2001, however, voters turned away from the CDU – as apparent payback for plunging the city into its most severe postwar financial crisis – and a new coalition government was formed by the opposition Sozialdemokratische Partei Deutschlands (SPD; Social Democratic Party of Germany) and the Partei des Demokratischen Sozialismus (PDS; Party of Democratic Socialism), the successor to the GDR's communist Sozialistische Einheitspartei Deutschland (SED; Socialist Unity Party of Germany).

National politics still seem to be the primary concern for the 77% of voters who turn out every three years, and the real hot gossip in Berlin lately has been the semi-fiasco of the 2005 federal elections. While Berliners still favoured the SPD by a 10% margin, the overall national result saw the CDU and SPD so close that neither party leader would concede defeat. After weeks of discussion a so-called Great Coalition between the two parties was formed; SPD head Gerhard Schröder stepped down and CDU chief Angela Merkel is now resident in the Kanzleramt (chancellery) as Germany's first female chancellor. Merkel is also the first East German to hold the post – ironic considering she represents the party furthest from the traditional left-wing politics of many eastern voters.

The next local elections in Berlin are set for 2006 and should prove an interesting test of the peoples' reactions to the new compromise regime.

ENVIRONMENT

THE LAND

In 1920, seven cities and countless distinct communities were amalgamated into Gross-Berlin (Greater Berlin), making it one of the largest cities in the world, with an area of 87,000 hectares and a population of nearly four million. Today, Berlin is still Germany's largest city, both in terms of population (just under 3.4 million) and area.

Berlin now covers a total of 889 sq km; its north–south length measures 38km, while from east to west it stretches for 45km. Most visitors never stray outside the central districts to see the full extent of the city, but just try walking from Friedrichshain to Charlottenburg and you'll realise it's bigger than the transport system makes it feel.

The city lies in the heart of the vast North German Plains and, apart from rivers and lakes, lacks distinctive geographical features. As such, the city's development can be almost entirely credited to its architects. Some of the rare hills in the area, like the Teufelsberg in the Grunewald, are actually *Trümmerberge* (rubble mountains) made from debris gathered during the post-WWII clean-up.

Berlin's historical importance as a trade centre stems from the two rivers that cross here. These are the 343km-long Havel, which has its headwaters in Mecklenburg about 110km northwest of Berlin, and its tributary the Spree, which joins it in Spandau. On its course, the Havel travels through 5900 hectares of canals and lakes, including the Wannsee – these are some of the city's most popular summertime spots, with beaches around the lakes and beer gardens overlooking the canals throughout town.

GREEN BERLIN

Despite being such an immense and busy city, Berlin is a relatively green city, with parks, forests, lakes and rivers taking up about one-third of its space. Nearly every neighbourhood has its own park, and forest cover stands at an impressive 18% of the city's total area, thanks to a successful tree-planting campaign during the last two decades. Of the city's 415,000 urban trees, most are linden (lime) and maple trees; others are oak, plane and chestnut. The eastern district of Hohenschönhausen has the most trees: 134 per kilometre of road, compared to a city average of 78.

Cycling in the Spreeboganpark (p103)

Sadly, the local fauna hasn't fared so well since WWII. Construction and a growing population have about halved the number of existing species, and low ground-water levels have dried up biotopes, threatening the survival of birds, reptiles, amphibians and fish. Only about 33 fish species still inhabit the city's rivers and lakes, the most common being perch, pike, roach and bream.

On the positive side, mammals thrive in the leafy forest belt surrounding Berlin, where populations of wild rabbits, foxes, martens and even boar have increased enormously (see the boxed text, below).

Berlin has some of the highest air pollution levels in Germany – higher than any other big city in former West Germany, though still lower than in some eastern cities such as Dresden, Halle or Chemnitz. Pollution and acid rain are increasingly doing damage to Berlin's surrounding forests, and the most recent survey in 2002 showed that just one in five trees remained healthy. In 1991, Berlin joined the International Climate Convention, pledging to reduce total CO_2 emissions by a quarter before 2010; by 1998 emissions were already down by 18%.

Berlin's drinking water is fine, though the water quality of its lakes and rivers is not. The Havel lakes, including the Wannsee, are prone to excessive algae growth, and the Spree River and Landwehrkanal, which flow right through the city, are badly polluted. The only relatively clean lakes in the area are those in the Grunewald.

Despite such problems Berlin is, in many ways, a very ecologically minded city. The state government has a strong record of investing in ambitious initiatives – such as the

PIG IGNORANCE

Berlin is hardly truffle country, but the city's leafy outer suburbs have become a paradise for wild boar in recent years. The districts most affected are Grunewald, Zehlendorf, Wilmersdorf, Reinickendorf and Spandau, where many a resident has woken up to find their garden trashed by porcine marauders.

The population explosion is said to have been caused by mild winters and an abundance of acorns and other foods, driving numbers of them to scavenge for more easily-obtained foods in the city. Many have developed a taste for lawns, flower beds and scraps scavenged from compost heaps and garbage bins. According to a report in the *Berliner Morgenpost*, wild pigs even wait regularly on the steps of one school to beg for food at break times.

Reactions to the problem are mixed; even the most green-minded Berliners start screaming 'cull' the moment they see their lovingly tended geraniums massacred by careless trotters. In response, the Senate has published an information pamphlet on city boars, giving information on their diet and habits, and encouraging people to be more tolerant of their piggy visitors. Failing that, the pigs are fair game outside populated areas, and licensed hunters bag around 1000 hapless porkers a year.

Programme for the Protection of Land and Endangered Species, which seeks to balance the objectives of nature and conservation with urban development – industry has been given particularly strict emission-reducing targets, a state-wide energy-saving campaign was launched in 1994, and solar power has been adopted on a massive scale.

Awareness also happens at a local level, and the success of the city's energy-saving programmes is largely due to people's willingness to contribute as individuals. Bicycle lanes abound, there are solar-powered parking voucher dispensers and recycling is the norm – even U-Bahn and S-Bahn stations have colour-coded *Trennmüll* (sorted rubbish) bins. The city has a comprehensive and efficient public transport system, which the majority of people use regularly, and driving is discouraged through restrictive parking regulations.

Greenpeace (www.greenpeace-berlin.de) is very active in Germany, and another important and similarly radical environmental group is the Grüne Liga (www.grueneliga.de). The Green Party has also traditionally been strong in Berlin, and won 12.4% of primary votes in the 2005 national elections, compared to 8.9% in 1994.

URBAN PLANNING & DEVELOPMENT

Even today, Berlin is a work in progress. Cranes have been an everyday sight on the skyline virtually since the end of WWII, but it was reunification that signalled the start of the large-scale building and reconstruction programmes that are still going on today.

So far, the dramatic Friedrichstadtpassagen have breathed new life into languishing Friedrichstrasse, the New Synagogue on Oranienburger Strasse symbolises the rebirth of Jewish culture in Berlin, and the long-debated Holocaust Memorial has finally become a poignant reality. The most prominent development, though, is Potsdamer Platz, where a sparkling new urban district has sprung up, featuring Daimler-City, the Sony Center and the new Potsdamer Platz rail station.

Further prestige projects are emerging around this area, with international companies vying for office space around Leipziger Platz and along Ebertstrasse. Pariser Platz has already been snapped up by embassies, the big banks and the Academy of Arts, and is once again becoming Berlin's 'reception room'.

Of course there's only so much space in the city, and the constant rebuilding has

OCCUPIED BERLIN

Squatting has always been a key facet of Berlin's counter-culture, and in 2004 the innocent-looking building at Yorckstrasse 59 became the focus of a particularly prominent case, as residents and supporters began a sustained anti-repossession campaign. Despite citywide protests, regular demonstrations and protracted negotiations with the owners, Kreuzberg local council and the police, the matter dragged on without resolution for over a year, until the courts finally had the squatters evicted in the summer of 2005.

Not content to let the issue lie, activists promptly occupied a set of empty rooms in the Künstlerhaus Bethanien (p126), sparking a whole new row. It's not hard to spot the impact the whole saga has had on life in Kreuzberg – graffiti all over the district still proclaims support for 'Yorck 59'.

had a knock-on effect on some older areas. Even one of the few remaining sections of the Berlin Wall – including the graves of over 1000 citizens who died trying to escape to the West – was recently demolished, despite vocal protests, as the Haus am Checkpoint Charlie museum simply couldn't afford to maintain it. Many old GDR *Plattenbau* (plate building) blocks have also succumbed to progress, though one company has set up an innovative business recycling them as luxury houses in rural western locations!

In housing terms, too, all this development has its drawbacks, and it's now much harder to find affordable lodgings in the centre of town; families in particular almost invariably live in the outlying districts. As buildings are increasingly subdivided, many more people are living in single apartments – 50% of Berlin's population now live alone, and the German tradition of the *Wohngemeinschaft* (shared house, or WG) is becoming a relative rarity in the inner city. Yet, some long-term squatted houses still survive in Friedrichshain and Kreuzberg, the old favourite haunts of the squat scene. See p15 for more on Berlin living, and the boxed text on above for squat politics.

Arts

Arts

The arts are fundamental to everything Berlin holds dear, and the sheer scope of creative activity in the city is astounding. Half the reason Berliners are always so busy is because of the efforts required to keep up with the ever-changing cultural kaleidoscope of trends, events and publications, and with a history of international excellence in most fields, expectations and standards are always set high. The city itself provides an iconic setting for any number of books, films, paintings and songs, its unmistakeable presence influencing artists and residents just as it does those canny visitors who take the time to dive in.

VISUAL ARTS

Berlin is one of Europe's great art cities, with dozens of fine exhibition spaces and a particular reputation for encouraging contemporary and alternative art. Besides the main museums, the best spots are the gallery quarters around the Hackesche Höfe and Auguststrasse in Mitte, Zimmerstrasse near the former Checkpoint Charlie, and the established Charlottenburg scene around the Ku'damm, Uhlandstrasse and Fasanenstrasse. High points of the art calendar include the Berlin Biennale (p12) and Art Forum Berlin (p11).

TOP FIVE ART MUSEUMS & GALLERIES

- Neue Nationalgalerie (p108) The best big-name modern art
- Berlinische Galerie (p123) Modern pieces with a local flavour
- Gemäldegalerie (p107) Canvas classics from across six centuries
- Kunst-Werke Berlin (p96) Edgy, alternative, out-there contemporary works
- Alte Nationalgalerie (p79) A healthy dose of true-blue Romanticism

Art & History

Fine art only really began to flourish in Berlin in the late 17th century, when self-crowned King Friedrich I founded the Academy of the Arts at the instigation of court sculptor Andreas Schlüter (1660–1714). Schlüter repaid the favour with several outstanding sculptures, including the *Great Elector on Horseback* (1699), now in front of Schloss Charlottenburg (p110), and the haunting *Masks of Dying Warriors* in the courtyard of the Zeughaus (p74) on Unter den Linden.

The arts languished again under Friedrich's successor, Soldier King Friedrich Wilhelm I, but took a turn towards greatness when his son, Friedrich II (Frederick the Great), ascended the throne in 1740. Friedrich drew heavily on the artistic, architectural and decorative expertise of Georg Wenzeslaus von Knobelsdorff (1699–1753), a student of Pesne. Knobelsdorff is most famous for designing the Staatsoper Unter den Linden (p77) and Schloss Sanssouci (p268) in Potsdam.

In many ways, Nineteenth-century styles reflected the new political and economic ideas coming from England and France, which resonated especially with the educated middle classes and found expression in neoclassicism. One major artist of the period was Johann Gottfried Schadow (1764–1850), whose most famous work is the *Quadriga* – the horse-drawn chariot that crowns the Brandenburg Gate (Brandenburger Tor; p74).

Another important neoclassical sculptor was Christian Daniel Rauch (1777–1857), a student of Schadow. Rauch had a talent for representing idealised, classical beauty in a realistic fashion. His most famous work is the 1851 monument of Friedrich the Great on horseback (p76) which stands outside the Humboldt Universität.

A student of Rauch, the sculptor Reinhold Begas (1831–1911) developed a neobaroque, theatrical style that was so ostentatiously counter-neoclassical that he met with a fair amount of controversy in his lifetime. The Neptune fountain (1891; p93) outside the Marienkirche is a Begas work, as is the Schiller monument (p77) on Gendarmenmarkt.

Brandenburger Tor (p74) at dusk

In painting, Romanticism gradually overtook neoclassicism in popularity. One reason for this was the awakening of a nationalist spirit in Germany – spurred by the Napoleonic Wars – during the reign of Friedrich Wilhelm III (1797–1840). Romanticism was the perfect form of expression for the idealism and emotion that characterised the period. The genre's leading light was Caspar David Friedrich (1774–1840), whose evocative works are a highlight of the Alte Nationalgalerie. Paintings by Karl Friedrich Schinkel, Berlin's dominant neoclassical architect, are also here, and at the Neuer Pavillon of Schloss Charlottenburg (p112); for more on the man see the boxed text, p42.

A parallel development during the period 1815 to 1848, was the so-called Berliner Biedermeier, a more conservative and painstakingly detailed style. There was also an early interest in paintings that chronicled Berlin's constantly evolving cityscape, which sold especially well among the middle classes.

Into the 20th Century

As the first tendrils of modernity reached Berlin, a lithographer named Heinrich Zille (1858–1929) became the first prominent artist to evoke the social development of the city, creating an instantly recognisable style in his drawings of everyday life and real people. Zille was acknowledged even during his lifetime as one of the definitive documenters of his time, and since his death his prolific photographic work has also come to be seen as a valuable historical record.

In 1903 Zille was accepted into the Berlin Secession, a group of young artists who had come together in 1892 to protest at the forced closure of an exhibition displaying pictures by Edvard Munch. Led by Max Liebermann (1847–1935) and Walter Leistikow (1865–1908), member artists were not linked by a common artistic style, but by a rejection of reactionary attitudes towards the arts that stifled new forms of expression. They preferred scenes from daily life to historical and religious themes, shunned studios in favour of natural outdoor light, and were hugely influential in inspiring new styles.

Liebermann himself evolved from a painter of gloomy naturalist scenes to an important representatives of 'Berlin impressionism'. In the early 1900s, Lovis Corinth (1858–1925) and

27

TOTALLY GROSZ

In this age of stuffed sharks, performance piercing and plastified corpses, it's hard to imagine the furore that a straightforward painting could cause in the 1920s. The work of Berliner George Grosz, however, requires a pretty small leap of imagination – the ferocious satire of his paintings still has the power to shock, if not offend. Just look at the steaming turd filling the brainpan of the fat capitalist in the famous *Pillars of Society* (1926) in the Neue Nationalgalerie, and it's easy to see why Germany was scandalised!

Max Slevogt (1868–1932) joined the group, as did Käthe Kollwitz (1867–1945), still regarded as Germany's finest female artist, whose keen social and political awareness lent a tortured power to her work.

After WWI, this liberal tradition allowed Berlin to evolve into the centre of contemporary German and international art. Radical movements proliferated, and Dadaism, cofounded by George Grosz (1893–1959), emerged as a prevalent form. Dadaists rejected traditional art in favour of collage and montage, and considered chance and spontaneity to be determining artistic elements. The first Dada evening, in 1917, was by all accounts a chaotic affair, with Grosz urinating on the pictures, Richard Huelsenbeck declaring that too few people had been killed for art, and the police trying to close the whole thing down.

Parallel movements had expressionist artists like Max Beckmann (1884–1950) and Otto Dix (1891–1969) who examined the threats of urbanisation, while Wassily Kandinsky, Paul Klee, Lyonel Feininger and Alexej Jawlensky formed the 'The Blue Four' in 1924, and went on to work and teach at the Bauhaus art school.

The Bauhaus style was based on practical anti-elitist principles bringing form and function together, and had a profound effect on all modern design – visit the Bauhaus Archiv (p106) for ample examples. The movement itself was founded in Weimar and then based in Dessau, in the state of Saxony-Anhalt, south of Berlin. Many of its most influential figures, however, worked in Berlin, and in 1932 the renowned art school moved wholesale to the capital to escape Nazi pressure.

As it turned out this was just a short reprieve, and the impact on the whole Berlin arts scene once the Nazis took over in 1933 was devastating. Many artists left the country, others ended up in prison or concentration camps, their works classified as 'degenerate' and confiscated or destroyed. The art promoted instead was pretty terrible, favouring straightforward forms and epic styles. Propaganda artist Mjölnir defined the typical look of the time with block Gothic scripts and idealised figures.

After WWII, Berlin's art scene was as fragmented as the city itself. In the east, artists were forced to toe the 'socialist-realist' line, which Otto Nagel and Max Lingner frequently managed to hurdle by feigning conformity while maintaining aesthetic and experimental aspects in their work. In the late '60s, East Berlin established itself as an arts centre in the German Democratic Republic (GDR) with the formation of the Berliner Schule (Berlin School). Members such as Manfred Böttcher and Harald Metzkes succeeded in freeing themselves from the confines of officially sanctioned socialist art in order to embrace a more multifaceted realism. In the '70s, when conflicts of the individual in society became a prominent theme, underground galleries flourished in Prenzlauer Berg and art became a collective endeavour.

In postwar West Berlin, artists eagerly absorbed abstract influences from France and the USA. Pioneers included Zone 5, which revolved around Hans Thiemann, and surrealists Heinz Trökes and Mac Zimmermann. In the 1960s, politics was a primary concern and a new style called 'critical realism' emerged, propagated by artists like Ulrich Baehr, Hans-Jürgen Diehl and Wolfgang Petrick. The 1973 movement, Schule der Neuen Prächtigkeit (School of New Magnificence), had a similar approach. In the 1980s, expressionism found its way back onto the canvasses of painters like Salomé, Helmut Middendorf and Rainer Fetting, a group known as the Junge Wilde (Young Wild Ones).

Contemporary Berlin

After the Wende (the turning point that led to the collapse of the GDR), fuelled by the sense of change, Berlin's arts scene developed into one of the most exciting and dynamic in Europe. Today the city is still considered an international centre of contemporary art, taking the title of Unesco City of Design in 2005. The Neue Nationalgalerie (p108) in particular hosts excellent thematic exhibitions by major local and international artists. Other pioneering galleries include **Galerie Wohnmaschine** (Map pp340–1; ☎ 3087 2015; Tucholskystrasse 35) and **Galerie Eigen + Art** (Map pp340–1; ☎ 280 6605; Auguststrasse 26). Kunsthaus Tacheles (p96) is home to numerous smaller-scale alternative artists' studios.

Nowhere is this grass-roots art scene better represented than in the proliferation of graffiti all over town, which not only fulfils the usual function as an outlet for teenage rebellion and radical protest, but also has a visible influence on many more institutionalised projects, such as shop fronts and school playgrounds. Wandering around the side streets of Friedrichshain and Kreuzberg is a great introduction to the many styles and themes that plaster Berlin buildings, and you'll quickly start to recognise recurring tags.

Public art is indeed a big feature of the city artscape, strongly informed by the graffiti aesthetic and often actively seeking to capture the guerilla element that gives illegal 'writing' its edge. One of the most popular installations of recent years was the Chaos Computer Club's *Blinkenlights,* an interactive project using lit windows in the Haus des Lehrers on Alexanderplatz to create a giant pixel-like display. For maximum public involvement, viewers with mobile phones could send messages and pictures or even play simple games on the huge 'screen'.

Surprisingly, despite an active community of over 4500 artists living and working here, few individuals have made the breakthrough from this vibrant local arena to the international stage. One name to look out for is Italian-German rising star, Monica Bonvicini, whose large-scale installations examine the nature of space and destruction. In 2005 she won the Nationalgalerie's prestigious New Art Prize, holding her own against fellow Berlin residents John Bock, Angela Bulloch and Anri Sala. On the more commercial side, Jim Rakete is one of Germany's best-known photographers, and also used to manage music acts such as Nina Hagen in the 1980s.

FILM

In 1895, Germany's first commercial film projection took place in Berlin. The city soon became synonymous with film-making in Germany, at least until the outbreak of WWII. With filming having resumed in Potsdam in 1992, Berlin has become the second-most important film centre in Germany (behind Munich), with a prolific experimental scene lurking in the shadows of the big names.

Berlin also plays host to most German premieres of international movies, and stages the single most important event on Germany's film calendar, the International Film Festival (p9). Better known as the Berlinale, it was founded in 1951 on the initiative of the western Allies, and features screenings of around 750 films, with some of them competing for the prestigious Golden and Silver Bear trophies. In 2006 the top prize (and two other awards) went to Jasmila Zbanic's hard-hitting low-budget drama *Grbavica,* which deals with mass rapes during the 1992–95 siege of Sarajevo.

TOP FIVE BERLIN FILMS

Berlin itself has 'starred' in many films, providing an iconic and evocative backdrop for everything from historical dramas to modern thrillers (and of course *Cabaret*).

- *Berlin: Sinfonie einer Grosstadt* (*Berlin: Symphony of a City*; Walter Ruttmann; 1927) Ambitious for its time, this fascinating silent documentary captures a day in the life of Berlin in the '20s.
- *Der Himmel über Berlin* (*Wings of Desire*; Wim Wenders; 1987) An angelic love story swooping around the old, bare no-man's-land of Potsdamer Platz.
- *Lola rennt* (*Run Lola Run*; Tom Tykwer; 1997) The geography's largely fictional, but the city's unmistakeable in this inventive, energetic MTV-generation movie.
- *Good Bye Lenin!* (Wolfgang Becker; 2003) This hugely successful comedy tells the story of a young East Berliner replicating the GDR for his mother after the fall of the Wall.
- *Gespenster* (*Ghosts*; Christian Petzold; 2005) A haunting study of modern urban alienation, flitting around anonymous corners of Tiergarten.

Since 1971 the International Forum of New Cinema, which showcases more radical and alternative films, has taken place alongside the more traditional competition.

Berlin's pioneering role in movie history is undeniable. America had Edison, France the Lumière brothers, and Berlin had Max Skladanowsky, a former fairground showman whose 1895 'bioscope' – a prototype film projector – paved the way for the first era of film making in Germany. By 1910, Berlin had 139 *Kinematographentheater* (which give us the German word for cinema, *Kino*) showing mostly slapstick, melodramas and short documentaries. The city now has more cinemas than ever (around 265), from multiplexes to tiny single-screen venues – see p214 for more details.

The 1920s and early '30s were a boom time for Berlin cinema, with Marlene Dietrich seducing the world and the mighty UFA studio producing virtually all of Germany's celluloid

Film Museum (p105), Potsdamer Platz

output. The two dominant directors of the time were Georg Wilhelm Papst, whose use of montage and characterisation defined the Neue Sachlichkeit (New Objectivity) movement, and Fritz Lang, whose seminal works *Metropolis* (1926) and *M* (1931) brought him international fame. After 1933, however, film makers found their artistic freedom, not to mention funding, increasingly curtailed, and by 1939 practically the entire industry had fled abroad.

Postwar Productions

Like most of the arts, the film industry has generally been well funded in Berlin since 1945, and particularly large subsidies were offered in the 1970s to lure film makers back to the city. It worked, and the leading lights of the Junge Deutsche Film (Young German Film) – directors such as Rainer Werner Fassbinder, Volker Schlöndorf, Wim Wenders and Werner Herzog – magically reappeared from Munich at the promise of more cash.

Fassbinder, perhaps the most talented and challenging of the group, died in an accident in 1982, but the other three have remained at the forefront of German cinema. Herzog, best known for his work with psychotic actor Klaus Kinski, is still an active documentary director and producer. Wenders has been highly acclaimed for USA-based films such as *Paris, Texas* (1984), *Buena Vista Social Club* (1999) and *Don't Come Knocking* (2005). Schlöndorf, with consistent foreign and domestic successes under his belt, now runs Potsdam's Babelsberg complex, once the domain of the great UFA studios. Even cinematographer Michael Ballhaus, a former Fassbinder collaborator, has carved out a distinguished international career, working regularly with Martin Scorsese.

As befits a city with such a chequered past, recent history has always been an issue for Berlin film makers, from early postwar *Trümmerfilme* ('rubble films') to the latest wave of post-*Wende Ostalgie* (GDR nostalgia). Some of the best films about the Nazi era include East Germany's first postwar film, *Die Mörder sind unter uns* (The Murderers Are Among Us; 1946); Fassbinder's *Die Ehe von Maria Braun* (Maria Braun's Marriage; 1979); *Rosenstrasse* (2003), about a group of women fighting for the release of their Jewish husbands (see boxed text, p97); and *Der Untergang* (Downfall; 2004), critically acclaimed for Bruno Ganz's stunning performance as Hitler in his final days.

Since reunification, however, few serious critical feature films have dealt with the GDR era, perhaps because of the proximity of the events and a reluctance among audiences to engage with their implications. Hannes Stöhr's *Berlin Is In Germany* (2001) provides a thoughtful take on reunification, but movies that deal with the division era itself tend to be light-hearted comedy-dramas. Director Leander Haussmann has carved himself a neat niche as the king of *Ostalgie* with his films *Sonnenallee* (1999), *Herr Lehmann* (Berlin Blues; 2003) and *NVA* (2005). However, Haussmann was outdone at his own game by *Good Bye Lenin!* (2003), Wolfgang Becker's witty tale of a son trying to re-create the minutiae of GDR life to reassure his sick mother. This very German film was an unexpected worldwide smash, with nominations at both the Golden Globes and the Academy Awards.

Current Trends

With its fundamentally commercial infrastructure and a series of recent hits, the Berlin film community has not been as badly affected as some by the city's financial crisis. As with so many aspects of Berlin culture, the city's strength lies in its diversity, involving people from all backgrounds in the creative process. The focus is overwhelmingly on evocative, serious cinema with strong social themes. The alternative scene has thrived for years, putting on dozens of seasons and events around town.

Women in particular have taken an unusually active role in the film industry here since the heyday of Marlene Dietrich, and many of the most ground-breaking and challenging films have been driven by women: directors Jutta Brückner, Sylke Enders and Doris Dörrie, and producer Ewa Karlstrom, are all active in Berlin, as is legendary director Margarethe von Trotta, who has been an influential figure since the early days of the Junge Deutsche Film. TV director Franziska Meyer Price is the latest to enter the arena, with the comedy *Ich bin ein Berliner* (2005), while Karlstrom's former colleague, Katja von Garnier, has successfully followed her male counterparts to America.

Berlin's major minority is very well represented on screen, and films by and about the Turkish community attract increasing critical interest. The most significant so far is Fatih Akin's powerful drama *Gegen die Wand* (English title *Head On;* 2003), an incisive and un-flinching look at the pressures facing Turkish Germans, which won the Golden Bear prize at the 2004 Berlinale. Very relevant themes are also addressed in Elmar Fischer's *Fremder*

DOCUMENTING EVIL

'I filmed the truth as it was then. Nothing more.'

Leni Riefenstahl

Films made during the Nazi period bring their own historical dilemma, none more so than the works of brilliant Berlin director Leni Riefenstahl (1902–2003).

A former actress, Riefenstahl caught the regime's attention with her first feature as director, *Das blaue Licht* (The Blue Light; 1932), and was recruited to make 'informational' films. Considered a vital part of the Third Reich propaganda machine, Riefenstahl's epics depicted Nazi events such as the 1936 Olympics. Her visually stunning *Triumph des Willens* (Triumph of the Will; 1934), a documentary about Hitler that centres on the Nuremberg rallies, is one of the most controversial pieces in cinematic history.

After the war, Riefenstahl maintained that she had held no fascist sympathies, protesting both her right as a film maker to record such events and her lack of choice in the matter under the Nazis. Demonised by the Allies and the industry, she spent four years in a French prison. In 1954, in an attempt to clear her reputation, she completed *Tiefland*, an allegorical, supposedly antifascist fairy tale she had started work on in 1944; with no distributor willing to touch it, however, her cinematic career was effectively over.

From then on Riefenstahl concentrated mainly on photography, producing several books about the Sudanese people, which went some way towards refuting accusations of racism. In 1992 she published her autobiography, and subsequently found herself the subject of a number of documentaries, including *Leni Riefenstahl: Die Macht der Bilder* (The Power of the Image; 1993) and *The Wonderful Horrible Life of Leni Riefenstahl* (2003). Despite a consistently high public profile she made only one more film, the nature documentary *Impressionen unter Wasser* (Impressions Under Water; 2002).

In September 2003 Leni Riefenstahl died in Germany, aged 101, leaving no real answers in the debate over art and complicity. Her fascination as an ambivalent figure has by no means disappeared – Anja Gronau is the most recent theatre director to address her complex life on stage, and none other than Jodie Foster is reportedly planning a full-length biopic.

Freund (The Friend; 2003), which examines crosscultural relationships in the context of the 9/11 terrorist attacks, and in Bettina Braun's documentary *Was lebst du?* (What Do You Live?; 2005), which follows four young Turkish men in Cologne. Even Berlin's tiny Korean community is portrayed in Henrike Goetz's debut feature film *Make My Day* (2004).

The city is also becoming popular as a location for major international productions. Jodie Foster has already declared herself a fan, having filmed much of *Flight Plan* (2005) here with Swabian director Robert Schwentke.

THEATRE

Since the Wende, major artistic, structural and personnel changes have swept Berlin's theatrical landscape on a regular basis. Today, Berlin has no fewer than 47 dedicated theatre houses, offering a wide variety of settings for the 9600-odd productions staged every year. The major stages have traditionally been very well subsidised, and hence often play disappointingly safe with their schedules, leading to some colourful rows over cultural policy and official appointments. However, the current directors of the city's leading venues are, for the most part, presiding over a boom period, with a lively fringe scene flourishing around them.

Enfant terrible Frank Castorf is the man behind much of this new wave, igniting a creative firestorm at the Volksbühne (p212) and bringing in fellow provocateur Christoph Schlingensief as his sidekick. Meanwhile, Claus Peymann has restored pomp to the Berliner Ensemble (p211). Bernd Wilms, who made the Maxim Gorki Theater (p211) into one of the most respected theatres in town, moved to the Deutsches Theater (p211) in 2001, and maintains a weighty presence despite political pressure on his post, while up-and-coming director Armin Petras has taken over at the Gorki. Also part of the new generation are Thomas Ostermeier and Jens Hillje, codirectors of the Schaubühne am Lehniner Platz (p212).

Dramatic History

Surprisingly, Berlin's theatre scene had rather modest beginnings. The first quality productions weren't staged until the arrival of such stellar dramatists as Gotthold Ephraim Lessing and Johann Wolfgang von Goethe in the middle of the 18th century. One of the first impresarios was August Wilhelm Iffland (1759–1814), who took over the helm of the Royal National Theatre in 1796 and was noted for his natural yet sophisticated productions.

Iffland's act proved hard to follow: when he died in 1814, Berlin theatre languished until Otto Brahm became director of the Deutsches Theater in 1894. Dedicated to the naturalistic style, Brahm coaxed psychological dimensions out of characters and sought to make their language and situations mirror real life. The critical works of Gerhart Hauptmann and Henrik Ibsen were staples on his stage throughout the 1890s.

In 1894, Brahm hired a young actor named Max Reinhardt (1873–1943), who became perhaps the most famous and influential director in German theatre ever. Born in Vienna, Reinhardt began producing, and eventually inherited the reins of the Deutsches Theater from Brahm. Stylistically, Reinhardt completely broke the naturalist mould favoured by his old mentor and became known for his lavish productions, using light effects, music and other devices. In 1919 he opened the Grosse Schauspielhaus, now the Friedrichstadtpalast (p210).

Reinhardt's path later crossed that of another seminal theatre figure, Bertolt Brecht (1898–1956), who moved to Berlin in 1924. The two worked together briefly at the Deutsches Theater, until Brecht developed his own unique style of so-called 'epic theatre', which, unlike 'dramatic theatre', forces its audience to detach themselves emotionally from the play and its characters and to reason intellectually.

Over the next decade Brecht developed this theory and its 'alienation techniques' in plays like *Die Dreigroschenoper* (The Threepenny Opera; 1928). A staunch Marxist, he went into exile during the Nazi years, surfaced in Hollywood as a scriptwriter, then left the USA during the communist witch-hunts of the McCarthy era. He wrote most of his best plays during his years in exile: *Mutter Courage und ihre Kinder* (Mother Courage and Her Children; 1941), *Leben des Galilei* (The Life of Galileo; 1943), *Der gute Mensch von Sezuan* (The Good Woman of Sezuan; 1943) and *Der kaukasische Kreidekreis* (The Caucasian Chalk Circle; 1948) are considered among the finest examples of his extraordinary style.

TOLLER & PISCATOR

The names of playwright Ernst Toller (1893–1939) and producer Erwin Piscator (1893–1966) no longer mean much to the average theatregoer, but they were key figures of their time, and their single collaboration, the Berlin premiere of Toller's play *Hoppla, wir leben!* (Whoops, We're Alive!), was arguably the biggest theatrical event of the 1920s.

From the start the two men clashed. Toller was a committed socialist with humanist leanings, traumatised by WWI and the years he spent in prison after the short-lived 1919 Munich revolution, and the play was based on his experience of postwar society and the problems of political activism. Piscator, on the other hand, was a radical communist aiming to establish 'total theatre' as an extreme, agitatory form of political engagement – the premiere was carefully timed to coincide with the 10th anniversary of the Russian Revolution.

Piscator's revolutionary production methods, using elaborate multisectioned sets, revolving stages, music and film clips, were actually ideally suited to Toller's vision of a world swamped in new technology, and had a profound influence on modern documentary theatre. However, the play's indeterminate ending was not the radical statement Piscator wanted to make; he rewrote it to have the lead character commit suicide, a crass stroke that undermined Toller's thoughtful attempt to examine the issues of political commitment and progress. The two never spoke again, and Toller reinstated his original ending for every subsequent run of the play.

Brecht returned to East Berlin in 1949 and founded the Berliner Ensemble with his wife, Helene Weigel, who directed it until her death in 1971. *Mother Courage and Her Children* premiered successfully in 1949 at the Deutsches Theater, but for much of the rest of his lifetime the great playwright was both suspected in the East for his unorthodox aesthetic theories and scorned in the West for his communist principles.

At the same time as Brecht was experimenting in prewar Berlin, new expressionistic approaches to musical theatre came from classically trained composers, including Hanns Eisler and Kurt Weill, who collaborated with Brecht on *The Threepenny Opera* and *The Rise and Fall of the City of Mahagony*. On the more mainstream variety circuit, champagne, cancan and long-legged showgirls were all the rage, and Mischa Spoliansky was among the leading lights of the cabaret stages.

After WWII, artistic stagnation spread across German theatre for more than two decades. In West Berlin the first breath of recovery came in 1970 with the opening of the Schaubühne am Halleschen Ufer under Peter Stein. The theatre, which later moved to the Ku'damm and became the Schaubühne am Lehniner Platz, rapidly developed into one of Germany's leading stages. In East Berlin, the Volksbühne grew to be a highly innovative venue, along with the Deutsches Theater. Taking advantage of relative political and artistic freedoms granted by the government, they provided platforms for political exchange and contributed to the peaceful revolution of 1989.

DANCE

Dance is alive and kicking up its heels in Berlin, which has three state-sponsored ballet troupes (attached to the three opera houses) and a thriving independent scene. Today new and innovative groups attract a growing audience, with performances often staged in unconventional settings. Leading venues are the Sophiensaele (p214) and Hebbel am Ufer (p211).

Sascha Waltz is the undisputed lady of the dance in Berlin right now, and has returned to lead her own troupe again after sharing the high-profile directorship of the Schaubühne with Thomas Ostermeier, though she still collaborates regularly with her former colleague. Waltz has probably done more than anyone else to shake up the contemporary dance scene here, and any performance with her involvement is worth catching. Elsewhere, US choreographer Meg Stuart is currently the artist in residence at the Volksbühne, bringing movement and music to the city's most provocative stage.

Historically, ballet arrived under Friedrich II, who brought Italian star Barberina to the city in 1744. The first royal company was formed in 1811, and eccentric American dancer Isadora Duncan opened her own school here in 1904. It was in the 1920s, however, that dance really took off. Berlin even gave birth to a new form, so-called 'grotesque dance'; influenced by Dadaism, it was characterised by excessive, often comical expressiveness. One of its prime practitioners was Valeska Gert, but even more influential was Mary Wigman, who regarded body and movement as tools to express the universal experience of life. Her style inspired some of today's leading German choreographers, including Pina Bausch and Reinhild Hoffmann.

Ballet also experienced a postwar renaissance under the Russian immigrant Tatjana Gsovsky, though it came and went quicker than the theatre revival. Initially working without a permanent stage, Gsovsky choreographed a number of memorable productions, including *Hamlet* (1953) and *The Idiot* (1954), at the Theater des Westens, before becoming ballet director at the Deutsche Oper. Sadly her impetus hasn't lasted, and today's ballet troupes concentrate on audience-pleasing classical repertoires such as *Swan Lake* and *The Nutcracker*.

In a more participatory vein, ballroom is definitively back in Berlin, and all kinds of clubs and other venues do very nicely with midweek tango and salsa sessions catering for the sustained Latin craze. If you'd rather swing your own hips than watch the pros stretch theirs, look out for the many classes on offer around town.

MUSIC

Germany's contemporary music scene has many centres, but Berlin is still the big one for most of today's multifarious styles and genres. It boasts at least 2000 active bands, countless DJs and the country's leading orchestras, not to mention the three great state-funded opera houses. Like the city itself, music here is constantly evolving, changing shape and redefining itself, and Berlin continues to be a fertile breeding ground for new musical trends.

The Classics

For centuries Berlin was largely eclipsed by Vienna, Leipzig and other European cities when it came to music. In 1882, however, the Berliner Philharmonisches Orchester (p206) was established, gaining international stature under Hans von Bülow and Arthur Nikisch. In 1923, Wilhelm Furtwängler became artistic director, a post he held (with interruptions during and shortly after the Nazi years) until 1954. His successor, the legendary Herbert von Karajan, was an autocratic figure who established a position of real dominance on the world stage and remained director until 1989. He was fol-

FIVE TOP BERLIN TRACKS

With over 420 songs namechecking Europe's coolest city, your iPod never had it so good!

- *Berlin* (Lou Reed) In Berlin, by the Wall… Lou falls in love
- *Dickes B* (Seeed) Reggae ode to the 'Big B'
- *Berlin Berlin* (Marlene Dietrich) The ultimate diva sings her city's praises
- *I Hate Berlin* (Second Decay) There's no pleasing some people
- *Take My Breath Away* (Berlin) Er, maybe not

lowed by Claudio Abbado and, in 2002, flamboyant British conductor Sir Simon Rattle, who won a Grammy with the orchestra before he had even officially started in the post.

The pulsating 1920s drew numerous musicians to Berlin, including Arnold Schönberg and Paul Hindemith, who taught at the Academie der Künste and the Berliner Hochschule, respectively. Schönberg's atonal compositions found a following here, as did his experimentation with noise and sound effects. Hindemith explored the new medium of radio and taught a seminar on film music.

Today the classical scene is considerably less high profile, but look out for composer Wolfgang Rihm, tenor Peter Schreier's oratorio performances and director Andreas Homoki's fresh productions at the Komische Oper (p209).

Jazz, Rock & Pop

Jazz and popular music came into their own here in the 1920s, providing the staple diet of the city's clubs, cabarets and drinking dens. Contemporary singer Max Raabe has carved out a niche for himself by recreating the typical sounds of the period with his Palast Orchestra, and is a regular fixture in Berlin. Modern jazz, too, is very much alive in the city; in particular, local lad Til Brönner is known as one of Germany's best contemporary jazz trumpeters.

The 1920s also generated the Berlin *Schlager* – silly but entertaining songs with titles like *Mein Papagei frisst keine harten Eier* (My Parrot Doesn't Eat Hard-boiled Eggs). Singing groups such as the Comedian Harmonists built their success on this music, and it still survives today, especially as part of satirical *Kabarett* performances.

Not content with these early innovations, Berlin has spearheaded most of Germany's popular music revolutions. In the late '60s, Tangerine Dream helped to propagate the psychedelic sound. A decade later Nina Hagen, born in East Berlin, followed her adopted father, writer Wolf Biermann, to West Germany and soon became the diva of German punk. Hagen also laid the groundwork for the major musical movement of the '80s, NDW or Neue Deutsche Welle (German New Wave), which gave the stage to Berlin bands like Ideal, the Neonbabies and UKW, and now provides the raw material for dozens of revival nights.

Gig and show posters

Back in the GDR, where access to Western rock and other popular music was restricted, bands such as Die Puhdys and Rockhaus kept alive a vibrant underground scene. West Berlin attracted a slew of international talent: David Bowie and Iggy Pop both spent stints living at Hauptstrasse 155, while Nick Cave owned a club here, and U2's classic albums *Achtung Baby* (recorded in Berlin) and *Zooropa* both use Zoo Station as a central motif.

Today, hundreds of indie, punk, alternative and gothic bands gig to appreciative audiences. Berlin group Rosenstolz have enjoyed considerable commercial success, thanks to some radio-friendly rock ballads, and are currently one of Germany's top names, along with part-Berlin combo Wir Sind Helden. Local rock veterans Element of Crime, led by singer-turned-author Sven Regener, also recently came back on the scene with a new album, and actress Julia Hummer has bucked the usual formula of the singing soap star by producing a rather well-received debut.

Electronic crossover is a growing by-product of the indie and dance scenes. Former art school 'fake band' (as they describe themselves), Chicks on Speed, and early '90s survivors Stereo Total have attracted cult followings with their pop-punky tunes, while local duo 2raumwohnung's bittersweet but catchy dance melodies have nudged them swiftly into the big time.

Techno & Beyond

Techno may have its roots in Detroit-based house music, but it was from Berlin that it conquered the world, using the huge impetus of the Wende to tap into the simultaneous explosion of the UK rave scene and the popularity of ecstasy. The scene also spawned the famous Love Parade (p11).

The most important proponents of the Berlin techno sound include Dr Motte, cofounder of the Love Parade and 'godfather of techno'; Westbam, who has also had commercial success with housier sounds; Ellen Allien, star act of the bpitch control record label; and Monica Kruse, another 'DJane' who's moved into producing. The Tresor record label, a spin-off of the legendary (but now homeless) club's success, has become an international brand with a full range of merchandising.

Pure techno is being sidelined, however, as more and more splinter genres of electronic music successively percolate into the club scene. House is not as ubiquitous here as it is in the rest of Europe and the USA, but does it dominate hipper spaces such as the Sage Club (p200), with more commercial trance playing to younger clubbers and certain gay crowds. Local boy and international superstar Paul van Dyk still DJs here regularly, but names you'll see slightly more often include Highfish, ED 2000 and André Galluzzi.

DESIGNER LABEL

Innovation is what Berlin is all about, and some record labels here have done just as much as individual artists to create and define new sounds. Compost, Kitty-Yo and Bungalow are all names to watch, but foremost among the trailblazers is !K7, founded in the mid-'80s by 'the mighty' Horst Weidenmüller.

Originally started as Studio !K7, to produce videos about punk, !K7 branched out with the 3Lux and X-Mix series of coordinated digital film clips and DJ mixes, but then abandoned the less popular visual element. The defining moment came in 1995 with the launch of the DJ Kicks series, eclectic compilations mixed by DJs according to their own tastes rather than a prescribed brief; the signing of Austrian duo Kruder and Dorfmeister also marked the label's transition from Detroit-based tech-house to a broader embracing of the underground scene.

Since then the label has been a byword for musical innovation: DJ Kicks reaches a huge international audience, www .k7.com explores Internet broadcasting and !K7 Records is putting out actual artist albums (as distinct to compilations) for the first time. The ambition, scope and anti-mainstream ethos of !K7 makes it one of the best and most challenging independent companies around, and its resolutely leftfield vision is as varied and changeable as Berlin itself.

Unsurprisingly, given Berliners' love of blazing beats, drum and bass also commands a dedicated following, with clubs such as Icon (p203) and Watergate (p202) thundering away every weekend. Indigenous DJs such as Bleed, Metro and Appollo are all well in touch with their audience, but the real highlights are the frequent special guests, who come from as far away as London and San Francisco to play here. Breakbeat is also coming onto the scene, thanks to its popularity in the UK; the charmingly named German-Scandinavian label Shitkatapult provides regular nights at Maria am Ufer (p203), and local boy T.Raumschmiere pops up frequently on Berlin flyers. For those who like it really rough, hardcore grime is on offer at occasional events in Cafe Moskau (p199) and elsewhere.

On the other side of the equation, some of the finest exports of Berlin come from a jazz/ breaks angle (electrojazz and breakbeats, favouring lush grooves, obscure samples and chilled rhythms) – offbeat producers and remix masters Jazzanova are the undisputed champions of the downtempo scene, encompassing artists such as Micatone, Andre Langenfeld, Terranova and Fauna Flash. Head to the Bohannon Club (p199) and look out for Sonarkollektiv Records or the Berlin Lounge compilation (2001, Wagram Music) for a glimpse of this particular corner of Berlin nightlife.

As elsewhere, soul, R&B and black music of all shades is very much in vogue, though few other European cities offer such a thriving reggae-dancehall scene. Such a Sound is among the longest-running of the many sound systems, while Seeed is probably the biggest reggae group in Germany right now and Ohrbooten are coming up fast with their injection of Berliner *Schnauze* (wit) into the rasta vibe. Homegrown hip hop lags behind Cologne and other German cities, but is still a distinct presence, as illustrated on the *Rap City Berlin* DVD.

These days most of the foreign artists moving here are also part of the electronic community. Particularly notable residents include Canadian techno innovator Richie Hawtin, filthy-minded Canadian songstress Peaches, and Chilean minimalist master Ricardo Villalobos. Thanks to this ever-fluid mix of talents and visions, constant experimentation ensures that genres are invented, deconstructed, reinvented and combined here quicker than anyone can even define them, giving rise to anything from laptop-driven sample noise by artists like Funkstörung, Pole and Thomas Fehlmann, to full-on dirty disco house from the likes of Namosh. And just when you thought you'd exhausted all the possibilities, the city still finds ways of trying something new: you can now refresh those tired ears with *Berlin – Soundtrack of the City* (Ampelmann Musik, 2005), a compilation of everyday noises from around town!

LITERATURE

Since its beginnings, Berlin's literary scene has reflected a peculiar blend of provincialism and worldliness. As with the other arts, Berlin didn't emerge as a centre of literature until relatively late, reaching its zenith during the dynamic 1920s. Overall, the city was less a place that generated influential writers than one where they came to meet each other, exchange ideas and be intellectually stimulated.

Today there are several literary organisations and author forums serving the same purpose, including the **Literaturforum im Brechthaus** (Map pp340–1; ☎ 282 2003; Chausseestrasse 125), which awards bursaries and prizes such as the Alfred-Döblin-Preis for unpublished work; the **Literarisches Colloquium Berlin** (☎ 816 9960; Am Sandwerder 5); and **literaturWERKstatt** (Map pp332–3; ☎ 485 2450; Kulturbrauerei), which organises regular large events such as the 2000 'literature train' from Portugal to Russia.

First Words

Berlin's literary history began during the Enlightenment in the late 18th century, an epoch dominated by humanistic ideals. A major author was Gotthold Ephraim Lessing (1729–81), noted for his critical works, fables and tragedies, who wrote the play *Minna von Barnhelm* (1763) in Berlin.

The Romantic period, which grew out of the Enlightenment, was marked by a proliferation of literary salons, where men and women from all walks of life came together to discuss philosophy, politics, art and other subjects. Literary greats working in Berlin during this era included Friedrich and August Wilhelm von Schlegel, and the Romantic poets Achim von Arnim, Clemens Brentano and Heinrich von Kleist.

During the realist movement in the mid-19th century, novels and novellas gained in popularity, thanks to increased interest from the newly established middle class. Historical novels and works critical of society also caught on, such as those by Wilhelm Raabe (1831–1910), who examines various aspects of Berlin life in *Chronik der Sperlingsgasse* (Chronicle of Sperling Lane; 1857). The Berlin society novel was raised to an art form under the pen of Theodor Fontane (1819–98). Most of his works are set around Brandenburg and Berlin, and show both the nobility and the middle class mired in their societal confinements.

Naturalism, a spin-off of realism, took things a step further after 1880, painstakingly recreating the milieu of entire social classes, right down to the local dialect. In Berlin, Gerhart Hauptmann (1862–1946) was a key practitioner of the genre, and many of his plays and novels focus on social injustice and the harsh life of workers – subjects so provocative that several of his premieres ended in riots. An 1892 production of his *Die Weber* (The Weavers), depicting the misery of Silesian weavers, even prompted the Kaiser to cancel his subscription at the Deutsches Theater. In 1912, Hauptmann won the Nobel Prize for Literature.

Modernism & Modernity

In the 1920s, renowned as a period of experimentation and innovation, Berlin became a magnet for writers from around the world. *Berlin Alexanderplatz*, by Alfred Döblin (1878–1957), provided a dose of big-city lights and the underworld during the Weimar Republic, and other notables from this era include the political satirists Kurt Tucholsky (1890–1935) and Erich Kästner (1899–1974). However, many such artists left Germany after the Nazis came to power, and those who stayed often went into 'inner emigration', keeping their mouths shut and working underground, if at all.

In West Berlin, the postwar literary scene didn't revive until the arrival of Günter Grass in the late 1950s. His famous *Die Blechtrommel* (The Tin Drum; 1958) traces recent German history through the eyes of a child who refuses to grow up; written in

TOP FIVE BERLIN BOOKS

- *Berlin Alexanderplatz* (Alfred Döblin; 1929) This stylised meander through the seamy 1920s is still a definitive Berlin text.
- *Goodbye to Berlin* (Christopher Isherwood; 1939) Another brilliant, semiautobiographical perspective on Berlin's 'golden age', seen through the eyes of gay Anglo-American journalist Isherwood.
- *Russendisko* (Russian Disco; Wladimir Kaminer; 2000) This collection of texts from Berlin's favourite Russian immigrant presents a whole host of unusual characters.
- *Boxhagener Platz* (Torsten Schulz; 2005) An unusual comedy whodunnit, set in 1968 Friedrichshain, with an 80-year-old protagonist sniffing out a murderer.
- *Berliner Verhältnisse* (Berlin Circumstances; Raul Zelik; 2005) Tipped as the next great Berlin novel, this is a witty look at the modern life of the city and its 30-somethings.

a variety of styles, the book is an enjoyable but significant retrospective of the Nazi years and the postwar period, and quickly made Grass a household name. He has followed up with an impressive body of novels, plays and poetry, becoming the ninth German to win the Nobel Prize for Literature in 1999. Together with Hans-Magnus Enzensberger, Ingeborg Bachmann and the Swiss writer Max Frisch, Grass paved the way for the political and critical literature that has been dominant since the 1960s.

In the mid-1970s, a segment of the East Berlin literary scene began to detach itself slowly from the party grip. Authors such as Christa Wolf (1929–) and Heiner Müller (1929–95) belonged to loose literary circles that regularly met in private houses. Wolf is one of the best and most controversial East German writers, while Müller had the distinction of being unpalatable in both Germanies; his dense, difficult works include *Der Lohndrücker* (The Man Who Kept Down Wages) and the *Germania* trilogy of plays.

Literary achievement stagnated at first after the Wende, as writers from the east and west began a process of self-examination. Only Heiner Müller and Botho Strauss stood out amid the creative void. In the late 1990s, Berlin's literary scene finally picked up steam. Newer books dealing with the past are characterised not by analytical introspection but by emotionally distanced, nearly grotesque, imagery. Examples here include Thomas Brussig's *Helden wie wir* (Heroes Like Us; 1995) and Ingo Schulze's *Simple Stories* (1998). Bernhard Schlink, a former Berliner now living in the USA, caused perhaps the biggest furore with his novel *Der Vorleser* (The Reader; 1995), which approaches issues of collective and individual responsibility through an unusual relationship between a teenage boy and a woman accused of war crimes.

Current Trends

History is still the focus of much writing about Berlin, fact and fiction, especially in works by outsiders. Interesting recent volumes include Helga Schneider's *The Bonfire of Berlin: A Lost Childhood in Wartime Germany* (2005), one of many wartime memoirs, and Bernd Cailloux's *Das Geschäftsjahr 1968/69* (The Financial Year 1968–69; 2005), an insightful examination of youth revolt and culture during this turbulent period.

On the fictional side, Thomas Brussig continues his engagement with the GDR era in *Wie es leuchtet* (How It Shines; 2004), depicting the fall of the Wall (and the triumph of the 1990 World Cup). Local author Horst Bosetzky spins more populist yarns, turning out a whole series of historical novels and *Krimis* (mysteries) set in his native city; he also co-wrote *Haste schon jehört?* (Have You Heard?; 2005), a highly entertaining collection of strange stories from the corners of Berlin life.

Since 2000, a whole new clutch of cult authors have come to the forefront of the literary scene with novels about Berlin itself. Element of Crime frontman Sven Regener's *Herr Lehmann* (2001), a boozy trawl through the Wende, has already been made into a film, and *Wedding* (2003), by comedy writer Horst Evers, is an entertaining and slightly surreal collection of humorous texts centred on domestic life in Berlin's least popular residential district. Turkish writer Yadé Kara addresses the crucial questions of multiculturalism and identity in *Selam Berlin* (2003), while Raul Zelik's *Berliner Verhältnisse* is already an instant cult classic.

The runaway success story, however, has been the rise of Russian-born author Wladimir Kaminer, whose stranger-than-fiction collections *Russendisko* (2000) and *Schönhauser Allee* (2003) established both the author and his Russian disco parties as a firm part of the Berlin scenescape. With another seven books under his belt, a full line of Russendisko merchandise and a regular column in *Zitty,* Kaminer looks set to be Berlin's next enduring media darling.

Of course not all new writers get – or want – a book deal, and the underground literary scene is as lively as in any other medium. To catch the latest unpublished authors, look out for readings by individuals and groups such as the Surfpoeten (Surf Poets), a collective of young Berlin writers; Kaffee Burger (p200), Kalkscheune (p205) and the Acud arts centre (p204) are favourite locations.

Architecture ▪

Architecture

The definition of a great city is different for each of us. For some it's simply about the many ways it entertains us with its sights, restaurants, shops, bars, theatres and clubs. Others detect urban greatness in a city's impact on the senses – the velocity, the smells, the beauty and the noise all being parts in the grand vision of how it sees itself, and how it wants to be seen. But it's through a careful appraisal of architecture – the buildings, public spaces and streets themselves – that a city speaks with its most intimate voice of the secrets it holds. How a city is built reveals much of its soul.

After visiting Berlin in 1891, Mark Twain remarked, 'Berlin is the newest city I've ever seen'. What was new to Twain then was an

energetic colossus, thrust into greatness by the madness of construction following the founding of the German empire in 1871. While still preserving the grandeur of the palaces and regal estates wrought by centuries of Prussian rulers, this new Berlin was built to foment revolutions in technology and learning, and to exploit the successes of its middle class merchants and manufacturers. From a hotchpotch of loosely affiliated villages, Berlin became, almost overnight in terms of its history, *the* powerhouse of European endeavour and expression.

Then came WWII, near obliteration and the horrifying bifurcation into East and West. What was so quickly laid to waste in the 'counter-blitzkrieg' of the victorious powers was (not quite as quickly) rebuilt from the rubble, with little else in mind than to restore the hopes of Berliners and once again to provide them with a sense of civility. This massive reconstruction, naturally, took on decidedly different forms of expression in the Allied zones and in the 'worker's paradise' being touted in the socialist East. The contrast between western European sensibilities and Moscow's penchant for bombast could not have been made more evident.

Then, following reunification, Berlin again hurled its prodigious energies into a veritable orgy of new construction to signal to the world that it was poised to reposition itself at the centre of European commerce, thought and creativity. The removal of the Berlin Wall quite literally opened up vast areas of empty space that hadn't been touched since WWII. Large sections of the historic centre were a blank canvas awaiting the visions of architects, urban planners and futurists.

And so Berlin became a virtual laboratory of architectural possibilities, as evidenced by the enormity of the Potsdamer Platz and Government Quarter undertakings, and the return of diplomatic courtiers and corporate headquarters. Berlin has indeed become an overnight showcase for the world's elite architects – IM Pei, Frank Gehry and Renzo Piano among them. Their corporate palaces and governmental centres rose to signal that Berlin was once again the heart, soul and primary engine of the nation and its people.

MODEST BEGINNINGS

Berlin, as Mark Twain implies, is essentially a creation of modern times, despite its medieval roots. Very little survives from the days of its founding in the early 13th century, although the rebuilt Nikolaikirche (Church of St Nicholas; p94), Berlin's oldest church, offers a good introduction to medieval building techniques. Excavations revealed that it has Romanesque origins, but when the Gothic style became all the rage, it was converted to a three-nave hall church, topped by a pair of slender spires.

Not far behind in age are the Marienkirche (Church of St Mary's; p93), first mentioned in 1294, and the Franziskaner Klosterkirche (Franciscan Abbey Church; p93), although the latter only survives as a picturesque ruin. All three churches were built in a style called *Backsteingotik* (Brick Gothic) in reference to the red bricks used in their construction. A hint of residential medieval architecture survives in the pint-sized Kolk (p137) neighbourhood in Spandau, with its half-timbered houses and section of town wall.

Not many traces remain from the Renaissance, which reached Berlin in the early 16th century. The single most important structure from that period, the Berliner Stadtschloss (Berlin City Palace; 1540), was demolished by the GDR government in 1951. Thankfully, the hideous Palast der Republik (Palace of the Republic; p91) built in its place is being torn down as well, paving the way for a possible reconstruction of the historic royal palace.

Renaissance survivors include the Jagdschloss Grunewald (p146), the Zitadelle Spandau (p138) and the ornately gabled Ribbeckhaus (p82), which is the oldest extant residential building in Berlin from this period.

GOING FOR BAROQUE

Berlin's first architectural heyday was in the mid-17th century. This was the age of baroque, a style merging architecture, sculpture, ornamentation and painting into a single *Gesamtkunstwerk* (complete work of art). In northern Germany it retained a formal and precise bent, never quite reaching the exuberance achieved further south.

The emergence of baroque architecture is linked to the period of absolutism following the Thirty Years' War (1618–48), when central European feudal rulers asserted their power by building grand residences. In Berlin, this role fell to Great Elector Friedrich Wilhelm, who brought in an army of architects, engineers and artists to systematically expand the city. When they were done, Berlin had grown three new quarters – the Dorotheenstadt, Friedrichstadt and Friedrichswerder – a fortified town wall, and a grand tree-lined boulevard known as Unter den Linden (p73).

His father may have laid the groundwork, but Berlin didn't truly acquire the stature of an exalted residence until Friedrich III came to power in 1688. His appetite for grand structures only grew bolder after he had himself crowned *King* Friedrich I in 1701, and during his reign Berlin gained two major baroque buildings. In 1695, shortly before his death, Johann Arnold Nering began constructing the Zeughaus (armoury), which now houses the Deutsches Historisches Museum (DHM; German Historical Museum; p74), and the Schloss Lietzenburg, a summer palace for Friedrich's wife, Sophie Charlotte, which was renamed Schloss Charlottenburg (Charlottenburg Palace; p110) after her death in 1705. Johann Friedrich Eosander then expanded the latter structure into a three-wing palace inspired by Versailles, topping it with a domed central tower.

But across town, construction of the Zeughaus proved to be fraught with obstacles. After Nering's death, Martin Grünberg took over, but had to resign in 1699. The baton then passed to Andreas Schlüter, who added the celebrated masks of dying warriors to the central courtyard with remarkable effect. Schlüter, however, turned out to be more skilled as a sculptor than as an architect, for part of his structure collapsed, and

IM Pei Bau (p74)

41

the whole project subsequently passed over to Jean de Bodt. The square, two-storey structure was finally completed in 1706.

Since 1999, the Zeughaus has been undergoing a major modernisation, which has seen the return of a dramatic glass-and-steel roof covering the so-called Schlüter courtyard (the original was shattered in 1945). From here a subterranean walkway leads to the museum's modern extension, the IM Pei Bau (IM Pei Building; p74), named after its Chinese-American architect. Fronted by a transparent, spiralling staircase shaped like a snail shell, it is a harmonious interplay of glass, natural stone and light, and is an excellent example of Pei's muted postmodernist approach.

Meanwhile, back in the early 18th century, two formidable churches were taking shape south of the Zeughaus on Gendarmenmarkt, the central square of Friedrichstadt, and the home of immigrant Huguenots. These were the Deutscher Dom (German Cathedral; p78) by Martin Grünberg, and the Französischer Dom (French Cathedral; p78) by Louis Cayart – the latter modelled on the Huguenots' destroyed mother church in Charenton. Both churches received their splendid domes in 1785, courtesy of Carl von Gontard.

Friedrich I's son, Friedrich Wilhelm I, wasn't much into fiddling with Berlin's skyline. He was a pragmatic fellow who loved soldiers more than art and architecture, and thus saw nothing wrong with converting sections of Tiergarten park (p103) and the Lustgarten (Pleasure Garden; p81) into military exercise grounds. His most lasting architectural legacy though, was a new city wall, which hemmed in Berlin until 1860.

Under the rule of his son, Friedrich II – better known as Frederick the Great – Berlin finally achieved a measure of cultural and political importance. When not busy on the battlefield, 'Old Fritz' (or 'Old Freddy'), as he was also known, sought greatness through building and embracing the ideals of the Enlightenment. He dreamed of creating a 'Forum Fridericianum', a cluster of cultural venues in the heart of town. Together with his childhood friend, architect Georg Wenzeslaus von Knobelsdorff, he hatched plans for the master design, which blended late baroque and neoclassical elements in a style called 'Frederician Rococo'.

Although never completed, the beautiful ensemble included the Staatsoper Unter den Linden (State Opera House; p77), an early neoclassical design; the Sankt-Hedwigs-Kathedrale (St-Hedwig-Cathedral; p77), inspired by Rome's Pantheon; the Alte Königliche Bibliothek (Old Royal Library; p73), a baroque confection; and the Humboldt Universität (Humboldt University; p75), originally a palace for the king's brother Heinrich. Knobelsdorff also added the Neuer Flügel (New Wing; p112) to Schloss Charlottenburg, although Schloss Sanssouci (Sanssouci Palace; p271) in Potsdam is considered his crowning achievement.

After Knobelsdorff's death in 1753, two architects continued in his tradition: Philipp Daniel Boumann – who designed Schloss Bellevue (Bellevue Palace; p102) for Frederick's youngest brother, August Ferdinand – and Carl von Gontard, who added the domed towers to the Deutscher Dom and Französischer Dom.

PRUSSIA'S BUILDING MASTER: KARL FRIEDRICH SCHINKEL

No single architect stamped his imprimatur on the face of Berlin more than Karl Friedrich Schinkel (1781–1841). The most prominent and mature practitioner of German neoclassicism, Schinkel was born in Neuruppin in Prussia, and learned his craft under the father-and-son team of Friedrich and David Gilly at the Baukademie (Building Academy) in Berlin. He enriched his formal education with a two-year trip to Italy (1803–05) to study the classics up close, only to return to a Prussia caught in the grip of Napoleonic occupation. Unable to practise his art, he scraped by as a romantic painter, and furniture and set designer.

Schinkel's career took off as soon as the French exited Berlin. His job as a Prussian civil servant took him from humble surveyor all the way to chief building director for the entire state. He travelled tirelessly throughout the land, designing buildings, supervising construction and even developing principles for the protection of historical monuments.

His travels in Italy notwithstanding, Schinkel actually looked to classical Greece for inspiration. From 1810 to 1840 his vision very much defined the look of Prussia, even garnering Berlin the nickname 'Athens on the Spree'. In his buildings Schinkel strove for the perfect balance between functionality and beauty, achieved through clear lines, symmetry and a masterful sense for aesthetics. Driven to the end, Schinkel fell into a coma in 1840 and died the following year in Berlin.

THE SCHINKEL TOUCH

If Frederick the Great had begun to dabble in neoclassicism, the style would reach its pinnacle during the long reign of his great-nephew, Friedrich Wilhelm III. A reaction against baroque flamboyance, it brought a return to classical design elements such as columns, pediments, domes and restrained ornamentation that had been popular throughout antiquity.

No single style has had a more lasting effect on Berlin's cityscape than neoclassicism, thanks in large part to one man: Karl Friedrich Schinkel, arguably Prussia's greatest architect (see the boxed text, opposite). Schinkel's first commission was the Mausoleum (p112), built for Queen Luise in Schloss Charlottenburg's park, although he didn't really make his mark until 1818, with the Neue Wache (New Guardhouse; p76), originally an army guardhouse and now a war memorial.

Nearby, the Altes Museum (Old Museum; p80), with its colonnaded front, is considered Schinkel's most mature work. Other neoclassical masterpieces include the magnificent Schauspielhaus (now the Konzerthaus; p79) on Gendarmenmarkt, and the small Neuer Pavillon (New Pavilion; p112), in the palace garden of Schloss Charlottenburg. Schinkel's one main departure from neoclassicism is the Friedrichswerdersche Kirche (p75), which was inspired by a popular Gothic Revival in early-19th-century England.

After Schinkel's death several of his disciples kept his style alive, notably Friedrich August Stüler, who built the Neues Museum (New Museum; p81), the Alte Nationalgalerie (Old National Gallery; p79) and the Matthäuskirche (Church of St Matthew; p108).

THE HOBRECHT PLAN

The onset of industrialisation in the middle of the 19th century saw Berlin's population explode, as hundreds of thousands flocked to the capital city in hope of improving their lot in the factories. Between 1850 and 1900, the number of inhabitants surged from 511,000 to 2.7 million.

Berlin quickly began bursting at the seams. To combat the acute housing shortage and improve canals and other infrastructure, an 1862 commission, helmed by chief city planner James Hobrecht, drew up plans for an expanded city layout. It called for two circular ring roads, bisected by diagonal roads radiating in all directions from the centre – much like the spokes of a wheel. The real estate between the roads was broken down into large lots and sold to speculators and developers. In a move uncharacteristic of Prussian bureaucracy, the commission imposed practically no building codes to regulate construction; the only restrictions called for building heights not to exceed 22m and for courtyards to measure at least 5.34 sq metres so that fire trucks could turn around.

Ruthless developers pounced on such lax regulations faster than a lion on a wounded hyena. The result of the Hobrecht plan was the uncontrolled proliferation of *Mietskasernen* – sprawling tenements, four or five storeys high, wrapped around as many as five inner courtyards. Yes, they did provide shelter for the incoming masses, but only by cramming entire families into tiny, dark and depressing flats. Sometimes these even doubled as woodshops, sewing studios and other small businesses. Sure, it vastly improved Berlin's transportation and sewer systems, but the Hobrecht plan's principal legacy was the ring of working-class districts with high-density housing (such as Prenzlauer Berg, Kreuzberg and Friedrichshain) that almost encircled central Berlin by 1900.

THE GRÜNDERZEIT

The founding of the German empire in 1871 under Kaiser Wilhelm I ushered in the so-called *Gründerzeit* (Foundation Years), which architecturally went hand in hand with Historicism. This retro approach to architecture merely recycled earlier styles, sometimes even blending several together in an aesthetic hotchpotch called Eclecticism. Public buildings from this period reflect the confidence of the new Germany and tend towards the ostentatious. The most prominent examples of Historicism are the Reichstag (p102) by Paul Wallot, and the Berliner Dom (Berlin Cathedral; p80) by Julius Raschdorff, both in neo-Renaissance style; Franz Schwechten's

Anhalter Bahnhof (p122, now ruined) and the Kaiser-Wilhelm-Gedächtniskirche (Memorial Church; p115, also ruined), both examples of neo-Romanesque; and the neobaroque Staatsbibliothek zu Berlin (State Library; p77) and Bodemuseum (p80) by Ernst von Ihne. The Theater des Westens (p209), meanwhile, takes even Eclecticism to new heights.

It was Otto von Bismarck who turned his attention to the residential development of the western city, and Charlottenburg in particular. He widened the Kurfürstendamm (p113), lining it and its side streets with attractive townhouses for the middle classes. Like the *Mietskasernen*, they were four or five storeys high and wrapped around a central courtyard, but there the similarities ended. Courtyards were large, allowing light to enter the roomy flats, some of which had as many as 10 rooms. These days, some harbour charming old-Berlin-style B&Bs, such as the Hotel-Pension Funk (p258) or Hotel Askanischer Hof (p257).

Berlin's upper crust, meanwhile, sought refuge in the fashionable villa colonies of Grunewald and Dahlem, far away from the claustrophobic centre. Bankers, academics, scientists, entrepreneurs and plenty of famous folk – including writers Gerhart Hauptmann and Lion Feuchtwanger – were among those attracted to Berlin's own 'Beverly Hills'.

THE BIRTH OF MODERNISM

The *Gründerzeit* was not a time of experimentation, but a few progressive architects still managed to make their mark, mostly in industrial and commercial design. On Leipziger Platz, Alfred Messel created a prototype of the department store in 1906 with the Warenhaus Wertheim (destroyed in WWII); then the largest such store in Europe, it had huge display windows, classical lines and a spacious interior layout.

The main pre-WWI trailblazer, though, was Peter Behrens (1868–1940) who is sometimes called the 'father of modern architecture'. Elements characterising modernism include a simplification of forms, the almost complete lack of ornamentation, and a preference for glass, concrete and steel as main building materials.

Le Corbusier, Walter Gropius and Ludwig Mies van der Rohe all worked in Behrens' office at one time or another. From 1907 to 1914, he worked as artistic consultant for the AEG electrical company in Berlin. His most famous building is the 1909 AEG Turbinenhalle (Map pp330–1; AEG Turbine Factory; Huttenstrasse 12-16, Tiergarten), an airy, functional and light-flooded 'industrial cathedral' with exposed structural beams. It is essentially a frill-free reinterpretation of Schinkel's classical lines, replacing stone columns with steel trusses, and an ornamented triangular gable with an unadorned polygonal one. The building is considered an icon of early industrial architecture.

THE WEIMAR YEARS

WWI put creativity on hold, but it flourished all the more during the years of the Weimar Republic (the 1920s), a dizzying era of unbridled experimentation in nearly all areas of society. The spirit of innovation lured some of the finest avant-garde architects to Berlin, including Bruno and Max Taut, Le Corbusier, Ludwig Mies van der Rohe, Erich Mendelsohn, Hans Poelzig and Hans Scharoun. In 1923 they formed an architectural association called Der Ring (The Ring). Members were united not by a single architectural vision, but by the desire to break with traditional aesthetics (especially the backward-looking Historicism) and to create a modern, streamlined and more functional – yet human-scale – approach to building.

Their theories were put into practice when Berlin experienced another housing shortage. With the encouragement of chief city planner, Martin Wagner, Ring members devised a new form of social housing called *Siedlungen* (housing estates). Avoiding the mistakes made with the claustrophobic *Mietskasernen*, these large residential developments went far beyond providing a roof over people's heads. Many were quasi-self–contained colonies, incorporating gardens, schools, shops and other communal areas which promoted social interaction.

Together with Bruno Taut, Wagner himself designed the Hufeisensiedlung (Horseshoe Colony; p141) in southern Neukölln, an eye-catching horseshoe-shaped structure wrapped around a central garden. Other famous *Siedlungen* were the garden-like Onkel-Toms-Hütte

(1926–32; Argentinische Allee, Zehlendorf), near the Grunewald forest; the Siemensstadt (1929–31), near Spandau; and the Weisse Stadt (1929–30), in the northwestern district of Reinickendorf. Taut's Flamensiedlung (Flemish Colony; p133), in Prenzlauer Berg, is also an outgrowth of this approach to residential living.

In non-residential architecture, various styles flourished. Erich Mendelsohn was one of the leading exponents of architectural expressionism, which takes an organic, sculptural approach. Among his finest works is a solar observatory, the Einsteinturm (Einstein Tower; 1924) in Potsdam, which is characterised by its dynamic, flowing structure. Mendelsohn's other major Berlin commission, the Universum Kino (Universum Cinema; 1928), today's Schaubühne Theater (p212), marked his transition to the more linear 'form follows function' approach of the Neue Sachlichkeit (New Objectivity) movement that emerged in the mid-1920s.

Other good examples of this latter style include Hans Poelzig's masterpiece, the 1931 Haus des Rundfunks (House of Broadcasting; Masurenallee 8-14, Charlottenburg) and Emil Fahrenkamp's Shell-Haus (p109). Also working in Berlin was Alfred Grenander, who, as head architect of the Berlin U-Bahn system, designed many of the city's beautiful stations, including the ones at Krumme Lanke (1929) and Onkel-Toms-Hütte (1929), both in Zehlendorf.

NAZI MONUMENTALISM

Modernist architecture had its legs cut out from under itself as soon as Hitler came to power in 1933. The new regime immediately shut down the Bauhaus School, one of the most influential forces in 20th-century architecture. Founded by Walter Gropius in 1919, it had moved to Berlin from Dessau only in 1932. Many of its visionary teachers, including Gropius, Mies van der Rohe, Wagner and Mendelsohn, went into exile in the USA where they found a more welcoming climate for their visions.

Back in Berlin, the Hitler era ushered in a period of architectural monumentalism – basically an inflated reinterpretation of neoclassicism. In 1937, he appointed Albert Speer as chief architect and put him in charge of redesigning Berlin into the 'Welthauptstadt Germania', the future capital of the Reich. At its core would be two major intersecting thoroughfares, the North–South axis stretching from the Reichstag to Tempelhof, and the East–West axis connecting the Brandenburg Gate (Brandenburger Tor) with Theodor-Heuss-Platz (then Adolf-Hitler-Platz) in Charlottenburg. At the top of the North–South axis, near today's Reichstag, Speer planned the Grosse Halle des Volkes (Great Hall of the People), which would have accommodated 150,000 people and been topped by a dome measuring 250m in diameter.

The axes and the hall were never realised, but a number of surviving Nazi-era buildings offer a hint of what Berlin might have looked like had history taken a different turn. One of the most prominent Third Reich relics is the Olympic area in western Charlottenburg. Walter and Werner March designed the coliseum-like Olympiastadion (p118), along with the adjacent Maifeld (p118). Another major Third Reich architect was Ernst Sagebiel, whose legacy survives in the chunky Reichsluftfahrtsministerium (Reich Aviation Ministry; p124), now home to the Federal Ministry of Finance, and the Flughafen Tempelhof (Tempelhof Airport; p124), once the largest airport in Europe. Heinrich Wolff designed the Reichsbank (p75; Werderscher Markt, Mitte) which, along with a modern extension by the young design team of Thomas Müller and Ivan Reimann, now houses the Federal Foreign Office.

In the Diplomatenviertel (Diplomatic Quarter; p106) south of the Tiergarten park – another Speer idea – the giant embassies of two Nazi allies also reflect the pompous grandeur in vogue at the time. The 1942 Italian Embassy (Map p346; Hiroshimastrasse 1) occupies its restored historical digs built by Friedrich Hetzelt, Hermann Göring's favourite architect. Inspired by the Palazzo della Consulta in Rome, it is an interpretation of a Renaissance palace whose bombast is only slightly tempered by the flamingo-pink paint job.

Across the street, the 1940 Japanese Embassy (Map p346; Tiergartenstrasse 24-27) looks very much like a foreboding fortress. It is almost an exact replica of the Nazi-era original by Ludwig Moshamer. Only the elliptical structure along Hiroshimastrasse, which houses a conference room, is a nod to modern architecture. The golden sun above the main entrance symbolises imperial Japan.

The bombing raids and street fighting of WWII destroyed or damaged about half of Berlin, leaving around 25 million cubic metres of rubble, most of which was cleared by the so-called *Trümmerfrauen* (rubble women). A memorial in their honour stands in front of the Rotes Rathaus (p94). Many of Berlin's modest hills are in fact *Trümmerberge* (rubble mountains), piled up from wartime debris and then reborn as parks and recreational areas. The best-known ones are the Teufelsberg (p119) in Wilmersdorf, and Mont Klamott in the Volks-park Friedrichshain (p130). Among the first new postwar structures was the Sowjetisches Ehrenmal (Soviet War Memorial; p143) in Tiergarten park, built with red marble reputedly scavenged from Hitler's destroyed Reichskanzlei (Reich Chancellery) on Vossstrasse.

THE DIVIDED CITY

After WWII, Berlin developed into two separate cities long before being physically sepa-rated by the Wall. The clash of ideologies and economic systems between the Western Allies and the Soviet Union also transferred into the architectural arena. East German architecture reflected that country's new Moscow-oriented, socialist political order, in stark contrast to the modernist aspirations of the democratic West.

EAST BERLIN

The most prominent architect in the GDR was Hermann Henselmann, the mastermind of the Karl-Marx-Allee (called Stalinallee until 1961; p129) in Friedrichshain. Built between 1952 and 1965, it became East Berlin's first 'socialist boulevard', and was supposed to reflect East German innovation and ingenuity. In reality, its design is doubly derivative – having been directly inspired by the monumental *Zuckerbäckerstil* (wedding-cake style) of which Stalin was such a fan – and, far from innovative, the Zuckerbäckerstil was merely a socialist reinter-pretation of good old-fashioned neoclassicism. The Russische Botschaft (Russian Embassy; p77) on Unter den Linden is another example of this preposterous 'neo-neoclassicism'.

After Stalin's death in 1961, even East Berlin slowly began embracing modern architec-ture, most notably on Alexanderplatz (p91), which had been devastated in WWII. Based on a carefully crafted 'socialist master plan', the square was enlarged, turned into a pedestrian zone, and developed into East Berlin's commercial hub and architectural showcase. The only prewar buildings restored rather than demolished were Peter Behrens' Berolinahaus (1930) and the Alexanderhaus (1932) just north of the railway tracks.

Other significant buildings orbiting Alexanderplatz include Henselmann's **Haus des Lehrers** (House of Teachers; p91) and the Kongresshalle (Congress Hall; 1964), now joined into the Ber-lin Congress Centre. Henselmann also drafted plans for the Fernsehturm (TV Tower; p92).

The behemoth parallel to the square's northeastern flank, is the 220m-long 1970 Haus der Elektroindustrie (Map pp340–1; House of the Electrical Industry). Completely reno-vated, it now serves as the Berlin seat of the Federal Ministry for the Environment, Nature Conservation and Nuclear Safety. Patches of colour and large letters spelling out a quote from Alfred Döblin's novel *Berlin Alexanderplatz* enliven the façade.

WEST BERLIN

In West Berlin, by contrast, urban planners sought to eradicate any hint of the monumen-talism so closely associated with the Nazi period. Instead, the goal was to rebuild the city in a modern, rhythmic and organic manner, and to create wide-open spaces as a metaphor for a free society.

A classic example of this approach is the 1954–57 Hansaviertel (Hansa Quarter; Map pp330–1), built in an area northwest of Tiergarten park which had been obliterated by wartime bombing. It's a loosely-structured leafy neighbourhood, with 3500 residents in a mix of high-rises and single-family homes. The Hansaplatz U-Bahn station anchors the area's commercial centre, along with a church, school and library. The Hansaviertel was the product of an architectural exposition, the Internationale Bauausstellung, or 'Interbau', held in 1957. Attracting 54 renowned architects from 13 countries – including Gropius, Luciano

Baldessari, Alvar Aalto and Le Corbusier – it represents the pinnacle of architectural vision in the 1950s.

Interbau also produced several interesting structures outside the Hansaviertel, including the Haus der Kulturen der Welt (House of World Cultures; p100), originally a congress hall, designed by Hugh A Stubbins as the American contribution to the exposition; and the Corbusierhaus (p117), a giant apartment complex of unflinching angularity by the French architect Le Corbusier, who thought of a house as a 'machine for living'.

Haus der Kulturen der Welt (p100)

Meanwhile, in another wartime wasteland southeast of Tiergarten park, a further major development was beginning to take shape: the Kulturforum (p106). This cluster of museums and concert halls was part of Hans Scharoun's vision of a cultural belt stretching from Museumsinsel to Schloss Charlottenburg. Of course the construction of the Berlin Wall in 1961 put an end to such visionary plans, and rather than being a central link between the eastern and western city halves, the Kulturforum found itself rubbing up against the concrete barrier.

Construction proceeded nevertheless, with Scharoun's Philharmonie (p109) the first piece in the Kulturforum puzzle to be completed in 1963. This amazing concert hall is considered a masterpiece of sculptural, expressionistic modernism. Like many of Scharoun's buildings it was essentially designed from the inside out, adapting the façade to the shape of the hall rather than the other way around. Scharoun also drew up the plans for the Staatsbibliothek zu Berlin (State Library; p109) on Potsdamer Strasse, and the Kammermusiksaal (Chamber Music Hall; p109), but didn't live to see their completion.

Mies van der Rohe's Neue Nationalgalerie (New National Gallery; p108) also has a commanding presence within the Kulturforum. This temple-like art museum takes the shape of a 50m-long glass-and-steel cube perching on a raised granite podium. Its coffered rib-steel roof seems to defy gravity with the help of eight steel pillars and a floor-to-ceiling glass front.

PARALLEL DEVELOPMENTS

Alexanderplatz and the Kulturforum may have been celebrated prestige projects, but both Berlins also had to deal with more pragmatic issues, such as the need for inexpensive, modern housing to accommodate growing populations. This led to several urban planning mistakes on both sides of the Wall in the 1970s and '80s, most notably in the birth of soulless, monotonous satellite cities that could accommodate tens of thousands of people.

In West Berlin, Gropius drew up the plans for the Grosssiedlung Berlin-Buckow in southern Neukölln, which was renamed Gropiusstadt (p141) after his death. The Märkisches Viertel in Reinickendorf, northwest Berlin, is another such development. On the other side of the Wall, Marzahn, Hohenschönhausen and Hellersdorf became three new city districts consisting almost entirely of high-rise *Plattenbauten*. This fast and inexpensive building technique involved precast concrete slabs and was much favoured throughout East Germany. Although equipped with modern conveniences such as private baths and lifts, these giant developments suffered from a paucity of open space, green areas and leisure facilities. They were indeed the ultimate 'machines for living'.

CRITICAL RECONSTRUCTION

While giant housing developments mushroomed on the peripheries, much of the central city was suffering from decades of decay and neglect. This was especially true of neighbourhoods languishing in the shadow of the Berlin Wall, and none more so than Kreuzberg. To kick-start revitalisation in these areas the Berlin Senate decided, in 1978, to hold another international building exposition and competition – the Internationale Bauausstellung (BA).

This time there would be a shift away from demolition and redevelopment to a blending of two architectural principles: the first was 'careful urban renewal', which would focus on preserving, renovating and reusing existing buildings; the second was to be 'critical reconstruction', which meant filling vacant lots with new buildings that reinterpret the traditional layout or design of surrounding structures. The goal was to reknit the urban fabric that had been destroyed by Speer's megalomania, wartime bombing and poor postwar planning.

Under the leadership of Josef Paul Kleihues, the royalty of international architecture descended upon Berlin to take up the challenges of Interbau. Their ranks included Rob Krier, James Stirling, Rem Koolhaas, Charles Moore, Aldo Rossi and Arata Isozaki, as well as Germans such as OM Ungers, Gottfried Böhm, Axel Schultes and Hans Kollhoff. Collectively, they introduced a new aesthetic to Berlin, moving away from the harsh modernist look and replacing it with a more diverse, decorative and innovative postmodernist approach. Time magazine called it 'the most ambitious showcase of world architecture in this generation'.

One area that got particular attention was the Fraenkelufer in Kreuzberg, where Hinrich and Inken Baller created innovative apartment buildings inspired by Art Nouveau and expressionism. Elsewhere, a more austere, neo-rationalist approach ruled, especially in Aldo Rossi's residential buildings at Wilhelmstrasse 36, and on Rauchstrasse south of Tiergarten park.

Interestingly, reconstruction and restoration were also a focus in East Berlin. In Prenzlauer Berg, which had been as neglected as Kreuzberg, Husemannstrasse (p131) was seriously spruced up in the '80s, and looked better than ever in its newly sparkling, late-19th-century glory. Around the same time, construction began of the Nikolaiviertel (Nikolai Quarter; p94), a small medieval 'theme park', cobbled together from original and reconstructed historical buildings and anchored by the Nikolaikirche. All this activity – in both city halves – was at least in part motivated by Berlin's 750th birthday celebrations in 1987.

THE NEW BERLIN

Reunification presented Berlin with both the challenge and the opportunity to redefine itself architecturally. The tearing down of the Wall opened up huge gashes of empty space where the two city halves would have to be physically rejoined. Critical reconstruction again became the guiding principle. In rejection of anything too clever, avant-garde or monumental, city planning director Hans Stimmann imposed numerous design parameters – on things such as building height and façade materials – which left even the most imaginative architects hamstrung. New development was to seek inspiration in the classic Prussian tradition, not go bold or make a clean cut with the past.

POTSDAMER PLATZ

The biggest and grandest of the post-1990 Berlin developments is Potsdamer Platz (p103), a complete reinterpretation of the famous historic square that was the bustling heart of the city until WWII. From an ugly wasteland created by the Wall has sprung a dynamic urban quarter swarming with shoppers, revellers, travellers, cineasts, diners, suits and residents.

An international roster of renowned architects collaborated on Potsdamer Platz, which is divided into DaimlerCity (p105), the Sony Center (p105) and the Beisheim Center (p104). In keeping with the restrictive tenets of critical reconstruction, the master plan follows the layout of a 'European city', complete with a dense irregular street grid, squares, and medium-height structures. An exception is the trio of high-rises facing the intersection of Potsdamer Strasse and Ebertstrasse, which form a kind of visual gateway. The result is pleasant, if a bit contrived, but definitely not the kind of bold 21st-century architecture that makes you go 'wow!'

The Sony Center, with its dramatic tented plaza and svelte glass skin, is among the more successful structures here. Its futuristic feel contrasts sharply with the more subdued Kollhoff-Haus opposite. Clad in a mantle of reddish-brown clinker bricks on a greyish-green granite base, its height descends in two steps away from the intersection. It's attractive, but still a bit on the dull side.

Other architects involved in redeveloping Potsdamer Platz included Arata Isozaki, who created the waffle-patterned, coffee-coloured Berliner Volksbank; Rafael Moneo, who conceived the sleek, minimalist Grand Hyatt Hotel (p256); and Richard Rogers (best known for the Centre Pompidou in Paris), who planned the Potsdamer Platz Arkaden (p236), a three-storey shopping mall. Engulfed by all these modern structures stands the sole survivor from the original Potsdamer Platz, the Weinhaus Huth (p106).

Even less imagination has been poured into the adjacent Leipziger Platz (p105), where critical reconstruction has been anything but critical: the square's reincarnation follows the original octagon to a tee, lining it with nondescript office blocks which are little more approachable and inviting than a prison.

PARISER PLATZ

Pariser Platz (p76) experienced a similar fate as that of Potsdamer Platz. Reconstructed from the ground up, it is a formal square framed by bank buildings and embassies with homogeneous façades that project an introspective rather than open flair.

At least two of the architects had the last laugh here though, by putting all their outrageous creativity on the inside. The DZ Bank (2000), by California-based deconstructivist Frank Gehry, for instance, conceals a vast atrium as bizarre as a sci-fi movie behind a bland mantle. At its centre floats an enormous free-form stainless-steel sculpture – a fish? a horse's head? – harbouring a conference room. Daylight streams in through the curving glass roof, with its steel girders as intricate as a spider's web.

Michael Wolford's British Embassy (2000) – in its historic location with the main entrance facing Wilhelmstrasse – comes close to matching Gehry's whimsy. Wolford has broken up what would be a monotonous sandstone façade with a protruding blue glass cube and purple cylinder, both hinting at the colourful and art-filled interior.

The newest arrival on the square, the Akademie der Künste (2005) by Günter Behnisch, is the only Pariser Platz building with a glass front. Behnisch had to fight tooth and nail to get approval for this departure from the critical reconstruction rule that all of the square's façades had to be clad in yellow or grey stone. He argued that, as the square's only public building, transparency was key; the building had to feel open and inviting, and it does.

The last gap on Pariser Platz is being filled by the US Embassy, which plans on opening for business in 2008. The design, by the Los Angeles firm of Moore, Ruble and Yudell, seems to stay closely within the trajectory of critical reconstruction with its simple stone façade facing the square.

Flanking the Brandenburg Gate, the Haus Liebermann and Haus Sommer by Kleihues closely resemble Stüler's original 19th-century structures, while the Adlon Hotel is practically an exact copy of the 1907 original.

DIPLOMATENVIERTEL

Some of Berlin's most exciting new architecture is clustered in the revitalised Diplomatenviertel (Diplomatic Quarter; p106) on the southern edge of Tiergarten park, where many countries rebuilt their embassies on their historic pre-WWII sites.

One of the most extravagant structures here is the 2000 Austrian Embassy (Map p346; Stauffenbergstrasse 1), by Viennese architect Hans Hollein. It consists of three linked, but visually very different, components: a curved front building, clad in patina-green copper; a terracotta entrance with an overhanging roof; and a grey concrete cube. Next door, the 2001 Egyptian Embassy (Map p346; Stauffenbergstrasse 6-7), with its shiny, reddish-brown façade ornamented with scenes from ancient Egypt, exudes an almost temple-like dignity.

The 2000 Mexican Embassy (Map pp338–9; Klingelhöferstrasse 3) is an avant-garde work by Teodoro González de Léon and Francisco Serrano. Two soaring, slanted curtains of slender concrete pillars protect the glass front and main entrance. The building doubles as a cultural institute.

Just north of here, the 1999 Nordic Embassies (Map pp338–9; Rauchstrasse 1) are among the most outstanding architectural contributions to the New Berlin. It's a compact compound uniting the representative offices of Denmark, Sweden, Finland, Iceland and

Norway behind one dramatic turquoise façade made of copper lamellas. Although forming a harmonious whole, each country occupies its own building designed to reflect its cultural identity. The complex is entered through the Felleshus, the only building shared by all embassies, which is also used for cultural events.

REGIERUNGSVIERTEL

More cutting-edge architecture awaits in the northeastern corner of the Tiergarten, where Germany's political power is concentrated in its new Regierungsviertel (federal government quarter; p100). Arranged in linear east–west fashion are the Bundeskanzleramt (Federal Chancellery; p100), the Paul-Löbe-Haus (p101) and the Marie-Elisabeth-Lüders-Haus (p101). Together with the Kanzlergarten (chancellor's garden p100), the Kanzlerpark (chancellor's park) and the Spreebogenpark (p103) they form the *Band des Bundes* (Ribbon of the Federation), which represents a symbolic linking of the formerly divided city halves.

Overlooking all these shiny new structures is the Reichstag (p102), which received a complete makeover courtesy of Lord Norman Foster, completed in 1999. Its crowning glory is, quite literally, a modern high-tech glass cupola, with a ramp spiralling up around a central mirrored cone. With this dazzling addition, Foster managed to inject levity into this mammoth building burdened with a rather weighty history. It is now one of Berlin's most beloved landmarks and tourist magnets.

North of here, is Berlin's first-ever central railway station, the brand-new Hauptbahnhof (Map pp330–1; Invalidenstrasse, Tiergarten), completed just in time for the 2006 soccer World Cup. Designed by the Hamburg firm of Gerkan, Marg und Partner, it is one of the largest railway stations in Europe. A glass-and-steel roof allows natural light to flood the main hall, which is flanked by two 46m-high arched structures.

MORE ARCHITECTURAL TROPHIES

In Kreuzberg, the deconstructivist Jüdisches Museum (p125) by Daniel Libeskind, is among the most daring and provocative structures in the New Berlin. With its irregular, zigzagging floor plan and shiny zinc skin pierced by gash-like windows, it is not merely a museum, but a powerful metaphor for the troubled history of the Jewish people. Visually it is at least as powerful as the new Holocaust Memorial (p75), which was finally completed in 2005 and consists of a giant field of 2711 concrete steles.

One of the less successful developments was the Friedrichstadtpassagen (p78), a trio of luxurious shopping complexes, including the glamorous Galeries Lafayette. Intended to restore bustling street life to Friedrichstrasse, they fail in their mission by hiding their jewel-like interiors behind bland, postmodern façades.

Other remarkable new buildings include the Dutch Embassy (Map pp340–1; Klosterstrasse 50), a starkly geometric glass cube by Rem Koolhaas, intended to embody 'Dutch openness', with a large terrace offering good views of the Spree River.

Across town, in Charlottenburg, several new structures have added some spice to the rather drab postwar architecture in the Ku'damm area. The Ludwig-Erhard-Haus (p116), home of the Berlin stock market, is a great example of the organic architecture of British architect Nicholas Grimshaw. A row of 15 arched steel girders form the building's skeleton, which has garnered it the nickname 'armadillo'. Nearby, Kleihues' Kantdreieck (p115) establishes a visual accent on Kantstrasse by virtue of its rooftop metal 'sail'.

Other buildings worthy of a look here include Helmut Jahn's Neues Kranzler Eck (p116) and the 2001 Ku'damm Eck (Map p344; Kurfürstenstrasse 227), a corner building with a gradated and rounded façade festooned with an electronic billboard and sculptures by Markus Lüppertz.

So much has been accomplished since reunification, yet Berlin remains a work in progress, even if all the headline-grabbing mega-projects are completed. The next big project may be the rebuilding of the Berliner Stadtschloss (Royal City Palace) on its original site, currently being cleared by the demolition of the GDR-era eyesore, the Palast der Republik (Palace of the Republic; p91).

History ■

History

THE RECENT PAST

Berlin had a rough entry into the 21st century. In 2001 the city finally plunged into the deep financial crisis that had been looming for years. Accused of mismanagement, excessive spending and corruption during his 15-year period in office, mayor Eberhard Diepgen of the centre-right CDU (Christian Democratic Union) was forced to resign. Klaus Wowereit, representing the centre-left SPD (Social Democrat Party), became his successor after the 2001 elections, and formed an unprecedented governing coalition with the postcommunist PDS (Party of Democratic Socialism, recently renamed Linkspartei or Left Party). The next elections take place in September 2006.

Even after five years in office, however, the so-called 'Red-Red Coalition' has not yet been able to improve Berlin's balance sheet. Painful, across-the-board spending cuts, federal subsidies and other measures have so far done little or nothing to kick-start the city's economic engine or bring down the unemployment rate. Some economic branches are blooming, though, such as fashion, design and tourism. It helps, but just not enough.

Multiculturalism and the integration of immigrants have been other hot topics around dinner tables in recent years. In early 2005, a wave of 'honour killings' of young Muslim women wishing to live a western lifestyle, shocked not only Berliners but the world as well. Schools in Kreuzberg where every single student is of Turkish descent have raised the spectre of *Parallelgesellschaften* (parallel societies) and challenged Berliners' legendary tolerance. For more on this subject, see the boxed text on p13.

But the news isn't all dire. Berlin continues to take shape, with the opening of the Holocaust Memorial (p75), the Akademie der Künste (Academy of Arts; p73) and the Hauptbahnhof (Main Train Station; Map pp330–1) being just three of the most high-profile recent additions. And in 2006, the entire city was awash with World Cup fever, with Berliners ready to welcome the global community in with open arms and hearts, to put aside their worries for a month and do what they do best…party!

FROM THE BEGINNING

MEDIEVAL BERLIN

Berlin is very much an accidental capital, whose birth was a mere blip on the map of history. Some time in the 13th century, itinerant merchants founded a pair of trading posts called Berlin and Cölln near today's Nikolaiviertel (p94). It was a profitable spot along a major medieval trade route, about halfway between the fortified towns of Köpenick (p138) and Spandau (p137). Supported by the local ruler, the Ascanian margrave of Brandenburg, the settlements flourished and, in 1307, decided to merge into a single town for political and security purposes.

Things looked good until 1319, when the death of the Ascanian ruler created a power vacuum. It left the fledgling town vulnerable to robber barons eager to fatten their coffers by attacking traders and cities. Despite such adversity, Berlin managed to expand its rights and independence, even becoming a player in the Hanseatic League in 1359.

Such confidence became a thorn in the side of Elector Friedrich of Hohenzollern, who was installed as Brandenburg's new ruler by Sigismund, one of the kings in the Holy Roman Empire, in 1417. Although he helped Berliners defeat the robber barons, he also eliminated

TIMELINE	**3000 BC**	**AD 1307**
	First agricultural settlements	Trading posts of Berlin and Cölln join to form a city

many of their hard-won political and economic liberties. The Hohenzollern clan would remain in power, without interruption, until 1918.

REFORMATION & THIRTY YEARS WAR

The Reformation, kick-started in 1517 by the monk Martin Luther in nearby Wittenberg, was slow to arrive in Berlin. Eventually, though, the wave of reform reached Brandenburg, leaving Elector Joachim II (ruled 1535–71) no choice but to subscribe to Protestantism. On 1 November 1539, the court celebrated the first Lutheran-style service in the Nikolaikirche in Spandau (p138). The event is still celebrated as an official holiday in Brandenburg, the German state that surrounds Berlin, although not in the city state of Berlin itself.

Berlin prospered for the ensuing decades until drawn into the Thirty Years' War (1618–48), a conflict between Catholics and Protestants that left Europe's soil drenched with the blood of millions. Elector Georg Wilhelm (ruled 1620–40) tried to maintain a policy of neutrality, only to see his territory repeatedly pillaged and plundered by both sides. By the time the war ended, Berlin lay largely in shambles – broke, ruined and decimated by starvation, murder and disease.

ROAD TO A KINGDOM

Stability finally returned during the long reign of Georg Wilhelm's son, Friedrich Wilhelm (ruled 1640–88). Also known as the Great Elector, he took several steps which helped chart Brandenburg's rise to the status of a European powerhouse. His first order of business was to increase Berlin's safety by turning it into a garrison town encircled by fortifications. He also levied a new sales tax, using the money to build three new neighbourhoods (Friedrichswerder, Dorotheenstadt and Friedrichstadt), a canal linking the Spree and the Oder rivers (thereby cementing Berlin's position as a trading hub), as well as the Lustgarten (p81) and Unter den Linden (p73).

But the Great Elector's most lasting legacy was replenishing Berlin's population by encouraging the settlement of refugees. In 1671, 50 Jewish families arrived from Vienna, followed in 1685 by Huguenots from France, who had been expelled by Louis XIV's anti-Protestant regime. The Französischer Dom (French Cathedral) on Gendarmenmarkt (p78) serves as a tangible reminder of Huguenot influence. Between 1680 and 1710, Berlin saw its population nearly triple to 56,000, making it one of the largest cities in the Holy Roman Empire.

The Great Elector's son, Elector Friedrich III, was a man of great ambition and had a penchant for the arts and sciences. Together with his beloved wife, Sophie Charlotte, he presided over a lively and intellectual court, founding the Academy of Arts in 1696 and the Academy of Sciences in 1700. One year later, he advanced his career by promoting

Friedrich Wilhelm on horseback in front of Schloss Charlottenburg (p110)

1417	1685
Friedrich of Hohenzollern becomes Elector of Brandenburg, kicking off 500 years of uninterrupted Hohenzollern rule	Berlin's population grows quickly when large numbers of French Huguenot refugees arrive

JEWS IN BERLIN

Great Elector Friedrich Wilhelm's seemingly generous invitation to Jewish refugees from Vienna to come to Berlin in 1671 may have been at least partly motivated by their wealth and financial power, but still, compared with treatment commonly meted out in the Middle Ages, his policy was distinctly enlightened.

Jewish families resided in Berlin from its early trading days, but their position depended on a religious technicality that allowed them to charge interest on money lent, a practice forbidden to Christians. As a result the corrupt Brandenburg nobility relied on local Jews to prop up their extravagant lifestyles, their dependence spurring massive resentment towards a people they regarded as inferior. Of course, it was easy enough to find an outlet for this hostility – any time their debts climbed too high, the rulers could find a pretext to expel the entire Jewish community from the city, inviting them back later on payment of substantial *Schutzgeld* (protection money).

Such expulsion was common practice, but with anti-Semitism the status quo, there were many far worse incidents. Untold numbers of Berlin Jews were subjected to brutally inventive torture and execution, often for the flimsiest of reasons. In 1510, for example, 38 Jews were tortured and burned for stealing the host from a church, simply because the real (Christian) perpetrator's confession was deemed too straightforward to be true. Pogroms were also regular occurrences, as the Jews were scapegoated for everything from food shortages to the plague.

Disturbingly, Berlin was by no means an isolated example, with states all over Europe following similar practices. In fact, by 1700 the city was even regarded as relatively liberal due to its high number of foreigners, and in 1812, King Friedrich Wilhelm III was among the first European rulers to grant Jews civic equality. Large Jewish communities remained in the region right up until 1935. An excellent place to learn more about the Jewish people's slow and obstacle-strewn path to equality is the Jüdisches Museum (Jewish Museum; p125).

---

himself to King Friedrich I (elector 1688–1701, king 1701–13) of Prussia, making Berlin a royal residence and the capital of the new state of Brandenburg-Prussia.

THE AGE OF PRUSSIA

All cultural and intellectual life screeched to a halt under Friedrich's son, Friedrich Wilhelm I (ruled 1713–40). He was frugal, boorish and, frankly, a bit odd. His main obsession was building an army of 80,000, which earned him the nickname *Soldatenkönig* (Soldier King). His brutal conscription methods launched a mass exodus of thousands of able-bodied men and their families, seriously cramping Berlin's economic development until he rescinded the draft in 1730. Even the Lustgarten was turned into an exercise ground for the king's beloved soldiers, who never even saw action on the battlefield.

The army did, however, come in handy for his son and successor Friedrich II (ruled 1740–86), better known to English speakers as Frederick the Great and to his subjects as *der alte Fritz* (Old Freddy). He set his covetous eyes on Silesia, in today's Poland, and before long the new king was engaged in a series of wars with Russia and Austria before finally achieving his goal in 1763. When not busy on the battlefield, Freddy was actually quite a culturally sensitive fellow who sought greatness through building. His grand architectural masterplan for Unter den Linden, although never completed, gave Berlin the Staatsoper (State Opera House; p77), Sankt-Hedwigs-Kathedrale (p77), the Humboldt Universität (Humboldt University; p75) and other major attractions.

Reiterdenkmal Friedrich Des Grossen (p76)

1740	1806
Frederick the Great starts transforming Berlin into an architectural showcase and centre of the Enlightenment	Napoleon marches into Berlin and occupies the city for three years

Frederick also embraced the ideas of the Enlightenment, abolishing torture, guaranteeing religious freedom, and introducing legal reforms. Some of the brightest minds of the day flocked to town during his reign, including the philosopher Moses Mendelsohn, the poet Gotthold Emphraim Lessing, the all-around talent Wilhelm von Humboldt and his brother Alexander, a naturalist and explorer. Intellectual salons, organised by women such as Henriette Herz and Rahel Levin, provided an open forum of discussion for anybody, regardless of social standing or religious background. Berlin flourished as a great cultural centre and even became known as Spree-Athen (Athens on the Spree).

NAPOLEON & REFORMS

After the death of Frederick the Great, Prussia went into a downward spiral, culminating in its defeat by Napoleon's forces at Jena, around 400km southwest of Berlin, in 1806. On 27 October in 1806 Napoleon marched through the Brandenburg Gate (Brandenburger Tor; p74), signalling the beginning of a three-year occupation of Berlin. The humiliation was compounded by the financial burden of astronomical war reparations and from citizens having to billet thousands of French troops in their homes. But Napoleon also provided the opportunity for Berliners to have their first taste of self-government, instituting a city administration with elected leaders.

When the French eventually left, it seemed there was no going back to the old system. Public servants, academics and merchants now questioned the right of the nobility to rule. Friedrich Wilhelm III (ruled 1797–1840) reacted with a string of token reforms – such as lifting restrictive guild regulations, abolishing bonded labour and granting Jews civic equality – but meaningful constitutional reform was not forthcoming, and power continued to be centred in the Prussian state.

The ensuing period of political stagnation was oddly paired with an intellectual flourishing in the cafés and salons. The newly founded Universität zu Berlin (Humboldt Universität) quickly grew in status, attracting such luminaries as Hegel and Ranke to its faculty. This was also the age of Karl Friedrich Schinkel, whose many projects – from the Neue Wache (New Guardhouse; p76) to the Altes Museum (Old Museum; p80) – still beautify Berlin.

REVOLUTION(S)

The ascent of Friedrich Wilhelm IV (ruled 1840–61) to the throne in 1840 revived hopes for reform, but in the end he proved just as reactionary as his father. In 1848 Berlin got caught up in the region-wide bourgeois revolutions, calling for a national German state and demanding basic, democratic rights. Faced with demonstrations in his own backyard, the king made some concessions, including the right to assemble, and freedom of the press. However, the following day, soldiers opened fire on 10,000 people who had gathered in celebration and all hell broke loose. Sheltered merely by barricades, people fought with pitchforks, axes, stones and other improvised weapons. After a night of hostilities that left over 200 dead, the king ordered his troops back and ostensibly proclaimed support for liberalism and nationalism. An elected Prussian national assembly met on 1 May but disagreements between the different factions kept it weak and ineffective, and it dissolved in December. The revolution was dead.

The political revolution may have failed, but the 'industrial revolution' certainly didn't. With manufacturing trades already well established by the 18th century, Berlin developed into a centre of technology and industry right from the dawn of the Industrial Age. The building of the German railway system (the first Berlin to Potsdam track opened in 1838) led to the founding of more than 1000 factories, including electrical giants AEG and Siemens. In 1841, August Borsig built the world's fastest locomotive, besting even the British in a race.

1810	1838
Wilhelm von Humboldt founds the Universität zu Berlin, renamed Humboldt Universität in 1949	Berlin's first train embarks on its maiden voyage from Berlin to Potsdam

BIRTH OF AN EMPIRE

When Friedrich Wilhelm IV suffered a stroke in 1857, his brother Wilhelm became first regent and then, in 1861, King Wilhelm I (ruled 1861–88). Unlike his brother, Wilhelm had his finger on the pulse of the times and was less averse to progress. One of his key moves was to appoint Otto von Bismarck as Prussian prime minister in 1862.

Bismarck's big dream was to create a Prussian-led unified Germany. An old-guard militarist, he waged war against Denmark (with Austria as his ally) over Schleswig-Holstein in 1864, then beat Austria itself in 1866, forming the North German Confederation the following year. He isolated France, manoeuvred it into declaring war on Prussia in 1870, then surprised Napoleon III by securing the support of most southern German states. By 1871, Berlin stood as the proud capital of a unified Germany. On 18 January, the king was crowned Kaiser at Versailles, with Bismarck as his 'Iron Chancellor'. The German Empire ('Deutsches Reich'– Germany's official name until 1945) was born.

The early years of the German Empire – a period called *Gründerzeit* (Foundation Years) – were marked by major economic growth, fuelled in part by a steady flow of French reparation payments. The population boomed as hundreds of thousands of people poured into Berlin to find work in the factories. Housing shortages were solved by building countless *Mietskasernen* (literally 'rental barracks'), labyrinthine tenements built around successive courtyards, where entire families subsisted in tiny and poorly ventilated flats without indoor plumbing.

New political parties formed to give a voice to the proletariat, most prominently the Sozialdemokratische Partei Deutschlands (SPD, Social Democratic Party of Germany). Founded in 1875, it captured 40% of the Berlin vote only two years later. Bismarck, who was no fan of democratic ideals, quickly passed a law making the party illegal, but this did nothing to diminish its popularity. In the end, the Iron Chancellor's deep-rooted aversion to real reform prompted his downfall. Soon after Wilhelm II (ruled 1888–1918) came to power, a rift arose between the Kaiser, who wanted to extend the social security system, and Bismarck, who wanted to enact ever-stricter antisocialist laws. Finally, in March 1890, the Kaiser excised his renegade chancellor from the political scene.

WWI & REVOLUTION (AGAIN)

The assassination of Archduke Franz Ferdinand, the heir to the Austrian throne, on 28 June 1914, triggered a series of diplomatic decisions which led to the bloodiest European conflict since the Thirty Years' War. In Berlin and elsewhere, initial euphoria and faith in a quick victory soon gave way to despair as casualties piled up in the battlefield trenches and stomachs grumbled on the home front. When peace came with defeat in 1918, it also ended domestic stability, ushering in a period of turmoil and violence.

On 9 November 1918, Kaiser Wilhelm II abdicated, bringing an inglorious end to the monarchy and 500 years of Hohenzollern rule. Power was transferred to the SPD, the largest party in the Reichstag, and its leader, Friedrich Ebert. This would not go unchallenged. Shortly after the Kaiser's exit, prominent SPD member Philipp Scheidemann stepped to a window of the Reichstag to announce the birth of the German Republic. Two hours later, Karl Liebknecht of the Spartakusbund (Spartacist League) proclaimed a socialist republic from a balcony of the royal palace on Unter den Linden. The struggle for power was on.

Founded by Liebknecht and Rosa Luxemburg, the Spartacist League sought to establish a left-wing Marxist-style government; by year's end it had merged with other radical groups into the Communist Party of Germany. The SPD's goal, meanwhile, was to establish a parliamentary democracy.

Supporters of the SPD and Spartacist League took their rivalry to the streets, culminating in the Spartacist Revolt in early January. On the orders of Ebert, government forces quickly

1862	1888
The Hobrecht Plan promotes the proliferation of huge tenements to combat a housing shortage	Kaiser Wilhelm II, the last German monarch, begins his reign

quashed the uprising. Liebknecht and Luxemburg were arrested and murdered en route to prison; their bodies were dumped in the Landwehrkanal.

THE WEIMAR REPUBLIC

In July 1919, the federalist constitution of the fledgling republic – Germany's first serious experiment with democracy – was adopted in the town of Weimar, where the constituent assembly had sought refuge from the chaos of Berlin. It gave women the vote and established basic human rights, but it also gave the chancellor the right to rule by decree – a concession that would later prove critical in Hitler's rise to power.

The so-called Weimar Republic (1920–33) was governed by a coalition of left and centre parties, headed by President Friedrich Ebert and later Paul von Hindenburg – both of the SPD, which remained Germany's largest party until 1932. The republic, however, pleased neither communists nor monarchists. Trouble erupted as early as March 1920 when right-wing militants led by Wolfgang Kapp forcibly occupied the government quarter in Berlin. The government fled to Dresden, but in Berlin a general strike soon brought the 'Kapp Putsch' to collapse.

THE 'GOLDEN' TWENTIES

The giant metropolis of Berlin as we know it today came into existence 1920 when the government amalgamated the region's towns and villages (Charlottenburg, Schöneberg, Spandau, etc) under a single administration. Overnight Berlin became one of the world's largest cities, with around 3.8 million inhabitants.

Otherwise, the 1920s began as anything but golden, marked by the humiliation of a lost war, social and political instability, hyperinflation, hunger and disease. Around 235,000 Berliners were unemployed, and strikes, demonstrations and riots became nearly everyday occurrences. Economic stability gradually returned after the introduction of a new currency, the *Rentenmark*, in 1923, and the passage of the Dawes Plan in 1924, which limited the crippling reparation payments imposed on Germany after WWI.

For the next few years Berlin experienced a cultural and artistic heyday that rivalled, perhaps even exceeded, events in Paris. It became a cauldron of experimentation, a hub of hedonism, a centre of tolerance and, yes, decadence. Bursting with creative energy, it was a laboratory for anything new and modern, drawing giants of architecture (including Bruno Taut, Martin Wagner, Hans Scharoun and Walter Gropius), fine arts (George Grosz, Max Beckmann and Lovis Corinth) and literature (Bertolt Brecht, Kurt Tucholsky, WH Auden and Christopher Isherwood). In 1923, Germany's first radio broadcast hit the airwaves over Berlin, and in 1931 TV had its world premiere here.

The fun came to an instant end when the US stock market crashed in 1929, plunging the entire world into economic depression. Within weeks, half a million Berliners were jobless, and riots and demonstrations again ruled the streets. The volatile, increasingly polarised political climate led to frequent confrontations between communists and members of a party that had only just begun to gain momentum – the Nationalsozialistische Deutsche Arbeiterpartei (National Socialist German Workers' Party, NSDAP, or Nazi Party), led by a failed Austrian artist named Adolf Hitler.

HITLER'S RISE TO POWER

Hitler's NSDAP gained 18% of the national vote in the 1930 elections. Buoyed by his success, Hitler challenged President Paul von Hindenburg of the SPD in 1932, winning 37% of the second-round vote. A year later, on 30 January 1933, faced with failed economic reforms and persuasive right-wing advisors, Hindenburg appointed Hitler Reichskanzler

1919	1920
Communist Spartacist Revolt is violently suppressed; birth of the Weimar Republic	Berlin becomes Germany's largest city after independent towns and villages are amalgamated into a single administrative unit

(Reich chancellor). That evening, Nazi supporters celebrated their rise to power with a torch-lit procession through the Brandenburg Gate.

The following month, Hitler blamed the 27 February fire that had mysteriously broken out at the Reichstag on communists, and persuaded Hindenburg to grant him emergency powers so he could 'protect the people and the state'. On 24 March, parliament met at Berlin's Kroll Opera House (destroyed in WWII) to pass the 'Enabling Law' – essentially assigning Hitler dictatorial powers and making itself redundant. The Nazi dictatorship had officially begun.

BERLIN UNDER THE NAZIS

The totalitarian Nazi ethos had immediate, far-reaching consequences for the entire population. Left-leaning parties, including the SPD and communist groups, were banned, along with trade unions. Freedom of the press ceased to exist. Terror was the rule of the day.

Hitler's brown-shirted thugs of the Sturmabteilung (storm troopers; SA) went after opponents with a vengeance, arresting, torturing and murdering countless people. Improvised concentration camps sprang up almost immediately, such as the one at the Wasserturm in Prenzlauer Berg (p133). North of Berlin, construction began on a large formal concentration camp in Sachsenhausen (p272). The brutality of Hitler's henchmen knew no bounds: during the so-called Köpenick Blood Week alone, in June 1933, almost 100 people were murdered (see p140 for more). On 10 May, right-wing students burned 'un-German' books on Bebelplatz (p73), prompting countless intellectuals and artists to rush into exile.

Jews, of course, were a main target right from the start. In April 1933, Joseph Goebbels, *Gauleiter* (district leader) of Berlin and newly appointed Minister of Propaganda, announced a boycott of Jewish businesses. By autumn, hundreds of Jewish professors had lost their jobs and more than half of Berlin's 40 synagogues had closed. The Nuremberg Laws of 1935 revoked German citizenship for Jews and outlawed marriage between Jews and people deemed as 'Aryans'.

Hitler demanded absolute loyalty and had no qualms about turning against anyone even remotely perceived as wanting to challenge his authority. The SA, for instance, had grown

Jüdisches Museum and park (p125)

1933	1936
Hitler is appointed chancellor; the Reichstag burns; by June the National Socialists are the only political party in Germany	Berlin Olympics showcase Nazi power and are a PR coup

ALBERT SPEER

A key tenet in Hitler's agenda was an extensive construction programme in Berlin, creating monumental buildings that were to reinforce the restored pride of the German nation. The man he hired to plan it all was Albert Speer (1905–81), a brilliant architect who worked closely with Hitler and eventually became his armaments minister in 1942, in charge of – among many other things – orchestrating forced labour from concentration camps.

Hitler and Speer's ultimate vision was to transform Berlin into a larger-than-life world capital for the new Nazi empire. 'Germania' was to be centred on the Great Hall, a proposed assembly hall in a domed structure that would have dwarfed the Reichstag. Sizeable tracts of land around Tiergarten and central Berlin were bulldozed to make room for these ambitious architectural projects, and Speer got as far as building the huge Reichskanzlei (Hitler's office), but WWII soon put paid to his efforts.

Having survived to see his dream bombed to the ground, Speer served 20 years in Spandau prison. On his release, he wrote *Inside the Third Reich* (1970), a detailed account of the day-to-day operations of Hitler's inner circle. Read it alongside Gitta Sereny's biography *Albert Speer: His Battle with Truth* (1996) for an insight into the complicated life of this controversial Nazi figure.

into a huge organisation and become an obstreperous bunch by 1934. With rumours of revolt circulating, on 30 June the elite SS troops (Schutzstaffel, Hitler's personal guard) rounded up and executed scores of high-ranking SA officers, including their leader, Ernst Röhm, in the SS barracks in Lichterfelde – an event that went down in history as the 'Night of the Long Knives'. Later that year, after Hindenburg's death, Hitler merged the position of president and chancellor and made himself supreme Führer (leader).

The international community, meanwhile, turned a blind eye to the situation in Germany, perhaps because many leaders were keen to see some order restored to the country after decades of political upheaval. Hitler's success at stabilising the shaky economy, especially the eradication of unemployment through public works programmes, also garnered him some admirers. The 1936 Olympic summer games in Berlin were a PR triumph, as Hitler launched a charm offensive to distract the world from the everyday terror of his regime. On 1 August athletes from 49 nations marched into the imposing Olympiastadion (p118) in western Charlottenburg. Germany took home the lion's share of medals (42), beating the Americans by seven.

Terror and persecution resumed as soon as the closing ceremony's last fireworks had evaporated into the night sky. For Jews, the horror escalated on 9 November 1938, with the *Reichspogromnacht* (often called *Kristallnacht*, or Night of Broken Glass). Nazi thugs shattered the windows of Jewish businesses and shops throughout Berlin and all of Germany, looting and torching many of them. In the aftermath, all Jewish businesses were transferred to non-Jews through forced sale at below-market prices. Jews had begun to emigrate after 1933, but this event set off a stampede. Very few of those who remained in Berlin – about 60,000 – were still alive in 1945.

WWII

On 1 September 1939 Germany invaded Poland, kicking off the 20th century's second pan-European conflict. This time the war was not greeted with pleasure in Berlin, whose people still remembered the hunger years of WWI and the early 1920s. Again the hostilities brought food shortages and increasing political oppression.

Belgium, the Netherlands and France fell quickly to Germany and, in June 1941, Hitler attacked the USSR, opening up a new front. Though successful at first, 'Operation Barbarossa' soon ran into problems, forcing Hitler's troops to retreat. With the defeat of the

1938	1939
Kristallnacht – Jewish businesses and institutions all over Berlin are attacked	Germany invades Poland, WWII begins

German 6th army at Stalingrad (today Volgograd) the following winter, morale flagged at home and on the fronts.

The fate of Jews deteriorated after the outbreak of war. At Hitler's request, a conference in January 1942 on Berlin's Wannsee (p145) came up with the *Endlösung* (Final Solution): the decision to systematically annihilate all European Jews in what came to be known as the Holocaust. Gays, Roma and Sinti (commonly referred to as Gypsies), priests, dissidents and other regime opponents were targeted as well. In the end more than six million people perished in dozens of concentration camps, most of them in Eastern Europe. About 500,000 survived to be freed by Soviet and Allied soldiers in 1945. In Berlin, the new Holocaust Memorial (p75) is one of many commemorating this grim period in history.

Resistance to Hitler was rare. The most famous act was the 20 July 1944 assassination attempt led by Claus Graf Schenk von Stauffenberg. A high-ranking officer in the military, Stauffenberg had access to the Wolfschanze (one of Hitler's military headquarters near Görlitz, about 215km east of Berlin), and personally placed a briefcase packed with explosives below the conference table near Hitler's seat. The bomb detonated but Hitler escaped with minor injuries thanks to the solid oak table which shielded him from the blast. Stauffenberg and his co-conspirators were shot that night at the army headquarters in the Bendlerblock in Berlin (p107). Hundreds of others, many of them completely unaffiliated with the coup, were later executed at Plötzensee prison (p136). Both locations are now memorial sites.

The Battle of Berlin

With the Normandy invasion of June 1944, Allied troops arrived in formidable force on the European mainland, supported by unrelenting air raids on Berlin and most other German cities. In the last days of the war Hitler, broken and paranoid, ordered the destruction of all remaining German industry and infrastructure, a decree that was largely ignored.

The final Battle of Berlin began in mid-April 1945. More than 1.5 million Soviet soldiers barrelled towards the capital from the east, reaching Berlin on 21 April and encircling it on

Sowietisches Ehrenmal, Treptower Park (p143)

1942	1945
Nazi leaders agree on total annihilation of the European Jewry in a conference on Berlin's Wannsee	Battle of Berlin devastates the city; Hitler commits suicide; the Yalta conference divides Berlin between the Allies

25 April. Two days later they were in the city centre, fighting running street battles with the remaining troops, many of them boys and elderly men. On 30 April the fighting reached the government quarter where Hitler was ensconced in his bunker behind the Chancellery, with his long-time mistress Eva Braun – whom he'd married just a day earlier. That afternoon, Hitler shot Braun and then himself.

Two days later Berlin surrendered to the Soviets. Red Army soldiers stormed the Reichstag and set it alight. On 7 May 1945, Germany capitulated. Peace was signed at the US military headquarters in Reims (France) and at the Soviet military headquarters in Berlin-Karlshorst, now a museum (p150).

The Aftermath

WWII took an enormous toll on Berlin and its people, as the civilian population had borne the brunt of the bombings. Entire neighbourhoods lay in smouldering rubble, with more than half of all buildings and one-third of industry destroyed or damaged. At least 125,000 Berliners had lost their lives. With around one million women and children evacuated, only 2.4 million people were left in the city in May 1945 (compared to 4.3 million in 1939), two-thirds of them women. It fell to them to do much of the initial clean-up, earning them the name *Trümmerfrauen* (rubble women). Over the following years, enormous amounts of debris were piled up into so-called *Trümmerberge* (rubble mountains), artificial hills such as the Teufelsberg in the Grunewald (p119).

Some small triumphs came quickly after the shooting stopped: U-Bahn service resumed on 14 May 1945, newspaper printing presses began rolling again on 15 May, and the Berliner Philharmonie gave its first postwar concert on 26 May.

POLITICS OF PROVOCATION

In line with agreements reached at the Yalta Conference in February 1945, Germany was divided into four zones of occupation. Berlin was sliced up into 20 administrative areas. The British sector encompassed Charlottenburg, Tiergarten and Spandau; the French got Wedding and Reinickendorf; and the Americans were in charge of Zehlendorf, Steglitz, Wilmersdorf, Tempelhof, Kreuzberg and Neukölln – all these areas later formed West Berlin. The Soviets, meanwhile, held on to eight districts in the east, including Mitte, Prenzlauer Berg, Friedrichshain, Treptow and Köpenick; the future East Berlin. The Soviets also occupied the zone surrounding Berlin, leaving West Berlin completely encircled by territories under Soviet control.

In July and August of that year, the victorious powers met in Schloss Cecilienhof (p271) in Potsdam to discuss the future of Germany. Friction between the Western Allies and the Soviets quickly emerged. For the Western Allies, a main priority was to help Germany get back on its feet by kick-starting the devastated economy. The Soviets, though, insisted on massive reparations and began brutalising and exploiting their own zone of occupation. Tens of thousands of able-bodied men and POWs ended up in labour camps deep in the Soviet Union. In the Allied zones, meanwhile, democracy was beginning to take root as Germany elected state parliaments in 1946–47.

An escalation of tensions led to a showdown in June 1948, when the Allies introduced the Deutschmark in their zones without having consulted the Soviets. Furious, the USSR issued its own currency, the Ostmark, and used the incident as a pretext for an economic blockade of West Berlin. The goal was to bring all of Berlin under its control but the Allies would have none of it. Led by Lucius D Clay, the US commander in Berlin, their response was quick and effective: Berlin would be supplied from the air. The Berlin Airlift miraculously saved the city from being absorbed into the Soviet empire (see boxed text on p62 for more).

1948	1949
Soviets blockade West Berlin, Western Allies begin the Berlin Airlift	Formation of the Bundesrepublik Deutschland (BRD, West Germany) and the Deutsche Demokratische Republik (DDR, East Germany)

THE BERLIN AIRLIFT

The ruined city of Berlin was still digging itself out from the rubble of WWII when the Soviets began their bid for total domination on 24 June 1948. The military leadership ordered a complete blockade of all rail and road traffic into the city. Berlin would be entirely cut off; everyone assumed it would be a matter of days before the city submitted to the Soviets.

Faced with such provocation, many in the Allied camp urged responses that would have been the opening barrages of WWIII. In the end wiser heads prevailed, and a mere day after the blockade began the US Air Force launched 'Operation Vittles'. The British followed suit on 28 June with 'Operation Plane Fare'. (France did not participate because its planes were tied up with rather less humanitarian missions in Indochina.)

For about 11 months Allied planes supplied the entire city, bringing in coal, food and machinery. Every day, around the clock, determined pilots made treacherous landings at Berlin's airports, sometimes as frequently as one per minute. On one day alone – the 'Easter Parade' of 16 April 1949 – they flew 1400 sorties, delivering 13,000 tons of supplies. By the end of the airlift they had flown a total of 200 million kilometres in 278,000 flights, and delivered 2.5 million tons of cargo. The operation cost the lives of 79 people, and is commemorated by the Luftbrückendenkmal (Airlift Memorial; p124) at Tempelhof airport.

Given the ever-escalating Allied effort and increasing international condemnation, the Soviets backed down in May 1949, and Berlin's western sectors were free once again. The whole debacle had only strengthened the relationship between Germany and the Western Allies – Berliners now regarded them not as occupational forces but as *Schutzmächte* (protective powers).

THE TWO GERMAN STATES

In 1949 the division of Germany – and Berlin – was formalised. The western zones evolved into the Bundesrepublik Deutschland (BRD, Federal Republic of Germany or FRG) with Konrad Adenauer as its first chancellor and Bonn on the Rhine River as its capital. The Marshall Plan pumped millions of dollars into reconstruction in West Germany, and helped usher in an economic boom called the *Wirtschaftswunder* (economic miracle) that began in the 1950s and lasted through most of the 1960s. The policies of its architect, economics minister Ludwig Erhard, encouraged investment and capital formation, and beckoned guests workers from southern Europe (mainly Turkey, Yugoslavia, and Italy) to address a manual labour shortage. This created many of the ethnic communities that characterise Berlin and other German cities today.

The Soviet zone, meanwhile, grew into the Deutsche Demokratische Republik (DDR, German Democratic Republic or GDR), making East Berlin its capital and Wilhelm Pieck its president. From the outset, though, the Sozialistische Einheitspartei Deutschlands (SED, Socialist Unity Party of Germany) led by party boss Walter Ulbricht dominated economic, judicial and security policy. In order to oppress any dissent, the notorious Ministry for State Security, or Stasi, was established in 1950 and had its headquarters in Lichtenberg (p149). Regime 'enemies' were incarcerated at the super-secret Stasi Prison (p149) nearby.

Movement between the two Berlins remained fairly open; West Berliners went east to visit friends or see a play, East Berliners came across to stock up on consumer goods or catch a movie. Starting in 1951, however, the GDR imposed restrictions on West Berliners wanting to travel outside the city. Suddenly, visiting family in Leipzig or Magdeburg required applying for a permit.

THE 1953 UPRISING

By 1953, the first signs of discontent had appeared in the GDR. Production bottlenecks stifled industrial output, heavy industry got priority over consumer goods, and increased demands on industrial workers bred bitterness. Furthermore, the death of Stalin that year

1953	1961
Soviet tanks crush a workers' uprising in East Berlin	Construction of the Berlin Wall begins

had raised hopes of reform but brought no real changes. Poverty and economic tensions merely prompted the SED to raise production goals even higher.

Strikes and calls for reform turned to civil unrest in urban and industrial centres, culminating in violence on 17 June 1953. Construction workers on Berlin's Karl-Marx-Allee got the ball rolling, but demonstrations quickly spread, eventually involving at least 10% of the workforce. It didn't do any good, of course. Soviet tanks quickly quashed the uprising, leaving scores dead (many of them executed) or condemned to lifelong prison terms.

THE WALL GOES UP

As the GDR government became evermore oppressive, the trickle of refugees to the West swelled into a stream. Eventually, the exodus of mostly young and well-educated people strained the GDR economy to such a degree that the SED built a wall to keep them in. Construction of the Berlin Wall, the Cold War's most potent symbol, began on the night of 13 August 1961. The inner-German border was fenced off, heavily guarded and mined.

Haus Am Checkpoint Charlie (p125)

This stealthy act left Berliners stunned. Formal protests from the Western Allies, as well as massive demonstrations in West Berlin, were ignored. Tension reached a boiling point on 25 October, as US and Soviet tanks faced off at Checkpoint Charlie (p123). The Berlin Wall subsequently became the setting of countless escape attempts, of which the most spectacular are detailed in the Haus am Checkpoint Charlie Museum (p125). By the time the Wall collapsed on 9 November 1989, almost 200 people had been killed trying to get across it (see boxed text on p136).

The building of the Wall marked a new low in East–West relations worldwide, and tense times were to follow. In 1963, US President John F Kennedy made a visit to West Berlin, praising locals for their pro-freedom stance in his famous *'Ich bin ein Berliner'* speech at the Rathaus Schöneberg, and putting the city firmly on the front line of the Cold War.

RAPPROCHEMENT

The era of Erich Honecker (1912–94), who succeeded Walter Ulbricht as general secretary of the SED in 1971, opened the way for rapprochement with the West and international recognition of the GDR. A major breakthrough came in September 1971, with the signing of the Four Power Agreement in the Kammergericht in Schöneberg (p119). It charged the governments of West Berlin and the GDR with finding ways to regulate access between the rest of West Germany and West Berlin, and to secure the right of West Berliners to visit East Berlin and the GDR. Negotiations resulted in the Transit Agreement of 1972, which regulated the right of GDR citizens to visit West Germany, but only in family emergencies.

1967	1972
The police killing of an unarmed student during a protest radicalises the student movement	In the Basic Treaty the BRD and GDR officially recognise each other's sovereignty and borders

Anyone visiting East Berlin, meanwhile, was saddled with a compulsory exchange of Deutschmarks for the weak Ostmark based on a 1:1 exchange rate.

Still, the talks had gone so well that both sides agreed to take things a step further and create a comprehensive treaty between the two Germanys. In the Basic Treaty, signed in December 1972, the two countries recognised each other's independence and sovereignty, accepted each others' borders, and committed to normalising their official relations by, among other things, setting up 'permanent missions' in Bonn and East Berlin, respectively.

STUDENT UNREST & TERRORISM

In West Germany the two major parties, the CDU and the SPD, formed a so-called 'grand coalition' in 1966. The absence of parliamentary opposition was among the factors fuelling an increasingly radical student movement with Berlin's Freie Universität (Free University; FU; p144) at its centre. At sit-ins and protests, students demanded an end to the Vietnam War and a reform of Germany's dated university system and teaching programs. These demonstrations were a thorn in the side of the government and crack-downs sometimes turned violent.

On 2 June 1967 police shot and killed unarmed student Benno Ohnesorg near the Deutsche Oper in Charlottenburg, during a protest against the visit of the Shah of Iran. It was the first demonstration Ohnesorg had attended. His death was a key event in the history of the student movement and brought into the fold scores of people who had previously remained on the sidelines. Another pivotal moment came a year later, on 11 April 1968, when Rudi Dutschke – the movement's charismatic leader at the FU – was shot in the head by a young worker outside his organisation's office on Kurfürstendamm. He survived, but students blamed the right-wing publishing house of Axel Springer for inciting the event, having run such headlines as 'Stop Dutschke Now!' (also see boxed text, p19).

By 1970 the movement had fizzled, but not without having shaken up the country and bringing many changes, including university reforms, politicisation of the student body and, eventually, the formation of the Green Party (Dutschke was a founding member).

Some of the most radical students, though, felt these accomplishments hadn't gone far enough and went underground. Berlin became the germ cell of the terrorist Rote Armee Fraktion (RAF, Red Army Faction), led by Ulrike Meinhof, Andreas Baader and Gudrun Ensslin. Throughout the 1970s the RAF abducted and assassinated prominent business and political figures throughout Germany. By 1976, however, Meinhof and Baader had committed suicide (both in prison) and remaining members found themselves in jail, in hiding, or seeking refuge in the GDR. Eventually that country's demise would expose them to West German attempts to bring them to justice.

THE WALL COMES DOWN

The *Wende* (turning point) began in September 1989, when East Germans starting defecting to the West after Hungary opened its border with Austria. The SED responded by tightening travel restrictions, but nothing could stop the flow of people seeking refuge in West German consulates and embassies in East Berlin, Warsaw, Prague and Budapest.

Supported by church leaders, the *Neues Forum* (New Forum) of opposition groups emerged, leading calls for human rights and an end to the SED political monopoly. By this time East Germany was losing about 10,000 citizens a day, and on 4 November 1989, about 500,000 demonstrators gathered on Berlin's Alexanderplatz demanding political reform.

The replacement of Honecker by Egon Krenz did not stave off the day of reckoning. On 9 November 1989, SED spokesperson Günter Schabowski told GDR citizens in a televised

1989	1991
The Berlin Wall is torn down	Members of the Bundestag (German parliament) vote to reinstate Berlin as Germany's capital

press conference that all travel restrictions to the West had been lifted. Asked when exactly this move would take effect, Schabowsky stared at his notes, then stuttered, mistakenly, 'Right away'. The misunderstanding, however, was only with regard to the date, not the actual lifting of the restrictions.

Soon thereafter, tens of thousands rushed through border points in Berlin, watched by perplexed guards, who did nothing to intervene. West Berliners went into the streets to greet the visitors, and tears and champagne flowed. Amid scenes of wild partying, mile-long parades of Trabants (cars manufactured in the GDR) the two Berlins came together again, united to the sound of – would you believe it – David Hasselhoff crooning *Looking for Freedom*.

REUNIFICATION

Government representation and opposition groups soon met for round-table discussions to hash out a course for the future. In March 1990, free elections in the GDR brought to power an alliance headed by the CDU's Lothar de Maizière. The SPD, which took an equivocal view of reunification, found itself punished by voters. The old SED administrative regions were abolished and the original states (Brandenburg, Mecklenburg-Western Pomerania, Saxony, Saxony-Anhalt and Thuringia) revived. The newly united city of Berlin became a separate city-state. Economic union took force in mid-1990, and in August 1990 the Unification Treaty was signed in the Kronprinzenpalais (p76) on Unter den Linden. A common currency and economic union became realities in July 1990. Also in July,

WHAT'S IN A DATE?

The public holiday to mark German reunification was originally proposed for 9 November, the day the Berlin Wall fell, as it was felt this would have the most resonance with the public. Unfortunately, this also happened to be the date of both Hitler's 1923 Munich coup, and the infamous *Kristallnacht* (Night of Broken Glass) attacks on Jews in 1938, making it a potential rallying day for neo-Nazis and a PR disaster waiting to happen. But the 9 November also has positive connotations: it was on this day in 1918 that the monarchy ended in Germany with the abdication of Kaiser Wilhelm II, and the first German republic was established. Still, in the end, Germany's national holiday was set on the less evocative, but much more tactful date of the anniversary of administrative reunification in 1990 – 3 October.

Pink Floyd replayed the original set of their 1980's album *The Wall* to a crowd of 200,000 (and TV audiences of millions worldwide) on Potsdamer Platz.

In September 1990 the BRD and the GDR, the USSR, France, United Kingdom and the United States met in Moscow to sign the Two-Plus-Four Treaty, ending postwar occupation zones and paving the way for formal German reunification. One month later the East German state was dissolved; in December Germany held its first unified post-WWII elections.

In 1991, a small majority (338 to 320) of members in the Bundestag (German parliament) voted in favour of moving the government to Berlin and of making Berlin the German capital once again. On 8 September 1994 the last Allied troops stationed in Berlin left the city after a festive ceremony.

THE BERLIN REPUBLIC

In 1999 the German parliament moved from Bonn to Berlin, convening its first session in the restored Reichstag building on 19 April. The ministries quickly followed, as did diplomats, government agencies, industrial associations and lobbyists – an estimated total of 15,000 people. A *Regierungsviertel* (government quarter) around the Reichstag sprang up, with new offices for parliamentarians, sleek embassies and, most notably, the striking Chancellery.

1994	1999
The last Allied troops leave Berlin	German parliament returns from Bonn to take up residence in Berlin's restored Reichstag

Elsewhere, too, the face of Berlin has greatly changed since reunification. An architectural frenzy has rejuvenated most of the central areas, restoring the Mitte district to its rightful place as the city's heart. The cultural vibrancy of the 1920s has returned with a vengeance, transforming Berlin from a political curiosity to a vital presence among European capitals. The city exudes a new sophistication and a greater internationalism than ever before, and signs of creative energy, construction and modernisation abound wherever you look.

But not everything is rosy in Berlin or the new Germany. Scandals surrounding the financial dealings of former chancellor, Helmut Kohl, and his unification government rocked the political establishment in 2000, and shook many people's faith in politicians, and the Berlin Senate's overenthusiastic investment has effectively bankrupted the city. Whatever its domestic problems, however, Berlin seems to have put its worst days firmly behind it.

TOP FIVE BOOKS ON BERLIN'S HISTORY

- *Berlin Rising: Biography of a City* (Anthony Read and David Fisher; 1994) An excellent social history, tracing the life of the city from its beginnings to post-Wall times.
- *Berlin* (David Clay Large; 2001) A smooth and engaging narrative history of Berlin, framed by the two unifications in 1871 and 1990.
- *Berlin Diary: Journal of a Foreign Correspondent 1934–41* (William Shirer; 1941) One of the most powerful works of reportage ever written. Shirer's portrait of the city he loved, grew to fear and eventually fled is a giant of the genre.
- *The Last Division: Berlin and the Wall* (Ann Tusa; 1996) A saga of the events, trials and triumphs of the Cold War, the building of the Wall and its effects on the people and the city.
- *Stasiland* (Anna Funder; 2003) A highly readable account of what life was like in the GDR, the ultimate Big Brother state, as told through the fate of several individuals.

2001	2006
Klaus Wowereit of the SPD (Social Democratic Party) becomes Berlin's (first openly gay) mayor	Berlin welcomes the World Cup 2006, bringing the best football players and their fans to the city

Sights ■

Sights

Berlin is a German city-state surrounded by a region known from medieval times as the *Mark* (March) of Brandenburg, now the *Bundesland* (federal state) of Brandenburg. In 2001, Berlin's previous 23 administrative *Bezirke* (districts) were reduced to 12 in an effort to curb bureaucracy (see the boxed text, p22). In most cases this has meant merging existing districts, a behind-the-scenes move with no impact on visitors as the old district names – Mitte, Charlottenburg, Kreuzberg etc – continue to be used by locals. The old district names are also the divisions we've used in organising this book.

We start out by profiling the eight central districts, beginning with **Mitte**, the city's historic core, and then moving in an anticlockwise direction. Next up is **Tiergarten** – with its giant park, government quarter and Potsdamer Platz. **Charlottenburg**, the heart of the western city, is up next, with its fun shopping and magnificent Schloss Charlottenburg. From here it's south to **Wilmersdorf**, a residential district anchored by the sprawling Grunewald forest. East of here is **Schöneberg**, known for its throbbing gay quarter and great farmers market, and **Kreuzberg**, where Checkpoint Charlie and the Jewish Museum are major attractions. We then cross the Spree back into former East Berlin and the emerging district of **Friedrichshain** with its bubbly nightlife and monumental German Democratic Republic (GDR) architecture. The central loop concludes with **Prenzlauer Berg**, a newly gentrified district centred on Kollwitzplatz.

The outer districts have been grouped together by compass direction, starting with the **Northern Districts** (Pankow and Wedding), then again moving anticlockwise to the **Western Districts** (Spandau), the **Southern Districts** (Köpenick, Neukölln, Treptow and Zehlendorf) and finally the **Eastern Districts** (Lichtenberg-Hohenschönhausen and Marzahn-Hellersdorf).

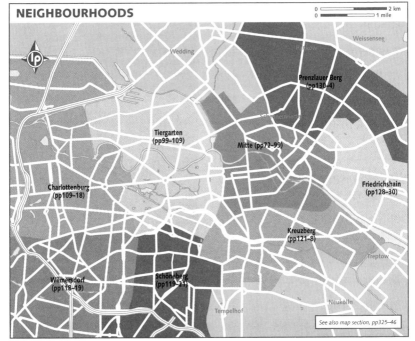

68

ITINERARIES

One Day

Get up early to beat the crowds to the dome of the **Reichstag** (p102), then head south and snap a picture of the **Brandenburger Tor** (Brandenburg Gate; p74) before exploring the maze of the **Holocaust Memorial** (p75) and continuing on to **Potsdamer Platz** (p103), Berlin's showcase of urban renewal. Walk east on Leipziger Strasse or hop on the U-Bahn to Stadtmitte to ponder Cold War history at **Checkpoint Charlie** (p123) and check out the dazzling **Friedrichstadtpassagen** (p78). Grab a quick bite, then saunter over to beautiful **Gendarmenmarkt** (p77) and north to **Unter den Linden** (p73). Follow this classic boulevard east, peeking inside the **Neue Wache** (New Guardhouse; p76) and checking out Nefertiti at the **Altes Museum** (Old Museum; p80) and the Pergamon Altar at the **Pergamon Museum** (p82). Spend the rest of the day soaking in the atmosphere of the **Scheunenviertel** (p95), where you should have no trouble sourcing favourite spots for dinner, drinks and dancing.

Three Days

Follow the one-day itinerary, then devote the morning of day two to **Schloss Charlottenburg** (p110). Miss neither the **Neuer Flügel** (New Wing; p112) nor a spin around the lovely **Schlossgarten** (p112). Hop on the U-Bahn to Bahnhof Zoo, then study the legacy of the late photographer Helmut Newton at the **Museum für Fotografie** (p116). Follow up with some shopping along and around the **Kurfürstendamm** (p237), perhaps taking time out from commerce for a visit to the **Kaiser-Wilhelm-Gedächtniskirche** (p115). Take the U-Bahn to the **Jüdisches Museum** (Jewish Museum; p125), then conclude the day in **Prenzlauer Berg** with dinner (p185) and a pubcrawl (p197).

On day three, indulge your aesthetic sensibilities with fine art at the **Gemäldegalerie**

Glass dome of the Reichstag (p102)

(Picture Gallery; p107) or the **Neue Nationalgalerie** (New National Gallery; p108) at the Kulturforum, then escape the city bustle by heading to Wannsee, where you might steer towards the romantic **Pfaueninsel** (Peacock Island; p147) and **Schloss Glienicke** (p148), then watch the sunset from the **Grunewaldturm** (Grunewald Tower; p118).

One Week

If you've got the luxury of a week, take one day to visit the magnificent **Schloss Sanssouci** (Sanssouci Palace; p268) in Potsdam, the German version of Versailles; it's just a quick S-Bahn ride away from the central city. Another day might be spent studying Berlin's Nazi and Cold War past by seeking out such places as the **East Side Gallery** (p128), the **Topographie des Terrors** (Topography of Terror; p127), the **Gedenkstätte Normannenstrasse** (Stasi Museum; **p149**), the **Alliierten Museum** (Allied Museum; p144), the **Gedenkstätte Deutscher Widerstand** (German Resistance Memorial; p107) or even the **Sachsenhausen concentration camp** (p272). If you're the type who likes venturing way off the well-worn tourist track, consider a trip to the **Erholungspark Marzahn** (p152), the **Zitadelle Spandau** (Spandau Citadel; p138) or down to **Köpenick** (p138), perhaps combined with a cruise on the **Müggelsee** (p139).

On your last day shop till you drop. Hit the Ku'damm and the **KaDeWe** (p240) in the morning, then forage for Berlin-designed duds and accessories in the Scheunenviertel (p232) and along Kastanienallee (p245). For your farewell dinner, treat yourself to a gourmet meal at **Margaux** (p170) in Mitte or **Die Quadriga** (p177) in Wilmersdorf.

ORGANISED TOURS

Walking Tours

Several companies offer scheduled guided English-language tours of Berlin, all of them excellent with well-informed and sharp-witted guides who provide lively commentary and are eager to answer your questions. Look for their flyers in hostels, hotels and the tourist offices.

BREWER'S BERLIN TOURS

☎ 2248 7435, 0177-388 1537; www.brewersberlin tours.com; tours €10-12

Founded by Terry Brewer, an ex-intelligence officer and official guide to the Allied Forces, this is the tour company offering the legendary All Day Berlin marathon which runs eight hours or more. Nightlife tours are available also. If you want to meet the man himself, book a Tuesdays with Terry tour. Tours depart from outside the Australian Ice Cream Shop at the corner of Georgenstrasse and Friedrichstrasse (Map pp340–1).

INSIDER TOUR

☎ 692 3149; www.insidertour.com; tours €10-12, bike tour incl bicycle €22, discounts for students, under 26, seniors & WelcomeCard holders

This popular company's daily (twice daily April to October) Famous Insider Tour offers an excellent and insightful introduction to all the city's major sights. Its extended summer repertory includes the always intriguing Third Reich and Iron Curtain tours, as well as the spot-on pub crawl. If you like to combine your sightseeing with a little exercise, try its Berlin by Bike tour. Pick up its free Insider Guide or download it from the website. Tours depart from outside McDonald's on Hardenbergplatz in Charlottenburg (Map p344) or from outside Coffeemamas below the S-Bahn station Hackescher Markt (Map pp340–1).

NEW BERLIN TOURS

☎ 0179-973 0397; www.newberlintours.com; general tour free, speciality tours adult/student €10/8

General walking tours are offered twice daily for free by this newish outfit. The guides work for tips, though, and most work really hard, so don't be stingy. Its bike tour is also free if you bring your own bike, or staff will rent you one for €7. Speciality tours cover sites relating to Berlin's Nazi

and communist past as well as a pub-crawl, but these cost money. It also publishes a free Berlin guide in print and online. Tours depart from outside Dunkin' Donuts on Hardenbergplatz in Charlottenburg (Map p344) and from outside Starbucks on Pariser Platz (Map pp340–1).

ORIGINAL BERLIN WALKING TOURS

☎ 301 9194; www.berlinwalks.de; tours €12-15, discounts if under 26 or with WelcomeCard, free if under 14

This well-established outfit runs a daily (twice daily April to October) Discover Berlin Walk, which gives a thorough general introduction to Berlin's must-see sights. Its equally fascinating Infamous Third Reich Sites and Jewish Life in Berlin tours are offered on a limited schedule, as are guided excursions to Potsdam and Sachsenhausen concentration camp. Tours depart from outside the taxi ranks on Hardenbergplatz in Charlottenburg (Map p344) and from outside Häagen-Dazs opposite S-Bahn station Hackescher Markt (Map pp340–1).

Bicycle Tours

Berlin is flat and bike-friendly with lots of bike paths and quiet side streets for stress-free riding. Bike tours let you cover a lot of ground quickly without wearing out any shoe leather. You'll be stopping every few hundred metres for photo ops and to be showered with stories and history. Both companies listed below offer two English-language tours that last about four to five hours. One is a general sightseeing tour, the other a Berlin Wall tour, which retraces the path of the Wall and focuses on sights that loomed large in Cold War history. Reservations are recommended.

BERLIN ON BIKE Map pp332-3

☎ 4404 8300; www.berlinonbike.de; Knaack-strasse 97; tours incl bike €15, with own bike €11, discounts for Welcome-Card holders; ☯ mid-March–early November; ⊙ Eberswalder Strasse)

Tours depart from the office in Court 4 of the Kulturbrauerei.

FAT TIRE BIKE TOURS Map pp340-1

☎ 2404 7991; www.fattirebiketoursberlin.com; Panoramastrasse 1a; tours incl bike & insurance adult/concession €20/17; ☯ Mar-Nov; ⊙ ⊠ Alexanderplatz

Tours depart from the office below the TV Tower, where you also can hire bikes, surf the Internet and wash your smalls.

Bus Tours

The most popular sightseeing tours work on the 'hop on, hop off' principle and there's very little difference between operators. Buses navigate central Berlin on routes designed to pass all the major attractions including Kurfürstendamm, Brandenburg Gate, Schloss Charlottenburg, Unter den Linden and Potsdamer Platz. The entire loop takes about two hours without getting off. Taped commentary usually comes in – count em – eight languages.

Buses make their rounds at 15-minute intervals (less frequently from November to March) from about 10am until 5pm or 6pm every day. Besides the main departure points mentioned below, you can start your tour at any of the other stops around town. Tickets cost about €20 for adults and €10 or €15 for children and are sold on the bus.

Most companies also run one or two traditional city tours daily where you see the sights without getting off the bus; the cost of these is about €25. Combination boat and bus tours, as well as organised trips to Potsdam, Dresden and the Spreewald, are also available.

For full details, call, check the website or look for flyers in hotel lobbies and at the tourist offices.

BBS BERLINER BÄREN STADTRUNDFAHRT Map pp340-1 & Map p344
☎ 3519 5270; www.bbsberlin.de
Tours start on the corner of Kurfürstendamm and Rankestrasse and on Alexanderplatz, opposite the Park Inn Hotel.

BEROLINA SIGHTSEEING Map p344
☎ 8856 8030; www.berolina-berlin.com
Tours start at Kurfürstendamm 220.

BVB Map p344
☎ 683 8910; www.bvb.net
Departures from Kurfürstendamm 225.

BVG TOP TOUR Map p344
☎ 2562 5569; www.bvg.de; adult/child 6-14 €15/10
Open-top double-decker with live German and English commentary. Route starts at

Kurfürstendamm 19, just outside the Kurfürstendamm U-Bahn station.

SEVERIN & KÜHN Map p344
☎ 880 4190; www.severin-kuehn-berlin.de
Board at Kurfürstendamm 216.

TEMPELHOFER REISEN
Map pp340-1 & Map p344
752 4057; www.tempelhofer.de
Starts at Unter den Linden 14 and Kurfürstendamm 231, outside the Wertheim department store.

Boat Tours

A lovely way to experience Berlin on a warm summer day is from the deck of a boat cruising the city's rivers, canals and lakes. Tours range from one-hour spins around Museumsinsel taking in the historic sights (from €5) to longer trips into the green suburbs (from €12) and dinner cruises. Narration is in English and German. Food and drink are sold on board, or bring along a picnic. Small children usually travel for free, while those under 14 and seniors can expect a 50% discount. The season runs roughly from April to October. Our map section indicates embarkation points that are served by one of the following companies:

Berliner Wassertaxi (Map pp340–1; ☎ 6588 0203; www.berliner-wassertaxi.de, in German)

Reederei Bruno Winkler (☎ 349 0011; www.reederei winkler.de)

Reederei Riedel (☎ 693 4646; www.reederei-riedel.de)

Stern & Kreisschiffahrt (☎ 536 3600; www.sternund kreis.de)

Speciality Tours

BERLINER UNTERWELTEN Map pp332-3
☎ 4991 0518; www.berliner-unterwelten.de; adult/concession €9/7, under 12 free; German tours noon, 2pm & 4pm Sat, Sun & Mon, English tours 11am & 1pm Sat & Mon, Spanish tours 3pm Sat
Dive into Berlin's dark and dank underbelly on a tour of two WWII-era underground bunkers built around U-Bahn station Gesundbrunnen. One was renovated in the 1980s as shelter in case of civil disaster or atomic attack. You'll see hospital beds, bathrooms, filter systems and cases filled with war detritus, from helmets to buttons to

condoms. Tours are operated by a nonprofit organisation dedicated to preserving and restoring these subterranean refuges. Other tours, including one of the nearby Flakturm (air raid tower), are also offered. Tickets are available on a first-come-first-served basis from its office inside the U-Bahn station Gesundbrunnen (take Humboldthain, Brunnenstrasse exit).

TRABI SAFARI Map pp340-1

☎ 2759 2273; www.trabi-safari.de; Gendarmenmarkt, cnr Markgrafenstrasse; 2/3/4 passengers per person €35/30/25

The tinny Trabant (Trabi for short) was the archetypal GDR-made automobile. This company gives you a shot at exploring Berlin behind the wheel – or as a passenger – of this venerable relic. Choose from the Classic tour covering major Berlin sights or come face to face with eastern Berlin's socialist flair on the Wild East tour. You'll be following your guide who delivers live commentary (in English by prior arrangement) that's piped into your car. Tours last 90 minutes.

MITTE

Eating p168; Shopping p232; Sleeping p251

Even cynics can't deny it: Mitte has magnetism. 'Middle', as the name translates, is indeed the glamorous heart of Berlin, a high-octane cocktail of culture, commerce and history. This is where you'll likely concentrate your time, where you come to play and learn, to admire and marvel, and to be astounded and bewildered.

Berlin's most famous and beloved landmarks are here; from the Brandenburg Gate and the Berliner Dom to the TV Tower on Alexanderplatz, which still can't quite shake its Stalinist aesthetic. You'll probably prefer the looks of Unter den Linden, the city's grand boulevard and a ribbon of splendid architecture wrought by some of the genre's finest practitioners. Nearby Gendarmenmarkt is justifiably considered Berlin's most beautiful square. Catch a glimpse of the city's medieval roots on a stroll through the Nikolaiviertel or its dark Third Reich days while stumbling around the brand-new Holocaust Memorial. The bust of Nefertiti, the Pergamon Altar and the paintings of Caspar David Friedrich are among the blockbusters on view in the giant treasure chests of Museumsinsel. Squeeze in some shopping along elegant Friedrichstrasse or in the Scheunenviertel, a warren of energetic bars, great places to eat, progressive galleries and idiosyncratic boutiques. Mitte will quite literally spoil you for choice.

Orientation

Mitte, formerly in East Berlin, forms an administrative unit with Tiergarten, the seat of the federal government, to the west and working-class Wedding to the northwest. It's small and compact and eminently walkable.

Mitte's top sights line up like Prussian soldiers for inspection along Unter den Linden, which stretches west–east from the Brandenburg Gate to Museumsinsel from where it continues as Karl-Liebknecht-Strasse to just beyond Alexanderplatz.

Friedrichstrasse, flanked by shops, hotels and restaurants, is the main north–south artery. South of Unter den Linden it leads to the Gendarmenmarkt area and onward to Checkpoint Charlie and Kreuzberg. Following it north takes you to the historic theatre

TRANSPORT

Bus 100, 200 and the Tegel airport–bound express bus, TXL, run along Unter den Linden to Alexanderplatz; No 240 runs along Torstrasse along the northern edge of the Scheunenviertel.

S-Bahn S5, S7 and S9 travel from Zoo station to Friedrichstrasse, Hackescher Markt (for Scheunenviertel) and Alexanderplatz; S1 and S2 also stop at Friedrichstrasse and Unter den Linden.

Tram M4, M5 and M6 connect Alexanderplatz with Hackescher Markt; M1 connects Museumsinsel with Scheunenviertel and Prenzlauer Berg via Friedrichstrasse, Oranienburger Strasse, Rosenthaler Strasse and Kastanienallee; M2 runs north from Hackescher Markt along Prenzlauer Allee.

U-Bahn Weinmeisterstrasse (U8), Rosa-Luxemburg-Platz (U2) or Oranienburger Tor (U6) will take you to Scheunenviertel. Stadtmitte (U2, U6) runs to Gendarmenmarkt and go to Friedrichstrasse or Französische Strasse (U6) for Unter den Linden. U2, U5 or U8 has trains to Alexanderplatz.

MITTE TOP FIVE

- Make a date with Nefertiti and her entourage at the Altes Museum (p80).
- Stock up on uniquely Berlin fashions, music and knick-knacks while boutique-hopping around the Scheunenviertel (p232).
- Meditate upon the design and immensity of the Holocaust memorial (p75).
- Feast your eyes on the architecture of Unter den Linden (below) and Gendarmenmarkt (p77).
- Let the sights drift by you while sipping a cool drink on the deck of a river cruiser (p71).

district around U-/S-Bahn Friedrichstrasse, with easy access to post-performance drinks in the Scheunenviertel anchored by the Hackesche Höfe. The Prenzlauer Berg district is just north of here, while Alexanderplatz is the gateway to eastern districts including Friedrichshain, just down Karl-Marx-Allee. Berlin's first settlement once stood southwest of here in the Nikolaiviertel and the southern half of Museumsinsel.

ALONG UNTER DEN LINDEN

Berlin's most splendid boulevard extends for about 1.5km from the Brandenburg Gate to the Schlossbrücke. Before being developed into a showpiece road, Unter den Linden was merely a riding path connecting the Berliner Stadtschloss with the Tiergarten, once the royal hunting grounds. Under Elector Friedrich Wilhelm (r 1640–88), the eponymous linden trees were planted and a century later the harmonious ensemble of baroque, neoclassical and rococo structures was completed. WWII brought heavy destruction, but restoration has, for the most part, been careful and authentic.

AKADEMIE DER KÜNSTE Map pp340-1

☎ 200 570; www.adk.de; Pariser Platz 4; admission & hr vary; 🚇 Unter den Linden, 🚌 100, 200, TXL
With roots in the Prussian Academy of Arts, founded in 1696 by King Friedrich I, the Academy of Arts is one of the oldest cultural institutions in town. In May 2005 it moved to spectacular new digs in its historic location on Pariser Platz, which it had been kicked out of in 1937 by Hitler architect Albert Speer. Designed by Günter Behnisch, today's building has a transparent, lighthearted quality thanks to the ample use of glass and open spaces. Readings, discussions, workshops and other events take place here as well as at the Acadamey's other branch in Tiergarten (Map pp330–1; Hanseatenweg 10).

ALTE KÖNIGLICHE BIBLIOTHEK

Map pp340-1
Bebelplatz; 🚇 Hausvogteiplatz, Französische Strasse, 🚌 100, 200
The Alte Königliche Bibliothek (Old Royal Library) is a handsome 1775 baroque building whose elegantly curved façade has garnered it the nickname *Kommode* (chest of drawers). Now part of the Humboldt Universität, it originally housed the royal library before that fast-growing collection migrated across Unter den Linden to the much larger Staatsbibliothek (p77) in 1914.

BEBELPLATZ Map pp340-1

🚇 Hausvogteiplatz, Französische Strasse, 🚌 100, 200
Named for August Bebel, the cofounder of the Social Democratic Party (SPD), Bebelplatz is best known as the square where the Nazis organised their first official book burning on 10 May 1933. Works by Bertolt Brecht, Thomas Mann, Karl Marx and other so-called 'subversive' writers went up in flames on this day. It was a portentous event that marked the end of the cultural greatness Berlin had achieved over the previous two centuries. A poignant memorial by Micha Ullmann, consisting of an underground library with empty shelves, keeps the memory alive.

Bebelplatz was to be the focal point of Frederick the Great's pet project, the Forum Fridericianum, an intellectual and artistic centre inspired by ancient Rome. Alas, the king's costly war exploits left his coffers too strained to fully realise such grandiose visions but several buildings still got built, including the Alte Königliche Bibliothek (above) on the square's western side with the Staatsoper Unter den Linden (p77) opposite and St-Hedwigs-Kathedrale (p77) in the southeast corner. Next to the church looms the new Grand Hotel de Rome, an ultra luxurious hospitality temple housed in seriously altered digs previously occupied by the GDR state bank. The hotel is part of a bigger development called Operncarré that also includes housing, offices and stores.

TOP FIVE HISTORIC BUILDINGS

- Berliner Dom (p80)
- Brandenburg Gate (below)
- Reichstag (p102)
- Schloss Charlottenburg (p110)
- Zitadelle Spandau (p138)

Detail of Berliner Dom (p80)

BRANDENBURGER TOR Map pp340-1
Pariser Platz; admission free; 🕙 11am-6pm Apr-Oct, to 5pm Nov & Jan-Mar, to 4pm Dec; 🚊 Unter den Linden, 🚌 100, 200, TXL
The recently restored landmark Branden-burger Tor (Brandenburg Gate), a symbol of division during the Cold War, now epitomises German reunification. It was against this backdrop in 1987 that then–US president Ronald Reagan uttered the now famous words: 'Mr Gorbachev – tear down this wall'. Two years later, the Wall was history.

The 1791 structure by Carl Gotthard Langhans is the only surviving one of 18 city gates. Johann Gottfried Schadow's **Quadriga**, a sculpture of the winged goddess of victory piloting a horse-drawn chariot, proudly perches atop the curtain of Doric columns. Napoleon kidnapped the lady in 1806 and kept her in Paris for years. But as his fortunes waned, she was freed by a gallant Prussian general and triumphantly returned to Berlin in 1814.

The gate's north wing contains the **Raum der Stille** (Room of Silence; Map pp340–1),

where the weary and frenzied can sit and contemplate peace. In the south wing is a **BTM tourist office** (p301).

The Brandenburg Gate's main side over-looks **Pariser Platz** (p76), while on the west it borders the newly named **Platz des 18. März**, which commemorates the bloody quashing of a pro-democracy demonstration on 18 March 1848.

DEUTSCHE GUGGENHEIM BERLIN
Map pp340-1
☎ 202 0930; www.deutsche-guggenheim.de; Unter den Linden 13-15; adult/concession/family €4/3/8, free Mon; 🕙 11am-8pm Fri-Wed, to 10pm Thu; 🚇 Französische Strasse, 🚌 100, 200
If you've seen any other Guggenheim museum, especially those in New York and Bilbao, this small, minimalist gallery space – a joint venture between Deutsche Bank and the Guggenheim Foundation – is likely to be disappointing. Curators mount sev-eral exhibits a year featuring international contemporary artists of some renown, such as Eduardo Chillida, Georg Baselitz and Gerhard Richter. Free tours are held at 6pm daily and there's a nice shop and an even better café on site.

DEUTSCHES HISTORISCHES MUSEUM & IM PEI BAU Map pp340-1
☎ 203 040; www.dhm.de; Unter den Linden 2, IM Pei Bau: Hinter dem Giesshaus 3; adult/under 18 €4/free; 🕙 10am-6pm; 🚌 100, 200, TXL
The pink building opposite the Kron-prinzenpalais is the baroque **Zeughaus**, a former royal armoury completed in 1706. Already a history museum during GDR times, it became the German Historical Mu-seum in 1991 only to be closed a few years later for a mega renovation. If all went according to schedule, a wealth of docu-ments, painting, books, posters, furniture, machines and other objects should once again be chronicling 2000 years of German history by the time you're reading this. The period from the 1st century BC to the end of WWI in 1918 will be covered upstairs, while downstairs exhibits focus entirely on the rest of the 20th century, including the Third Reich and Cold War eras. The building's glass-covered central court-yard features the famous 22 sculptures of dying warriors by baroque artist Andreas Schlüter.

Temporary exhibits occupy the museum's extension, the so-called **IM Pei Bau** designed by the 'Mandarin of Modernism' IM Pei. It's a truly striking space – starkly geometric, yet imbued with a sense of lightness achieved through an airy atrium and generous use of glass.

FRIEDRICHSWERDERSCHE KIRCHE

Map pp340-1

☎ 2090 5577; www.smb.spk-berlin.de; Werderscher Markt; admission free; ⏱ 10am-6pm; ⊕ Hausvogteiplatz

With its twin square towers and phalanx of slender turrets punctuating the roofline, the neogothic Friedrichswerdersche Kirche (1830) is a perky presence on the Werderscher Markt, a short stroll southeast of Bebelplatz. Inspired by English churches, Karl Friedrich Schinkel dreamt up this playful design, which has housed a showcase of 19th-century sculpture since 1987.

Works by all of the period's heavyweights, including Johann Gottfried Schadow, Christian Daniel Rauch and Christian Friedrich Tieck, fill the softly lit nave. The upstairs firmly trains the spotlight on Schinkel himself with a comprehensive exhibit about his life and accomplishments.

The chunky structure southeast of here, by the way, housed the Reichsbank during the Third Reich and the central committee of the Sozialistische Einheitspartei Deutschland (SED; Socialist Unity Party of Germany) in GDR times. In united Germany, the building with its modern extension is home of the Auswärtiges Amt (Federal Foreign Office).

HOLOCAUST MEMORIAL Map pp340-1

Denkmal für die ermordeten Juden Europas; ☎ 7407 2929; www.holocaust-mahnmal.de; Ebertstrasse; admission free, tours adult/concession €3/1.50; ⏱ memorial 24hr, information centre 10am-8pm, tours 10.30am & 2pm Sat & Sun; ⏸ Unter den Linden

It took 17 years of discussion, planning and construction, but on 8 May 2005 the memorial to the Jewish victims of the Nazi-planned genocide of WWII was finally dedicated. Colloquially known as Holocaust Memorial, it occupies a space the size of a football field on high-profile real estate just south of the Brandenburg Gate. New York architect Peter Eisenmann conceived a vast grid of 2711 rectangular concrete blocks of varying height positioned on undulating ground as though it were some giant cemetery. You're free to access this maze at any point and make your individual journey through it. If it feels sober and unemotional at first, spend some time to contemplate the design, feel the coolness of the stone and watch the interplay of light and shadow.

To learn more about this gruesome period in history, visit the Ort der Information (information centre) below the memorial; the entrance is on its eastern side. A graphic timeline of Jewish persecution during the Third Reich is followed by rooms documenting the fate of individuals and entire families. In one darkened room, the names of the victims and their dates of birth and death are projected onto all four walls while a sombre voice reads their short biographies. It takes almost seven years to commemorate all victims in this fashion.

HUMBOLDT UNIVERSITÄT Map pp340-1

☎ 20 930; Unter den Linden 6; ⏹ 100, 200, TXL; ⏺ M1, 12

The students and faculty of the Humboldt Universität, Berlin's oldest university, are up against it to uphold their alma mater's illustrious legacy. Marx and Engels both studied here and the long list of famous professors includes the Brothers Grimm and Nobel Prize winners Albert Einstein, Max Planck and the nuclear scientist Otto Hahn.

Founded in 1810 by the diplomat, linguist and philosopher Wilhelm von Humboldt, the university occupies a former royal palace. Statues of the man and his famous explorer brother Alexander flank the main entrance.

KOMISCHE OPER Map pp340-1

☎ 4799 7400; www.komische-oper-berlin.de; box office Unter den Linden 41, entrance on Behrensstrasse 55; ⏸ Unter den Linden, ⏹ 100, 200, TXL

The Komische Oper (Light Opera) is one of Berlin's three opera houses. A theatre has stood in this spot since 1764, but the core of the structure dates only to 1892. After WWII, the original interior – a richly festooned baroque extravaganza – was largely restored, clashing with the decidedly functional '60s façade.

KRONPRINZENPALAIS Map pp340-1

Unter den Linden 3; 100, 200, TXL, M1, 12

The Kronprinzenpalais (Crown Princes' Palace) was merely a townhouse until Philipp Gerlach got his hands on it in 1732 and converted it into a residence for crown prince and future king Frederick the Great. Various other royals resided here until the demise of the monarchy in 1918.

Soon after Prussia's former first family moved out, the National Gallery happily moved in. Crowds flocked to see works by the finest artists of the day – Lovis Corinth, Otto Dix and Paul Klee among them – until the Nazis closed the show in 1937. 'Degenerate art', they sneered, while secretly stashing much of it away in their own collections.

The building was bombed to bits in WWII but faithfully re-created in the late 1960s to serve as the GDR's guesthouse for visiting dignitaries. Yes, Indira Gandhi slept here. On 31 August 1990 the palais captured the headlines again when the agreement paving the way to German unification was signed here.

The Crown Princes' Palace is connected to what used to be the Crown Princesses' Palace, built for the three daughters of Friedrich Wilhelm III in 1811. In its current incarnation as the Opernpalais, it houses a restaurant-café famous for its cake selection, as well as a pub and cocktail bar. It's great in summer when the beer garden is in full swing but pretty stuffy otherwise.

NEUE WACHE Map pp340-1

Unter den Linden 4; admission free; 10am-6pm; 100, 200, TXL

Built in 1818, the neoclassical Neue Wache (New Guardhouse) was Schinkel's first major Berlin commission and is now a memorial to the 'victims of war and tyranny'. Inspired by a classic Roman fortress, it's the double row of columns supporting a tympanum embellished with allegorical war scenes that gives the building a certain gravitas.

The inner courtyard was covered up in 1931 leaving only a skylight, which now spotlights Käthe Kollwitz's heart-wrenching sculpture *Mother and her Dead Son,* also known as *Pietà.* Buried below the austere room are the remains of an unknown soldier and a resistance fighter as well as soil from nine European battlefields and concentration camps.

PARISER PLATZ Map pp340-1

Unter den Linden, 100, 200, TXL

The Brandenburg Gate stands sentinel over this elegant square, where embassies, banks and a luxury hotel have snapped up Berlin's priciest real estate. Created in 1734, Pariser Platz' first brush with prestige came in the late 19th century, when it was considered the city's grand *Wohnzimmer* (living room), where luminaries from the arts and politics went to work and play. Badly destroyed during WWII, the square and gate were trapped just east of the Berlin Wall during the Cold War, reduced to the haunt of machine gun–toting border guards.

Some of the world's finest architects have left their mark on the 'new' Pariser Platz. Frenchman Christian de Portzamparc designed the French embassy (Map pp340–1) and Los Angeles–based Frank Gehry the DZ Bank (Map pp340–1). The architectural firm of Moore Ruble Yudell, also of LA, created the new US Embassy, which is expected to fill the square's last gap in 2008. German architect Günter Behnisch designed the glass-fronted Akademie der Künste (Academy of Arts, p73), which reopened in 2005. See the Architecture chapter for more details about the new Pariser Platz buildings (p49).

In the southeastern corner, the Hotel Adlon (now called the Adlon Kempinski, p251) was the first building to return to Pariser Platz in 1997. In its earlier incarnation, the former grande dame of Berlin caravanserais gave shelter to such celebs as Charlie Chaplin, Greta Garbo and Thomas Mann. Architecture critics have scoffed at this fairly faithful replica of the 1907 original but this doesn't seem to bother the presidents, diplomats, actors and merely rich, who regularly shack up here these days. Remember Michael Jackson dangling his baby out the window? It happened at the Adlon.

REITERDENKMAL FRIEDRICH DES GROSSEN Map pp340-1

Unter den Linden, near Bebelplatz; 100, 200, TXL

Seemingly surveying his domain, Frederick the Great cuts an imposing figure on horseback in this famous 1850 monument, which kept Christian Daniel Rauch busy for a dozen years. The plinth features a who's who of famous German military men, scientists, artists and thinkers as well as scenes from the king's life. The early GDR leaders didn't think much of the man and exiled the statue to Potsdam until Honecker restored it to its original spot in 1980.

RUSSISCHE BOTSCHAFT Map pp340-1

☎ 226 6320; Unter den Linden 63-65; 🚇 Unter den Linden, 🚌 100, 200, TXL

The hulking Russische Botschaft (Russian Embassy) is a white behemoth built in Stalin-era *Zuckerbäckerstil* (wedding-cake style). A tall wall allows only glimpses of the compound but if you are interested in this type of monumental architecture, swing by Karl-Marx-Allee (p129) in Friedrichshain, which is lined with them.

SANKT-HEDWIGS-KATHEDRALE

Map pp340-1

☎ 203 4810; www.hedwigs-kathedrale.de; Behrenstrasse 39; admission free; 🕙 10am-5pm Mon-Sat, 11am-5pm Sun; 🚇 Französische Strasse, 🚌 100, 200, TXL

Nothing less than the Pantheon in Rome inspired architect Knobelsdorff's design for St-Hedwig-Cathedral (1773), whose giant copper dome overlooks Bebelplatz. Frederick the Great named the church in honour of the patron saint of Silesia, which he just happened to have conquered.

St Hedwig was Berlin's only Catholic house of worship until 1854 and has been the mother church of the Berlin archdiocese since 1929. During WWII it was a centre of Catholic resistance under Father Bernard Lichtenberg, who died en route to Dachau in 1943 and is buried in the crypt. Like so many buildings around here, the church was blown to bits during WWII and now features a subdued, modern interior.

STAATSBIBLIOTHEK ZU BERLIN

Map pp340-1

☎ 2660; www.sbb.spk-berlin.de; Unter den Linden 8; 🕙 9am-9pm Mon-Fri, to 5pm Sat; 🚇 🚈 Friedrichstrasse, 🚌 100, 200, TXL

The original sheet music of Beethoven's 9th Symphony, medieval maps drawn by Nicolas von Kues, poems penned by the Persian writer Hafez – this is just a tiny sampling of the amazing archive of over 10 million books, periodicals and other printed matter amassed by the Staatsbibliothek (State Library). Founded in 1661 by the Great Elector Friedrich Wilhelm, the collection outgrew even its mammoth

current quarters built in 1914 by Ernst von Ihne, making it necessary to build a **second branch** (p109) in the 1970s. The original has a pretty inner courtyard with a café. Free 90-minute tours run at 10.30am every first Saturday of the month. In order to access the reading rooms and collection, you need a library card that costs €10 per month (€25 per year) and comes with age and residency restrictions.

STAATSOPER UNTER DEN LINDEN

Map pp340-1

☎ 203 540; www.staatsoper-berlin.org; Unter den Linden 7; 🚇 Hausvogteiplatz, Französische Strasse, 🚌 100, 200, TXL

The Staatsoper (State Opera House) on Bebelplatz is one of Berlin's earliest neoclassical structures, completed in 1743 as Frederick the Great's court opera to plans by Georg Wenzeslaus von Knobelsdorff. It's hard to imagine that this beautiful building, fronted by a curtain of Corinthian columns, was completely destroyed three times, the first time by a major fire in 1843 and twice during WWII. Today it is the most prestigious of Berlin's three opera houses and well respected throughout Europe (also see p209) .

GENDARMENMARKT & AROUND

Once a thriving marketplace, graceful Gendarmenmarkt is Berlin's most beautiful square. The twin structures of Französischer Dom (French Cathedral) and Deutscher Dom (German Cathedral) frame Schinkel's Schauspielhaus (now Konzerthaus) to form a superbly harmonious architectural trio. In recent years, luxury hotels and fancy restaurants have sprouted around the square, giving it an increasingly metropolitan flair.

Gendarmenmarkt was created in 1700 as the centrepiece of Friedrichstadt by Elector Friedrich III, later King Friedrich I. The new quarter was primarily settled by Huguenots, French Protestants expelled from France in 1685 by Louis XIV. Gendarmenmarkt derives its name from the *Gens D'arms* – a Prussian regiment of Huguenot soldiers – stationed here in the 18th century.

A magnificent **statue of Friedrich Schiller** (Map pp340–1) by Reinhold Begas stands in the middle of the square. Squirreled away by the Nazis, it ended up in West Berlin, from where it returned across the Wall in 1988 following an exchange of artworks between the two German states.

While in the area, you might want to make a quick detour one block north to the Stadtmodellausstellung (City Model Exhibit; Map pp340–1; ☎ 9020 5009; Behrensstrasse 42; admission free; ⏰ 10am-6pm) where large-scale architectural models give you a sense of what central Berlin will eventually look like.

DEUTSCHER DOM Map pp340-1

☎ 2273 0431; Gendarmenmarkt 1; admission & tours free; ⏰ 10am-10pm Tue Sep-May, 10am-7pm Tue Jun-Aug, 10am-6pm Wed-Sun year round; ⓔ Französische Strasse, Stadtmitte

One in the trio of Gendarmenmarkt beauties, the Deutscher Dom (German Cathedral), a 1708 work of Martin Grünberg, wasn't much of a looker until getting its dazzling galleried dome courtesy of Carl von Gontard in 1785. Since 1996 it's been used for exhibitions organised by the *Bundestag*, the German parliament. At the time of writing there was a hopelessly academic historical survey of German parliamentarianism that regularly bored groups of teenaged school children to tears.

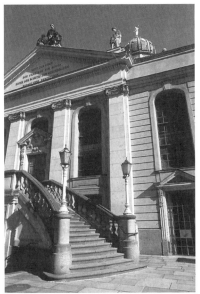

Französischer Dom (this page)

FRANZÖSISCHER DOM & HUGENOTTENMUSEUM Map pp340-1

☎ 229 1760; www.franzoesische-kirche.de; Gendarmenmarkt; adult/concession/family €2/1/3.50; ⏰ noon-5pm Tue-Sat, 11am-5pm Sun; ⓔ Französische Strasse

The Französischer Dom (French Cathedral) was built as a place of worship for the Huguenots, who settled in Berlin in the late 17th century. Completed in 1705, it closely follows the design of the group's main church in Charenton, which was destroyed in 1688. The Gontard-designed domed tower – matching that of the Deutscher Dom – was added 1785.

On the ground floor, the Hugenottenmuseum (Huguenots Museum) chronicles the Huguenots' story with descriptions in French and German. Once restoration of the **tower** is complete, you will again be able to climb its spiralling staircase to the top for tremendous city views.

FRIEDRICHSTADTPASSAGEN

Map pp340-1

Friedrichstrasse btwn Französische Strasse & Mohrenstrasse; ⓔ Französische Strasse, Stadtmitte

Even if Gucci and Prada don't quicken your pulse, a stroll through this trio of spectacularly designed shopping complexes (called Quartiers) linked by a subterranean passageway will wow you. Their opening in the mid-'90s helped Friedrichstrasse reclaim its historic position as one of Berlin's luxury hubs, a distinction that had been interrupted by WWII and communism.

Quartier 207 is the Berlin branch of the famous French department store Galeries Lafayette. Parisian architect Jean Nouvel designed its spectacular centrepiece, a translucent glass funnel that reflects light like some mutated hologram. Designed by a team led by Henry Cobb, **Quartier 206** Map pp340–1) is a stunning Art Deco–inspired symphony in glass and marble helmed by a tented glass roof. The patterned coloured marble floors are as dizzying as they are dazzling. A nice café on the ground floor invites a rest.

Cologne-based OM Ungers came up with **Quartier 205** (Map pp340–1), whose lofty light court is visually anchored with an installation by John Chamberlain and framed by upmarket fast-food eateries.

KONZERTHAUS BERLIN Map pp340-1

☎ 203 090; www.konzerthaus.de; Gendarmen-markt 2; ◉ Französische Strasse, Stadtmitte

One of Schinkel's finest accomplishments, the Konzerthaus (1821), originally called the Schauspielhaus, rose up from the ashes of Carl Gotthard Langhans' National Theater. It is the unifying element of Gendarmenmarkt, visually linking the German and French Cathedrals. Schinkel kept the few remaining outside walls and columns that hadn't been consumed by flames and added a grand staircase leading to a raised columned portico. WWII, of course, took its toll, but since its reopening in 1984 the Konzerthaus has once again been a shining beacon of Berlin culture. It's truly a fabulous building, both inside and out, and it's well worth attending a concert here or taking a guided tour (€3 per person; usually offered at 1pm Saturdays). Also see p206.

MUSEUM FÜR KOMMUNIKATION

Map pp336-7

☎ 202 940; www.museumsstiftung.de; Leipziger Strasse 16; adult/concession €3/1.50, under 15 free; ⏰ 9am-5pm Tue-Fri, 11am-7pm Sat & Sun; ◉ Mohrenstrasse, Stadtmitte

The ultra-rare Blue Mauritius stamp, the world's first telephone and three cheeky robots are among the main draws of the Museum für Kommunikation (Museum of Communication). Founded in 1898, it is the world's oldest postal museum but actually covers the gamut of telecommunication technology up until the Internet age. The most precious exhibits are in the 'treasure chamber' in the basement, while other galleries trace the evolution of various gadgets, from telephones and answering machines to TVs and PCs.

As interesting as the exhibits is the building's sumptuous architecture, especially its galleried and heavily-ornamented light court. At night, clever illumination makes it glow like a blue crystal. A café, shop and free Internet access are also available.

STASI – DIE AUSSTELLUNG Map pp340-1

☎ 2324 7951; www.bstu.de; Mauerstrasse 38, enter on Französische Strasse; admission free; ⏰ 10am-6pm Mon-Sat; ◉ Französische Strasse, Mohrenstrasse, ◉ Unter den Linden

They hid tiny cameras in watering cans and flowerpots, stole keys from school children to install listening devices in their homes and collected body-odour samples from suspects' groins. Stasi – Die Ausstellung (Stasi – The Exhibit) engagingly reveals the GDR's Ministry for State Security as an all-pervasive power with an all-out zeal and twisted imagination when it came to controlling, manipulating and repressing its own people.

Unfortunately all exhibits are detailed in German only, but a comprehensive English-language booklet is available free (so far) for the asking at the reception desk.

MUSEUMSINSEL

The sculpture-studded Schlossbrücke (Palace Bridge) leads to the little Spree island where Berlin's settlement began in the 13th century. Its northern half, Museumsinsel (Museum Island), is a fabulous treasure-trove of art, sculpture and objects spread across four grand old museums with a fifth one, the Neues Museum (New Museum), soon to be rebuilt. Collectively they became a Unesco World Heritage Site in 1999.

Museumsinsel is the result of a late-18th-century fad among European royalty to open up their private collections to the public. The Louvre in Paris, the British Museum in London, the Prado in Madrid and the Glyptothek in Munich all date back to this time. Back in Berlin, not to be outdone, Friedrich Wilhelm III and his successors followed suit, thereby creating one of the world's great museum-going experiences.

ALTE NATIONALGALERIE Map pp340-1

☎ 2090 5577; www.smb.spk-berlin.de; Bodestrasse 1-3; adult/concession €8/4, incl same-day admission to Altes Museum & Pergamon Museum €12/6, under 16 free, last 4hr Thu free; ⏰ 10am-6pm Tue-Sun, to 10pm Thu; ◉ Hackescher Markt, ◉ 100, 200, TXL, ◉ M1,12

The Alte Nationalgalerie (Old National Gallery), a sensitively restored Greek-temple building by Friedrich August Stüler, is an elegant setting for this exquisite collection of 19th-century European art. The wall-sized paintings by Franz Krüger and Adolf Menzel glorifying Prussia's military are hard to ignore, but they don't overshadow the insightful portraits by Philipp Otto Runge and the mystical landscapes of Caspar David Friedrich and, yes, Karl Friedrich Schinkel (there's just no escaping the man).

Another focus is on French Impressionists, including Monet and Renoir, and sculpture by Johann Gottfried Schadow and Christian Daniel Rauch. The gorgeously restored rotunda showcases the emotionally charged sculptures of Reinhold Begas, while the marble stairwell is decorated with Otto Geyers' patriotic frieze of German greats.

ALTES MUSEUM Map pp340-1

☎ 2090 5577; www.smb.spk-berlin.de; Am Lustgarten; adult/concession €8/4, incl same-day admission to Alte Nationalgalerie & Pergamon Museum €12/6, under 16 free, last 4hr Thu free; ☯ 10am-6pm Tue-Sun, to 10pm Thu; ⓇHackescher Markt, ⓈM1,12

Schinkel's imposing neoclassical Altes Museum (Old Museum, 1830) was the first exhibition space to be built on Museumsinsel. It's a monumental work fronted by a phalanx of Ionic columns that gives way to a rotunda festooned with sculptures of Zeus and his celestial entourage. Art and sculpture from ancient Greece dominate the galleries on the main floor, although you'll also find a few Roman pieces thrown into the mix, including a portrait of Caesar and Cleopatra. The most striking objects from the Antiquities Collection, though, are on display next door at the Pergamon Museum.

To meet the current 'star' of the Altes Museum, venture upstairs where a selection from the **Egyptian Museum** is housed until the completion of the Neues Museum in 2009. And here she is, the famous **bust of Nefertiti**, she of the long graceful neck and stunning good looks (even after all these years – about 3300, give or take a century or two).

The bust was part of the treasure trove German archaeologists unearthed between 1911 and 1914 while sifting through the dirt around the Nile city of Armana. They had stumbled upon the royal city built by Neferteti's husband, Akhenaten (r 1353–1336 BC), the renegade pharaoh who broke with tradition and raised the previously obscure sun god Aten to the status of supreme deity. Most of the items on display at the museum date to this period, including statues of the king and the royal family along with objects from everyday life. A major highlight from a later period is the so-called Berlin Green Head (500 BC), which is an almost expressionistic sculpture carved from green stone.

BERLINER DOM Map pp340-1

☎ 202 690; www.berliner-dom.de; Am Lustgarten; adult/concession €5/3, under 14 free; ☯ church & crypt 9am-8pm Mon-Sat, noon-8pm Sun Apr-Sep, to 7pm Oct-Mar, viewing gallery 9am-8pm Apr-Sep, to 5pm Oct-Mar, last admission 1hr before closing; Ⓡ ⓇHackescher Markt, ⓐ 100, 200, TXL, ⓈM1, 12

The Berlin Cathedral cuts a majestic figure in its prime spot on Museumsinsel. Completed in 1905 in ornate Italian Renaissance style, this was where the royal Hohenzollerns – the Prussian royal family – came to worship and be buried; their city palace stood just across the street on Schlossplatz. Wartime destruction kept the Dom closed until 1993 but restoration has now more or less concluded.

It's as splendid on the inside as it is on the outside, thanks to the efforts of several artists. Christian Daniel Rauch contributed the baptismal font, Guido Reni the Petrus mosaic and Friedrich August Stüler the altar table. The organ, a 1904 work by Wilhelm Sauer, has over 7200 pipes and is among the largest in Germany.

Niches in the northern and southern apses hold the ornate sarcophagi of various Hohenzollerns, including a pair carved by Andreas Schlüter for Friedrich I and his second wife Sophie Charlotte.

A central copper dome tops the colossal structure whose dimensions are best appreciated by climbing the 270 steps to the **viewing gallery**. Besides giving you nice views over Mitte, the view also gives you good close-ups of the amazing design details.

Concerts, guided tours and readings take place throughout the year. Ask at the box office or check the website or listings magazines for details.

BODEMUSEUM Map pp340-1

☎ 2660; www.smb.spk-berlin.de; Am Kupfergraben/Monbijoubrücke; ⓇHackescher Markt, ⓐ 100, 200, TXL, ⓈM1,12

If all goes according to plan, the Bodemuseum on the northern tip of Museumsinsel will have reopened following a nearly-six-year facelift by the time you're reading these words. The 1904 building is an imposing neobaroque work by Ernst-

Altes Museum (opposite page) and Lustgarten (this page)

Eberhard Ihne, who also designed the Staatsbibliothek zu Berlin (p77) on Unter den Linden. It again presents a stunning collection of sculpture from the Middle Ages to the late 18th century, including priceless late Gothic works by Tilman Riemenschneider and the *Pazzi Madonna*, an early Renaissance sculpture by Italian artist Donatello. Under the same roof is a broad sampling from the Museum of Byzantine Art. Ivory carvings from Constantinople (today's Istanbul) and religious icons from Russia are among the highlights here. Numismatic fans should look for the Coin Cabinet on the ground floor. Admission hours and prices were not available at the time of writing.

LUSTGARTEN Map pp340-1
Am Lustgarten; 🚊 Hackescher Markt, 🚌 100, 200, TXL, 🚋 M1 or 12

The Lustgarten (Pleasure Garden) fronting the Altes Museum looks like a peaceful patch of green, but it has actually seen quite a few ups and downs. Its life began rather placidly as a garden that supplied the nearby palace kitchen with fruit and vegetables, including Berlin's first-ever potatoes. Things got more interesting after the Thirty Years' War (1648), when the Great Elector had it turned into a real

pleasure garden with statues, grottoes and fountains among which to frolic. Such 'frivolity' was not tolerated by his austere grandson, Friedrich Wilhelm I (aka the Soldier King) who, naturally, turned the little park into an exercise ground for his beloved troops. It fell to Schinkel to completely redesign the grounds in 1830 in order to create a worthy complement to his then brand-new Altes Museum. Alas, the Nazis paved it over one more time, but in the late 1990s it was restored to its Schinkel-era appearance.

NEUES MUSEUM Map pp340-1
Bodestrasse; 🚊 Hackescher Markt, 🚌 100, 200, TXL, 🚋 M1, 12

With space getting tight in the Altes Museum, Friedrich August Stüler got the nod to build a second gallery, which opened in 1859 as the prosaically named Neues Museum (New Museum). WWII reduced it to rubble but it is now being painstakingly rebuilt. This immense undertaking is expected to take until 2009 whereupon Queen Nefertiti and her entourage from the Egyptian Museum (currently at the Altes Museum, opposite) will be moving into their new digs. She will be joined by the collections of the Museum of Pre- and Early History in Charlottenburg (p112).

PERGAMON MUSEUM Map pp340-1

☎ 2090 5555; www.smb.spk-berlin.de;
Am Kupfergraben 5; adult/concession €8/4, incl
same-day admission to Altes Museum & Alte
Nationalgalerie €12/6, under 16 free, last 4hr
Thu free; ⏰ 10am-6pm Tue-Sun, to 10pm Thu;
🚇 Hackescher Markt, 🚌 100, 200, TXL,
🚊 M1,12

If you only have time for one museum
while in Berlin, make it the Pergamon. It's
a veritable feast of classical Greek, Babylonian, Roman, Islamic and Middle Eastern
art and architecture excavated by German
archaeologists at the turn of the 20th
century.

The giant complex, which was only
completed in 1930, actually harbours three
important collections under one roof: the
Collection of Classical Antiquities, the Museum of Near Eastern Antiquities and the
Museum of Islamic Art. Each one is worth
seeing at leisure, but if you're pressed
for time, make a beeline to the following
highlights.

The museum's namesake and undisputed crowd magnet is the **Pergamon Altar**
(165 BC) from Asia Minor (in today's Turkey). It's a gargantuan raised marble shrine
surrounded by a vivid frieze of the gods
doing battle with the giants. Walk up its
steps for close-ups of the Telephos Frieze,
which depicts the life story of the legendary founder of Pergamon.

The next room presents another key exhibit: the immense **Market Gate of Miletus** (2nd
century AD), a masterpiece of Roman architecture. Beyond the gate lies the collection
of the Museum of Near Eastern Antiquities
and another civilisation entirely: Babylon
during the reign of King Nebuchadnezzar
II (604–562 BC). It's impossible not to be
awed by the reconstructions of the **Ishtar
Gate**, the Processional Way leading up to it
and the façade of the king's throne hall. All
are sheathed in glazed bricks glistening in a
luminous cobalt blue and ochre. The strid-
ing lions, horses and dragons, which represent major Babylonian gods, are so striking
that you can almost hear the roaring and
fanfare. Another collection highlight is the
intricate temple façades from Uruk, with
their multihued clay inlays and detailed
brick reliefs.

Finally, in the Museum of Islamic Art,
keep an eye out for the fortress-like 8th-
century caliph's palace from Mshatta in
today's Jordan. Crowds also gather for
a peek inside the 17th-century Aleppo
Room, taken from the house of a Syrian
merchant, with its rich, painted, wood-
panelled walls.

Try to budget at least two hours for this
amazing museum.

SCHLOSSPLATZ

Nothing of today's Schlossplatz evokes
memory of the magnificent edifice that
stood here from 1451 to 1951: the Berliner
Stadtschloss (Berlin City Palace), for centuries the primary residence of the ruling
Hohenzollern family. Despite international
protests, the GDR government demolished
the barely war-damaged structure, which it
considered a 'symbol of Prussian militarism',
in 1951. In its stead was put the country's
political nerve centre, anchored by the Palast
der Republik, the Staatsratsgebäude and the
Marx Engels Forum. It was a decision even
some East Berlin political honchos later ad-
mitted regretting.

MARSTALL & RIBBECKHAUS Map pp340-1

Breite Strasse; ⓢ Spittelmarkt, Klosterstrasse,
🚌 148

Southeast of Schlossplatz, the neobaroque
Neuer Marstall (New Stables; Map pp340–1)
is a 1901 work by Ernst von Ihne that once
sheltered royal horses and carriages. In
1918, revolutionaries hatched their plans
to bring about the end of the Hohenzollern
monarchy here. One of the bronze reliefs
on the northern façade shows Karl Liebknecht proclaiming (unsuccessfully) the
German socialist republic on November 9.
In 2005, the building found a new purpose
as the secondary home of the **Hochschule für
Musik Hanns Eisler** (p206), a prestigious music
academy. You can now hear concerts in the
Krönungskutschensaal, the hall once filled
with royal wedding carriages.

The Neuer Marstall is an extension of the
Alter Marstall (Old Stables; Map pp340–1),
built by Michael Matthias Smids in 1670,
making it Berlin's oldest baroque building.
It rubs shoulders with the **Ribbeckhaus** (Map
pp340–1), a rare Renaissance structure
with four pretty gables and a highly ornate
sandstone portal. The latter two buildings
are now home to public libraries.

(Continued on page 91)

1 *Art Nouveau-style courtyard of Hackesche Höfe (pp95-6), Mitte* 2 *Schlossgarten Charlottenburg (p112), Charlottenburg* 3 *Lounging in front of the Berlin Wall (p136), Mitte* 4 *Plaza and fountain at the entrance to the Berliner Dom (p80), Mitte*

1 *Reichstag and its famous glass dome (p102), Tiergarten* **2** *Pariser Platz (p76) and Brandenburger Tor Quadriga (p74), Mitte* **3** *The ancient Greek Pergamon Altar in the Pergamon Museum (p82), Mitte* **4** *Entrance Hall of Alte Nationalgalerie (pp79-80), Mitte*

1

Deutscher Dom (p78) and
nzerthaus (p79) on
ndarmenmarkt, Mitte
ove Parade (p11), Tiergar-
3 Sculpture outside Neue
tionalgalerie (pp108-9),
rgarten

2

3

1 *Main Gate of Schloss Char-tenburg (pp110-12), Charlot-tenburg* 2 *Kantdreieck build-(p115), Charlottenburg* 3 *Gc Gallery (p112), Schloss Charl-tenburg, Charlottenburg*

1 *Steiff in Berlin toy shop (p239), Charlottenburg* 2 *Ludwig Erhard Haus (p116), Charlottenburg* 3 *The famous elephant gates at Berliner Zoo & Aquarium (p114), Charlottenburg* 4 *Erotik Museum (p114), Charlottenburg*

1 *Marheineke Markthalle (pp242-3), Kreuzberg* **2** *East Side Gallery (pp128-9), Friedrichshain* **3** *Jüdisches Museum (pp125-6), Kreuzberg* **4** *Checkpoint Charlie booth (p123), Kreuzberg*

1 Schloss Köpenick (p140)
2 Sowjetisches Ehrenmal (p103),
Mitte 3 Model historical ships at
the Deutches Technikmuseum
(pp123-4), Kreuzberg 4 Statue at
the Reconciliation Chapel, near
Gedenkstätte Berliner Mauer
(pp135-6), Wedding

ВЕЧНАЯ СЛАВА
ГЕРОЯМ ПАВШИМ
В БОЯХ С НЕМЕЦКО
ФАШИСТСКИМИ
ЗАХВАТЧИКАМИ
ЗА СВОБОДУ И
НЕЗАВИСИМОСТЬ
СОВЕТСКОГО
СОЮЗА

1941
1945

1 *Schlossbrücke (p79) with Berliner Dom (p80) in the background, Mitte* **2** *A serene moment on the Landwehrkanal (p122), Kreuzberg* **3** *People relaxing in the Grunewald (p118), Wilmersdorf* **4** *Jellyfish at Aquadom and Sealife Berlin (p92), Mitte*

(Continued from page 82)

SITE OF THE FORMER PALAST DER REPUBLIK Map pp340-1

Schlossplatz; ⊟ 100, 200

By the time you're reading this there will likely be a huge vacant lot across from the Berliner Dom in the spot where the GDR-era Palast der Republik (Palace of the Republic) once stood. After more than a decade of heated debate, demolition of the concrete, steel and orange glass monstrosity finally began in January 2006.

The GDR's 'palace' occupied the site of the historical Berliner Stadtschloss (Berlin City Palace), demolished in 1951 by the East German government despite an international outcry. The current plan foresees a rebuilding of the palace shell with a modern interior that could be used for a variety of purposes such as a museum, a hotel, a library, meeting space etc. Have a look at the scale model in the Infocenter (Hausvogteiplatz 3; admission free; ☺ 9.30am-6pm). The projected price tag: a billion euros. However, with the Berlin city government broke, no private investors in sight and a national government focused on other priorities, it's anyone's guess as to when reconstruction might actually take place.

It took, after all, 25 years after the original Schloss had been razed before the Palast der Republik opened for business in 1976. The multipurpose building, which could accommodate up to 5000 people, quickly became a feature in the cultural life of East Berlin. The GDR parliament (the Volkskammer) met in the Kleiner Saal (Small Hall) but the other sections were open to the public. Stars like Harry Belafonte performed in the Grosse Halle (Big Hall), also used for congresses and balls. The sweeping foyer contained a gallery showcasing the works of contemporary GDR artists, a variety theatre and restaurants.

After reunification the place was immediately boarded up since it was seriously contaminated with asbestos. In 1993, a French artist covered the structure with cloth painted like the old Schloss façade, sparking the movement to rebuild the historical landmark. The saga continues…

STAATSRATSGEBÄUDE Map pp340-1

Schlossplatz 1; ⊕ Spittelmarkt, ⊟ 100, 200, TXL, 147

The only piece of the Berlin City Palace spared demolition was the arched portal from which Karl Liebknecht proclaimed (in vain) a German socialist republic in 1918. In honour of the Marxist martyr, the GDR politicos had the section incorporated into the Staatsratsgebäude (National Council Building, 1964), the top political institution of the GDR government. In 2005, the building became the Berlin campus of the European School of Management & Technology.

ALEXANDERPLATZ & AROUND

Formerly East Berlin's main commercial hub, Alexanderplatz – 'Alex' for short – was first called Ochsenmarkt (ox market) and renamed in honour of Tsar Alexander I, who visited Berlin in 1805. Today it is light years away from the low-life district Alfred Döblin called 'the quivering heart of a cosmopolitan city' in his 1929 novel *Berlin Alexanderplatz*.

Badly bombed in WWII, it got its current socialist look in the 1960s courtesy of GDR city planners. The TV Tower, the 123m-high Interhotel Stadt Berlin and the Centrum Warenhaus (now Kaufhof), once the GDR's largest department store, all date back to those days. Other landmark relics include the Brunnen der Völkerfreundschaft (Fountain of Friendship among the Peoples) and the Weltzeituhr (World Time Clock). Off to the side is the Haus des Lehrers (House of Teachers) with a frieze by Walter Womacka, which is now part of the adjacent Berlin Congress Centre.

Although plans to turn Alexanderplatz into a skyscraper-studded mini-Manhattan had to be shelved (for now) for lack of cashed-up investors, the square is gradually changing anyway. In 2005/06, the Kaufhof department store got a complete Josef Paul Kleihues–designed makeover. It traded its traditional honeycomb façade for a sleek travertine-glass skin and gained a glass-domed central light court. Nearby, the 1929 Berolinahaus by Peter Behrens is being converted into a branch of the C&A clothing store, which opened its first shop on Alexanderplatz in 1911.

And not far away, in an area bounded by Alexanderstrasse, Dirckseenstrasse and Grunerstrasse, the new Alexa Shopping Mall is taking shape. The Portuguese-French investors hope to be open for business in early 2007 with about 200 stores, a huge food court, a multiplex cinema and a fitness centre.

Sights

MITTE

AQUADOM & SEALIFE BERLIN
Map pp340-1

☎ 992 800; Spandauer Strasse 3; adult/student/child €13.50/12.60/10; ⏱ 10am-7pm (last admission) Apr-Aug, 10am-6pm Sep-Mar; 🚇 Hackescher Markt, Alexanderplatz, 🚌 100, 200, TXL, 🚊 M4, M5, M6

This entertaining aquarium takes you on a virtual journey along the Spree, Havel and Elbe Rivers into the frigid waters of the North Atlantic. Along the way you'll meet the aquatic denizens living in the various habitats, which have been re-created in 30 tanks, including a 360-degree aquarium where a giant school of mackerel makes its merry rounds. Other crowd favourites include smile-inducing sea horses, the otherworldly jellyfish and a big tank with manta rays and small sharks. Kids can test their knowledge by answering quiz questions throughout. All labelling is in English and German.

Visits conclude with what is billed as the big highlight: a very slow lift ride through a 16m-tall cylindrical aquarium teeming with tropical fish. It's right in the lobby of the Radisson SAS Hotel, from where you could sneak a free preview.

Ephraim-Palais (this page)

EPHRAIM-PALAIS Map pp340-1

☎ 2400 2121; www.stadtmuseum.de; Poststrasse 16; adult/concession €3/1.50; ⏱ 10am-6pm Tue & Thu-Sun, noon-8pm Wed; 🚇 Klosterstrasse, 🚌 148

The 1762 Ephraim-Palais, on the southern edge of the Nikolaiviertel, is considered one of Berlin's most beautiful buildings. Originally the home of the court jeweller and coin minter Veitel Heine Ephraim, it sports an elegantly curving rococo façade decorated with frolicking cherubs and gilded wrought-iron balconies.

The present structure is in fact a complete replica of the original, torn down in 1936 to make room for the widening of Mühlendamm. Fortunately, sections of the precious façade survived in storage in West Berlin until given to the eastern city in 1984 to be used in the construction of the Nikolaiviertel.

These days, the palais presents changing exhibits focusing on aspects of art and the cultural history of Berlin as well as the graphics collection of the Stadtmuseum (City Museum). Architectural highlights include the oval staircase and the Schlüterdecke, an ornate ceiling, on the 1st floor.

FERNSEHTURM Map pp340-1

☎ 242 3333; www.berlinerfernsehturm.de; Panoramastrasse 1a; adult/child under 16 €7.50/3.50; ⏱ 9am-midnight Mar-Oct, 10am-midnight Nov-Feb; 🚇 🚊 Alexanderplatz

The Fernsehturm (TV Tower) is Berlin's tallest structure, soaring skyward for 368m. From the panorama platform at a lofty 203m, you'll be able to pinpoint the city's major landmarks, marvel at the size of the Tiergarten park and compare the layout of the former eastern and western city halves. Upstairs, the Telecafé serves coffee, snacks and full meals (€6 to €13) as it makes a full revolution within 30 minutes.

Built in 1969, the tower was intended to demonstrate the technological superiority of the GDR, but ironically it became a source of embarrassment. In sunlight, the steel sphere below the antenna produces the reflection of a giant cross – not a welcome sight in a secular land where crosses had been removed from church roofs. West Berliners gleefully dubbed the phenomenon 'the Pope's revenge'.

The Fat Tire Bike Tours office on the north side of the tower base sells discounted tickets for €5.50.

FRANZISKANER KLOSTERKIRCHE

Map pp340-1

☎ 636 1213; Klosterstrasse 73a; admission free, except for some events; ☺ noon-6pm Tue-Sun; ⊙ Klosterstrasse

The husk of its ancient church is all that is left of the 1250 Franciscan monastery on Klosterstrasse. After 1534 it became a prestigious grammar school where pupils such as Karl Friedrich Schinkel and Otto von Bismarck prepared for their illustrious careers.

Destroyed in the final days of WWII, the ruins offered silent testimony against war and fascism in GDR days. After years of restoration, it reopened in June 2005 and now serves as a cultural venue for concerts, exhibits and other events.

Behind the ruins, at Littenstrasse 12-17, looms a branch of the **Landgericht Berlin** (state courthouse, Map pp340-1), which has handsome Art Nouveau staircases.

HISTORISCHER HAFEN BERLIN

Map pp340-1

☎ 2147 3257; www.historischer-hafen-berlin.de; Märkisches Ufer; exhibit adult/concession/family €2/1/5, under 6 free; ☺ 2-6pm Tue-Fri, 11am-6pm Sat & Sun May-Oct; ⊙ Märkisches Museum

Laced by rivers, canals and lakes, it's not surprising that Berlin has a long history in inland navigation and even had the busiest river port in Germany until WWII. The Historischer Hafen (Historical Harbour), at the southern tip of Museumsinsel, is an outdoor museum with over 20 boats, barges and tugboats, many still operational. One boat doubles as a café in summer while another contains a small exhibit documenting 250 years of river shipping on the Spree and Havel.

MARIENKIRCHE Map pp340-1

☎ 242 4467; Karl-Liebknecht-Strasse 8; admission free; ☺ 10am-6pm Apr-Oct, to 4pm Nov-Mar; ⊛ Hackescher Markt, Alexanderplatz, ⊟ 100, 200, TXL, ⊞ M4, M5, M6

The 13th-century Marienkirche (St Mary's Church) is considered Berlin's second-oldest church after the Nikolaikirche. It's filled with art treasures, the oldest being the bronze baptismal font from 1437. Other eye-catchers are the baroque alabaster pulpit by Andreas Schlüter (1703) and the badly faded Dance of Death wall fresco in the vestibule, created after the plague epidemic of 1484. Call about

TOP FIVE VIEWS

- Fernsehturm (opposite)
- Glockenturm (p118)
- Grunewaldturm (p118)
- Panorama Punkt (p104)
- Reichstag (p102)

English-language tours, usually offered at 1pm on Saturday and Sunday.

MÄRKISCHES MUSEUM Map pp340-1

☎ 3086 6215; www.stadtmuseum.de; Am Köllnischen Park 5; adult/concession €4/2; ☺ 10am-6pm Tue & Thu-Sun, noon-8pm Wed; ⊙ Märkisches Museum

Berlin's main history museum – a 1908 work by Ludwig Hoffmann – occupies a unique architectural jumble that borrows elements from several actual buildings in the region. The tower, for instance, is modelled on that of the cathedral in Ratzeburg and the ornate gables recall St Catherine's Church in Brandenburg.

Exhibits help you understand how the tiny trading village of Berlin-Cölln evolved into today's modern metropolis. Rooms are organised by theme rather than chronology. An armoury, a magnificent Guild Hall and a collection of religious sculptures, for instance, represent medieval times. A highlight is the Kaiserpanorama (emperor's panorama), basically a 3-D slide show that was a form of mass entertainment in the early 20th century. If you happen to visit on a Sunday, don't miss the quirky automatophones, historic mechanical musical instruments that are wound up and launched on their cacophonous journey at 3pm (separate admission, €2/1).

In the little Köllnischer park just south of the museum you can meet the city's official symbols, Thilo, Maxi and Schnute, three real-life **brown bears** (admission free; ☺ 8am-5pm Apr-Sep, 9am-3pm Oct-Mar) that reside in the bear pit.

MARX-ENGELS-FORUM Map pp340-1

Bounded by Karl-Liebknecht-Strasse, Spandauer Strasse, Rathausstrasse & the Spree River; ⊛ Hackescher Markt, ⊟ 100, 200, TXL, ⊞ M4, M5, M6

A twice-life-size sculpture of Karl Marx and Friedrich Engels anchors this sterile square, which Erich Honecker inaugurated in 1986 by hailing the duo as the 'greatest sons of the German people'. Also part of the ensemble are reliefs showing people living happily under socialism and others deploring the inhumanity of capitalism.

MOLKENMARKT Map pp340-1

Intersection of Mühlendamm, Stralauer Strasse & Spandauer Strasse; Ⓜ **Klosterstrasse,** 🚌 **148**
Berlin's oldest market square, the Molkenmarkt, had its heyday in the 13th century but is now thoroughly engulfed in roaring traffic. Only a few historic buildings survived war and redevelopment, including the baroque **Palais Schwerin** (Map pp340–1; Molkenmarkt 3) and the **Münze**, where coins have been minted since 1937. A decorative frieze depicts the evolution of metallurgy and coin minting.

Looming above it all is the **Altes Stadthaus** (Map pp340–1; Klosterstrasse 47) with its elegant domed tower. Built in 1911 as an extension of the Red Town Hall and later used by the GDR's Ministerrat (council of ministers), it now houses offices of the Berlin senate. In 2004 a copy of the lost statue of the goddess Fortuna returned to its historic spot atop the dome.

MUSEUM KNOBLAUCHHAUS
Map pp340-1

☎ 2345 9991; www.stadtmuseum.de; Poststrasse 23; Ⓜ **Klosterstrasse,** 🚌 **148**
The 1761 Knoblauchhaus is the oldest residential building in the Nikolaiviertel and at the time of research was closed for renovation. It was the home of the prominent Knoblauch family, which included politicians, the founder of a first aid society and the architect of the original synagogue on Oranienburger Strasse (p97). As patrons of the arts, the Knoblauchs enjoyed tea and talk with people such as Schinkel, Schadow and Begas in this very house.

MUSEUM NIKOLAIKIRCHE Map pp340-1

☎ 2472 4529; www.stadtmuseum.de; Nikolaikirchplatz; admission by donation; ⏰ 10am-6pm Tue & Thu-Sun, noon-8pm Wed; Ⓜ **Klosterstrasse,** 🚌 **148**
Lording it over the Nikolaiviertel are the twin spires of the late-Gothic Nikolaikirche (1230), Berlin's oldest church. It received a significant drubbing during WWII but was faithfully rebuilt in the 1980s and reopened as a museum. The exhibit focuses on the

church's role in local history. Of greater interest, perhaps, are baroque epitaphs of prominent Berliners on its walls and pillars.

NEPTUNBRUNNEN Map pp340-1

Spandauer Strasse; 🚇 **Hackescher Markt, Alexanderplatz,** 🚌 **100, 200, TXL,** 🚋 **M4, M5, M6**
This fountain, between Marienkirche and Rotes Rathaus, was designed by Reinhold Begas in 1891 and originally stood on Schlossplatz between the palace and the Marstall. It shows Neptune holding court over a quartet of buxom beauties symbolising major rivers: the Rhine, Elbe, Oder and Vistula.

NIKOLAIVIERTEL Map pp340-1

Bounded by Rathausstrasse, Spandauer Strasse, Mühlendamm & the Spree River; Ⓜ **Klosterstrasse,** 🚌 **148**
Just behind the Rotes Rathaus, the twee Nicholai Quarter occupies the area of Berlin's first settlement dating back to the early 13th century. Despite its Disney-esque patina, it is a fairly successful attempt by GDR architects to re-create Berlin's medieval core, a prestige project undertaken in celebration of the city's 750th anniversary in 1987. The result is a maze of narrow, cobbled lanes lined with historic buildings, some original, most reconstructed. The Ephraim-Palais and Nikolaikirche contain small museums (also described in this section).

It's a nice place for strolling but you won't find too many Berliners patronising the pricey cafés, restaurants and cutesy shops. Also here is the restaurant-pub **Zum Nussbaum**, a favourite watering hole of humorist and local legend Heinrich Zille (1858–1929).

ROTES RATHAUS Map pp340-1

☎ 902 60; Rathausstrasse 15; admission free; ⏰ 9am-6pm Mon-Fri; Ⓜ **Klosterstrasse,** 🚌 **148**
The hulking Rotes Rathaus (Red Town Hall) has been Berlin's power nexus since 1860 and is currently occupied by governing mayor Klaus Wowereit and his city government, the Senate. The moniker 'red', by the way, was inspired by the colour of the red-brick façade and not the political leanings of its occupants. A terracotta frieze (1879) running along the building's length illustrates city history until 1871. The two bronze sculptures near the main entrance

honour the men and women who helped rebuild the city – literally with their hands – after WWII. For security reasons, access is restricted to certain areas.

SAMMLUNG KINDHEIT & JUGEND
Map pp340-1

Childhood & Youth Collection; ☎ 275 0383; Wallstrasse 32; adult/concession/family € 2/1/2.50; ⊗ 9am-5pm Tue-Fri, 10am-6pm Sat & Sun; ⊚ Märkisches Museum

This museum takes you on a sometimes entertaining, sometimes pedantic journey through the history of growing up in Germany, Berlin in particular. Nostalgia buffs can squeeze behind the wooden desks of a re-created 1912 classroom or discover the purpose of an *Eselskappe* (donkey hat) that had to be worn by undisciplined kids. In the Scriptorium you can test your penmanship using quill and ink. The big collection of toys from the past two centuries brings smiles to faces young and old.

SCHEUNENVIERTEL

North of Alexanderplatz, the Scheunenviertel (Barn Quarter) is one of the city's liveliest areas, teeming with restaurants, bars and nightclubs, especially around the Hackescher Markt, along Oranienburger Strasse and in such restored courtyard complexes as the Hackesche Höfe. Alte Schönhauser Strasse and Neue Schönhauser Strasse are hip shopping streets, lined with dozens of trendy boutiques. Auguststrasse has become a famous art mile with leading galleries like Eigen + Art and the Kunst-Werke Berlin being major art-scene hubs. Since reunification, the Scheunenviertel has also reprised its historic role as Berlin's Jewish quarter with the New Synagogue as its most visible symbol.

ANNE FRANK ZENTRUM Map pp340-1

☎ 3087 2988; Rosenthaler Strasse 39; adult/concession/family €3.50/2/6; ⊗ 10am-6pm Tue-Sun; ⊚ Hackescher Markt

This small but poignant exhibit allows peeks into the life of Anne Frank, the German-Jewish girl famous for her diary written while hiding from the Nazis in Amsterdam. At time of writing it had temporarily moved to Karl-Liebknecht-Strasse 7 but should by now have returned to its permanent location in the Museum Blindwerkstatt Otto Weidt, next to the Hackesche Höfe.

GROSSE HAMBURGER STRASSE
Map pp340-1

⊚ Hackescher Markt

The Grosse Hamburger Strasse is a key street in Berlin's Jewish history. The city's first Jewish Cemetery, the **Alter Jüdischer Friedhof**, once occupied the grassy area near the corner with Hackescher Markt. Over 12,000 people were buried here between 1672 and 1827, including Veitel Heine Ephraim (see Ephraim-Palais, p92) and the Enlightenment philosopher Moses Mendelssohn. The latter is honoured with a memorial tombstone (not the original one), which stands solitary and silent as a reminder of the destruction wrought upon the sacred grounds by the Gestapo in 1943.

Nearby, in the space where Grosse Hamburger Strasse 26 is, a plaque marks the site of the city's first **Jewish seniors home** (Map pp340–1). In 1942 the Nazis turned the building into a deportation centre. A haunting sculpture by Will Lammert shows a group of fatigued women standing in abject resignation to their fate. Bombs flattened the building and it was never rebuilt. Every year, the names of all 55,696 Berlin Jews who perished at the hands of the Nazis are read out aloud here on Holocaust Memorial Day (27 January).

The building at Grosse Hamburger Strasse 27 originally housed a **Jewish boys school** (Map pp340–1) founded in 1788 at the instigation of Moses Mendelssohn; he's honoured by a plaque. The Nazis closed the school but it survived the war intact. Today, both boys and girls – Jewish or not – once again hit the books in its hallowed rooms.

On the opposite side of the street is the **Missing House** (Map pp340–1; 1990), an installation and memorial by French artist Christian Boltanski. The 'missing house' in question was a neobaroque apartment building that stood at Grosse Hamburger Strasse 15/16 until it was destroyed by a direct bomb hit.

HACKESCHE HÖFE Map pp340-1

www.hackesche-hoefe.com; ⊚ Hackescher Markt

One of Berlin's biggest tourist magnets, the Hackesche Höfe (1907) is a warren of eight beautifully restored courtyards filled

TOP FIVE QUIRKY MUSEUMS

- Berliner Medizinhistorisches Museum (Berlin Medical History Museum; p98)
- Deutsches Currywurst Museum (p114)
- Erotik Museum (p114)
- Ramones Museum (p126)
- Zucker Museum (Sugar Museum; p136)

with upmarket cafés, galleries, boutiques and entertainment venues. The nicest one is Hof 1 (enter from Rosenthaler Strasse), whose façades are emblazoned with intricately patterned Art Nouveau tiles designed by August Endell.

Court VII offers access to the **Rosenhöfe**, really just a small, single courtyard with a sunken rose garden. Sculpted filigree metal balustrades, vaguely resembling flowers and botanical tendrils, give this place a whimsical quality.

HANDWERKERVEREINSHAUS (SOPHIENSAELE) Map pp340-1

☎ 2859 9360; Sophienstrasse 18; ⊕ Weinmeisterstrasse

This handsome building, now a performance venue called **Sophiensaele** (p214), looms large in the history of Berlin's workers' movement. It was built in 1905 as the clubhouse of the Handwerkerverein, the city's first workers association, which became a germ cell of the labour movement. Its large assembly halls hosted numerous political gatherings, especially in the aftermath of WWI when members of the Spartacus League, including Karl Liebknecht and Wilhelm Pieck, rallied the troops in support of a socialist revolution. This, of course, failed. Liebknecht was soon murdered, but Pieck later became the GDR's first president.

HECKMANNHÖFE Map pp340-1

www.heckmann-hoefe.de; Oranienburger Strasse 32; ⊛ Oranienburger Strasse

For our money, this former machine factory is the nicest of the Scheunenviertel courtyard complexes. Ivy-clad brick buildings house cafés, unique shops and the teensy candy-making shop called Bonbonmacherei (p233). Benches, a pretty fountain and a small playground invite lingering beneath the looming dome of the New Synagogue.

KUNSTHAUS TACHELES Map pp340-1

☎ 282 6185; www.tacheles.de; Oranienburger Strasse 54-56; ⊕ Oranienburger Tor

It may look like a crumbling ruin – and it is – but the Tacheles is still one of the most dynamic and beloved art and cultural spaces in town. Originally a department store, the building was later used by the Nazis before being badly damaged by WWII bombs. The East German government targeted it for demolition but never fully followed through with it, so it was still left standing when the Wall fell in 1989. A few months later, dozens of artists 'discovered' it and turned it into a giant art squat. Although it has lost some of its anarchic edge, it's still a chaotic, graffiti-covered warren of studios and galleries, including a cinema, café and beer garden. There's always something going on here – theatre, readings, happenings, parties – just check the listings mags or the website.

KUNST-WERKE BERLIN Map pp340-1

☎ 243 4590; www.kw-berlin.de; Auguststrasse 69; adult/concession €6/4; ⊗ noon-7pm Tue-Sun, to 9pm Thu; ⊛ Oranienburger Strasse

This nonprofit institution keeps the finger on the pulse of the contemporary art scene in Berlin and beyond through changing exhibits, workshops and events. Founded in 1990 and housed in a converted margarine factory, it helped shape the Scheunenviertel into one of the city's art hubs. Café Bravo, inside a glass-and-steel cube by US artist Dan Graham, is a suitably edgy place for a respite.

MUSEUM BLINDENWERKSTATT OTTO WEIDT Map pp340-1

☎ 2859 9407; www.blindes-vertrauen.de; Rosenthaler Strasse 39; admission €1.50; ⊗ noon-8pm Mon-Fri, 11am-8pm Sat & Sun; ⊛ Hackescher Markt

This small museum honours the courage of Otto Weidt, a broom and brush maker who protected many of his blind and deaf Jewish workers from the Nazis. Weidt hid an entire family in a room behind a cabinet in his workshop, provided food and false papers, bribed Gestapo officials into releasing Jews scheduled for deportation and even went to Auschwitz to help his girlfriend escape from the camp. The exhibit, which occupies three rooms of the original workshop, is suitably called 'Blind Trust – Life in Hiding at the Hackescher Markt, 1941–1943'. A highlight is a videotaped interview with a pair of survivors reporting on their experiences at the workshop during the war.

NEUE SYNAGOGUE & CENTRUM JUDAICUM Map pp340-1

☎ 2840 1250; www.cjudaicum.de; Oranienburger Strasse 28-30; adult/concession €3/2, tours €1.50/1; ⏲ 10am-8pm Sun & Mon, to 6pm Tue-Thu, to 5pm Fri Apr-Sep, 10am-6pm Sun-Thu, to 2pm Fri Oct-Mar, dome closed Oct-Mar, tours 4pm Wed, 2pm & 4pm Sun; 🚇 Oranienburger Strasse

The gleaming gold dome of the rebuilt New Synagogue is the most visible symbol of Berlin's revitalised Jewish community. Designed in Moorish-Byzantine style by Eduard Knoblauch, the 1866 original seated 3200 people and was Germany's largest synagogue. Thanks to its beauty and rich décor, it became an instant landmark.

During the 1938 *Kristallnacht* pogroms, a local police chief prevented SA thugs from setting it on fire, an act of courage commemorated by a plaque. The Nazis still managed to desecrate it, although services continued until 1940 when it was appropriated for storage. Allied bombs nearly destroyed the building in 1943.

With the consent of East Berlin's small Jewish community, the GDR government demolished most of the ruins in 1958, although they kept the main façade as a memorial. In 1988, Honecker announced that his government intended to rebuild the synagogue but his regime collapsed before he got around to it. The united German government adopted the plan, though, and the New Synagogue was inaugurated in May 1995.

Today it's not mainly a house of worship (although prayer services are held in a small room upstairs) but a museum and information centre. Permanent displays document the building's history and architecture as well as the lives of the people who worshipped here. Exhibits include a model of the synagogue, a Torah scroll and an eternal lamp from the original structure, unearthed during excavations in 1989. Guided tours take you behind the building where a glass-and-steel structure props up the remaining ruins of the sanctuary and a stone band in the ground traces the enormous outline of the original synagogue. Upstairs is a space for special exhibits. The dome is accessible from April to September.

SOPHIE-GIPS-HÖFE & SAMMLUNG HOFFMANN Map pp340-1

☎ 2849 9121; Sophienstrasse 21; tours €6; ⏲ 10am-4pm Sat by appointment only; 🚇 Weinmeisterstrasse

Just past the **Handwerkervereinshaus** a tunnel-like entrance leads to the quiet and dignified Sophie-Gips-Höfe, whose trio of courtyards contains galleries and the popular **Barcomi's** (☎ 2859 8363; Sophienstrasse 21, 2nd courtyard; snacks €2-5; ⏲ 9am-10pm) café. Formerly, this handsome 19th-century brick complex housed a sewing-machine factory; in GDR days, medical equipment

Sights

MITTE

THE BRAVE WOMEN OF ROSENSTRASSE

Rosenstrasse is the site of a little-known episode in the history of WWII that marked one of the most courageous acts of civilian protest. It was at Rosenstrasse 2–4 where hundreds of Berlin women stood in gallant defiance of the Nazis in freezing rain and subzero temperatures during the brutal winter of 1943. These women had one thing in common: they were Christians whose Jewish husbands had been rounded up and corralled in this former Jewish welfare office for shipment to Auschwitz.

Outraged and despairing, the wives gathered in protest outside their husbands' temporary jail in peaceful but agonising testament, demanding the release of their men. They stayed through day and night, their grim vigil tearing at the conscience of every German soul. And miraculously, on 11 March of that year, Goebbels himself ordered the release of every prisoner, clearly fully aware that shooting down a bunch of unarmed German women was not good PR.

Today a1994 red sandstone sculpture by Inge Hunzinger called *Block der Frauen* (Block of the Women; Map pp340–1) stands on the site of the protest while nearby two information pillars offer historical background. In 2003, renowned filmmaker Margarethe von Trotta turned the incident into a feature film called *Rosenstrasse*.

was produced here. Take note of the neon-light installation by Gunda Förster in the connecting walkways.

One of the complex's main draws is the **Sammlung Hoffmann**, a showcase of contemporary art gathered by Erika and Rolf Hoffmann in more than 30 years of collecting. Every Saturday the Hoffmans open their private two-storey apartment/gallery for guided tours, complete with felt slippers. Actual displays change once a year but may include works by Frank Stella, Lucio Fontana and scores of lesser-known artists from around the world.

SOPHIENKIRCHE Map pp340-1

☎ 308 7920; www.sophien.de; Grosse Hamburger Strasse 29; ⊖ Weinmeisterstrasse
The baroque Sophienkirche is a simple single-nave, galleried confection with a delicate stucco ceiling and an ornate tower. Concerts played on its fancy organ take place sporadically. The first parish church in the Spandauer Vorstadt, it was completed in 1713 with funds provided by Sophie Luise, the third wife of King Friedrich I. The queen, however, was sadly missing from its inaugural service, having been banished from Berlin by her stepson and newly crowned Friedrich Wilhelm I. The enchanting churchyard has some fine-looking tombstones shaded by ancient trees.

ORANIENBURGER TOR & AROUND

BERLINER MEDIZINHISTORISCHES MUSEUM Map pp330-1

☎ 450 536 122; www.charite.de/ch/patho/WebpageBMM; Charité Hospital Mitte, Schumannstrasse 20-21; adult/concession/family €4/2/8; 10am-5pm Tue-Sun, to 7pm Wed; ⊖ Hauptbahnhof-Lehrter Bahnhof
Rudolf Virchow (1821–1902) was a famous doctor, researcher and professor whose pathology collection forms the basis of this highly unusual museum. Think of it as a 3-D medical textbook. Crammed into glass cases are hundreds of organs showing the havoc various diseases can wreak on them: inflamed appendices, cancer-stricken lungs, broccoli-like skin tumours, a colon the size of an elephant trunk. If you think this is

bad, skip the last row, which features two-headed babies and deformed foetuses not even the makers of *Alien* could imagine.

Virchow first displayed his grisly collection in 1899 in the same building, an adjunct to his Institute of Pathology. His lecture hall – a preserved ruin – is used for special events. Another floor presents changing exhibits. The museum is in the hospital campus' northwestern corner, which is accessible from Schumannstrasse, Luisenstrasse and Invalidenstrasse.

BRECHT-WEIGEL GEDENKSTÄTTE
Map pp340-1

☎ 283 057 044; Chausseestrasse 125; tours adult/concession €3/1.50; tours half-hourly 10-11.30am Tue, Wed & Fri, 10am-noon & 5-6.30pm Thu, 9.30am-1.30pm Sat, hourly 11am-6pm Sun; ⊖ Oranienburger Tor, Zinnowitzer Strasse
Bertolt Brecht, one of Germany's seminal 20th-century playwrights, lived in this house not far from his theatre, the Berliner Ensemble, from 1953 until his death in 1956. You'll see Brecht's office, his large library with everything from classics to crime stories, and the tiny bedroom where he died. Decorated with Chinese artwork, it's been left as though he'd just stepped out for a moment, leaving his hat and woollen cap hanging on the door.

Downstairs are the cluttered living quarters of his actress wife Helene Weigel, who continued to live here until her death in 1971. The couple are buried at the Dorotheenstädtischer Friedhof next door.

Call ahead to find out about the English-language tours. The basement restaurant serves Austrian food prepared from Weigel's recipes (mains €7 to €15).

DOROTHEENSTÄDTISCHER FRIEDHOF Map pp340-1

Chausseestrasse 126; ⊖ Oranienburger Tor, Zinnowitzer Strasse
This cemetery wins, hands down, the award for the most celebrity corpses in Berlin. A veritable pantheon of German greats lie buried here, including architects Schadow and Schinkel (who designed his own tombstone), composers Paul Dessau and Hanns Eisler, and writers Heinrich Mann and Bertolt Brecht plus his wife Helene Weigel. Brecht lived in a house just north of here, allegedly to be close to his idols, the phi-

losophers Hegel and Fichte, who are also interred here.

HAMBURGER BAHNHOF Map pp330-1

☎ 3978 3439; www.hamburgerbahnhof.de; Invalidenstrasse 50-51; adult/concession €8/4, under 16 free, last 4hr Thu free; ⊙ 10am-6pm Tue-Fri, 11am-8pm Sat, to 6pm Sun; ⊚ Zinnowitzer Strasse, ⊚ Lehrter Bahnhof/Hauptbahnhof, 🚌 147, 245

Andy Warhol's smiling *Mao*, Cy Twombly's luminous abstractions, Joseph Beuys' provocative installations – they're all part of the collection at Berlin's premier contemporary art museum, which picks up where the **Neue Nationalgalerie** (p108) leaves off (about 1950). Fans of Beuys will get their fill as the entire western wing is dedicated to the *enfant terrible* of German late-20th-century art. Other exhibits change periodically but you're likely to spot works by Robert Rauschenberg, Roy Lichtenstein, Anselm Kiefer and Keith Haring.

At least as interesting as the art (and to some, perhaps even more so) is the architecture of the building, a former late-neoclassical train station converted by Josef Paul Kleihues. The main hall, a lofty affair with exposed iron girders, provides a perfect setting for megasized canvases, installations and sculptures. The gleaming-white façade exudes great elegance and surprising dignity, especially at night when a light installation by the late Dan Flavin bathes the building in mystical blues and greens.

In 2004, the museum space expanded into the adjacent Rieckhallen, a series of interconnected industrial halls previously used by a shipping company. Encased in black corrugated metal like a giant container, they now present exhibits drawn from the prestigious collection of Friedrich Christian Flick, a German industrialist with a passion for modern and contemporary art. Displays change periodically but may include works by such living heavyweights as Bruce Naumann, Paul McCarthy, Rodney Graham and Jason Rhoades, along with those who pushed the artistic envelope earlier in the 20th century – among them Sol Lewitt, Marcel Duchamp, Nam June Paik and Sigmar Polke.

The museum also presents a busy calendar of concerts, lectures, films and meet-the-artists sessions.

MUSEUM FÜR NATURKUNDE

Map pp332-3

☎ 2093 8591; www.museum.hu-berlin.de; Invalidenstrasse 43; adult/concession/family €3.50/2/7; ⊙ 9.30am-5pm Tue-Fri, 10am-6pm Sat & Sun; ⊚ Zinnowitzer Strasse

With over 25 million items, the collection of the Humboldt University-affiliated Museum für Naturkunde (Natural History Museum) is one of the largest in the world. Only a tiny fraction can be displayed, of course, but it includes some showstoppers. Note that at the time of writing sections of the museum were closed during a renovation expected to last until 2007. This includes the Dinosaur Hall, normally home to the museum's biggest stars: a 23m-long and 12m-tall brachiosaurus, and an ultrarare fossilised archaeopteryx.

There's still plenty to see in the other galleries, though, including the largest piece of amber ever found, meteorites from Mars and neat historic dioramas. Children are delighted by 'Bobby' (1925–35), a stuffed gorilla and former Berlin Zoo denizen that was the first such animal raised in captivity to adulthood.

TIERGARTEN

Eating p172; Shopping p236; Sleeping p256

Named for the sprawling urban park, the Tiergarten district is a vital link between the city's former western and eastern halves. After reunification, it received the lion's share of new construction and harbours two of Berlin's most headline-grabbing megadevelopments: the **Regierungsviertel** (Government Quarter) and **Potsdamer Platz**, both tourist magnets of the first rank. In May of 2006, Berlin's first-ever central train station, the sparkling **Hauptbahnhof**, opened in northern Tiergarten. In the quiet streets south of the park, meanwhile, black limousines are a common sight in the **Diplomatenviertel** (Diplomatic Quarter), which is also distinguished by some fine contemporary architecture. East of here, the stellar collections of the **Kulturforum** continue to quicken the pulse of art aficionados.

Tiergarten park itself started out as the private hunting grounds of the Great Elector, Friedrich Wilhelm (r 1640–88) and became a park, masterfully landscaped by Peter Lenné, in the 18th century. During the frigid winter of 1946–47, Berliners chopped down virtually all the trees for firewood.

TIERGARTEN TOP FIVE

- Keep an eye on the politicians during a leisurely riverside saunter through the Regierungsviertel (below).
- Spend a summery afternoon of strolling, lazing, picnicking or carousing in Tiergarten park (p103).
- Burn up the pixels in your digicam from Foster's breathtaking glass dome atop the Reichstag (p102).
- Feel your spirits soar during an afternoon of art appreciation at the Gemäldegalerie (p107) or Neue Nationalgalerie (p108).
- Treat your ears and eyes to a concert at the magnificent Philharmonie (p109).

ORIENTATION

Most of the Tiergarten district is taken up by the park, which extends from Zoo station to the Brandenburg Gate, bisected by Strasse des 17 Juni. Germany is governed from the new Regierungsviertel to the northeast, and the Kulturforum and Potsdamer Platz are off its southeastern corner. The Diplomatenviertel is west of here. Moabit and the new Hauptbahnhof are north of the Spree.

REGIERUNGSVIERTEL & AROUND

Berlin's new government quarter has sprung up in the Spreebogen, a horseshoe-shaped bend of the Spree River. Called the Band des Bundes (literally 'Ribbon of the Federation') it comprises several buildings running in an east–west direction and symbolically joining the two city halves across the Spree. At its centre is the Reichstag, now home to the German parliament, the Bundestag.

A great way to explore the government quarter is on a stroll along the newly created **river promenade**, which allows for interesting perspectives on the shiny new buildings.

BUNDESKANZLERAMT Map pp330-1
Willy-Brandt-Strasse 1; closed to the public;
🚊 Hauptbahnhof-Lehrter Bahnhof, 🚌 100
The vast Bundeskanzleramt (Federal Chancellery), an edgy design by Axel Schultes and Charlotte Frank, is the most prominent building in the Band des Bundes. The complex centres on a nine-storey-high white cube with circular openings that

quickly inspired Berliners to nickname the place 'washing machine'. Views from the upper floors, which contain the chancellor's offices and private residence, are reportedly stupendous. Also here are the cabinet meeting room and a supersecure, special-access-only floor.

Two lower elongated office blocks – one 335m, the other 204m long – flank the cube, giving the compound an 'H' shape if seen from above. To the west, the cube gives way to the Kanzlergarten (Chancellor's Garden) and, across the Spree River, to the Kanzlerpark.

The entire Chancellery complex is closed to the public but you're free to take a gander at the forecourt with the rusted-steel sculpture called 'Berlin' by the late Basque artist Eduardo Chillida. For fine views of the exterior, head north to the Moltkebrücke (bridge) or take a stroll along the new river promenade.

HAUS DER KULTUREN DER WELT
Map pp330-1
☎ 397 870; www.hkw.de; John-Foster-Dulles-Allee 10; admission varies; 🕙 10am-9pm Tue-Sun; 🚌 100
The extravagant Haus der Kulturen der Welt (House of World Cultures) by Hugh Stubbins was the American contribution to the 1957 Interbau, an architecture exhibition that brought top international talent to Berlin. Originally a congress hall, its most striking design element is the gravity-defying parabolic roof, which flops upon the top of the building like a giant manta ray. Berliners have nicknamed the 'pregnant oyster'. Alas, the architect's vision outdis-

TRANSPORT

Bus 100 goes through Tiergarten park to the government quarter; M29 follows Landwehrkanal into Kreuzberg; 200 travels along the southern park edge to Potsdamer Platz; 123 connects Potsdamer Platz with the Government Quarter and Hauptbahnhof; TXL for Tegel airport stops near the Reichstag.

S-Bahn S1 and S2 stop at Potsdamer Platz and at Unter den Linden (for the Government Quarter); S5, S7 and S9 go to Hauptbahnhof-Lehrter Bahnhof, also for the government quarter.

U-Bahn Served by U2 for Potsdamer Platz; U9 to Hansaplatz for northwestern Tiergarten park.

Bundeskanzleramt (opposite page)

tanced the technology of the time, causing the roof to partly collapse in 1980. After being rebuilt, it was reincarnated in 1989 as a cultural centre with a busy programme of art exhibits, lectures, seminars, concerts and other performances from around the world. The reflecting pool features Henry Moore's sculpture *Divided Oval: Butterfly*, whose curvy outline echoes the building's.

Computerised chime concerts ring out at noon and 6pm daily from the 68-bell, black marble and bronze **carillon** – the largest in Europe – just east of here. On Sundays at 3pm from May to September, a carillonneur gives live concerts, which are followed by guided tours of the tower.

MOABIT Map pp330–1
Along Turmstrasse & Alt-Moabit; ⓔ Turmstrasse, Hauptbahnhof-Lehrter Bahnhof
Originally settled by French Huguenots, Moabit has become home to a multicultural mix of blue-collar Berliners, immigrants and government employees. The **Bundesinnenministerium** (Federal Ministry of the Interior; Map pp330–1) occupies futuristic riverfront digs at Alt-Moabit 98, and such residential developments as **Die Schlange** (The Snake; Map pp330–1) have attracted scores of government desk jockeys. In far eastern Moabit, the sparkling new Hauptbahnhof, Berlin's new central train station, opened in 2006.

Moabit's few charms can be explored on an easy stroll. From U-Bahn station Turmstrasse, the area's commercial spine, head northwest to the **Arminius Markthalle** (Map pp330–1; Bremer Strasse 9), the nicest of Berlin's turn-of-the-20th-century market halls. South of here, along the road called Alt-Moabit, is 1835's **St Johanniskirche** (Map pp330–1), an early work by Schinkel fronted by an arcaded Italianate portico. Farther east lies the vast **Justizzentrum** (Centre of Justice; Map pp330–1), which incorporates courts and a fortresslike prison that has hosted such top crooks as Red Army Faction (RAF) terrorists, Erich Honecker and Stasi director Erich Mielke.

PAUL-LÖBE-HAUS & MARIE-ELISABETH-LÜDERS-HAUS
☎ 2270; www.bundestag.de; Konrad-Adenauer-Strasse & Schiffbauerdamm; 🚇 Hauptbahnhof-Lehrter Bahnhof
This pair of sparkling buildings facing each other on the Spree north of the Reichstag houses conference rooms and offices for the members of parliament and their staff. A double bridge connects the two across the river in a visual symbol of reunification.

Designed by Stefan Braunfels, both structures echo the themes of the **Bundeskanzleramt** (Federal Chancellery; opposite) just to the west. The **Paul-Löbe-Haus** (Map pp330–1) has the shape of a double-sided comb and is seven storeys high. Like a bowling alley built for giants, an atrium extends across the entire 200m length of the building.

The equally striking **Marie-Elisabeth-Lüders-Haus** (Map pp330–1) contains the parliamentary library and other government-related institutions. Its most eye-catching design elements include a massive tapered stairway, a flat roofline jutting out like a springboard over a plaza, and a cube with giant circular windows containing the library reading room.

Underground tunnels connect both structures to the Bundestag inside the Reichstag. The whimsical-looking building just north of the Paul-Löbe-Haus houses a day-care centre, mostly for the kids of government employees.

Paul Löbe and Marie-Elisabeth Lüders, by the way, were both strong voices of democracy before and after WWII. The Nazis, predictably, imprisoned them.

Tours of either building are free but require advance registration. Check the website (click through to English/Information Counter/Visit Us) for details.

REICHSTAG Map pp330-1

☎ 2273 2152; www.bundestag.de; Platz der Republik 1; admission free; ⏰ lift to cupola 8am-midnight, last entry 10pm; 🚌 100

Just north of the Brandenburg Gate, the Reichstag has been the seat of the Bundestag, the German parliament, since 1999 following a complete renovation by Lord Norman Foster. The British star architect turned the 1894 building by Paul Wallot into a state-of-the-art parliamentary facility, preserving only the historical shell and adding its most striking contemporary feature: the glistening glass dome.

The quick lift ride to the top is one of the highlights of any Berlin visit, as much for the 360-degree panorama of the city as for the close-ups of the dome and the mirror-clad funnel at its centre. The lift drops you at an outdoor viewing platform where there's also a pricey **restaurant** (☎ 2262 9933; ⏰ 9am-midnight). From here you can climb the spiralling ramp inside the dome itself, which, by the way, sits right above the Plenary Hall. At the top, displays document the history of the building.

There's always a queue for the lift, so prepare for a wait. Only the disabled, people with baby strollers and those with restau-

rant reservations can proceed directly via a separate entrance on the left. Note that the dome is closed for cleaning for several days four times a year, although you can still access the viewing platform. Other areas of the Reichstag, including the Plenary Hall, may only be seen on guided tours or during lectures, which are usually in German and must be booked far in advance in writing. Check the website (click to English/Information Center/Visit Us) for details.

The Reichstag has been the setting of numerous milestones in German history. After WWI, Philipp Scheidemann proclaimed the German republic from one of its windows. The Reichstag fire on 27 February 1933 allowed Hitler to blame the communists and seize power. A dozen years later, the victorious Soviets nearly obliterated the building. Restoration – without the dome – wasn't finished until 1972. At midnight on 2 October 1990 the reunification of Germany was enacted here. In the summer of 1995, the Reichstag again made worldwide headlines when Christo (a Bulgarian artist famous for wrapping public places) and his wife, Jeanne-Claude, wrapped the edifice in fabric for two weeks. Lord Norman set to work shortly thereafter.

SCHLOSS BELLEVUE & BUNDESPRÄSIDIALAMT Map pp330-1

☎ 20 000; www.bundespraesident.de; Spreeweg 1; closed to the public; 🚆 Bellevue; 🚌 100

This freshly renovated, chalk white, neoclassical palace on the northwestern edge of Tiergarten is the official residence of the German president, at the time of writing, Horst Köhler. It was built in 1785 by Philipp Daniel Boumann for the youngest brother of Frederick the Great, then became a school under Kaiser Wilhelm II and a museum of ethnology under the Nazis.

The president and his staff have their offices in the 1998 **Bundespräsidialamt** just south of the palace. This is essentially Germany's version of the 'oval office', which in this case refers to the elliptical shape of the building, which is mantled in glass and polished black granite.

Architecture fans might also like a look at the 300m-long undulating housing development called **Die Schlange** (The Snake), which sits northeast of the palace across the Spree.

SIEGESSÄULE Map pp330-1

☎ 391 2961; www.monument-tales.de; Grosser Stern; adult/concession €2.20/1.50; ⌚ 9.30am-6.30pm Mon-Fri, to 7pm Sat & Sun Apr-Oct, 10am-5pm Mon-Fri, to 5.30pm Sat & Sun Nov-Mar; 🚌 100

Like arms of a starfish, five large roads merge into the roundabout called Grosser Stern at the heart of the Tiergarten. At its centre is the landmark Siegessäule (Victory Column), a triumphal column commemorating success-ful 19th-century Prussian military exploits, notably over Denmark (1864), Austria (1866) and France (1871). The large gilded lady on top (she stands 8.3m tall) predictably repre-sents the goddess of Victory, although locals simply call her 'Gold-Else'. Film fans might remember her from a key scene in Wim Wenders' 1985 flick *Wings of Desire*. The Nazis moved the entire column from its previ-ous location outside the Reichstag in 1938 and also added a level, making it soar to an impressive 67m. And yes, you can climb to the top. Tickets also give access to the small museum and discounts at the adjacent café and beer garden.

The Siegessäule has become a symbol of Berlin's gay community (the city's larg-est gay publication is named after it) and marks the terminus of the annual Christo-pher St Parade. The park around here is a popular cruising spot for gay men, espe-cially around the Löwenbrücke.

Also in the immediate vicinity are a few more **monuments** to Prussian glory, notably the one of Otto von Bismarck designed by Reinhold Begas northeast of the column.

SOWJETISCHES EHRENMAL Map pp330-1

Strasse des 17 Juni; 🚇 Unter den Linden, 🚌 100

Just west of the Brandenburg Gate, the So-viet War Memorial commemorates the Red Army soldiers who died fighting in the epic Battle of Berlin. Two Russian tanks said to have been the first to enter the city in 1945 flank the monument. The reddish marble was allegedly scavenged from the ruins of Hitler's chancellery on Wilhelmstrasse. (More of this marble may have been used in building the Soviet War Memorial in Treptower Park; p143.)

SPREEBOGENPARK Map pp330-1

North of Otto-von-Bismarck-Allee;

🚇 Hauptbahnhof-Lehrter Bahnhof

This triangular park north of the chancel-lery was the final piece in the puzzle of the government quarter to be completed in June 2005. It's a simple, geometric space of lawns dappled with beech and oak trees and offering views of the river, the Hum-boldthafen (Humboldt Harbour) and the glass hall of the new Hauptbahnhof. The park's pedestrian-only Gustav-Heinemann-Brücke (bridge) links the train station with the government quarter.

STRASSE DES 17 JUNI Map pp330-1

🚇 Unter den Linden, Tiergarten, 🚌 100

This broad boulevard originally connected the Berlin City Palace on Unter den Linden with Schloss Charlottenburg and was called Charlottenburger Chaussee. In 1937 Hitler doubled its width and turned it into a triumphal road called, rather mundanely, East-West Axis. Its present name com-memorates the 1953 workers' uprising in eastern Berlin (p62), which brought the GDR to the brink of collapse.

TIERGARTEN Map pp330-1

🚇 Tiergarten, Bellevue, 🚌 100

Berlin's 'green lung' bristles with huge shady trees, groomed paths, woodsy groves and lakes and meadows, and is great for a jog, picnic or stroll. At 167 hectares, it is one of the world's largest city parks, bisected by the Strasse des 17 Juni. In spring, when the rhododendrons erupt in full bloom, the area around Rousseau Island is an oasis from city stresses. On sunny sum-mer weekends, the park becomes a giant grilling party as friends and families gather on the lawns for all-day picnics.

POTSDAMER PLATZ & AROUND

A showcase of urban renewal, Potsdamer Platz is perhaps the most visible symbol of the 'New Berlin' and a major tourist attrac-tion. The historical Potsdamer Platz was a busy traffic hub that became synonymous with metropolitan life and entertainment in the early 20th century. In 1924, Europe's first (hand-operated) traffic light was installed here, a replica of which was recently hoisted in the same spot. WWII sucked all life out of Potsdamer Platz and the area soon plunged into a coma, bisected by the Wall until re-unification.

In the 1990s, the city tapped an interna-tional cast of star architects, including Arata Isozaki, Rafael Moneo, Richard Rogers and

Helmut Jahn, to design 'Potsdamer Platz – The Sequel' based on a master plan by Renzo Piano. Hamstrung by city-imposed building guidelines, the final product is anything but avant-garde but still a pleasant and human-scale cityscape.

Berliners and visitors have by and large embraced the development, which consists of three sections: DaimlerCity, the Sony Center and the Beisheim Center. Daimler-City, which stretches south of Potsdamer Strasse, was the first to be completed in 1998. The Sony Center, wedged between Potsdamer Strasse, Ben-Gurion-Strasse and Bellevuestrasse, followed in 2000. The last in the trio, the Beisheim Center, was inaugurated in 2004 and occupies the triangle created by Lenné-, Bellevue- and Ebertstrasse.

For a birds-eye view of the area, you can take what is billed as the world's fastest elevator to the observation deck of the **Panorama Punkt** (Map p346; ☎ 2529 4372; www.panoramapunkt.de; Potsdamer Platz 1; adult/concession €3.50/2.50; ☼ 11am-8pm, last admission 7.30pm, closed Mon Nov-Mar).

BEISHEIM CENTER Map p346
Ⓔ ⓡ Potsdamer Platz
The last section in the Potsdamer Platz area to be completed was the Beisheim Center occupying the triangle created by Lenné-, Bellevue- and Ebertstrasse. Here, Otto Beisheim, one of the wealthiest men in Europe, spent €460 million of his own money to immortalise himself in steel and stone. The Beisheim Center consists of five buildings containing luxury apartments, offices and two top-end hotels, the Ritz-Carlton (p256) and the Marriott. The complex was inspired by classic American skyscraper design; the Ritz-Carlton, for instance, conceived by Hilmer & Sattler and Albrecht, is modelled on the Rockefeller Center in New York.

DAIMLERCHRYSLER CONTEMPORARY
Map p346
☎ 2594 1420; Weinhaus Huth, Alte Potsdamer Strasse 5; admission free; ☼ 11am-6pm;
Ⓔ ⓡ Potsdamer Platz
Fans of 20th-century abstract, conceptual and minimalist art should pop into this loft-like gallery, a quiet and elegant space. Ring the bell to be buzzed in.

Changing exhibits show off new acquisitions or selections from the corporation's collection, which ranges from Bauhaus artists like Oscar Schlemmer and Max Bill to international hot shots such as Andy Warhol and Jeff Koons.

Sony Center (opposite page)

DAIMLERCITY Map p346

Btwn Potsdamer Strasse, Landwehrkanal & Linkstrasse; ⊙ ⓡ Potsdamer Platz
DaimlerCity centres on an open plaza, the **Marlene-Dietrich-Platz**, and features architecture by, among others, Rafael Moneo, Arata Isozaki and Renzo Piano. The large pond on its southern end is great for dipping one's toes on a hot summer day.

The complex is home to a large shopping mall, the **Potsdamer Platz Arkaden** (p236), and packed with entertainment options, including a musical theatre, a casino, several nightclubs, cinemas and scores of restaurants and bars.

DaimlerChrysler also sponsored several **sculptures** dotted around DaimlerCity. These include Keith Haring's *The Boxers* on Eichhornstrasse, Jeff Koons' *Balloon Flower* on Marlene-Dietrich-Platz, Mark Di Suvero's *Galileo* within the pond, Auke de Vries's *Gelandet* (Landed) on Schellingstrasse and Robert Rauschenberg's *The Riding Bikes* on Fontaneplatz.

FILMMUSEUM BERLIN Map p346

☎ 300 9030; www.filmmuseum-berlin.de; Potsdamer Strasse 2; adults/concession/family €6/4/14; ⏱ 10am-6pm Tue-Sun, to 8pm Thu; ⊙ ⓡ Potsdamer Strasse

A multimedia journey through German film history and a behind-the-scenes look at special effects are what await visitors to the Filmmuseum Berlin. The museum kicks off with an appropriate sense of theatre as it sends you through a warped mirror room conjuring visions of *The Cabinet of Dr Caligari*.

Major themes include pioneers and early divas, silent-era classics such as Fritz Lang's *Metropolis*, Leni Riefenstahl's groundbreaking Nazi-era documentary *Olympia* (see boxed text, p31), German exiles in Hollywood and post-WWII movies. Stealing the show as she did in real life, though, is *femme fatale* Marlene Dietrich with a selection of costumes, personal finery, photographs and documents.

The museum is part of the **Filmhaus**, which also harbours a film school, the **Arsenal** cinemas (p214), a library, a museum shop and a bistro.

In the spring of 2006 the brand-new **Fernsehmuseum** (Museum of TV) was scheduled to open on the 3rd and 4th floor of the Filmhaus. It should present a visually

TOP FIVE FREEBIES

- Enjoy fine views of the city and the warped mirror funnel of the Reichstag (p102) dome.
- Grab a picnic for a mellow afternoon in Schlossgarten Charlottenburg (p112), the Tiergarten (p103) or any of Berlin's many other fine parks.
- Cold War history comes alive on a visit to Checkpoint Charlie (p123), the Allierten Museum (Allied Museum; p144) and the East Side Gallery (p128).
- See the best of historic architecture on a stroll along Unter den Linden (p73) and Gendarmenmarkt (p77).
- Delve into the dark depths of WWII history at locations including the Holocaust Memorial (p75), the Topographie des Terrors (p127), Gedenkstätte Deutscher Widerstand (p107) and Museum Karlshorst (p150).

stimulating romp through seven decades of German TV back to the earliest image experiments in the late 1920s and even allow visitors to watch milestone shows in full length.

LEIPZIGER PLATZ Map p346

⊙ ⓡ Potsdamer Platz
Just like Potsdamer Platz, this historical square has been resurrected from the former wasteland of the GDR death strip. Leipziger Platz was first laid out in 1734 and later became one of Berlin's most beautiful squares courtesy of the urban planning 'dream team' of Schinkel & Lenné. The new incarnation replicates the square's original octagonal shape, which is outlined by a series of modern office buildings, including the Canadian embassy. The square is bisected by the busy Leipziger Strasse, which will eventually be flanked by greenery. The hulking building just east of here houses the **Bundesrat** (Federal Council; Map pp336–7), the body of the German legislative branch of government that represents the interests of the *Länder*, or federal states.

SONY CENTER Map p346

www.sonycenter.de; Potsdamer Strasse; ⊙ ⓡ Potsdamer Platz
Designed by Helmut Jahn, the Sony Center is one of the most spectacular new developments in Berlin. At its core is a central plaza dramatically canopied by a tentlike

Sights

TIERGARTEN

Bicycle statue Weinhaus Huth (this page)

glass roof supported by steel beams emanating like the spokes of a bicycle wheel. After dark it sparkles in a light show of changing colours.

With plenty of sitting areas, free wi-fi and a fun fountain, the plaza has become a popular place for hanging out and people-watching. The buildings around it contain restaurants, stores, a multiplex cinema and Sony's European headquarters.

Also integrated into the complex is the opulent **Kaisersaal**, the only surviving room of the prewar Hotel Esplanade, the erstwhile belle of Bellevuestrasse. It was moved 75m to its current location with the help of some wizardly technology and completely restored as a gourmet restaurant (p173). Sections of the historic hotel's façade have also been incorporated and are visible from Bellevuestrasse.

WEINHAUS HUTH Map p346
Alte Potsdamer Strasse 5; ⊙ 🚇 **Potsdamer Platz**
This dignified structure, dwarfed by its postmodern neighbours, is the only eyewitness to the original incarnation of Pots-

damer Platz. Designed in 1912 by Conrad Heidenreich and Paul Michel, it was one of the first steel-frame buildings in town and miraculously survived both WWII and the Berlin Wall. Behind the shell-limestone façade a restaurant, **Diekmann im Weinhaus Huth** (p172), operates once again while on the 4th floor are the breezy galleries of the **DaimlerChrysler Contemporary**.

KULTURFORUM & AROUND
This cluster of top-notch museums and concert venues off the southeastern edge of the Tiergarten was master-planned in the 1950s by Hans Scharoun, one of the era's premier architects. Most of the buildings weren't completed until the 1980s.

BAUHAUS ARCHIV/MUSEUM FÜR GESTALTUNG Map pp338-9
☎ 254 0020; www.bauhaus.de; Klingelhöferstrasse 14; adult/concession €6/3; ⌚ 10am-5pm Wed-Mon; 🚇 Nollendorfplatz, 🚌 100, M29
Walter Gropius himself, the founder of the Bauhaus school (1919–33), designed the avant-garde building housing the Bauhaus Archive/Museum of Design, whose gleaming white shed roofs look a bit like the smokestacks of an ocean liner.

Exhibits behind this striking silhouette document the enormous influence the Bauhaus movement exerted on all aspects of modern architecture and design. The collection includes everything from study notes to workshop pieces to photographs, models, blueprints and documents by such notable Bauhaus members as Klee, Kandinsky, Schlemmer and Feininger. Prized collection highlights include the original model of Gropius' 1925 Bauhaus building in Dessau and a reconstruction of Lázló Moholy-Nagy's kinetic *Light-Space-Modulator*, a clever sculpture that manages to combine colour, light and movement.

DIPLOMATENVIERTEL Map p346
btwn Stauffenberger- & Klingelhöferstrasse & Landwehrkanal; 🚌 **200**
After WWI several embassies began moving into the quiet, villa-studded colony south of the Tiergarten, which had long been popular with Berlin's cultural elite; the Brothers Grimm and the poet Hoff-

man von Fallersleben were among those residing here in the 19th century. It was Hitler's chief architect, Albert Speer, who first coined the term Diplomatenviertel and arranged for other countries, including allies Italy and Japan, to move to the district. WWII practically obliterated the area, which remained in a state of quiet decay while the embassies all set up in Bonn, the new West German capital. Reunification sparked a construction boom and the quarter has become a showcase of great contemporary architecture. For details, see the Architecture chapter, p49. For a suggested walking tour, see p157.

GEDENKSTÄTTE DEUTSCHER WIDERSTAND Map p346

☎ 2699 5000; www.gdw-berlin.de; Stauffenbergstrasse 13-14; admission free; ☉ 9am-6pm Mon-Fri, to 8pm Thu, 10am-6pm Sat & Sun; ⊚ Mendelssohn-Bartholdy-Park, ⊟ 200

The German Resistance Memorial Center addresses an often-ignored facet of Third Reich history: homegrown resistance against the Nazi terror regime. Photographs, documents and explanatory panels show how both ordinary and prominent Germans risked their lives and livelihoods to thwart Hitler's mob. It's actually quite a long list that included the artists Ernst Barlach and Käthe Kollwitz, scientists such as Carl von Ossietzky, Dietrich Bonhoeffer and other theologians, exiles including Thomas Mann and the university students Hans and Sophie Scholl, to name just a few.

The exhibit is in the historic Bendlerblock, a vast complex that housed the Wehrmacht high command from 1935 to 1945. In these very rooms, a group of high-ranking officers, led by Claus Schenk Graf von Stauffenberg, plotted the bold but ultimately ill-fated assassination attempt on Hitler on 20 July 1944. Stauffenberg and his main co-conspirators were shot that evening in the building's courtyard, where a memorial now honours their courage and legacy. In the aftermath of the foiled coup, over 600 people were arrested and 110 executed, many at Plötzensee Prison, now the Gedenkstätte Plötzensee (p136) site.

Panelling is in German only, but you can ask for an excellent and free English-language audio-guide.

GEMÄLDEGALERIE Map p346

☎ 266 2951; www.smb.spk-berlin.de; Matthäikirchplatz 8; adult/concession incl same-day admission to Kunstgewerbemuseum, Kupferstichkabinett, Neue Nationalgalerie & Musikinstrumenten-Museum €8/4, under 16 free, last 4hr Thu free; ☉ 10am-6pm Tue-Sun, to 10pm Thu; ⊚ ⊞ Potsdamer Platz, ⊟ 148, 200, M29, M41

If you only have time for one art museum, make it the Gemäldegalerie (Picture Gallery), a spectacular showcase of European painting from the 13th to the 18th centuries in a glorious building designed by Munich architects Hilmer & Sattler.

The collection is famous for its exceptional quality and breadth. It's especially strong when it comes to Dutch and Flemish masters, such as Van Dyk, Hals and Rubens. It also boasts one of the world's largest Rembrandt collections, with 16 paintings on display, including the famous *The Man with the Golden Helmet*. Other highlights include works by Cranach, Dürer, Holbein and other Germans. The Italians are represented by Botticelli, Raffael, Titian and many others, while the French collection includes paintings by Watteau and de la Tour. Gainsborough and Reynolds are among the British artists represented here, while the Spaniards field such heavy hitters as Goya and Velázquez. The galleries radiate out from the lofty Great Hall, which has the dimensions and solemnity of a cathedral.

Admission includes an excellent English-language audio-guide. Budget at least two hours.

KUNSTGEWERBEMUSEUM Map p346

☎ 266 2951; www.smb.spk-berlin.de; Tiergartenstrasse 6; adult/concession incl same-day admission to Gemäldegalerie, Kupferstichkabinett, Neue Nationalgalerie & Musikinstrumenten-Museum €8/4, under 16 free, last 4hr Thu free; ☉ 10am-6pm Tue-Fri, 11am-6pm Sat & Sun; ⊚ ⊞ Potsdamer Platz, ⊟ 200, M29

The cavernous Kunstgewerbemuseum (Museum of Applied Arts) brims with decorative objects from the Middle Ages to the present. The vast collections here range from gem-encrusted reliquaries to Art Deco ceramics and modern appliances.

If you want to explore the museum chronologically, start in the medieval section on the ground floor, where church riches dominate. Here, the most precious items include the famous Guelph treasure, with a domed reliquary said to have contained the head of St George, and the baptismal font of Emperor Friedrich Barbarossa.

On the same floor, the Renaissance is represented with delicate Venetian glass, colourful earthenware called majolica, rich tapestries, elegant furniture and other objects reflective of the exalted lifestyle at court or in a patrician household.

From there it's off to the upper floor, which focuses on the baroque, neoclassical, Art Nouveau and Art Deco periods. It's an eclectic collection that includes historical board games, amazing works in ivory and exquisite porcelain. The Chinese Room from the Graneri Palace in Turin, Italy, is another highlight.

In the basement, the New Collection showcases international 20th- and 21st-century glass, ceramics, jewellery and utilitarian products, including furniture by Michael Thonet, Charles Eames, Philippe Starck and other top practitioners.

KUPFERSTICHKABINETT Map p346
☎ 266 2951; www.smb.spk-berlin.de; Matthäikirchplatz 8; adult/concession incl same-day admission to Kunstgewerbemuseum, Gemäldegalerie, Neue Nationalgalerie & Musikinstrumenten-Museum €8/4, under 16 free, last 4hr Thu free; ☼ 10am-6pm Tue-Fri, 11am-6pm Sat & Sun; Ⓔ ☒ Potsdamer Platz, ⬛ 200, M29

The Kupferstichkabinett (Museum of Prints & Drawings) has one of the world's finest and largest collections of art on paper, including hand-illustrated books, illuminated manuscripts, drawings and prints produced mostly in Europe from the 14th century onward. All the household names are represented, from Dürer to Botticelli, Rembrandt to Schinkel, Picasso to Giacometti.

Because of the light-sensitive nature of these works, only a tiny fraction of the collection can be shown in special exhibits at any given time. This is also the reason for the protective glass casings and muted lighting.

MATTHÄUSKIRCHE Map p346
☎ 261 3676; Matthäikirchplatz; tower admission €1; ☼ noon-6pm Wed-Sun; Ⓔ ☒ Potsdamer Platz, ⬛ 200, M29

Standing a bit lost and forlorn within the Kulturforum, the Matthäuskirche is a

neo-Romanesque confection designed by Friedrich August Stüler in 1846. Its attractive façade features alternating bands of red brick and ochre tiles. During the Third Reich, it was supposed to be dismantled and transplanted to Spandau to make room for Albert Speer's Germania (see the boxed text, p59). Fortunately the war – and history – took a different turn. Climb the tower for good views of the Kulturforum and Potsdamer Platz.

MUSIKINSTRUMENTEN-MUSEUM
Map p346

☎ 254 810; www.mim-berlin.de; Tiergartenstrasse 1; adult/concession incl admission to Kunstgewerbemuseum, Gemäldegalerie, Neue Nationalgalerie & Kupferstichkabinett €8/4, under 16 free, last 4hr Thu free; ☼ 9am-5pm Tue, Wed & Fri, to 10pm Thu, 10am-5pm Sat & Sun; Ⓔ ☒ Potsdamer Platz, ⬛ 200, M29

Harpsichords, medieval trumpets, shepherds' bagpipes and other historical instruments may not start a stampede for tickets. But what about the flute Frederick the Great played to entertain his guests? Or a glass harmonica invented by Benjamin Franklin? Or Johann Sebastian Bach's cembalo?

The superb collection of Berlin's Musikinstrumenten-Museum (Musical Instrument Museum) includes all these plus hundreds more treasures from the 16th century to today. There are historical paintings and porcelain figurines, Steinway pianos and curiosities such as a musical walking stick. At several listening stations you can hear what some of the more obscure or antiquated instruments sound like.

A crowd favourite is the Mighty Wurlitzer (1929), an organ with more buttons and keys than a troop of beefeater guards. It is cranked up at noon on Saturday. At 11am on Saturdays, the museum offers guided tours (€2). Classical concerts, many free, take place year-round (ask for a free schedule or check the website).

NEUE NATIONALGALERIE Map p346
☎ 266 2951; www.smb.spk-berlin.de; Potsdamer Strasse 50; adult/concession incl same-day admission to Kunstgewerbemuseum, Kupferstichkabinett, Gemäldegalerie & Musikinstrumenten-Museum €8/4, under 16 free, last 4hr Thu free; ☼ 10am-6pm Tue & Wed, to 10pm Thu-Sun; Ⓔ ☒ Potsdamer Platz, ⬛ 200, M29

The first of the Kulturforum museums to open, the Neue Nationalgalerie (New National Gallery) opened in 1968 as Berlin's main repository of visual art by 20th-century European artists working until 1960. It's housed in a spectacular 'light temple of glass', a late masterpiece of Ludwig Mies van der Rohe (also see p47).

All major genres are represented: cubism (Picasso, Gris Leger), surrealism (Dalì, Miró, Max Ernst), new objectivity (Otto Dix, George Grosz), Bauhaus (Klee, Kandinsky) and, above all, German expressionism (Kirchner, Nolde, Schmitt-Rottluff). Highlights include the warped works of Otto Dix (eg *Old Couple*, 1923), the 'egghead' figures of George Grosz, and Kirchner's chaotic *Potsdamer Platz* (1914) peopled by a demimonde of prostitutes and revellers. Of special significance is the group of 11 Max Beckmann paintings, which trace the artist's development between 1906 and 1942.

Galleries in the basement are usually reserved for the permanent collection, while the glass-encased ground level hosts special travelling exhibitions, such as the attendance record–breaking MoMA show in 2004.

PHILHARMONIE & KAMMERMUSIKSAAL Map p346
☎ 254 880; www.berliner-philharmoniker.de; Herbert-von-Karajan-Strasse 1; tours €3/2; ☼ tours 1pm daily (in German); ⊘ ⊠ Potsdamer Platz, ⊟ 200, M29

Berlin's premier classical concert venue, the Hans Scharoun–designed Philharmonie boasts almost otherworldly acoustics. This is achieved through a complicated floor plan of three pentagonal levels twisting and angling upward around a central orchestra pit. The audience sits in terraced blocks with perfect views and sound emanating from every angle. From the outside, the 1963 structure with its upward-turning corners looks a bit like a postmodern Chinese teahouse. In 1981 the honey-coloured aluminium façade was added. It is the permanent base of the Berliner Philharmoniker, one of the world's leading orchestras (p206).

The adjacent **Kammermusiksaal** (Chamber Music Hall), also based on a design by Scharoun, is essentially a smaller version of the Philharmonie.

SHELL-HAUS Map p346
Reichspietschufer 60; ⊘ Mendelssohn-Bartholdy-Park

Looking like a giant upright staircase, the eye-catching Shell-Haus is one of the most famous office buildings created during the Weimar Republic. Designed by Emil Fahrenkamp in 1931, it was one of Berlin's earliest steel-frame structures that is concealed beneath a skin of travertine. Its extravagant silhouette is best appreciated from the southern bank of the Landwehrkanal. Recently renovated, it's now the headquarters of Berlin's gas company GASAG.

STAATSBIBLIOTHEK ZU BERLIN
Map p346

☎ 2660; www.sbb.spk-berlin.de; Potsdamer Strasse 33; ☼ 9am-9pm Mon-Fri, to 7pm Sat; ⊘ ⊠ Potsdamer Platz, ⊟ 200, M29

The hulking building between Kulturforum and Potsdamer Platz houses part two of the State Library with books published after 1955, ie picking up where the collection at the main branch on Unter den Linden (p77) leaves off. Called 'Stabi' for short, the building was designed by Hans Scharoun and has been open since 1978. Free 90-minute tours (in German) run at 10.30am every third Saturday of the month. In order to access the reading rooms and collection, you need a library card that costs €10 per month (€25 per year) and comes with age and residency restrictions.

CHARLOTTENBURG
Eating p174; Shopping p237; Sleeping p256

Until reunification, this 300-year-old district was the glittering centre of West Berlin, an intense cauldron of exciting nightlife, shopping, eating and sleeping. Things have definitely quietened down since reunification when the wave of attention swapped over to Mitte (even taking Nefertiti and her royal entourage from the Egyptian Museum with it). But Charlottenburg's other main draws are in no danger of migrating. Shopaholics can still get their fix on Kurfürstendamm, Kantstrasse and their side streets. Schloss Charlottenburg continues to delight art fans, 'royal' groupies and garden buffs. Even now that the Egyptian queen has moved on, the

TRANSPORT

Bus Zoo station is the main hub for sightseeing favourites 100 and 200 (see p291); M19, M29, X10 travel along Kurfürstendamm; 145 and X9 for Schloss Charlottenburg; 139 for the Funkturm and trade fair grounds (via Kantstrasse).

S-Bahn S5, S7 and S9 serve Zoo station and Savignyplatz from Friedrichshain, Alexanderplatz, the government quarter and Scheunenviertel.

U-Bahn Zoo station is the main hub served by the U2 from Mitte, Tiergarten, Schöneberg, Schloss Charlottenburg and Olympic Stadium; Uhlandstrasse is the western terminus of the U1 to Schöneberg, Kreuzberg and Friedrichshain.

museum landscape is as rich and varied as ever and even set to grow with the addition of the cheeky Deutsches Currywurst Museum (scheduled for autumn 2006), which pays homage to the famous sausage snack.

The burgher of Charlottenburg generally is a refined specimen; well educated, moneyed, sophisticated and, if the bevy of delis and speciality stores is an indication, very much into food and drink. Excellent places to observe the species at play are the bars and restaurants around Savignyplatz.

The main reasons to venture further west, where things get increasingly more suburban, is to do business at the ICC trade show grounds or to catch a game or concert at the Olympiastadion.

ORIENTATION

Charlottenburg, which forms an administrative unit with Wilmersdorf, is an expansive district stretching from the Olympiastadion in the west to Zoo station in the east. It is bordered by Spandau in the west and Tiergarten and Schöneberg in the east. Berlin International Airport at Tegel is just beyond its northern boundaries. Main arteries include Kurfürstendamm, the famous shopping and entertainment mile; Kantstrasse, which culminates at the trade show grounds; and Hardenbergstrasse/Otto-Suhr-Allee, which goes to Schloss Charlottenburg. The Olympic Stadium area is about 6km west of Zoo station.

SCHLOSS CHARLOTTENBURG

Schloss Charlottenburg is an exquisite baroque palace and one of the few sites in Berlin where you can get a sense of the splendour of the royal Hohenzollern clan. The grand edifice you see today has rather

Schloss Charlottenburg (this page)

modest origins as the petite summer residence of Sophie-Charlotte, wife of Elector Friedrich III. Originally called Schloss Lietzenburg, it was designed by Arnold Nering and expanded in the vein of Versailles by Johann Friedrich Eosander after the Elector became King Friedrich I in 1701. Later royals dabbled with the place, most notably Frederick the Great who hired Georg Wenzeslaus von Knobelsdorff to add the spectacular Neuer Flügel (New Wing, 1746). In the 1780s, Carl Gotthard Langhans built the Schlosstheater (Palace Theatre), which now houses the Museum für Vor- und Frühgeschichte (Museum of Pre- and Early History).

Reconstruction became a priority after WWII and when it was finished in 1966, the restored **equestrian statue of the Great Elector** (1699) by Andreas Schlüter had also returned to the courtyard.

Schloss Charlottenburg is about 3km northwest of Zoo station, backed by a lavish park and surrounded by several worthwhile museums. Each of the palace buildings charges separate admission, but the **Kombinationskarte Charlottenburg** (adult/concession €7/5) is good for one-time admission on a single day to all sections except the lower floor of the Altes Schloss. Seeing the entire complex takes at least a day. Crowds often get huge on weekends and during summer holidays, so show up as early as possible.

ALTES SCHLOSS Map pp330-1

☎ 3209 1440; Spandauer Damm; www.spsg.de; adult/concession incl guided tour & upper floors €8/5, upper floors only €2/1.50; ☾ 10am-5pm Tue-Sun Apr-Oct, 11am-5pm Nov-Mar, last tour at 5pm; ◉ Sophie-Charlotte-Platz, then 🚌 309, ◉ Richard-Wagner-Platz, then 🚌 145

Also known as the Nering-Eosander Building after its two architects, this is the central, and oldest, section of the palace. On the lower floor are the baroque living quarters of Friedrich I and Sophie-Charlotte, which must be visited on a 50-minute tour (in German only, but free English pamphlets are available).

Each room is an extravaganza in stucco, brocade and overall opulence. Highlights include the Oak Gallery (Room 120), a wood-panelled festival hall drenched with family portraits; the lovely Oval Hall (Room 116) with views of the French gardens

CHARLOTTENBURG TOP FIVE

- Get an eyeful of royal pomp while exploring Schloss Charlottenburg, especially the exquisite Neuer Flügel (p112).
- Ponder the absurdity of war at the Kaiser-Wilhelm-Gedächtniskirche (p115).
- Take a fun journey through history at the Story of Berlin (p116).
- Indulge in tasteful titillation at the Museum für Fotografie (p116) or the Erotik Museum (p114).
- Plunge headlong into the shopping frenzy of Kurfürstendamm (p237).

and the Belvedere; the Audience Chamber (Room 101), filled with Belgian tapestries; Friedrich I's bedchamber, with the first-ever bathroom in a baroque palace (Room 96); the fabulous Porcelain Chamber (Room 95), smothered in Chinese and Japanese blueware from floor to ceiling; and the Eosander Chapel (Room 94), with its *trompe l'oeil* arches.

Before or after the tour, you are free to explore the apartment of Friedrich Wilhelm IV upstairs. It's filled with paintings, vases, tapestries, weapons, Meissen porcelain and other items essential to a royal lifestyle. A highlight here is the Silberkammer (Silver Chamber) featuring a sampling of a 2600-piece silver table setting, a wedding gift for Crown Prince Wilhelm. Completed in 1914, WWI and the demise of the monarchy ensured that no royal would ever use the table setting.

BELVEDERE Map pp330-1

☎ 3209 1445; Spandauer Damm; www.spsg.de; adult/concession €2/1.50; ☾ noon-5pm Tue-Fri, 10am-5pm Sat & Sun Apr-Oct, noon-4pm Tue-Sun Nov-Mar; ◉ Sophie-Charlotte-Platz, then 🚌 309, ◉ Richard-Wagner-Platz, then 🚌 145, or ◉ 🚆 Jungfernheide

This pint-size palace in the far northeastern corner of the Schloss gardens got its start in 1788 as a teahouse for Friedrich Wilhelm II. Here he enjoyed reading, listening to chamber music and holding spiritual sessions with fellow members of the mystical Order of the Rosicrucians. These days, the late-rococo vision by Carl Gotthard Langhans makes an elegant backdrop for porcelain masterpieces by the royal manufacturer KPM.

Sights

CHARLOTTENBURG

MAUSOLEUM Map pp330-1

☎ 3209 1446; Spandauer Damm; www.spsg.de; admission €1; ⏰ 10am-5pm Tue-Sun Apr-Oct; ⓔ Sophie-Charlotte-Platz, then 🚌 309, ⓔ Richard-Wagner-Platz, then 🚌 145

Framed by trees, near the palace garden's carp pond, the neoclassical Mausoleum (1810) serves as the final resting place of Queen Luise, for whom Christian Daniel Rauch conceived an especially ornate marble sarcophagus. The temple-like structure was twice expanded to make room for other royals, including Luise's husband, Friedrich Wilhelm III who's in another Rauch tomb. Kaiser Wilhelm I and his second wife Auguste are among those buried in the crypt.

MUSEUM FÜR VOR- UND FRÜHGESCHICHTE Map pp330-1

☎ 3267 4840; Spandauer Damm; www.smb .spk-berlin.de; adult/concession € 3/1.50, incl same-day admission to Museum Berggruen & Museum für Fotografie/Helmut Newton Sammlung €6/3, under 16 free, last 4hr Tue free; ⏰ 9am-5pm Tue-Fri, 10am-5pm Sat & Sun; ⓔ Sophie-Charlotte-Platz, then 🚌 309, ⓔ Richard-Wagner-Platz, then 🚌 145

In the former palace theatre (Langhans Building), the Museum für Vor- und Frühgeschichte (Museum of Pre- and Early History) sheds light on the cultural evolution of Europe and parts of Asia from the Stone Age to the Middle Ages. Pride of place goes to the Trojan antiquities (some originals, some replicas) unearthed by Heinrich Schliemann in 1870. Upstairs in gallery 3, the focus is on Europe with a preserved Neanderthal skull being a highlight. Also keep an eye out for the Berliner Goldhut, a famous Bronze Age hat made of a thin layer of gold.

The museum is to move to the Neues Museum on Museumsinsel (p81) upon its scheduled 2009 completion.

NEUER FLÜGEL Map pp330-1

☎ 3209 1440; Spandauer Damm; www.spsg.de; adult/concession incl audio-guide €5/4; ⏰ 10am-5pm Tue-Sun Apr-Oct, 11am-5pm Nov-Mar; ⓔ Sophie-Charlotte-Platz, then 🚌 309 or ⓔ Richard-Wagner-Platz, then 🚌 145

The reign of Fredrick the Great saw the 1746 addition of the Neuer Flügel (New

Wing), designed by Knobelsdorff. Here you'll find some of the palace's most beautiful rooms, including the confectionlike White Hall, a former banquet room; the Golden Gallery, a rococo fantasy draped in pale apple green wall coverings, golden filigree ornamentation and mirrors; and the Concert Room filled with 18th-century paintings by French masters such as Watteau, Boucher and Pesne.

To the right of the staircase are the Winterkammern (Winter Chambers) of Friedrich Wilhelm II, decorated in a comparatively austere early neoclassical style. Noteworthy here are the Gobelin tapestries and the Schinkel-designed bedroom of Queen Luise.

You're free to explore on your own, but it's worth following the two audio tours included in the admission price.

NEUER PAVILLON (SCHINKEL PAVILLON) Map pp330-1

☎ 3209 1443; Spandauer Damm; www.spsg.de; adult/concession with guided tour €2/1.50; ⏰ 10am-5pm Tue-Sun, last tour 5pm; ⓔ Sophie-Charlotte-Platz, then 🚌 309, ⓔ Richard-Wagner-Platz, then 🚌 145

Considered modest as far as Prussian kings go, Friedrich Wilhelm III (r 1797–1848) hired Schinkel to design this small summer palace inspired by a Neapolitan villa. It now houses works by early-19th-century Berlin artists, including Carl Blechen, Eduard Gaertner and Schinkel himself, alongside furnishings, porcelain and sculpture from the same period.

SCHLOSSGARTEN CHARLOTTENBURG Map pp330-1

Spandauer Damm; admission free; ⓔ Sophie-Charlotte-Platz, then 🚌 309, ⓔ Richard-Wagner-Platz, then 🚌 145

The sprawling park behind Schloss Charlottenburg is a favourite spot with Berliners and visitors for strolling, jogging or whiling away a lazy afternoon. It was originally laid out in French baroque style, but this was changed when natural English gardens became all the rage at the turn of the 18th century. After WWII, a compromise was struck: the area adjacent to the palace is in the French style and the English park is behind the carp pond.

AROUND SCHLOSS CHARLOTTENBURG

Besides the dazzling splendour of Schloss Charlottenburg, there are four museums in the immediate vicinity.

ABGUSS-SAMMLUNG ANTIKER PLASTIK BERLIN Map pp330-1

☎ 342 4054; www.abguss-sammlung-berlin.de; Schlossstrasse 69b; admission free; ⊙ 2-5pm Thu-Sun; ◉ Sophie-Charlotte-Platz, then 🚌 309, ◉ Richard-Wagner-Platz, then 🚌 145

If you are a fan of classical sculpture or simply enjoy the sight of naked guys without noses or other pertinent body parts, make this small collection a definite stopover. With works spanning 3500 years created by cultures as diverse as the Minoan, Roman or Byzantine, you will be able to trace the evolution of this ancient art form. The shop sells plastercast copies of many popular sculptures.

BRÖHAN MUSEUM Map pp330-1

☎ 3269 0600; www.broehan-museum.de; Schlossstrasse 1a; adult/concession € 4/2; ⊙ 10am-6pm Tue-Sun; ◉ Sophie-Charlotte-Platz, then 🚌 309, ◉ Richard- Wagner-Platz, then 🚌 145

Karl Bröhan (1921–2000) was a man with a passion for furniture and furnishings from the Art Nouveau, Art Deco and functionalism periods. These decorative styles were very much in vogue during the period from 1889 to 1939 and are considered the midwives of modern design. Bröhan was also an extremely generous man: on his 60th birthday, he donated his entire prized collection to the city of Berlin.

On the ground floor you can wander past outstanding period rooms, each fully furnished and decorated with lamps, porcelain, glass, silver, carpets and other items by such famous designers as Hector Guimard, Émile Ruhlmann and Peter Behrens.

Upstairs, the museum's picture gallery has great works by Berlin Secession painters, including Hans Baluschek, Willy Jaeckel and Walter Leistikow.

Henry van de Velde (1863–1957), the multitalented Belgian Art Nouveau artist, gets his own room on the top floor, which is also used for special exhibitions.

HEIMATMUSEUM CHARLOTTENBURG-WILMERSDORF Map pp330-1

☎ 902 913 201; www.heimatmuseum-charlotten burg.de; Schlossstrasse 69; admission free; ⊙ 10am-5pm Tue-Fri, 11am-5pm Sat & Sun; ◉ Sophie-Charlotte-Platz, then 🚌 309 or ◉ Richard-Wagner-Platz, then 🚌 145

More dynamic than most, this local history museum mounts as many as 10 changing exhibits annually, highlighting the traditions, buildings and people that shaped this district, women in particular. The biggest crowds turn out for its Easter and Christmas shows.

MUSEUM BERGGRUEN Map pp330-1

☎ 326 9580; www.smb.spk-berlin.de; Schlossstrasse 1; adult/concession incl same-day admission to Museum für Vor- und Frühgeschichte & Museum für Fotografie/Helmut Newton Sammlung €6/3, under 16 free, last 4hr Thu free; ⊙ 10am-6pm Tue-Sun; ◉ Sophie-Charlotte-Platz, then 🚌 309, ◉ Richard- Wagner-Platz, then 🚌 145

This intimate museum is a delicacy for fans of classical modern art, especially of Picasso, Klee, Matisse and Giacometti. Picasso is especially well represented with more than 100 paintings, drawings and sculpture from all his major creative phases. The early Blue and Rose periods (eg *Seated Harlequin,* 1905) give way to his bold cubist canvases (eg the portrait of George Braque, 1910) and the mellow creations of his later years (eg *The Yellow Pullover,* 1939).

Elsewhere it's off to the delicate and emotional world of Paul Klee, with a selection of 60 works created between 1917 and 1940. There are also paper cutouts by Matisse and Giacometti's famous sculptures alongside a sprinkling of African art that inspired both Klee and Picasso.

KURFÜRSTENDAMM & AROUND

The 3.5km-long Kurfürstendamm is a ribbon of commerce with origins as a bridle path leading to the royal hunting palace in the Grunewald forest. Known as Ku'damm for short, the boulevard got its current look in the 1880s courtesy of Bismarck who had it widened, paved and lined with fancy residential buildings. The 1920s added the luxury hotels and shops, art galleries, restaurants, theatres and other entertainment venues that still characterise the Ku'damm today. Recent updates have brought some striking new architecture, including Helmut Jahn's Neues Kranzler Eck.

BAHNHOF ZOO Map p344

🚇 🚈 Zoologischer Garten

For decades, Bahnhof Zoo (Zoo Station) was the gateway to Berlin for millions of people arriving in the city by train from other parts of Germany and Europe. No more. Since the opening of the Hauptbahnhof in Tiergarten (p292) long-distance trains bypass this legendary station, which inspired the U2 song 'Zoo Station', featured on their album *Achtung Baby*. In the 1980s Bahnhof Zoo was the haunt of drug pushers and child prostitutes, an era graphically portrayed in *Wir Kinder vom Bahnhof Zoo* (The Children of Bahnhof Zoo, published in English as *Christiane F*), the 1981 biography of the teenager Christiane F.

BERLINER ZOO & AQUARIUM Map p344

☎ 254 010; adult/child/student zoo or aquarium €11/5.50/8, zoo & aquarium €16.50/8.50/13, family tickets available; 🚇 🚈 Zoologischer Garten

An exotic Elephant Gate marks the gateway to the Berlin Zoo (www.zoo-berlin .de; Hardenbergplatz 8; 🕙 9am-6.30pm mid-Mar–mid-Oct, 9am-5pm mid-Oct–mid-Mar), Germany's oldest animal park and home to some 14,000 furry and feathered denizens from around the world. Founded by King Friedrich Wilhelm IV in 1844, its original cast of critters, including bears and kangaroos, hailed from the royal family's private zoo on the Pfaueninsel (see p147). These days, perennial crowd pleasers include cheeky orang-utans, endangered rhinos, playful penguins and such classics as giraffes, zebras and elephants. Bao Bao, a rare giant panda donated by China, enjoys celebrity status among zoo connoisseurs.

Also worth a visit is the adjacent Aquarium (www.aquarium-berlin.de; Budapester Strasse 32; 🕙 9am-6pm year-round), which has three floors of fish, amphibians, insects and reptiles, including the famous crocodile hall. Elsewhere you can commune with poison frogs, watch slithering octopus or meet a real-life 'Nemo' in the clownfish tank.

DEUTSCHES CURRYWURST MUSEUM
Map p344

☎ 8871 8630; www.currywurstmuseum.de; Kurfürstendamm 46; 🕙 10am-10pm; call for admission; 🚇 Uhlandstrasse

Expected to open in the autumn of 2006, this quirky museum is a paean to the quintessential Berlin snack food, the iconic *Currywurst*, invented here in 1949. The multimedia exhibit takes not only a historical look at the sausage but also includes a 3-D animation tracking its journey through the human body. If you haven't lost your appetite, you can buy a spicy wiener in the on-site Imbiss or a T-shirt in the shop. For more on the *Currywurst*, see the boxed text on p179.

EROTIK MUSEUM Map p344

☎ 886 0666; Joachimstaler Strasse 4; adult/concession € 5/4, over 18 only; 🕙 9am-midnight; 🚇 🚈 Zoologischer Garten

Relax, it's just sex… Berlin's Erotik Museum is the brainchild of Beate Uhse, Germany's late sex-toy marketing queen. For over-18s only, the displays range from from wacky to sophisticated, raunchy to romantic and tell the story of physical pleasure through the ages and around the world. There's artsy stuff like fine examples of Japanese Shunga art (with their exaggerated genitalia), Chinese sex-ed 'wedding tiles' and Balinese fertility demons, but also life-size dioramas on such topics as fetishism, sadism and masochism. Erotic films from the early days of cinema and historic chastity belts elicit lots of giggles. Other exhibits focus on the work of gay-movement pioneer Magnus Hirschfeld and of Frau Uhse herself. A garish adult store is attached.

EUROPA-CENTER Map p344

www.europa-center-berlin.de; Breitscheidplatz; 🚇 Kurfürstendamm

Now looking rather dated, the Europa-Center was Berlin's first high-rise when it opened in 1965. The 20-storey-tall shopping, restaurant and office temple stands on the site of the Romanisches Café, a legendary hangout of artists and intellectuals – Brecht to Sinclair Lewis to George Grosz – during the heady Golden Twenties. Step inside for a look at the artsy waterlily fountain and the psychedelic Flow of Time Clock by Bernard Gitton, which measures time via a series of

Erotik Museum (opposite page)

JÜDISCHES GEMEINDEHAUS Map p344
☎ 880 280; Fasanenstrasse 79-80;
Ⓤ Uhlandstrasse

The Jüdisches Gemeindehaus (Jewish Community Centre) has been a Berlin mainstay since 1959. You can take your pick between browsing through German and international Jewish periodicals in the library, surfing the Web in the Internet café or eating kosher cuisine at the upstairs **Gabriel's** restaurant (p175).

The centre stands on the site of a once-majestic Moorish-style synagogue destroyed by the Nazis during the *Kristallnacht* pogroms of 9 November 1938. Only the portal has survived. A broken Torah roll in the courtyard commemorates the event. A few steps further a memorial wall records the names of concentration camps and Jewish ghettos.

KAISER-WILHELM-GEDÄCHTNISKIRCHE Map p344
☎ 218 5023; Breitscheidplatz; admission free;
Ⓨ Memorial Hall 10am-4pm Mon-Sat, hall of worship 9am-7pm; Ⓢ Ⓡ Zoologischer Garten, Ⓡ Kurfürstendamm

The Kaiser Wilhelm Memorial Church (1895) stands quiet and dignified amid the commercialism engulfing Breitscheidplatz and Kurfürstendamm. Destroyed in 1943 by Allied bombs, the husk of the neo-Romanesque church's west tower is one of Berlin's most haunting and enduring landmarks. It is now home to a **Gedenkhalle** (Memorial Hall), whose mosaics, marble reliefs, liturgical objects and photos from before and after the bombing hint at the church's one-time opulence.

The adjacent octagonal **hall of worship**, added in 1961, has intensely midnight blue windows and a giant golden Jesus figure 'floating' above the altar.

KANTDREIECK Map p344
Kantstrasse 155; Ⓤ Uhlandstrasse

The award-winning 1994 'Kant Triangle' is Josef Paul Kleihues' most famous Berlin commission. The attractive office building combines a five-storey triangular glass-and-slate base with a 36m-high square tower. At the top is the landmark triangular 'sail', which shifts in the wind like a giant metal weather vane.

vials and spheres filled with phosphorous liquid. There's a **BTM tourist office** (p301) on the ground floor of the centre's Budapester Strasse (north) side.

The complex flanks bustling **Breitscheidplatz**, where everyone from footsore tourists to seasoned street performers gathers around the quirky **Weltbrunnen** (World Fountain, 1983) by Joachim Schmettau. Made from reddish granite it shows a world split open with sculptures of humans and animals clustering in various scenes. Naturally, Berliners have found a nickname for it: Wasserklops (water meatball).

FASANENSTRASSE Map p344
Ⓤ Uhlandstrasse

Nowhere does the aura of Charlottenburg's late-19th-century bourgeois grandeur survive better than on this quiet, leafy avenue lined by palatial townhouses. Sneak a peek into some of their foyers to discover stucco ceilings, romantic murals, marble fireplaces, and creaky wrought-iron or brass lifts resembling giant birdcages.

At Fasanenstrasse 23 is the **Literaturhaus** where you can attend readings, check out the gallery, browse the bookshop or enjoy a light meal at the **Café Wintergarten** (p174). Not to be missed is the **Käthe-Kollwitz-Museum** next door.

115

TOP FIVE FOR CHILDREN

- Fancy yourself a pirate, princess or boat captain at the Kindermuseum Labyrinth (p136).
- Meet Bao Bao the panda bear and other beloved critters at the Berliner Zoo & Aquarium (p114).
- Be transported back in time and discover what Berlin might have looked like in the Middle Ages at the Museumsdorf Düppel (p147)
- Push buttons, pull knobs and engage in experiments at the Spectrum science centre, part of the Deutsches Technikmuseum (p123).
- Head to the Müggelsee (p139) or Wannsee (p145) for a splash in the lake and a fun boat ride.

KÄTHE-KOLLWITZ-MUSEUM Map p344

☎ 882 5210; www.kaethe-kollwitz.de; Fasanenstrasse 24; adult/concession €5/2.50; ⊙ 11am-6pm Wed-Mon; ⊙ Uhlandstrasse

This exquisite museum is dedicated to Käthe Kollwitz (1867–1945), one of Germany's greatest woman artists (see boxed text p132). Lithographs, graphics, woodcuts, sculptures and drawings are the core of this private collection. Amassed by the late painter and gallery owner Hans Pels-Leusden, it shows the socialist artist's work in all its haunting complexity. Highlights include the antihunger lithography *Brot* (Bread, 1924) and the woodcut series *Krieg* (War, 1922–23). Among her favourite themes were motherhood and death; sometimes the two are strangely intertwined as in works that show death as a nurturing figure, cradling its victims. The collection also includes sculpture, self-portraits and a copy of the Kollwitz memorial by Gustav Seitz, also seen on Kollwitzplatz in Prenzlauer Berg. Special exhibits supplement the permanent collection twice annually.

English-language audio guides cost an additional €3.

LUDWIG-ERHARD-HAUS Map p344

Fasanenstrasse 83-84; ⊙ ⊞ Zoologischer Garten

Structure, space, skin – the building philosophy of British architect Nicholas Grimshaw is perfectly illustrated in his 1997 Ludwig-Erhard-Haus, a prime example of 'organic' architecture. The armadillo inspired the hi-tech design, with its 'rib cage' of steel girders clad in a 'skin' of glass. It houses the Berlin Stock Exchange and the Chamber of Commerce & Industry.

MUSEUM FÜR FOTOGRAFIE/HELMUT NEWTON SAMMLUNG Map p344

☎ 3186 4825; Jebensstrasse 2; adult/concession incl same-day admission to Museum Berggruen & Museum für Vor- und Frühgeschichte €6/3, under 16 free, last 4hr Thu free; ⊙ 10am-6pm Tue-Sun, to 10pm Thu; ⊙ ⊞ Zoologischer Garten, ⊞ 100

Helmut Newton, the celebrated if controversial *enfant terrible* of fashion photography, donated a sizable collection of his images to the city of Berlin shortly before his fatal car accident in January 2004. They form the core exhibit of the brand-new Museum of Photography in a former art library behind Zoo Station. Newton was born in Berlin in 1920 and studied photography here with famed fashion photographer YVA before fleeing from the Nazis in 1938. His work reflects a lifelong fascination – some might say obsession – with the female body. He's perhaps best known for his provocative large-scale photographs of nude women, but even many of his landscapes and still lifes are sexually charged. Besides presenting a selection of Newton works, the exhibit is also a bit of a shrine to the man, displaying his cameras, his partially recreated office in Monte Carlo and his library.

NEUES KRANZLER ECK Map p344

Cnr Kurfürstendamm & Joachimstaler Strasse; ⊙ Kurfürstendamm

The New Kranzler Eck is a sleek office-and-retail complex framed by Kantstrasse, Kurfürstendamm and Joachimstaler Strasse. Helmut Jahn, the Chicago-based architect of the Sony Center (p105), creatively combined existing structures, including an old insurance building and a department store, with a soaring steel-and-glass tower with a cool, angular geometry. A walkway leads to shops and a courtyard with two giant birdcages. Of the historic Café Kranzler that stood on this spot, only the rotunda remains.

STORY OF BERLIN Map p344

☎ 8872 0100; www.story-of-berlin.de; Kurfürstendamm 207-208; adult/concession/family €9.30/7.50/21; ⊙ 10am-8pm, last admission & bunker tour 6pm; ⊙ Uhlandstrasse

Inside the Ku'damm Karree shopping mall, the Story of Berlin is a local history museum with a 21st-century hi-tech twist.

You'll be outfitted with headsets whose narration (in English or German and backed by sound effects) activates as you enter any of the 20 exhibition rooms. Each encapsulates a different epoch in the city's fascinating history, from its founding in 1237 to its days as the Prussian capital, the Golden Twenties and the dark days of the Third Reich. The Cold War period comes creepily to life during a tour of a still fully functional atomic bunker beneath the building. Budget at least two hours for this multimedia exhibit.

DAS VERBORGENE MUSEUM Map p344

☎ 313 3656; Schlüterstrasse 70; adult/concession €1.50/0.50; ☒ 3-7pm Thu & Fri, noon-4pm Sat & Sun during exhibits only; ☒ Savignyplatz
Founded by a pair of feminist artists and art historians, the small Verborgene Museum (Hidden Museum) gets its name not from having an obscure location but from its artistic focus: the largely forgotten works by early-20th-century women artists, mostly from Germany. Past exhibits have highlighted the photography of Helmut Newton mentor Else Simon (aka YVA) and the works of Bauhaus artist Gertrud Arndt and the architect Lucy Hillebrand. Call or check the listings magazines for current shows.

WESTERN CHARLOTTENBURG
FUNKTURM

☎ 3038 1905; Hammarskjöldplatz; ☒ 10am-11pm Tue-Sun, 11am-9pm Mon; adult/concession €3.60/1.80; ◉ Kaiserdamm, Theodor-Heuss-Platz, ☒ MesseNord/ICC
The Funkturm (radio tower), part of the trade-fair grounds, is by far the most visible structure in western Charlottenburg. Its filigree outline, which bears an uncanny resemblance to Paris' Eiffel Tower, soars 138m into the Berlin sky (150m with antenna) and has been transmitting signals since 1926. From the viewing platform at 125m or the restaurant at 55m you can enjoy sweeping views of the Grunewald and the western city, as well as the AVUS, Germany's first car-racing track, which opened in 1921; AVUS stands for Automobil-, Verkehrs- und Übungsstrecke (auto, traffic and practice track). The Nazis made

it part of the autobahn system, which it still is today.

GEORG KOLBE MUSEUM

☎ 304 2144; Sensburger Allee 25; www.georg -kolbe-museum.de; ☒ 10am-5pm Tue-Sun; adult/ concession €4/2.50, under 12 free; ☒ Heerstrasse
Georg Kolbe (1877–1947) was one of Germany's most influential sculptors in the first half of the 20th century. A member of the Berlin Secession, he distanced himself from traditional sculpture and became a chief exponent of the idealised nude.

After his wife's death in 1927, Kolbe's figures took on a more solemn and emotional air, whereas his later works focus on the athletic male, an approach that found favour with the Nazis.

The attractive museum, in Kolbe's former studio, shows sculptures from all phases of the artist's life alongside temporary exhibits often drawn from his rich personal collection of 20th-century sculpture and paintings. The sculpture garden is an oasis of tranquillity and there's a nice museum café as well.

CORBUSIERHAUS

Flatowallee 16; ☒ Olympiastadion
This honeycomb-like housing estate just south of the Olympic Stadium was French architect Le Corbusier's (1887–1965) contribution to the 1957 International Building Exhibition (Interbau). It represents his attempt to address the post-WWII housing shortages all over Europe, but especially in bomb-ravaged Berlin. Some 575 flats are crammed into the 17-storey structure standing on stilts, its monotonous exterior brightened by a few colour accents. This was the third in a series of complexes he called Unitè d'Habitation (housing unit); the others are located in Marseille and Nantes.

Le Corbusier's original plan called for the complex to be an autonomous vertical village, complete with a post office, shops, a school and other infrastructure. In Berlin, though, this vision never came to fruition because of lack of funding, and the architect later distanced himself from the project.

If you'd like to stay in an original Le Corbusier, you can rent an apartment here (see p259).

OLYMPIASTADION & GLOCKENTURM

Stadium ☎ 2500 2322; www.olympiastadion
-berlin.de; Olympischer Platz 3; ⏰ 10am-7pm
Apr-Oct, to 4pm Nov-Mar; adult/concession €3/2,
tours €6/5; 🚇 Olympiastadion. **Glockenturm**
☎ 305 8123; www.glockenturm.de; Am Glockenturm; adult/conc €2.50/1.50; ⏰ 9am-6pm;
🚇 Pichelsberg

The Olympic Stadium, built for the 1936
Olympic Games, is one of the best examples
of Nazi-era monumentalist architecture. Afri-
can-American runner Jesse Owens won four
gold medals here, shattering Hitler's theory
that Aryans were all-powerful *Übermenschen*
(a super race). Designed by the brothers
Walter and Werner March, the coliseumlike
structure replaced an earlier stadium completed by their father Otto in 1913.

From 2000 to 2004, the structure went
from crumbling to state-of-the-art during a
major facelift to prepare it for its close-up
during the football (soccer) World Cup of
2006. Complete with a jaunty, luminescent
roof construction several games were
scheduled to be hosted here, including the
final. At other times, bleachers are packed
with fans of Berlin's Bundesliga football
club Hertha BSC or such blockbuster bands
as U2.

On nonevent days, you can explore
the stadium on your own or by joining a
guided tour offered several times daily (call
for times). An audio-guide (in English) for
an extra €2 is a worthwhile investment.
Tours take you into sections that are otherwise off-limits, such as the locker rooms,
warm-up areas and VIP areas.

The **Maifeld**, a vast field west of the
stadium, was used for Nazi mass rallies
(it holds about 250,000 people) and the
equestrian competitions during the 1936
Olympic Games. It later became the
drilling ground for British Allied troops,
which, until 1994, had their headquarters
nearby. Soaring above the field is the 77m
Glockenturm (Clock Tower), which offers good
views over the stadium, the city and the
Havel River. Check out the Nazi-era bell;
it weighs 2.5 tonnes and was rung only
twice – to signal the start and the finish of
the Olympic Games. A recent renovation of
the tower added a glass lift (elevator) and
a new ground-floor exhibit on the Olympic
Games of 1936.

Northwest of the Maifeld, the **Waldbühne**
(see p209) is a lovely outdoor amphitheatre

originally built for the Olympic gymnastics
competition. It's now a beloved summer
venue for concerts, films and other cultural
events.

WILMERSDORF

Eating p177; Shopping p239; Sleeping p259

Affluent, sedate and bourgeois, Wilmersdorf does not exactly teem with traditional tourist sights, although it redeems
itself with the vast **Grunewald**. The former
royal hunting terrain is now a sprawling
forest and formidable outdoor playground
hemmed in by the Havel River and the
magnificent villas of Berlin fat cats. Back
in town, whatever after-dark sparkle you
can find is likely to be concentrated around
Ludwigkirchplatz.

Orientation

Sprawling Wilmersdorf segues into Charlottenburg to the north and Zehlendorf to
the south. The Grunewald forest takes up
about half of its area. Hotels, restaurants
and cafés abound in the eastern reaches
where Wilmersdorf rubs up against Charlottenburg and Schöneberg.

GRUNEWALDTURM

☎ 300 0730; Havelchaussee 61; tower ascent
€0.50; ⏰ 10am-dusk, in summer sometimes to
midnight; 🚇 Wannsee, then 🚌 218

With its turrets and ornate details, the
56m neogothic Grunewaldturm, near the
Havel River, has a dreamy 'Rapunzel' quality, even if it was originally dedicated to
decidedly unromantic Kaiser Wilhelm I. It
was designed in 1899 by Franz Schwech-
ter to mark what would have been the

emperor's 100th birthday; that's Wilhelm in marble in the domed hall in the upper part of the tower. It's worth climbing the 204 steps to the top for views over the Havel River, all the way to the **Pfaueninsel** (p147).

If the tummy rumbles, the tower restaurant serves pretty decent food, including breakfast (until 3.30pm).

TEUFELSBERG
Teufelsseechaussee; 🚇 Heerstrasse
It may have a terrifying name, but at 115m high, the Teufelsberg (Devil's Mountain) in the northern Grunewald isn't exactly the Matterhorn. It is, however, the tallest of Berlin's 20 'rubble mountains' built by locals, most of them women, during the cleanup of their bomb-ravaged city after WWII. It took 20 years to pile up 25 million cubic metres of debris.

The hill that was borne from destruction is now a fun zone, especially in snowy winters when you'll find hordes of squealing kids tobogganing or even skiing down its gentle slopes. Older ones try their climbing skills or explore the terrain on mountain bikes, while in autumn colourful kites flutter through the air like swarms of butterflies. The little lake at the bottom of the hill is the **Teufelssee** (not suitable for swimming). Just north of the lake is the Teufelsfenn moor.

SCHÖNEBERG
Eating p178; Shopping p240; Sleeping p260
Wedged in between staid Wilmersdorf and zany Kreuzberg, Schöneberg has a radical pedigree rooted in the squatter days of the 80s but now flaunts a comfortable, gentrified, though still left-leaning, identity. The KaDeWe department store ranks as a key attraction with the bars and cafés around Winterfeldtplatz, the district's heart and soul, a close second. People from all over town turn out for the bountiful farmers' market held here every Saturday. The gay crowd gathers nearby along Motzstrasse and Fuggerstrasse and has done so since the 1920s, a period vividly chronicled by one-time area resident Christopher Isherwood in *Goodbye to Berlin*. One local party gal who liked to hang with the 'boyz' was Marlene Dietrich. She's buried in southern Schöneberg not far from Rathaus

Schöneberg, the town hall where John F Kennedy exulted 'Ich bin ein Berliner!' back in 1961.

ORIENTATION
Schöneberg is hemmed in by Charlottenburg and Wilmersdorf to the west, Tiergarten to the north, Steglitz to the south and Kreuzberg to the east. Key U-Bahn stations are Wittenbergplatz for the KaDeWe, and Nollendorfplatz for Winterfeldtplatz and the 'gay triangle' between Eisenacher- Motz- and Fuggerstrasse. The major thoroughfares, Potsdamer Strasse and Hauptstrasse, feel considerably more downmarket.

TRANSPORT
Bus M19 and M29 travel from the Ku'damm to the KaDeWe; M19 continues to U-Bahn Mehringdamm in western Kreuzberg, M29 goes to eastern Kreuzberg.

S-Bahn S41, S42 and S45 stop at Schöneberg and Innsbrucker Platz.

U-Bahn Nollendorfplatz is the main hub served by U1 from Kurfürstendamm and Kreuzberg; U2 from Zoo Station, Mitte and Prenzlauer Berg; U3 from Wilmersdorf; and the short intra-Schöneberg U4.

ALTER ST MATTHÄUS-KIRCHHOF
Map pp338-9
☎ 781 1297; Grossgörschenstrasse 12; ⏱ 8am-7pm; ♿ 🚇 Yorckstrasse, 🚇 Kleistpark
This pretty cemetery, created in 1856, was a favourite among Berlin's late-19th-century bourgeoisie and is filled with opulent gravestones and memorials. Celebrities buried here include the Brothers Grimm and the physician and politician Rudolf Virchow. A memorial tombstone honours Claus Schenk Graf von Stauffenberg and his fellow conspirators who were executed by the Nazis after their failed assassination attempt on Hitler in 1944. Their bodies were initially buried here, but members of the SS had them exhumed, cremated and their ashes scattered.

The cemetery office has a pamphlet with names and grave locations of these and other famous Berliners.

GRAVE OF MARLENE DIETRICH

Map pp338-9

☎ 7560 6898; Stubenrauchstrasse 43-45; ☼ 24hr; ⊖ �ⓡ Bundesplatz

To pay homage to Marlene Dietrich (1901–92), you have to travel to the little Städtisches Friedhof III (Municipal Cemetery III) in southern Schöneberg. This is where the 'Blue Angel' makes her final home in a not terribly glamorous plot not far from her mother's. Her tombstone says simply 'Marlene' along with the inscription: 'Here I stand on the marker of my days.' Look for the map inside the cemetery entrance to locate the grave, which is near the Fehlerstrasse (north) side of the grounds. From the U- or S-Bahn station, walk southwest on Südwestkorso to Stubenrauchstrasse. In 2004, avant-garde fashion photographer Helmut Newton was buried four plots away from the grande dame.

KAMMERGERICHT Map pp338-9

☎ 901 50; Elssholzstrasse 30-33; ⊖ Kleistpark

West of Kleistpark, the imposing 1913 Kammergericht (Courts of Justice) was the site of the notorious show trials of the Nazi Volksgerichtshof (People's Court) against the participants – real and alleged – in the July 1944 assassination attempt on Hitler. Led by the fanatical judge Roland Freisler, hundreds of people were handed their death sentences by this court before being executed at Plötzensee prison, now the Gedenkstätte Plötzensee memorial site (p136). Freisler, alas, was crushed to death by a falling beam in the court building during an air raid in February 1945, thereby avoiding what would undoubtedly have been a starring role at the Nuremberg Trials.

After the war, the Allies confiscated the building and used it first as the seat of the Allied Control Council, and then, until 1990, as the headquarters of the Allied Air Control. Since 1997, after extensive renovations, it is once again being used as a courthouse.

HEINRICH-VON-KLEIST PARK & AROUND Map pp338-9

Potsdamer Strasse; ⊖ Kleistpark

East of the Kammergericht, this little park gets a romantic quality thanks to the graceful sandstone Königskolonnaden (Royal Colonnades). Richly ornamented with sculptures of angels and gods, they were designed in

1780 by Carl von Gontard (he of Gendarmenmarkt churches fame. They originally stood near today's Rotes Rathaus in Mitte but were displaced by road construction in 1910.

South of the park is the Café Neues Ufer (☎ 7895 7900; Hauptstrasse 157), one of Berlin's oldest lesbian and gay hangouts. Back in the late 1970s, when it was still known as Anderes Ufer, it also drew a slew of artists, including David Bowie and Iggy Pop, who shared an apartment next door at Hauptstrasse 155. One of Bowie's seminal albums, Heroes, was inspired by his Berlin stay.

NOLLENDORFPLATZ & AROUND

Map pp338-9

⊖ Nollendorfplatz

Paintings and photographs from the early 20th century show Nollendorfplatz as a bustling urban square filled with cafés, theatres and people on parade. It was just this kind of liberal and libertine flair that drew British author Christopher Isherwood, whose writings inspired the movie Cabaret, to this area in the 1920s. The apartment building where he rented his modest room still stands nearby at Nollendorfstrasse 17.

To Isherwood, 'Berlin meant boys' and boys he could find aplenty in such famous bars as the Eldorado, haunt of a demimonde that included Marlene Dietrich and chanteuse Claire Waldorff. The Nazis, of course, put an end to the fun, but not for good. Although the Eldorado never made a comeback, the area south of Nollendorfplatz, especially Motzstrasse, reprised its role as Berlin's gay mecca after the war and continues to be a major gay nightlife hub today.

Since 1989, a pink granite triangle plaque at the south entrance of Nollendorfplatz U-Bahn station commemorates the gay and lesbian victims of the Third Reich. Although rarely talked about, homosexuals suffered tremendously under the Nazis. They were socially ostracised and had to wear pink triangles on their clothing. Many were imprisoned, deported to concentration camps, tortured and murdered.

The main building to survive since the wicked 1920s is the Metropol Theater with its ornate and erotic frieze. It started life in 1906 as the Neue Schauspielhaus (New Theatre) and was later taken over by Erwin

Königskolonnaden (colonnade) with Kammergericht (opposite page) in the background

Piscator (p33). In late 2005, it was revived as the Goya nightclub (p202).

From Nollendorfplatz, it's only a short walk south on Maassenstrasse to **Winterfeldtplatz**, where a popular farmers market is held on Wednesdays and Saturdays. Cafés, eateries and speciality boutiques orbit the square, which is overlooked by the **St-Matthias-Kirche**.

RATHAUS SCHÖNEBERG Map pp338-9
John-F-Kennedy-Platz; ⊕ Rathaus Schöneberg
The Rathaus Schöneberg (Town Hall) was the seat of the West Berlin government from 1948 to 1990, but it is a single day in 1963 for which the building is best remembered. President John F Kennedy was in town and he was going to speak. From the steps of the Rathaus, the silver-tongued orator flayed the forces of darkness to the east and applauded the powers of light in the west, concluding with the now famous words: 'All free men, wherever they live, are citizens of Berlin. And therefore, as a free man, I take pride in the words: Ich bin ein Berliner.' The adoring crowd of half a million cheered his words all the way into the history books.

The Rathaus clock tower holds a copy of the **Liberty Bell**, presented to the city in 1950 by the then US army commander in Berlin,

General Lucius D Clay. More than seven million Americans had donated money towards this replica of the Philadelphia original.

A popular **flea market** takes place at weekends outside the town hall (p240).

KREUZBERG
Eating p181; Shopping p241; Sleeping p261
Kreuzberg has always had a split personality. The western half around Viktoriapark (a popular summer hangout) has tended towards the upmarket in recent years. The main strip, Bergmannstrasse, lined with convivial cafés and stores, is a popular playground for the mostly upwardly mobile young folks living around here.

The ambience feels almost sedate compared to eastern Kreuzberg, sometimes still referred to by its pre-Wende postal code SO36. This one-time anarchist stronghold, famous for violent brawls with police on May Day, still nurtures a countercultural edge. Mostly, though, it's a multicultural mosaic dominated by Turkish immigrants and Germans of Turkish descent and it's even nicknamed Little Istanbul. The area around Kottbusser Tor (Kotti, for short) is a hub of the community. Nearby Oranienstrasse is a well-known nightlife hub, although the

121

TRANSPORT

Bus M29 from Potsdamer Platz for Checkpoint Charlie and Oranienstrasse; 140 between western and eastern Kreuzberg via Tempelhof Airport, Gneisenaustrasse and Kottbusser Tor.

S-Bahn S1, S2 and S26 stop at Yorckstrasse in western Kreuzberg.

U-Bahn Served by U1 from Charlottenburg, Schöneberg and Friedrichshain; U6 and U8 from Mitte; U7 from Schöneberg and Neukölln.

newer riverside haunts along Schlesische Strasse attract a hipper crowd.

Separating the two halves is the Landwehrkanal, whose idyllic banks lend themselves to strolling and picnicking. Northern Kreuzberg, meanwhile, feels more like an extension of Mitte and harbours the district's heavyweight attractions: the Jewish Museum and Checkpoint Charlie.

If you're not prone to vertigo and would like a cool view over the city, you can sway 150m above ground in a hot-air balloon – tethered safely to the ground – with **Berlin Hi-Flyer** (Map pp336–7; ☎ 01805 708 708; www .air-service-berlin.de; cnr Wilhelmstrasse & Zimmerstrasse; adult/concession €19/10; ☺ 10am-10pm Sun-Thu, to 12.30am Fri & Sat Mar-Nov, 11am-6pm Sun-Thu, to 7pm Fri & Sat Dec-Feb, weather permitting; ⊖ Kochstrasse).

ORIENTATION

Kreuzberg forms an administrative unit with Friedrichshain across the Spree, which once separated West and East Berlin. Other surrounding districts are Mitte to the north, Schöneberg to the west and Tempelhof and Neukölln to the south. The Landwehrkanal traverses the district before emptying into the Spree. Viktoriapark and Bergmannstrasse are south of the canal, near U-Bahn station Mehringdamm, while SO36 is north of the water centred around Kottbusser Tor and Görlitzer Platz stations.

ABGEORDNETENHAUS Map pp336-7
House of Representatives; ☎ 2325 2325; Niederkirchner Strasse 5; admission free; ☺ 9am-3pm Mon-Fri; ⊖ ☒ Potsdamer Platz
The stately neo-Renaissance structure across from the Martin-Gropius-Bau,

technically placing it in Mitte, has been a political power nexus since its late-19th-century days as the house of the Prussian Parliament. Under the Nazis, it went through a stint as a courthouse before being turned into an air force officers club by Luftwaffe chief Göring, whose ministry was only steps away (Former Reichsluftfahrtsministerium, p124). After reunification, it became the seat of Berlin's state parliament. Free changing exhibits are held in the foyer and on the mezzanine level.

ANHALTER BAHNHOF Map pp336-7
Askanischer Platz; ☒ Anhalter Bahnhof
Only a forlorn fragment of the entrance portal is left of the Anhalter Bahnhof, once Berlin's finest and busiest railway station, surrounded by luxury hotels and bustling cafés. Marlene Dietrich departed from here for Hollywood, and the king of Italy and the tsar of Russia were among the official visitors to Berlin arriving at this station. Although badly bombed in WWII, Anhalter Bahnhof remained operational for years but was eventually eclipsed by Ostbahnhof. Not even vociferous protests by Berliners could halt its demolition in 1960.

BERGMANNSTRASSE Map pp336-7
⊖ Platz der Luftbrücke, Gneisenausstrasse, Südstern
Bergmannstrasse, which runs through the heart of western Kreuzberg from Mehringdamm to Südstern, is a fun road teeming with funky second-hand stores,

KREUZBERG TOP FIVE

- Glean some insights into 2000 years of Jewish life in Germany at the captivating Jüdisches Museum (p125).
- Marvel at the ingenuity demonstrated by GDR escapees at the Haus am Checkpoint Charlie (p125).
- Enjoy a leisurely picnic on the Landwehrkanal banks with supplies gathered at the exotic Türkenmarkt (Turkish Market; p243).
- Explore the artistic visions of homegrown artists at the extraordinary Berlinische Galerie (Berlin Gallery; opposite).
- Make an in-depth exploration of the bars along Schlesische Strasse (p194), then party till breakfast time at the Watergate club (p202).

boutiques, bookshops, restaurants and cafés. Be sure to swing by Marheinekeplatz where the **Marheineke Markthalle** (p242), one of Berlin's few surviving historic market halls, is a main attraction. The red-brick **Passions-kirche** (Map pp336–7), also on the square, often hosts classical and jazz concerts.

Further east you'll pass a cluster of **cemeteries** from the 18th and 19th centuries. Gustav Stresemann, chancellor during the Weimar Republic, is one of the better-known people buried here. Other names you might recognise are the architect Martin Gropius, the sculptor Adolf Menzel and Schiller's girlfriend, Charlotte von Kalb.

BERLINISCHE GALERIE Map pp336-7
☎ 7890 2600; www.berlinischegalerie.de; Alte Jakobstrasse 124-128; admission €5/4; ☻ 10am-6pm; ⊕ Kochstrasse, Hallesches Tor, Moritzplatz

The reopening of the Berlinische Galerie (Berlin Gallery) in October 2004 brought the city yet another step closer to being one of the world's great capitals of art. After languishing in storage for seven years for lack of suitable exhibition space, the stellar collection of homegrown artists of international renown moved into the modernist digs of a former glass warehouse around the corner from the Jewish Museum. Two floors cover all major artistic movements since the late 19th century, from Berlin Secessionism (Lesser Ury, Max Liebermann) to New Objectivity (Otto Dix, George Grosz) and contemporary art by such 'Junge Wilde' (Young Wild Ones) members as Salomé and Rainer Fetting. Temporary exhibits inject additional impulses as do the occasional lecture or movie screening.

CHAMISSOPLATZ Map pp336-7
⊕ Platz der Luftbrücke

This gorgeous square, with its park and stately 19th-century buildings, was virtually unscathed by WWII. Walking around here will warp you right back to another era, an effect that hasn't been lost on film directors who often use these streets as backdrops for films. A restored **Café Achteck** *pissoir,* an ornate public men's toilet, octagonal in shape and painted poison-frog green, adds another layer of old-time authenticity. On Saturdays the entire neighbourhood turns up for the organic farmers market held on the square from 8am to 1pm.

CHECKPOINT CHARLIE Map pp336-7
Intersection of Friedrichstrasse & Zimmerstrasse; ⊕ Kochstrasse

Alpha, Bravo, Charlie… The English phonetic alphabet inspired the name of the third Allied checkpoint in post-WWII Berlin. A symbol of the Cold War, Checkpoint Charlie was the main gateway for Allies, other non-Germans and diplomats between the two Berlins from 1961 to 1990. It was here US and Soviet tanks faced off in October 1961, pushing the world to the brink of WWIII.

To commemorate this historical spot, Checkpoint Charlie has been partially reconstructed. There's a US Army guardhouse (the original is in the Alliierten Museum, p144) and a copy of the famous sign warning 'You are now leaving the American sector' in English, Russian, French and German. That original is now at the **Haus am Checkpoint Charlie Museum** next door.

A new office district – with buildings designed by Philip Johnson and other international architects – has sprouted up all around this former death strip.

> ## TOP FIVE COLD WAR SITES
> - Alliierten Museum (p144)
> - East Side Gallery (p128)
> - Gedenkstätte Berliner Mauer (p135)
> - Gedenkstätte Hohenschönhausen (Stasi Prison; p149)
> - Haus am Checkpoint Charlie (p125)

DEUTSCHES TECHNIKMUSEUM BERLIN Map pp338-9
☎ 902 540; www.dtmb.de; Trebbiner Strasse 9; adult/concession €4.50/2.50; ☻ 9am-5.30pm Tue-Fri, 10am-6pm Sat & Sun; ⊕ Möckernbrücke, Gleisdreieck

The giant German Museum of Technology is a fantastic place to keep kids entertained for hours. Its 14 departments are loaded with interactive stations, demonstrations and exhibits that examine technology through the ages. There's an entire hall of vintage locomotives and rooms crammed with historic printing presses, early film projectors, old TVs and telephones and lots more. A highlight is the reconstruction of the world's first computer, the Z1 (1938) by Konrad Zuse. All throughout, you'll have plenty of opportunity to push buttons and pull knobs or to watch the friendly museum staff explaining and demonstrating various machines. You may even get to print business cards, make paper, grind corn or step behind the microphone of a mock TV studio.

A **new wing**, opened in December 2003, holds the museum's stellar collections on aviation and navigation. Among the exhibits are several original naval vessels, including a WWII-era Biber, a one-man U-Boat used to attack anchoring ships. Most soldiers sent on such a mission died. The aviation section chronicles 200 years of German flight, from experimental hot-air balloons to the Berlin Airlift (p62). A C-54 Skymaster plane, better known as a *Rosinenbomber* (candy bomber), that was used in the airlift graces the museum's roof.

Outside, in the sprawling **Museumspark**, you can explore working windmills, a waterwheel, an engine shed and an historical brewery.

Be sure to save some time and energy for the adjacent **Spectrum** (enter from Möckernstrasse 26; admission included). At this fabulous science centre, you can participate in around 250 experiments that playfully explain the laws of physics and other scientific principles. If you ever wondered why the sky's blue or how a battery works, this is the place to get the low-down.

FLUGHAFEN TEMPELHOF Map pp336-7
Platz der Luftbrücke; ⊖ Platz der Luftbrücke
When it eventually closes down, as has been planned for years, Tempelhof Airport can look back on a long history as one of Europe's oldest airfields. Aircraft have taken to the skies above Tempelhof since aviation pioneer Orville Wright came to town in 1909. The commercial airport opened in 1923, Lufthansa started its operations here in 1926, and in the 1930s Nazi architect Ernst Sagebiel expanded the airport into one of the world's largest structures. But Tempelhof surely had its finest hour during the 1948 Berlin Airlift (see the boxed text p62) when Allied planes took off and landed here every few minutes, saving West Berlin from being absorbed into the Soviet empire.

The **Luftbrückendenkmal** (Airlift Memorial; Map pp336–7) right outside the airport honours all those who participated in keeping the city fed and free. Berliners have nicknamed it *Hungerharke* (hunger rake), a moniker inspired by the monument's trio of spikes that represent the three air corridors used by the western Allies. The names of 79 airmen and other personnel who died during this colossal effort are engraved in the plinth.

FORMER REICHSLUFTFAHRTS-MINISTERIUM Map pp336-7
Leipziger Strasse 5-7; ⊖ Kochstrasse
A short walk west of Checkpoint Charlie looms the giant building that was once Hermann Göring's Reich Aviation Ministry. Designed by Ernst Sagebiel (who also built Tempelhof Airport), it is one of the few architectural relics from the Third Reich that – quite ironically – got through the Allied pounding relatively unscathed. It took less than a year to build this huge complex honeycombed with over 2000 offices. After the war, the building housed several GDR ministries and in 1990 became headquarters of the Treuhand-Anstalt, the agency charged with privatising East German companies and property. It is now the home of the Federal Finance Ministry.

FRIEDHÖFE VOR DEM HALLESCHEN TOR Map pp336-7
☎ 622 1063; bounded by Mehringdamm, Blücherstrasse, Zossener Strasse & Baruther Strasse; admission free; ☼ 8am-sunset; ⊖ Mehringdamm
Founded in 1735, this is Berlin's oldest continuously used cemetery complex. It is also one of the most picturesque and filled with beautiful tombstones, many of artistic merit. Famous Berliners buried here include the architect Georg Wenzeslaus von Knobelsdorff, the painter Antoine Pesne, the writer and literary-salon patron Henriette Herz, the poet and painter ETA Hoffmann and the composer Felix Mendelssohn-Bartholdy.

GRUSELKABINETT BERLIN Map pp336-7
☎ 2655 5546; www.gruselkabinett-berlin.de; Schöneberger Strasse 23a; adult/child €7/5; ☼ 10am-7pm Sun, Tue & Thu, to 3pm Mon, to 8pm Fri, noon-8pm Sat; ⊖ Anhalter Bahnhof
This 'horror cabinet' is housed within a WWII air-raid shelter, once part of a network of bunkers, including Hitler's, which extended for miles beneath the city. A

small exhibit in the basement has displays on the bunker's history along with wartime-era newspapers, recordings of Allied plane attacks and a smattering of actual belongings left behind by those once holed up here during the bombing raids.

Other exhibits are more hokey than historical, but seem to score well with teenaged school groups thanks perhaps to the eccentric couple who run the place. On the ground floor, groaning dummies demonstrate the niceties of medieval surgery techniques, and upstairs you'll be spooked by creepy characters while exploring a dark and dank maze. Things can get pretty scary and perhaps too intense for tender souls or little kids.

HAUS AM CHECKPOINT CHARLIE (MAUERMUSEUM) Map pp336-7

☎ 253 7250; www.mauermuseum.de; Friedrich-strasse 43-45; adult/concession €9.50/5.50; ☑ 9am-10pm; ⊙ Kochstrasse

The Cold War years are engagingly if haphazardly chronicled in this private museum, with a strong emphasis on the history and horror of the Berlin Wall. The exhibit is strongest when documenting the courage and ingenuity some GDR citizens displayed in their escapes to the West using hot-air balloons, tunnels, concealed compartments in cars and even a one-man submarine.

Elsewhere the focus is on historic milestones involving the city, including the Berlin Airlift, the 1953 workers' uprising, the construction of the Wall and reunification. There's even an original remnant from the white borderline across which US and Soviet tanks faced off at Checkpoint Charlie in 1961.

Other rooms hold exhibits about human-rights heroes (Gandhi, Lech Walesa etc) and the world's main religions.

Displays are in various languages, including English, and a café and store are also on site.

JÜDISCHES MUSEUM Map pp336-7

☎ 2599 3300; www.jmberlin.de; Lindenstrasse 9-14; adult/concession/family incl same- & next-day admission to Museum Blindenwerkstatt Otto Weidt €5/2.50/10; ☑ 10am-10pm Mon, to 8pm Tue-Sun, last admission 1hr before closing; ⊙ Hallesches Tor, Kochstrasse, ☒ 265

One of Berlin's must-do sights, the Jüdisches Museum (Jewish Museum) is

the largest in Europe. It chronicles 2000 years of Jewish history in Germany with an emphasis on contributions to culture, art, science and other fields. It's an engaging presentation with listening stations, videos, documents 'hidden' in drawers and other multimedia devices.

The 14 sections cover every major period from the Roman days to the Middle Ages, the Enlightenment and Emancipation to the Holocaust and, ultimately, to the re-emergence of the Jewish community in Germany. There are exhibits about individuals, such as the philosopher Moses Mendelssohn, and others about Jewish family and holiday traditions.

Facade of the Jüdisches Museum (this page)

Only one section deals directly with the Holocaust, but its horrors are poignantly reflected by the architecture. Designed by Daniel Libeskind, the building serves as a metaphor for the tortured history of the Jewish people. Zinc-clad walls rise skyward in a sharply angled zigzag ground plan that's an abstract interpretation of a star. Instead of windows, irregular gashes pierce the building's gleaming skin.

The visual symbolism continues on the inside. There's no direct entrance to the museum, which instead is reached through

125

an adjoining baroque building. A steep staircase descends to a trio of stark, intersecting walkways, each a so-called 'axis'. The Axis of Exile leads to the Garden of Exile & Emigration, a disorienting field of tilted concrete columns not unlike the new Holocaust Memorial (p75). The Axis of the Holocaust leads to the Holocaust-Tower, one of the museum's several 'voids' – tomblike empty spaces that symbolise the loss of humanity, culture and life. Only the Axis of Continuity leads to the actual exhibit, but it too is a cumbersome journey along an upward sloping walkway and several steep flights of stairs. Libeskind's architecture is a powerful language indeed.

Enquire about guided tours in English (€3). There's a café-restaurant in the main building and the museum is wheelchair accessible.

KREUZBERG MUSEUM Map pp336-7

☎ 5058 5233; Adalbertstrasse 95a; www .kreuzbergmuseum.de; admission free; ⓨ noon-6pm Wed-Sun; ⓔ Kottbusser Tor
Still a work in progress, this museum chronicles the ups and downs of one of Berlin's most colourful districts. A permanent exhibit expected to open in late 2005 was to document Kreuzberg's 19th-century heyday as a centre of manufacturing and trading, highlight aspects of the district's legacy as a hotbed of left-wing protest and discuss the role immigrants have played in shaping the area. A historical print shop is also part of the museum.

KÜNSTLERHAUS BETHANIEN

Map pp336-7
☎ 616 9030; www.bethanien.de; Mariannenplatz 2; admission varies, often free; ⓨ 2-7pm Wed-Sun; ⓔ Görlitzer Bahnhof, Kottbusser Tor
This beautiful building, designed by a trio of Schinkel students, began life in 1847 as a hospital and even employed the later writer and poet Theodor Fontane as a pharmacist. Today it's both a sanctuary and creative laboratory for emerging artists from around the globe, with 25 studios and three exhibition spaces. Check the listings magazines for upcoming shows and events. In mid-2005, a group of squatters who had been evicted from a building at Yorckstrasse 59 took over an empty wing of the Künstlerhaus. For more on the subject, see the boxed text on p24.

MARTIN-GROPIUS-BAU Map pp336-7

☎ 254 860; www.gropiusbau.de; Niederkirchner Strasse 7; admission varies; ⓨ usually 10am-8pm Wed-Mon; ⓔ ⓡ Potsdamer Platz
One of the most beautiful exhibition spaces in Berlin, the Martin-Gropius-Bau began life in 1881 as a museum of arts and crafts and is now a fitting venue for travelling shows of international stature. Designed by the great-uncle of Bauhaus founder Walter Gropius, it's a three-storey cube inspired by the elegance and symmetry of Italian Renaissance palaces. A light-filled atrium and façades richly adorned with mosaics and terracotta reliefs are among the distinctive design features. Badly damaged during WWII, the building languished in the shadow of the Wall (there's still a short stretch of the Wall running east along Niederkirchner Strasse) until restored just in time for its 100th anniversary. See the listings magazines or the website for current exhibits.

RAMONES MUSEUM Map pp336-7

www.ramonesmuseum.com; Solmsstrasse 30; admission free; ⓨ noon-6pm Sat & Sun; ⓔ Gneisenaustrasse
One of their songs was *Born to Die in Berlin*. But fact is that the legacy of The Ramones, one of the seminal US punk bands in the '70s and '80s, is kept very much alive in the German capital, thanks to superfan Florian Hayler. His collection of memorabilia forms the basis of this little 'shrine', which opened in September 2005. Crammed into two rooms are vintage T-shirts, signed album covers, Marky Ramone's sneakers and drumsticks, Johnny Ramone's jeans and lots of other original flotsam and jetsam along with posters, flyers, photographs and articles.

SCHWULES MUSEUM Map pp336-7

☎ 693 1172; www.schwulesmuseum.de; Mehringdamm 61; adult/concession €5/3; ⓨ 2-6pm Wed-Mon, to 7pm Sat; ⓔ Mehringdamm
The nonprofit Gay Museum is exhibition space, research centre and community hub rolled into one. Since 1985 volunteers have collected, catalogued and displayed materials on gay history, art and culture. In late 2004, this resulted in a permanent exhibit entitled 'Self-Confidence and Perseverance: 200 Years of Gay History'. The focus is on Berlin between 1790 and 1990. This is presented

Topographie des Terrors (this page)

alongside temporary exhibits as well as an extensive archive and library, which includes plenty of English-language publications. Check the listings magazines for upcoming lectures, literary salons and other events.

The museum is in the back courtyard; enter to the left of the Café Melitta Sundström.

TOPOGRAPHIE DES TERRORS

Map pp336-7

☎ 2548 6703; www.topographie.de; Niederkirchner Strasse 8; admission free; ☺ 10am-8pm May-Sep, to dusk Oct-Apr; ⓔ ⓡ Potsdamer Platz, ⓔ Kochstrasse

In the wasteland along Niederkirchner Strasse once stood some of the most feared institutions of the Third Reich: the Gestapo headquarters, the SS central command, the SS Security Service and, after 1939, the Reich Security Main Office. From their desks, Nazi thugs hatched Holocaust plans and issued arrest orders for political opponents; many of them suffered torture and death in the notorious on-site Gestapo prison. Today the buildings are gone (signs explain what was where) and a ghostly air hangs over the bleak, abandoned grounds, whose creepiness is furthered by a short stretch of Berlin Wall.

Since 1997, this has been the setting for a harrowing open-air exhibit called Topographie des Terrors (Topography of Terror),

which is an excellent primer on the Third Reich years with particular focus on the brutal institutions that wielded power from this site. Displays are in German, but you can borrow a free audio-guide in English from the information kiosk, which also sells an excellent catalogue (€3). Some images in the exhibit may be too graphic for children.

A permanent documentation centre has been delayed for years and is currently projected to open in 2009. We're not placing any bets.

VIKTORIAPARK Map pp336-7

Btwn Kreuzbergstrasse, Methfesselstrasse, Dudenstrasse & Katzbachstrasse; ⓔ Platz der Luftbrücke

Many people know Karl Friedrich Schinkel as one of Berlin's most influential architects but few realise that he's also responsible – at least indirectly – for giving Kreuzberg its name. After Napoleon's defeat by the Prussians in 1815, Schinkel was asked to commemorate this triumph with a **memorial** to be installed atop a hill *(berg)* called Tempelhofer Berg. He came up with a pompous cast-iron spire standing taller than a giraffe, which is dramatically decorated with battle scenes and supported by a cross-shaped base. '*Kreuz*' is the German word for 'cross' and so this is what actually inspired the renaming of the hill and thus the district.

Since the late 19th century, most of the Kreuzberg, which rises 66m, has been given over to the rambling Viktoriapark. Its most distinctive feature is an artificial **waterfall**, which tumbles down a narrow, rock-lined canal on the park's northern side. It empties into a pool anchored by a **fountain** showing Neptune frolicking with an ocean nymphet. In these times of empty city coffers, the water spectacle is rarely on.

In fine weather, the park is a peaceful spot for strolling along treelined paths, lounging on the lawn, taking the kids to the playground or relaxing in the **Golgatha beer garden** (p194). On New Year's Eve, the entire hill becomes party central with thousands of revellers watching the fireworks and partying till dawn.

FRIEDRICHSHAIN

Eating p183; Shopping p244; Sleeping p262

Friedrichshain exudes a unique, gritty charm. Unlike Mitte and Prenzlauer Berg, it has not gone through gentrification and retains a relaxed, bohemian, down-home spirit. True gentrification may never happen for Friedrichshain either, for unlike its northern cousins, this district is not blessed with great beauty. Sure, there are pockets of pleasantness such as the Volkspark Friedrichshain, the happening nightlife zone around Boxhagener Platz or the fanciful Oberbaumbrücke (bridge). But in the end it'll be hard to shake that working-class roughness that's dominated here well over a century. And maybe that's a good thing.

Friedrichshain's conventional tourist sights are limited to the East Side Gallery, the longest remaining stretch of the Berlin Wall, and the Karl-Marx-Allee, the epitome of Stalinist pomposity. Those willing to dig deeper, though, will find a fledgling art scene, underground everything (clubs, restaurants, bars, galleries) and the quiet promise of an exciting urban future for the district.

ORIENTATION

Friedrichshain is the smallest of Berlin's districts. It is bounded to the south by the Spree River, across which it is administratively paired with Kreuzberg. The Volkspark Friedrichshain is on its northern border with Prenzlauer Berg, while the main thoroughfare, the monumental Karl-Marx-Allee, links it with the districts of Mitte to the northwest and Lichtenberg further east.

128

TRANSPORT

Bus 140 for Ostbahnhof from Kreuzberg; 200 for Volkspark Friedrichshain from Mitte; 240 for Boxhagener Platz from Prenzlauer Berg via Ostbahnhof.

S-Bahn S3, S5, S7 and S9 stop at Ostbahnhof, Warschauer Strasse and Ostkreuz; S8, S41 and S42 stop at Frankfurter Allee and Ostkreuz.

Tram Served by M5 and M6 from Alexanderplatz via Mollstrasse and Landsberger Allee; M8 from Scheunenviertel; M10 from Prenzlauer Berg; M13 from ⓢ ⓡ Warschauer Strasse for Boxhagener Platz.

U-Bahn Served by U1 from Charlottenburg, Schöneberg and Kreuzberg; U5 from Alexanderplatz along Karl-Marx-Allee.

Boxhagener Platz is east of Warschauer Strasse, a major north–south route that ends at the Oberbaumbrücke leading to Kreuzberg. The East Side Gallery runs parallel to the Spree.

CAFÉ SYBILLE Map pp332-3

☎ 2935 2203; Karl-Marx-Allee 72; ☽ 10am-8pm; admission free; ⓤ Weberwiese, Strausberger Platz

One of the most popular cafés in East Berlin until the fall of the Wall, Café Sybille closed in 1997, but was given a new lease on life in 2001 when it was taken over by the Förderverein Karl-Marx-Allee (Friends of Karl-Marx-Allee). Not merely a spot for coffee and cake, it now functions as an information centre about the boulevard, with an exhibit about its history. The group has installed 39 information markers chronicling milestones on both sides of the street between Strausberger Platz and Proskauer Strasse. Some have been vandalised, but they're a good base for a self-guided tour of this historic boulevard.

EAST SIDE GALLERY Map pp336-7

Mühlenstrasse; ⓢ ⓡ Warschauer Strasse, Ostbahnhof

The East Side Gallery is the longest, best-preserved and most interesting stretch of the Berlin Wall and the one to see if you have little time. Running parallel with the Spree between Stralauer Platz and Oberbaumbrücke, the 1300m-section was turned into an open-air gallery by dozens of artists from around the globe after the collapse of Communism. Now a symbol of both history and renewal, it is swathed in an eclectic hotchpotch of political statements, surreal imagery and truly artistic visions. Famous paintings include Birgit Kinder's *Test the Best,* showing a Trabi bursting through the Wall, and *The Mortal Kiss* by Dimitrij Vrubel, which has Erich Honecker and Leonid Brezhnev locking lips. The better works are near the Ostbahnhof end.

KARL-MARX-ALLEE Map pp332-3
www.kma-berlin.de; btwn Alexanderplatz & Frankfurter Tor; ⓈAlexanderpIatz, Schillingstrasse, Strausberger Platz, Weberwiese, Frankfurter Tor
The monumental Karl-Marx-Allee, leading southeast from Alexanderplatz, is one of the most impressive vestiges of the former East Berlin. This was the GDR's 'first socialist boulevard' and a source of considerable national pride. It provided modern flats for thousands of people and also served as a backdrop for military parades. Until the early 1970s, this was also the 'Ku'damm of the East', lined with shops, cafés, restaurants and the glamorous Kino Kosmos. For more on the boulevard's history, see the boxed text, below.

Now newly restored and protected as a historic monument, Karl-Marx-Allee is undergoing a moderate renaissance with bars and businesses bringing new life to the giant boulevard. Its greater importance, though, lies in being a unique open-air showcase of GDR architecture and as a metaphor for the inflated sense of importance and grandeur of that country's regime.

It may seem like a long walk, but the best way to appreciate this unique boulevard is on foot. If you're pushed for time, walk 1km or so east of Strausberger Platz. En route, information markers provide excellent historical background in German and English. The documentary exhibit at the Café Sybille is another place to learn more about this street.

OBERBAUMBRÜCKE Map pp336-7
ⓈSchlesisches Tor, Ⓢ Ⓡ Warschauer Strasse
The Oberbaumbrücke (1896), one of Berlin's most picturesque bridges, links Kreuzberg and Friedrichshain across the Spree. With its jaunty towers and turrets, crenellated walls and arched walkways, it almost resembles a medieval drawbridge. Neglected during the Cold War, it was restored for over €100 million, which included a new railway viaduct designed by bridge-meister Santiago Calatrava. Rising from the river

LIFE IN A GDR 'PALACE'

When the GDR government decided to build a showpiece road for their capital, they didn't pick prestigious Mitte but humble working-class Friedrichshain for its setting. The reasons were both historical and practical. It was along today's Karl-Marx-Allee that the Red Army had clawed its way into Berlin block-by-block in the waning days of WWII, leaving a dusty heap of destruction in its wake. All that needed doing was to clean up and start building anew. It was like a blank canvas on which to doodle.

And so they created Karl-Marx-Allee, or rather Stalinallee as it was called until 1961, which was built in two phases between 1952 and 1965. A team of six architects designed the first and architecturally more inspired section between Strausberger Platz and Frankfurter Tor. Their leader was Hermann Henselmann, widely consider the top architect in East Germany.

Following the diktat of the GDR honchos, Henselmann emulated a style called 'national tradition', which blended the so-called Zuckerbäckerstil (wedding-cake style) – then all the rage in Moscow and Leningrad – with more classical, Schinkel-inspired elements.

The result was a 90m-wide boulevard flanked by *Volkspaläste* (people's palaces), concrete behemoths up to 300m long. Honeycombed with flats boasting hot water and central heating, they were viewed with awe by people still largely living like postwar troglodytes. Fancy tiles made in Meissen porcelain covered the façades, which would have been be impressive if they'd been able to keep them from falling off all the time. The first residents, who moved in on 7 January 1953, were SED party faithful along with a few token workers who'd helped build the palaces. Henselmann himself lived at Strausberger Platz 19, in a fancy apartment with polished parquet floors, until his death in 1995.

Phase two of Karl-Marx-Allee (1959–65) – between Strausberger Platz and Alexanderplatz – has a decidedly more modern look and marks the first large-scale use of Plattenbau construction using prefab building blocks that would become an aesthetic epidemic throughout the GDR. Façades, it would seem, were always more important in the GDR than what was going on behind them.

south of the bridge is a giant aluminium sculpture called **Molecule Man** by American artist Jonathan Borofsky (p143).

VOLKSPARK FRIEDRICHSHAIN

Map pp332-3

Am Friedrichshain & Friedenstrasse; 🚌 200

Created in 1840 as a refuge for Friedrichshain's working-class folks, this is Berlin's oldest public park and still a fun place to while away a sunny afternoon. Besides expansive lawns, it has playgrounds, tennis courts, a free half-pipe for skaters and fun events including a summer outdoor film series (p214).

A main draw is the 1913 **Märchenbrunnen** (Fairytale Fountain) in the southwest corner. It's a neobaroque fantasy in stone with several water basins inhabited by sandstone figures of turtles, frogs and other animals, many inspired by the Brothers Grimm fairytales. In the warmer months, the area is a popular gay cruising spot.

After WWII the park's landscape changed forever with the creation of a pair of **Bunkerberge** (rubble mountains) made from 2 million cu metres of wartime debris piled atop two demolished flak towers. The taller one (78m) is nicknamed Mont Klamott.

On the park's southern edge is the **Friedhof der Märzgefallenen**, a cemetery for the 183 victims of the revolutionary riots in March 1848, a tumultuous time now also commemorated on the square west of the Brandenburg Gate.

The park's two GDR-era memorials have also survived reunification. Southeast of the fountain, along Friedenstrasse, the **Denkmal der Spanienkämpfer** (Memorial to the Fighters in Spain) commemorates the German soldiers who lost their lives fighting fascism in the Spanish Civil War (1936–39). In the northeastern corner, the **Deutsch-Polnisches Ehrenmal** (German-Polish Memorial) honours the joint fight of Polish soldiers and the German resistance against the Nazis during WWII.

PRENZLAUER BERG

Eating p185; Shopping p245; Sleeping p263

Aging divas know that a facelift can quickly pump up a drooping career, and it seems the same can be done with entire neigh-bourhoods. No other district besides Mitte and Tiergarten has been rejuvenated more since the Wende than Prenzlauer Berg, which has been transformed from war-scarred backwater to hipster haven in less than a decade. Popular fun zones include the see-and-be-seen **Kastanienallee** and the considerably less polished **Helmholtzplatz** for 20-somethings, and the well-established **Kollwitzplatz** and **Wasserturm** area for those beyond college age. The area around Schönhauser Allee U-Bahn station belongs in the up-and-coming category.

Although not a particularly leafy part of town, Prenzl'berg is best explored on a gentle meander along its quiet streets flanked by stately apartment buildings shimmering in freshly applied pastels. Take the time to pop into the occasional deli, café, bar, restaurant or boutique for some local flavour. Just be prepared to share the turf with a small army of chic mamas and papas pushing baby strollers, for this is the district with the highest birth rate (which also explains the inordinate number of playgrounds).

ORIENTATION

Prenzlauer Berg, which was absorbed into the Pankow administrative district in 2001, borders Mitte and Friedrichshain to the south and Wedding to the west. There are three main north–south roads: Greifswalder Strasse, Prenzlauer Allee and Schönhauser Allee. Kastanienallee links the district with Mitte.

TRANSPORT

Bus 148 from Prenzlauer Allee for Potsdamer Platz via Alexanderplatz

S-Bahn S8, S41 and S42 stop at Schönhauser Allee, Prenzlauer Allee, Greifswalder Strasse, Landsberger Allee and Storkower Strasse.

Tram M1 from Museumsinsel and Scheunenviertel via Rosenthaler Platz, Kastanienallee and Schönhauser Allee; 12 from Scheunenviertel via Kastanienallee to Eberswalder Strasse; M5, M6, M8 from Friedrichshain; M4 from Alexanderplatz along Greifswalder Strasse.

U-Bahn U2 from Charlottenburg, Schöneberg and Mitte stops at Senefelderplatz, Eberswalder Strasse and Schönhauser Allee.

BERLINER PRATER Map pp332-3

☎ 247 6772; Kastanienallee 7-9; ⏰ from 4pm Mon-Fri, from noon Sat, from 10am Sun; Ⓜ Eberswalder Strasse

The Berliner Prater has been serving beer and entertainment since 1852 when it was a popular stopover for people heading out for a day in the countryside. In the early 20th century, the Prater became a hot spot of the local workers movement. August Bebel and Rosa Luxemburg were among those who fired up the crowds with rousing speeches here. Today, the Prater serves as a secondary stage of the Volksbühne theatre (p212), with its provocative, off-beat productions. In summer, the beer garden is one of the finest in town (p197).

GETHSEMANEKIRCHE Map pp332-3

☎ 445 7745; Stargarder Strasse 77; Ⓜ Schönhauser Allee

This statuesque red-brick church is an 1893 neo-Gothic work by August Orth, one of the top church architects of the late 19th century. It was one of dozens of churches Emperor Wilhelm II had built to 'create a bulwark against socialism, communism and atheism' which, they feared, were fomenting in Prenzlauer Berg and other working-class districts.

Ironically, rather than stifling such movements, the Gethsemane church encouraged them. Its congregation can look back on a proud tradition of dissent and as a place that has always protected nonconformists and freethinkers, both during the Third Reich as well as in GDR times. The church made headlines in 1989 when a peaceful gathering of regime opponents was brutally quashed by the Stasi.

Today, as well as being an active parish it occasionally hosts concerts and is at the centre of an increasingly lively section of Prenzlauer Berg surrounded by boutiques, cafés and speciality stores.

HUSEMANNSTRASSE Map pp332-3

btwn Danzigerstr & Käthe-Kollwitz-Platz; Ⓜ Eberswalder Strasse

Nostalgia for the 'good old days' spurred the East Berlin government to have this entire street restored into a living museum of 19th-century Berlin, complete with cutesy shops, an old-time post office and atmospheric pubs. The project's comple-

tion was timed to coincide with the city's 750th anniversary in 1987. Although it was deemed a success, the sparkling reconstruction only highlighted the dismal condition of the surrounding streets. Husemannstrasse, which was named after a Nazi resistance fighter, still makes for a nice stroll today, even if most shops along here have that commercial and tourist-oriented feel.

JÜDISCHER FRIEDHOF Map pp332-3

☎ 441 9824; Schönhauser Allee 23-25; admission free; ⏰ 8am-4pm Mon-Thu, 8am-1pm Fri, entry up to 30min before closing; Ⓜ Senefelderplatz

Berlin's second Jewish cemetery dates to 1827 and hides its leafy grounds behind a thick wall along Schönhauser Allee. Many prominent Berliners are interred here, including the composer Giacomo Meyerbeer and the artist Max Liebermann. WWII brought vandalism and bomb damage but the restored grounds are still dotted with exemplary tombstones and memorials. About 60 of them are displayed in a new Lapidarium (*lapis* is Latin for stone) built on the foundation of the former memorial hall. Men must cover their heads in the cemetery; free yarmulkes may be borrowed at the entrance for this.

Also restored was the so-called Judengang, a 10m-wide ritual pathway through which funeral processions originally entered the grounds. It runs for 400m between Kollwitzplatz and Senefelder Platz along the cemetery's eastern wall. The gate is usually closed.

KOLLWITZPLATZ Map pp332-3

Ⓜ Senefelderplatz

Among trendy bars and restaurants, this leafy square was named for the artist Käthe Kollwitz who lived in the neighbourhood for over 40 years (see boxed text, p132). A 1958 bronze sculpture by Gustav Seitz of the artist is the main feature of the square's little park. It's not terribly flattering, showing Kollwitz as an elderly woman, tired but dignified. Children often leave the excellent nearby playground to clamber around this larger-than-life sculpture or sit in her maternal lap. To see Kollwitz's own works, visit the Käthe-Kollwitz-Museum (p116) in Charlottenburg. A good time to visit is during the Saturday farmers' market when the entire neighbourhood seems to gather.

KÄTHE KOLLWITZ

Considered among the finest women's artists of the 20th century, Käthe Kollwitz (1867–1945) is best known for her deeply moving, often heart-wrenching works that capture the depth of human hardship, suffering and sorrow. Through her sculpture and graphic works she expressed a deep kinship with and concern for the suppressed and poor in a timeless, haunting manner that rings as true now as it did then.

Kollwitz was born Käthe Schmidt in Königsberg (today's Kaliningrad, Russia) and, encouraged by her father, attended art schools in Berlin, Munich, Florence and Paris. Upon her return to Berlin in 1891, she married Karl Kollwitz, a physician with a practice on Weissenburger Strasse (today's Kollwitzstrasse), right in the heart of the Prenzlauer Berg working-class ghetto.

Kollwitz's outlook on life and approach to art were greatly influenced by the misery and poverty she observed daily while walking the streets or assisting her husband at work. Her impressions were compounded by personal tragedies, most lingeringly the deaths of her son in the battlefields of WWI and of her grandson in WWII. It is no coincidence that one of her most poignant works is *Mother and Her Dead Son*, on view at the Neue Wache (p76) in Mitte.

Kollwitz became a member of the Berlin Secession (p27), joining in 1919 the faculty of the prestigious Academy of Arts. The Nazis forced her resignation in 1933, but didn't see anything wrong with adapting some of her work for propaganda purposes. Despite being a staunch pacifist and committed socialist, she remained in Berlin until evacuated to the Harz Mountains in May 1943. She died in 1945, shortly before the end of the war.

KULTURBRAUEREI Map pp332-3

www.kulturbrauerei-berlin.de; Knaackstrasse 97;
Ⓢ Eberswalder Strasse

Towers and turrets, gables and arches are not usually the stuff of industrial sites. But for this former brewery, renowned architect Franz Schwechten pulled out all the stops back in 1889. The result is this fanciful complex of 20 ornate red and yellow brick buildings framing a series of courtyards.

The last bottle of beer was filled in 1967 and the place more or less lingered until 1991 when it was reborn as the Kulturbrauerei (literally 'cultural brewery'), a lively cultural centre with a motley mix of theatre, concert and dance venues, galleries, a nightclub, restaurants, a multiplex cinema, a supermarket and the bike touring company Berlin on Bike (p70).

The **Sammlung Industrielle Gestaltung** (Collection of Industrial Design; ☎ 4431 7868; adult/concession €2/1; Ⓨ 1-8pm Wed-Sun), near the entrance on Knaackstrasse, showcases East German product design alongside artefacts from the 1920s and '30s and also has a classy gift shop.

MAUERPARK & BERNAUER STRASSE

Map pp332-3
Btwn Eberswalder Strasse, Schwedter Strasse, Gleimstrasse & Malmöer Strasse; admission free;
Ⓨ 24hr; Ⓢ Eberswalder Strasse

Not your typical leafy urban oasis, the Mauerpark (Wall Park) occupies a section of 'death strip' right along the former border between East and West Berlin. A small section of the **Berlin Wall** has become a favourite canvas of graffiti artists, although the park's benches and trashcans prove to be pretty popular too. On Sunday, a popular flea market lures treasure seekers from around town (p246).

The Wall ran north–south along Schwedter Strasse, then continued west on Bernauer Strasse. Some of the most spectacular escape attempts took place along here. Success stories include the day when 57 people burrowed their way to freedom in 1964. Others were less lucky: it was here where a despondent Ida Siekmann leapt to her death from a 3rd-floor window. Multilingual panels set up along the street recall these and other historical moments. For more about the Wall, it's well worth visiting the Gedenkstätte Berliner Mauer (p135) about 1km west of the Mauerpark.

Behind the mound on the southern end is the **Friedrich-Ludwig-Jahn-Sportpark**, the stadium where Stasi chief Erich Mielke used to cheer on his beloved Dynamo Berlin football (soccer) team. Just north of here, the new **Max-Schmeling-Halle** is the home base of Berlin's successful men's basketball team Alba Berlin.

PRENZLAUER BERG MUSEUM

Map pp332-3
☎ 902 953 917; Prenzlauer Allee 227; admission free; Ⓨ 10am-6pm Tue, Wed & Sun, noon-8pm Thu; Ⓢ Senefelderplatz, Ⓜ M2

This little museum presents changing exhibits highlighting some aspect of the district's fascinating history. A recent documentation called Hops & Malt, for instance, chronicled Prenzlauer Berg's legacy as a beer-brewing centre. Permanent displays focus on the history of the school complex itself as well as on the Jewish school in Rykestrasse.

SYNAGOGE RYKESTRASSE Map pp332-3
☎ 880 280; Rykestrasse 53; ◉ Senefelderplatz
This stately synagogue, built in 1904 in neo-Romanesque style, is the largest in Germany, with seating for around 2000 worshippers. It was the only Jewish house of worship in Berlin that survived the 1938 *Kristallnacht* pogroms, most likely thanks to its courtyard location behind an apartment building inhabited by non-Jews.

Nazi thugs still managed to thoroughly vandalise the interior and later converted the rooms into horse stables. Restored after the war, it served as the sole synagogue of East Berlin's 200-person Jewish congregation. These days, police keep an eye on the place 24/7. It's closed to the public, although you can get a peek at the ornate façade through the wrought-iron gates.

VITRA DESIGN MUSEUM Map pp332-3
☎ 4862 3204; www.design-museum.de; Christinenstrasse 18/19; ◉ Senefelderstrasse
If all goes according to plan, the curtain will go up in autumn 2006 on the Berlin branch of this cutting-edge design museum, an offshoot of the mothership in Weil am Rhein in southern Germany. It will be part of the Pfefferberg which, like the Kulturbrauerei, is an ex-brewery turned cultural complex. A new, white and sharply geometrical entrance pavilion on Christinenstrasse will give access to two floors of exhibits in an original 19th-century brewery building. For updates, consult the website or check with the tourist office.

WASSERTURM Map pp332-3
Cnr Knaackstrasse & Rykestrasse; ◉ Senefelder Platz
Locals affectionately call this handsome brick water tower 'Dicker Hermann' (fat Hermann), but the beloved 1873 landmark also went through a dark spell in its history. Soon after Hitler came to power, the SA turned the adjacent boiler and engine room into an improvised concentration camp where they imprisoned and tortured

communists, Jews and regime opponents of all stripes. A plaque commemorates this period of unspeakable terror. After the war, the tower was converted into flats; the boiler and engine room is now a children's day-care centre.

ZEISS GROSSPLANETARIUM & AROUND Map pp332-3
☎ 4218 4512; www.astw.de; Prenzlauer Allee 80; adult/concession €5/4; show times vary; ◉ ⓡ Prenzlauer Allee
The people of East Berlin were not allowed to see what was across the Wall, but at least they could gaze at the entire universe at this fine planetarium. At its 1987 opening, the Zeiss Grossplanetarium was one of the most modern and largest star theatres in Europe. Today, it presents an imaginative schedule of traditional narrated shows (in German), sci-fi film screenings, classical music 'under the stars' and children's programming.

The planetarium is near a pair of interesting housing developments. East of its landmark silvery dome, **Ernst-Thälmann-Park** is not only a park, but also a model of a high-rise housing development built for the GDR elite in the mid-'80s. North of here, between Sültstrasse and Sodtkestrasse, is the 1930 **Flamensiedlung** (Flemish Colony). Inspired by Dutch architecture, Bruno Taut and Franz Hillinger sought to create mass housing without the suffocating density and dreariness that typified the tenement blocks. They added green courtyards, balconies and other features to the designs to help break the monotony and create much-needed open spaces.

Zeiss Grossplanetarium (this page)

NORTHERN DISTRICTS

PANKOW

Pankow, Berlin's northernmost district, was once the preferred residential area of the East German intellectual and power elite, which helps explain the many villas. These days, it preserves a pleasant, slow-paced atmosphere but is modest in terms of visitor attractions. Part of its appeal lies in the forests and parks that cover more than one-third of its area. In 2001 it was administratively joined with Prenzlauer Berg.

TRANSPORT

Bus 107 connects ◎ ⊛ Pankow with central Pankow and the palace; 245 connects Zoo station with Bernauer Strasse.

S-Bahn S2 connects Pankow with Friedrichstrasse and Potsdamer Platz; S8 connects Pankow with Prenzlauer Berg and Friedrichshain.

Tram M1 connects Pankow with Scheunenviertel and Prenzlauer Berg; main lines through Wedding are M13 and 50 to Charité Campus Virchow-Klinikum.

U-Bahn Pankow is the northern terminus of the U2; Wedding's hub Osloer Strasse is served by the U8 and U9.

Orientation

Pankow's Jewish cemetery is in Weissensee, right on the border with Prenzlauer Berg at the terminus of bus 200. The Niederschönhausen neighbourhood with the Schloss is towards the northern end of Pankow about 6km north of Alexanderplatz.

JÜDISCHER FRIEDHOF WEISSENSEE

Map pp332–3

☎ 925 0833; Herbert-Baum-Strasse 45; ☼ 8am-5pm Sun-Thu Apr-Oct, to 4pm Sun-Thu Nov-Mar, to 3pm Fri year-round; ⊛ 200 to Michelangelostrasse

First laid out in 1880, this enormous Jewish cemetery is the final resting place of more than 115,000 people, including such prominent players as the painter Lesser Ury and publisher Samuel Fisher. Bauhaus fans should check out the cubist tomb designed by Walter Gropius for Albert Mendel. For locations consult a chart near the entrance.

Also here is a monument honouring the victims of the Holocaust.

MAJAKOWSKIRING

Admission free; ☼ 24hr; ◎ ⊛ Pankow, then ⊛ 107 or ⊛ M1, 50

During GDR days, this oval ring road, southwest of Schloss Niederschönhausen, was 'celebrity central'. The party top brass lived side by side with prominent artists, scientists and writers, including Christa Wolf, Arnold Zweig and Hanns Eisler. Nicknamed the 'Städtchen' (little town), it was completely sealed off from the public, lest anyone saw the (relatively) lavish villas and overall luxury in which their rulers wallowed while denying almost everyone else basic amenities such as a car or telephone. The GDR's first president, Wilhelm Pieck, lived at No 29.

SCHLOSS NIEDERSCHÖNHAUSEN

Ossietzkystrasse; ☼ park 8am-sunset; ◎ ⊛ Pankow, then ⊛ 107 or ⊛ M1, 50

If you could peel away the many layers of alterations wrought upon Niederschönhausen Palace, you'd get to a modest, two-storey country home built in the 17th century. Elector Friedrich III (later to be King Friedrich I) acquired it in 1691 and had it enlarged by the same architectural team of Nering and Eosander who would later build his Schloss Charlottenburg. An audition, perhaps?

From 1740 to 1797, Frederick the Great's estranged wife Elisabeth Christine lived here and some 150 years later it became the residence of Wilhelm Pieck, the GDR's first president. Its last official role was as a state guesthouse for visiting dignitaries: yes, Mikhail and Fidel slept here. After the GDR's demise, several so-called round-table discussions, paving the way to reunification, took place here.

So all in all it's quite a historic site but unfortunately, at least for now, the Schloss remains closed to the public. You can see it from the outside – though it does look pretty dreary and forlorn – and at least enjoy a stroll through the romantic Peter Lenné–designed Schlosspark where the little Panke River flows. Some of the trees here are reported to be over 1000 years old. Kids tend to gravitate toward the big playground.

WEDDING

If you listen very closely, you'll hear faint murmurings about Wedding being the next 'hot' district, but for now at least few signs lend substance to the rumour. Scarred by industry and devoid of grand historic buildings or happening nightlife, *der Wedding* (the article is proper use in German) is still a no-nonsense, roll-up-your-sleeves kind of place. Still, those with an interest in WWII and Cold War history will find a handful of intriguing sights.

Orientation

Wedding is a sprawling district that extends east of Berlin International Airport in Tegel, north of Tiergarten and Mitte and west of Prenzlauer Berg. Seestrasse and Osloer Strasse are major east–west arteries, while Beusselstrasse, Chausseestrasse and the latter continuation, Müllerstrasse, are important north–south thoroughfares. The Berlin Wall once ran along Bernauer Strasse. Plötzensee is about 4.5km northwest of here.

ANTI-KRIEGS-MUSEUM Map pp330-1
☎ 4549 0110; www.anti-kriegs-museum.de; Brüsseler Strasse 21; admission free; ☼ 4-8pm; ◉ Amrumer Strasse, Seestrasse

The Anti-War-Museum may be small but it has a big – and timely – message. Erich

Friedrich, who founded it in 1925, was an avowed peacenik and author of the book *War against War* (1924). After Nazis trashed his museum in 1933, he emigrated to Belgium and later joined the French resistance. His grandson, Tommy Spree, reopened the museum in 1982 with objects from both world wars. A staircase descends to an air-raid shelter equipped with bunk beds, gas masks and a 'gas bed' for babies. The Peace Gallery presents changing exhibits.

GEDENKSTÄTTE BERLINER MAUER
Map pp332-3
☎ 464 1030; www.berliner-mauer-dokumentations zentrum.de; Bernauer Strasse 111; admission free; ☼ 10am-6pm Apr-Oct, to 5pm Nov-Mar; ◉ Bernauer Strasse, ◉ Nordbahnhof

The fascinating if horrifying history of the Berlin Wall is the theme of this memorial site, which combines a documentation centre, an art installation and a chapel. A small but hi-tech exhibit chronicles the events leading up to that fateful day in August 1961 when the first bricks were laid. From a viewing platform you'll have a fine perspective on the short section of Wall that's been integrated into a surprisingly sober and unemotional artistic re-creation of the death strip. Since it doesn't really convey the brutality of this artificial border, additional displays focusing on the personal

Gedenkstätte Berliner Mauer (this page)

THE BERLIN WALL

Shortly after midnight on 13 August, 1961 construction began on a barrier that would divide Berlin for 28 years. The Berlin Wall was a desperate measure by a GDR government on the verge of economic and political collapse to stem the exodus of its own people: 2.6 million of them had already left for the west since 1949.

Euphemistically called the 'Anti-Fascist Protection Barrier', this grim symbol of oppression stretched for 160km, turning West Berlin into an island of democracy within a sea of socialism. Continually reinforced and refined over time, its cold concrete slabs – which you could touch or paint on the western side – backed up against a dangerous no-man's-land of barbed wire, mines, attack dogs and watchtowers staffed by loyal border guards ready to gun down anyone trying to escape.

More than 5000 people attempted an escape but only about 1600 made it across; most were captured, and 191 were killed – the first only a few days after 13 August. The full extent of the cruelty of the system became blatantly clear on 17 August 1962 when 18-year-old Peter Fechtner was shot during his attempt to flee and was then left to bleed to death while East German guards looked on.

At the end of the Cold War this potent symbol was eagerly dismantled. Memento seekers chiselled away much of it and entire sections ended up in museums around the world. Most of it, though, was unceremoniously recycled for use in road construction. Today little more than 1.5km of the Wall is left.

devastation the Wall wrought on so many people should soon be up as well. The nearby **Versöhnungskapelle** (Reconciliation Chapel), with its simple but radiant design, is a good spot to reflect upon it all.

GEDENKSTÄTTE PLÖTZENSEE
Map pp330-1

☎ 344 3226; www.gedenkstaette-ploetzensee.de; Hüttigpfad; admission free; 9am-5pm Mar-Oct, to 4pm Nov-Feb; Beusselstrasse, TXL, 123, 126

Nearly 3000 people were executed at Plötzensee prison during the Third Reich, about half of them German resistance fighters. The room where the beheadings and hangings took place is now a hauntingly simple memorial. Housed in a plain brick shed, only a steel bar with eight hooks pierces its emptiness. Next door, an exhibit documents the Nazis' perverted justice system, which gleefully handed out death sentences like candy at a parade.

The extent of their cruelty knew no bounds. The families of the condemned even had to pay for the cost of the execution, while executioners received a bonus for each murder. They were particularly busy in 1944 when many of the conspirators of the failed assassination attempt on Hitler on 20 July of that year – and their (mostly uninvolved) relatives and friends, a total of 110 people – were hanged here, a process the Führer had allegedly captured on film.

An excellent, free, English brochure is available at the desk. Sections of the origi-

nal prison are now a juvenile detention centre.

KINDERMUSEUM LABYRINTH
Map pp328-9

☎ 4930 8901; www.kindermuseum-labyrinth .de; Osloer Strasse 12; adult/child/family €3.80/3.30/9.90; 1-6pm Tue-Sat, 11am-6pm Sun; Osloer Strasse, Pankstrasse

Highly interactive, this place inside an old factory is more like an educational playground than a conventional museum, which should please tots tremendously. They can play boat captain, build castles or dress up like pirates or princesses. Not every activity is suitable for non-German speakers, but there's enough to keep everyone entertained. Bring some thick socks or slippers as shoes may not be worn inside.

ZUCKER MUSEUM Map pp330-1

☎ 3142 7574; www.dtmb.de/zucker-museum; Amrumer Strasse 32; admission free; 9am-4.30pm Mon-Thu, 11am-6pm Sun; Amrumer Strasse, Seestrasse

Those with a sweet tooth might like to check out the quirky Zucker Museum (Sugar Museum), which celebrated its 100th birthday in 2004, making it the world's oldest exhibit of its kind. You'll learn all about the origin of sugar and its chemistry; find out about its uses in the production of vinegar, pesticides and even interior car panelling; and also discover its role in the slave trade.

WESTERN DISTRICTS

SPANDAU

Spandau is a congenial mix of green expanses, rivers, industry and almost rural residential areas wrapped around a medieval core famous for its 16th-century fortress, the Spandauer Zitadelle. Older than Berlin by a few years, Spandau thrived as an independent city for nearly 800 years and only became part of Berlin in 1920. Its people, though, continue to feel as Spandauers first, Berliners second. To this day, they talk about 'going to Berlin' when heading to any other city district.

www.lonelyplanet.com

oldest neighbourhood and exudes medieval village flair with its romantic narrow lanes, crooked, half-timbered houses and 78m-long section of **town wall**. A must-see jewel is the church of **St Marien am Behnitz** (☎ 353 9630; Behnitz 9; admission free; ⏲ 3-5pm Mon-Thu, 2-5pm Sun). A recent top-to-bottom makeover of the 1848 church saw the return of the handpainted murals, decorative stucco and stained-glass windows that had been destroyed during a botched 1960s restoration job. Try catching a concert here – the acoustics are tremendous.

LUFTWAFFENMUSEUM

☎ 3687 2604; www.luftwaffenmuseum.de; Flugplatz Gatow, Gross Gliencker Weg; admission free; ⏲ 9am-5pm Tue-Sun, last admission 4pm; ⊕ Rathaus Spandau, then 🚌 135 to Seekorso

About 9km south of Altstadt Spandau, the Luftwaffenmuseum (German Air Force Museum) occupies the grounds of the former military airport Berlin-Gatow. Built in 1934–35 as a Nazi air-force academy, it fell under British control after the war, becoming an important lifeline during the 1948 Berlin Airlift (see the boxed text, p62). When the Royal Air Force left in 1994, the Bundeswehr turned much of the airport into a museum.

An old hangar houses a permanent exhibition on the history of the Luftwaffe, while other rooms focus on airport history or present changing exhibits. Uniforms and

Sights

WESTERN DISTRICTS

TRANSPORT

Bus 145 connects Schloss Charlottenburg with central Spandau.

S-Bahn S5 and S75 connect Spandau with Charlottenburg, Mitte and Friedrichshain.

U-Bahn U7 serves central Spandau from Charlottenburg, Wilmersdorf, Schöneberg, Kreuzberg and Neukölln.

Orientation

Central Spandau is about 10km northwest of Zoo station. Nearly all its sights cluster in the Altstadt served by the U7. The Luftwaffenmuseum is about 9km south of here in the rural suburb of Gatow.

GOTISCHES HAUS Map p343

☎ 333 9388; Breite Strasse 32; admission free; ⏲ 10am-6pm Mon-Fri, to 5pm Sat; ⊕ Altstadt Spandau

The original owners of the late-medieval Gothic House must not have been hurting for money, for they built their home of stone not wood, as was customary at the time. One of the oldest residential buildings in Berlin, this Altstadt gem now houses the Spandau **tourist office** and changing historical exhibits. The nicest room has an ornate net-vaulted ceiling.

KOLK Map p343

⊕ Altstadt Spandau

Separated from the Altstadt by the busy Strasse am Juliusturm, the Kolk is Spandau's

---

THE LAST PRISONER

Spandau not only inspired the name of that mediocre '80s band Spandau Ballet but, more importantly, will forever be associated with the prison where several top Nazis sentenced at the Nuremberg Trials were interned. The so-called 'Allied War Criminal Prison' was built expressly for this purpose and jointly administered by all four Allies. Responsibility for the inmates rotated between them every month with a flag outside indicating who called the shots at any given time. Despite going to all this trouble, the prison only held a total of seven inmates, including such Nazi honchos as Karl von Dönitz, Albert Speer and Rudolf Hess. By 1966 all but Hess had been released but the Allies kept the prison open just for him until he died in 1987 at age 93. To prevent the place from becoming a neo-Nazi shrine, it was demolished soon thereafter.

miscellaneous memorabilia are on display in the nearby former control tower.

Plane buffs will have a field day here with over 100 craft from all eras and various countries on display inside the hangar and on the runways. Biplanes from WWI, a Russian-made MiG-21, the Messerschmidt ME-163 Komet and an Antonov An-14 used by the GDR airforce are just some of the highlights.

NIKOLAIKIRCHE Map p343

☎ 333 5639; Reformationsplatz; admission free, tower €1; ⏱ noon-4pm Mon-Thu, 11am-3pm Sat, 2-4pm Sun, tower tours noon & 1pm Sat, 2pm & 3pm Sun Apr-Oct; ⦿ Altstadt Spandau

The graceful Nikolaikirche (Church of St Nicholas) in the heart of the Altstadt played a pivotal role during the Reformation. In 1539 it hosted the first public Protestant worship service in Brandenburg whose ruler, Elector Joachim II, was a supporter of the reformer Martin Luther. That's the elector immortalised in bronze outside the church.

The Nikolaikirche was first mentioned in a record of 1240 but the structure you see today dates from the 15th century. The walls of the west tower, which doubled as fortress and watchtower, are up to 3m thick. Guided tower tours are sometimes offered at weekends. You can also climb to the top for impressive views.

The church itself is a three-nave Gothic hall design filled with important treasures, including the bronze baptismal font (1398) and the baroque pulpit (1714). Pride of place, though, goes to the late-Renaissance altar (1582) whose centre panel depicts the Last Supper. For great views, you can climb up the tower on weekends in the warmer months.

ZITADELLE SPANDAU Map p343

☎ 354 9440; Strasse am Juliusturm; adult/concession €2.50/1.50, incl museum, tower & galleries; ⏱ 9am-5pm Tue-Fri, 10am-5pm Sat & Sun; ⦿ Zitadelle

The Zitadelle Spandau (Spandau Citadel, 1594), on a little island in the Havel River, is one of the most important and best-preserved Renaissance fortresses in the world. Protected by a moat and the river, its symmetrical layout is classic textbook: a square with each corner protected by an arrowhead-shaped bastion.

The citadel's most prominent feature is the Juliusturm, a crenellated tower that can be climbed for decent views over the Havel and Spree Rivers and the Altstadt. From 1874 to 1919 the tower sheltered a good chunk of the reparation payments France had to make to Prussia after losing the war of 1870–71.

History buffs eager to learn more about Spandau should drop into the Stadtgeschichtliches Museum Spandau (Spandau City History Museum) in the New Armoury. The fortress also harbours numerous artist studios and creative workshops. Two galleries, one in the Bastion Kronprinz, the other in the Palas (once the residential wing), present changing art exhibits throughout the year.

In winter, thousands of bats hang out in the citadel's catacombs to escape the freezing winter. The Berliner Artenschutz Team, an organisation dedicated to protecting endangered species, offers guided tours (☎ 3675 0061; adult/concession €8/6) in summer. Registration is mandatory.

SOUTHERN DISTRICTS
KÖPENICK

A 20-minute S-Bahn ride away, Köpenick is the perfect antidote to the wonderful but exhausting urban velocity of central Berlin. Occupying a scenic spot at the confluence of the Spree and Dahme rivers, about 15km southeast of Alexanderplatz, it's famous for its many lakes and forests, a handsome baroque castle and an old town centre that has withstood the ravages of time, war and

TRANSPORT

Bus 104 runs to Neukölln and Treptow from Wilmersdorf, Schöneberg and Kreuzberg. In Zehlendorf, X10 and 115 run along Clayallee; from ⓇWannsee take 316 for Schloss Glienicke and 218 for Pfaueninsel and north through Grunewald.

S-Bahn S3 for Köpenick; S8, S9, S41, S42 for Treptower Park; S41, S42, S45 for Neukölln; S1 for Zehlendorf.

Tram From S-Bahn station Köpenick: M62 and M68 for Altstadt; 60 and 61 for Müggelsee from Altstadt; 62 north goes to Mahlsdorf.

U-Bahn U3 for northern Zehlendorf; U7 and U8 for Neukölln.

modernism. It can claim Berlin's largest lake (Müggelsee), largest forest (Köpenicker Stadtforst) and highest natural elevation (Müggelberge, 115m). A leisurely ramble, relaxed boat ride or cooling dip in the water will quickly restore balance to an overstimulated brain.

Orientation & Information

Köpenick's pint-sized Altstadt sits in a strategic spot right at the convergence of the Spree and Dahme rivers. It's about 1.5km south of S-Bahn station Köpenick along Bahnhofstrasse and Lindenstrasse and served by tram 62 or 68 (get off at Rathaus Köpenick). Schloss Köpenick is just south on a little island in the Dahme, with the Kietz fishing quarter visible across the water looking east. Friedrichshagen and the Müggelsee are about 3.5km further east of the Altstadt.

Tourist office (☎ 6548 4340; www.berlin-tourismus-online.de; Alt-Köpenick 34; ⏰ 9am-6pm Mon-Fri) Guided one-hour Altstadt tours leave from here at 10am on Saturday (€5).

ALTSTADT & KIETZ

Many of the cobblestone streets in Köpenick's Altstadt still follow their original, medieval layout. The oldest street is Böttcherstrasse but for the best parade of historic houses go to Strasse Alt-Köpenick, which is lined with baroque beauties.

The most imposing building in the Altstadt is undoubtedly the 1904 **Rathaus** (Town Hall; ☎ 6172 3351; Alt-Köpenick 21; admission free; ⏰ 8am-6pm Mon-Fri, 10am-6pm Sat), a red-brick, neogothic jumble, which gets a fairytale quality from its frilly turrets, soaring tower and stepped gable. A **bronze statue** of the Hauptmann of Köpenick guards the entrance (see boxed text, p140).

Continue south to the Schloss Köpenick (p140) and then east across the bridge to the tiny Kietz neighbourhood, which has origins as a medieval fishing village. Its peaceful little lanes are still flanked by the nicely restored but modest homes of the former fisherfolk.

FRIEDRICHSHAGEN

Stern und Kreis Boat Tours ☎ 536 3600; 🚇 Friedrichshagen, then 🚋 60 or 61
Friedrichshagen is a pretty, historic suburb first settled by Bohemian families brought

SOUTHERN DISTRICTS TOP FIVE

- Share your picnic with peacocks on the enchanting Pfaueninsel (p147).
- Look deep into the Russian soul at the Sowjetisches Ehrenmal (p143).
- Travel around the world and back in time at the Museen Dahlem (p147).
- Discover the garden that inspired the painter Max Liebermann at the Liebermann-Villa (p146).
- See what a young royal with vision, money and Schinkel by his side can accomplish at Schloss Glienicke (p148).

here by Frederick the Great to grow mulberry trees needed in silk production. In the late 19th century, the town became a literary hub for poets and writers, including Gerhart Hauptmann. Its main drag is **Bölschestrasse**, just south of the S-Bahn station Friedrichshagen, which is a showcase of two centuries' worth of buildings rendered lively by cafés and stores. The Marktplatz opposite the Christopherus-Kirche sports a rare statue of Frederick the Great as a young man. On Sunday, a **flea market** right by the S-Bahn station invites ferreting for GDR memorabilia and other bric-a-brac.

Bölschestrasse deadends at the northern shore of the **Grosser Müggelsee**, at 4km long and 2.5km wide Berlin's largest lake. Berlin's last private brewery, the Berliner Bürgerbräu, is here in a protected building complex, as are the landing docks of Stern & Kreis Schiffahrt whose boats ply the lake from May to October. One ferry makes its journey across to the southern bank from where an easy forest trail leads to the tiny **Teufelssee** (Devil's Lake) and the landmark **Müggelturm** (Müggel Tower; admission €1; ⏰ 10am-sunset), which you can climb for sweeping views.

In summer, crowds pack the beaches at **Seebad Friedrichshagen**, just east of the boat landing docks, and **Strandbad Müggelsee** on the eastern shore in the medieval fishing village of Rahnsdorf. Picturesque Rahnsdorf is worth an excursion in its own right for its network of little canals, garnering it the nickname *Neu-Venedig (New Venice)*, complete with Rialto Bridge. The prettiest section is about 1km south of the Wilhelmshagen S-Bahn station via Schönblicker Strasse.

HAUPTMANN VON KÖPENICK

There was nothing fairytale about the legendary incident in 1906 when an unemployed cobbler named Wilhelm Voigt dressed up as an army captain, marched upon Köpenick town hall, arrested the mayor, confiscated the city coffers and disappeared with the loot. Although quickly caught and convicted, he became quite a celebrity for his chutzpah and for having made such a laughing stock of Prussian authority.

In 1930, German author Carl Zuckmeyer immortalised Voigt in the play *Der Hauptmann von Köpenick*, whose movie version was nominated for an Academy Award as Best Foreign Language Film in 1957. Back in Köpenick, the **Heimatmuseum** (Local History Museum; ☎ 6172 3351; Alter Markt 1; admission free; ☼ 8am-6pm Mon-Fri, 10am-6pm Sat & Sun), in a 17th-century half-timbered gem in the Altstadt, has dedicated an entire exhibit to the town's most (in)famous son. The story is also re-enacted every summer during a raucous festival.

GEDENKSTÄTTE KÖPENICKER BLUTWOCHE

☎ 6172 3351; Puchanstrasse 12; admission free; ☼ 10am-noon & 1-6pm Thu, hr may be expanded, call ahead; ☒ Köpenick

Soon after Hitler became chancellor in January 1933, his henchmen in the SA launched a brutal crackdown on Köpenick's communists, social democrats and other political opponents. In the week of 21–26 June alone, hundreds of people were arrested and tortured; 90 ended up dead, the youngest just 18.

The atrocities went down in history as the *Köpenicker Blutwoche* (Köpenick's Bloody Week). Most of the violence took place in the prison of the **Amtsgericht Köpenick** (municipal courthouse), which today houses a small memorial exhibit, including a reconstructed cell. The victims were raised to martyr status during the GDR era and given a monument on the Platz des 23 April, a riverside square about 750m south of the courthouse. The name of the square, by the way, refers to the date in 1945 when the Red Army arrived in Köpenick.

GRÜNAUER WASSERSPORTMUSEUM

☎ 674 4002; www.stadtmuseum.de; Regattastrasse 191; admission free; ☼ 2-4.30pm Sat Apr–mid-Oct; ☒ Grünau, then ☒ 68 to Wassersportallee

The Water Sports Museum is in the Köpenick suburb of **Grünau**, a handsome colony founded in 1749 on the western bank of the Dahme River, about 4km south of the Altstadt. This section of the river, called **Langer See**, was the site of the Olympic regattas in 1936, which is a major focus of the museum's exhibits. Through its hotchpotch collection of flags, medals, clothing, newspaper articles, photos, boats and boat accessories the museum also tells the general history of water sports in the region.

It's fun if you happen to be interested in this sort of thing, but probably not worth the trip out here otherwise. The lack of English panelling doesn't help matters either.

SCHLOSS KÖPENICK

☎ 266 2951; www.smb.spk-berlin.de; Schlossinsel; adult/concession €4/2, under 16 free, last 4hr Thu free; ☼ 10am-6pm Tue-Sun; ☒ Köpenick, then ☒ 62 or 68

South of the Altstadt, on the little Schlossinsel (Palace Island) in the Dahme, the graceful Köpenick Palace is fairly modest, at least by royal standards. Built in baroque style between 1677 and 1682, it served as a royal residence as well as a prison and a teaching seminary before becoming a museum in 1963. Since 1990, it has been a subsidiary of the Kunstgewerbemuseum (Museum of Applied Arts) at the Kulturforum (p107). The recently restored rooms present a rich and eclectic collection of decorative furniture, tapestries, porcelain, silverware, glass and other items from the Renaissance, baroque and rococo periods. Highlights include four lavishly panelled rooms and the stunning **Wappensaal** (Coat of Arms Hall). It was in this very hall that, in 1730, a military court meted out questionable justice against two soldiers accused of attempted desertion. The verdicts? The guillotine for Captain Hans and the throne – eventually – for Captain Friedrich. He just happened to have the good fortune to be the son of King Friedrich Wilhelm I.

NEUKÖLLN

Neukölln has an image problem. Major sections of Berlin's poorest district are plagued by unemployment, a pervasive drug culture and an unintegrated immigrant population. The pale and downtrodden shuffle around Hermannplatz and the main commercial drag, Karl-Marx-Strasse, lined by cut-rate import stores and downmarket chains. Yet there's another side to Neukölln. Adventurous urbanites willing to go beyond the grit and grime will find plenty of intriguing, even handsome, pockets in such suburbs as Britz, Buckow and Rudow.

Orientation

Northern Neukölln is basically an extension of Kreuzberg's 'Little Istanbul' with Hermannplatz at its centre. Southwest of here is the Volkspark Hasenheide, which is popular for recreation and picnics, but also infested with drug dealers. Karl-Marx-Strasse heads south from here, changing its name a couple of times before reaching the high-rises of Gropiusstadt after about 4.5km. Northeast of here is the considerably more human-scale suburb of Britz.

GROPIUSSTADT

Johannisthaler Chaussee, Lipschitzallee, Wutzkyallee, Zwickauer Damm

On the southern edge of Berlin, Gropiusstadt is a classic example of modern urban planning gone bad. This test-tube district built from 1963 to 1973 is a glass and concrete jungle with 18,500 flats in high-rises up to 31 storeys tall. It has little in common with Bauhaus guru Walter Gropius' original plans for a modern model city with plenty of green and open spaces. By the late '70s, the quality of life here had reached a nadir and Gropiusstadt had devolved into a hub of drugs, violence, social isolation and despair. It's a period vividly described in the autobiography of Christiane F, who grew up in the project and became a teenage heroin addict.

Despite some improvements, this is still a bleak part of town. There are no real attractions here for visitors, but if you just want to get a feel for the place, get off at any of the four U-Bahn stations and take a stroll. The Johannisthaler Chaussee station gives access to the **Gropius-Passagen**, a megamall that is among the largest in Germany.

HUFEISENSIEDLUNG

Lowise-Reuter-Ring; Parchimer Allee, then 250m walk north

Anyone interested in modern architecture should swing by the Hufeisensiedlung (Horseshoe Colony), an innovative 1920s housing project by architects Bruno Taut

and Martin Wagner and not far from Schloss Britz. It features about 1000 balconied flats in a three-storey-high literally horseshoe-shaped building wrapped around a little park and is considered one of the earliest attempts to humanise high-density housing.

KÖRNERPARK

6809 2876; Schierker Strasse; admission free; park 24hr, gallery noon-8pm Tue-Sun Apr-Oct, 11am-5pm Nov-Mar; Neukölln, Hermannstrasse
Tucked away among residential streets not far from Rixdorf, this 'hidden' Neukölln jewel is an elegant sunken baroque garden complete with cascading fountain and sweeping staircases leading to an orangery housing a café and art gallery. You'd never guess it was all built on an actual gravel pit! In summer, join the locals for classical, jazz and world music concerts. If the park wasn't in the flight path of Tempelhof airport, you'd swear you were in Charlottenburg.

PUPPENTHEATER-MUSEUM BERLIN

Map pp336-7
687 8132; www.puppentheater-museum.de; Karl-Marx-Strasse 135, rear bldg; adult/child €2.60/2.10, shows €5; 9am-4pm Mon-Fri, 11am-5pm Sun; Karl-Marx-Strasse
A wonderful diversion, not only for tots, the Puppet Theater Museum transports you to a fantasy world inhabited by an international cast of hand puppets, marionettes, shadow puppets, stick figures and all manner of dolls, dragons and devils. Many of them perform during regular shows geared towards both kids and adults.

RIXDORF

Richardplatz; Karl-Marx-Strasse, Neukölln
The contrast between the cacophonic bustle of Karl-Marx-Strasse and the quiet streets of Rixdorf, a tiny historic village centred on Richardplatz, seems almost surreal given that they're only steps apart. Weavers from Bohemia first settled here in the early 18th century and some of the original buildings still survive, including a **blacksmith** (Map pp336–7; Richardplatz 24), now a women's centre, and a **farmhouse** (Map pp336–7; Richardplatz 3A). Even these structures are mere saplings, though, compared to the **Bethlehemskirche** (Map pp336–7;

TOP FIVE WWII SITES

- Berliner Unterwelten Museum (p71)
- Gedenkstätte Deutscher Widerstand (p107)
- Haus der Wannsee Konferenz (p145)
- Holocaust Memorial (p75)
- Sowjetisches Ehrenmal (opposite)

Richardplatz 22), which has origins in the 15th century.

SCHLOSS BRITZ

☎ 6097 9230; www.schloss-britz.de; Alt-Britz 73; gallery adult/concession € 4/3, tours € 2/1, park free; gallery ⊙ 2-6pm Tue-Thu, 2-8pm Fri, 11am-6pm Sat & Sun, tours 2-5.30pm Wed, park 9am-dusk; ⊙ Parchimer Allee, then walk west about 500m or bus M46

Not really a palace but a large country estate, Schloss Britz has a pedigree going back to the 16th century but, having been toyed with repeatedly, now sports more of a French Renaissance look. In recent years, it has emerged as a hub for highbrow culture in largely lowbrow Neukölln and frequently hosts concerts and exhibits in its historical rooms, the former horse barn or the park. Tours of the interior offer a look at the lifestyle of a wealthy family in the late 19th century. In fine weather, the pretty park is a relaxing place for a stroll or a picnic.

TREPTOW

Treptow, a former border district hugging the western Spree bank, is synonymous with the Treptower Park, which becomes Plänterwald further south. It's a lovely patch of green with shady paths for strolling, lawns for picnicking as well as the giant Soviet War Memorial. Treptow has been a popular weekend getaway since the early 19th century when people would party in riverside restaurants or take a spin on the Spree, a tradition continued by Stern und Kreisschiffahrt boats (p71) to this day. Southern Treptow, meanwhile, has staked its future on the Adlershof, a successful science and technology centre.

Orientation

Treptower Park and the Plänterwald dominate northern Treptow, stretching south for several kilometres and encompassing the

Soviet War Memorial and the Archenhold Observatory. A walk along the Spree passes by the Treptowers, the traditional Zenner restaurant and the Insel der Jugend (Island of Youth). Adlershof is about 6.5km south of the S-Bahn station Treptower Park.

ANNA SEGHERS GEDENKSTÄTTE

☎ 677 4725; Anna-Seghers-Strasse 81; adult/concession €2/1; ⊙ 10am-4pm Tue & Thu & by appointment; ⊛ Adlershof

Anna Seghers (1900–83) is best known for her chilling novel The Seventh Cross (1941), which was turned into a movie starring Spencer Tracy in 1944. A committed communist, she spent the Nazi years in exile in France and Mexico before renting this modest flat upon her return in 1955. It's a simply furnished place, which almost seems to drown in thousands of books. A Remington typewriter sits silently on her desk; paintings by her friend, Mexican muralist Diego Riviera, decorate a wall. A small exhibit documents Seghers' life and work.

ARCHENHOLD-STERNWARTE

☎ 534 8080; www.astw.de; Alt-Treptow 1; museum adult/concession €2.50/2, tours €4/3; ⊙ 2-4.30pm Wed-Sun, tours 8pm Thu, 3pm Sat & Sun; ⊛ Plänterwald

Germany's oldest astronomical observatory, in the southeastern corner of Treptower Park, is the place where Albert Einstein first introduced his theory of relativity in 1915. The observatory's other major claim to fame is its 21m-long refracting telescope, the longest in the world, built in 1896 by astronomer Friedrich Simon Archenhold. It's sometimes open for stargazing – call or check the schedule posted on the website. Exhibits in the foyer impart nuggets about the planetary system, astronomy in general and the history of the observatory. Kids love having their picture taken next to a good-sized meteorite chunk.

GRENZWACHTURM Map pp336-7

Schlesischen Busch, cnr Pushkinallee & Schlesische Strasse; ⊙ Schlesisches Tor

East German border guards, machine-guns at the ready, used to keep an eye on the Berlin Wall and the infamous 'death strip' from the top of this ugly grey concrete box. The only original GDR guard tower still in situ, it's now a memorial surrounded by a green patch. The structure itself is currently closed, although you're free to walk around the grounds.

SOWJETISCHES EHRENMAL
Map pp336-7
Treptower Park; admission free; ⏱ 24 hr; 🚇 Treptower Park
At the heart of Treptower Park, the monumental Soviet War Memorial (1949) is quite a sight. The gargantuan complex was built on the graves of 5000 Soviet soldiers killed in the Battle of Berlin and attests both to the immensity of the wartime losses and to the overblown self-importance of the Stalinist state.

For the full effect, approach from the north where the first thing you see is an epic statue of Mother Russia grieving for her dead children. Two mighty walls fronted by kneeling soldiers flank the gateway; the red marble used here was supposedly scavenged from Hitler's ruined chancellery. Beyond lies a massive plaza lined by sarcophagi representing the then 16 Soviet republics, each decorated with war scenes and Stalin quotes. This all culminates in a mausoleum topped by a 13m-high statue of a Russian soldier clutching a child, his great sword resting on a shattered swastika. The socialist-realism mosaic inside the plinth shows grateful Soviets honouring the fallen.

To reach the monument from the S-Bahn station, head southeast for 750m on Puschkinallee, then enter the park through the stone gate.

TREPTOWERS Map pp336-7
An den Treptowers 3; www.allianz-berlin.de; tours ⏱ 2-6pm 2nd Sat of month; 🚇 Treptower Park
Near where the Landwehrkanal meets the Spree, the Treptowers is a new office complex with Berlin's tallest office building, the 30-storey Allianz Tower. Its foyer and hallways are filled with contemporary art, which can be seen on free guided one-hour tours (in German), although unfortunately only on one day a month.

Always on view is the landmark sculpture **Molecule Man** by American artist Jonathan Borowsky in the river outside the tower. It shows the outline of three bodies in embrace, which is meant as a symbol of the joining together of the three districts of Kreuzberg, Friedrichshain and Treptow across the former border.

ZEHLENDORF
Only Köpenick is greener than Zehlendorf, a fresh-air mosaic of forest, rivers and lakes. It's home to a big university, the Freie Universität, but most students prefer heading back to their pad somewhere more central, leaving the villa-studded suburbs of Dahlem and Wannsee to Berlin's upper crust.

For nonlocals Zehlendorf is a welcome refuge from urbanity. Museums, such as exquisite non-European collections in Dahlem, are as much a lure as the expansive Grunewald and Wannsee. In summer, these are ideal for strolling, swimming and other outdoor pursuits. Throw a couple of palaces, important historical sites and a botanical garden into the mix, and you've got yourself one mighty fine district.

Orientation
Zehlendorf is located in the far southwest corner of Berlin and is bordered by Wilmersdorf to the north, Schöneberg to the east and Potsdam to the west.

TOP FIVE ESCAPES
- Botanischer Garten & Museum (p144)
- Erholungspark Marzahn (p152)
- Grunewaldturm (p118)
- Pfaueninsel (p147)
- Müggelsee (p139)

Botanischer Garten (p144)

The university, Museen Dahlem and Botanical Gardens cluster in Dahlem in northern Zehlendorf. The other main suburb is Wannsee in the city's far southwestern corner, just outside Potsdam which counts the forest, palace and romantic Pfaueninsel among its main attractions.

ALLIIERTEN MUSEUM

☎ 818 1990; www.alliiertenmuseum.de; Clayallee 135; admission free; ☼ 10am-6pm Thu-Tue; Ⓜ Oskar-Helene-Heim, then any bus or 10-min walk north on Clayallee

The Alliierten Museum (Allied Museum) documents the history and challenges faced by the Western Allies in Berlin after WWII and during the Cold War. Exhibits are presented chronologically in two buildings and the central yard. Start a tour in the former Outpost cinema for US troops, where the 1948 Berlin Airlift (see the boxed text, p62) is a major focus. Then it's off to the Cold War years, presented in all their drama at the nearby Nicholson Memorial Library. A highlight here is the partial reconstruction of the Berlin Spy Tunnel, built in 1953–54 by US and British intelligence services to tap into the central Soviet telephone system. The original was 2m wide and 450m long and recorded half a million calls until a double agent blabbed to the Soviets. The museum concludes with an overview of the events leading to the collapse of communism and the fall of the Berlin Wall.

Some of the most interesting objects are in the museum yard. They include the original guard cabin from Checkpoint Charlie, a Hastings plane used during the Berlin Airlift, the restaurant car of a French military train, a small section of the Wall and a GDR guard tower.

All explanatory panelling is in German, English and French. Disabled access is good.

BOTANISCHER GARTEN & MUSEUM

☎ 8385 0100, recorded message (in German) 8385 0027; www.bgbm.org; Königin-Luise-Strasse 6-8; adult/concession/family gardens & museum €5/2.50/10, museum only €2/1/4; ☼ garden 9am-dusk, latest 9pm; museum 10am-6pm; Ⓡ Botanischer Garten

Entered from Unter den Eichen or Königin-Luise-Platz, Berlin's stunning botanical garden is a symphony of perfume and colour. One of the largest such places in Europe, it is over 100 years old and boasts some 22,000 plant species from around the world. Highlights include a large pond framed by swamp plants and the Grosse Tropenhaus (Giant Tropical Greenhouse), the largest in the world, which holds a small bamboo forest. Other greenhouses are filled with orchids, bamboo, cacti, 'flesh-eating' plants and giant Victoria water lilies. Sight-impaired visitors can visit a special smell-and-touch garden.

Near the Königin-Luise-Platz entrance, the Botanisches Museum (Botanical Museum) complements the garden by providing scientific background information about plants.

Both the garden and museum are operated by the Freie Universität Berlin.

BRÜCKE MUSEUM

☎ 831 2029; www.bruecke-museum.de; Bussardsteig 9; adult/concession €4/2; ☼ 11am-5pm Wed-Mon; Ⓜ Oskar-Helene-Heim, then 🚌 115 to Pücklerstrasse

In 1905 Karl Schmidt-Rottluff, Erich Heckel and Ernst Ludwig Kirchner founded the artist group Die Brücke (The Bridge, 1905–13), which rejected traditional art taught in the academies. Instead, they turned the art world on its head with ground-breaking visions that paved the way for German expressionism. Shapes and figures that teeter on the abstract – without ever quite getting there – with bright, emotional colours and a warped perspective characterise the style of Die Brücke.

It was Schmidt-Rottluff's idea to bring the works of Brücke members together under a single roof. He got things going in the 1960s by donating his personal collection, which has since been steadily expanded. Housed in a Bauhaus-inspired building by Werner Düttmann, this is a small museum where quality matters more than quantity. Combine your visit here with a stroll over to the Grunewaldsee and the Jagdschloss Grunewald.

FREIE UNIVERSITÄT BERLIN

☎ 8381; www.fu-berlin.de; Kaiserwerther Strasse 16-18 (administration), Garystrasse 35-39 (Henry-Ford-Bau); Ⓜ Dahlem-Dorf, Thielplatz

The Free University was founded in 1948 in reaction to the growing restrictions on

Domäne Dahlem alternative farm (this page)

academic freedoms imposed on students and faculty at the Humboldt University, then in the Soviet sector. Lectures started in the spring of 1949 and were initially held in empty villas throughout Dahlem; today it has about 35,000 students. In the 1960s, it played a leading role in the country's student movement, which sparked major nationwide academic and political reforms.

FREILICHTMUSEUM DOMÄNE DAHLEM

Dahlem Estate Open-Air Museum; ☎ 666 3000; www.domaene-dahlem.de; Königin-Luise-Strasse 49; adult/concession €2/1, under 6 free, Wed free; 🕙 10am-6pm Wed-Mon; ◉ Dahlem-Dorf

A favourite with children, this large farming estate turned open-air museum transports you back to preindustrial Berlin. It's a big, historical complex attached to an actual working farm whose organic products – vegetables, flowers, eggs, meats, etc – are sold in a little shop on site. The main exhibits occupy a restored 1560 manor, one of Berlin's oldest buildings, and focus on the region's agricultural history, rural handicrafts and beekeeping.

Volunteers demonstrate spinning, weaving, pottery making, furniture painting and other retrocrafts. An organic farmers market takes place from noon to 6pm on Wednesday and 8am to 1pm Saturday. The

museum also hosts hugely popular festivals. Check the website or call for upcoming events.

GLIENICKER BRÜCKE

www.glienicker-bruecke.de; 🚇 Wannsee, then 🚌 316

It's 125m long and connects Berlin and Potsdam across the Havel River. But the Glienicke Bridge is world famous mostly for being the setting of secret agent exchanges between the Soviets and the US during the Cold War. Despite its prominent role in countless spy novels and feature films, only three exchanges actually took place, the last one in 1986.

GRAVE OF HEINRICH VON KLEIST

Bismarckstrasse btwn No 2 & 4; 🚇 Wannsee

The Romantic poet Heinrich von Kleist (1777–1811) and his mistress Henriette Vogel (1780–1811) committed murder-suicide on 21 November 1811 in a spot on the southern shore of the Kleiner Wannsee, just south of Wannseebrücke.

Kleist, now one of Germany's most revered literary figures, never enjoyed success in his lifetime. At the time of his death, he was penniless and estranged from his family who had hoped he would pursue a military career. Henriette, who was married to a Prussian civil servant, suffered from advanced stages of cancer.

Both are buried on a rise about halfway between the road and the lake, although the tombstone only mentions Kleist.

HAUS DER WANNSEE KONFERENZ

☎ 805 0010; www.ghwk.de; Am Grossen Wannsee 56-58; admission free; 🕙 10am-6pm; 🚇 Wannsee, then 🚌 114 to Jugenderholungsheim

In January 1942 a group of elite Nazi officials met in a stately villa on Lake Wannsee to discuss the 'Final Solution', the systematic deportation and annihilation of the European Jews. The same building now houses the haunting Wannsee Conference Memorial Exhibit.

You can stand in that fateful room where discussions took place, study the minutes of the conference (taken by Adolf Eichmann) and look at photographs of those involved, many of whom lived to a ripe old age. The other rooms chronicle, in a thorough and graphic fashion, the horrors

Jagdschloss Glienicke (this page)

leading up to and perpetrated during the Holocaust. English-language pamphlets may be borrowed from the desk, which also sells various books and booklets on the subject.

JAGDSCHLOSS GLIENICKE

☎ 805 010; Königstrasse 36b; ⍟ Wannsee, then ⊟ 316

This hunting lodge on the Glieniecker See was built by the Great Elector in 1684 but was later demoted to an army hospital and even a wallpaper factory. Prince Carl, who lived in nearby Schloss Glienicke (p148), had it restored in French neobaroque style in 1859. Since 1962 it has served as an international conference and education centre. A fire destroyed the roof in 2003. Across the lake you can see Park Babelsberg with **Schloss Babelsberg**, which is about a 2km walk away via Parkbrücke.

JAGDSCHLOSS GRUNEWALD

☎ 8149 7348; Hüttenweg 100; adult/concession €2/1.50; ⍟ 10am-5pm Tue-Sun mid- May–mid-Oct, 10am-5pm Sat & Sun mid-Oct–mid-May, tours 11am, 1pm & 3pm; ⍟ Oskar-Helene-Heim, then ⊟ X10 or 115 to Königin-Luise-Strasse/Clayallee, then 25min walk west through forest

Prussian rulers loved to hunt and the Grunewald forest was one of their favour-ite stomping grounds ever since Elector Joachim II first got the dogs running back in 1542. He also picked a scenic spot near the Grunewaldsee (lake) to build this snowy white Jagdschloss (hunting lodge) in Renaissance style. The oldest existing royal abode in town, it was originally called 'Haus am Grünen Walde' (House in the Green Woods) and thus gave the entire forest its name.

These days its rooms are filled with paintings from the 15th to the 18th centuries, including exquisite oils of the royal family by Lucas Cranach the Elder. Otherwise, many of the decorative objects and paintings have hunting themes, often with graphic depictions not suitable for the queasy.

While you're here, you might like a stroll around the Grunewaldsee (swimming allowed). Watch your step: this is doggie paradise and pooper-scoopers haven't exactly caught on yet.

LIEBERMANN-VILLA AM WANNSEE

☎ 8058 3830; www.max-liebermann.de; Colomierstrasse 3; adult/conc €6/4; ⍟ 11am-6pm Fri-Mon & Wed, to 8pm Thu; ⍟ Wannsee, then ⊟ 114 to Colomierstrasse

From 1910 until his death in 1935, the painter Max Liebermann spent his summers in this villa – nicknamed his 'Little

Versailles' – with its large and lush garden overlooking the Wannsee. The garden, with its teahouse, benches, flower boxes, sundial and other elements, inspired some 400 oil paintings, pastels and prints. Villa and garden have been undergoing a multiyear restoration and should have reopened by the time you're reading this (call ahead to make sure). Liebermann's restored studio and a selection of works decorating the walls of the living room and bedroom provide unique insight into the man, his artistic vision and contribution to German art. Downstairs, a nice lake-view café invites lingering on a sunny day.

MUSEEN DAHLEM

☎ 830 1438; www.smb.spk-berlin.de; enter Lansstrasse 8; adult/concession €6/3, under 16 free, last 4hr Thu free; ⊗ 10am-6pm Tue-Fri, 11am-6pm Sat & Sun; ⊖ Dahlem Dorf

The huge museum complex combines four extraordinary collections under one roof. The **Ethnologisches Museum** (Museum of Ethnology) has one of the world's largest and most prestigious collections of pre-industrial non-European art and objects. It's impossible to describe fully the museum's extraordinary collection. Budget at least two hours to walk through its labyrinth of halls – it's an eye-opening journey of discovery that'll fly by in no time.

The main thematic groupings cover cultures from Africa, East Asia, the South Sea islands and North America. The Africa exhibit is particularly impressive with its wealth of masks, ornaments, vases, musical instruments and other objects of ceremonial and everyday life, most hailing from Cameroon, Nigeria and Benin. Note the high level of artisanship, for instance, of the beaded throne given to Kaiser Wilhelm II by King Njoya of Cameroon. The South Seas hall, meanwhile, impresses with its cult objects, outriggers and other vessels from New Guinea, Tonga and other South Pacific islands.

If you're travelling with kids, be sure to take them to Arnimallee 23 for the **Junior-Museum** (⊗ 1-6pm Mon-Fri, 11am-6pm Sat & Sun), which is technically part of the Ethnologisches Museum, where touch-intensive and interactive changing exhibits will help broaden their horizons.

Otherwise, plunge on to the fascinating **Museum für Indische Kunst** (Museum of Indian

Art) to feast your eyes on two millennia of art from India, Southeast Asia and Central Asia. The most prized items are exquisite terracottas, stone sculptures and bronzes as well as wall paintings and sculptures scavenged from Buddhist cave temples along the Silk Route.

Also here is the **Museum für Ostasiatische Kunst** (Museum of East Asian Art), which displays ceramics, bronzes, lacquerware, jade objects and graphics from China, Japan and Korea. Highlights include a Japanese tearoom and a 16th-century Chinese imperial throne made of lacquered rosewood with mother-of-pearl inlay.

The newest arrival is the **Museum Europäischer Kulturen** (Museum of European Cultures), which was relocated to this complex in April 2005. It collects objects from daily life throughout Europe starting with the 18th century. The inaugural exhibit focuses on the aftermath of, and challenges people faced during, WWII.

The entire museum complex is wheelchair-accessible.

MUSEUMSDORF DÜPPEL

☎ 802 6671; Clauertstrasse 11; adult/concession €2/1; ⊗ 3-7pm Thu, 10am-5pm Sun Apr-Oct, admission until 1hr before closing; ⊛ Zehlendorf, then ⊟ 115

The Museumsdorf Düppel (Düppel Museum Village) is a window to what Berlin looked like in the Middle Ages. Over a dozen reed-thatched buildings have been re-created on the grounds of an actual 12th-century settlement surrounded by fields and woods. Museum volunteers grow threatened plant species like the Düppel rye and breed such endangered animals as the Skudde (a type of sheep) and the Düppeler Weideschwein (Düppel pasture pig). Demonstrations of various old-time crafts such as blacksmithing and pottery take place on Sunday.

PFAUENINSEL

☎ 8058 6831; www.spsg.de; adult/concession ferry €2/1, palace €3/2.50, Meierei €2/1.50; ⊗ ferry 8am-9pm May-Aug, 9am-7pm Apr & Sep, 9am-6pm Mar & Oct, 10am-4pm Nov-Feb, palace 10am-5pm Tue-Sun Apr-Oct, Meierei tours 11am-3pm Sat & Sun; ⊖ Wannsee, then ⊟ 218

As if lifted from a fairytale, the dreamy Pfaueninsel (Peacock Island) in the Havel River makes for a most enchanting city escape. The island was the romantic fantasy of King Friedrich Wilhelm II who, in 1797, hired court architect Johann Gottlieb Brendel to build a **mock-medieval palace**, where he liked to frolic with his mistress. Tours take you into the equally exotic interior of this snowy white building.

The **park** with its ancient trees is well worth a ramble. The prolific Peter Lenné designed it in 1822 when the island served as a summer retreat for the family of Friedrich Wilhelm III. The numerous animals brought here at the time later became the inaugural denizens of the Berlin Zoo, also created by Lenné. Fortunately, the namesake peacocks still strut their stuff on the island.

On your strolls you're likely to bump into a clutch of other buildings. Standouts include the **Kavaliershaus** with its Gothic facade and the **Meierei** (dairy), part of a farming estate oddly embedded within a faux monastery ruin. Tours of the richly decorated upstairs festival hall are available on weekends.

Since the island is a nature preserve, the *verboten* list is rather long and includes smoking, cycling, swimming, animals and radios. Picnicking, though, remains legal and this is a nice place to do it. There are no cafés or restaurants on the island.

SCHLOSS GLIENICKE

☎ 805 3041; www.spsg.de; Königstrasse 36; adult/concession €2/1.50, incl tour €3/2.50, in winter with tour only €2/1.50, Casino €1; ☒ 10am-5pm Sat, Sun & hols late Apr–mid-Oct, tours 11am, 1pm & 3pm Sat, Sun & hols mid-Oct–Mar, Casino 10am-5pm mid-May–mid-Oct; ☒ Wannsee, then ☒ 316
Glienicke Palace, at the far southwestern tip of Berlin, is the result of what happens when a rich, royal kid goes to Italy and falls in love with the country. Prince Carl of Prussia (1801–83), a son of Friedrich Wilhelm III, was only 21 when he returned to Berlin giddy with dreams of building his own Italian villa. He hired Schinkel to turn an existing estate – surrounded by a rambling, romantic garden designed by Peter Joseph Lenné – into an elegant, antique-looking compound.

When Schinkel was through, he had indulged the prince's love of antiquities by expanding the existing mansion, converting the former billiard house into the **Casino**, an Italian villa with a double pergola, and building two pavilions, the **Kleine Neugierde**

(literally 'Small Curiosity') and **Grosse Neugierde** ('Big Curiosity'). The latter sits in an especially scenic spot overlooking the Havel river, Schloss Babelsberg and the outskirts of Potsdam. A stroll through the park is a true delight, as beautiful vistas open up at every bend in the path.

The palace itself is richly decorated with marble fireplaces, rare woods and fine furniture. It's open for tours at weekends. The opening of the **Hofgärtnermuseum** (Royal Court Gardeners' Museum) was planned for April 2006. It offers insight into the lives and practices of landscape artists like Lenné who created parks and gardens for royal families in Berlin and beyond. There's also a restaurant with a lovely terrace.

EASTERN DISTRICTS
LICHTENBERG-HOHENSCHÖNHAUSEN

This double district is a prime destination for East German history buffs. You can walk around the office of Erich Mielke, the head of the Ministry of State Security (Stasi for short) and breathe the musty air in tiny cells of the prison where he used to lock up real and imagined regime opponents. Both are chilling evidence of the machinations of the ultimate 'Big Brother' state.

These days, life's still tough in Lichtenberg-Hohenschönhausen, a veritable petrie dish of discontent that has spawned large numbers of both neo-Nazis and neocommunists. Giant high-rise ghettos in classic GDR prefab characterise vast stretches of the district, especially in Hohenschönhausen. Pockets of delight include the sprawling animal park, which is bigger than the zoo in Charlottenburg but with fewer

TRANSPORT

Bus 195 from ☒ Marzahn to Erholungspark Marzahn and Mahlsdorf.
S-Bahn S5, S7, S75 for Lichtenberg; S7 for Marzahn.
Tram M6 from Scheunenviertel/Mitte to Marzahn via Landsberger Allee; M4 from Alexanderplatz to Hohenschönhausen.
U-Bahn U5 for Lichtenberg and Hellersdorf.

THE STASI – FEAR & LOATHING IN THE GDR

The walls had ears. Modelled after the Soviet KGB, the GDR's Ministerium für Staatssicherheit (Ministry for State Security, 'Stasi' for short) was founded in 1950. It was secret police, central intelligence agency and bureau of criminal investigation, all rolled into one. Called the 'shield and sword' of the paranoid SED leadership – which used it as an instrument of fear and oppression to secure its power base – the Stasi grew steadily in power and size over the four decades of its existence. By the end, it had 91,000 official full-time employees plus 173,000 IMs (*inoffizielle Mitarbeiter,* unofficial informants) recruited among regular people to spy and snitch on their coworkers, friends, family and neighbours. By the time the system collapsed, there were files on six million people.

The Stasi's all-pervasiveness is unimaginable. Its methods knew no limits with wire-tapping, videotape observation and opening of private mail being the more conventional techniques. Perhaps the most bizarre form of Stasi terror was the conservation of a suspected 'enemy's' body odour. Samples taken during interrogations – usually by wiping the unfortunate victim's crotch with a cotton cloth – were stored in hermetic glass jars. If a person needed to be identified, specially trained groin-sniffing dogs – euphemistically known as 'smell differentiation dogs' – sprang into action.

Expand your knowledge about the horrors and absurdities of the Stasi visit **Stasi – Die Ausstellung** (p79), the **Gedenkstätte Normannstrasse** (below) or the **Gedenkstätte Hohenschönhausen** (below).

---

animals, and a tidy little baroque palace on the same grounds.

Orientation

Lichtenberg is east of Friedrichshain and linked to Hohenschönhausen to the north. The Stasi headquarters are just off Frankfurter Allee. The zoo is on the district's eastern edge, Karlshorst near its southern edge.

GEDENKSTÄTTE HOHENSCHÖN-HAUSEN (STASI PRISON)

☎ 9860 8230; www.stiftung-hsh.de; Genslerstrasse 66; adult/concession tours €3/1.50, Wed free, exhibit admission free; 🕑 tours (in German) 11am & 1pm Mon-Fri, hourly 10am-4pm Sat & Sun; 🚊 Landsberger Allee, then 🚊 M5 to Freienwalder Strasse, then 10min walk east

Ten minutes walk east of the Freienwalder Strasse tramstop is this memorial site in a feared former Stasi prison commemorating the suffering of thousands of victims of political persecution in Eastern Germany after WWII. The complex can only be seen on guided tours, which are led by former prisoners and reveal the full extent of the unspeakable terror and cruelty perpetrated here on many thousands of people, many of whom were completely innocent.

You'll learn all about the prison's three frightening incarnations. Right after the war, the Soviets used the place to process prisoners destined for the Gulag. More than 3000 of the men, women and

children interned here died – usually by freezing to death in their unheated cells – until the Western Allies intervened in October 1946.

The Soviets then made it a regular prison, dreaded especially for its 'U-Boat', a tract of damp, windowless, subterranean cells outfitted only with a wooden bench and a bucket. Prisoners were subjected to endless interrogations, beatings, sleep deprivation and water torture. *Everybody* signed a confession sooner or later.

In 1951, the Soviets handed over the prison to the folks at the GDR Ministry for State Security (Stasi), who happily adopted their mentors' methods. Suspected enemies of the regime, including participants in the 1953 workers uprising, were locked up in the U-Boat until a new, much bigger cellblock was built, with prison labour, in the late '50s. Psycho-terror now replaced physical torture: inmates had no idea of their whereabouts and suffered total isolation and sensory deprivation. Only the collapse of the GDR in 1989 and the resulting demise of the Stasi put an end to the horror.

GEDENKSTÄTTE NORMANNEN-STRASSE (STASI MUSEUM)

☎ 553 6854; www.stasimuseum.de; Ruschestrasse 103, House 1; adult/concession €3.50/3; 🕑 11am-6pm Mon-Fri, 2-6pm Sat & Sun; 🚇 Magdalenenstrasse

Anyone interested in GDR history, and the Stasi in particular, will find a visit to this museum – housed in the actual headquarters of the Ministry for State Security – very rewarding. Most interesting here is the 'lion's den', the offices from which Erich Mielke, who headed the Stasi from 1957 to 1989, wielded his power. Mielke knew not only the dirt about every GDR citizen, but he also had secret files of all the GDR government honchos, including Honecker, which explains his longevity in office. All the furniture is simple, functional and, above all, original.

Other rooms are filled with Stasi memorabilia, including cunning surveillance devices (hidden in watering cans, rocks, even neckties), and exhibits explaining the GDR's political system and the extent of its repressiveness. Truly chilling is the original prisoner transport van, with five tiny, lightless cells, displayed in the foyer. Panelling is in German only, but an English-language booklet is available for €3.

Ruschestrasse is right there when you exit the U-Bahn station. Head north for 100m, then turn right into the big building complex and walk straight towards House 1.

MUSEUM BERLIN-KARLSHORST
☎ 5015 0810; www.museum-karlshorst.de; Zwieseler Strasse 4; admission free; ☸ 10am-6pm Tue-Sun; ⓡ Karlshorst

In the waning days of WWII, this building served as the headquarters of the Soviet army. On 8 May 1945, German commanders signed the unconditional surrender of the Wehrmacht here. The war was over.

Since 1995, a joint Russian-German exhibit commemorates this fateful day and the events leading up to it. Documents, photographs, uniforms and various knick-knacks illustrate such topics as the Hitler-Stalin Pact, the daily grind of life as a WWII soldier and the fate of Soviet civilians during wartime. You can stand in the Great Hall where the surrender was signed and see the office of Marshal Zhukov, the first Soviet supreme commander after WWII when the building became the seat of the Soviet Military Administration. Outside is a battery of Soviet weapons, including a Howitzer canon and the devastating *Katjuscha* multiple rocket launcher, also known as the 'Stalin organ'.

The museum is about a 10- to 15-minute walk from the S-Bahn station; take the Treskowallee exit, then turn right onto Rheinsteinstrasse.

TIERPARK & SCHLOSS FRIEDRICHSFELDE
Tierpark: ☎ 515 310; www.tierpark-berlin.de; adult/child/student €10/5/7.50; ☸ 9am-5pm mid-Oct–mid-Mar, 9am-7pm mid-Mar–mid-Sep, 9am-6pm mid-Sep–mid-Oct, ticket office closes 1hr earlier; ⓞ Tierpark
Schloss: ☎ 2400 2162; www.stadtmuseum.de; Am Tierpark 125; tours on top of Tierpark fees €2; ☸ tours hourly 1-4pm Tue-Sun; ⓞ Friedrichsfelde or Tierpark

Tierpark Friedrichsfelde opened in 1955 and at last count had almost 10,000

GDR history lives on through the trusty Trabant

CHARLOTTE VON MAHLSDORF – THE GRANDE 'DAME' OF THE GDR

The Gründerzeit Museum wouldn't be much different from any other collection of period rooms had its founder not been the GDR's most famous transvestite. Charlotte von Mahlsdorf, neé Lothar Berfelde, was born in 1928 and developed a fervent passion for dresses and bric-a-brac when only a small child, much to the consternation of her Nazi father. Papa Berfelde's efforts to whup his son into manhood ended abruptly when she bludgeoned him to death with his own revolver at the tender age of 15.

Upon release from prison, Charlotte was now free to fully indulge her zeal for collecting furniture and *objets d'art* from the late 19th century. Eventually this evolved into the Gründerzeit Museum, which opened in 1960 as a modest two-room display in the partially destroyed historic Mahlsdorf estate. Charlotte set to work restoring the building and grew her collection to an impressive 23 rooms. The museum also became a gathering place for East Germany's gay scene, apparently becoming a thorn in the side of the government which threatened to make it state property in the '70s. Charlotte ended up giving many of her best things away rather than risking their confiscation until the harassment suddenly stopped in 1976 (rumour has it because she agreed to become a Stasi informant).

In 1992 the united German government awarded her the Cross of the Order of Merit. That same year, though, neo-Nazi attacks on the estate prompted Charlotte to relocate to Sweden. She died unexpectedly on a visit to Berlin in 2002, shortly after publishing her autobiography, *I am my Own Woman*. Her life was adapted into a 1992 feature film by Rosa von Praunheim and a 2004 Broadway play by Doug Wright that won Tony and Pulitzer awards.

---

animals representing over 1000 species from all continents, most of them living in open-moated habitats. Star residents include such rare, hoofed animals as wild horses, oryx antelopes and Vietnamese sika stags, which are extinct in the wild. Be sure to visit the **Alfred-Brehm-Haus** with its tigers and lions; the **Dickhäuterhaus** where the elephants (including some little ones born in the zoo) and rhinos reside; and the **Schlangenfarm**, which has more slithering, poisonous snakes than even Harry Potter could handle.

Before becoming a zoo, the grounds were the Peter Lenné–designed park of **Schloss Friedrichsfelde**. This late-baroque pleasure palace was the fancy of Benjamin Raulé, a Dutch trader and royal counsellor, but was later appropriated by King Friedrich I after Raulé fell out of favour and was jailed in the Zitadelle Spandau. After an intense restoration, the palace reopened in 2003. It can only be visited on tours (in German) that let you sneak peeks into the lives and lifestyles of its many owners. Fans of decorative arts will appreciate the exquisite wall coverings, baroque glass, handpainted porcelain, historical portraits, silverware and other items that might once have belonged to palace residents.

Note that it's not possible to see the palace without paying admission to the Tierpark.

MARZAHN-HELLERSDORF

Marzahn and Hellersdorf are satellite cities put up quickly in the 1970s and early 80s to combat an acute housing shortage in East Berlin. Row upon row of prefab housing developments – so-called *Plattenbauten* – rush skyward for up to 21 storeys like concrete stalagmites. These days it's hard to fathom that these *Arbeiterschliessfächer* (workers' lockers), as the tiny but modern flats were nicknamed, were actually in hot demand in GDR times. Too great was the lure of private baths, central heating, lifts and parking aplenty.

Perspectives quickly changed after re-unification and any who could escape such desolation did, leaving behind the old and socially weak. To stem the exodus the city has pumped millions into making the district more liveable. The single most visible result – and worth the trip out here – is the Erholungspark with its exotic gardens. Otherwise, Marzahn-Hellersdorf still has a long way to go.

Orientation

Marzahn-Hellersdorf is on the far eastern edge of Berlin surrounded by Brandenburg in the east, Köpenick in the south, Lichtenberg in the west and Hohenschönhausen in the north. It's about 9km east of Alexanderplatz via Landsberger Allee. The Erholungspark Marzahn is smack-dab in the middle and the district's only large patch of green.

ERHOLUNGSPARK MARZAHN

☎ 546 980; www.erholungspark-marzahn.de; Eisenacher Strasse 98; adult/concession €2/1; ☺ park: 9am-dusk, Japanese & Oriental Gardens: 1pm-dusk Mon-Fri, 9am-dusk Sat & Sun Apr-Oct; ⓡ Marzahn, then ⓑ 195 direction Mahlsdorf
This sprawling Erholungspark (recreational park), which opened in 1987 in celebration of Berlin's 750th anniversary, offers a breath of fresh air amid the Plattenbauten colonies of eastern Berlin suburbia. You can wander among the rhododendrons and take the kids to the playground or animal preserve, but the biggest draw here is the foursome of exotic gardens.

The Chinese Garden is the largest of its kind in Europe (2.7 hectares) and a collaborative effort between Berlin and its sister city Beijing. At its centre is a lake embedded in a hilly landscape. At the authentic teahouse you can sample green tea or participate in a traditional tea ceremony (reservations required, ☎ 0179-394 5564).

The Japanese Garden, designed by Yokohama-based priest and professor Shunmyo Masuno, uses water, rocks and plants to create an oasis of tranquillity and spirituality.

The tropical Balinese Garden is inside a greenhouse, which recreates a traditional family home in a jungle setting complete with ferns, orchids and frangipani tree. Great in winter!

The newest is the lovely Oriental Garden, a rectangular walled courtyard featuring a central gazebo with a fountain that feeds water into four beautifully tiled pools. These in turn are surrounded by roses, jasmine, oranges, oleander and other fragrant greenery.

GRÜNDERZEIT MUSEUM

☎ 567 8329; www.gruenderzeitmuseum.de; Hultschiner Damm 333; adult/concession €4.50/3.50; ☺ 10am-6pm Wed & Sun; ⊕ Mahlsdorf, then ⓡ 62 to Alt-Mahlsdorf
Inside an 18th-century country manor, this museum is the life's work of Charlotte von Mahlsdorf (1928–2002), born Lothar Berfelde, the GDR's most famous transvestite and gay icon (see the boxed text p151). It presents a series of late 19th-century period rooms decked out in the bourgeois style popular during the early years of the German empire, ie the Gründerzeit (roughly 1880 to 1900). Besides furnished living rooms, there's also a kitchen, servant's quarters and, most famously, the Mulackritze, a gay dive whose interior was moved here from its original location at Mulackstrasse 15 in the Scheunenviertel in Mitte. There's also a small collection of mechanical instruments that are sometimes put through their paces.

Walking Tours ∎

Walking Berlin

Berlin is a great city for walking. It's reasonably compact and divided into defined districts, each sprinkled with intriguing sights and attractions. This chapter outlines five self-guided tour options (for Organised Tours, see p70). 'Berlin Blockbusters' is a sweeping introduction to the city's main sights. If you want to see how the cityscape has evolved since reunification, follow the 'Contemporary Architecture' tour. Finally, there's a trio of tours taking you into Berlin's most appealing and interesting neighbourhoods – Charlottenburg, Kreuzberg and Prenzlauer Berg – covering the main attractions plus a few less obvious surprises. Happy trails!

BERLIN BLOCKBUSTERS

This day-long meander takes in all of Berlin's must-see sights, plus some fabulous lesser-known places. Along the way, you'll be treated to great views, tremendous architecture, interesting nosh spots and plenty of places you might recognise from the history books.

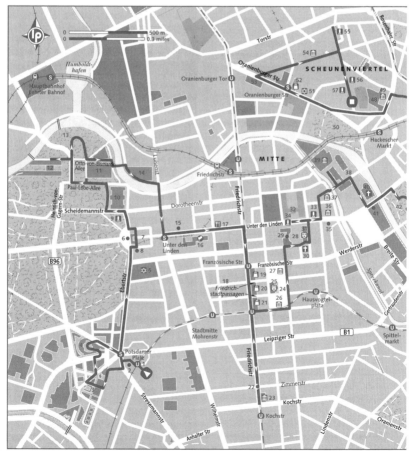

From Potsdamer Platz it winds through the new Government Quarter to Unter den Linden, into historic Berlin, and ends at the Scheunenviertel.

Kick off your tour at **Potsdamer Platz 1** (p103), Berlin's newest quarter and a showcase of contemporary architecture. Check out the short section of **Berlin Wall 2** at the top of Stresemannstrasse, the public art in **DaimlerCity 3** (p105), and the tented plaza at the **Sony Center 4** (p105). Continue north on Ebertstrasse to the sombre **Holocaust Memorial 5** (p75), where you should take time to wander among the concrete blocks to get the full visual and emotional impact. Next, get your camera ready for the majestic **Brandenburg Gate** (6; Brandenburger Tor; p74), the ultimate symbol of German reunification. It anchors **Pariser Platz 7** (p76), a harmoniously proportioned square where you should pop into the **DZ Bank 8** (p49) and ask nicely for permission to gawk at Frank Gehry's stunning atrium. Continue north on Ebertstrasse, past the moving **Wall Victims Memorial 9**, which honours those who died trying to escape the sinister clutches of the GDR. The hulking **Reichstag 10** (p102), where the German parliament meets, looms nearby. It's well worth joining the inevitable queue for the lift to the rooftop glass dome, from where you can enjoy terrific views over the historic city and Tiergarten park. Back on level ground, walk north towards the **Paul-Löbe-Haus 11** (p101), where members of parliament keep their offices. To the west of Paul-Löbe-Allee is the **Bundeskanzleramt 12** (p100), the office and residence of current chancellor, Angela Merkel. Head north across Otto-von-Bismarck-Allee to the brand-new **Spreebogenpark 13** (p103), which overlooks the Spree River, then continue east along the north side of the Paul-Löbe-Haus and cross a little pedestrian bridge over the Spree. Take the stairs down to the river promenade and follow it past the **Marie-Elisabeth-Lüders-Haus 14** (p101) – another striking new government building – to Luisenstrasse, then go south, back over the river. From the bridge, you'll have good views back to the Reichstag. Continuing down Luisenstrasse takes you to **Unter den Linden 15** (p73), Berlin's grand historic boulevard. Walk east and soon you'll spy, on your right, the **Russische Botschaft** (16; Russian Embassy; p77), a monumental confection in white marble. Nearby, the elegant **Café Einstein 17** (p172) makes a stylish refuelling spot.

Hook a right onto Friedrichstrasse to get to the ultradeluxe **Friedrichstadtpassagen 18** (p78), where you should check out architect Jean Nouvel's shimmering cone inside the **Galeries Lafayette 19** (p234), and Henry Cobb and IM Pei's coloured marble fantasy in **Quartier 206 20**. The food court in **Quartier 205 21** offers plenty more options for fighting off any hunger pangs. If you'd like a dose of Cold War history, carry on for another 500m to the site of **Checkpoint Charlie 22** (p123), the most famous ex-border crossing

WALK FACTS

Start Potsdamer Platz (Ⓢ Ⓡ Potsdamer Platz)
Finish Hackesche Höfe (Ⓡ Hackescher Markt)
Distance 12km
Duration 5-6 hours, without museums

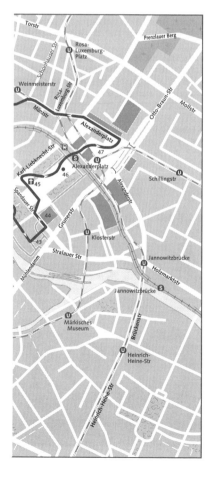

between East and West Berlin. The nearby **Haus am Checkpoint Charlie 23** (p125) has good exhibits about the history of the Berlin Wall and the ingenious people who escaped across it.

Otherwise proceed from Quartier 205 by turning left on Mohrenstrasse to get to **Gendarmenmarkt 24** (p77), Berlin's most beautiful square, which is anchored by Schinkel's **Konzerthaus 25** (p79) and the sumptuous towers of the **Deutscher Dom 26** (p78) and the **Französischer Dom 27** (p78).

Walk north on Markgrafenstrasse, then east on Behrenstrasse to **Bebelplatz 28** (p73), site of the infamous Nazi book burnings in 1933. A trio of stately 18th-century buildings orbits this handsome square: the **Alte Königliche Bibliothek 29** (p73), **Sankt-Hedwigs-Kathedrale 30** (p77) and the **Staatsoper Unter den Linden 31** (p77).

Bebelplatz spills back out onto Unter den Linden, where you'll be hit with a parade of historic buildings, including the **Humboldt Universität 32** (p75) and Schinkel's **Neue Wache 33** (p76). Also take a peak at Christian Daniel Rauch's epic **Reiterdenkmal Friedrich des Grossen** (**34**; statue of King Frederick the Great; p76). The ornate building further ahead on the south side of Unter Den Linden is the **Kronprinzenpalais 35** (p76), a one-time royal palace, while the pink building opposite is the Zeughaus, an armoury converted into the **Deutsches Historisches Museum** (**36**; German Historical Museum; p74). Also check out its **new wing 37** designed by IM Pei.

Continue on to Bodestrasse, then east and across the bridge to **Museumsinsel 38** (p79), a cluster of world-class repositories of art and sculpture. If you have only time for one, make it the **Pergamon Museum 39** (p82), where the giant Pergamon Altar and the luminous Ishtar Gate from Babylonian times are the undisputed highlights.

Looming before you is the city's magnificent cathedral, the **Berliner Dom 40** (p80), the burial place of many Hohenzollern royals. The cathedral's gallery is another spot offering excellent city views. Across from the cathedral once stood the hideous GDR-era **Palast der Republik 41** (p91), whose demolition began in early 2006 and was expected to take well into 2007. There's talk about replacing the structure with a replica of the royal city palace that once occupied the spot.

Beyond the Dom, turn right for the **Marx-Engels-Forum 42** (p93), and walk past the statue of Karl Marx and Friedrich Engels to the **Nikolaiviertel** (**43**; Nikolai Quarter; p94), a re-created medieval village built on the general area where Berlin was founded in the 13th cen-

Gendarmenmarkt (p77)

tury. Wander among the cutesy, cobbled lanes, perhaps popping into the Gothic **Museum Nikolaikirche** (p94) for its free historical exhibit and ornate epitaphs.

Make your way towards the **Rotes Rathaus** (44; Red Town Hall; p94), home of the city government, to the **Marienkirche 45** (p93), which is Berlin's oldest operating church and is filled with artistic treasures. Continue east, perhaps catching a ride up the **Fernsehturm** (46; TV Tower; p92), to the aesthetically challenged **Alexanderplatz 47** (p91), once the commercial heart of East Berlin.

From here follow Münzstrasse to the **Scheunenviertel** (p95), Berlin's historic Jewish quarter and now among the most vibrant parts of town, with great eating, shopping and nightlife. Turn left on Neue Schönhauser Strasse, which is lined with fun boutiques, and left again on Rosenthaler Strasse to get to the **Hackesche Höfe 48** (p95), a beautifully restored series of interlinked courtyards filled with cafés, shops and entertainment venues. Also here is the **Museum Blindenwerkstatt Otto Weidt 49** (p96), which tells the story of Berlin's equivalent of Oskar Schindler.

Pick up Oranienburger Strasse, the Scheunenviertel's main entertainment drag, and follow it north, perhaps pausing for a break in the riverside **Monbijoupark 50**. Soon you'll arrive at the sparkling **Neue Synagoge** (51; New Synagogue; p97), the most visible symbol of Berlin's Jewish renaissance. Immediately adjacent is the entrance to the **Heckmannhöfe 52** (p96), another creatively adapted courtyard complex. Continuing on Oranienburger Strasse soon takes you to the **Kunsthaus Tacheles 53** (p96), a graffiti-riddled ruin, reborn as a cultural and artistic centre. The grungy beer garden in the back still preserves its counter-cultural vibe.

Cross the street and go northeast, via Auguststrasse for a bit of gallery-hopping. Contemporary art fans should pop into **Kunst-Werke Berlin 54** (p96), a super-edgy exhibition space with a sleek café.

When you get to Grosse Hamburger Strasse, turn left to reach Koppenplatz, where you see a table and two chairs, one knocked over, on a bronze floor made to look like wooden parquet. It's an installation called **Der verlassene Raum** (55; *The Deserted Room*) by Karl Biedermann. The quotes chiselled into a band framing the 'floor' are excerpts from a collection of poems published in 1947 by Nobel Prize winner Nelly Sachs.

Backtrack south on Grosse Hamburger Strasse, to the site of the **Alter Jüdischer Friedhof 56** (p95). In 1943 the Nazis completely desecrated what was Berlin's first Jewish cemetery here. A single tombstone stands where the philosopher Moses Mendelssohn is believed to have been buried. Across the street is the **Missing House 57**, a memorial installation on the site of a bombed-out apartment building. Signs bearing the names of former residents are affixed to the façade outside of each person's flat.

South of here, Grosse Hamburger Strasse runs into Oranienburger Strasse, an ideal place to conclude this tour with a coffee or beer at one of the many cafés and bars. After 12km, you've certainly earned it.

CONTEMPORARY ARCHITECTURE

Berlin has always embraced cutting-edge architecture, but never as intensely as in the period since reunification. The tearing down of the Berlin Wall quite literally opened up huge swaths of empty land, giving the city the chance to remould its looks and image in stone, steel and glass. This tour covers three major areas: the government quarter, the diplomatic quarter and Potsdamer Platz.

Start at the **Reichstag 1** (p102), the historic anchor of the *Band des Bundes* (Ribbon of the Federation), as the new federal-government quarter is called. Walk north to the ultramodern **Paul-Löbe-Haus 2** (p101) then turn right on Paul-Löbe-Allee and head down the to the Spree River. Following the paved river promenade north gets you good views of the dramatic **Marie-Elisabeth-Lüders-Haus 3** (p101) across the water. For a closer look, detour over the foot bridge, otherwise continue west along the north side of the Paul-Löbe-Haus. This takes you first past the **Swiss Embassy** (4; Otto-von-Bismarck-Allee 4), which has linked its original historic wing to a jarringly postmodern extension. However, your attention will likely be drawn a bit further south to the humungous **Bundeskanzleramt** (5; Federal Chancellery; p100), where the chancellor and her cabinet hatch their plans for the future of the country.

Make your way south to John-Foster-Dulles-Allee, passing the **Haus der Kulturen der Welt 6** (p100), with its bizarre roofline that made headlines in 1957. There's a café inside. As you continue west, look across the Spree at the new megahousing development for government employees, called **Die Schlange** (7; The Snake; p102) on account of its undulating outline. Turn left on Spreeweg, past **Schloss Bellevue 8** (p102), home of the German president, to his office building, the elliptical **Bundespräsidialamt 9** (p102).

Head south to Grosser Stern roundabout, with the **Siegessäule 10** (p103) at its centre, then continue south along Hofjägerallee, where you'll soon spy the turquoise-panelled façade of the **Nordic Embassies 11** (p49). The complex looks stunning at night, when it's lit like a giant crystal. Next door is the equally impressive **Mexican Embassy 12** (p49), fronted by a curtain of slanted concrete columns. This is followed by the new **national headquarters of the CDU 13**, one of Germany's main political parties. The extravagant building resembles an ocean liner encased in a wedge-shaped glass hall.

Across the street is the **Bauhaus Archiv 14** (p106), designed by the 'godfather' of modern architecture, Walter Gropius. It's worth taking a look inside the museum, or maybe grabbing a quick cuppa in its café, before continuing east on Von-der-Heydt-Strasse. Turn north on Hiroshimastrasse, which is punctuated by a pair of embassies: the beige **Japanese Embassy 15** (p45) and the pink **Italian Embassy 16** (p45). Both originally date to the Nazi era, which helps explains their bombastic style and proportions.

Continue east on Tiergartenstrasse, past the new **South African Embassy 17** at No 18, to Stauffenbergstrasse and the **Austrian Embassy 18** (p49). Its immediate southern neighbour is the **Egyptian Embassy 19** (p49), easily recognised by the Pharaonic encryptions decorating its reddish-brown tile façade.

Beyond here, the diplomatic quarter gives way to the **Kulturforum 20** (p106), an

WALK FACTS

Start Reichstag (🚌 100 or Ⓤ Unter den Linden)
Finish Potsdamer Platz (Ⓢ Ⓤ Potsdamer Platz)
Distance 5.5km
Duration 2½ hours, without museums

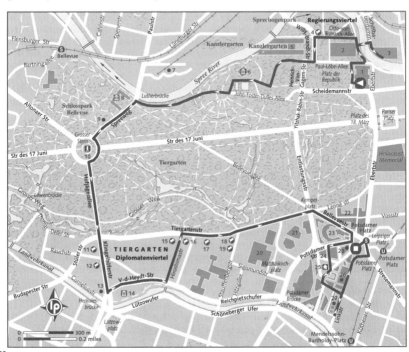

artistic showcase created between 1961 and 1987. The most striking building here is the 1963 **Philharmonie 21** (p109) by Hans Scharoun, with its idiosyncratic roofline. From here, the tour moves on to Potsdamer Platz, a veritable treasure trove of contemporary architecture. Coming from Bellevuestrasse, the **Beisheim Center 22** (p104) on your left was inspired by American mid-century high-rise architecture. On your right is the **Sony Center 23** (p105), with its dramatic, tented plaza and Helmut Jahn's soaring glass skyscraper. South of Potsdamer Strasse, the **DaimlerCity 24** (p105) complex is a reflection of the creative talents of several world-renowned architects, including Rafael Moneo, who designed the sleek **Grand Hyatt 25** (p256); Renzo Piano, who created the **DaimlerChrysler Building 26** (p104); Arata Isozaki, who's responsible for the **Berliner Volksbank building 27**; and Hans Kollhoff's towering **Kollhoff-Haus 28**, with its distinctive reddish-brown brick mantle. Potsdamer Platz is filled with eateries and cafés in case hunger strikes.

CHARLOTTENBURG

Charlottenburg has been chic and upmarket since it was developed in the late 19th century, and was the centre of West Berlin until the Wall's collapse. This tour meanders through its commercial core, taking you past historic landmarks, museums, shopping areas and the design district.

Bahnhof Zoo (1; Zoo Station; p114) takes its name from the **Berlin Zoo 2** (p114), a beloved animal park a short walk east along Budapester Strasse. En route you pass the **Zoo-Palast 3**, the cinema that used to host the Berlin International Film Festival, and the ruined **Kaiser-Wilhelm-Gedächtniskirche 4** (p115), a poignant symbol of the destructive powers of war.

The Gedächtniskirche overlooks **Breitscheidplatz 5**, a buzzy square where crowds gather around the whimsical **Weltbrunnen 6** (p115). A modern counterpoint to the church is the **Europa-Center 7** (p114), a soaring shopping and restaurant complex that was Berlin's first high-rise when it opened in 1965. Inside is a **BTM tourist office 8** (p301).

Breitscheidplatz is the eastern terminus of Berlin's major shopping street, the **Kurfürstendamm 9** (p113) – better known as Ku'damm. Follow it west to the corner of Joachimstaler Strasse, where Helmut Jahn's **Neues Kranzler Eck 10** (p116) soars skyward in all its glimmering glass glory. This retail and office complex replaced the venerable Café Kranzler, one of the western city's most traditional coffee houses, of which only the rooftop rotunda remains.

Continue on Ku'damm, then hook south, down fashionable **Fasanenstrasse 11** (p115), lined with fancy galleries and proud townhouses. The Literaturhaus, at No 23, hosts readings and literary discussions and also houses a gallery, a book store and the sophisticated **Café Wintergarten 12** (p174). Next door, the **Käthe-Kollwitz-Museum 13** (p116) displays some of the finest works by one of the 20th century's most important female artists. It is followed by the Villa Grisebach, home of the prestigious **Galerie Pels-Leusden 14** and an auction house – note the frilly iron grill work and witch's hat slate turret on this building.

Continue south to Lietzenburger Strasse, then head west one block and north along Uhlandstrasse where, on the left side of the street, you'll see an entrance to the Ku'damm Karree. The main point of interest in this otherwise nondescript shopping

Schloss Charlottenburg (p110)

mall is the excellent **Story of Berlin 15** (p116), a fun museum that takes an 'edutaining' multi-media approach to presenting city history.

Take the Ku'damm exit out of the mall and stroll another two blocks west to Bleib-treustrasse where Charlottenburg's newest museum, the **Deutsches Currywurst Museum 16** (p114) is expected to open in autumn 2006 with exhibits celebrating the famous sausage snack invented in Berlin in 1949. Cutting north on Bleibtreustrasse leads you to the **Savignypassage 17**. In the 1980s this became the very first place in Berlin where the support archways of the elevated S-Bahn tracks were converted into galleries, stores and restaurants – a concept since copied throughout the city, especially in Mitte. Follow the pedestrian-only passageway past a stretch of restaurants, cafés and shops to **Savignyplatz 18**. This green expanse, bisected by the roaring Kantstrasse, has been Charlottenburg's eating and nightlife hub since long before the Wall collapsed. Just east of here, on Kantstrasse, is a small interior design district anchored by **Stilwerk 19** (p239), a multilevel atrium-style mall, brimming with upmarket design stores as well as a restaurant and jazz club.

Continue east on Kantstrasse, where you'll soon spy Josef Paul Kleihues' landmark **Kant-dreieck 20** (p115), with its unmistakeable metal 'sail'. A quick detour south on Fasanenstrasse takes you to the **Jüdisches Gemeindehaus 21** (p115), built on the site of a synagogue destroyed during the 1938 *Kristallnacht* pogroms. From here follow Fasanenstrasse back north, perhaps examining the façade of the 1896 **Theater des Westens 22** (p209), which looks majestic despite being an architectural jumble of baroque, neoclassical and Art Nouveau elements. Further north on Fasanenstrasse, the **Delphi Filmpalast 23** (p207) was a hugely popular dance hall before it was totally destroyed by WWII bombs and then reborn in 1949 as Germany's then most modern cinema. In the basement is a popular jazz club called Quasimodo. Continue north

WALK FACTS

Start & Finish Zoo Station (Ⓤ Ⓢ Zoologischer Garten)
Distance 4km
Duration 2 hours, without museums

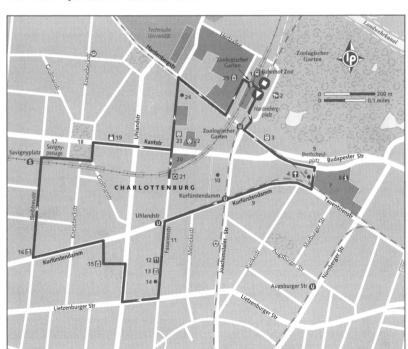

past the extravagant **Ludwig-Erhard-Haus 24** (p116) to Hardenbergstrasse. Take a right, then a left into Jebensstrasse, for close-ups of the controversial genius of photographer Helmut Newton, whose personal collection forms the core of the newish **Museum für Fotografie 25** (p116). This is just steps from Zoo station, where this tour concludes.

KREUZBERG

Kreuzberg is a district of contrasts and is filled with intriguing places, as you will discover on this leisurely walk. Travel from the charming western section, which wraps around the Viktoriapark, to the epicentre of Turkish Berlin in eastern Kreuzberg, via the idyllic Landwehrkanal.

From Mehringdamm U-Bahn station head south, perhaps grabbing a *Currywurst* (spicy sausage) at **Curry 36 1** (p183), a legendary sausage stand. Veer right onto Yorckstrasse, stopping for a peek inside the **Bonifatiuskirche 2**, a neo-Gothic church whose spiky twin towers are wedged between historic apartment buildings. Just past the church, look for two giants buttressing a balcony above an ornate iron gate – these sculptures point the way to the picturesque 19th-century **Riehmers Hofgarten 3**, an elegant block-sized complex wrapped around a leafy, cobbled courtyard. A section of it is taken up by the **Hotel Riehmers Hofgarten** (p261), a jewel among Berlin's boutique hotels.

Walk through the courtyard, exit onto Grossbeerenstrasse and then turn left (if the gate's closed, walk to the corner of Grossbeerenstrasse and Yorckstrasse, then turn left). Sauntering one block further south takes you to the foot of the Kreuzberg, the district's namesake hill, which is draped in the lawns and trees of the rambling

WALK FACTS

Start (Ⓤ Mehringdamm)
Finish Oranienstrasse (Ⓡ Görlitzer Bahnhof)
Distance 6km
Duration 2½-3 hours

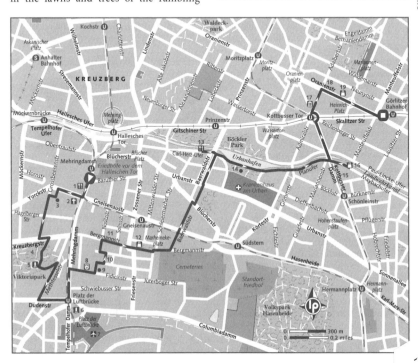

Shoppers at Okomarkt Domane, Dahlem, Zehlendorf

Viktoriapark 4 (p127). Gentle paths meander to the top, where Schinkel's **Kreuzberg memorial 5** (p127) commemorates Prussian military victories. Views from up here are pretty good, especially in winter when you can spy numerous landmarks through the leafless trees. Make your way back downhill, ending up on Methfesselstrasse. Follow it south to Dudenstrasse, then turn left to arrive at the Platz der Luftbrücke, easily recognised by the **Luftbrückendenkmal 6** (p124), which commemorates the Berlin Airlift of 1948–49 and those who died making it happen. The Nazi-built **Tempelhof airport 7** (p124) behind the memorial served as a pivotal landing site for Western Allied planes during the airlift, but flights into here have been limited lately and its days may be numbered.

Walk north on Mehringdamm, then turn right on Fidicinstrasse, past the English-language theatre **Friends of Italian Opera 8** (p212), and the windowless brick **Wasserturm 9** (Water Tower) which looks very much like Rapunzel's tower, but is now a local cultural centre.

Turn left on Kopischstrasse and follow it to **Chamissoplatz 10** (p123), a pretty and historic square, anchored by a pint-sized park and hemmed in by stately 19th-century buildings decorated with wrought-iron balconies. One block north, **Bergmannstrasse 11** (p122) is western Kreuzberg's charismatic main drag. Teeming with restaurants, cafés and an eclectic range of stores, it culminates in Marheinekeplatz, where the bustling **Marheineke Markthalle 12** (p242) is one of Berlin's few surviving late-19th-century market halls.

Continue a bit on Bergmannstrasse, then hook a left onto Baerwaldstrasse and head north until reaching the scenic Landwehrkanal. To your left, in an old half-timbered customs house, is the **Altes Zollhaus 13** (p181), which serves classic German food. Turn right and follow the canal to a widening at **Urbanhafen 14**, where the lawns invite lounging for a spell. Follow the waterfront as far as **Kottbusser Damm 15**, the bustling main street of Turkish Kreuzberg, aka 'Little Istanbul'. Grocers, bakeries, supermarkets, shops, department stores and cafés – all with a distinctive oriental flair – line both sides of the road. On Tuesday and Friday afternoons, the Maybachufer banks come alive with fruit, vegetables and gossip during the colourful **Türkenmarkt** (16; Turkish Market; p181).

Head north to Kottbusser Tor U-Bahn station, then take Adalbertstrasse, which runs past the **Kreuzberg Museum 17** (p126) to **Oranienstrasse 18**, a lively, multicultural strip whose cafés, eateries and stores put the 'fun' in funky. End your tour strolling down here, browsing such stores as **Die Imaginäre Manufaktur 19** (p242), which sells unique items made by blind people, and maybe staying for a drink or bite to eat.

PRENZLAUER BERG

This tour takes you through one of Berlin's prettiest neighbourhoods, with its origins as a 19th-century workers' slum little more than a memory. You'll get a sense of its past, visit sights and places that define the lifestyle of the local population, and encounter plenty of opportunities to grab a cuppa or a bite.

Start on **Senefelderplatz 1** (take the southern U-Bahn exit), a triangular patch of green named after the inventor of lithography, Aloys Senefelder (1771–1834); there's a monument to the man in the square's little park. Oh yeah, and that weird-looking green thing nearby is one of Berlin's few remaining late-19th-century *pissoirs* (urinals), nicknamed Café Achteck for their octagonal shape.

Head north on Schönhauser Allee to the **Jüdischer Friedhof 2** (p131), which has graves dating back to 1827, including that of the painter Max Liebermann. Turning right on Wörther Strasse takes you straight to **Kollwitzplatz 3** (p131), the heart of southern Prenzlauer Berg. The little park in the middle has a busy children's playground and a huge bronze sculpture of the square's namesake, the artist Käthe Kollwitz. There's a good **ice cream vendor 4** on Kollwitzstrasse.

French-flavoured **La Poulette 5** (p185), which does delicious bargain lunches, is recommended. More cafés await at the foot of the **Wasserturm 6** (p133), reached via Knaackstrasse. To bone up on Prenzl'berg history, study the **information column 7** at the corner of Knaackstrasse and Kolmarer Strasse, or check out the latest exhibits at the nearby **Prenzlauer Berg Museum 8** (p132).

From here turn north on Rykestrasse, saying hello to the policeman guarding the **Synagoge Rykestrasse 9** (p133), Germany's largest Jewish house of worship. Swing a left on Wörther Strasse to get back to Kollwitzplatz, then cut north on **Husemannstrasse 10** (p131), a historic showpiece road spruced up by the East German government in the late 1980s.

Heading left on Sredzkistrasse, you'll soon spy the slender tower of the **Kulturbrauerei 11** (p132), a historic ex-brewery that has morphed into a popular cultural venue with stages, a museum, a restaurant and a multiplex cinema. Enter from Sredzkistrasse, walk through the complex, exit on Knaackstrasse and turn left.

From the Kulturbrauerei, cross Danziger Strasse and follow Lychener Strasse (itself home to some good watering holes and casual eateries) to **Helmholtzplatz 12**, a park-like square that draws a bizarre mix of families, down-and-outs and hipsters. Its bars, cafés and shops have become the preferred haunts of the quasi-alternative scene that made Kollwitzplatz such a trendy commodity a few years ago.

Circle the perimeter of Helmholtzplatz, checking out the cool stores, then pick up Lychener Strasse again, make your way to Stargarder Strasse and turn left. This lovely street, which has its share of interest shops and nosh spots, runs past the **semanekirche 13** (p131), a beautiful

WALK FACTS

Start Ⓤ Senefelderplatz
Finish Ⓤ Eberwalder Strasse
Distance 7km
Duration 3 hours

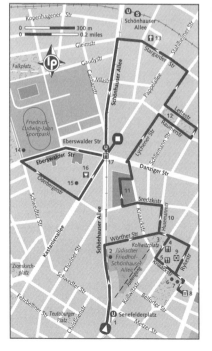

church framed by restored 19th-century buildings. In the late 1980s, this was one of the centres of the dissident movement that spurred the collapse of the East German government.

A short walk west takes you to Schönhauser Allee, a bustling thoroughfare and shopping strip. Follow it south, then turn right on Eberswalder Strasse, which leads to the **Mauerpark 14** (p132) – a not terribly attractive park that does, however, contain a small section of the Berlin Wall. Bargain-hunting hipsters turn out here in droves for the Sunday flea market.

Continue southeast on Oderberger Strasse, another entertaining street dotted with bars, restaurants and boutiques selling knick-knacks, clothing and accessories. This runs into Kastanienallee, which offers more of the same. If the door at Kastanienallee 12 is open, sneak a peek into the **Hirschhof 15**, a garden and playground 'guarded' by a bizarre stag sculpture assembled from recycled materials; it's in the third of three successive courtyards. Just north is the **Prater 16** (p197), a beer garden-cum-restaurant-cum-theatre venue. Finish up at U-Bahn station Eberswalder Strasse with a famous *Currywurst* (spicy sausage) from **Konnopke's Imbiss 17** (p187).

Eating

Eating

Foodies find lots to like about Berlin these days. Although once considered a culinary wasteland, getting good grub in the city is no longer a challenge. Wherever you look, clever young chefs, many brimming with ideas collected abroad, give the local cuisine scene an adventuresome new edge. Quality is up, way up, as much in humble cafés as in Michelin-starred haunts.

These days, Berlin is absorbing international food trends faster than a sponge on acid. One of the latest waves is 'wellness' food, which translates into any dish that's light, healthy, and uses fresh ingredients. Vietnamese restaurants are all the rage, while pan-Asian restaurants have become so ubiquitous that one almost wishes someone would invent a vaccine. Meanwhile, vegetarians will be happy to discover that asking for tofu, tempeh and *seitan* no longer earns blank stares from clueless servers.

One of life's little luxuries is a leisurely breakfast, and Berliners have just about perfected the art – especially on Sundays when many cafés dish out lavish buffets. Another favourite guilty pleasure – and a Berlin tradition – is the *Currywurst* (see boxed text, p179). If there ever was a fast food with cult status, this humble sausage is it. The döner (doner kebab), the popular Western version of which was invented here some 20 odd years ago by a Turkish immigrant, comes a close second though.

Opening Hours

One thing's for sure: you'll never go hungry in Berlin. Most restaurants and cafés are open daily, roughly from 11am to 11pm. Actual hours vary widely, though, depending on the location, time of year, the weather and even the mood of the proprietor. Practically all but the top nosh spots serve food throughout the day, although tables are predictably most crowded from 12.30pm to 2pm for lunch, and from 7.30pm to 10.30pm for dinner. If you get the midnight (or 3am) munchies, you'll usually find some döner, falafel or sausage shop still doing brisk business, especially at weekends.

Hotels usually stop serving breakfast at 10am, although trendier joints will keep the buffet open until a more hangover-friendly 11am or even noon. But don't worry too much if you've overslept: most self-respecting Berlin cafés serve breakfast until well into the afternoon.

How Much?

Thankfully, eating out is not a budget-buster in Berlin. It's easy to fill up remarkably well for just a few euros, and even the gourmet restaurants dole out great value. Many places now offer a weekday 'business lunch', which usually includes an appetiser, main course and drink for a fixed price. In these pages, we've given you a scrumptious spread of options to match all tastes and budgets. For bargain-basement grab-and-go suggestions, check the Cheap Eats sections under each neighbourhood.

Booking Tables

Reservations are essential at the top eateries, and recommended for midrange restaurants – especially at dinnertime. Berliners are big fans of eating out and tend to linger at the table, so if a place is full at 8pm it's likely to stay that way for at least a couple of hours.

PRICE GUIDE

The following breakdown is a rough guide. A meal is defined as an appetizer, a main course and one drink at dinnertime.

€€€	over €30 a meal
€€	€20 to €30 a meal
€	under €20 a meal

Foodhall at the KaDeWe department store (p240)

Tipping

Restaurant bills include a service charge and tipping is not compulsory. If you're satisfied with the service, add about 5% to 10%. It's customary to tip as you're handing over the money, rather than leaving change on the table. For example, say '30, *bitte*' if your bill comes to €28 and you want to give a €2 tip. If you have the exact amount, just say '*Stimmt so*' (that's fine).

If you're eating out as a group, it's perfectly fine for each party to pay separately (*getrennt*). Usually the server will go from person to person and calculate the amount each owes – to which you then add a tip at your discretion.

Self Catering

Several supermarket chains compete for shoppers throughout Berlin. Kaiser's and especially Reichelt have fresh meat, cheese and deli counters, and usually an attached bakery. Discount chains include Aldi, Lidl, Plus and Penny Markt, which all offer good quality and a decent assortment in an often helter-skelter warehouse-style setting. For the ultimate selection, the food hall of the KaDeWe department store (p240) is simply unbeatable, but the prices reflect this. Farmers' markets and small Turkish corner stores are also good food sources.

Try the following places for stocking up after hours, and on Sundays:

Edeka (Map pp340–1; ⌚ 6am-10pm Mon-Sat, 8am-10pm Sun) Inside Friedrichstrasse train station.

Lidl (Map pp338–9; ⌚ 8am-9pm) Inside Innsbrucker Platz U-Bahn station.

Lidl (Map pp336–7; ⌚ 8am-10pm) Basement, Ostbahnhof train station.

Rewe (Map pp336–7; ⌚ 8am-10pm) Basement, Ostbahnhof train station.

Spar Express (Map pp332–3; Schönhauser Arkaden; ⌚ 6am-midnight Mon-Sat, 8am-10pm Sun; Ⓢ Schönhauser Allee)

Ullrich (Map p344; Hardenbergstrasse 25; ⌚ 9am-10pm Mon-Sat, 11am-7pm Sun; Ⓢ Ⓡ Zoologischer Garten)

...wash with hip restaurants where ...or is fabulous, the crowd cosmopoli... ...d the menu stylish. Sure, some places may be more sizzle than substance, but few people seem to mind. You'll find a veritable UN of cuisines represented here, from African to Vietnamese. Gourmets should focus on the Gendarmenmarkt area, where several innovative chefs have earned a Michelin star. If you're craving typical Berlin fare, head to the rather sedate Nikolaiviertel.

BETH CAFÉ Map pp340–1   Kosher €

☎ 281 3135; Tucholskystrasse 40; mains €3-10; ☽ noon-8pm Sun-Thu, ⊛ Oranienburger Strasse
This kosher café-bistro, with a smoking ban and a pretty inner courtyard, is perfect for enjoying a leisurely lunch of lox on toast, various salads, gefilte fish or other staples of Jewish cuisine. It's affiliated with the congregation of Adass Jisroel, which also operates Kolbo (Map pp340–1; Auguststrasse 77-78; ☽ 2.30-6pm Mon-Thu, 10.30am-2pm Fri), a small kosher market nearby.

BOCCA DI BACCO

Map pp340–1   Italian €€€
☎ 2067 2828; Friedrichstrasse 167; mains €17-25; ☽ noon-midnight Mon-Sat, 6pm-midnight Sun; ⊛ Französische Strasse
The mother ship in Charlottenburg (Map p344; ☎ 211 8687; Marburger Strasse 5; ⊛ Wittenbergplatz) has nourished the famished for over a quarter of a century, but the Mitte branch gets thumbs up too, including those of such A-listers as Steven Spielberg and Matt Damon. The lounge is perfect for discrete ogling while anticipating a culinary feast revolving around choice meats, pasta and vegetables.

BORCHARDT

Map pp340–1   Franco-German €€€
☎ 8188 6262; Französische Strasse 47; mains €15-30, three-course menu €46; ⊛ Französische Strasse
Named after a caterer to the Prussian court, this Mitte institution is on the speed dial of politicians, actors and other power crowd types. This generally makes for top-notch people-watching in the open dining room, with ceilings as lofty as the chef's ambitions. The Wiener schnitzel – thin, juicy and huge – is reputedly among the best in town.

TOP FIVE MITTE EATS

- Margaux (p170)
- Mandala Suites (opposite)
- Manngo (p170)
- Vino e Libri (p171)
- W-Imbiss (p171)

CANTAMAGGIO Map pp340–1   Italian €€

☎ 283 1895; Alte Schönhauser Strasse 4; mains €13-20; ☽ dinner Mon-Sat; ⊛ Rosa-Luxemburg-Platz
The rather plain décor does little to distract diners from the delicious homemade pasta and more substantial market-fresh mains at this convivial trattoria. Well established since long before tourists 'discovered' the Scheunenviertel, tables here are always crowded, sometimes with actors and directors from the nearby Volksbühne.

ENGELBRECHT Map pp340–1   French €€€

☎ 2859 8585; Schiffbauerdamm 6/7; mains €16-24; ☽ noon-11.30pm Mon-Fri, 6-11.30pm Sat & Sun; ⊛ Friedrichstrasse
Bertolt Brecht used to be a regular when this was still the legendary Trichter restaurant. Now it's a French brasserie injected with a dose of German severity – think ebony furniture, ivory walls and expressionist art. The menu too is a cross between the two nations, with occasional excursions into Italy or Austria. Beef goulash with hazelnut gnocchi is a typical offering.

GOOD TIME Map pp340–1   Thai €€

☎ 2804 6015; Chausseestrasse 1; mains €9-17; ☽ noon-midnight; ⊛ Oranienburger Tor
Take a trip to Thailand without packing your bags at this warm and friendly restaurant, whose décor invites dreams of faraway places. The kitchen turns out superior cooking, thanks largely to freshly flown-in ingredients. Some dishes show Indonesian inflections (satay chicken and the like) but it's the fragrant coconut-based curries that steal the show.

HASIR Map pp340–1   Turkish €€€

☎ 2804 1616; Oranienburger Strasse 4; mains €19-28; ☽ 11.30am-midnight; ⊛ Hackescher Markt
The flagship branch of this small, family-run chain is a glamorous bazaar tucked into a courtyard around the corner from the

Hackesche Höfe. The kitchen produces fire-works of flavours, from feta-filled artichoke hearts to clay-pot braised leg of lamb and loaves of *kuver*, a kind of flat bread served piping hot from the oven.

Smaller, more casual and less expensive branches are in **Wilmersdorf** (Map p344; ☎ 217 7774; Nürnberger Strasse 46; ⊕ Augsburger Strasse), **Schöneberg** (Map pp338–9; ☎ 215 6060; Maassenstrasse 10; ⊕ Nollendorfplatz) and **Kreuzberg** (Map pp336–7; ☎ 614 2373; Adalbertstrasse 10; ☽ 24hr; ⊕ Kottbusser Tor).

HONIGMOND

Map pp340–1   Central European €€

☎ 2844 5512; Borsigstrasse 28; lunch buffet €6.50, mains €8.50-12; ☽ 7.30am-1am Mon-Fri, 8am-1am Sat & Sun; ⊕ Oranienburger Tor

Dark wood, candlelight and an old piano give this restaurant its cosy charm. It was a favourite among GDR dissidents (includ-ing punk chanteuse Nina Hagen and her adopted father, protest songwriter Wolf Biermann) until the Stasi cancelled the fun in 1987. Revived in 1995, it now gets good crowds for its lunch buffet and such stick-to-the-ribs specialities as *Königsberger Klopse* (meat balls in caper sauce).

ISHIN MITTE Map pp340–1   Sushi €-€€

☎ 2067 4829; Mittelstrasse 24; maki & nigiri €2.50-6.20, platters €6.50-16.50; ☽ 11am-8pm Mon-Fri, 11am-6pm Sat; ⊕ ℞ Friedrichstrasse

This big sushi parlour often bustles with business types, and the look is more office cafeteria than restaurant. But never mind, you're here for the sushi, freshly prepared by a small army of Japanese chefs cutting, chop-ping and assembling behind a long bar. The quality is high, the portions generous and the free hot green tea a welcome bonus.

KASBAH Map pp340–1   Moroccan €€

☎ 2759 4361; Gipsstrasse 2; mains €9-15; ☽ dinner Tue-Sun; ⊕ Weinmeisterstrasse, Rosenthaler Platz

The tantalising melange of cumin, corian-der and cinnamon wafting through this exotic salon will perk up even the most jaded proboscis. Eating here is a sensory ritual: rinse your hands with rose water before digging into *tagine* (a stew), *b'stilla* (stuffed filo) or other traditional North African dishes, then cap it all off with a pal-ate-cleansing mint tea. *Bismillah!*

KUCHI Map pp340–1   Sushi & Pan-Asian €€€

☎ 2838 6622; Gipsstrasse 3; mains €7-23; ☽ noon-midnight (later on weekends); ⊕ Weinmeisterstrasse

Sushi purists might shudder at Kuchi's 'extreme' creations, but clued-in scenesters gobble 'em up like M&Ms. An inside-out roll named My Best Friends Roll – featuring salmon wrapped around vegetable tempura – is considered a classic. *Yakitori* (grilled skewered chicken), tempura, stir-fries, *donburi* (rice bowl) and savoury noodle soups take you into more traditional culi-nary territory. The branch in **Charlottenburg** (Map p344; ☎ 3150 7815; Kantstrasse 30; ℞ Savignyplatz) has a takeaway attached.

LAGANO Map pp340–1   Italian €€

☎ 2021 4377; Kronenstrasse 55-58; mains €5-8; ☽ 11am-midnight Mon-Fri, 1pm-midnight Sat & Sun; ⊕ Stadtmitte

This place screams trendy, with its see-and-be-seen glass front, soft jazz, free wi-fi, big lounge and a menu of 'lifestyle food'. Fortunately, there's substance behind the trappings. The pizza, pasta and salads are creative, delicious, and healthily prepared right in front of you. Homemade noodles with trout, fennel, leeks and lemon? Pizza with shrimp and rucola? Fast food never tasted this good.

MANDALA SUITES

Map pp340–1   Breakfast €€

☎ 202 920; Friedrichstrasse 185-190; buffet €20, incl beverages; ☽ 6.30am-11am Mon-Fri, 7am-noon Sat & Sun; ⊕ Stadtmitte

Like froth on a cappuccino, the breakfast sky-lounge of this mod Kleihues-designed hotel floats above the rooftops, offering a quiet and elegant retreat. The buffet is opulent, first-rate and constantly refreshed, but the views – and perhaps the sleek Bauhaus-inspired furnishings – are just as memorable. Reservations essential.

TOP FIVE QUICK EATS

- Curry 36 (p183)
- Dada Falafel (p171)
- Dolce Pizza (p180)
- Dolores (p172)
- Schlemmerbuffet Zach (p172)

Eating

MITTE

Bocca di Bacco (p168)

MANNGO

Map pp340–1   Vietnamese €

☎ 2804 0558; Mulackstrasse 29; mains €5;
🕙 noon-midnight Mon-Fri, 4pm-midnight Sat;
Ⓔ Rosa-Luxemburg-Platz, Weinmeisterstrasse

If Monsieur Vuong (right) is too trendy, chic or crowded for your taste, head around the corner to this sweet little restaurant. The *pho* (noodle) soups are as authentic as anything this side of Hanoi, the curries delicious and the service friendly. Try one of the freshly-squeezed juices or finish up with a seductively sweet Vietnamese coffee.

MARGAUX

Map pp340–1   Gourmet €€

☎ 2265 2611; Unter den Linden 78, enter on Wilhelmstrasse; mains €28-45; 🕙 noon-2.30pm & 7-10.30pm Tue-Sat; Ⓡ Unter den Linden

It took culinary *wunderkind* Michael Hoffman only one year to wow the Michelin testers with his '*cuisine avant-garde classique*'. What may sound like an oxymoron actually translates into first-rate ingredients, refined flavours and artistic presentation. And somehow, the divine dishes taste even better against those lush back-lit onyx walls.

MONSIEUR VUONG

Map pp340–1   Vietnamese €

☎ 3087 2643; Alte Schönhauser Strasse 46; mains €6.40; 🕙 noon-midnight; Ⓔ Rosa-Luxemburg-Platz, Weinmeisterstrasse

Despite the pepper-red walls, good-looking clientele and beautiful dishware, this bustling eatery only looks expensive. The Vietnamese fare – soups and two or three main courses daily – is made to order, and is uniformly delicious, as are the fruit cocktails and exotic teas. No reservations, so be prepared to queue or, better yet, come during the afternoon off-hours.

NOODLE KITCHEN

Map pp340–1   pan-Asian €€

☎ 238 283 464; Karl-Liebknecht-Strasse 3; mains €10-15; 🕙 5pm-midnight; Ⓡ Hackescher Markt

Hotel restaurants rarely reach most-favourite status with foodies, but this contender at the Radisson SAS has generated a buzz. It doesn't even feel like a hotel restaurant, with its savvy looks and a contemporary menu of stir-fries, noodle soups, barbecued meats, satays, and sushi, that takes 'fresh' to a whole new level. Outside tables have views of the Spree and Berliner Dom.

PAN ASIA

Map pp340–1   pan-Asian €€

☎ 2790 8811; Rosenthaler Strasse 38; 2-course lunch €6.50, mains €6-13; 🕙 noon-midnight; Ⓡ Hackescher Markt

Manga films, light projections and long communal tables account for the hipster quotient at this high-energy restaurant next to the Hackesche Höfe.

The menu predictably hopscotches from Thailand to China, via Japan and Vietnam, and back. Fresh ingredients and healthy, low-fat cooking techniques make it a favourite with waist-watchers. There's courtyard seating in summer and killer bathroom décor.

ROSMINI PASTA-MANUFAKTUR

Map pp332–3   Italian €€

☎ 2809 6844; Invalidenstrasse 151; mains €9-16; 🕙 dinner daily; Ⓔ Rosenthaler Platz

The walls are white, the furniture pine and the décor simple at this low-key trattoria, which specialises in fresh pasta – handmade daily on the premises. Chef Massimo finds endless ways to pair his product with vegetables, meats, fish and sauces, so you'll never know what's on the menu. There's a great wine list or try their delicious micro-brew imported from Italy.

VAU Map pp340–1 Gourmet €€€
☎ 202 9730; Jägerstrasse 54; lunch €12 per course; dinner mains €35, menus from €75; ⏰ noon-2.30pm & 7-10.30pm Mon-Sat; ⊕ Hausvogteiplatz

In the same locale where Rahel Varnhagen held her literary salons a couple of centuries ago, Michelin-starred chef Kolja Kleeberg now pampers a Rolls-Royce crowd of diners with his fanciful gourmet creations. The dining room is a composition of glass, steel, slate and wood, and is a perfect foil for imaginative cuisine, featuring only hand-selected, seasonal ingredients. Reservations essential.

VINO E LIBRI Map pp332-3 Italian €€
☎ 4405 8471; Torstrasse 99; mains €8-16; ⏰ dinner; ⊕ Rosenthaler Platz

Two of civilization's greatest treasures – wine and books – form the name, décor and soul of this *ristorante*, run with charm and panache by a Sardinian family. The pizza is excellent, but chef Bruno truly shines when it comes to experimental flavour combinations. The strawberry salmon and tagliatelle with wild boar in a chocolate-based sauce are truly excellent. Wife Debora, meanwhile, keeps the service running as smoothly as a well-oiled machine.

W-IMBISS Map pp332-3 Fusion €
☎ 4849 2657; Kastanienallee 49; dishes €4-10; ⏰ 12.30pm-midnight; ⊕ Rosenthaler Platz, ⊞ M1, M12

With his pencil-thin moustache and funky hat, Gordon W has the gangster look down pat, but in real life the eccentric Canadian is a culinary performance artist *par excellence*. Watch him chop, knead and toss his progressive nosh – all made with first-class ingredients – in the tiny kitchen which takes up half his tiki-inspired restaurant. The naan pizzas are a great snack, but to truly understand Gordon's genius order the daily special – usually some fish marinated in secret spices. For a vitamin high, slug down a fresh apple and wheatgrass cocktail.

YOSOY Map pp340–1 Spanish €€
☎ 2839 1213; Rosenthaler Strasse 37; tapas €3-6, mains €9-15; ⏰ 11am-midnight; ⊞ Hackescher Markt

This buzzy tapas bar transports you straight to Andalusia, with its sunny walls, Moorish tiles and mix of tourists, Spanish expats and Iberophile Berliners. There's a fine menu of mains, including *filete de toro* (bull fillet), but regulars prefer sipping sherry and grazing on classic tapas such as Serrano ham, tuna-stuffed peppers and marinated squid. Service can sometimes be stretched thin.

ZOE Map pp340–1 International €€
☎ 2404 5635; Rochstrasse 1; mains €8.50-16; ⏰ noon-midnight Mon-Fri, 6pm-midnight Sat & Sun; ⊕ Weinmeisterstrasse

Dressed in virginal white, Zoe seems to take minimalist décor to its extreme, but fortunately plenty of creativity flows out of the kitchen with its duelling chefs. One's in charge of Mediterranean, the other of Asian cuisine; the results are exquisite in both cases. Say hi to Zoe, the owner's dog, an adorable Doberman-German shepherd blend. Free wi-fi.

CHEAP EATS
BECKER'S FRITTEN
Map pp340–1 Snacks €
Oranienburger Strasse 43a; snacks €1.80-4; ⏰ noon-1am Sun-Thu, noon-4am Fri & Sat; ⊕ Oranienburger Tor

The simple spud takes centre stage at this bright orange takeaway wagon. The place is often mobbed by hungry hipsters lusting after a heaped helping of that great guilty pleasure: French fries. Enjoy them piping hot, fresh and paired with delicious sauces, from tangy mayo to sassy satay.

DADA FALAFEL
Map pp340–1 Middle Eastern €
☎ 2759 6927; Linienstrasse 132; meals €3-4; ⏰ 10-2am; ⊕ Oranienburger Tor

This tiny takeaway would be a mere blip on busy Oranienburger Strasse, were it not for their scrumptious falafel and *shwarma* sandwiches. One bite and you're hooked, we swear. The décor alone is worth a gander: check out the tentacled chandelier and the expressionist mural.

Eating

MITTE

171

DOLORES Map pp340–1 Californian €

☎ 2809 9597; Rosa-Luxemburg-Strasse 7; dishes €3.50-4.50; ⏰ 11.30am-10pm Mon-Fri, 1-10pm Sat; ⊕ ⬤ Alexanderplatz

This hole-in-the-wall proves that healthy fast food does not have to be an oxymoron. The specialty here is the *burrito*, a plate-sized flour *tortilla* (soft, thin bread) freshly stuffed with meat (the lime *cilantro* chicken is yummy), rice, beans, veggies, sour cream, cheese, salsa or any combination thereof. Eat in or take away.

PICCOLA ITALIA Map pp340–1 Italian €

☎ 283 5843; Oranienburger Strasse 6; dishes €1.50-7; ⏰ until 1am Sun-Thu, until 3am Fri & Sat; ⬤ Hackescher Markt

There's usually a line out the door of this teensy pizzeria, and for good reason: the pies are tasty, toothsome, generously topped and cheap. If the weather permits, grab one and head across the street to Monbijoupark. Pasta dishes are available too.

SCHLEMMERBUFFET ZACH

Map pp332-3 Middle Eastern €

☎ 283 2153; Torstrasse 125; dishes €1.10-7; ⏰ 24hr; ⊕ Rosenthaler Platz

If there were a doner Oscar, this clean and friendly *Imbiss* would be a serious contender. Portions are huge, the meat (veal or chicken) is perfectly slivered, the bread is toasted to perfection, the salads are fresh and the yogurt sauce garlicky. In the wee hours the place often gets mobbed by clubbers, cabbies and other night owls.

TIERGARTEN

Most of Tiergarten's eating options are as exalted as you'd expect from a neighbourhood teeming with diplomats, politicians and business executives. Quality has improved significantly in recent years, even at Potsdamer Platz, although for the real gems you should venture beyond the glitz.

CAFÉ AM NEUEN SEE

Map pp338-9 Café €€

☎ 254 4930; Lichtensteinallee 2; dishes €5-15; ⏰ daily Mar-Oct, Sat & Sun Nov-Feb; ⊕ ⬤ Zoologischer Garten

This lakeside Bavarian-style beer garden in Tiergarten park is a pretty place on a warm summer night, even if it can get more packed than a U2 concert. Delicious beers go well with rustic sausages, grilled meats and, of course, pizza. Romantic types can even rent a boat and take their sweetie for a spin.

CAFÉ EINSTEIN STAMMHAUS

Map pp338-9 Austrian €€

☎ 261 5096; Kurfürstenstrasse 58; breakfast €5-15, mains €10-22; ⏰ 9-1am; ⊕ Nollendorfplatz

Schnitzels, noodles and warm apple strudels – you'll find them all at this classic Viennese coffee house in a lavish garden villa. Marble table tops, jumbo-sized mirrors and cosy banquettes create a stylish look, although we wouldn't mind if the staff laid off the snootiness. The villa, by the way, was once owned by Henny Porten, Germany's earliest superstar actress, who fled Nazi Germany after refusing to divorce her Jewish husband. The branch in *Mitte* (Map pp340–1; ☎ 204 3632; Unter den Linden 42; ⬤ Unter den Linden) has less flair but better people-watching.

DESBROSSES

Map p346 French €€

☎ 337 776 340; Potsdamer Platz 3; 2-course business lunch €13, mains €10-22; ⏰ 6.30am-midnight; ⊕ ⬤ Potsdamer Platz

The Ritz-Carlton may be brand-new but its restaurant is a 140-year-old brasserie moved here piece by piece from the Burgundy region of France. The onsite bakery churns out crusty breads, which are an ideal complement to the unpretentious cuisine, turned out in an open kitchen with a race car-red enamel oven. Seafood fans can put together a feast at the raw bar.

DIEKMANN IM WEINHAUS HUTH

Map p346 Franco-German €€

☎ 2529 7524; Alte Potsdamer Strasse 5; weekday lunch €10, mains €15-18; ⏰ noon-1am; ⊕ ⬤ Potsdamer Platz

Rows of tables draped in crisp white linen welcome you to this elegant restaurant inside the only prewar Potsdamer Platz building. It's famous for its oysters, but even if slimy molluscs turn you off, you're sure to find a favourite among such menu items as pike perch, roast venison or *coq au vin* (chicken stewed in wine).

Yosoy restaurant (p171)

EDD'S

Map pp338-9   Thai €€

☎ 215 5294; Lützowstrasse 81; mains €8-22;
🕑 11.30am-3pm & 6pm-midnight Tue-Fri, 5pm-midnight Sat, 2pm-midnight Sun; ⊖ Kurfürstenstrasse

Thai restaurants may have proliferated like rabbits on Viagra, but Edd's not worried. His grandma used to cook for Thai royals and he's regaled Berlin foodies for over three decades. Most nights he is still at the helm of the kitchen, producing such palate-pleasers as twice-roasted duck, chicken steamed in banana leaves, and curries that are culinary poetry. Reservations essential.

JOSEPH ROTH DIELE

Map pp338-9   German €

☎ 2636 9884; Potsdamer Strasse 75; dishes €4-7;
🕑 10am-midnight Mon-Fri; ⊖ Kurfürstenstrasse

Named for an Austrian Jewish writer forced into exile by the Nazis, this quirky retreat time-warps you back to the 1920s, when Roth used to live next door. Walls decorated with bookshelves and quotes from his works draw a literary, intellectual crowd, and conversation rarely seems to flag in such a stimulating setting. Come here for coffee and cakes or some good, homestyle cooking.

KAISERSAAL

Map p346   Franco-German €€€

☎ 2575 1454; Bellevuestrasse 1, Sony Center; mains €20-30; 🕑 dinner; ⊖ 🚊 Potsdamer Platz

Emperor Wilhelm II used to dine in this magnificent neo-rococo hall when it was still part of the Hotel Esplanade, the grandest of the old Potsdamer Platz hotels. Now the Kaiser's life-size likeness keeps an eye on patrons savouring the fantastic creations of Jörgen Sodemann, whose classic cuisine sparkles with flavour and artsy presentation.

LEI E LUI

Map pp330-1   International €€

☎ 3020 8890; Wilsnacker Strasse 61; mains €7-15; 🕑 noon-midnight Mon-Fri, 2pm-midnight Sat & Sun; ⊖ Turmstrasse

The Italian name conjures visions of pasta and polenta, but owner-chef Karen Kaiser's repertory travels far beyond Italy, to the cuisines of Morocco, the Caribbean, Spain and Thailand. The lively décor is an equally eclectic proposition that somehow manages to find harmony in red velvet sofas, crystal chandeliers and oversized mirrors. Because it is located off the tourist track, the quality remains high and prices are reasonable.

THE CULINARY INSIDE TRACK

For foodies, visiting a new city can be an exciting yet scary prospect. Where to focus one's culinary attentions? How to avoid – horror of all horrors! – a bad meal? In comes Henrik Tidefjärd – a gourmet, raconteur and tour guide all wrapped into one affable package. The multilingual Swede specialises in taking small groups of people (never more than nine) on what he has dubbed a 'Gastro-Rallye'. This involves a lively evening, stopping at three or four of Berlin's hippest restaurants for one course at each. In between, Henrik will give you a crash-course on what makes Berlin tick, peppering you with bits of history, tasty insights and secret tips. You're also free to pick his brain about whatever racy and quirky trivia you've been dying to know about the city. In the end you'll almost feel like an insider yourself; a very well-fed insider, that is.

Tours start at €59 per person, include all food and drink, and must be booked at least one day in advance. For details call ☎ 4372 0701 or check www.berlinagenten.com.

SCHLEUSENKRUG

Map pp338-9   Beer Garden €

☎ 313 9909; Müller-Breslau-Strasse at the Tiergarten locks; breakfast & mains €4.50-10; ⏲ 10am-11pm; ⊖ ⊛ Zoologischer Garten

Follow a jog in Tiergarten with breakfast at this classic beer garden, sitting pretty right by a lock on the Landwehrkanal. Later in the day the place starts jumping with people from all walks of life chatting, hoisting mugs of foamy beer and feasting on grilled organic sausages and other hearty fare.

CHEAP EATS

GOSCH Map p346   Fish €

☎ 2529 6820; Alte Potsdamer Strasse; sandwiches €2-3.50, mains €6-13; ⊖ ⊛ Potsdamer Platz

Only the brisk North Sea wind is missing from this stylish bistro, a clone of the original branch on the Frisian island of Sylt. Come here for a take-away sandwich or pick your *poisson* (fish) at the counter, then wait while it's turned into a delicious meal. Also in Charlottenburg (Map p344; ☎ 8868 2800; Kurfürstendamm 212; ⊖ Uhlandstrasse).

SALOMON BAGELS

Map p346   Deli €

☎ 2529 7626; Potsdamer Platz Arkaden; dishes €2-8; ⏲ 9am-8pm; ⊖ ⊛ Potsdamer Platz

At this chic shopping mall café, with its extravagant chairs and chandeliers, the lowly bagel goes spiritual – the owners actually regard them as 'wisdom that's fit to eat'. From plain to pumpkin seed, all bagels are made fresh and packaged into delicious sandwiches, including the classic lox and cream cheese version. They serve breakfast too.

CHARLOTTENBURG

While the culinary spotlight remains trained on flashy Mitte, clued-up Berliners know that some of the finest eating is done in subdued Charlottenburg. The crowd is a bit older here, more affluent and discerning, which translates into higher quality – and prices. The most fashionable haunts are around Savignyplatz, while west, along Kantstrasse, is a gaggle of more casual but excellent Asian and Spanish eateries. The residential streets south of Schloss Charlottenburg yield some great off-the-beaten-track finds.

CAFÉ WINTERGARTEN IM LITERATURHAUS

Map p344   Café €€

☎ 882 5414; Fasanenstrasse 23; mains €8-16; ⏲ 9.30am-midnight; ⊖ Uhlandstrasse

Everyone from book rats to artists gather at this lovely Art Nouveau villa. When the weather plays along, the garden is ideal for a light lunch or a leisurely afternoon of coffee, cake and chat. Or come to prepare for your shopping spree with breakfast under the graceful stucco-ornamented ceilings.

CASSAMBALIS

Map p344   Mediterranean €€

☎ 885 4747; Grolmanstrasse 35; mains €9-24; ⏲ noon-midnight; ⊖ Uhlandstrasse

Owner, Costas Cassambalis, pairs his passion for art and food in this congenial brasserie, popular with everyone from Charlottenburg literati to guests of the adjacent Hecker's Hotel (p257). Walls are swathed in his favourite paintings, including some created by patrons. Regulars swear by the grilled sea bream and the tender beef roulade. There's a great antipasti buffet too.

ENGELBECKEN Map pp338-9 — Bavarian €€

☎ 615 2810; Witzlebenstrasse 31; mains €8-16;
☯ 4pm-midnight Mon-Sat, noon-midnight Sun;
Ⓢ Sophie-Charlotte-Platz

It's no Munich beer hall, but this corner restaurant still lays on Bavarian charisma with a trowel. Squeeze behind a scrubbed wooden table and pick from a menu that features all the usual suspects: *Weisswurst* (veal sausage) with chewy pretzels, roast pork with dumplings and red cabbage, apple strudel with custard… All meats are hormone-free.

FRANZISKUSHOF LADEN

Map p344 — German €

☎ 8867 5176; Mommsenstrasse 63; mains €3-5;
☯ 11am-3pm Mon-Fri; Ⓡ Savignyplatz

Devotees of thoughtful German home-cooking should check this lunch hotspot-cum-butcher shop. It's the fundraiser for a Franciscan-run farming monastery in Brandenburg. Its mission: to help reintegrate people who've fallen on tough times. All meals are made with organic meats and the produce is grown on the farm.

GABRIEL'S Map p344 — Kosher €€

☎ 882 6138; Fasanenstrasse 79; mains €10-17, buffet €18; ☯ 11.30am-3.30pm & 6.30-11pm Sun-Fri, 11.30am-3.30pm Sat; Ⓢ Ⓡ Zoologischer Garten

Inside the Jewish Community Centre, this is Berlin's oldest certified *glatt* kosher restaurant (previously known as Arche Noah). The menu features lots of traditional favourites such as *kreplach* (Jewish ravioli), gefilte fish and beef brisket. Reservations are required for the Sabbath meal.

HARD ROCK CAFÉ Map p344 — American €€

☎ 884 620; Meinekestrasse 21; mains €8-17;
☯ noon-11pm; Ⓢ Uhlandstrasse, Kurfürstendamm

This place gets a quick mention in case you're keen to add to your T-shirt collection or simply crave a great burger. Otherwise, it's the same predictable mix of rock memorabilia, loud music and fast service.

JULES VERNE Map p344 — International €€

☎ 3180 9410; Schlüterstrasse 61; breakfast €4-10, 2-course lunch €5.50-8; dinner mains €8.50-17; ☯ 8-1am; Ⓡ Savignyplatz

Jules Verne was a well-travelled man, so it's only fitting that a restaurant bearing his name would feature a global menu. The

French *flammekuche* (Alsatian 'pizza') and Austrian schnitzel are both good, although the top seller is North African–style couscous. It's also popular for breakfast, which you can enjoy until 3pm along with plenty of international newspapers and magazines.

LA CALETA Map p344 — Spanish €€

☎ 8862 7475; Wielandstrasse 26a; mains €10-18;
☯ dinner Mon-Sat; Ⓡ Savignyplatz

In Spanish, *caletas* are little bays where fish find refuge, and that's just how owner Señor Bonfiglio would like guests to feel at his romantic restaurant. In two beautiful dining rooms patrons enjoy food from around the Iberian peninsula. The paella Valenciana (€13) is just one dish showcasing his culinary authority, but any meal is elevated with a glass of *rioja*, *ribera* or other delicate *vino* from the extensive list.

MARCHÉ Map p344 — International €

☎ 882 7578; Kurfürstendamm 14-15; meals €5-10;
☯ 8am-10pm; Ⓢ Kurfürstendamm

If you need a break from Ku'damm shopping, lug your bags to this self-service bistro, tucked away in the basement of a former liqueur factory. Pick from salad, vegetable, pasta and cake buffets, or have a hot meal prepared in front of you, but do leave room for some creamy Mövenpick ice cream. Smoke-free sections and a playground are additional perks.

MAR Y SOL Map p344 — Spanish €€

☎ 313 2593; Savignyplatz 5; tapas €2-4, mains €10-18; ☯ dinner; Ⓡ Savignyplatz

This is a top spot for tapas and beautifully captures the sultry mood of Andalusia. On balmy nights, tables on the fountain-studded tiled patio are a hot commodity, while in winter the action moves into the rustically elegant dining room. Either way, you'll be happy munching on *manchego* (sheep's milk cheese), bacon-wrapped dates, Serrano ham, garlic prawns and other tastebud ticklers.

TOP FIVE CHARLOTTENBURG EATS

- Engelbecken (left)
- Jules Verne (left)
- Mar y Sol (above)
- Moon Thai (p176)
- Stella Alpina (p177)

Cassambalis (p174)

MEXICO LINDO

Map p344   Mexican €€

☎ 312 8218; Giesebrechtstrasse 19; mains €6-16;
☾ dinner; Ⓜ Adenauerplatz

Tex-Mex restaurants are a dime a dozen, but for a splendid introduction to real Mexican food head to this festive *cantina* drenched in bold art and colours. Relax with a margarita before choosing from *ceviche* (marinated seafood cocktail), *fajitas* (sautéed beef or chicken strips), *quesadillas* (cheese-filled corn tortillas) or other dishes prepared so authentically that even the Mexican embassy are clients.

MOON THAI

Map p344   Thai €€

☎ 3180 9743; Kantstrasse 32; mains €6.50-14;
☾ noon-midnight; Ⓢ Savignyplatz

This single-room restaurant exudes a feel-good ambience, with its orange walls accented by carvings, drums, woven textiles and other imported Thai art. It's a family affair, with at least two generations preparing a huge repertory of classic dishes. The Moon Thai duck is excellent and even the *seitan* (cooked wheat gluten) dishes strut their stuff when paired with fresh vegetables and bold spices.

MR HAI & FRIENDS

Map p344   Vietnamese €€

☎ 3759 1200; Savignyplatz 1; lunch special €8, mains €8-16; ☾ 11-1am; Ⓢ Savignyplatz

Tables are squished together as tightly as lovers at this trendy Vietnamese place, where dishes are dressed in intricate and sometimes provocative flavours. Feel your anticipation grow as you watch the cooks fussing over grills and steamy woks in a glass-encased show kitchen. From soups to noodles to crispy duck, it's all freshly prepared with top ingredients and know-how.

NU Map p344   Pan-Asian €€

☎ 8870 9811; Schlüterstrasse 55; 2-course weekday lunch €6, mains €8-18; Ⓢ Savignyplatz

With its sexy waitresses, manga flicks and trendy communal tables, we were afraid that Nu was more about good looks than good food. Fortunately, not so. The kitchen delivers almost invariably with convincing results. The two-course lunch specials are a steal.

SCHWARZES CAFÉ Map p344   Café €

☎ 313 8038; Kantstrasse 148; dishes €4.50-9;
☾ 24h; Ⓜ Ⓢ Zoologischer Garten, Savignyplatz

Not many cafés have shown as much staying power as this rambling multi-floor icon, founded in 1978 by 15 women. It's great for a bite, a beer or breakfast – no matter where the hands of the clock are sitting. The toilets are a hoot, the little garden idyllic.

STELLA ALPINA Map p344 Italian €€
☎ 322 2805; Suarezstrasse 4; 2-course weekday lunch €7.50, mains €6-18; ⏰ noon-midnight; Ⓞ Sophie-Charlotte-Platz

After a day of museum hopping around Schloss Charlottenburg, you deserve a good meal, and you'll get one at this congenial northern Italian trattoria. Their pizza is reputedly among the best in town but the chef also puts in an inspired performance with any of the veal, lamb and fish dishes. It has delicious weekday lunches too.

CHEAP EATS
LON MEN NOODLE HOUSE
Map p344 Taiwanese €
☎ 3151 9678; Kantstrasse 33; soups €2.40-6.50; ⏰ noon-midnight; Ⓡ Savignyplatz

On days when a brisk breeze whips across Berlin, a bowl of steamy soup can be as welcome a sight as your best friend. This tiny and unassuming kitchen churns out authentic broths, paired with thin or wide rice noodles and vegetables, meats or wontons. Most are pretty spicy, but you can ask the cooks to lay off the heat.

WILMERSDORF
Sedate Wilmersdorf isn't a famous food-lovers' destination, although there are some true gems waiting for those wishing to completely escape the tourist track. If it's variety you're after, head to Pariser Strasse, the main eats street, lined with a tasty mix of Tex-Mex, Indian, Spanish, German and other cuisine outlets.

DIE QUADRIGA
Map p344 Gourmet €€€
☎ 2140 5650; Eislebener Strasse 14, inside Brandenburger Hof Hotel; menus €55-115; ⏰ dinner Mon-Fri; Ⓞ Augsburger Strasse

This intimate dining shrine is a Berlin highlight. Michelin-starred chef, Bobby Bräuer, has a knack for picking only the finest ingredients and whipping them up into gimmick-free meals. Enjoy them in the elegant setting of a 1920's salon, complete with Frank Lloyd Wright chairs and live piano music (some nights). The wine list features the 850 best German wines. Reservations required.

JIMMY'S DINER Map p344 American €
☎ 886 0607; Pariser Strasse 41; mains €6.50-10; ⏰ 3pm-open end; Ⓞ Spichernstrasse, Uhlandstrasse

If you're hunting for a juicy burger but want to avoid the Hard Rock Café herd, give Jimmy's a shot. Founded in 1987 and named after the owner's golden retriever, this is a veritable 'diner-saur' in town. No half-baked culinary stunts here; so just settle into a Naugahyde booth and order up some classic grub, thoughtfully served until the wee hours.

LONG AN Map p344 Vietnamese €€
☎ 2196 2055; Prager Strasse 2a; mains €6-12; ⏰ 6-11.30pm Mon-Thu, noon-11.30pm Fri-Sun; Ⓞ Spichernstrasse

This place really spices up Wilmersdorf. Tables are usually packed, and the food is why. The cooks here really understand the mysteries of lemongrass, coriander, mint, tamarind and other exotic spices and turn them into dishes so good you'll be tempted to lick the plate. Prices are reasonable and the servers are not stingy with the smiles.

NAMASKAR Map p344 Indian €€
☎ 8868 0648; Pariser Strasse 56; lunch specials €5-7, mains €10-18; ⏰ 5pm-midnight Mon, noon-midnight Tue-Sun; Ⓞ Spichernstrasse

Never mind the tacky green Astroturf underneath the sidewalk tables, this is one classy restaurant serving some of the best Indian

BERLIN'S BEST...
Asian Mao Thai (p185)
Celebrity Spotting Margaux (p170)
Exotic Flair Kasbah (p169)
German Altes Zollhaus (p181)
Gourmet Die Quadriga (left)
Italian Vine e Libri (p171)
Lunch La Poulette (p185)
Sushi Sasaya (p187)
With Kids Marché (p175)

Eating

WILMERSDORF

cuisine in town. Fortunately, the interior is considerably more stylish, with servers clad in clay-coloured robes (called *salwar kameez*) floating among the saffron-yellow walls. The marinated shrimp served in the *kadhai* (sort of an Indian wok) are a speciality.

QBA Map p344 — Cuban €€

☎ 8855 1754; Konstanzer Strasse 1; mains €8-18; ☟ dinner; ⊕ Adenauerplatz

Fans spin lazily beneath smoke-stained ceilings, the furniture has seen better days and Fidel and Che stare down upon the bubbly crowd. QBA looks as if a tornado has lifted the place straight out of Havana and whirled it all the way to Berlin. The fiery fare, tasty cocktails and respectable cigar selection all keep the customers happy. Also in Mitte (Map pp340–1; ☎ 2804 0505; Oranienburger Strasse 45; ⊕ Oranienburger Tor).

TRATTORIA TOSCANA

Map pp338-9 — Italian €€

☎ 862 1620; Badensche Strasse 33; mains €8-17; ☟ 11.30am-midnight Tue-Sun; ⊕ Berliner Strasse

Although a bit out of the way, every step will be rewarded when you arrive in Romeo Brandi's culinary realm. Sharing his passion for good food comes naturally to this charismatic Neapolitan. Flavours are woven together like fine tapestries into such dishes as tagliatelle with truffles, which involves must-see tableside pyrotechnics in a hollowed-out parmesan wheel. Reservations advised.

CHEAP EATS

BIER'S CURRY 195 Map p344 — Sausages €

☎ 881 8942; Kurfürstendamm 195; snacks €2-3.50; ☟ 11-5am; ⊕ Uhlandstrasse

A much-loved institution, this sausage parlour satisfies the proletarian hunger pangs of deep-pocketed locals, who have the option of washing down their franks with a bottle of Dom Perignon (€150). It's also a popular hangout for off-duty chefs, who often keep the place jumping until the wee hours.

SUSHI BERLIN Map p344 — Sushi €

☎ 881 2790; Pariser Strasse 44; nigiri €1.50-2.50, maki €2.50-7.50; ☟ noon-midnight Mon-Sat, 4-11pm Sun; ⊕ Spichernstrasse

This squeaky-clean hole-in-the-wall, in business since 1991, claims to be Berlin's oldest

sushi bar. Perhaps, but what really matters is that the fishy morsels here are super-fresh, expertly cut and affordably priced. You can save by ordering combinations (€11 to €18).

SCHÖNEBERG

If you're not sure what you're hungry for, take the U-Bahn to Nollendorfplatz and start walking south. Chances are you'll end up at one of the two dozen or so eateries between the station and Hauptstrasse. Expect a great range in tastes – Turkish, Indian, Nepalese, Thai, Greek, and then some – but not in price: practically all are quite reasonable on the wallet.

BUDDHA HAUS Map pp338-9 — Tibetan €€

☎ 7050 9959; Akazienstrasse 27; mains €5-15; ☟ noon-midnight; ⊕ Eisenacher Strasse

A haze of good smells greets you the moment you step into this cheerful eatery, with its natural brick walls, lampion-style lights and soothing music. The menu is a spectrum of flavours packaged into healthfully prepared stews, soups, sautés, *momos* (stuffed breads), curries and other appetising dishes. Vegetarians will be happy here as well. In summer, tables spill out into the courtyard.

HAKUIN Map pp338-9 — Vegetarian €€€

☎ 218 2027; Martin-Luther-Strasse 1; mains €15-19; ☟ dinner Tue-Sun, lunch Sun; ⊕ Wittenbergplatz

No matter how hectic the day, as soon as you step inside this Zen Buddhist-run restaurant, stress evaporates as fast as light drizzle on summer asphalt. Dishes eschew meat, make ample use of organic ingredients and have such poetic names as *Surabaya* (an array of Indonesian savoury dishes with rice) or *Kabuki* (a smorgasbord of Japanese delicacies). Smoking is a no-no.

TOP FIVE SCHÖNEBERG EATS

- Dolce Pizza (p180)
- Ousies (opposite)
- Petite Europe (opposite)
- Storch (p180)
- Trattora á Muntagnola (p180)

GETTING VERSED IN *WURST*

Its aroma wafting from many a street corner catches your nose like a crisp left hook. It's been ravenously gobbled up by chancellors, Madonna and George W, and has even been celebrated in popular song. 'It', of course, is the humble *Currywurst*, the iconic treat that's as much a part of Berlin's cultural tapestry as the Brandenburg Gate.

To the uncouth or uninitiated, we're talking about a smallish fried or grilled *wiener* sliced into bite-sized ringlets, swimming in a spicy tomato sauce, dusted with curry powder and served on a flimsy paper plate with a plastic tooth-pick for stabbing. Sound prosaic? Well, what remains a mystery to many outsiders resonates deeply in the discerning German's soul. The *Wurst* itself is subtly spiced and served with or without its crunchy epidermis. The sauce is redolent with mysterious spices, and the paper plate is the perfect expression of German egalitarianism.

The people of Hamburg might disagree, but Berliners know that their city is the true birthplace of this beloved calorie bomb. The first sausage officially hit the curry at the steaming *Imbiss* (snack bar) of Herta Heuwer on September 4, 1949 – later receiving patent No 721319. From here it started its triumphal course to snack stands across the nation. In the German capital, *Currywursts* are so ubiquitous that they're even sold by roving street vendors with steaming mini-kitchens strapped around their bellies.

What exactly went into Herta's sauce will never be known, as in 1999 she took the secret to her grave. Her contribution to culinary history has garnered her a plaque at Kantstrasse 101, however, where her Imbiss once stood. And, as if to cement Berlin's claim to being the German *Currywurst* capital, the **Deutsches Currywurst Museum** (p114) was expected to open in late 2006.

There's always a healthy debate about where to find the best dog in town, but we're going to stick our necks out and share our very own favourite top three, which are **Konnopke's Imbiss** (p187), **Witty's** (p180) and **Curry 36** (p183).

For more, check out *Best of the Wurst* (2004), a hilarious short film made by a Korean American woman about her quest to get to know Berlin and its people one sausage at a time. See it for free on **iFilm** (www.ifilm.com).

LA COCOTTE

Map pp338-9   French €€

☎ 7895 7658; Vorbergstrasse 10; mains €8-15;
◷ 6pm-1am; ◉ Eisenacher Strasse

The look of the place, and the food on your plate, are so French you may actually have to pinch yourself to remember you're still in Berlin. The menu is more country-style than *haute*, with such flavour-intense dishes as *coq au vin*, boar ragout and goulash all making appearances. Choose between sitting inside the charming Art Nouveau building or outside on the petite terrace.

OUSIES

Map pp338-9   Greek €€

☎ 216 7957; Grunewaldstrasse 16; dishes €3.50-14; ◷ dinner; ◉ Eisenacher Strasse

It's a tight squeeze at this perennially popular neighbourhood haunt, but that just adds to the Hellenic flair of this so-called *ouzeria,* the Greek version of a Spanish tapas bar. Build your meal from such classics as *tsaziki* or *dolmades*, or go exotic with *spetsofai,* a hearty sausage, or *eleosalata,* a black olive paste, cuddling up with tomato and feta cheese. Reservations advised.

PAPAYA AM KLEISTPARK

Map pp338-9   Thai €€

☎ 8149 4254; Hauptstrasse 159; mains €6-13;
◷ noon-midnight; ◉ Kleistpark

Phornphilai and Michael run this contemporary Thai bistro with great charm and aplomb. Bathed in soft colours and simply furnished, it's the go-to place for tastebud temptations from the north-east of Thailand. Everything's prepared as authentically as possible, considering we're in Berlin and not Khon Kaen. A typical dish is sticky rice with chicken and, of course, papaya.

PETITE EUROPE

Map pp338-9   Italian €

☎ 781 2964; Langenscheidtstrasse 1; mains €4.50-12; ◷ dinner; ◉ Kleistpark

This earthy little eatery has the defining hallmarks of a genuine and trusted neigh-bourhood spot: no-nonsense food and a relaxed, friendly ambience. Night after night, tables fill up with patrons hungry for home-made pastas and wood-fired pizzas. It's not a unique kind of food that you'd travel too far out of your way for, although you probably wouldn't be disappointed if you did.

SHIMA   Map pp338-9   pan-Asian €€

☎ 211 1990; Schwäbische Strasse 5; mains €9-18;
⊗ 6.30pm-1am; ⊜ Eisenacher Strasse

This restaurant-lounge combination took foodies on a culinary spin around Asia long before the Pan-Asian concept caught fire in Berlin. Indian *chapati* (bread) to Korean *kimchee* (fermented cabbage), Japanese tempura to Thai curry or Indonesian chicken satay – almost everything is spirited in flavour and fanciful in presentation. The lounge serves more than 100 cocktails.

STORCH   Map pp338-9   Alsatian French €€

☎ 784 2059; Wartburgstrasse 54; flammekuche €8, mains €14-20; ⊗ dinner; ⊜ Eisenacher Strasse

The floors are worn smooth here from the legions of patrons eager to nibble on crusty *flammekuche* (the Alsatian spin on the pizza) or dig into stuffed goose, wild-boar *ragout* or other robust mains. Owner Volker Haupt-vogel – whose mellow demeanour belies his punk-rocker past – is often around to greet patrons with disarming charm.

TIM'S CANADIAN DELI

Map pp338-9   Café €

☎ 2175 6960; Maassenstrasse 14; mains €5-13;
⊗ 8-1am; ⊜ Nollendorfplatz

When the sun's out, there are few better places for breakfast than this corner café's convivial outdoor tables and benches, with views of the Winterfeldtplatz. At other times, it's the bison burgers, bagels, steaks and other feel-good food that keep the cash register ringing. The good-value lunches for a mere €5, including soft drink, exude a magnetic pull on wallet-watchers.

TRATTORIA Á MUNTAGNOLA

Map pp338-9   Italian €€

☎ 211 6642; Fuggerstrasse 27; pizza €5.50-9.50, pasta €9.50-11.50, mains €15-20; ⊗ dinner;
⊜ Viktoria-Luise-Platz, Wittenbergplatz

The owners here hail from the deep Italian south, a rural region called Basilicata, whose sun-baked hills have spawned a rustic cuisine with feisty flavours. Olive oil, *prosciutto*, even sorrel, dandelions and fennel are imported straight from the Boot and turned into crispy pizzas, homemade pastas and mouth-watering meat dishes. The lasagne, braised lamb and fried calamari are all top choices. Kids are welcome.

CHEAP EATS

DOLCE PIZZA

Map pp338-9   Italian €

☎ 2005 1585; Maassenstrasse 6; pizza €1.50-10;
⊗ 11am-10pm; ⊜ Nollendorfplatz

It's no secret: this is the best pizza in Schöneberg. Queues can sometimes be discouragingly long, but if you hang in there you'll be rewarded with a thin and crispy crust, fresh and imaginative toppings and swift and friendly service. There's great ice cream next door. There's also a branch in **Kreuzberg** (Map pp336–7;
☎ 7889 5998; Hagelberger Strasse 16;
⊗ noon-9pm Mon-Fri, 4-9pm Sat & Sun;
⊜ Mehringdamm).

HISAR

Map pp338-9   Middle Eastern €

S-Bahnhof Yorckstrasse; dishes €2.50-5; ⊗ 10am-midnight; ⊕ Yorckstrasse

It may be off-the-beaten track, but tried-and-true Hisar is, beyond doubt, one of the best doner kebab stands in this here town. You will no doubt be glad you made the pilgrimage.

RANI

Map pp338-9   Indian €

☎ 215 2673; Goltzstrasse 32; dishes €3.50-7;
⊗ 11am-1am; ⊜ Nollendorfplatz

In an area crowded with Indian restaurants, Rani has defied the odds and stayed popular even after many years in business. Curries here are simple but satisfying, and are best paired with a tangy *lassi* (yogurt drink), especially on a balmy day when the pavement tables make for good people-watching.

WITTY'S

Map p344   Sausages €

☎ 853 7055; Wittenbergplatz; snacks €2-4; ⊗ 11-1am; ⊜ Wittenbergplatz

If there is such as thing as healthy fast food, you'll probably find it at this 'doggeria' across from the KaDeWe department store. Sink your teeth into one of Witty's certified organic sausages and you'll quickly discover the reason for its cult status. Dipping their crispy French fries into one of the homemade sauces – mayonnaise, peanut or garlic – is heavenly.

KREUZBERG

Kreuzberg is 'back', or so goes conventional wisdom, although we doubt that it was ever really out. Fact is, this multicultural cauldron has a lot going on in the gastro department. Not much gourmet cuisine here (though there is some to be found) but plenty of bohemian cafés, old-school pubs, casual 'donerias' and the great *Türkenmarkt* (Turkish Market) for fresh anything. The main drags are Bergmannstrasse in western Kreuzberg, and Oranienstrasse and Schlesische Strasse in eastern Kreuzberg.

ALTES ZOLLHAUS
Map pp336-7   German €€€
☎ 692 3300; Carl-Herz-Ufer 30; 3-/4-/5-course meals €38/43/48, mains €20-25; ⏰ dinner Tue-Sat; ◉ Prinzenstrasse
A customs house in an earlier incarnation, this elegant half-timbered jewel hugs an idyllic spot right on the Landwehrkanal. Try scoring a garden table or else make do with the somewhat stuffy interior, which is still a suitable setting for the upmarket and innovative German cuisine, laced with Mediterranean touches, prepared by chef Herbert Beltle. First-timers can't go wrong with the roast duck.

TOP FIVE KREUZBERG EATS
- Austria (below)
- Bar Centrale (below)
- Café Jacques (p182)
- Henne (p182)
- Le Cochon Bourgeois (p182)

AUSTRIA Map pp336-7   Austrian €€
☎ 694 4440; Bergmannstrasse 30; mains €13-18; ⏰ dinner; ◉ Gneisenaustrasse
With its collection of deer antlers, Romy Schneider posters and rustic floors, this place looks like a hunting lodge designed in Hollywood. Clichés aside, the *Wiener schnitzel* (€16.50) – thin, tender and huge – is indeed worthy of an Oscar, and is best paired with a cool Kapsreiter beer. Thursday's traditional special, suckling pig, brings out the devotees in droves.

BAR CENTRALE
Map pp336-7   Italian €€
☎ 786 2989; Yorckstrasse 82; appetisers & pastas €7-14, mains €15-18; ◉ Mehringdamm
Send your tastebuds on a tailspin at this upmarket yet down-to-earth restaurant serving creative Italian (not a pizza in sight). You

Time for a doner kebab, Kreuzberg

could easily build a meal from the antipasti alone: grilled baby calamari, truffled foie gras and tuna *carpaccio* are just some of the tempting selections. Berlin mayor Klaus Wowereit, so he tells us, is a regular here.

CAFÉ JACQUES
Map pp336-7   Mediterranean €€

☎ 694 1048; Maybachufer 8; mains €7.50-15; ⏲ dinner; ⓞ Schönleinstrasse

Fresh flowers, flattering candlelight, delicious wine – this café might just be the perfect spot for a casual date. But, frankly, you only have to be in love with good food to enjoy this Gallic charmer. The blackboard menu lists lots of Mediterranean supper choices rooted either in French or North African cuisine. The couscous is excellent.

CHANDRA KUMARI
Map pp336-7   Sri Lankan €€

☎ 694 1203; Gneisenaustrasse 4; mains €5-13; ⏲ noon-midnight; ⓞ Mehringdamm

Blending a bouquet of coriander, cumin, coconut and other big flavours, the food here is so perky it may get you off your Prozac. Organic vegetables and hormone-free meats end up in rich curries paired with fragrant rice, pancake-like *appe*, or noodle-like *iddi-appe*. The undecided should order a *Reistafel* (a number of small Indonesian-style dishes served with rice) to try a variety of tastes.

HENNE
Map pp336-7   German €

☎ 614 7730; Leuschnerdamm 25; half chicken €6; ⏲ dinner Tue-Sun; ⓞ Moritzplatz

You know those restaurants with menus a mile-long, where it takes forever to make up your mind? Well, you won't have that problem at this Berlin institution, whose name *is* the menu: roast chicken it is, take it or leave it. It's a concept that's been a cult since 1907, so who are we to argue? There's garden seating in summer. Reservations recommended.

HORVÁTH
Map pp336-7   Gourmet €€€

☎ 6128 9992; Paul-Lincke-Ufer 44a; 3-course menu €30, mains €18-24; ⏲ 6pm-midnight Tue-Sun; ⓞ Kottbusser Tor, Schönleinstrasse

Eastern Kreuzberg may still feel more grunge than gourmet, but this food tem-

ple could mark a turning point for the neighbourhood. Local star chef, Wolfgang Müller, treats his foodie patrons to such culinary flights of fancy as caramelized potato soup with frogs legs, or Barbary duck with shitake mushrooms. For the full survey of his skills, order the 10-course small-plate menu (€60).

IL CASOLARE
Map pp336-7   Pizza €

☎ 6950 6610; Grimmstrasse 30; pizza €4.70-7.50; ⏲ noon-midnight; ⓞ Kottbusser Tor

We almost don't want to recommend this place, because its popularity has given the staff a serious case of attitude, but alas, there's a pair of reasons to put up with them: the canal-side setting and the pizza – thin, crispy, cheap and wagon-wheel sized. Toppings range from classic to crude (horse meat anyone?) and the wine flows freely. Smiles cost extra. The I Due Forni branch in Prenzlauer Berg (Map pp332–3; ☎ 4401 7333; Schönhauser Allee 12; ⓞ Senefelderplatz) is equally popular.

KUCHEN KAISER
Map pp336-7   International €

☎ 6140 2697; Oranienplatz 11-13; mains €4.50-10; ⏲ 9am-midnight; ⓞ Moritzplatz, Kottbusser Tor

The 'emperor of cakes' (as the name, none too humbly, translates) started feeding the sugar cravings of royals, celebrities and mere mortals in 1866. Yummy cakes remain a primary draw for the sundry crowd of old-timers and hipsters, only now they've got competition from the great selection of breakfasts (served until 4pm) and the creative crossover cuisine of chef Ahmad Shadabudin.

LE COCHON BOURGEOIS
Map pp336-7   French €€€

☎ 693 0101; Fichtestrasse 24; mains €18-22; ⏲ 6pm-midnight Tue-Sat; ⓞ Südstern

A century ago, a grocer occupied the lovingly redecorated rooms of the 'Bourgeois Pig', where you can now indulge in the solid but clever Franco-German cuisine of chef Hannes Behrmann. Enjoy the ambience of candlelight, fresh flowers and live piano music, while digging into aromatic lamb, duck or fish creations. The *crème brûlée* (caramelised custard) is the perfect coda to a delightful meal.

MORGENLAND

Map pp336-7   Café €

☎ 611 3291; Skalitzer Strasse 35; breakfast €5.50-7, buffet €9, mains €5-12; ☽ 9am-1am Mon-Fri, 10am-1am Sat & Sun; ⊕ Görlitzer Bahnhof

This eastern Kreuzberg café is a breakfast institution, especially on Sunday when everyone from red-eyed night owls to churchgoers invade for the table-bending brunch (reservations advised). At other times it's a relaxed café with pan-European food – pasta to lamb to fried fish. There's a nice terrace in summer.

SEEROSE

Map pp336-7   Vegetarian €

☎ 6981 5927; Mehringdamm 47; small/big plate €3.50/5; ☽ 10am-10pm Mon-Sat, noon-9pm Sun; ⊕ Mehringdamm

Vegetarians in the know flock to this little café which tempts tastebuds with delicious, fresh and wholesome casseroles, soups, salads, pastas and pressed juices. Order at the buffet-style counter, then wait for the friendly staff to bring out your food while being showered by Beethoven or other classics.

WELTRESTAURANT MARKTHALLE

Map pp336-7   German €€

☎ 617 5502; Pücklerstrasse 34; mains €7.50-16; ☽ 9am-midnight; ⊕ Görlitzer Bahnhof

This mellow pub has a century-old pedigree and new-found fame as a location for the 2003 Berlin cult flick Herr Lehmann. Come for breakfast (served until 5pm), fresh and creative salads at lunchtime, or a heaping helping of Schweinebraten (roast pork), the favourite dish of the film's title character. It pairs exceptionally well with a mug of foamy Berliner Bürgerbräu, brewed just a few miles away in Köpenick.

CHEAP EATS

CURRY 36 Map pp336-7   Sausages €

☎ 251 7368; Mehringdamm 36; snacks €1.50-5; ☽ 9am-4am Mon-Sat, 11am-3am Sun; ⊕ Mehringdamm

Don't let the prosaic name deter you, this Imbiss makes some of best Currywurst in town, and has around-the-clock queues to prove it. Service is swift and friendly, and the sausage has a nicely spiced bite to it.

HABIBI Map pp336-7   Middle Eastern €

☎ 6165 8346; Oranienstrasse 30; snacks €2.50-5; ☽ 10am-3am; ⊕ Kottbusser Tor

This small snack chain is the granddaddy of Berlin's falafel and shwarma circuit. Its late hours make it a favourite spot to restore balance to the brain after an extended bar-hop. Order a freshly pressed carrot juice for an additional energy jolt.

It also has another branch at Körtestrasse 35 (Map pp336–7; ⊕ Südstern) and a further two in Schöneberg: Winterfeldtplatz 24 (Map pp338–9; ⊕ Nollendorfplatz) and Akazienstrasse 9 (Map pp338–9; ⊕ Eisenacher Strasse).

SESAM Map pp336-7   Middle Eastern €

☎ 694 6801; Gneisenaustrasse 22; dishes €2.50-7; ☽ noon-3am; ⊕ Gneisenaustrasse

In a neighbourhood swarming with falafel and shwarma joints, Sesam stands out from the pack. The brightly coloured walls and tile mosaics are cheerful and welcoming, but it's the tasty trio of sauces (garlicky yogurt, yellow sweet and sour, and spicy red) accompanying all dishes that keeps this place humming until the wee hours.

FRIEDRICHSHAIN

Friedrichshain does bars best, to be sure, but that doesn't mean that no decent bites are in sight. You'll find plenty of down-to-earth eateries sprinkled around Boxhagener Platz and its side streets. And, thanks to a local populace teeming with starving students and artists, your hard-earned euros will stretch further here than in any of the other central districts.

ALARABI

Map pp336-7   Middle Eastern €

☎ 2977 1995; Krossener Strasse 19; mains €4-8; ☽ 10am-midnight; ⊕ ⊞ Warschauer Strasse, ⊕ Frankfurter Tor

Candlelight, exotic décor and a small fleet of shishas (water pipes) turns this cosy corner eatery into a warm and welcoming refuge. Free sesame seed dip with pita bread arrives while you peruse the menu, which is especially strong on appetisers (the €9 platter is enough for two). The service can be a bit challenged when it's crowded.

MISERIA & NOBILTÀ

Map pp336-7   Italian €€

☎ 2904 9249; Kopernikusstrasse 16; mains €10-20; ☼ dinner; ◉ ⓡ Warschauer Strasse, ◉ Frankfurter Tor

When Eduardo Scarpetti penned the comedy *Poverty and Nobility* in 1888, he didn't know that, over a century later, it would inspire the name of this popular family-run trattoria. Thanks to the gracious owners, you'll definitely feel more king than pauper here, when digging into their deftly prepared – and daily changing – southern Italian compositions. Bring a good appetite.

NOI QUATTRO

Map pp332-3   Italian €€

☎ 2404 5622; Strausberger Platz 2; mains €8-18; ☼ noon-midnight Mon-Sat, 10am-midnight Sun; ◉ Strausberger Platz

Top-notch *nuova cucina italiana* (new Italian cooking) with a view of the 'worker's palaces' – where else but Berlin can you get this? Noi Quattro doesn't shine with fancy décor but instead puts its emphasis on premium-quality ingredients and delightful, if occasionally out-there, creations including chocolate tagliatelle with foie gras and kumquats, wild boar with gingerbread pasta, or caramelised goat cheese may all make appearances on the seasonally changing menu.

PAPA NO Map pp336-7   Pan-Asian €

☎ 2007 8821; Warschauer Strasse 81; lunch €5, meals under €10; ☼ noon-midnight; ◉ Frankfurter Tor

No is a form of traditional Japanese musical drama, known for its slow, minimalist movements. Frankly, we think it's a bit of an odd choice for a name because this is one hip and energetic eatery. The menu stretches beyond Nippon nosh to include authoritatively spiced curries, Thai soups, chicken satay and other Asian classics. They do free delivery within a 5km radius.

PAPAYA Map pp336-7   Thai €

☎ 2977 1231; Krossener Strasse 11; mains €6.50-14.50; ☼ noon-midnight; ◉ ⓡ Warschauer Strasse, ◉ Frankfurter Tor

You can watch the chefs stirring up a storm in the open kitchen at this bustling café, which is a favourite fuel stop for scenesters ready to launch themselves into a night on the razzle. Perkily spiced, coconut-based *tom ka* soups, tangy *pad thai* noodles, toothsome Thai basil chicken and other classics are all delicious hangover preventions. If tables are full, just head across the street to the sister property called **Malago** (Map pp336–7; ☎ 2123 8848; Krossener Strasse 15) which, not coincidentally, is the Thai word for – you guessed it – papaya.

PI-BAR

Map pp336-7   Vegetarian & Fish €€

☎ 2936 7581; Gabriel-Max-Strasse 17; mains €7-17; ☼ 4pm-midnight Mon-Sat, 10am-midnight Sun; ◉ ⓡ Warschauer Strasse, ◉ Frankfurter Tor

It didn't take long for the Pi-Bar crew to capture the hearts and tummies of locals and visiting revellers. The cooks make wonderful casseroles, risottos, stir-fries and other dishes that taste fresh and vivid, yet use only vegetables and fish. The décor is Friedrichshain funky, with ample sofas, flattering light flitting from paper lamps, and colour-drenched walls.

SMART DELI

Map pp336-7   Sushi €€

☎ 0160-9653 9686; Grünberger Strasse 90; meals €10-20; ☼ noon-8pm Mon-Sat; ◉ Samariterstrasse

This trendy little *Imbiss*, run by a pair of charming Japanese women, is a great place to get a protein fix without depleting your travel budget. Sushi morsels start at €3.50 and are consumed while crowding around stand-up tables. You can also stock up on manga comics, imported Japanese lifestyle magazines and Hello Kitty candy.

UMSPANNWERK OST

Map pp332-3   Modern German €€

☎ 4280 9497; Palisadenstrasse 48; mains €8-16; ☼ 11.30am-11pm; ◉ Weberwiese

This industrial-chic restaurant doesn't try to hide its past as a transformer station – it embraces it. There's still plenty of energy buzzing about the large dining room, hemmed by brick walls and huge arched windows. Watch the cooks prepare seasonally changing pasta and meat selections in an open kitchen, then repair downstairs for an after-dinner theatre or jazz performance (p208).

Eating

FRIEDRICHSHAIN

CHEAP EATS

NIL Map pp336-7   Sudanese €

☎ 2904 7713; Grünberger Strasse 52; dishes €2-4;
🕒 11-2am; ⊖ 🚇 Warschauer Strasse

If you're tired of the usual doner sandwich,
give this exotic outpost a try. Most people
just order a *tamiya,* the Sudanese spin on
the falafel paired with salad, yoghurt and
peanut sauce. For a more in-depth investigation, order the Sudan Teller, which comes
with intricate spiced *fohl* (beans), eggplant
salad and curd cheese tinged with fenu-
greek and cumin.

TIGRIS

Map pp336-7   Middle Eastern €

☎ 2935 1212; Simon-Dach-Strasse 11; snacks €2-5;
🕒 11am-midnight; ⊖ 🚇 Warschauer Strasse

Tigris' tasty falafel and *shwarma* sandwiches are favourites with people out on
the night-time prowl along this well-
trodden party lane. In summer, the pavement tables offer a great vantage point
for people-watching.

PRENZLAUER BERG

You'll find some good restaurants dotted
around this increasingly chi-chi district,
with promising new challengers appearing all the time. Possibilities cluster around
the Wasserturm, Kollwitzplatz and Helmholtzplatz, although you're perhaps more
likely to find a personal favourite along the
residential streets connecting them, such
as Lychener Strasse, Schliemannstrasse or
Rykestrasse. A clutch of innovative upmarket eateries have recently sprung up near
Schönhauser Allee station.

DREI

Map pp332-3   Californian €€

☎ 4171 5718; Lychener Strasse 30; mains €11-17;
🕒 6pm-midnight Mon-Sat, 10am-midnight Sun;
⊖ Eberswalder Strasse

A bar, lounge and restaurant in one (hence
the name, 'three'), this snazzy place helped
launch Helmholtzplatz' evolution into a
hipster haunt. The menu is loaded with
interesting items, pairing healthy ingredients
with low-fat cooking techniques. Coconut
chicken, ostrich filets and mussels in lemongrass broth are typical entries. Even waist-
watching Beverly Hills belles would approve.

TOP FIVE PRENZLAUER BERG EATS

- Gugelhof (below)
- Mao Thai (below)
- Neugrüns Köche (p186)
- Sasaya (p187)
- Trattoria Paparazzi (p187)

The branch in **Charlottenburg** (Map p344;
☎ 5471 0271; Savignyplatz 2; 🕒 lunch &
dinner daily; 🚇 Savignyplatz) serves a two-
course 'express lunch' for only €7.

GUGELHOF

Map pp332-3   Alsatian French €€

☎ 442 9229; Knaackstrasse 37; mains €8-14;
🕒 dinner Mon-Fri, 10am-midnight Sat & Sun;
⊖ Senefelderplatz

This unpretentious place is a favourite
among Berlin politicos, and not just since Bill
Clinton popped by a few years ago. You'll
often spot familiar faces hunkered over the
plain wooden tables and, like the rest of
the crowd, fortifying themselves on hearty
choucroute (a sauerkraut-based stew), cheese
fondue, *flammekuche* (a pizza-like dish) and
other Alsatian soul food.

LA POULETTE Map pp332-3   French €€

☎ 4403 8012; Knaackstrasse 30-32; mains €12-24,
3-course lunch €8; 🕒 noon-2am; ⊖ Senefelderplatz

The name means 'little chicken' and refers
to the chef's daughter. That's her smiling
down at diners from the flowery mural
behind the bar. It's this personal touch
that gives La Poulette an edge among the
trendy cafés surrounding the Wasserturm.
That, and the incredibly good-value lunches
which allow you to sample fancy creations
at pauper's prices.

MAO THAI Map pp332-3   Thai-Chinese €€

☎ 441 9261; Wörther Strasse 30; mains €8.50-20;
🕒 noon-midnight daily; ⊖ Senefelderplatz

If you love Thai food, your tastebuds will
do cartwheels at this sophisticated Siam
outpost. The duck is the signature dish, but
even simple *pad thai* noodles demonstrate
surprising complexity. The classy art and
furniture, all imported from Thailand, provide eye candy, as do the artistic garnishes –
even a lowly radish tastes better when
carved into a bird.

Eating

PRENZLAUER BERG

Mao Thai (p185)

MASSAI

Map pp332-3   Eritrean €€

☎ 4862 5595; Lychener Strasse 12; mains €7-12.50; ☯ dinner daily; ⊕ Eberswalder Strasse

Everything is exotic about this East African bar and restaurant: the décor, with its woven tables, tent and cylindrical lamps; the harp-like music; and certainly the menu that flaunts zebra steak and crocodile filet alongside lamb, beef, chicken and vegetarian dishes. All food is served family-style on a traditional platter and scooped up with *injera,* spongy bread that soaks up every bit of flavour.

NEUGRÜNS KÖCHE

Map pp332-3   German/Mediterranean €€

☎ 4401 2092; Schönhauser Allee 135a; 3-/4-course menu around €27/31; ☯ dinner Mon-Sat; ⊕ Eberswalder Strasse

When this place opened for business in 2005, it was an instant runaway hit. The formula is deceptively simple: take fresh, regional, organic ingredients and turn them into two different multi-course menus nightly. One features updated German fare (veal ragout strudel, pork cutlet with lemon mashed potato), the other goes Mediterranean (braised beef, sage gnocchi, buffalo mozzarella).

OKI

Map pp332-3   Japanese & German €€

☎ 4985 3130; Oderberger Strasse 23; mains €8-17; ☯ 3-11pm Tue-Sun; ⊕ Eberswalder Strasse

Fusion cuisine can be a bit of a hit or miss affair, so our sceptics' antenna went on alert when we heard about a restaurant that was pairing Japanese and northern German foods. No need to worry, Oki's cooks perform successful feats of culinary alchemy. Try such playful treats as seared ahi tuna on a bed of bacon-braised cucumber, or fish soup dotted with caramelised apple chunks.

RICE QUEEN

Map pp332-3   Pan-Asian €

☎ 4404 5800; Danziger Strasse 13; mains €5-8; ☯ dinner; ⊕ Eberswalder Strasse

The bright and colourful décor will most likely cheer you up even on the grimmest of winter nights, while the posters of Chinese horoscope animals are great conversation starters. But the main reason to pay a visit to Rice Queen is the intriguing flavour bombs produced by chef Garry Chan. His restless palate and adventurous kitchen draws inspiration from the cuisines of Malaysia, China, Thailand and Indonesia, usually with tantalizing results.

SALSABIL

Map pp332-3　　　　　　　　　　　Arabic €

☎ 4403 3846; Raumerstrasse 14; mains €5-7;
🕒 dinner Tue-Sat; ❻ Eberswalder Strasse

Sweet smoke wafting from water pipes
blends smoothly with the fragrant aroma
of succulent lamb, fluffy couscous and
mysteriously spiced vegetables at this
relaxed eatery. For the complete pasha
feel, surrender to the sumptuous languor
of the private alcoves with thick pillows
and low tables. Also try the exotic juices,
like *gallab*, a rich blend of dates, almonds
and rose water.

SASAYA

Map pp332-3　　　　　　　　　　Japanese €€

☎ 4471 7721; Lychener Strasse 50; mains €5-25;
🕒 noon-3pm & 6-10.30pm Thu-Tue; ❻ 🚇 Schönhauser Allee

Chef Isao Sasaki hails from the island of
Hokkaido, honed his craft in New York and
now pursues his passion for creative Japanese with great fanfare in Berlin. The space
is minimalist, the food is not. Everything
we tried had perfect pitch – sushi to salads,
tempura to fish. Tables fill quickly with
Japanese expats and plugged-in locals, so
make reservations.

TRATTORIA PAPARAZZI

Map pp332-3　　　　　　　　　　　Italian €€

☎ 440 7333; Husemannstrasse 35; pizza & pasta
€8-12, other mains €15-18; 🕒 dinner;
❻ Eberswalder Strasse

When Doris Burneleit opened her first
restaurant in 1987, deep inside East Berlin, she'd never set foot in Italy, nor had
she had any formal training as a chef. Yet
she proved to be such a magician in the
kitchen that even the Italian ambassador
became a fan. She still pampers the *cog-
noscenti* in artistic country-style digs. The
malfatti (cheese and spinach dumplings) is
a speciality.

TOP FIVE BREAKFAST CAFÉS

- Café Wintergarten im Literaturhaus (p174)
- Jules Verne (p175)
- Kuchen Kaiser (p182)
- Mandala Suites (p169)
- Morgenland (p183)

VILLA RODIZIO

Map pp332-3　　　　　　　　　　Brazilian €€

☎ 4404 6900; Milastrasse 2; all-you-can-eat
rodizio €15, mains €8-17; ❻ Eberswalder Strasse

Not only carnivores and low-carb diet devotees favour this restaurant inside a gabled
and turreted mini-palace. Dinner can stretch
to two hours as you divide your attention
between the salad and appetizer buffet and
six courses of meat – bacon-wrapped turkey
to succulent lamb – grilled on skewers and
then cut at the table by *cortadores*.

CHEAP EATS

INTERSOUP

Map pp332-3　　　　　　　　International €

☎ 2327 3045; Schliemannstrasse 31; soups €4-6;
🕒 6pm-3am; 🚇 Prenzlauer Allee

At this 'den of liquidity' you can lounge in
grandma's sofas while keeping a cold or
hangover at bay with a plate of hot, steamy
soup. There's usually a delicious dozen on
the menu, ranging from tangy Thai broth to
stick-to-the-ribs pea soup. The red lanterns
were scavenged from Café Kranzler in Charlottenburg. It's self-service and the opening
hours can vary.

KONNOPKE'S IMBISS

Map pp332-3　　　　　　　　　　Sausages €

☎ 442 7765; Schönhauser Allee 44a; Currywurst
€1.50; 🕒 5.30am-8pm Mon-Fri, noon-6.30pm Sat;
❻ Eberswalder Strasse

In the history of *Currywurst* in Berlin, this
humble kitchen is legend. Times were tough
when Max and Charlotte Konnopke opened
their first shack beneath the elevated U-
Bahn tracks in 1930. Since then, the family
has weathered war and the GDR to churn
out millions of what many consider the best
wiener in town. Eat 'em while they're hot.

OUTER DISTRICTS

SPANDOWER ZOLLHAUS

Map p343　　　　　　　　　　　　German €€

☎ 333 4841; Möllentordamm 1; mains €5.50-
14.50; 🕒 3pm-midnight Mon-Sat, 11am-midnight
Sun; ❻ Altstadt Spandau

If you're in the market for German comfort
food, make a beeline to this friendly and
unpretentious restaurant inside one of the
oldest buildings in historic Spandau. The
Zollhaus Ente (duck) is a perennial favourite,
served nice and moist off the bone with a

tan as perfect as George Hamilton's. Or go the whole hog with a belt-loosening portion of *Eisbein* (roast pork knuckle).

VILLA RIXDORF Map pp336-7   German €€

☎ 6808 6000; Richardplatz 6, Neukölln; mains €4-12; ⏰ 11am-midnight; Ⓜ Karl-Marx-Strasse

This jewel, where elegant chandeliers dangle from ceilings adorned with delicate stucco ornamentation, feels light years away from bustling Berlin. It's quaint, quiet and remarkably good value. The kitchen produces classic, unpretentious German fare, served in big portions.

KROKODIL   International €-€€

☎ 6588 0094; Gartenstrasse 46-48, Köpenick; mains €6-12; ⏰ 5pm-midnight Mon-Sat, 11am-midnight Sun in summer, 3pm-midnight Sat, 11am-midnight Sun in winter; 🚉 Köpenick, then 🚌 167

In an idyllic spot right on the river Dahme, not far from the Köpenick Altstadt, this delightful place is perfect for kicking back at sunset with a cold beer in hand. Capacity crowds turn out for the Sunday brunch and weekend live music (reservations definitely advised). The food – consisting mostly of pasta, salads, casseroles and fish – is solid, but not the main reason to come. If you like it here, ask about rooms at the attached hostel.

SEEHASE   German €€

☎ 8049 6474; Am Grossen Wannsee 58-60, Zehlendorf; mains €6.50-17; ⏰ 11am-midnight; 🚉 Wannsee

The Wannsee is perfect for escaping sticky Berlin on a hot summer day, and this rustic, beloved lakeside lair is the ideal spot for capping it off. As the sun dips below the horizon, pick from a gamut of piscatorial delights – pike-perch to snapper – or go for one of the meaty German and Greek offerings.

Eating

OUTER DISTRICTS

Entertainment

Entertainment

Being entertained is what Berliners do best – even the most steadfast workaholic will have a life outside the office, and you can bet they won't be spending their evenings in front of the TV. The city's cultural and leisure opportunities span an almost impossibly broad range of tastes and interests, all at the highest level you'll find in Germany, and there's often little distinction between weekdays and weekends in terms of the quality of events.

Like most things in Berlin, the nature of the entertainment on offer varies from district to district. Since reunification the western side of town has increasingly come to seem like a backwater, catering for an older, more affluent public; Charlottenburg and Tiergarten are best known for their chic bars and theatres, while Wilmersdorf and Schöneberg are slightly less refined, but have a denser concentrations of venues, including the city's main gay area.

On the eastern side of the city, Mitte has reclaimed its status as the city's true centre, and is rapidly becoming a two-tier district. South of Oranienburger Tor you'll find the really exclusive haunts and cultural bastions, such as the Deutsches Theater, attracting more tourists, celebrities and better-heeled folk than even Tiergarten. Further north are the less elitist but equally fashionable haunts of the Berlin *Szene* (scene), as well as plenty of more down-to-earth venues extending up into lively, experimental Prenzlauer Berg.

Further east, the former squat district of Friedrichshain has boomed over the last few years, attracting a citywide reputation for its nightlife. The original spirit of the area still survives around Rigaer Strasse, where hard-core squatters run some pretty anarchic bar-clubs at a discreet distance from the main cocktail strips.

At the moment, however, it's Kreuzberg that dominates Berlin's entertainment scene, responding to Friedrichshain's growing popularity with a sudden surge of new, cool venues. Despite rising levels of fashionable sophistication, parts of the district defiantly retain the punky, alternative feel that made it famous in the 1960s, and you'll find some of the city's rowdiest bars and clubs centred on Oranienstrasse.

One thing you'll notice in every district, and arguably the real distinguishing feature of the Berlin entertainment scene, is the inventive use of the most unlikely spaces. The years of raves, squats and illegal parties have had a visible influence, and sites as diverse as breweries, vaults, swimming pools, kebab shops and even old U-Bahn tunnels have been commandeered in the name of fun. With surprises at every turn, it pays to keep your eyes open as you explore!

Newton Bar (p192), Mitte.

Listings

Zitty (€2.50) and *Tip* (€2.70) are the best of the listings magazines, full of insider tips and colourful articles, and they also produce regular annual guides to most aspects of city life. *Tip* tends to be more mainstream, while *Zitty* is younger and edgier. Monthly *Prinz* (€1.30) has its own dedicated Berlin edition, without quite the same local savvy. *Berlin Programm* (€1.60) and *Kultur Pur* (annual; €5) cover the arts in more detail. There are also dozens of free entertainment mags covering everything from nightlife to film and literature; try *Uncle Sally's, 030* or *Fresh* for club and music news. The freebie, *Siegessäule*, is the Berlin bible for all things gay and lesbian, and produces the biannual *Kompass* directory. *Sergej* magazine is strictly for men. The English-language *ExBerliner* (€2) also has a basic listings section.

The above publications are in German, but you should be able to make sense of the listings even with a minimal command of the language.

Tickets & Reservations

Outlets selling tickets to cultural and sporting events are scattered all over the city. A 15% commission charge usually applies to ticket sales. Hekticket (below) sells half-price theatre tickets from 4pm on the day of the performance; choices are limited to what's officially left unsold that day.

As well as the stores listed here, you can buy tickets in KaDeWe (p240) and the larger bookshop chains.

Box Office Theaterkasse (Map pp338–9; ☎ 2101 6960; Nollendorfplatz 7, Schöneberg; ⊖ Nollendorfplatz)

Hekticket Charlottenburg (Map p344; ☎ 230 9930; www.hekticket.de; Hardenbergstrasse 29d, Charlottenburg; ☷ 10am-8pm Mon-Sat, 2-6pm Sun; ⊖ ⊠ Zoologischer Garten)

Hekticket Mitte (Map pp340–1; ☎ 2431 2431; www .hekticket.de; Karl-Liebknecht-Strasse 12, Mitte; ☷ noon-7pm Tue-Fri, 10am-8pm Sat; ⊖ ⊠ Alexanderplatz)

Spectrum Theaterkasse Friedrichshain (☎ 427 9119; Ring-Center, Frankfurter Allee 111, Friedrichshain; ⊖ ⊠ Frankfurter Allee)

Spectrum Theaterkasse Mitte (Map pp340–1; ☎ 2463 8811; Berlin-Carré, Karl-Liebknecht-Strasse 13, Mitte; ⊖ ⊠ Alexanderplatz)

Theaterkasse Centrum (Map p344; ☎ 882 7611; Meinekestrasse 25, Charlottenburg; ⊖ Uhlandstrasse, Kurfürstendamm)

Theaterkasse Friedrichstrasse (Map pp328–9; ☎ 2840 8155; ⊠ Friedrichstrasse, Mitte; ☷ 8am-8pm Mon-Fri, 10am-6pm Sat)

Gay & Lesbian Berlin

Berlin has the biggest and also the most active gay and lesbian scene in Germany, and can even rival Amsterdam, with exclusive and mixed facilities available for pretty much any activity. See p295 for more information on the history of Berlin's gay scene and local gay issues. The scene is concentrated in three main districts: around Nollendorfplatz in Schöneberg; on Oranienstrasse in Kreuzberg; and around the northern end of Schönhauser Allee in Prenzlauer Berg.

Check with **Mann-O-Meter** (Map pp338–9; ☎ 216 8008; Bülowstrasse 106, Schöneberg), *Siegessäule* (above), and www.berlin.gay -web.de for the latest on a range of activities including the cruising scene, popular parties and the ins and outs of the lesbigay landscape.

BEST OF GAY BERLIN

With so much on offer for gays and lesbians, it's hard to know how best to organise your time. The following are some of our favourite ways to spend one gay day in Berlin:

- Laying your head at the **Eastside Pension** (p263).
- Relearning your history at the **Schwules Museum** (p126).
- Getting it and flaunting it on **Christopher Street Day** (p10).
- Drinking in the F'hain scene at **Himmelreich** (p196).
- Film nights and glamorous parties at **Kino International** (p215).
- Playing away (sport, that is) with **Vorspiel** (p230).
- Dancing away your Sunday at GMF in **Café Moskau** (p199).
- Steaming away your aches and pains at the **Treibhaus Sauna** (p229).

DRINKING

As you'd expect from the capital of beer-obsessed Germany, Berlin elevates drinking culture to a fine art, offering everything from spit 'n' sawdust *Kneipen* (pubs) to shiny-smart cocktail lounges. The emphasis is on style, atmosphere and inspiration, and some proprietors have gone to extraordinary lengths to come up with a unique concept for their own corner of the city scene. That said, you'll quickly be struck by the overwhelming prevalence of the colour red!

Unlike in UK-style pubs, table service is common and it's customary to keep a tab instead of paying each round separately. Most bars open in the early evening, between 5pm and 8pm, unless they serve food during the day. Happy hours are practically mandatory, usually falling between 5pm and 10pm; the website www.bartime .de (in German) has a handy search engine for dedicated discount drinkers.

If you really can't make your mind up, try the card game **Berliner Bar- und Clubquartett** (€11.80) for inspiration – essentially Top Trumps with bars; the 44 cards also double as discount coupons at each establishment. This can be found at Hugendubel (p238).

MITTE

AMBULANCE BAR Map pp340-1
☎ 281 2095; Oranienburger Strasse 27;
⏱ from 7pm; 🚇 Oranienburger Strasse
No first aid required: the Ambulance Bar is a healthly hip modern lounge space, with red lights, video screens and nightly 'DJ pleasures'.

BRAUHAUS LEMKE Map pp340-1
☎ 2472 8727; Dircksenstrasse 143; ⏱ from noon;
🚇 Hackescher Markt
There may be better ways of filling a railway arch than setting up a microbrewery pub-restaurant underneath it, but once you've supped on a few Lemke brews we defy you to think of one.

ERDBEER Map pp340-1
Max-Beer-Strasse 56; ⏱ from 6pm;
🚇 Rosa-Luxemburg-Platz
A cocktail bar for people who prefer pubs. The humble strawberry is king here, and the red colour scheme and pint-sized daiquiris rather pleasingly testify.

KÖH Map pp340-1
☎ 282 8420; Hackesche Höfe, Sophienstrasse 6;
⏱ from 5pm; 🚇 Hackescher Markt
Surely the classiest pool hall ever. This dapper establishment is a haven of sophistication for anyone who wants to shoot some stick without getting hustled. The beers slip down as easily as the balls, but you get the feeling Minnesota Fats might not approve.

NEWTON Map pp340-1
☎ 2061 2990; Charlottenstrasse 57; ⏱ 6pm-4am;
🚇 Französische Strasse, Stadtmitte
You don't get much posher than a Gendarmenmarkt address, and this chic brown bar has been a home from home for Mitte's well-heeled folk since forever. Despite the Helmut Newton nudes on the walls, it was actually named after Sir Isaac.

PIPS Map pp340-1
☎ 282 4512; Auguststrasse 84; ⏱ from 8pm Mon-Sat; 🚇 Oranienburger Tor
Gladys Knight may be MIA, but the '70s are far from forgotten at this refreshingly colourful dance bar. Strut your stuff to the cool sounds or line up at the long long bar for liquid refreshment.

REINGOLD Map pp340-1
☎ 2838 7676; Novalisstrasse 11;
🚇 Oranienburger Tor
Inside the metal cocoon flutters the butterfly heart of a beautifully opulent 1930s glamour lounge. Deep house and Latin sounds dominate the decks, and there are regular events and readings.

RUTZ Map pp340-1
☎ 2462 8760; Chausseestrasse 8; ⏱ Mon-Sat;
🚇 Oranienburger Tor
Dedicated oenophiles should seek out this classy wine merchant, bar and restaurant, which stocks no fewer than 1001 quality tipples from all over the world. Bottles start

around €8 and go all the way up to €1450; luckily, if you need help choosing, the staff know their stuff.

VILLA CAPRICE Map pp340-1
☎ 0176-295 1293; Dirckstrasse 37; ☽ from noon Mon-Sat; 🚇 Hackescher Markt
At first sight this appears simply to be a fashion-conscious cocktail bar with dubious floral wallpaper, but head downstairs and you'll find a relaxed dancefloor that grooves away into the night at weekends. Exhibitions and clothing sales also take place here.

WINDHORST Map pp340-1
☎ 2045 0070; Dorotheenstrasse 65; ☽ from 6pm Mon-Fri, from 9pm Sat; ⊕ 🚇 Friedrichstrasse
Tucked away between the Hotel Maritim and the US embassy, Windhorst is a small, smart cocktail bar of the classic American model, with an inventive range of house specials. Thankfully the big yellow 'BAR' sign is the only tasteless feature.

TIERGARTEN

KUMPELNEST 3000 Map pp338-9
☎ 8891 7960; Lützowstrasse 23; ☽ from 5pm; ⊕ Kurfürstenstrasse
You can't get much further removed from the studied elegance of Tiergarten's many hotel bars than this place. The Kumpelnest was once a brothel and has been famed since the 1980s for its wild, inhibition-free all-nighters, attracting a hugely varied public.

VICTORIA BAR Map pp338-9
☎ 2575 9977; Potsdamer Strasse 102; ☽ 6pm-2am; ⊕ Kurfürstenstrasse
Dedicated to serious boozing, everything from the drinks to the décor in this discreet cocktail lounge is top quality. They even run an occasional 'School of Drunkenness', with lectures on the merits of various key spirits!

CHARLOTTENBURG

EN PASSANT Map p344
☎ 3180 2469; Else-Ury-Bogen; 🚇 Savignyplatz
Hidden away under the S-Bahn station at Savignyplatz, this gallery-bar gets into its stride at night, when the arched ceiling is beautifully lit and all kinds of events are laid on.

GAINSBOURG Map p344
☎ 313 7464; Savignyplatz 5; 🚇 Savignyplatz
This cramped, American-style bar speaks to a 30-something intellectual crowd, and might well have appealed to Serge himself. Relax in the warmly lit interior while sipping one of the award-winning (and copyrighted) cocktails.

SCHLEUSENKRUG Map pp338-9
☎ 313 9909; Müller-Breslau-Strasse; ☽ 10-1am; ⊕ 🚇 Zoologischer Garten, Tiergarten
This traditional beer garden has been sloshing out the beers since 1954, standing guard over the lock at the far western end of the Tiergarten park.

OPEN ALL HOURS

Most bars in Berlin give their closing times as 'open end', but in practice this generally means between 1am and 3am during the week, and maybe 5am at weekends. So, what to do once you've been kicked out by homesick bar staff?

Help is at hand – there are still a handful of bars in Berlin that never close, keeping the great tradition of the 24-hour bender alive.

Under Hackescher Markt S-Bahn station, **am to pm** (Map pp340–1; Am Zwirngraben 2, Mitte) is the original 24/7 bar-club, and has a good claim to be the liveliest, packing them in to 80s music all night and spilling outside in summer.

On the other side of town, the **Schwarzes Café** (Map p344; ☎ 313 8038; Kantstrasse 148, Charlottenburg; 🚇 Savignyplatz) has been a nightowls' haven for years, and is usually packed with hungry souls all day as well.

Nearby, **Miró** (Map pp338–9; ☎ 3290 7404; Stuttgarter Platz 14, Charlottenburg; 🚇 Charlottenburg) is a little more unusual – it's the house bar of the Charlottenburger Hof art hotel, and beer-weary drinkers can join paying guests for the rather civilised breakfast buffet.

Our personal late-night highlight, though, has to be the Good Morning Vietnam sessions at **Delicious Doughnuts** (p199), which start at 5am most nights for the ideal morning wind-down.

Entertainment

DRINKING

WILMERSDORF

GALERIE BREMER Map p344
☎ 881 4908; Fasanenstrasse 37; ⏰ from 8pm Mon-Sat; ⓞ Spichernstrasse
A true Berlin classic – proprietor Rudolf van der Lak opened this tiny gallery-bar way back in 1955. It's named for his wife, artist Anja Bremer, who died in 1985. Sadly 'Rudi' opted for a change of pace at the age of 85, and handed over the reins to the ArtCultura collective, but it's still worth dropping by.

LEIBNIZ BAR Map p344
☎ 3276 4699; Leibnizstrasse 57; ⓞ Adenauerplatz
Run by Americans for Americans, but don't let that put you off – with 240 cocktails on the list, this cheery bar is a welcome break from the posy trend spots. If you think you can take it, spring €10 for a Leibniz Killer.

SCHÖNEBERG

GREEN DOOR Map pp338-9
☎ 215 2515; Winterfeldtstrasse 50; ⓞ Nollendorfplatz
One of Berlin's finest cocktail bars, tended by a long line of renowned mixologists. For that added feeling of exclusivity, you have to ring the bell to get in.

HAFEN Map pp338-9
☎ 211 4118; Motzstrasse 19; ⓞ Nollendorfplatz
A permanent fixture on the good-time gay circuit, the 'Harbour' pulls in all kinds of guys and gals with its friendly free-for-all vibe. It's also a popular warm-up venue for those heading to cruising dens such as Tom's Bar (right next door) and Mutschmanns.

HAR DIE'S KNEIPE Map p344
☎ 0172-302 3068; Ansbacher Strasse 29; ⏰ noon-3am; ⓞ Wittenbergplatz
A recent refit has smartened up this convivial gay pub considerably, but it remains a good place to meet locals, even in the day. It's staunchly gay, but everyone's welcome.

SCHNEIDER Map pp338-9
☎ 216 2635; Frankenstrasse 13; ⏰ from 4pm Mon-Fri, from 1pm Sat & Sun; ⓞ Viktoria-Luise-Platz
Venture into the leafy residential area south of Winterfeldtplatz to find this pleasant neighbourhood bistro-bar, which often has live music on weekend evenings.

SO & SO Map p344
☎ 2145 9766; Fuggerstrasse; ⏰ from noon; ⓞ Wittenbergplatz
S&S offers the next-best thing to drinking inside a lava lamp: trippy projections, cool DJs and strong cocktails. Less try-hard butch than the raucous places opposite, and so low-key you'll barely notice it is, at least nominally, a gay bar.

ZOULOU BAR Map pp338-9
☎ 784 6894; Hauptstrasse 4; ⏰ 7pm-6am; ⓞ Kleistpark
Nothing to do with Michael Caine or bloody spears – the theme here is more American than African, which is probably just as well if you've ever seen a Soweto speakeasy.

KREUZBERG

ARCANOA Map pp336-7
☎ 691 2564; Am Tempelhofer Berg 8; ⓞ Platz der Luftbrücke
Alternative and just a teensy bit New Age, Arcanoa caters primarily for an arty crowd with regular events, concerts and open-stage nights – including a 'medieval jam session'.

BARBIE DEINHOFF'S Map pp336-7
www.bader-deinhoff.de; Schlesische Strasse 16; ⓞ Schlesisches Tor
Absolutely, undeniably the last word in gender-fluid trash kitsch art – and that's saying something in Berlin. The name's a reference to the Baader-Meinhoff terrorist gang, there's a loose nautical theme and even the resident Barbies seem to have taken to piracy.

FOGO Map pp336-7
☎ 692 1465; Arndtstrasse 29; ⓞ Gneisenaustrasse
It may have sand on the floor, but this isn't your average faux-tropical cocktail bar. The decor is a riot of randomness, pitting Jesus, Buddha and Che Guevara against an onslaught of Hindi Aztec murals and plastic snakes. Even the menu is deceptive – it's 2-for-1 all day every day, so that €10 *mojito* is better value than it seems!

GOLGATHA pp336–7
☎ 785 2453; Dudenstrasse 48-64; ⏰ Apr-Oct; ⓞ 🚇 Yorckstrasse
This popular beer garden in the Viktoriapark has been around for years, and is still great for grilled snacks and cool drinks on a balmy night. A DJ springs into action after 10pm.

Würgeengel (this page)

bottle and ignited. Luckily for public order, they're far too tasty to throw at riot police.

SERENE Map pp336-7
☎ 6904 1580; Schwiebusser Strasse 2; ⏰ from 8pm Wed & Thu, from 9pm Sat; ⊖ Platz der Luftbrücke
Another Berlin first: a bar dedicated to the fine sport of table tennis. Thursday and Saturday are for ladies only, and the first Friday of the month is black-music night.

SOFIA Map pp336-7
☎ 0163-283 2519; Wrangelstrasse 93; ⏰ from 9am Mon-Sat, from 8pm Sun; ⊖ Schlesisches Tor
Sofia apparently started life as a kebab shop, but its new incarnation is rather more pleasing, offering comfy seats, moulded waterfall-effect decor and posters of one Ms Loren. Thanks to the friendly owners it's become a favoured, though by no means exclusive, lesbigay hangout.

SPINDLER & KLATT Map pp336-7
☎ 6956 6775; Köpenicker Strasse 16-17; ⏰ 8pm-1am Wed, Thu & Sun, 8pm-5am Fri & Sat; ⊖ Schlesisches Tor
The most fashionable thing to hit Kreuzberg since the *caipirinha*, this stunning club-restaurant takes the age-old concept of the converted warehouse and adds the unthinkable: discreet sophistication. Wispy drapes, riverside terrace, Asian fusion food and a dash of Oriental style – late nights have never been so chic.

WALDOHREULE Map pp336-7
☎ 3974 2060; Köpenicker Strasse 194; ⊖ Schlesisches Tor
Named after a type of owl, this friendly bar is packed with a mixed bunch of students, regulars and session drinkers, all admiring the neat stacking furniture, the tiny dance floor or the ancient GDR headlines on the walls.

WÜRGEENGEL Map pp336-7
☎ 615 5560; Dresdener Strasse 122; ⊖ Kottbusser Tor
The 'Exterminating Angel' pays homage to the 1962 Luis Buñuel movie, its dramatic blood-red velvet décor reminiscent of a *belle époque* brothel. The place is crammed the second the adjacent Babylon cinema closes.

HEINZ MINKI Map pp336-7
☎ 6953 3766; Vor dem Schlesischen Tor 3; ⏰ from 2pm Mon-Fri, from noon Sat & Sun; ⊖ Schlesisches Tor
On the dividing line with neighbouring Treptow, the endearingly named Minki is a snazzy red-brick lounge supplemented by a big walled garden, and is already a firm favourite with hipsters 'rediscovering' Kreuzberg.

KONRAD TÖNZ Map pp336-7
☎ 612 3252; Falckensteinstrasse 30; ⏰ Tue-Sun; ⊖ Schlesisches Tor
Another long-standing classic, Konrad Tönz takes retro to extremes, with kitsch '70s furniture, authentic wallpaper and possibly the last surviving mono DJ setup in Europe. Charles and Di gaze out obliviously amid the ageing magazine cut-outs on the walls.

MÖBEL OLFE Map pp336-7
☎ 6165 9612; Reichenberger Strasse 177; ⏰ Tue-Sun; ⊖ Kottbusser Tor
This sparsely decorated pub is good for at least a couple of hours after the regular places close. The table football's always busy, the beer's always excellent and the friendly crowd's mixed in every respect.

MOLOTOW COCKTAIL Map pp336-7
☎ 6956 9130; Oranienstrasse 189; ⊖ Kottbusser Tor
Worth a visit just for the eponymous house cocktail, a suitably lethal recipe served in a

FRIEDRICHSHAIN

BLOONA Map pp336-7

☎ 0179-490 9514; Gärtnerstrasse 12;
Ⓢ Samariterstrasse
The best thing about this lounge bar/restaurant is the, um, unusual cocktails on offer – try a Hello Kitty, an absinthe *caipirinha* or a Bitch Wallbanger.

COCKTAILS TO GO Map pp336-7

Warschauer Strasse; Ⓢ Ⓤ Warschauer Strasse
What do you get if you cross a cocktail bar with a kebab van? Probably something like this – surely the world's first cocktail kiosk. It's not exactly sophisticated, but at €2.50 a pop you won't give a Fuzzy Duck.

DACHKAMMER Map pp336-7

☎ 296 1673; Simon-Dach-Strasse 39;
Ⓢ Ⓤ Warschauer Strasse
Two concepts in one bar. Downstairs you get the traditional, rustic pub look, with hearty snacks and magazines; or trip upstairs for a fantastically convincing 1950's flashback in the multi-roomed cocktail bar.

DIE TAGUNG Map pp336-7

☎ 292 8756; Wühlischstrasse 29;
Ⓢ Ⓤ Warschauer Strasse
Ostalgie incarnate: it seems like half the paraphernalia from 50 years of the GDR has ended up here. The former basement Cube Club has struck out on its own as **Octopussy** (Map pp328–9; www.octopussy-club.de; Gürtelstrasse 36), with a programme of alternative sounds.

FEUERMELDER Map pp336-7

Krossener Strasse 21; Ⓥ from 3pm Mon-Sat, from noon Sun; Ⓢ Ⓤ Warschauer Strasse
Punks, rockers and other leather-clad folk gather in this loud bar to knock back beers and play pool, table football or the ancient fruit machines. It's popular with members of Berlin's active antifascist movement.

HIMMELREICH Map pp336-7

☎ 7072 8306; Simon-Dach-Strasse 36;
Ⓥ from 7pm Mon-Fri, from 2pm Sat & Sun;
Ⓢ Ⓤ Warschauer Strasse
Proving all those stereotypes about gays having good taste, this smart red-hued cocktail bar makes most of the competition look like a straight guy's bedsit.

ORANKE ORANGE Map pp332-3

☎ 214 0022; Karl-Marx-Allee 93; Ⓥ 4-11pm;
Ⓢ Weberwiese
Karl-Marx-Allee might not be the obvious spot for an open-air beach beer garden, but when the sun's out you can't fault the concept. Opening hours are extended on public holidays.

ROCKCAFÉ HALFORD Map pp336-7

☎ 9290 0182; Boxhagener Strasse 19-20; Ⓥ from 3pm; Ⓢ Frankfurter Tor
If you thought normal bouncers were scary, wait until you see the eight-foot monster biker on guard outside this old-school heavy metal pub… Luckily he's made of plastic, but after a few beers it's easy to get nervous.

SANATORIUM 23 Map pp332-3

☎ 4202 1193; Frankfurter Allee 23; Ⓥ from 2pm; Ⓢ Frankfurter Tor
There's only one word to describe this sharply styled lounge: cool. Very, very, very cool. The look is Oriental meets pop art in hospital, the vibe's relaxed and friendly, the DJs know their dubplates and the long, low seating is quite literally made for lounging.

STEREO 33 Map pp336-7

☎ 9599 9433; Krossener Strasse 24; Ⓥ Mon-Sat;
Ⓢ Ⓤ Warschauer Strasse
Linked with the smart Haifischbar in Kreuzberg, Stereo 33 is a close runner-up for the title of coolest bar in Friedrichshain. Modern, minimalist design, well-schooled DJs and bargain sushi all add to the appeal.

SUPAMOLLI

☎ 2900 7294; Jessnerstrasse 41; Ⓥ 8pm-7am Tue-Sun; Ⓢ Frankfurter Tor
This one-time squatter haunt has morphed into a relatively respectable venue bar with an eclectic programme of live concerts, theatre and films.

WASCHMASCHINEWSKY Map pp332-3

☎ 4201 9852; Bänschstrasse 25;
Ⓢ Samariterstrasse
Another new *Szene* favourite, buoyed by a combination of unique beer (bought direct from a tiny Polish brewery) and seething absinthe cocktails (shaken in a miniature washing machine at the bar).

PRENZLAUER BERG

BAR 55 Map pp332-3
☎ 4862 5515; Kollwitzstrasse 55; ⊕ Senefelder Platz
Another day, another bar with a number in its name. The really important figure here though, is in the volume – you can buy cocktails in litres here, which may well affect your mental arithmetic.

BECKETTS KOPF Map pp332-3
☎ 0162-237 9418; Pappelallee 64; ⊕ ⓡ Schönhauser Allee
Named for the great Irish playwright, whose visage does indeed grimace out from the window of this small but stylish cocktail bar, daring you to sup some absurd concoction as you hang around for that Godot guy. Other illustrious faces keep you company inside – just don't think of Happy Days…

DRUIDE Map pp332-3
☎ 4849 4777; Schönhauser Allee 42; ⊕ Eberswalder Strasse
With 300 cocktails, 40 different types of absinthe (the largest number in Germany) and DJs at weekends, there's plenty to make you sink into Druide's chintzy sofas, but little to get you up and out again.

FLUIDO Map pp332-3
☎ 4404 3902; Christburger Strasse 6; ☾ Tue-Sun; ⊕ Eberswalder Strasse
The after-hours den of choice for barstaff across the city, Fluido's understated deep-red design would scream 'sophisticated lounge' if screaming wasn't so darned vulgar.

FREIZEITHEIM Map pp332-3
☎ 0174-402 6444; Schönhauser Allee 157; ☾ Tue-Sun; ⊕ Eberswalder Strasse
The pom-pom curtains are your first hint as to the colourful retro flavour here, giving way to two floors of cocktails and glittery fabness. The 'microclub' in the basement goes gay on Tuesday, and lesbian on Thursday.

PRATER Map pp332-3
☎ 448 5688; www.pratergarten.de; Kastanienallee 7-9; ☾ from 4pm Mon-Fri, from noon Sat, from 10am Sun; ⊕ Eberswalder Strasse
Berlin's oldest beer garden is also one of the prettiest and is a great place for quaffing away beneath the chestnut trees. The complex includes a small stage operated by the Volksbühne, a cocktail bar, an old-fashioned restaurant and the popular Bastard club.

BERLIN KNEIPEN

Alt-Berlin (Old Berlin) nostalgia is as strong as ever, and old-fashioned *Kneipen* have their own tradition of hospitality, serving up cheap beer, strong schnapps, hearty food and raucous humour in smoke-filled surroundings. Most, however, are real *Kiezkneipen,* the private turf of neighbourhood denizens and local characters, so as a stranger you may not meet the warmest reception. Try the following reliable but non-exclusive haunts for a taste of the good old times.

E&M Leydicke (Map pp338–9; ☎ 216 2973; Mansteinstrasse 4, Schöneberg; ☾ from 4pm; ⊕ ⓡ Yorckstrasse) Founded in 1877, this old-fashioned pub and wine merchant still bottles its own flavoured schnapps and fruit wines on the premises.

Gambrinus (Map pp340–1; ☎ 282 6043; Linienstrasse 133, Mitte; ☾ noon-4am Mon-Sat, 3pm-4am Sun; ⊕ Oranienburger Tor) With its prime location this is inevitably a bit touristy, but the regulars are real Berliners and there's a huge collection of photos documenting turn-of-the-century Mitte.

Mommsen-Eck (Map pp344; ☎ 324 2580; Mommsenstrasse 45, Charlottenburg; ☾ from 8am Mon-Sat, 9-1am Sun; ⊕ Wilmersdorfer Strasse) The 'House of 100 Beers' celebrated its centenary in 2005 and still seems to be a fine example of its ilk – though it can get very crowded at mealtimes. The thick menu's a great read on its own, and they're not lying about the beers.

Zur Letzten Instanz (Map pp340–1; ☎ 242 5528; Waisenstrasse 14, Mitte; ⊕ Klosterstrasse) As the legalese menu suggests, the name of this historic pub – 'The Final Authority' – relates to the presence of the courtroom opposite, although how it came to be called this is another story (or two).

Entertainment

DRINKING

RAZZIA IN BUDAPEST Map pp332-3
☎ 4862 3620; Oderberger Strasse 38;
Ⓔ Eberswalder Strasse
Prenzlauer Berg meets Kreuzberg: this hip joint fuses retro sophistication with more than a touch of kitsch, offering tasselled lamp shades, chaise longues and electro DJs. Don't ask us what any of it has to do with Hungarian police raids.

ROTE LOTTE Map pp332-3
☎ 0172-318 6868; Oderberger Strasse 38;
Ⓔ Eberswalder Strasse
Right next door to Razzia, Lotte goes even further back to create a look perhaps best described as 'antique retro'. Occupying the plush seats in the front conservatory is a little like frequenting a 19th-century living room, though the rest's rather more prosaic.

SCHALL UND RAUCH Map pp332-3
☎ 443 3970; Gleimstrasse 23; ⏰ 9-2am;
Ⓔ Ⓡ Schönhauser Allee
A bistro by day, this trendy gay place turns into a chic cocktail bar when the moon gets high, with award-winning design and a young, buff following. The Sunday brunch (€7) has cult status.

SONNTAGS CLUB Map pp332-3
☎ 449 7590; Greifenhagener Strasse 28;
Ⓔ Ⓡ Schönhauser Allee
This friendly, relaxed, lesbigay café-bar project is open to all, and holds frequent events. There is also a piano just begging to have its ivories tickled.

TARANTINO'S Map pp332-3
☎ 4050 0355; Brunnenstrasse 163; Ⓔ Bernauer Strasse
What, no bloodstains? Hollywood's high priest of screen violence might be disappointed at the lack of gunplay here, but the style and atmosphere would doubtless strike a chord, as would the movie stills and mug shots. All together now: 'Ezekiel 25:17…'

VEB GETRÄNKEKOMBINAT Map pp332-3
☎ 445 5458; Lettestrasse 6; ⏰ 10-4am;
Ⓔ Ⓡ Schönhauser Allee
Formerly Wohnzimmer, little has changed here besides the GDR-inspired name, and the laid-back atmosphere still brings in the scene-conscious Prenzl'berg set for coffee, cakes and cocktails.

Reingold (p192)

SOUTHERN DISTRICTS
ANKERKLAUSE Map pp336-7
☎ 693 5649; Kottbusser Damm 104, Neukölln;
Ⓔ Kottbusser Tor
Ahoy there! This nautical Neukölln favourite occupies an old glass-panelled harbourmaster's house above the Landwehrkanal, and still packs 'em in at all hours.

LORETTA AM WANNSEE
☎ 803 5156; Kronprinzessinenweg 260, Wannsee;
⏰ from 11am; Ⓡ Wannsee
This huge beer garden near the lake has more than 1000 seats, perfect for capping off a hot summer day's swimming. A heated marquee keeps the action going in winter, too.

TABOU TIKI ROOM Map pp336-7
www.taboutikiroom.com; Maybachufer 39, Neukölln; ⏰ Tue-Sun; Ⓔ Schönleinstrasse
Could this be the start of a Neukölln revival? With enough Polynesian props to restage South Pacific, this entertainingly silly bar-club is already enticing Berlin's hipsters southeast for exotic music (sci-fi jazz, Hawaiian swing, rock n' roll, country…) and drinks with little umbrellas.

CLUBBING

The sun may not be shining, the weather may not be sweet, but if you just want to move those dancing feet Berlin is all you could ever want or need. This is Germany's club capital, the city where Euro techno came of age, the living heart of the European electronic scene and the spiritual home of the lost weekend – and nobody here ever parties in half measures...

Taste is no barrier to enjoyment either – whether you're into house, techno, drum and bass, punk, Britpop, dancehall, easy-listening, ska, folk or ballroom, you can find a place to party almost any night of the week. To get the best from the scene peruse the listings magazines (p191), consult www.nachtagenten.de, or sift through the myriad flyers in shops, cafés and bars – you'll find at least 130 different events on any given Saturday.

Getting into clubs is easier in unpretentious Berlin than in most European cities. In the few places with a dress code, imagination usually beats income, so you don't have to swathe yourself in labels. Admission at even the coolest places seldom exceeds €15.

Wherever you're going, though, don't bother showing up before midnight, and you needn't worry about closing times – the city's notoriously late nights have got even later lately, and with a growing number of daytime clubs it's quite possible not to go home at all on weekends!

MITTE

2BE Map pp340-1
☎ 2758 2682; www.2be-club.de; Ziegelstrasse 23; admission price varies; ⏱ from 11pm Fri & Sat; Ⓡ Oranienburger Strasse

2BE deals almost exclusively in black music, specifically hip-hop and dancehall nights, with the occasional big-name special event. Expect plenty of b-boy posing.

BAR 25 Map pp336-7
www.bar25.de; Holzmarktstrasse 25; admission free; ⏱ noon-2am; Ⓢ Ⓡ Jannowitzbrücke

Thanks to Yaam (see the boxed text, Parties p201), the Spreeside strip has become phenomenally popular for summer weekend after-parties, and Bar 25 is at the forefront of the craze, giving Berlin's avid crew of hardcore club casualties somewhere to waste away those pesky afternoons.

TOP FIVE CLUBS

- Berghain (p203)
- Kaffee Burger (p200)
- Maria am Ufer (p203)
- Watergate (p202)
- Café Moskau (below)

BOHANNON CLUB Map pp340-1
☎ 0160-9585 1766; Dircksenstrasse 40; admission €6-8; ⏱ from 8pm Thu, from 10pm Fri & Sat; Ⓡ Hackescher Markt

This basement club takes a while to warm up and maintains an unusually civilised air, hosting high-class genre-hopping DJs with as much emphasis on tunes as beats. It's linked to the Sonar Kollektiv record label, and downtempo legends Jazzanova now play their highly recommended midweek sessions here.

CAFÉ MOSKAU Map pp332-3
☎ 2463 1626; www.das-moskau.com; Karl-Marx-Allee 34; admission €8-10; Ⓢ Schillingstrasse

Recently vacated by the WMF (p200), this iconic former communist café has retained the much-loved GMF gay parties every other Sunday, and now runs changing club events, which almost invariably rank among the finest in the city.

DELICIOUS DOUGHNUTS Map pp340-1
☎ 2809 9279; Rosenthaler Strasse 9; admission €3-5; ⏱ from 10pm Thu-Sat; Ⓢ Weinmeisterstrasse

A tasty slice of Mitte nightlife, Doughnuts has perfected the cosy velvet lounge look and seems tailor-made for those nights when you just don't want to go home. It's a friendly place with a small but lively dance floor, table football and a tendency to stay open well into daylight hours.

GRÜNER SALON Map pp340-1
☎ 2859 8936; www.gruener-salon.de; Volksbühne, Rosa-Luxemburg-Platz; admission €3-15; ⏱ Tue, Thu-Sat; Ⓢ Rosa-Luxemburg-Platz

Smoky sophistication rules in the Volksbühne's intimate 'Green Salon', an elegant throwback to the wicked 1920s and the centre of Berlin's active ballroom-dancing scene. Its salsa, tango and swing nights are often preceded by dance lessons.

KAFFEE BURGER Map pp340-1

☎ 2804 6495; www.kaffeeburger.de; Torstrasse 60; admission €3-5; ☿ from 7pm Sun-Thu, from 9pm Fri & Sat; ⊕ Rosa-Luxemburg-Platz

The best alternative club in town, Kaffee Burger is decked out in what appears to be original 60s GDR living-room furniture and wallpaper. The indie, rock and punk parties and gigs are often preceded by literature and poetry readings; most importantly, however, this is the home of Wladimir Kaminer's legendary Russendisko (Russian disco), arguably the most fun you can have in Cyrillic.

MUDD CLUB Map pp340-1

☎ 2759 4999; www.muddclub.de; Grosse Hamburger Strasse 17; admission price varies; ☿ from 9.30pm Wed-Sun; ⓡ Hackescher Markt

Named after the legendary SoHo original which was a hub of the New York underground in the '70s and '80s. It's set back from the street and down a steep staircase. Russian and Slavic acts feature heavily amid the rock and indie line-ups.

OXYMORON Map pp340-1

☎ 2839 1886; www.oxymoron-berlin.de; Rosenthaler Strasse 40-41; admission €5-10; ☿ Fri & Sat; ⓡ Hackescher Markt

Located inside the Hackesche Höfe, this shape-shifting salon is a café-restaurant by day and a chic club after 11pm, with a variety of retro and electro nights and occasional 'extras' such as go-go dancers. Dress code is just on the smarter side of casual.

RIO Map pp332-3

rioberlin.de; Chausseestrasse 106; admission price varies; ☿ Sat; ⊕ Zinnowitzer Strasse

A challenge for every Szene junkie – the programme at this latest hotspot is so wilfully erratic it's sometimes hard to tell if it's open at all.

ROTER SALON Map pp340-1

☎ 2406 5806; www.roter-salon.de; Volksbühne, Rosa-Luxemburg-Platz; admission price varies; ☿ Mon, Wed-Sat; ⊕ Rosa-Luxemburg-Platz

The Grüner Salon's red counterpart ditches the sophistication and goes for a more rowdy retro atmosphere, hosting readings, live concerts and dance parties (including a truly stompin' northern soul all-nighter). Post-Volksbühne premiere bashes are especially well attended.

SAGE CLUB Map pp340-1

☎ 2787 6948; www.sage-club.de; Köpenicker Strasse 76; admission €5-10; ☿ Thu-Sun; ⊕ Heinrich-Heine-Strasse

Berlin's premier house club is not as exclusive as it could be, though door policy is selective at weekends. It's worth it just for the amazing garden area (with pool) and four dancefloors (with fire-breathing dragon); the sharp music and good-looking public aren't bad either.

SOPHIENCLUB Map pp340-1

☎ 282 4552; www.sophienclub.de; Sophienstrasse 6; admission €3-10; ☿ from 10pm Tue-Sat; ⊕ Weinmeisterstrasse

No-one could accuse this club of trendsetting, but that's just fine with the young crowds who gather here for regular doses of familiar '60s to '90s, funk, soul and Britpop tunes.

WEEK-END Map pp340-1

www.week-end-berlin.de; Am Alexanderplatz 5; admission €6-8; ☿ Thu-Sat; ⊕ ⓡ Alexanderplatz

Forget the underground, above ground is where it's at, and once you've gawped at the 270° views from the 12th-storey dancefloor here you might just think twice about all those basement bars. The crowd's hip, the bouncers can be picky and the line-ups are often high-profile.

WMF

☎ 2838 8850; www.wmfclub.de; admission €6-12; ☿ from 11pm Fri & Sat

This peripatetic Berlin classic was seeking out its eighth location at time of research – check the website for news. The music is mostly cutting-edge electro, though frequent special events provide plenty of variety – grime nights are the latest attraction.

TIERGARTEN

40 SECONDS Map p346

☎ 889 064 241; www.40seconds.de; Potsdamer Strasse 58; admission price varies; ☿ from 11pm Fri & Sat; ⊕ ⓡ Potsdamer Platz

Another club with a view, this time one that treats guests to a Potsdamer Platz panorama from the open roof terrace. If you're not so keen on the music, there's also a new restaurant, 40seatings, on the premises. Aimed at over-25s the whole place is, unsurprisingly, trendy as hell, and dressing up is recommended.

DIE 2 Map pp330-1

☎ 3983 8969; Rathenower Strasse 19; admission price varies; ☼ Wed-Sat; ⊕ Westhafen
Lesbians of all ages and styles gather here for the disco nights and Thursday's more sedate cultural programme of exhibitions and readings. Fans of small dogs also meet here once a month (no, we're not kidding).

KAPITAL Map pp338-9

Potsdamer Strasse 76; admission price varies; ⊕ Kurfürstenstrasse
A new high-capacity club catering for more populist strains of dance music. It hosts the kind of big names you might see on German MTV, plus gay nights, gigs and other events.

POLAR.TV Map pp330-1

☎ 246 2593; www.no-ufos.de; Heidestrasse 73; admission price varies; ☼ from 11pm Sat; ⊠ Hauptbahnhof (Lehrter Bahnhof)
Founded for the No UFOs club nights, this warehouse venue has a solid track record of pulling in energetic young crowds with the finest electro and techno sounds. Sister club Sternradio (Map pp340-1; ☎ 2462 95320; Alexanderplatz 5) is a bit more laid-back, and both establishments have outdoor seating for a breath of fresh air.

TROMPETE Map pp338-9

☎ 2300 4794; www.trompete-berlin.de; Lützow-platz 9; admission €5-11; ☼ from 7pm Thu, from 10pm Fri & Sat; ⊕ Nollendorfplatz
Actor Ben Becker is no stranger to blowing his own trumpet, and any club with his backing was never going to have problems getting publicity. Fortunately the crowds turn out even when BB isn't propping up the bar, and the weekly after-work lounge party is a consistent hit. You can almost hear the silent partners' sighs of relief.

CHARLOTTENBURG

ABRAXAS Map p344

☎ 312 9493; Kantstrasse 134; admission €3-5; ☼ from 10pm Tue-Sat; ⊠ Savignyplatz
It may look like a sex shop from the outside, but inside this little club is a hotbed of salsoul, hip-hop and funk cuts. The dance floor is packed from about 1am and the entire crowd generally seems to be on the pull.

BIG EDEN Map p344

☎ 882 6120; www.arena-berlin.de; Kurfürstendamm 202; admission €4-10; ☼ Thu-Sat; ⊕ Adenauerplatz
Virtually the only club of any size and standing on this side of town, originally owned by homegrown playboy Rolf Eden. It's hardly paradise but it's big, it's loud, and it does occasionally get some good DJs in.

PARTIES

Some of the best club nights in Berlin are independent of the venues they use and may move around, although they'll usually have one home residency where they can be found every week or month. There is also a thriving illegal party scene, relying on email lists or word of mouth and often using buildings outside the central districts.

Chicks De Luxe (www.chicksunited.de) The capital's biggest lesbian party packs out the Kino International (see p215) on a regular basis, and also moonlights in other venues.

Club Deewane (www.club-deewane.com) It's official: bhangra is big in Berlin. This is the original Bollywood party, bringing desi beats and colourful chaos to clubs such as Oxymoron (see opposite).

Karrera Club (☎ 7895 8410; www.karreraclub.de) Tim, Christian and Spencer must be the hardest-working DJs in Berlin, putting on indie and Britpop parties almost every night. Venues include Kaffee Burger (opposite), Mudd Club (opposite) and the Sophienclub (opposite).

Stadtbad (Map pp332-3; ☎ 449 4598; www.stadtbad-oderberger.de; Oderberger Str 57-59; ⊕ Eberswalder Strasse) Prenzlauer Berg's old municipal bathhouse is occasionally used as a party venue to help fund its restoration.

Yaam (Map pp336-7; ☎ 615 1354; www.yaam.de; Stralauer Platz 35, Friedrichshain) The granddaddy of all summer parties, this Caribbean Sunday session has been dishing up food, drink and dub-reggae music bizness for years. It's so popular it even has winter events at venues such as the Berlin Arena.

Entertainment

CLUBBING

SCHÖNEBERG

90 GRAD Map pp338-9

☎ 2300 5954; www.90grad.de; Dennewitzstrasse 37; admission €8-10; ☽ from 11pm Fri & Sat; ☺ Kurfürstenstrasse

Unimpressive from the outside, this squat black cube is actually as trendy as anything in Mitte, with a similarly elitist door policy and a backlist of celebrity visitors from George Clooney to Heidi Klum.

CONNECTION Map p344

☎ 218 1432; www.connection-berlin.de; Fuggerstrasse 33; admission price varies; ☽ Fri & Sat; ☺ Wittenbergplatz

This well-established gay disco is one of the most popular boozing and cruising spots in town, renowned for its dense warren of underground darkrooms. Upstairs there are three floors of men-only action, a mirrored dance floor and blaring techno.

GOYA Map pp338-9

☎ 2639 1430; www.goya-berlin.de; Nollendorfplatz 5; admission €10; ☽ Thu-Sat; ☺ Nollendorfplatz

Could this be the future of Berlin clubbing? This very exclusive new club-restaurant

Goya, in the Metropol Theater (this page)

project in the old Metropol theatre is funded almost entirely by public 'shareholders', who pay up to €4000 each for a stake and privileged member status. The music policy is eclectic, with a world flavour.

KREUZBERG

CLUB 103 Map pp336-7

www.103club.de; Falckensteinstrasse 47; admission €6-10; ☽ Fri & Sat; ☺ Schlesisches Tor

A highly rated new arrival, with no fewer than four big rooms at its disposal and plenty of lounging space in between. Head for the upper level – the glass-walled top dancefloor is the hottest spot in the place. The music policy is teasingly random.

PRIVATCLUB Map pp336-7

☎ 611 3302; www.monosound.de; Markthalle, Pücklerstrasse 34; admission price varies; ☽ Fri & Sat; ☺ Görlitzer Bahnhof

Down in the basement of the Weltrestaurant Markthalle (p183), an unshowy bunch of party people soak up the alternative soul, funk, easy, trash pop and indie sounds in this kitsch but cool lounge.

SCHWUZ Map pp336-7

☎ 629 0880; www.schwuz.de; Mehringdamm 61; admission €3-8; ☽ Fri & Sat; ☺ Mehringdamm

On Saturday, Melitta Sundström turns into the warm-up bar for this mainstream dance club in the SchwuZ gay centre. Come here to check out the flamboyant drag queens and get sweaty on the two dance floors.

SO36 Map pp336-7

☎ 6140 1306; www.so36.de; Oranienstrasse 190; admission €3-8; ☽ always on Sat & Sun, other nights vary; ☺ Kottbusser Tor

This long-running legend is Kreuzberg's punk heart, keeping the district's alternative ethos alive with its relentlessly offbeat live concerts and theme nights. Lesbigay events here are consistently popular, particularly Gayhane, a monthly 'homoriental' party with Turkish and German pop, transvestites and belly dancing.

WATERGATE Map pp336-7

☎ 6128 0394; www.water-gate.de; Falckensteinstrasse 49a; admission €6-12; ☽ from 11pm Fri & Sat; ☺ Schlesisches Tor

A cornerstone of just about everyone's weekend, Watergate has a fantastic location with a lounge overlooking the Spree and a floating terrace actually on it, opposite the colour-changing logo of the Universal Music building. Upstairs, the main floor hosts the notorious hard:edged drum and bass nights every other Friday, with more down-tempo events on Saturday and occasional weekdays. Don't worry about missing it – parties invariably run on into the morning, if not the afternoon!

FRIEDRICHSHAIN

BERGHAIN Map pp336-7
www.berghain.de; Am Wriezener Bahnhof; admission €10; ☿ Fri & Sat; ⓡ Ostbahnhof
The people behind the legendary but defunct Ostgut club have scored another huge hit with this vast post-industrial techno-electro hellhole. The upstairs Panoramabar became the coolest spot in the city within days of opening, and when the full club is open on Saturday it really is a sight and a half: three levels of concrete, speakers and partitions, full of hidden corners (including darkrooms) and packed with the most mixed crowd in Berlin. One warning – no cameras are allowed. Truly, truly essential.

BLACK GIRLS COALITION Map pp332-3
☎ 6953 4300; Samariterstrasse 32; admission price varies; ☿ from 10pm Mon-Sat; ⓔ Samariterstrasse
Don't be fooled by the word 'girls'; these are male wolves in expensive, very tight sheep's clothing. For the many regulars who pack into this tiny space, it's all about the monthly Roots Night, Berlin's trashiest trannie party.

CASSIOPEIA Map pp336-7
☎ 2936 2966; www.cassiopeia-berlin.de; Revaler Strasse 99; admission €4-6; ☿ Thu-Sat; ⓔ ⓡ Warschauer Strasse
One of several new squat-like venues along Revaler Strasse, Cassiopeia distinguishes itself by having a big courtyard and its own water-tower dancefloor. Music focuses on drum and bass, electro and hip hop, though some nights are still finding their feet.

MARIA AM UFER Map pp336-7
☎ 2123 8190; www.clubmaria.de; Stralauer Platz 33-34; admission €5-10; ☿ from 10pm Fri & Sat; ⓡ Ostbahnhof
Spiritual home to some of Berlin's most discerning clubbers – the DJs playing here

are invariably among the best in their field, whether it's breakbeat, down-tempo or some other strand of electronica. It's also now a key address for techno, hosting 'Tresor in exile' nights while the legendary club looks for a new venue. Live concerts often take place here on weekdays.

MATRIX/NARVA LOUNGE Map pp336-7
☎ 2936 9990; www.matrix-berlin.de; Warschauer Platz 18; admission €6-8; ☿ from 10pm; ⓔ ⓡ Warschauer Strasse
Side by side under Warschauer Strasse station, these two clubs aim at slightly different segments of the dancing public but regularly combine for big events, and share an indoor swimming pool. Matrix is more populist and commercial, while the Narva Lounge strives for a bit of affluent class.

RAUMKLANG Map pp336-7
☎ 2930 9800; www.raum-klang.de; Libauer Strasse 1; admission price varies; ☿ Thu-Sat; ⓔ ⓡ Warschauer Strasse
A brand new concept club offering what may well be the first sound system in Berlin specifically designed to prevent hearing damage at high volumes. Let your ears party to soul, breaks, beats and live bands in the coloured rooms, or chat freely in the quiet(ish) lounge. Over 21s only.

ROSIS Map pp336-7
www.rosis-berlin.de; Revaler Strasse 29; admission €5; ☿ Thu-Sat; ⓡ Ostkreuz
We're not sure if this derelict house was ever actually a squat, but it catches the Friedrichshain vibe spot-on – dim lighting, dank concrete, games, and a totally random music policy.

PRENZLAUER BERG

ICON Map pp332-3
☎ 4849 2878; www.iconberlin.de; Cantianstrasse 15; admission €3-10; ☿ from 11pm Tue, Fri & Sat; ⓔ Eberswalder Strasse
Along with Watergate, this sweaty, cavernous basement is Berlin's top location for seriously heavy-duty drum and bass – Recycle on Saturday is an eardrum-rinsing local institution. Friday is generally given over to special events, with some very strong nu-skool breakbeat and downtempo nights. International DJs seemingly queue up to get on the bill here.

SEX CLUBS

The hedonism of the 1920s is back – anything goes in Berlin, and we mean *anything*. While full-on sex clubs are most common in the gay scene, there are also several mixed and/or straight places catering for consenting adults rather than overpaying voyeurs.

Club Culture Houze (Map pp336–7; ☎ 6170 9669; www.club-culture-houze.de; Görlitzer Strasse 71, Kreuzberg; admission price varies; ☼ Wed-Mon; ◉ Görlitzer Bahnhof) The CCH democratically caters for all tastes, persuasions and fetishes, with two mixed and four men-only parties a week, plus regular lesbian events. Check listings *very* carefully before you set out.

Dark Side Club (Map pp336–7; ☎ 4606 8496; www.darkside-club.de; Nostitzstrasse 30, Kreuzberg; men/women/couples €25/8/25; ☼ Wed-Sat; ◉ Gneisenaustrasse) A specialist fetish club with a strict dress policy and code of conduct. Wednesday is a more relaxed erotic night (admission €5) ideal for the curious novice.

KitKat Club (☎ 7889 9704; www.kitkatclub.de; Bessemer Strasse 2-14, Schöneberg; admission €10-15; ☼ Thu-Sun; ☒ Papestrasse) The original Berlin den of decadence is still going strong, housed in a former brewery with the main club downstairs and the separate Penthouse above it. Most parties are open to all comers, subject to the erotic dress code; Saturday's Penthouze and the Sunday-morning Piep Show are infamous.

KNAACK Map pp332-3

☎ 442 7060; www.knaack-berlin.de; Greifswalder Strasse 224; tickets €5-18; ☼ Mon, Wed, Fri & Sat; ◉ Senefelderplatz
Part venue, part club, this 1953-vintage warren is known for its popular rock, punk and indie concerts, but the regular five-floor dance parties are pretty good too.

NBI Map pp332-3

☎ 4405 1681; www.neueberlinerinitiative.de; Kulturbrauerei, Schönhauser Allee 36; admission free–€6; ☼ from 6pm; ◉ Eberswalder Strasse
Newly rehoused in the Kulturbrauerei, it seems that what the nbi has lost in living-room charm it makes up for by having a proper-sized dancefloor and an expanded events programme.

PAX STUDIO Map pp332-3

☎ 0172-310 8500; Brunnenstrasse 154; admission price varies; ☼ from 6pm Sun-Thu, from 11pm Fri & Sat; ◉ Rosenthaler Platz
The GDR's flagship recording studio once saw the likes of the Puhdys coming in to cut tracks; the large back hall has now been converted into a dancefloor, while the corridor serves as a lounge. As you'd expect, the sound system's pretty good.

PULP MANSION Map pp340-1

www.pulp-mansion.de; Saarbrücker Strasse 36; admission €5-10; ☼ Fri & Sat; ◉ Senefelder Platz
One of those venues that really looks like it should be illegal, Pulp Mansion is hidden away down a twisting staircase in the back courtyard of the rather posh Backfabrik apartment block, with cracked tiles, dim lights and pounding techno, electro and house beats.

CULTURAL CENTRES

Cultural centres are an integral part of Berlin's entertainment scene, providing a forum for all kinds of local and international performers and genres. These multi-purpose venues rarely impose limits on their stages and on any given night you might come across cinema, dance, live music, theatre, art, literature readings and even circus acts.

ACUD Map pp332-3

☎ 449 1067; www.acud.de; Veteranenstrasse 21, Mitte; ◉ Rosenthaler Platz
Set up in a derelict house, this alternative arts centre hosts plays, exhibitions, parties and lots of lesser-known movies from around the world, shown in their original languages.

BEGINE Map pp338-9

☎ 215 1414; www.begine.de; Potsdamer Strasse 139, Schöneberg; ◉ Bülowstrasse
This women-only café and cultural centre has a somewhat radical 'herstory': it started out as a militant feminist squat during the 1980s and now puts on concerts, readings, films and other events with an intellectual bent.

HAUS DER BERLINER FESTSPIELE
Map p344

☎ 3025 4890; www.berlinerfestspiele.de; Schaperstrasse 24, Wilmersdorf; ❷ Spichernstrasse
The heavyweight among Berlin's many multi-discipline venues. The 1951 building lacks the historic splendour of the concert halls, but it's a bastion of highbrow culture across the board, accommodating just about every major arts festival to hit the city.

INSEL DER JUGEND
☎ 5360 8020; www.insel-berlin.com; Alt-Treptow 6, Treptow; ⧩ Plänterwald
The 'Island of Youth' is a former GDR youth club housed in a mock medieval castle on an island in the Spree. There's something for everybody, from workshops to live rock concerts to open-air cinema (June to September) and dance parties of all musical stripes.

KALKSCHEUNE Map pp340-1
☎ 5900 4340; www.kalkscheune.de; Johannisstrasse 2, Mitte; ⧩ Oranienburger Strasse
While it's not a centre per se, the Kalkscheune puts on as eclectic a variety of events as you'll find in Berlin. Favourites include ballroom dancing, live gigs, fashion shows, club events and singles nights.

KULTURBRAUEREI Map pp332-3
☎ 484 9444; www.Kulturbrauerei-berlin.de; Schönhauser Allee 36, Prenzlauer Berg; ❷ Eberswalder Strasse
The huge former Schultheiss brewery is now Prenzlauer Berg's cultural powerhouse, putting itself firmly at the centre of everything that goes on in art, shopping and nightlife. There are enough individual venues to fill a small village, including a multiscreen cinema, pool hall, art gallery, three bar-restaurants, three nightclubs, four live venues and two repertory theatres, most well-known in their own right. It even has its own Christmas market.

KUNSTHAUS TACHELES Map pp340-1
☎ 282 6185; www.tacheles.de; Oranienburger Strasse 54-56, Mitte; ❷ Oranienburger Tor
Punk politics and squat aesthetics still rule in this long-serving former department store, a hotbed of anti-mainstream cinema, dance, jazz, cabaret, readings, workshops, art, theatre and more.

PFEFFERBERG Map pp332-3
☎ 4438 3342; www.pfefferberg.de; Schönhauser Allee 176, Prenzlauer Berg; ❷ Senefelderplatz
Also converted from a brewery, Pfefferberg is rougher, readier and more alternative than the Kulturbrauerei, promoting a lot of cross-cultural and antifascist projects. The bare concrete Haus 13 club is a regular dance fixture at weekends.

SCHOKOFABRIK Map pp336-7
☎ 615 2999; www.schokofabrik.de; Mariannenstrasse 6, Kreuzberg; ❷ Kottbusser Tor, Görlitzer Bahnhof
Ladies of all persuasions frequent Kreuzberg's women-only cultural centre, which offers a *hamam* (Turkish bath), sport, fitness and beauty services, and dance classes – as well as the more conventional meetings and events.

TESLA Map pp340-1
☎ 2474 9777; www.tesla-berlin.de; Klosterstrasse 68-70, Mitte; ❷ Klosterstrasse
The palatial building formerly known as the Podewil cultural centre now houses this self-styled 'laboratory' for multimedia art, which devotes itself to highly experimental projects. As well as concerts, exhibitions and workshops, regular radiotesla productions explore the mysteries of the airwaves – don't expect any Britney Spears records…

TRÄNENPALAST Map pp340-1
☎ 2061 0011; www.traenenpalast.de; Reichstagsufer 17, Mitte; ❷ ⧩ Friedrichstrasse
In a retired border-crossing facility, the 'Palace of Tears' offers a variety of multicultural entertainment, from African jazz and Russian rock to Norwegian folk and Polish dance via German cabaret and the odd spot of 'comedy blues'.

URANIA Map pp338-9
☎ 218 9091; www.urania-berlin.de; An der Urania 17, Schöneberg; lectures €5; ❷ Nollendorfplatz
In contrast to the entertainment slant of most centres, the Urania promotes a very serious intellectual agenda, holding lectures by international experts on a broad spectrum of disciplines. The 'Philosophical Café' is a popular and regular discussion event, and the film and theatre programme is also highly recommended.

LIVE MUSIC

CLASSICAL

Classical music fans are truly spoilt in Berlin – not only is there a phenomenal range of concerts throughout the year, but almost all the major concert halls are architectural gems of the highest order. A trip to the Philharmonie or the Konzerthaus is a particular treat, although regular concert series are also organised in Berlin's castles (☎ 4360 5390 for information). Aficionados under 28 should look into the Classic Card (www.classiccard.de). Note that most venues take a summer hiatus (usually July and August).

BERLINER PHILHARMONIE Map p346

☎ 2548 8132; www.berliner-philharmoniker.de; Herbert-von-Karajan-Strasse 1, Tiergarten; tickets €7-120; ◉ Ⓜ Potsdamer Platz

The Philharmonie is arguably the finest place in Berlin to hear classical music, thanks to its supreme acoustics. The current director is the flamboyant and controversial conductor Sir Simon Rattle; expect to pay top dollar when he steps behind the baton with the Berliner Philharmoniker. The adjacent Kammermusiksaal (tickets €8 to 32) is a much smaller chamber-music venue with an annually appointed pianist in residence. There isn't a bad seat in either house.

BERLINER SYMPHONIKER

☎ 325 5562; www.berliner-symphoniker.de; tickets €20-35

Founded in 1966, the Berliner Symphoniker has no permanent home and performs mainly in the Philharmonie and the Konzerthaus. Israeli conductor, Lior Shambadal, is the man in charge. After going bankrupt in 2004, the orchestra is now run by the private Berolina-Orchester company.

C BECHSTEIN CENTRUM Map p344

☎ 3151 5201; www.bechstein.de; Stilwerk, Kantstrasse 17, Charlottenburg; Ⓜ Savignyplatz

Germany's most prestigious piano manufacturer holds free concerts at its flagship store in the Stilwerk centre about eight times a year, inviting world-class musicians to showcase its stunning instruments.

DEUTSCHES SYMPHONIE-ORCHESTER

☎ 2029 8711; www.dso-berlin.de; tickets €11-75

The DSO, conducted by former Los Angeles Opera director Kent Nagano, started life in 1946 and was financed by the USA until 1953. Like the Symphoniker, it has no permanent venue, performing regularly at the Philharmonie (left), the Tempodrom (p208) and other major stages.

HOCHSCHULE FÜR MUSIK HANNS EISLER Map pp340-1

☎ 9026 9700; www.hfm-berlin.de; Charlottenstrasse 55, Mitte; ◉ Stadtmitte

The gifted students at Berlin's top-rated music academy populate several orchestras, a choir and a big band, which collectively stage as many as 400 performances annually. Almost all events are free or low-cost. Also look for activity at Neuer Marstall (p82), a secondary outpost for the school.

KONZERTHAUS BERLIN Map pp340-1

☎ 203 090; www.konzerthaus.de; Gendarmenmarkt 2, Mitte; tickets €13-43; ◉ Stadtmitte, Französische Strasse

The lavish, Schinkel-designed Konzerthaus is one of Berlin's top classical venues and a tourist attraction in its own right. The 'house band' is the excellent Berliner Sinfonie-Orchester (www.berliner-sinfonie-orchester.de), helmed by Eliahu Inbal and regular guest director Michael Gielen. There are two auditoriums here, as well as a smaller music club.

UNIVERSITÄT DER KÜNSTE Map p344

☎ 3185 2374; www.hdk-berlin.de; Hardenbergstrasse 33, Charlottenburg; ◉ Ernst-Reuter-Platz

The University of the Arts puts on a variety of classical recitals in its main concert halls on Hardenbergstrasse and Bundesallee, as well as in other venues around town. Events are usually free or donation-based.

JAZZ

Harking back to the louche heyday of the 1920s, Berlin's jazz scene just keeps on jumpin', with several fancy places in Charlottenburg balanced out by some pleasingly insalubrious joints further east. Wherever you go, you're guaranteed a good mix of local and international performers presenting some very diverse interpretations of the core genre.

A-TRANE Map p344

☎ 313 2550; www.a-trane.de; Bleibtreustrasse 1, Charlottenburg; admission €5-20; ⊗ from 9pm; 🚇 Savignyplatz

This is everything a jazz club should be – intimate, loud and usually packed. The varied talent on display is invariably top-class and, despite the cosy tables, everyone is standing by the end of the evening. Entry is free on Monday when local boy Andreas Schmidt is playing, and after 12.30am on Saturday for the late-night jam session.

B-FLAT Map pp340-1

☎ 283 3123; www.b-flat-berlin.de; Rosenthaler Strasse 13, Mitte; admission €4-12; ⊗ from 8pm; 🚇 Weinmeisterstrasse

Modern jazz in all its variants dominates the programme here, with increasing doses of world, Latin and other beats. Wednesday is acoustic night (free entry) and Sunday is tango, while the film lounge takes over one Thursday a month.

BEBOP BAR Map pp336-7

☎ 6950 8526; www.bebop-bar.de; Willibald-Alexis-Strasse 40; ⊗ from 8.15pm; 🚇 Gneisenaustrasse

Tucked away in residential Kreuzberg, Bebop is a great little jazz bar with a really personal feel to it. Admission is decided by whoever's playing, and ranges from free to €8.

JUNCTION BAR Map pp336-7

☎ 694 6602; www.junction-bar.de; Gneisenaustrasse 18, Kreuzberg; admission €3-6; 🚇 Gneisenaustrasse

Live gigs 365 days a year – the Junction is famed for the musical maelstrom in its basement, where you'll find a rowdy crowd drinking in everything from jazz and blues to fusion, hip-hop and crossover. Nightly DJs follow the bands.

QUASIMODO Map p344

☎ 312 8086; www.quasimodo.de; Kantstrasse 12a, Charlottenburg; admission €7.50-13; ⊗ from 9pm; 🚇 🚇 Zoologischer Garten

Underneath the Delphi cinema, Berlin's oldest jazz club consistently attracts high-calibre national and international acts. Its petite size puts you close to the stage, but the low ceiling, black walls and smoky air can be just a tad claustrophobic.

SCHLOT Map pp332-3

☎ 448 2160; www.kunstfabrik-schlot.de; Chausseestrasse 18, Mitte; admission €3-15; ⊗ Thu-Tue; 🚇 Zinnowitzer Strasse

Schlot is an ambitious venue that opened immediately after reunification and quickly garnered an enduring reputation. As well as cutting-edge performances and workshops, look out for Horst Evers and co at Der Frühschoppen on Sunday, Berlin's finest *Kabarett* brunch.

UMSPANNWERK OST Map pp332-3

☎ 4208 9293; www.umspannwerk-ost.de; Palisadenstrasse 48, Friedrichshain; admission price varies; ☽ from 11.30am; ⊝ Weberwiese

Amazingly, this elegant-looking house was originally built as an electricity substation around the turn of the 20th century. Today it contains a restaurant (see p184), the Kneifzange Kabarett and the Berliner Kriminal Theater (p212), as well as this atmospheric cellar jazz club.

UNIQUE MUSICLOUNGE Map p344

☎ 315 1860; www.unique-music-lounge.de; Stilwerk, Kantstrasse 17, Charlottenburg; tickets from €15; ☽ 10am-midnight Mon-Sat, 11am-midnight Sun; ◉ Savignyplatz

Formerly Soultrane, this big club-restaurant in the stylish Stilwerk centre is definitely aiming for the upper end of the jazz market, with a smart set-up, pricey food and a programme that veers into soul, funk and pop. Go for the huge Sunday brunch.

BIG VENUES

Any time that big international acts and megastars roll into town, they'll probably play at one of these large venues. Touring productions such as *Lord of the Dance* and the Cirque de Soleil shows also have extended runs here.

ARENA Map pp336-7

☎ 533 2030; www.arena-berlin.de; Eichenstrasse 4, Treptow; ⊝ Schlesisches Tor, ◉ Treptower Park

Located on the south bank of the Spree, the midsized Berlin Arena easily holds its own against larger venues, particularly when the open riverside area is being used. The adjacent **Glashaus** hosts smaller gigs and some theatre; the **Club der Visionäre** and **MS Hoppetosse** bars are also part of the complex.

COLUMBIAHALLE Map pp336-7

☎ 698 0980; www.columbiahalle.de; Columbiadamm 13-21, Tempelhof; ⊝ Platz der Luftbrücke

Just opposite Tempelhof airport, this unfancy former sports centre hosts everything from international name artists to punk festivals and metal gigs. Next door, the smaller **ColumbiaClub** is more geared towards party nights.

MAX-SCHMELING-HALLE Map pp332-3

☎ 443 045; www.max-schmeling-halle.de; Am Falkplatz, Prenzlauer Berg; ⊝ Eberswalder Strasse

Built as part of Berlin's bid for the 2000 Olympics, this 8500-seat hall wasn't quite enough to get the edge over Sydney but is now home to the Alba basketball team (see p216) and also hosts concerts, theatre and conferences.

OLYMPIASTADION

☎ 254 6900; www.olympiastadion-berlin.de; Olympischer Platz 3, Charlottenburg; ◉ Olympiastadion

The historic Olympic Stadium has finally emerged from four years of renovation and is once again hosting Berlin's biggest sport and music events, though it'll take something to outdo the 2006 World Cup final. You can tour the building during the day (€6) or come for the spectacular weekly Ring of Fire lightshow (€10). Also see p118.

POSTBAHNHOF Map pp336-7

☎ 698 1280; www.fritzclub.com; Strasse der Pariser Kommune 3-10, Friedrichshain; ◉ Ostbahnhof

This latest addition to the gig circuit covers the same kind of territory as the Columbia venues, and is already pulling in plenty of high-profile international bands. Club nights with Radio Fritz DJs follow most weekend gigs.

TEMPODROM Map pp336-7

☎ 695 3385; www.tempodrom.de; Möckernstrasse 10, Kreuzberg; ◉ Anhalter Bahnhof

Housed on the grounds of the former Anhalter Bahnhof, the round Tempodrom puts on a range of large concerts, performances, musicals, circuses and the like. Look out for the popular **Liquidrom spa centre**, if and when it reopens.

VELODROM Map pp332-3

☎ 443 045; www.velodrom.de; Paul-Heyse-Strasse 26, Lichtenberg; ◉ Landsberger Allee

This cycle track is not merely for bikes – plenty of other top sporting and music events, as well as conferences, are held in the 11,000-seat main hall, run by the same company that administers the Max-Schmeling-Halle.

WALDBÜHNE

☎ 810 750; Am Glockenturm, Charlottenburg; ⊙ May-Sep; ⊚ Olympia-Stadion, ⊞ Pichelsberg

You can't beat a huge open-air amphitheatre in the woods for atmosphere: 22,000 people can and do pack into this place to enjoy films, rock, pop and classical concerts throughout the summer.

OPERA & MUSICALS

Not many cities afford themselves the luxury of three state-funded opera houses, but then opera has been popular in Berlin ever since the first fat lady loosed her lungs, and fans can catch some of the biggest and best performances in the country here. However, this interest has never translated into a great public passion for musicals, and there's no equivalent of London's West End here.

DEUTSCHE OPER Map pp338-9

☎ 343 8401; www.deutscheoperberlin.de; Bismarckstrasse 35, Charlottenburg; tickets €12-112; ⊚ Deutsche Oper

Berlin's largest opera house may look unsightly but its musical supremacy is seldom questioned, and the arrival of its first-ever female boss, Kirsten Harms, looks set to shake off a slightly stuffy image. All operas are performed in their original language. Expect a strong Mozart revival for the 2006–07 season under musical director Yves Abel.

HANSA THEATER Map pp330-1

☎ 3983 7474; www.hansatheater-berlin.de; Alt-Moabit 48, Tiergarten; ticket prices vary; ⊚ Turmstrasse

Head north of the Spree for a lively blend of modern musical theatre and revue shows, from Stephen Sondheim to Hildegard Knef.

KOMISCHE OPER Map pp340-1

☎ 4799 7400; www.komische-oper-berlin.de; Behrenstrasse 55-57, box office Unter den Linden 41, Mitte; tickets €8-93; ⊞ Unter den Linden

Musical theatre, light opera, operetta and dance theatre are the domain of Mitte's high-profile central venue. While plenty of parliamentarians pop in, there's no elitism here. Productions are drawn from many periods and all are sung in German.

NEUKÖLLNER OPER Map pp336-7

☎ 688 9070; www.neukoellneroper.de; Karl-Marx-Strasse 131-133, Neukölln; tickets €9-21; ⊚ Karl-Marx-Strasse

You don't need public funding to run a good venue – Neukölln's refurbished prewar ballroom is easily the most creative opera house in the city, with an actively anti-elitist repertoire pitting children's shows and experimental performances against rare operas by greats such as Mozart and Schubert.

STAATSOPER UNTER DEN LINDEN
Map pp340-1

☎ 2035 4438, tickets ☎ 2035 4555; www.staatsoper-berlin.de; Unter den Linden 5-7, Mitte; tickets €8-120; ⊚ Französische Strasse

Berlin's oldest opera house looms proudly on Unter den Linden in a neoclassical temple of the arts, with a pedigree as long as its busy programme. Life director, Daniel Barenboim, places much emphasis on lavish productions of baroque operas and works by later composers. All operas are performed in their original language.

THEATER DES WESTENS Map p344

☎ 319 030; www.theater-des-westens.de; Kantstrasse 12, Charlottenburg; tickets €27-85; ⊚ ⊞ Zoologischer Garten

Virtually the only place in town to get your Lloyd Webber fix, this is Berlin's traditional venue for German-language productions of big-name musicals, hosting both touring and home-grown companies. It's a good stage but quality varies widely and the cheapest seats tend to have lousy views.

Theater des Westens (this page)

CABARET

With the possible exception of Paris, few cities are as closely associated with cabaret as Berlin, and there are plenty of venues here dedicated to reviving the lively and lavish variety shows of the Golden Twenties. For the full experience you can often dine at your table.

BAR JEDER VERNUNFT Map p344
☎ 883 1582; www.bar-jeder-vernunft.de; Schaperstrasse 24, Wilmersdorf; tickets €14-30; Ⓜ Spichernstrasse, Uhlandstrasse

With an emphasis on entertainment rather than *varieté,* most performers visiting this exquisite Art Nouveau–style tent venue have cult followings and shows are often sold out in advance. The same people run the Tipi (Map pp330–1; ☎ 390 6650; www .tipi-das-zelt.de; Grosse Querallee, Tiergarten), a much larger tent with more mainstream appeal.

FRIEDRICHSTADTPALAST Map pp340-1
☎ 2326 2203; www.friedrichstadtpalast.de; Friedrichstrasse 107, Mitte; tickets €12-61; Ⓜ Oranienburger Tor

The Friedrichstadtpalast is the largest revue theatre in Europe and often sells out all 2000 seats. The ambitious scale of the glam, ritzy, Vegas-style productions – which feature an 80-strong corps of leggy dancers supported by excellent in-house musicians – ensures an entertaining evening.

SCHEINBAR VARIETÉ Map pp338-9
☎ 784 5539; www.scheinbar.de; Monumentenstrasse 9, Schöneberg; tickets €5-12; ⊙ shows 8.30pm; Ⓜ Ⓡ Yorckstrasse

Seeing the stage here should be no problem unless you lie down – the venue's so 'intimate' that you're never far away from the action. Most performers are newcomers hoping to get a break here before moving on to bigger things.

WINTERGARTEN VARIETÉ Map pp338-9
☎ 2500 8888; www.wintergarten-variete.de; Potsdamer Strasse 96, Tiergarten; tickets €15-55; Ⓜ Kurfürstenstrasse

This is the closest vaudeville has ever come to being cool. Every night top magicians, clowns, acrobats and artistes from around the world appear beneath the starry velvet ceiling. The line-up changes every few months and quality varies, but it's worth a peek.

KABARETT & COMEDY

Cabaret should not be confused with *Kabarett,* satirical comedy featuring a team of *Kabarettisten* in a series of stand-up monologues, songs or skits. The humour ranges from biting to surreal, and shows can be hilarious – if your German is up to it! As well as the dedicated venues listed here, it's worth checking out Der Frühschoppen, the regular *Kabarett* brunch at Schlot (p207).

BERLINER KABARETT ANSTALT
Map pp336-7
☎ 202 2007; www.bka-theater.de; Mehringdamm 32-34, Kreuzberg; tickets €5-20; Ⓜ Mehringdamm
Despite the name, *Kabarett* is only a small part of the programme at this intimate venue, which hosts comedy, plays, revues, dance, classical, jazz and even Turkish-Arabic club nights.

DIE WÜHLMÄUSE
☎ 3067 3011; www.wuehlmaeuse.de; Pommernallee 2-4, Charlottenburg; tickets €11.50-34; Ⓜ Theodor-Heuss-Platz
'The Voles' is one of Berlin's most professional comedy outfits, with a regular procession of quality, mainly *Kabarett,* acts making the trek out west.

DISTEL Map pp340-1
☎ 204 4704; www.distel-berlin.de; Friedrichstrasse 101, Mitte; tickets €9-23; Ⓜ Ⓡ Friedrichstrasse
The GDR's first *Kabarett* stage was founded in 1953 and continues in a similarly satirical vein today, though it must be much easier poking fun at a government that won't set the Stasi on you.

KOOKABURRA COMEDY CLUB
Map pp340-1
☎ 4862 3186; www.comedy-club.biz; Schönhauser Allee 184, Prenzlauer Berg; tickets €5-12; Ⓜ Rosa-Luxemburg-Platz
A stand-up club in the more modern understanding of the genre, attracting plenty of TV-hardened talent. Regular nights include a Sunday open stage and a monthly tribute to Charles Bukowski and Tom Waits.

QUATSCH COMEDY CLUB Map pp340-1

(☎ 3087 85685; www.quatschcomedyclub.de; Friedrichstrasse 107; ⊖ Oranienburger Tor)
Located in the basement of the Friederichstadtpalast (opposite), this is Berlin's top spot for stand-up.

CASINOS

CASINO BERLIN Map pp340-1

☎ 2389 4144; www.casino-berlin.de; Park Inn Hotel, Alexanderplatz, Mitte; admission €5, machines €1; ⏰ 11am-3am; ⊖ ⓡ Alexanderplatz
Craps with a view: Berlin's highest den of vice is way up on the 37th floor, offering all the usual card and random-chance games. There's a separate slot-machine area on the ground floor for those prone to vertigo.

SPIELBANK BERLIN Map p346

☎ 255 990; www.spielbank-berlin.de; Marlene-Dietrich-Platz 1, Tiergarten; Casino Royal admission €5; ⏰ 11.30am-3am; ⊖ ⓡ Potsdamer Platz
Parked next to the glass-fronted Potsdamer Platz Theater, the Spielbank claims to be Germany's largest casino, with tables and machines spread over three floors. The gaming areas are split into Casino Leger (casual) and Casino Royal (formal dress). Admission is to over 18s only throughout.

THEATRE

Get ready to smell the greasepaint; with over 100 stages around town, theatre is the mainstay of Berlin's cultural scene. Add in a particularly active collection of roaming companies and experimental outfits and you'll find there are more than enough offerings to satisfy all possible tastes.

Many theatres are closed on Monday and from mid-July to late August. Box offices generally keep at least office hours on days without performances. Good seats are often available on the evening itself, with unclaimed tickets sold 30 minutes before curtain. It's also fine to buy spare tickets from other theatregoers, though you should make sure they're legit. Some theatres offer discounts of up to 50% for students and seniors.

Friedrichstrasse and the Kurfürstendamm are Berlin's main drama drags; check www.berlin-buehnen.de and local listings magazines for smaller, experimental theatres around town.

MAJOR STAGES

BERLINER ENSEMBLE Map pp340-1

☎ 2840 8155; www.berliner-ensemble.de; Bertolt-Brecht-Platz 1, Mitte; tickets €2-30; ⊖ ⓡ Friedrichstrasse
Founded by Bertolt Brecht himself, this prestigious theatre has been supervised by director Claus Peymann since 1999. Despite plenty of big names and some modern Austrian works complementing the stock German classics (including many works by Brecht) and Shakespeare, the general consensus is that the programme lacks a bit of excitement. The building itself is gorgeous, and cheap tickets are usually available.

DEUTSCHES THEATER Map pp340-1

☎ 2844 1225; www.deutschestheater.de; Schumannstrasse 13a, Mitte; tickets €5-43; ⊖ Oranienburger Tor
Berlin's premier theatre has a long and rich tradition, but since reunification its pre-eminent reputation has waned – there's a sense of stagnation in the unadventurous programming, and you'll often be better off investigating the smaller Kammerspiele (studio theatre) next door, which stages some really innovative stuff. New director Michael Thalheimer is the latest man to try and create a buzz around the place.

HEBBEL AM UFER Map pp336-7

☎ 2590 0427; www.hebbel-am-ufer.de; box office Hallesches Ufer 32, Kreuzberg; tickets €8-15; ⊖ Hallesches Tor
In 2003 the Hebbel Theater merged with the nearby Theater am Hallesches Ufer and Theater am Ufer to create the HAU, which promptly won Theatre of the Year in 2004. With an emphasis on modern, experimental drama and dance on all three stages, the new entity is a serious presence on the avant-garde scene.

MAXIM GORKI THEATER Map pp340-1

☎ 2022 1115; www.gorki.de; Am Festungsgraben 2, Mitte; tickets €10-30; ⊖ ⓡ Friedrichstrasse
The smallest and least subsidised of the state-funded theatres, the Gorki habitually stages a good mix of traditional and modern pieces, and quality is uniformly high. Expect plenty of fresh contemporary works under new director Armin Petras.

SCHAUBÜHNE AM LEHNINER PLATZ
Map pp338-9
☎ 890 020; www.schaubuehne.de;
Kurfürstendamm 153, Wilmersdorf; tickets €13-35;
Ⓔ Adenauerplatz
West Berlin owes any cutting-edge theatrical credentials to this former 1920's cinema, rescued from bland obscurity under
the forceful leadership of choreographer
Sasha Waltz and director Thomas Ostermeier. Ostermeier is still in charge, joined
by playwright Jens Hillje, and Waltz remains a regular collaborator. The ambitious
and wide-ranging programme competes
with the Volksbühne (see below) far more
than the mainstream stages.

VOLKSBÜHNE AM ROSA-LUXEMBURG-
PLATZ Map pp340-1
☎ 2406 5777; www.volksbuehne-berlin.de; Rosa-
Luxemburg-Platz, Mitte; tickets €10-30; Ⓔ Rosa-
Luxemburg-Platz
Nonconformist, radical and provocative:
Volksbühne head and Dostoyevsky fan
Frank Castorf wouldn't have it any other
way, and his even more controversial
colleague Christoph Schlingensief seems
bent on outdoing him. The aggressively
modern ethos pulls in a predominantly
18- to 35-year-old audience from East
Berlin.
   Smaller, even more off-beat perform-
ances take place over at the Volksbühne am
Prater (Map pp332–3; Kastanienallee 7-9,
Prenzlauer Berg).

ENGLISH-LANGUAGE THEATRE
BERLINER GRUNDTHEATER
☎ 7800 1497; www.thebgt.de
Founded for the Edinburgh Fringe back in
1991, this part-time company stages annual
English-language productions in venues
around the city.

FRIENDS OF ITALIAN OPERA
Map pp336-7
☎ 691 1211; www.thefriends.de; Fidicinstrasse 40,
Kreuzberg; tickets €14; Ⓔ Platz der Luftbrücke
More *cosa nostra* than *Cosi fan tutti,* Berlin's oldest English-language stage takes
its name from a neat Mafia euphemism,
though audiences need little persuasion to
attend the nightly performances.

SPECIALIST THEATRE
BAMAH JÜDISCHES THEATER
Map pp338-9
☎ 251 1096; www.bamah.de; Am Steinplatz,
Hardenbergstrasse 12, Charlottenburg; tickets €22;
Ⓔ Ⓡ Zoologischer Garten
Berlin's main Jewish theatre stages traditional and modern Jewish works and other
relevant pieces to an appreciative audience,
without shying away from contentious issues and controversial material.

BERLINER KRIMINAL THEATER
Map pp332-3
☎ 4799 7488; www.kriminaltheater.de; Pali-
sadenstrasse 48, Friedrichshain; tickets €19-35;
Ⓔ Weberwiese
Part of the Umspannwerk Ost building, the
BKT is sadly not run by felons – instead it
specialises in whodunnits and other crime-
related plays. Naturally *Die Mausefalle* (The
Mousetrap) gets a frequent airing.

HACKESCHES HOFTHEATER
Map pp340-1
☎ 283 2587; www.hackesches-hoftheater.de;
Hackesche Höfe, Rosenthaler Strasse 40/41, Mitte;
tickets €8-14; Ⓡ Hackescher Markt
The Hoftheater keeps Yiddish culture
alive with a busy programme of theatre
and music, and also specialises in mime
performances (are we missing the connection?). The Yiddish Music Summer festival
draws major crowds here every year.

THEATERDISCOUNTER Map pp340-1
☎ 4404 8561; www.theaterdiscounter.de; Packhalle,
Monbijoustrasse 1, Mitte; Ⓡ Oranienburger Strasse
The central concept here is 'theatre on
the cheap'. Plays are stacked high and
sold fast, with minimal rehearsal times,
a rapid turnover and tickets available
for a very reasonable €10. Apparently
this cash'n'carry model works, as TD has
quickly become a one-stop shop for brand-
new experimental plays.

TIYATROM Map pp336-7
☎ 615 2020; www.tiyatrom.de; Alte Jakobstrasse
12, Kreuzberg; admission price varies;
Ⓔ Hallesches Tor, Moritzplatz
Naturally, Berlin's largest minority has
its own dedicated theatre, though you

might be surprised to find out that the city's principal Turkish stage already has 20 years of service behind it. If you don't speak Turkish or German you're gonna struggle.

CHILDREN'S & YOUTH THEATRE

CABUWAZI
☎ 530 0040; www.cabuwazi.de
The name stands for 'Chaotisch-Bunter WanderZirkus' (Chaotic and Colourful Travelling Circus), a not-for-profit programme that trains kids aged 10 to 17 as circus artistes. They stage performances at various venues; call or check listings magazines for shows.

GRIPS THEATER Map pp330–1
☎ 397 4740; www.grips-theater.de; Altonaer Strasse 22, Tiergarten; tickets €6-16; ⊜ Hansaplatz
The Grips is the best, and best-known, of Berlin's youth stages, producing high-quality topical and critical plays that are suitable for older children and teenagers. The regular productions of director Volker Ludwig's highly successful U-Bahn musical *Linie 1* are a definite highlight – keep an eye out for the equally acclaimed Korean adaptation!

THEATER AN DER PARKAUE
☎ 557 752; www.carrousel.de; Parkaue 29, Friedrichshain; adult/concession/child €11/9/7; ⊜ ⊛ Frankfurter Allee
Out on the far eastern side of town, this theatre has an intelligent programme of classics and new plays catering for teenagers and adults, as well as a dedicated children's department. The schedule is helpfully organised according to age group.

Puppet Theatre

DIE SCHAUBUDE Map pp332–3
☎ 423 4314; Greifswalder Strasse 81-84, Prenzlauer Berg; adult €5.50-12.50, child €3.60; ⊛ Greifswalder Strasse
Not just for the kiddiewinks – the professional puppeteers here take their art seriously, and evening shows are generally aimed at adults.

Performance at Die Schaubude (this page)

PUPPENTHEATER FIRLEFANZ
Map pp340–1
☎ 283 3560; www.puppentheater-firlefanz.de
Sophienstrasse 10, Mitte; adult €6-12, child €4-8; ⊝ Wed, Fri-Sun; ⊜ Weinmeisterstrasse
Traditional puppets and marionettes play to crowds of all ages here, next to the Hackesche Höfe.

DANCE

With the **Hebbel Am Ufer** (p211) consistently promoting experimental choreography, and Sasha Waltz back working at the **Schaubühne** (opposite), Berlin's independent dance scene has never been stronger. Though there are few dedicated venues, many theatres now include dance performances in their programmes; check listings for upcoming events.

In the mainstream, classical ballet is performed at the **Staatsoper Unter den Linden** (p209) and the **Deutsche Oper** (p209), while more modern interpretations crop up at the **Komische Oper** (p209). On a less highbrow level, the city's finest scantily clad show-girls strut their stuff at the **Friedrichstadtpalast** (p210).

DOCK 11 STUDIOS Map pp332-3

☎ 448 1222; www.dock11-berlin.de; Kastanienallee 79, Prenzlauer Berg; admission price varies; ⌚ shows Wed–Sun; ◉ Eberswalder Strasse
As well as an extensive programme of performances, Dock 11 runs courses and workshops during the week, teaching everything from ballet and street dance to Pilates and acrobatics.

SOPHIENSAELE Map pp340-1

☎ 2859 9360; www.sophiensaele.com; Sophienstrasse 18, Mitte; tickets €13; ◉ Hackescher Markt
Before heading off to rejuvenate the Schaubühne, Sasha Waltz transformed the Sophiensaele into Berlin's number-one spot for experimental and avant-garde dance. In her absence the emphasis is edging back towards theatre and performance art, but you can still expect to find some of the city's most exciting dance events here.

CINEMAS

The choice is astounding but, compared to the cost of other forms of entertainment, going to the movies can be pricey in Berlin, with Saturday-night tickets at the multiplexes costing as much as €9. Almost all cinemas also add a sneaky *Überlängezuschlag* (overrun supplement) of €0.50 to €1 for films longer than 90 minutes. Seeing a show on a *Kinotag* (film day, usually Monday to Wednesday) or before 5pm can save you up to 50%. Smaller, independent neighbourhood theatres are usually cheaper, and may offer student discounts.

Cinemas show mostly mainstream Hollywood movies dubbed into German. Many smaller screens show movies in their original language, denoted in listings by the acronym 'OF' (*Originalfassung*) or 'OV' (*Originalversion*); those with German subtitles are marked 'OmU' (*Original mit Untertiteln*).

SUMMER SCREENS

Claustrophobic film fans should love Berlin in the summertime, when numerous outdoor stages pop up around town. The repertoire is mostly made up of mainstream crowd pleasers. As well as the **Waldbühne** (p209), popular *Freiluftkinos* include the following:

Friedrichshain (Map pp332–3; ☎ 2936 1629; www.freiluftkino-berlin.de; Volkspark Friedrichshain)

Hasenheide (Map pp336–7; ☎ 283 4603; www.freiluftkino-hasenheide.de; Volkspark Hasenheide, Neukölln)

Insel der Jugend (p205)

Kreuzberg (Map pp336–7; ☎ 2936 1628; www.freiluftkino-kreuzberg.de; Mariannenplatz 2)

Museuminsel (Map pp340–1; ☎ 2062 8778; www.museuminselfestival.info; Bodestrasse, Mitte)

Those with young children should look out for the **Spatzenkino** (☎ 449 4750; www.spatzenkino.de) screenings of films aimed at young children.

Oh, and yes Pulp Fiction fans, you can buy beer along with your popcorn in most Berlin cinemas – just remember to return your empty bottles when you leave!

ARSENAL Map p346

☎ 2695 5100; www.fdk-berlin.de; Sony Center, Potsdamer Strasse 21, Tiergarten; adult/child €6.50/3; ◉ ◈ Potsdamer Platz
Eschewing the Hollywood fare that dominates the other Potsdamer Platz screens, nonmainstream movies from around the world (usually dubbed into English) can be seen at this excellent theatre in the Filmhaus.

BABYLON Map pp336-7

☎ 6160 9693; www.yorck.de; Dresdener Strasse 126, Kreuzberg; adult/concession €7/6; ◉ Kottbusser Tor
The popular Babylon is one of 13 Berlin cinemas making up the Yorcker family of broad-appeal art house screens, which also includes the **Central Cinema** (Map pp340–1) in the Hackesche Höfe and the enormous **Delphi-Filmpalast** (Map p344) on Kantstrasse.

CINEMAXX POTSDAMER PLATZ Map p346

☎ 2592 2111; www.cinemaxx.de; Voxstrasse 2, Tiergarten; adult/concession €7.30/5; ◉ ◈ Potsdamer Platz

This state-of-the-art megacomplex, part of a nationwide chain, is the primary venue of the **Berlinale International Film Festival** (p9). There are up to 20 movies on the programme at any given time here, and the big releases are often shown in their original language.

CINESTAR IM SONY CENTER Map p346

☎ 2606 6260; www.cinestar.de; Potsdamer Strasse 4, Tiergarten; adult/concession €7.50/5.50, IMAX €7.90/6.90; ⊕ Ⓡ Potsdamer Platz
No surprises here: it's yet another huge chain multiplex on Potsdamer Platz. This one has both standard and IMAX screens, and is the venue of choice for most international premieres thanks to the Sony Center's showy glass atrium.

DISCOVERY CHANNEL IMAX THEATER

Map p346

☎ 2592 7259; www.imax-berlin.de; Marlene-Dietrich-Platz 4, Tiergarten; adult/concession €8/6.70; ⊕ Ⓡ Potsdamer Platz
This big domed cinema screens the usual IMAX films and documentaries about travel, space and wildlife – many in 3D. Subtitles are a thing of the past here – for a €20 deposit you get your own radio receiver to hear the English version.

EISZEIT Map pp336-7

☎ 611 6016; www.eiszeit-kino.de; Zeughofstrasse 20, Kreuzberg; tickets €6-7; ⊕ Görlitzer Bahnhof
There's an excellent daily changing programme of obscure, alternative and experimental film fare at this tiny but long-running picture house.

FILMKUNST 66 Map p344

☎ 882 1753; Bleibtreustrasse 12, Charlottenburg; adult/concession €7/5; Ⓡ Savignyplatz
Charlottenburg's main independent art cinema is known for its regular seasons showcasing offbeat fare such as animation, shorts or Laurel and Hardy.

FILMKUNSTHAUS BABYLON Map pp340-1

☎ 242 5076; www.fkh-babylon.de; Rosa-Luxemburg-Strasse 30, Mitte; adult/concession €6.50/5.50; ⊕ Rosa-Luxemburg-Platz
Not to be confused with the Kreuzberg Babylon, this specialist screen has been at the centre of some controversy since 2005,

when fans started campaigning against the 'dilution' of its schedule with commercial programming.

FSK Map pp336-7

☎ 614 2464; www.fsk-kino.de; Segitzdamm 2, Kreuzberg; tickets €6.50; ⊕ Kottbusser Tor, Moritzplatz
Just off Oranienplatz, this high-calibre two-screen arthouse theatre shows plenty of European cinema. Unusually, the auditoriums have small fountains at the front, perhaps to encourage you to go to the toilet before the trailers end.

INTIMES Map pp336-7

☎ 2966 4633; Niederbarnimstrasse 15, Friedrichshain; adult/child €6/2.50; ⊕ Samariterstrasse
You wouldn't expect Berlin's alternative district to be without an alternative cinema, and this arthouse screen is just the ticket for offbeat releases and cult classics.

KINO INTERNATIONAL Map pp332-3

☎ 2475 6011; Karl-Marx-Allee 33, Mitte; adult/concession €7.50/6.50; ⊕ Schillingstrasse
With its camp cavalcade of glass chandeliers, glitter curtains and parquet floor, the Kino International is a show in itself, and also hosts regular club nights. Monday is 'MonGay' with homo-themed classics, imports and previews.

MOVIEMENTO Map pp336-7

☎ 692 4785; www.moviemento.de; Kottbusser Damm 22, Kreuzberg; adult/concession €6.50/5.50; ⊕ Hermannplatz
The oldest cinema in town, this three-screen independent place shows a good range of nonblockbuster mainstream foreign and German movies.

NEUE KANT Map p344

☎ 319 9866; www.neuekantkinos.de; Kantstrasse 54, Charlottenburg; adult/concession €7.50/6.50; ⊕ Wilmersdorfer Strasse
Originally built in 1912, the original Kant-Kino was rescued from closure by a group of industry professionals, including director Wim Wenders, and now screens a mix of popular and arthouse fare. The same body also runs the **Filmtheater** (☎ 3087 2510; www.hackesche-hoefe.org) in the Hackesche Höfe.

XENON Map pp338-9

☎ 782 8850; www.xenon-kino.de; Kolonnenstrasse 5-6, Schöneberg; tickets €6; Ⓞ Kleistpark
Built in 1909, the city's second-oldest movie theatre is dedicated entirely to lesbigay cinema, with lots of juicy imports and themed seasons.

SPORTS, HEALTH & FITNESS

Like many Germans, Berliners have a fairly ambivalent attitude towards fitness – gyms, spas and particularly solariums do a roaring trade, but no-one seems to mind heading off for a cigarette and a *Currywurst* afterwards. That said, Berlin is generally quick to catch on to the latest exercise trends, and the many sports on offer are taken pretty seriously by participants and spectators alike.

In terms of amenities, the city is as well-equipped as you'd expect from a European capital, although for larger and more specialised facilities you'll need to head outside the central districts.

WATCHING SPORT
American Football
BERLIN THUNDER
☎ 3006 4400; www.berlin-thunder.de; Olympiastadion; tickets €8-31.50; Ⓡ Olympiastadion
This unlikely import is quickly catching on in Berlin, largely thanks to Thunder's storming record – the team consistently tops the league and has two World Bowls to its name, having narrowly missed out on a third in 2005. Expect the best turnout for games against national rivals Frankfurt Galaxy.

Athletics
BERLIN MARATHON
☎ 302 5370; www.berlin-marathon.com
Every September you have the opportunity to watch or participate in Germany's principal contribution to the international marathon calendar. Over 50,000 people take part, and nine world records have been set here since 1977, so expect some stiff competition.

FLYING BLIND
The women's marathon record was broken here for the second year running in 2005, but the real star of the day was one Regina Vollbrecht, who crossed the line about an hour after the race winners yet still made the front page of the *Berliner Zeitung*. The reason? Ms Vollbrecht is blind. She ran the course behind a trainer holding a string, and managed to smash her own world record with a time of three hours and 22 minutes. Not only that, but she's a local girl, residing in the southern district of Tempelhof. For all its identity crises, Berlin is still a city that knows how to fête its heroes!

ISTAF
☎ 3038 4444; Olympiastadion; Ⓡ Olympiastadion
This international track-and-field meet is held in early September, shortly before the Berlin Marathon.

Basketball
ALBA BERLIN
☎ 01805-300 777; www.albaberlin.de; Max-Schmeling-Halle, Prenzlauer Berg; tickets €7.50-32
Berlin's top basketball team, founded in 1990, competes hard on a European level and has a solid winning record. Home games mostly take place at 3pm Saturday.

Cycling
BERLINER SECHSTAGERENNEN
☎ 4430 4430; www.sechstagerennen-berlin.de; Velodrom/Berlin Arena; tickets €26-40
Held in January, the Berlin Six-Day Event attracts more than 75,000 spectators for just under a week of hotly contested two-wheeled action.

Horse Racing
GALOPPRENNBAHN HOPPEGARTEN
☎ 03342-38 930; www.galopprennbahn-hoppegarten.de; Goetheallee 1, Dahlwitz-Hoppegarten; tickets €5-20; Ⓨ May-Oct; Ⓡ Hoppegarten
Built in 1868, this 50,000-capacity course is one of the smartest tracks on the European flat circuit. Around 10 high-profile meetings take place here every year, including one on the Day of German Unity, October 3. Look out for other, less serious special events – elephant races have been held here in the past!

PFERDESPORTPARK KARLSHORST

☎ 500 170; www.psp-sportpark.de; Treskowallee 129, Lichtenberg; tickets €2 Sat, free other times; ⓡ Karlshorst

This track dates to 1862, but was completely destroyed in WWII. After the war, it was rebuilt as the only trotting (trap-racing) course in the GDR. There's one meet a week, usually on Wednesday or Friday evening.

TRABRENNBAHN MARIENDORF

☎ 740 1212; www.berlintrab.de; Mariendorfer Damm 222-298, Tempelhof; tickets €2.50; ⓤ Alt-Mariendorf

Founded in 1913, this is the trotting course of choice for hobnobbing politicos and business folk. Races are usually held on Wednesday or Sunday, with a five-day derby week in August.

Ice Hockey

EHC EISBÄREN

☎ 9718 4040; www.eisbaeren.de; Sportforum Berlin, Steffenstrasse, Hohenschönhausen; tickets €15-30; ⓡ Hohenschönhausen

Traditionally the underdog, the Ice Bears have come into their own since the demise of rival West Berlin team the Capitals, and finally became national champions in 2005. Fervent fans ensure that every home game practically explodes with atmosphere.

Soccer

Call it what you want, football is king in Germany, and Berlin makes no exception. The game proliferates at every level, with 341 official clubs ranging from grassroots amateurs to heavyweight professional teams, and raging 2006 World Cup fever will doubtless linger on at least until Euro 2008.

DEUTSCHER FUSSBALL-BUND

Map pp328-9

☎ 896 9940; www.dfb.de; Humboldtstrasse 8a, Wilmersdorf;

The DFB (German National Soccer Association) holds two national-championship finals in Berlin every year. The main event is the hugely popular *DFB-Pokalendspiel* (DFB Cup final), played at the Olympic Stadium; tickets are hard to come by and should be ordered months in advance. In January you can also catch the annual indoor-soccer championship in the Max-Schmeling-Halle.

HERTHA BSC

☎ 300 928; www.herthabsc.de; Olympiastadion; tickets €10-55; ⓡ Olympiastadion

Berlin's long-standing Bundesliga (National League) team is one of the country's most high-profile clubs, usually found just below the top of the table. Kick-off at the Olympic Stadium is usually at 3.30pm every other Saturday.

The stadium is generally packed when big-name teams such as Bayern München come calling; otherwise, you should be able to get tickets without any trouble on match days.

UNION BERLIN

☎ 656 6880; www.fc-union-berlin.de; Stadion an der Alten Försterei, An der Wuhlheide, Köpenick; tickets €6-18; ⓡ Köpenick

It's a long way from the big leagues, but the former East's pride and joy has come into form lately, blasting eight goals in a single game in the 2005–06 season. The team holds the unswerving devotion of its supporters, and the 18,000-seat stadium in working-class Köpenick is seldom lacking in atmosphere.

Tennis

LADIES GERMAN OPEN

☎ 8957 5520; www.german-open.org; Rot-Weiss Tennis Club, Grunewald; tickets €15-65; ⓡ Grunewald

This very popular event takes place every May near the Hundekehlesee lake, and usually attracts high-ranking players. Previous winners include Martina Hingis, Conchita Martinez and Justine Henin-Hardenne. Tickets can be tough to get, especially for the later rounds.

Water Polo

WASSERFREUNDE SPANDAU 04

☎ 304 6866; www.spandau04.net; Deutsches Sportforum, Olympiastadion; tickets €6; ⓡ Olympiastadion

Want to follow a winning team? For about the last 20 years Spandau 04 have been the top dogs of the German *Wasserball* league, as well as producing some outstanding individual swimming and diving performances. The polo season runs from November to May.

OUTDOOR ACTIVITIES

Cycling

The countryside surrounding central Berlin offers many lovely cycling routes. Check at major book shops for guides with detailed route descriptions, and see p289 for details on bike rentals and taking your bike on public transport.

ADFC BERLIN Map pp332-3

☎ 448 4724; www.adfc-berlin.de; Brunnenstrasse 28, Mitte; ☺ noon-8pm Mon-Fri, 10am-4pm Sat; ⊖ Rosenthaler Platz

The Allgemeiner Deutscher Fahrradclub (General German Bicycle Club) is a great source of information for cyclists. They publish a **cycle route map** (*Radwegekarte*; €7.80) that shows all bike routes in Berlin. Members receive automatic third-party insurance, and you can take part in organised tours whether you join or not.

Golf

As you'd expect in a crowded city, the full-size traditional golf courses are outside Berlin, but there are a couple of smaller central ranges if you just want to practise your swing.

AIRPORT-GOLF-BERLIN Map pp330-1

☎ 4140 0300; www.airport-golf-berlin.de; Kurt-Schumacher-Damm 176, Reinickendorf; ☺ 9am-9pm; ⊖ Jakob-Kaiser-Platz

A convenient 40,000 sq metres of golfing goodness, clearly aimed at stressed businesspeople passing through Tegel airport. There's no course, but it does have fully featured separate driving, chipping and pitching areas, as well as putting greens. 15 balls will cost you €2.

ÖFFENTLICHES GOLF-ZENTRUM

Map pp330-1

☎ 2804 7070; www.golfzentrum-berlin.de; Chausseestrasse 94-98, Mitte; ☺ 7am-dusk; ⊖ Schwarzkopffstrasse

Part of the Sportpark Mitte, this is another good practice area offering 40 balls from €2, and tuition from around €20.

Ice Skating

Berlin has several well-maintained municipal ice rinks which are usually open from October to March. The cost is €3.30 per adult, or €1.60 for a child, per two-hour session, plus €2.50 to €5 to rent skates. Skating periods vary, but most rinks have three a day, usually lasting three hours.

In addition to the permanent rinks listed below, temporary open-air ice rinks set up shop in public areas in most parts of town each year – often as part of the Christmas markets, with music, mulled wine and Santa hats everywhere. The most popular spots include the western end of Unter den Linden, Potsdamer Platz (Map p346), Alexanderplatz (Map pp340–1) and Spandau (Map p343); there are also plenty of less crowded rinks tucked away in corners such as Wilmersdorfer Strasse (Map p344). Skating on all these surfaces is usually free, with skate hire available for around €2.50.

If it's cold enough to freeze, you may be able to venture out on some of the smaller lakes; try the Schlachtensee, southwest of the centre.

Online, www.eisbahnen-berlin.de and www.eissport-berlin.de have information on the city's various skating facilities.

EISSTADION NEUKÖLLN

☎ 6280 4403; Oderstrasse 182, Neukölln; ⊖ Hermannstrasse

A big, open ice arena southeast of the centre. Monday and Wednesday are 'Happy Days' here, with a 50% discount, and the last hour is half price for the remainder of the week.

ERIKA-HESS-EISSTADION

Map pp330-1

☎ 200 945 551; Müllerstrasse 185, Mitte; ⊖ Reinickendorfer Strasse

Up towards Wedding, this is a good indoor ice-skating rink offering courses and all the standard facilities.

HORST-DOHM-EISSTADION

Map pp338-9

☎ 823 4060; www.eissport-service.de; Fritz-Wildung-Strasse 9, Wilmersdorf; ⊖ ⊛ Heidelberger Platz

The city's largest ice rink enjoys a pretty location surrounded by trees, which looks great in the snow and at night. A 400m outer speed-skating ring encircles a second, more leisurely area.

(Continued on page 227)

1 *Fernsehturm (p92), Alexander-platz, Mitte* **2** *Outdoor diners at Hackescher Markt S-Bahn station (p95), Mitte* **3** *Illuminated ceiling of Sony Center (pp105-6), Potsdamer Platz, Tiergarten* **4** *The modern hall of worship and the Kaiser-WilhelmGedächtniskirche (p115), Charlottenburg*

1 *A cafe in Prenzlauer Berg (p197)*
2 *Sausage vendor on Friedrichstrasse (pp15-17), Mitte* **3** *Looking out on to Gendarmenmarkt from Newton (p192), Mitte* **4** *Tapas bar Yosoy (p171), Mitte*

1 *Various wines on the buffet table at Cassambalis (p174), Charlottenburg* 2 *Sushi making at Kuchi (p169), Mitte* 3 *Bocca di Bacco (p168), Mitte* 4 *Entrance to Borchardt (p168), Mitte*

1 *Bartenders working at Reingold (p192), Mitte*
2 *Country and Western bar playing at Kaffee Burger (p200), Mitte* 3 *Exterior of [Tagung (p196), Friedrichsh[* 4 *Berlin Philharmonie (p20[Tiergarten*

1 ...ie Schaubude puppet thea...(p213), Prenzlauer Berg ...elting it out at the Winter...ten Varieté (p210), Tiergar... 3 The opulent Komische ...er (p209), Mitte

1 *Stalls at Türkenmarkt (p243), Kreuzberg* **2** *KaDeWe department store (p240), Schöneberg* **3** *Galeries Lafyette (p234), Mitte* **4** *Ampelmann Galerie (p233), Mitte*

ohmarkt Strasse des 17
 (p237), Tiergarten
shions at Berlinomat
4), Friedrichshain
lypso shoe shop (p233),
e **4** Leysieffer chocolate
 (p239), Charlottenburg

225

1 *African Suite at Hecker's Hotel (p257), Charlottenburg* **2** *The cagey Lion's Room at Propeller Island City Lodge (p260), Wilmersdorf* **3** *Lobby of Honigmond Garden Hotel (p253), Mitte* **4** *Entrance to Brandenburger Hof (pp259-60), Wilmersdorf*

(Continued from page 218)

In-Line Skating & Skateboarding

In-line skating and skateboarding remain firm favourites with young Berliners, and there are plenty of outdoor ramps, pipes and parks scattered around the suburbs. Check out www.skate-spots.de for locations. Some of the best are at the old Radrennbahn in Weissensee, Grazer Platz in Schöneberg, the Gartenschau in Marzahn and Räcknitzer Steig in Spandau. There's a selection of popular free half-pipes in the Volkspark Friedrichshain (pp330–1).

SKATEHALLE BERLIN Map pp336-7

☎ 2936 0322; www.skatehalle-berlin.de; Revaler Strasse 99, Friedrichshain; Noon-9pm Mon-Tue, Noon-Midnight Wed-Fri, 11am-Midnight Sat, 11am-8pm Sun; adult/conc €5/3; 🅾 🚊 Warschauer Strasse

Opened in 2005 alongside the Cassiopeia club (p203), this is boarding heaven, offering budding Tony Hawks everything from corner ramps and curbcuts to London gaps and picnic tables, plus the biggest half-pipe in Germany.

Multisport

FREISPORTANLAGE AM SÜDPARK

☎ 361 5201; Am Südpark 51, Spandau; 🕙 10am-8pm May-Sep; 🚊 Spandau, 🚌 131, 134

A rare treat for outdoor sports fans, this 10,000 sq metre facility is absolutely free and incorporates tennis, volleyball, basketball and beach volleyball courts, an in-line skating area and table tennis. For the less energetic, there's also a café and mini-golf (€2). Allow at least half a day for a visit.

SPORTPARK MITTE Map pp330-1

☎ 0177-280 6861; www.beachmitte.de; Chausseestrasse 96; 🕙 from 10am Apr-Sep; 🅾 Schwartzkopffstrasse

If you do like to be beside the seaside, this sandy sports park is a slice of beach-life right in the centre of town. Strut your stuff day or night on one of the two dozen beach courts, which can accommodate volleyball, soccer, handball and more. Reservations recommended.

Running

Berlin is a great place for running because of its many parks. While the Tiergarten (Map pp330–1 & Map p346) is easily the most popular, thanks to its large size and central location, both the Volkspark Hasenheide (Map pp336–7) in Neukölln and the Grunewald in Wilmersdorf/Zehlendorf are also well trodden. The trip around the scenic Schlachtensee, in the Grunewald, is 5km.

If you prefer to run through historic surroundings, the gardens of Schlossgarten Charlottenburg (Map pp328–9) are delightful, though seasoned joggers might feel under-challenged.

Swimming

Berlin may be landlocked, but the surrounding area is peppered with picturesque lakes where swimming is allowed. If you prefer some amenities, however, try one of the public pools. Outdoor pools are usually open 8am to 8pm daily from May to September, depending on the weather; admission costs €4/2.50 per adult/concession. For details of indoor swimming centres see p230.

BADESCHIFF Map pp336-7

☎ 533 2030; www.arena-berlin.de; Eichenstrasse 4, Treptow; 🕙 8am-midnight; 🅾 Schlesisches Tor, 🚊 Treptower Park

Part of the Arena complex, this unusual pool actually floats on the Spree itself, offering some great views along the north bank. Unlike most other outdoor swim spots, it stays open throughout the winter, covered, heated and with added saunas.

SOMMERBAD KREUZBERG Map pp336-7

☎ 616 1080; Prinzenstrasse 113-119, Kreuzberg; 🅾 Prinzenstrasse

This is the city's most central, multicultural and popular facility, and is also known as the Prinzenbad (Princes' Pool). There are two 50m pools, a slide and an FKK (nudist) section, all packed the second the sun comes out.

SOMMERBAD OLYMPIASTADION

☎ 3006 3440; Osttor, Olympischer Platz, Charlottenburg; 🅾 Olympia-Stadion

Built for the 1936 Olympic Games, you can do your laps here in the 50m pool once used by the world's top athletes. You'll be watched by oversized sculptures and four gigantic clocks.

STRANDBAD WANNSEE
☎ 803 5612; Wannseebadweg 25, Zehlendorf; ℞ Nikolassee

Claiming to be the largest lakeside pool in Europe, 'Berlin's Lido' has been in business since 1907 and its kilometres of sandy beach can get about as crowded as the real thing. You can rent boats, take an exercise class, eat and drink at several restaurants, or just relax in the giant wicker chairs. The water quality is decent.

HEALTH & FITNESS
Climbing
MAGIC MOUNTAIN Map pp332-3
☎ 8871 5790; www.magicmountain.de; Böttger-strasse 20-26, Wedding; adult/concession €14/11; ℘ noon-midnight Mon-Wed & Fri, 10am-midnight Thu, 11am-midnight Sat & Sun; ℗ ℞ Gesundbrunnen

A very well-equipped indoor climbing centre for budding rock-scramblers of all ages and abilities, providing three walls, an artificial boulder, equipment shop and a full fitness set-up to complete your workout.

Gyms & Fitness Centres

Most Berlin gyms are membership-based, and many require you to sign a contract (often for 12 months), take an induction course, shell out a registration charge and pay monthly fees – hardly worth the hassle unless you're staying long-term. In less uptight places you can get a day pass for around €25. Some also offer free trial workouts before joining – it won't hurt to ask. Opening times are generally around 8am to 11pm, with slightly shorter hours at weekends.

ELIXIA Map pp340-1
☎ 2200 2700; www.elixia.de; Behrenstrasse 48, Mitte; ℗ Französische Strasse

Elixia offers 2500 state-of-the-art sq metres in a central location, with extensive cardio training, free weights and spa areas. There are eight more branches around the city.

FITNESS COMPANY Map pp340-1
☎ 279 0770; www.fitcom.de; Panoramastrasse 1a, Mitte; ℗ ℞ Alexanderplatz

One of Germany's largest gym companies, Fitcom has another eight outlets spread around central and suburban Berlin, including a full health club and a business-oriented centre with a pool. The firm also operates Jopp Frauen Fitness (☎ 210 111; www.jopp.de), a chain of women-only fitness centres with seven properties in town.

HIMAXX Map pp330-1
☎ 3906 6222; www.himaxx.net; Stromstrasse 11-17, Tiergarten; ℘ 4-9pm Mon-Thu, 3-9pm Fri, 11am-4pm Sat; ℗ Turmstrasse

Want to get fit quick? This specialist gym simulates high-altitude training conditions by reducing the amount of oxygen in the air, making you work that much harder and improve that much faster.

HOLMES PLACE LIFESTYLE CLUB
Map pp340-1
☎ 2062 4949; www.holmesplace.de; Quartier 205, Friedrichstrasse 67-71, Mitte; ℗ Französische Strasse

The latest venture of this luxury British chain boasts an exclusive address and twice the space of its nearest Elixia rival, not to mention a body-boggling choice of classes.

MOVEO Map pp336-7
☎ 6950 5254; www.moveoberlin.de; Am Tempelhofer Berg 7d, Kreuzberg; classes €12.80; ℗ Platz der Luftbrücke

Various forms of yoga (including *iyengar*, *hatha*, *kundalini*, *kripalu*) ensure physical and spiritual well-being for everyone from kids to expectant mothers at this low-key studio. Some classes are taught in English.

Saunas & Spas

Germans are far from prudish and saunas are usually mixed and nude – shyness is not an option! However, hours are set aside for women only, so call ahead. The cheapest saunas are those at public pools. Privately operated facilities usually have more amenities and may be positively luxurious.

Men should also note the distinction between 'normal' and men-only (ie gay) saunas, which tend to be full-on cruising venues.

ARS VITALIS Map pp338-9

☎ 788 3563; www.ars-vitalis.de; Hauptstrasse 19, Schöneberg; day pass €25; ⊕ Kleistpark
This combined gym and spa is one of Berlin's nicest sweat spots. If the huge range of classes (including jazz dance, yoga, t'ai chi and Pilates), separate ladies' area, three different types of sauna and a posse of trained masseurs aren't enough, in summer you can strike out onto the roof terrace.

GATE SAUNA Map pp340-1

☎ 229 9430; www.gate-sauna.de; Wilhelmstrasse 81, Mitte; admission €14; ⊗ 11-7am Mon-Thu, 24hr Fri-Sun; ⊕ Mohrenstrasse
This is one of the biggest and most active gay saunas, just southeast of the Brandenburg Gate. As well as two floors of modern saunas, steam rooms and massage areas, it has a bar, restaurant and video room, cabins and a swing (no, not the kiddies' kind).

SURYA VILLA Map pp332-3

☎ 4849 5780; www.ayurveda-wellnesszentrum.de; Rykestrasse 3, Prenzlauer Berg; classes €11, full day €165; ⊗ 10.30am-9pm; ⊕ Eberswalder Strasse
With four floors of massages, baths, saunas, yoga, *qi gong*, mantra singing, meditation, health food and other treatments, this *Ayurveda* (holistic) centre is a real treat for the strained and stressed.

THERMEN AM EUROPA-CENTER

Map p344
☎ 257 5760; www.thermen-berlin.de; Nürnberger Strasse 7, Schöneberg; day pass €14-29.80; ⊗ 10am-midnight Mon-Sat, 10am-9pm Sun; ⊕ Wittenbergplatz
If you're bored with your basic Swedish, check into this stylish facility near the Gedächtniskirche. It incorporates salt-rich indoor and outdoor pools, fitness rooms, beauty treatments, aqua-gymnastics, restaurant, a tanning terrace and nine (!) saunas.

TREIBHAUS SAUNA Map pp332-3

☎ 448 4503; www.treibhaussauna.de; Schönhauser Allee 132, Prenzlauer Berg; 3 hrs €10; ⊗ 1pm-7am Mon-Thu, 24hr Fri-Sun; ⊕ Eberswalder Strasse
This is one of the nicest gay saunas in town and is kitted out with full hi-tech equipment and an on-site sex shop. Admission includes a drink from the spacious bar.

Sports Centres

In the outer suburbs you'll find several large sports centres – combining any combination of pools, squash and tennis courts, fitness studios, saunas etc under one roof – as well as plenty of smaller, more specialised outlets. Prices depend on which facilities you use, and there are usually discount or membership schemes available for longer periods.

FEZ WUHLHEIDE

☎ 5307 1504; www.fez-berlin.de; An der Wuhlheide 197, Köpenick; admission €2, swimming, incl admission, €3.50; ⊛ Wuhlheide
It's a bit far from the centre but Köpenick's FEZ has plenty to offer, with a BMX track, dance studio and various courses supplementing the usual fitness and swimming facilities. An added highlight is the virtual space-station training, which you won't find in many gyms.

FITFUN Map p344

☎ 312 5082; www.squashclub-fitfun.de; Uhlandstrasse 194, Charlottenburg; squash per hr €6; ⊕ ⊛ Zoologischer Garten
Fitfun is a good central squash club, with 13 courts and a fully featured fitness setup, plus a canteen. Members arrange regular tournaments and practice nights.

SPOK SPORT- UND KULTURZENTRUM

☎ 740 7250; www.spok.de; Nordendstrasse 56, Pankow; ⊗ 8am-11pm; tram M1
A combination of indoor and outdoor sports facilities, including tennis, badminton, beach volleyball and football courts, plus swimming, gym and table tennis opportunities, as well as saunas, a running track and playground. Oh, and a beer garden.

SPORT- UND ERHOLUNGSZENTRUM

Map pp332-3
SEZ; ☎ 4208 7920; Landsberger Allee 77, Friedrichshain; ⊛ Landsberger Allee
Currently in the throes of a major renovation, parts of the huge SEZ complex are reopening gradually, with bowling lanes, a fitness area and a sports hall already finished. Final completion of the swimming area is scheduled for 2007.

TSB CITY SPORTS Map pp338-9

☎ 873 9097; www.citysports-berlin.com; Brandenburgische Strasse 53, Wilmersdorf; Ⓜ Konstanzer Strasse

One of the largest racket-sport facilities in town, TSB has courts for tennis, table tennis, squash and badminton, and also offers self-defence and dance courses.

Sports Clubs

If you're looking to play any kind of team game, your only option will usually be to join a relevant club. The best way to find one is by checking local magazines and notice boards. There are also several clubs catering for particular 'interest groups'.

RSC BERLIN

☎ 5321 7405; www.rsc-berlin.de

One of the oldest sports clubs for physically disabled people in Germany, founded in 1967. The core activities are wheelchair basketball, badminton and table tennis, with additional opportunities for physiotherapy. 'Pedestrians' are also welcome!

VORSPIEL

☎ 4405 7740; www.vorspiel-berlin.de

Boasting an impressive 1100 members, Berlin's lesbigay sports club is far from exclusive, and runs a huge range of different activities for players of all levels and preferences. As an added bonus, you get four free trial sessions before signing up. In time-honoured innuendo tradition, the name means 'foreplay'.

Swimming

Berlin has plenty of indoor pools in each district. Some may be closed on mornings when school groups take over, while others are reserved for specific groups – women, men, lap-swimmers, nudists, seniors – at certain times of the week. Tickets for almost all municipal pools are €4 per adult, or €2.50 concession (€2.50 before 8am and after 8pm).

Opening hours vary by day, and pool and season. For full information, contact the BBB (☎ 01803-102 020; www.berlinerbae derbetriebe.de) or pick up a pamphlet at any pool.

For details of outdoor swimming pools and lakes see p227.

BAD AM SPREEWALDPLATZ

Map pp336-7

☎ 6953 5210; Wiener Strasse 59h, Kreuzberg; sauna adult/concession €9/7; Ⓜ Görlitzer Bahnhof

This consistent local favourite has a wave pool, cascades, Jacuzzis and a slide, in addition to a 25m lap pool.

BLUB BADEPARADIES

☎ 606 6060; Buschkrugallee 64, Neukölln; admission €10.70-13.30; 🕙 10am-11pm; Ⓜ Grenzallee

A modern 'fun' pool with a whole lot of attractions, including a wave pool, waterfall, 120m slide, saltwater pool, hot whirlpools, sauna landscape and restaurants.

STADTBAD CHARLOTTENBURG

Map pp330-1

Alte Halle ☎ 3438 3860, Neue Halle ☎ 3438 3865; Krumme Strasse 10; sauna €11; Ⓜ Bismarckstrasse

The colourful 1898 Alte Halle (Old Hall) here is a protected monument, one of the few of its kind still in use. On nude bathing nights, the 25m, 28°C pool and sauna attract large numbers of gay men. The modern Neue Halle (New Hall) is more suited for serious swimmers and has a 50m lap pool.

STADTBAD NEUKÖLLN Map pp336-7

☎ 6824 9812; Ganghoferstrasse 5; sauna adult/concession €14/11; Ⓜ Rathaus Neukölln

Called the most beautiful pool in Europe at its opening in 1914, this is still one of Berlin's most impressive bathing temples, wowing swimmers with mosaics, frescoes, marble and brass. There are 25m and 20m pools, plus a sauna area.

Shopping

opping

Berlin may not traditionally rank among the world's great shopping cities but, frankly, that's quite an outdated perception. Fact is, Berlin is a great place to shop. The city's zest for life, boundary-pushing energy and experimental spirit translate into a cosmopolitan cocktail of unique boutiques that are a joy to explore. Shopping is one of life's great pleasures, a benign diversion that's as much about visual and mental stimulus as it is about actually buying stuff. Whether you're a penny-pincher or a power-shopper, you'll find plenty of opportunities to drop some cash in Berlin's multi-faceted neighbourhoods.

'Neighbourhoods' (or, as the locals say, *Kieze*) is a key word in understanding how to approach shopping in Berlin. There is no grand central shopping boulevard here, like London's Oxford Street or Broadway in Manhattan. The closest the German capital comes to having a retail spine is Kurfürstendamm and its extension, Tauentzienstrasse – and they still don't quite measure up. Perfecting the art of shopping in Berlin means venturing into the various *Kieze*, each of which has its own flair, identity and mix of stores calibrated to the needs, tastes and pockets of locals. Go to posh Charlottenburg for international couture and to Kreuzberg for second-hand fashions. In Mitte, ritzy Friedrichstrasse has cosmopolitan flair, while the Scheunenviertel and Prenzlauer Berg are hotbeds of hip local designers. Schöneberg has the big KaDeWe department store, but its side streets are lined with speciality boutiques.

Berliners, ever the individualistic bunch, prefer patronising small indie stores over generic chains any day. The latter are usually relegated to malls, which in turn are mostly banished to the suburbs – the snazzy Potsdamer Platz Arkaden in Tiergarten being the exception.

Note that many stores, especially smaller ones, do not accept credit cards.

Opening Hours

Stores are now permitted to welcome customers until 8pm from Monday to Saturday. In practice, though, only department stores, supermarkets, shops in major commercial districts (such as the Kurfürstendamm), and those in malls take full advantage of this change. These stores usually open around 9.30am. Boutiques and other smaller shops keep flexible hours, opening sometime mid-morning and generally closing at 7pm on weekdays and 4pm on Saturday. Stores are closed on Sunday, except for some bakeries, flower shops and souvenir shops. For a selection of supermarkets open after hours and on Sundays, see p167.

MITTE

Shopping in Mitte is spread out, but a lot of fun, with several distinct areas catering for all manner of tastes and budgets. If it's Berlin-made fashions and accessories you're after, concentrate your browsing in the Scheunenviertel – especially along Alte Schönhauser Strasse, Neue Schönhauser Strasse and inside the Hackesche Höfe. A string of cutting-edge galleries holds court on nearby Auguststrasse. For international couture and gift items, head to Friedrichstrasse – especially the elegant Friedrichstadtpassagen, anchored by the visually dazzling Galeries Lafayette. North of here is Dussmann, one of the city's best stores for books and music. Further east, Alexanderplatz has some mainstream stores which will soon get competition from the giant Alexa shopping mall taking shape south of the square.

1000 & 1 SEIFE
Map pp340-1   Cosmetics
☎ 2809 5355; Sophienstrasse 28-29, Rosenhöfe; ☷ 3-7pm Tue-Fri, 11am-2pm Sat; ⓇHackescher Markt

Soap guru Xenia Trost brews up her magical beauty bars in a tiny soap kitchen using only organic oils, spices and other natural ingredients. This results in such pioneering concoctions as *Zimt-Ziege* (with goat milk and cinnamon), *Lakritz* (fennel and anis) and *Ei-Avocado* (egg and avocado). Each bar is a little work of art.

AMERICAN APPAREL

Map pp340-1 Clothing

☎ 2809 6318; Münzstrasse 19; ⓨ 11am-8pm Mon-Sat; Ⓤ Weinmeisterstrasse

Brand-name bunnies probably won't appreciate AA's stylish but logo-free T-shirts, tank tops, skirts, shorts and underwear, all available for him and her in a rainbow of colours. Everything is designed, cut and sewn from pesticide-free cotton in a sweatshop-free facility in Los Angeles, giving you that guilt-free shopping experience. Also in **Charlottenburg** (Map p344; ☎ 2360 7456; Bayreuther Strasse 35; Ⓤ Wittenbergplatz).

AMPELMANN GALERIE SHOP

Map pp340-1 Souvenirs & Gifts

☎ 4404 8801; Court V, Hackesche Höfe; ⓨ 10am-10pm Mon-Sat, 11am-7pm Sun Apr-Nov, 11am-8pm Nov-Apr; Ⓢ Hackescher Markt

It took a vociferous grass-roots campaign to save the little *Ampelmann,* the endearing fellow on the pedestrian traffic lights who helped generations of East Germans safely cross the street. Now a beloved cult figure, his likeness fills an entire store's worth of T-shirts, towels, onesies, key rings, cookie cutters and many other products. Other branches are in the **DomAquarée** (Map pp340–1; ☎ 2758 3238; Karl-Liebknecht-Strasse 1; ⓨ 10am-8pm Mon-Sat, 11am-6pm Sun; Ⓤ Ⓢ Alexanderplatz) and in the basement of the **Potsdamer Platz Arkaden** (Map p346; ☎ 2592 5691; Alte Potsdamer Strasse; ⓨ 10am-8pm Mon-Sat; Ⓤ Ⓢ Potsdamer Platz).

BERLIN STORY

Map pp340-1 Books

☎ 2045 3842; Unter den Linden 40; ⓨ 10am-7pm daily; Ⓢ Unter den Linden, Ⓑ 100, 200, TXL

This central store is a one-stop-shop for Berlin-related maps, videos, magazines and books of all kinds (guides, history, architecture, cooking etc), many in English and other foreign languages. There's a huge selection in all, including posters, CDs, DVDs and souvenirs, such as authenticated pieces of the Wall, miniature Buddy Bears and Berlin logo T-shirts. A 25-minute film about the city's history and major sights runs for free at the rear of the premises, where there's also a historical exhibit.

TOP FIVE SHOPPING STRIPS

- Alte and Neue Schönhauser Strasse, Mitte (opposite) – latest trends hot off the sewing machine
- Bergmannstrasse, Kreuzberg (p241) – hip vintage duds, chic home accessories and groovy sounds
- Friedrichstrasse, Mitte (opposite) – all the big international names united on one glamour strip
- Kastanienallee and Oderberger Strasse, Prenzlauer Berg (p245) – neat knick-knacks and fashion-forward outfits
- Kurfürstendamm, Charlottenburg (p237) – mainstream chains meet *haute couture*

BONBONMACHEREI

Map pp340-1 Confectionery

☎ 4405 5243; Oranienburger Strasse 32, Heckmann-Höfe; ⓨ noon-8pm Wed-Sat; Ⓢ Oranienburger Strasse

The lost art of handmade sweets has been lovingly revived in this little basement store with its integrated show kitchen. Watch master candy-makers Katja and Hjalmar using antique equipment and traditional recipes to produce such tasty delights as tangy sour drops and green leaf-shaped *Maiblätter* (May leaves), a local speciality.

BUTTENHEIM LEVIS STORE

Map pp340-1 Clothing

☎ 2759 4460; Neue Schönhauser Strasse 15; ⓨ noon-8pm Mon-Fri, noon-7pm Sat; Ⓤ Weinmeisterstrasse

Fashion is fickle but some designs are timeless. Jeans, for instance, were invented in 1873 in San Francisco by Levi Strauss, a German immigrant hailing from the hamlet of Buttenheim. This retail space pays homage to the man and his product with a wide range of vintage styles and accessories to match. Changing art exhibits add further visual appeal.

CALYPSO Map pp340-1 Shoes

☎ 2854 5414; Rosenthaler Strasse 23; ⓨ noon-7pm Mon-Fri, noon-4pm Sat; Ⓤ Weinmeisterstrasse

You don't need a shoe fetish to love Calypso's assortment of funky, outrageous and even regular styles, but it helps. Rosemarie Mohamed's store is crammed to the rafters with head-turning footwear from the 1930s to the '90s, perfect for fighting current-fashion fatigue.

Shopping

MITTE

233

CARHARTT STORE

Map pp340-1   Men's Clothing

☎ 2809 7367; Rosenthaler Strasse 48; ☾ noon-8pm Mon-Fri, 11am-7pm Sat; ⊕ Weinmeisterstrasse

For the past 115 years Carhartt has built a reputation on making durable outfits for American working stiffs. Now the company has become the latest in a string of clothing purveyors making the crossover from work-wear to street-wear. Their jeans, outerwear, shirts and T-shirts have been given a slick urban edge and transition well from daytime to after-dark adventures. Stussy, Vans and other brands are available too.

CLAUDIA SKODA

Map pp340-1   Berlin Designer-wear

☎ 280 7211; Alte Schönhauser Strasse 35; ☾ noon-8pm Mon-Fri, noon-7pm Sat; ⊕ Weinmeisterstrasse

Berlin-born Claudia Skoda has been a fixture on the city's design scene since the 1970s, when she used to party with David Bowie and Iggy Pop. Deep-pocketed fashionistas from around town regularly make the pilgrimage to this Mitte boutique to peruse her latest creations. The signature material is knitwear, sometimes in bold colours, turned into innovative yet eminently wearable outfits.

Dussmann - Das Kulturkaufhaus (this page)

DNS RECORDSTORE

Map pp340-1   Music

☎ 247 9895; Alte Schönhauser Strasse 39-40; ☾ 11am-8pm Mon-Fri, 11am-6pm Sat; ⊕ Weinmeisterstrasse

This DJ's favourite is one of the best-stocked stores for electronic club sounds, from drum and bass and techno to trip-hop and acid, all nicely sorted in racks of vinyl. A handful of turntables are around if your ears are itching for a test-listen.

DUSSMANN – DAS KULTURKAUFHAUS

Map pp340-1   Music & Books

☎ 2025 1111; Friedrichstrasse 90; ☾ 10am-10pm Mon-Sat; ⊕ 🚅 Friedrichstrasse

It's easy to lose track of time as you browse through Dussmann's four floors of wall-to-wall books, DVDs and an astonishing selection of music CDs that leaves no genre unaccounted for. Unique services such as rentals of reading glasses and CD players are a definite bonus, as are the café and the Internet terminals (€1 per 10 minutes). High-profile authors occasionally stop by for readings and book signings.

GALERIES LAFAYETTE

Map pp340-1   Department Store

☎ 209 480; Friedrichstrasse 76; ☾ 10am-8pm Mon-Sat; ⊕ Französische Strasse

Part of the exclusive Friedrichstadtpassagen, this Berlin branch of the exquisite French fashion emporium is famous for the dramatic architecture of Jean Nouvel. The entire store is centred on a glass cone, shimmering with kaleidoscopic intensity. From here, three floors of concentric circles rise up, each featuring fancy clothing and accessories. Nubile young things should head to the top floor dedicated to designers *du jour,* both local and international. Foodies shouldn't miss the gourmet food hall in the basement.

JÜDISCHE GALERIE BERLIN

Map pp340-1   Art Gallery

☎ 282 8623; Oranienburger Strasse 31; ☾ 10am-6pm Mon-Thu, 10am-5pm Fri, 11am-3pm Sun; ⊕ Oranienburger Tor, 🚅 Oranienburger Strasse

This gallery, next to the New Synagogue, offers an excellent introduction to art produced by 20th-century Jewish artists. Although most are now Berlin-based, many actually hail from other parts of Germany, Eastern Europe and Israel.

CLOTHING SIZES

Measurements approximate only, try before you buy

Women's Clothing

Aus/UK	8	10	12	14	16	18
Europe	36	38	40	42	44	46
Japan	5	7	9	11	13	15
USA	6	8	10	12	14	16

Women's Shoes

Aus/USA	5	6	7	8	9	10
Europe	35	36	37	38	39	40
France only	35	36	38	39	40	42
Japan	22	23	24	25	26	27
UK	3½	4½	5½	6½	7½	8½

Men's Clothing

Aus	92	96	100	104	108	112
Europe	46	48	50	52	54	56
Japan	S		M	M		L
UK/USA	35	36	37	38	39	40

Men's Shirts (Collar Sizes)

Aus/Japan	38	39	40	41	42	43
Europe	38	39	40	41	42	43
UK/USA	15	15½	16	16½	17	17½

Men's Shoes

Aus/UK	7	8	9	10	11	12
Europe	41	42	43	44½	46	47
Japan	26	27	27½	28	29	30
USA	7½	8½	9½	10½	11½	12½

KINDERKAUFLADEN

Map pp340-1 — Kids

☎ 2790 8424; Steinstrasse 3; ☷ 11am-7pm Mon-Fri, 11am-6pm Sat; ☻ Weinmeisterstrasse

Babies and toddlers keen on making a fashion statement should drag their hip parents to this boutique, where a browse might turn up Amelia onesies, Kidscase jackets or shiny rubber booties. In the same spacious digs you'll find various transportation devices, cuddly toys, furniture (including beds) and other items essential to growing up in style.

KUNST- & NOSTALGIEMARKT

Map pp340-1 — Antiques & Collectibles

Am Kupfergraben; ☷ 10am-4pm Sat & Sun; ☻ ☷ Friedrichstrasse

Just west of Museumsinsel, this art and collectible market gets high marks for scenic location, but you're more likely to be fighting over that antique coaster set with Maggie from Brighton than Mimi from Berlin. Antique book collectors have plenty

of boxes to sift through and there's also a good sampling of furniture, bric-a-brac and Eastern Bloc detritus.

LUCCICO Map pp340-1 — Shoes

☎ 216 6517; Oranienburger Strasse 23; ☷ noon-8pm Mon-Fri, 11am-4pm Sat; ☷ Oranienburger Strasse

'Shoes till death', promises Luccico, one of Berlin's most popular purveyors of fashionable Italian footwear. The slogan may be a tad ominous but, given the high quality of the product, probably not entirely unfounded. Styles range from sleek boots to classic flats, via sexy sling pumps and comfy flip-flops. There are further branches in Mitte (Map pp340-1; ☎ 283 2372; Neue Schönhauser Strasse 18; ☻ Weinmeisterstrasse) and Prenzlauer Berg (Map pp332-3; ☎ 4172 5987; Schönhauser Allee 118; ☻ Schönhauser Allee), and the one in Kreuzberg (Map pp336-7; ☎ 691 3257; Bergmannstrasse 8; ☻ Mehringdamm, Gneisenaustrasse) sells left-over sizes at reduced prices.

O.K. Map pp340-1 — Souvenirs & Gifts

☎ 2463 8746; Alte Schönhauser Strasse 36-37; ☷ noon-8pm Mon-Fri, noon-4pm Sat; ☻ Weinmeisterstrasse

This is an import store with a twist. Instead of rattan chairs and Indonesian masks, O.K. stocks a potpourri of everyday items from around the world, mostly made from simple materials in developing nations. Recycled tyre ashtrays from Morocco, toothbrush holders from Iran and colourful rice-sack bags from Thailand go a long way to show that there's plenty of beauty in the ordinary.

RESPECTMEN

Map pp340-1 — Menswear

☎ 283 5010; Neue Schönhauser Strasse 14; ☷ noon-8pm Mon-Fri, noon-6pm Sat; ☻ Weinmeisterstrasse

Clothes make the man, as Mark Twain once quipped, and RespectMen can help bring out the suave, confident persona in you with their classic yet body-conscious business suits and accoutrements from socks to ties. Besides the house label, outfits by other select designers grace racks and shelves, including Drykorn, Firma, Evolution and Hüftgold.

SATURN Map pp340-1 Electronics & Music

☎ 247 516; Alexanderplatz 8; ☟ 10am-8pm Mon-Sat; ⊖ ⓡ Alexanderplatz

This is your standard go-to place for electronic appliances and accessories. Prices are quite good, although the service needs work. They also have some of the lowest prices in town for mainstream CDs, not to forget a bevy of special-purchase deals. Listen to *any* CD by scanning its barcode into a listening station. You'll also find them in the **Potsdamer Platz Arkaden** (Map p346; ☎ 259 240; Alte Potsdamer Strasse; ☟ 10am-8pm Mon-Sat; ⊖ ⓡ Potsdamer Platz).

SCHÖNHAUSER

Map pp340-1 Home Accessories

☎ 281 1704; Neue Schönhauser Strasse 18; ☟ noon-8pm Mon-Fri, 11am-6pm Sat; ⊖ Weinmeisterstrasse

Wedged in among stores striving to set the trends of tomorrow, Schönhauser is a flashback to the '60s and '70s or – as one might say – the 'Age of Orange'. Orange lamps, camps, chairs, tables – they've got it all here. That, plus a selection of groovy gift items and knickknacks for kitchen, bath and bedroom, all teetering between kitsch and collectible.

SOMMERLADEN

Map pp340-1 Vintage Designer-wear

☎ 0177-299 1789; Linienstrasse 153; ☟ 2-8pm Mon-Fri, noon-5pm Sat; ⊖ Rosa-Luxemburg-Platz

Dolce & Gabbana makes you swoon? Issey Miyake gets your blood flowing? Can't live without Diesel, Adidas or Miu Miu? Johanna Mattner specialises in these and many other fashionista favourites, all gently 'pre-worn' and at discounts as deep as the Grand Canyon. Those of the male persuasion can dig up treasure here as well.

YOSHIHARU ITO

Map pp340-1 Berlin Designer-wear

☎ 4404 4490; Rosa-Luxemburg-Strasse 5; ☟ noon-8pm Mon-Sat; ⓡ Oranienburger Strasse

This Tokyo-trained couture designer knows how to make you stand out in the crowd without having to wear flashy clothes. Over the past decade or so, Ito has built his considerable reputation on putting a personal spin on classic cuts, which are perfectly tailored and made of high-quality materials. Men's clothing is his main strength, but his latest women's line is turning heads as well.

TIERGARTEN

Taken up mostly by its giant namesake park, and the government and embassy quarters, Tiergarten has few spending temptations – *except* at Berlin's best shopping mall, right on bustling Potsdamer Platz.

ANTIKMARKT POTSDAMER PLATZ

Map p346 Antiques & Collectibles

Gabriele-Tergit-Promenade; ☟ 8am-3pm Sat, 10am-6pm Sun; ⊖ ⓡ Potsdamer Platz

This newish market snuggles up against the futuristic backdrop of DaimlerCity, with about 150 stalls helmed by mostly professional vendors hawking kitsch and collectibles. You could easily spend a leisurely couple of hours rummaging for antique furniture, vintage radios, GDR memorabilia, brass scales, music on vinyl and lots of other detritus from yesteryear. Just don't expect any bargains.

AVE MARIA

Map pp338-9 Religious stuff

☎ 262 1211; Potsdamer Strasse 75; ☟ noon-6pm Mon-Fri, noon-3pm Sat; ⊖ Kurfürstenstrasse

Ave Maria is a portal for the pious in a neighbourhood of sex shops, *donerias* and Turkish grocers. Specialising in frankincense (over 40 varieties!), it also stocks smiling Madonnas, Jesus T-shirts, pope candles and all manner of rosaries and crucifixes. Gregorian chants enhance the browsing experience, not just for the faithful but also for pagans in search of kitsch-cool knickknacks.

POTSDAMER PLATZ ARKADEN

Map p346 Shopping Mall

☎ 255 9270; Alte Potsdamer Strasse; ☟ 10am-8pm Mon-Sat; ⊖ ⓡ Potsdamer Platz

This pleasant indoor mall brims with mainstream chains such as H&M, Mango, Esprit (all clothing), Hugendubel (books) and Saturn (electronics). In between are smaller stores selling everything from eye-wear to cigars to tuxedos. The basement has Kaiser's and Aldi supermarkets, and lots of fast-food outlets. There's a post office at street level. Head upstairs for a bewildering – and mouth-watering – selection of Italian ice cream at Caffé & Gelato.

TOP FIVE 'UNIQUE BERLIN' STORES

- 1000 & 1 Seife (p232)
- Ampelmann Galerie Shop (p233)
- Die Imaginäre Manufaktur (p242)
- Bonbonmacherei (p233)
- Harry Lehmann (right)

CHARLOTTENBURG

Shopping in Charlottenburg is concentrated along Kurfürstendamm and its eastern extension, Tauentzienstrasse. The area around the Gedächtniskirche is chock-a-block with multiple outlets of H&M, C&A, Mango, Zara and other international chains flogging mass-produced fashions and accessories. To satisfy more exclusive label cravings, head to Ku'damm between Schlüterstrasse and Leibnizstrasse, where the marble-and-glass consumer temples of Versace, Hermès, Cartier and Bulgari will gladly help you max out that credit card. Kantstrasse, meanwhile, is the go-to zone for home designs, with the giant Stilwerk serving as its main magnet. Also take a wander along some of the side streets connecting Ku'damm and Kantstrasse, which are lined with numerous individualistic boutiques, bookstores and galleries.

BLEIBGRÜN Map p344   Shoes & Women's Clothing
☎ 882 1689; Bleibtreustrasse 29-30; ☽ 10.30am-6.30pm Mon-Fri, 10.30am-4pm Sat;
🖸 Uhlandstrasse
'Well-heeled' women with a passion for footwear should head to this little store, in one of the nicest side streets off Ku'damm. Try on everything from strappy sandals to kickbutt boots from such Italian shoe mavens as Merazzi or Giuseppe Zanotti. Complete the look with an equally stylish outfit at the affiliated boutique next door.

CAMERAWORK Map p344   Art Gallery
☎ 310 0773; Kantstrasse 149; ☽ 11am-6pm Tue-Sat; 🖲 Savignyplatz
This light and airy space is a perfect setting for the classic photographs by all the top practitioners. Among those represented are Diane Arbus, Man Ray, Irving Penn, Helmut Newton, David Lachapelle, Herb Ritts, Richard Avedon and Leni Riefenstahl. This is the only photography gallery traded on the stock market and the photos are for sale.

FLOHMARKT STRASSE DES 17 JUNI
Map pp330-1   Flea Market
Strasse des 17 Juni; ☽ 10am-5pm Sat & Sun;
🖲 Tiergarten
Berlin's biggest flea market is also a favourite with tourists, making bargains as rare as tulips in Tonga. Still, with its great selection of Berlin memorabilia, plus grandma's jewellery and furniture, it's definitely a fun browse. Running along Strasse des 17 Juni, west of the S-bahn station, it spills over into an arts and crafts market selling mostly new stuff.

GALERIE BROCKSTEDT
Map p344   Art Gallery
☎ 885 0500; Mommsenstrasse 59; ☽ 10am-6pm Tue-Fri, 10am-2pm Sat; 🖲 Savignyplatz
This well-respected commercial gallery has built a name for itself with art by modern masters, especially those working between the two world wars, including Otto Dix, George Grosz and Franz Radziwil. A secondary focus belongs to post-WWII realists, including Isabel Quintanilla and Francesco Lopez, and abstract German artists such as Willi Baumeister and Ernst Wilhelm Nay.

GLASKLAR Map p344   Glass
☎ 313 1037; Knesebeckstrasse 13-14; ☽ 11am-6.30pm Mon-Fri, 11am-4pm Sat;
🖲 Ernst- Reuter-Platz
Glasses for wine, water, tea, grappa, champagne and martini. Thick glasses fit for a peasant and delicate ones for festive dinner parties. Glasklar has nothing but floor-to-ceiling shelves of beverage vessels in their infinite, timeless variety. They're complemented by a smallish assortment of vases, ashtrays, teapots and bowls. Prices start at less than €1.

HARRY LEHMANN Map p344   Perfume
☎ 324 3582; Kantstrasse 106; ☽ 9am-6.30pm Mon-Fri, 9am-2pm Sat; 🖲 Wilmersdorfer Strasse
Time seems frozen at this endearing slice of 'Old Berlin', where the Lehmann family has been brewing perfumes from secret recipes since 1926. Dozens of scents are kept in big-bellied jars, and then syphoned into smaller flasks and sold by weight with prices starting at just €3 for 10g. Try the flowery Calypso, elegant Akazie or sensuous Lambada, or ask them to customise your own scent.

237

TOP FIVE MARKETS

- Flohmarkt am Arkonaplatz (p245)
- Flohmarkt am Mauerpark (p246)
- Flohmarkt Strasse des 17 Juni (p237)
- Türkenmarkt (p243)
- Winterfeldtmarkt (p241)

HAUTNAH Map p344 — Erotica

☎ 882 3434; Uhlandstrasse 170; ☽ noon-8pm Mon-Fri, 11am-4pm Sat; ◎ Uhlandstrasse

Those who worship at the altar of hedonism should check out Hautnah's three-floor emporium of erotica, stocked with everything girls and boys with imaginations might need for a naughty night. Expect frilly feather boas, latex bustiers, nurses' outfits, sex toys and some unprintable stuff but – surprise – also a decent wine selection to get you in the mood.

HEIDI'S SPIELZEUGLADEN

Map p344 — Toys

☎ 323 7556; Kantstrasse 61; ☽ 9.30am-6.30pm Mon-Fri, 9.30am-2pm Sat; ◎ Wilmersdorfer Strasse

In an age when kids master Nintendo before the alphabet, Heidi's may seem like an anachronism. For about 30 years she has specialised in low-tech, quality toys, from wooden trains to sturdy stuffed animals and 'edutaining' children's books. There's also a great selection of doll houses, play kitchens and toy stores to help spur kids' imaginations and social skills.

HUGENDUBEL

Map p344 — Books

☎ 214 060; Tauentzienstrasse 13; ☽ 10am-8pm Mon-Sat; ◎ Kurfürstendamm

This excellent all-purpose chain has a sweeping selection of books, including Lonely Planet titles and novels in English. You can browse as long as you like, or preview your purchase while comfortably ensconced in leather sofas, or even while enjoying a latte at the in-store café. There are smaller branches in Mitte (Map pp340–1; Friedrichstrasse 83; ◎ Französische Strasse) and Tiergarten (Map p346; Potsdamer Platz Arkaden; ◎ ⓡ Potsdamer Platz).

KARSTADT SPORT

Map p344 — Sports Gear

☎ 880 240; Joachimstaler Strasse 5-6; ☽ 10am-8pm Mon-Sat; ◎ ⓡ Zoologischer Garten

This multistorey department store has four floors of equipment and outfits for any sport – tennis to soccer to rock climbing to spelunking.

Hertha BSC football club paraphernalia at Karstadt Sport (this page)

KORSETT ENGELKE Map p344 Lingerie
☎ 324 4126; Kanstrasse 109; ⏱ 10am-1pm &
3-6.30pm Mon-Fri; ⓜ Wilmersdorfer Strasse
This store is a tantalising throwback to a
bygone era, even though the items it sells –
bras, bodices and other 'unmentionables' –
are unlikely to ever go out of fashion. No
matter whether you're tiny or titanic, staff
here can fix you up with the right size. If
not, the onsite seamstress will keep stitch-
ing until it fits.

LEYSIEFFER Map p344 Chocolates
☎ 885 7480; Kurfürstendamm 218; ⏱ 10am-8pm
Mon-Sat; ⓜ Uhlandstrasse
Leysieffer has been composing irresistible
chocolates for nearly a century. Its champagne truffles, nougat, dark chocolates and
other temptations, all artfully displayed at
this busy flagship store, make nice gifts for
the folks back home.

MARGA SCHOELLER BÜCHERSTUBE
Map p344 Books
☎ 8862 9320, 881 1112; Knesebeckstrasse 33;
⏱ 9.30am-7pm Mon-Wed, 9.30am-8pm Thu & Fri,
9.30am-4pm Sat; ⓜ Uhlandstrasse, ⓡ Savignyplatz
Founded in 1929, this well-regarded bookstore was once frequented by such literary
luminaries as Bertolt Brecht and Elias Can-
etti. Its sophisticated assortment includes
plenty of English titles, including new and
classic literature, self-help tomes, biographies and children's books. The super-helpful
staff can order anything that's not in stock.
Check for book signings and readings.

PLATTEN PEDRO Map pp330-1 Music
☎ 344 1875; Tegeler Weg 102; ⏱ 10am-6pm
Mon-Fri, 10am-1pm Sat; ⓜ Mierendorffplatz
It's a bit off the beaten track, but vinyl purists happily trek to this cultish store, packed
to the rafters with vintage albums, from pop
to punk to polka – and not a CD in sight!
Owner Pedro is happy to help you source
that special, hard-to-find tune from the
130,000 plus he's amassed over the years.

STEIFF IN BERLIN Map p344 Toys
☎ 8872 1919; www.steiffinberlin.de; Kurfürstendamm 220; ⏱ 10am-8pm Mon-Sat; ⓜ Uhlandstrasse
What do Happy the pig, Hoppel the bunny
and Sniffy the hedgehog all have in common? They're all creations of this famous
stuffed-animal company, founded in 1880

by Margarete Steiff, who also invented the
Teddy bear (named for US President Teddy
Roosevelt, whom she admired) in 1902.
Meet the entire menagerie at this delight-
ful store, including some highly collectable
limited-edition animals.

STILWERK Map p344 Interior Design
☎ 3151 5500; Kantstrasse 17; ⏱ 10am-8pm Mon-
Sat; ⓡ Savignyplatz
This four-floor emporium of good taste is
the ultimate playground for home designers.
Everything for home and hearth is here –
sugar bowls to chairs to kitchens – all by
such top international designers as Alessi,
Bang & Olufsen, Philippe Starck, Ligne Roset,
Gaggenau and many others. There's also a
restaurant, the jazz club Unique musicLounge
(p208) and the occasional piano concert.

VON KLOEDEN Map p344 Toys
☎ 8871 2512; Wielandstrasse 24; ⏱ 10am-7pm
Mon-Fri, 10am-4pm Sat; ⓜ Adenauerplatz,
Uhlandstrasse
Growing – and grown-up – minds will find
plenty of stimuli when perusing the over-
stuffed shelves of this venerable toy store,
which has supplied Berlin kids with quality,
low-tech toys, books and games since 1967.
Staff will bend over backwards to help you
ferret out just what you need from among
the huge assortment, which even includes
books in English.

WILMERSDORF
In Wilmersdorf most shopping is done along
the pedestrianised Wilmersdorfer Strasse,
just south of the U-Bahn station by that
name, but it's mostly department and chain
stores. Those with a sweet tooth, however,
will want to check out one Berlin original.

ERICH HAMANN SCHOKOLADE
Map p344 Chocolates
☎ 873 2085; Brandenburgische Strasse 17; ⏱ 9am-
6pm Mon-Fri, 9am-1pm Sat; ⓜ Konstanzer Strasse
Chocolate junkies in search of a classic Berlin souvenir should make the trip
out to this old-time chocolate factory, a
local institution since the Roaring Twenties. The packaging and the store haven't
changed since, and neither has the quality
of the product. The bitter varieties and the
chocolate bark are specialties, although the
handmade truffles also have their fans.

SCHÖNEBERG

Schöneberg's main draw is undeniably the KaDeWe, one of Europe's grandest department stores. The district's true character, though, reveals itself during a stroll from Nollendorfplatz to Hauptstrasse, via Maassenstrasse, Goltzstrasse and Akazienstrasse. Browse for everything from books to Berlin fashions, antiques to jewellery, shoes to Spanish wines, in dozens of unique and fun boutiques. On Saturday the farmers market on Winterfeldtplatz brings in fans from throughout the city.

FLOHMARKT RATHAUS SCHÖNEBERG

Map pp338-9   Flea Market
John-F-Kennedy-Platz; ⊗ **8am-4pm Sat & Sun;** ⊚ **Rathaus Schöneberg**
Pro and amateur vendors mix it up at this neighbourhood market, where you can hone your bargaining skills. It's not the trendiest of markets, but there's still plenty in store for those with a nose for treasure, and deals on clothing, books and toys are quite common. Savvy punters show up early for the best finds.

KADEWE Map p344   Department Store

☎ **21 210; Tauentzienstrasse 21-24;** ⊗ **10am-8pm Mon-Sat;** ⊚ **Wittenbergplatz**
Shopaholics will get their fix at this gigantic department store, the second-largest consumer temple in Europe, after Harrod's of London. The assortment is so vast, if they don't have it, it probably doesn't exist. Nowhere is this truer than in the legendary 6th-floor gourmet food hall, a culinary universe selling only the best of anything – aged gruyère to Porterhouse steaks, Veuve Cliquot to oysters, *chorizo* to *harissa* – from around the world. Don't expect any bargains. The name, by the way, stands for Kaufhaus des Westens (Department Store of the West).

LIEBLINGSLADEN

Map pp338-9   Women's Clothing
☎ **2191 2480; Hohenstaufenstrasse 67;** ⊗ **11am-7pm Mon-Fri, noon-5pm Sat;** ⊚ **Nollendorfplatz, Eisenacher Strasse**
Label lovers on a budget should get over to this little boutique to sift through the latest shipment of samples, overstock and last-season garments from such well-established

TOP FIVE BOOKSHOPS

- Another Country (opposite)
- Berlin Story (p233)
- Dussmann – Das Kulturkaufhaus (p234)
- Hugendubel (p238)
- Marga Schoeller Bücherstube (p239)

labels as Energie, Freesoul, BSA, Sabotage and No.li.ta – all sold at up to 70% off retail. Another major asset? The superfriendly owners who will happily help you source your next *Lieblingsstück* (favourite piece).

MARA SCHMUCK

Map pp338-9   Jewellery
☎ **215 2582; Grunewaldstrasse 15;** ⊗ **noon-7.30pm Mon-Fri, noon-3pm Sat;** ⊚ **Eisenacher Strasse**
This studio/shop combo has some pretty unique baubles for sprucing up necks, earlobes, wrists and other body parts. There's a good selection of inexpensive fashion jewellery, but the main reason to come here is for the edgy in-house creations made from a wide range of materials – pearls to stainless steel, titanium to plexiglass – that are often used in unconventional combinations.

MR DEAD & MRS FREE

Map pp338-9   Music
☎ **215 1449; Bülowstrasse 5;** ⊗ **11am-7pm Mon-Fri, 11am-4pm Sat;** ⊚ **Nollendorfplatz**
With a pedigree going back to 1983, this little place is a veritable institution on the Berlin music scene. Techno types should look elsewhere, though, for here the focus is clearly on rock, pop, country, indie, alternative, even jazz, soul and blues – much of it on import from the UK and US. Vinyl rules, with a few CDs thrown into the mix.

PRINZ EISENHERZ

Map p344   Books
☎ **313 9936; Lietzenburger Strasse 9a;** ⊗ **10am-8pm Mon-Sat;** ⊚ **Wittenbergplatz**
You won't find a better source than this for lesbigay literature, nonfiction and magazines in many languages, including, of course, English. Since moving to bigger digs, the lesbian section has grown considerably, as has the selection of videos, DVDs, postcards and calendars.

SCHROPP Map pp338-9   Books & Maps

☎ 2355 7320; Potsdamer Strasse 129; ☯ 9.30am-8pm Mon-Fri, 10am-4pm Sat; ◉ Bülowstrasse

In business for more than 250 years, Schropp fits the entire world onto its two floors, each crammed with every conceivable map, travel guide, dictionary and globe. Come here for some quality armchair travelling or to plan your next trip.

VAMPYR DELUXE

Map pp338-9   Clothing & Accessories

☎ 217 2038; Goltzstrasse 39; ☯ noon-7pm Mon-Fri, noon-5pm Sat; ◉ Eisenacher Strasse, Nollendorfplatz

If you like to stay ahead of the fashion curve, pop into this hip haven, chock-full of outfits and accessories from both emerging designers and established labels, many of them one-of-a-kind and many made locally. Vamp it up with handbags by Tita Berlin, sexy outfits for women by VampStar, cool leather wear by stylesucks.com and sassy undies by Gonzales.

WINTERFELDTMARKT

Map pp338-9   Farmers Market

Winterfeldtplatz; ☯ 8am-2pm Wed, 8am-4pm Sat; ◉ Nollendorfplatz

A Berlin institution, this market is ideal for stocking up on fresh produce, eggs, meat, flowers and other essentials for living *la dolce vita* in Berlin. On Saturdays, a smattering of vendors sell candles, jewellery, scarves and artsy-crafty stuff. Do as the locals do and cap off a spree with coffee or breakfast in a nearby café.

KREUZBERG

Kreuzberg has a predictably eclectic shopping scene. Bergmannstrasse in the western district and Oranienstrasse both offer a fun cocktail of vintage fashions, music and books, even though Oranienstrasse tends to be grittier and more downmarket. Nearby Kottbusser Damm is almost completely in Turkish hands with vendors selling everything from billowing bridal gowns to waterpipes and exotic teas and spices. On Tuesday and Friday, the Turkish Market lures crowds from outside the district with inexpensive fresh produce and other goods.

ANOTHER COUNTRY Map pp336-7   Books

☎ 6940 1160; Riemannstrasse 7; ☯ 11am-8pm Mon-Fri, 11am-4pm Sat; ◉ Gneisenaustrasse

Another Country is a welcoming 'culture club' owned by bearded and slightly eccentric Brit, Alan Raphaeline. Knowledgeable and always up for a chinwag, he presides over a meticulously sorted library/store of used English-language books, including a vast science fiction collection. You can borrow or buy, join the book club, come for film screenings and poetry readings, or simply hang out on the sofas.

ARARAT Map pp336-7   Paper & Gifts

☎ 693 5080; Bergmannstrasse 99a; ☯ 10am-8pm Mon-Sat; ◉ Gneisenaustrasse

Mt Ararat is where Noah's ark supposedly got stranded, and while there aren't any animals inside this store, you'll still find a boatload of enticing items to browse through. The focus is on top-quality paper products, from notebooks and photo albums to possibly the best range of greeting cards in town. It's a great place for last-minute gift ideas.

BAGAGE Map pp336-7   Bags

☎ 693 8916; Bergmannstrasse 13; ☯ 11am-8pm Mon-Fri, 10am-7pm Sat; ◉ Mehringdamm

In Berlin bags aren't just a transporting tool, they're a lifestyle statement. This little store stocks all the latest designs by local and international labels such as Crumpler, Schlepp, Kultbag and Luma. Materials of choice include recycled rubber, air mattresses and even GDR-era postal sacks, which are turned into innovative designs which capture the city's individualistic spirit nicely.

COLOURS Map pp336-7   Vintage Clothing

☎ 694 3348; 1st fl, rear Bergmannstrasse 102; ☯ 11am-7pm Mon-Fri, 11am-6pm Sat; ◉ Mehringdamm

This huge loft has great used duds going back to the days when Madonna was first singing about virgins, plus a smaller selection of new street-wear and clubwear threads for today's hip young things. Most items are clean, in good condition and priced by the kilo (€14, or €10 during Happy Hour, 11am–2pm Wednesday). There's good range of accessories too. It's

TOP FIVE MUSIC STORES

- Dussmann – Das Kulturkaufhaus (p234)
- Mr Dead & Mrs Free (p240)
- Platten Pedro (p239)
- Scratch Records (opposite)
- Space Hall (opposite)

in the back courtyard, upstairs on the right. In Schöneberg there's an affiliated outfit, **Garage** (Map pp338–9; ☎ 211 2760; Ahornstrasse 2; ⏰ 11am-7pm Mon-Fri, 11am-6pm Sat; ⊕ Nollendorfplatz).

DIE IMAGINÄRE MANUFAKTUR

Map pp336-7   Gifts & Housewares
☎ 2588 6616; Oranienstrasse 26; ⏰ 9am-5pm Mon-Wed & Fri, 10am-5.30pm Thu; ⊕ Kottbusser Tor, Görlitzer Bahnhof
Blind and sight-impaired craftspeople have been hand-making traditional brooms and brushes in this mini factory-cum-store for nearly 130 years. Since 1998, the product palette has been expanded to include more contemporary, even extravagant, designs. As well as other products, you'll find lamp shades, toys and cat entry doors. The store is worth a visit for the original 1920's interior alone.

FASTER, PUSSYCAT!

Map pp336-7   Clothing
☎ 6950 6600; Mehringdamm 57; ⏰ 11am-8pm Mon-Fri, 11am-6pm Sat; ⊕ Mehringdamm
Russ Meyer's 1965 camp classic about go-go dancers gone bad inspired the store's name, and some of the fashions here also teeter towards the outrageous (check out the wigs). But there's also plenty of smart street-wear and accessories. Gear from Spanish label Skunkfunk shares rack space with Gsus jackets and Pace jeans, all ready to be paired with Kickers shoes and Alprausch bags.

FOTO BRAUNE

Map pp336-7   Photography
☎ 623 7055; Karl-Marx-Strasse 7; ⏰ 9am-7pm Mon-Fri, 10am-3pm Sat; ⊕ Hermannplatz
The store may be small, but what it lacks in size it makes up for with great, up-to-date service and knowledgeable staff. Just about all your photographic needs

are well catered for, from digital to black & white and Super 8 film. They also buy, sell and repair cameras. It's technically in Neukölln.

GROBER UNFUG Map pp336-7   Comics
☎ 6940 1490; www-grober-unfug.de; Zossener Strasse 32-33; ⏰ 11am-7pm Mon-Fri, 11am-4pm Sat; ⊕ Gneisenaustrasse
Berlin's coolest comic store can easily keep devotees worshipping for hours among the books, DVDs, soundtracks and knick-knacks. At street level you'll find mostly German stuff, while upstairs you can drool over the mega-selection of indie and mainstream imports from the US, Japan and elsewhere. Also upstairs is a gallery with original drawings. There's a smaller branch in Mitte (Map pp340–1; ☎ 281 7331; Weinmeisterstrasse 9; ⊕ Weinmeisterstrasse)

HAMMETT Map pp336-7   Books
☎ 691 5834; Friesenstrasse 27; ⏰ 10am-8pm Mon-Fri, 9am-4pm Sat; ⊕ Gneisenaustrasse
Amateur sleuths won't be able to resist a browse around this bookshop, where shelves are packed with classic and contemporary mysteries, detective and crime stories. Named after one of the genre's finest, Dashiell Hammett, it also has a good selection of English-language titles, hundreds of used books and a children's corner. Look out for book signings and readings.

LUNAMARO Map pp336-7   Home Accessories
☎ 6940 1396; Bergmannstrasse 105; ⏰ 10am-8pm Mon-Sat; ⊕ Mehringdamm
Tucked into a courtyard off busy Bergmannstrasse, the poetic-sounding Lunamaro awakens longings for far-away places. Clay figurines from Mexico, hammocks from Brazil, candles from South Africa, pillows from India and other exotic items will add a touch of fairy tale to your flat until your next blue-sky holiday.

MARHEINEKE MARKTHALLE

Map pp336-7   Market Hall
Marheinekeplatz; ⏰ 7.30am-7pm Mon-Fri, 7.30am-2pm Sat; ⊕ Gneisenaustrasse
Market halls used to be all the rage in Berlin…oh, about a hundred or so years ago.

Shoppers and stalls inside Marheineke Markthalle (opposite page)

Now only three of them are left plying their trade, including this gem where the aisles are piled high with fruit and vegetables, cheeses, meats and sausages, alongside such everyday necessities as hiking socks and yarn. Prices are low however the quality varies.

MOLOTOW

Map pp336-7   Berlin Designer-wear
☎ 693 0818; Gneisenaustrasse 112; ⏲ 2-8pm Mon-Fri, noon-4pm Sat; ⊖ Mehringdamm
Open since 1986, Molotow was among the first stores to promote fashion made in Berlin by fledgling designers. Outfits – for both men and women – range from the sedate to quite experimental and come with a whole range of accessories to complete the look. All in all, a fun place to dawdle.

SCRATCH RECORDS Map pp336-7   Music
☎ 6981 7591; Zossener Strasse 31; ⏲ 11am-7pm Mon-Wed, 11am-8pm Thu & Fri, 11am-4pm Sat; ⊖ Gneisenaustrasse
A small but choice selection of soul, funk, electro, R&B, jazz and soundtracks on vinyl (in the back) and CD (in front) – much of it hard-to-find imports, forms the core of Scratch Records. The in-the-know staff will be only too happy to help you source a

new favourite. Even the discount bin holds the occasional treasure.

SPACE HALL Map pp336-7   Music
☎ 694 7664; www.space-hall.de; Zossener Strasse 33; ⏲ 11am-8pm Mon-Fri, 11am-4pm Sat; ⊖ Gneisenaustrasse
Space Hall is nirvana for fans of electronica, with an entire basement filled with everything from techno to drum and bass, breakbeat to trance, most of it for the turntable brigade. The ground floor has a bit of everything – punk to crossover – or head upstairs for house tunes. A dozen or so players stand by for easy pre-purchase listening.

TÜRKENMARKT

Map pp336-7   Outdoor Market
Maybachufer; ⏲ noon-6.30pm Tue & Fri; ⊖ Schönleinstrasse
Heaps of fruit and vegetables, mountains of bread loaves, buckets spilling over with olives, handmade feta spreads and cheeses – Berlin's Turkish Market is as good as anything you'll find this side of Istanbul. Quality is high, prices are low and helpful smiles abound. Grab your loot and head west along the canal to carve out your picnic spot in the little park at the Urbanhafen.

FRIEDRICHSHAIN

Friedrichshain's students and starving artists don't yet support a major shopping scene, but there are some Berlin-designer and second-hand gems to be found around Boxhagener Platz, which also hosts a decent Sunday flea market. Along Karl-Marx-Allee, retail activity concentrates around Frankfurter Allee U-Bahn station, which is also where you find the excellent Berlinomat, a store featuring exclusively local designers (see boxed text, below).

DAZU Map pp336-7 — Bags
☎ 4431 0600; www.ichichich-berlin.de; Kopernikusstrasse 14; ⏲ 4-8pm Thu-Fri, noon-4pm Sat or by appointment; ⊖ ⓡ Warschauer Strasse
Lui Gerdes designs big, sturdy bags that trade under the tongue-in-cheek label 'Ichl-chlch' (MeMeMe) and are sold in this little showroom/shop shared with hat-maker Helena Ahonen. Each bag is handmade, colourful and unique, although all are from the same basic material: truck tarpaulin. Ask about custom designs. They're also available at Lieblingsladen (p240) and other indie boutiques.

EAST OF EDEN Map pp332-3 — Books
☎ 423 9362; Schreinerstrasse 10; ⏲ noon-7pm Mon-Fri, noon-4pm Sat; ⊖ Samariterstrasse
This living-room-type bookstore is full with used novels, nonfiction, cookbooks and other printed matter, mostly in English but with a few German and French works as well. They also host the occasional poetry reading, usually featuring local wordsmiths.

FLOHMARKT AM BOXHAGENER PLATZ
Map pp336-7 — Flea Market
Boxhagener Platz; ⏲ 9am-4pm Sun;
⊖ ⓡ Warschauer Strasse, ⊖ Frankfurter Tor
This one-time sizzling market has become a victim of its own success, as pros have displaced impecunious locals hoping to beef up their budget. Although still popular, the assortment has become a bit tired, but that just means you have to dig a little harder for the cool finds. Conclude your hunting session with coffee or breakfast at a neighbourhood café.

MONDOS ARTS
Map pp332-3 — Ostalgiana
☎ 4201 0778; Schreinerstrasse 6; ⏲ 10am-7pm Mon-Fri, 11am-4pm Sat; ⊖ Samariterstrasse
Cult and kitsch stuff from the GDR is the bread and butter of this funky store named after Mondos, a brand of GDR-made condoms. It's fun to have a look even if you didn't grow up drinking Red October beer, falling asleep to the Sandmännchen (little sandman) TV show or listening to rock by the Puhdys.

PRACHTMÄDCHEN
Map pp336-7 — Men & Women's Clothing
☎ 9700 2780; Wühlischstrasse 28; ⏲ 11am-8pm Mon-Fri, 11am-4pm Sat; ⊖ ⓡ Warschauer Strasse, ⊖ Frankfurter Tor, Samariterstrasse
Pia and Penelope are keeping Friedrichshain scenesters and others looking good in Emily the Strange vixen-wear, fresh and bright T-shirts and hoodies by Blutsgeschwister and comfy Skunkfunk from

A PLATFORM FOR DESIGN

Creativity is king in Berlin, a city where individualism trumps conformity and thinking outside the box is nurtured and encouraged. It's only natural that such an experimental climate would spawn a design culture that is an expression, even a reflection of Berlin's idiosyncratic spirit. Jörg Wichmann and Theresa Meirer have tapped into this dynamism and created a showcase for homegrown designers with Berlinomat (☎ 4208 1445, Frankfurter Allee 89; ⏲ 11am-8pm Mon-Fri, 10am-6pm Sat; ⊖ ⓡ Frankfurter Allee), a mini-department store tucked in among the Stalinist behemoths of Frankfurter Allee. In halogen-flooded snowy-white rooms, they present the latest visions from a pool of about 140 creatives working in fashion, accessories, furniture and jewellery. Don't expect stodgy couture: the Berlin look is down-to-earth, slightly irreverent, with a fresh edge you won't find in Paris or Milan. Products here are innovative, fairly priced and made for every-day use, not special occasions. Showered by electronic beats you can inspect sassy jeans by Hasipop, cult GDR era-style sneakers by Zeha, bags made of milk cartons by MilkBerlin and lots of other unique items you won't find on the high street back home. A cool lounge serves pick-me-ups in case all that browsing leaves you exhausted. A small selection of Berlinomat designers can also be found on the top floor of the Galeries Lafayette department store in Mitte (p234).

Spain. Don't leave without checking out their own Prachtmädchen line of jewellery and accessories. Prices are lower than you'd find for similar frocks elsewhere in town.

PRENZLAUER BERG

Kastanienallee is a hotbed of Berlin-made fashions, with several designer stores lined up just south of the U-Bahn station Eberswalder Strasse. Oderberger Strasse, around the corner, also yields some good possibilities. A definite highlight is the Mauerpark, which is home to an excellent Sunday flea market, and the nearby Flohmarkt am Arkonaplatz isn't bad either. The area further north, around the Schönhauser Allee Arkaden, can be placed in the up-and-coming category. Keep an eye out for some idiosyncratic boutiques mixed in among the bargain stores along Schönhauser Allee and down such side streets as Stargarder Strasse.

BIODROGERIE ROSAVELLE

Map pp332-3   Cosmetics
☎ 4403 3475; Schönhauser Allee 10-11; ⏱ 9am-8pm; ⊜ Rosa-Luxemburg-Platz

Good vibrations are guaranteed at this beautiful, Feng Shui-designed drugstore that stocks a huge assortment of natural cosmetics for man, woman and child. If you're from overseas, you'll find that top-performing products by Dr Hauschka, Weleda, Logona, Lavera and other Euro-brands sell for a lot less here than at home. Ask about their manicures and beauty treatments.

COLEDAMPF'S CULTURCENTRUM

Map pp332-3   Kitchenware
☎ 4373 5225; Wörther Strasse 39; ⏱ 10am-8pm Mon-Fri, 10am-6pm Sat; ⊜ Senefelderplatz

The ultimate chef's playground, this store is stuffed with everything from the functional to the frivolous. From shiny copper pans to ravioli cutters, ice-tea glasses to espresso pots, you're sure to find something you can't live without among the 8000 or so items stocked here. A second branch is in Wilmersdorf (Map p344; ☎ 883 9191; Uhlandstrasse 54-55; ⏱ 10am-8pm Mon-Fri, 10am-4pm Sat; ⊜ Spichernstrasse).

TOP FIVE BERLIN DESIGN STORES

- Berlinomat (opposite)
- East Berlin (below)
- Gestatten, der Konk (p246)
- Thatchers (p247)
- Tausche (p247)

EAST BERLIN

Map pp332-3   Berlin Designer-wear
☎ 2472 4189; Kastanienallee 13; ⏱ 2-8pm Mon-Wed, noon-8pm Thu & Fri, 11am-8pm Sat; ⊜ Eberswalder Strasse

Local design guru, Cora Schwind, fills this fun store with trendy big-city clothes for the fashion conscious. Short- and longsleeved T-shirts, hoodies and sweaters are decorated with her signature logos, such as an eagle or an abstraction of the TV Tower. Stock up on her hand-painted wrist cuffs, leather bags and belts, and other accessories to acquire that ultimate Berlin look. A second shop is located in Mitte (Map pp340–1; Alte Schönhauser Strasse 33-34; ⊜ Weinmeisterstrasse).

EISDIELER

Map pp332-3   Berlin Designer-wear
☎ 285 7351; Kastanienallee 12; ⏱ noon-8pm Mon-Fri, noon-6pm Sat; ⊜ Eberswalder Strasse

Not simply flavour of the month – the urban street-wear designed by this five-guy co-op is as cool as the ice cream that used to be sold in this store before they took it over. Besides T-shirts, jeans and other clothes created under the Eisdieler label, each one has his own line as well. There's a second store in Mitte (Map pp340–1; Auguststrasse 74; ⏱ noon-6pm Tue-Sat).

FLOHMARKT AM ARKONAPLATZ

Map pp332-3   Flea Market
Arkonaplatz; ⏱ 10am-5pm Sun; ⊜ Bernauer Strasse

This smallish flea market feeds the retro frenzy with lots of groovy furniture, accessories, clothing, vinyl and books from the 1960s and '70s. Fuel up with croissants and latte in a nearby café, then join the throngs of Berlin hipsters poking around for stylish finds. Prices are moderate. The

Shoppers at a flea market

adjacent little park invites a browsing break. This market is easily combined with a visit to the Flohmarkt am Mauerpark (below).

FLOHMARKT AM MAUERPARK

Map pp332-3   Flea Market
Bernauer Strasse 63, Mauerpark; ⏰ 10am-5pm Sun; ⓔ Eberswalder Strasse
This flea market, right on the one-time border, is still wonderfully 'old-school' – you know, the kind not deluged with professional marketeers. For now it's mostly locals cleaning out their closets, which keeps prices low; often ridiculously so. The outdoor café and 'beach' bar are welcome refuelling pits. The Flohmarkt am Arkonaplatz (p245) is just a short walk away.

GESTATTEN, DER KONK

Map pp332-3   Berlin Designer-wear
☎ 4365 9667; Raumerstrasse 36; ⏰ 11am-8pm Mon-Fri, 11am-6pm Sat; ⓔ Eberswalder Strasse
Esther Perbandt, Von Wedel & Tiedeken and Majaco may not yet be household names, but on Berlin's fashion scene their innovative designs are among the most closely watched. This sleek white showroom brings them and a few others together under one roof – handy for putting together your own unique outfit. The house label Schultze & Lotz is being crafted right on site.

IN'T VELD – SCHOKOLADEN

Map pp332-3   Chocolates
☎ 4862 3423; Dunckerstrasse 10; ⏰ noon-7pm Mon-Fri, 11am-4pm Sat; ⓔ Eberswalder Strasse
The Greeks call it 'food of the gods'. It produces happiness-inducing endorphins. Entire movies extol its magical qualities. Chocolate is clearly one of the most popular guilty pleasures available anywhere in the world, as this tiny store aptly demonstrates. Cluizel from France, Scharffenberger from California, Equateur from Ecuador and dozens more are beautifully displayed here, along with hand-made truffles and cocoa powders for hot chocolate. Also in **Schöneberg** (Map pp338-9; ☎ 4862 3423; Winterfeldtstrasse 45; ⓔ Nollendorfplatz).

FUCK FASHION

Map pp332-3   Clothing & Accessories
☎ 4471 6932; Schönhauser Allee 72b; ⏰ 10am-8pm Mon-Fri, 10am-4pm Sat; ⓔ ⓡ Schönhauser Allee
Youthful hipsters flock to this store, jam-packed with the latest fashion must-haves. The last time we checked, this included

sexy lingerie by Pussy Deluxe and Vive Maria, shoes by Onitsuka Tiger, skatewear by Serial Killer and T-shirts by Toxico and Skunkfunk. A glass case holds silver jewellery for every body part – eyebrows to unmentionables. There's also a branch in **Charlottenburg** (Map p344; ☎ 8871 0491; Joachimstaler Strasse 39/40; ❸ ❿ Zoologischer Garten).

LUXUS INTERNATIONAL
Map pp332-3   Gifts & Accessories

☎ 4432 4877; Kastanienallee 101; ❂ noon-8pm Mon-Fri, 11am-6pm Sat; ❸ Eberswalder Strasse
There's no shortage of creative spirits in Berlin, but not many of them can afford to open their own store. In comes Luxus International, which rents them a shelf or two to display everything from necklaces to handbags, ashtrays to lamps. You never know what you'll find but you can bet it's a Berlin original.

MONT K
Map pp332-3   Outdoor & Camping

☎ 448 2590; Kastanienallee 83; ❂ 10am-8pm Mon-Fri, 10am-4pm Sat; ❸ Eberswalder Strasse
If you're into climbing something other than stairs – say, the Matterhorn or Kilimanjaro – Mont K will set you up with everything from backpacks to tents and crampons. The young, in-the-know sales team is happy to divulge an arsenal of peak-bagging tips.

RUNGE & GRAF
Map pp332-3   Tea

☎ 4004 3273; Käthe-Niederkirchner-Strasse 15; ❂ 10am-8pm Mon-Sat; ❒ 200, ❒ M4
If you consider fine tea one of life's indispensable pleasures, you'll find kindred spirits in Michael Graf and Anja Runge at their little emporium. Choose from hundreds of varieties imported from around the world, including many rare and valuable crops, plus tea pots, tea cups, caddies, infusers and other accoutrements.

SCHÖNHAUSER ALLEE ARKADEN
Map pp332-3   Shopping Mall

☎ 4471 1711; Schönhauser Allee 79-80; ❂ 8am-8.30pm Mon-Sat; ❸ ❿ Schönhauser Allee
This mid-size mall has revitalised the traditional but once moribund shopping district

around Schönhauser Allee. It's nicely designed, with more than 100 retailers, mostly of the chain variety, plus a post office and supermarket.

TAUSCHE
Map pp332-3   Bags

☎ 4020 1770; www.tausche-berlin.de; Raumerstrasse 8; ❂ noon-8pm Mon-Fri, 10am-6pm Sat; ❸ Eberswalder Strasse
Berlin-made, Tausche messenger-style bags are practical, durable, stylish and kitted out with exchangeable flaps, which zip off and on in seconds. Bags come in seven sizes and start at €40, two flaps included. Additional ones can be purchased individually as can various inserts, depending on whether you need to carry a laptop, a camera, workout clothes or baby diapers. How handy is that?

THATCHERS
Map pp340-1   Berlin Designer-wear

☎ 2462 7751; Kastanienallee 21; ❂ noon-8pm, noon-6pm Sat; ❸ Eberswalder Strasse
Well known veterans of the Berlin designer scene, Ralf Hensellek and Thomas Mrozek specialise in making professional women look good in well-tailored clothing that's feminine but not fussy, sexy but not vulgar. Their smart dresses, skirts and shirts go easily from office to dinner to nightclub, but they won't go out of fashion by the next season. Also located at Court IV of the **Hackesche Höfe** (Map pp340–1; ☎ 2758 2210; Rosenthaler Strasse 40-41; ❂ 11am-8pm Mom-Fri, 11am-6pm Sat; ❿ Hackescher Markt).

UHRANUS
Map pp332-3   Gifts & Accessories

☎ 7072 8400; Kastanienallee 31; ❂ noon-8pm Mon-Fri, noon-6pm Sat; ❸ Eberswalder Strasse
Diesel watches, Funk sunglasses and Alprausch bags are among the must-have accessories you can lay your hands on at this sassy little store, which also has plenty of other cool gift items for your hard-to-please friends back home. The name, by the way, is a play on the German words for 'watch' (*Uhr*) and the planet Uranus. There's a second branch, also found in **Prenzlauer Berg** (Map pp332–3; ☎ 4479 3901; Schönhauser Allee 69; ❸ Schönhauser Allee).

VOPO RECORDS

Map pp332-3   Music

☎ 442 8004; Danziger Strasse 31; ⏳ noon-8pm
Mon-Fri, noon-4pm Sat; Ⓤ Eberswalder Strasse
Punk, metal and hardcore fans could get lost
for hours perusing the selection of CDs and
vinyl here, although if you're into electronica,
hip-hop and ska, you also stand a good
chance of digging up some choice finds.
Prices are moderate and the try-before-
you-buy policy is a welcome asset. They also
sell T-shirts and concert tickets.

Sleeping

Sleeping

Berlin continues to sizzle and an ever-growing stream of visitors has, of late, enticed every international chain from Best Western to Ritz-Carlton to build flagship houses in the German capital. On the budget end, the city's hostel scene, already one of the buzziest in Europe, continues to grow apace with new places constantly upping the ante in terms of comfort and facilities. Privately-run midrange places, meanwhile, have been forced to keep up with the competition or risk falling by the wayside. All this activity translates into increased quality as well as quantity. In fact, at last count, Berlin could put heads on more than 80,000 beds. So no matter whether you're a cash-strapped student, a pennywise family or a high-flying business exec, you're likely to find a place to your liking.

Accommodation Styles

Berlin has no shortage of big luxury hotels, most of which have popped onto the hospitality scene only in the past decade. Usually of the international chain variety, they offer top-notch everything but can rarely shake that generic, corporate feel. You're likely to find hipper digs among the city's new crop of designer and boutique hotels, which boast such Zeitgeist-capturing features as in-room bathtubs, lobbies that double as lounges and furniture by Philippe Starck. A subgroup especially popular in Berlin, are so-called *Kunsthotels* (art hotels), which are designed by artists and/or liberally sprinkled with original art.

If you're more the old-fashioned type, check into one of Berlin's charismatic *Hotel-Pensions* or simply *Pensions*. These typically occupy one or several floors of historic residential buildings and offer local colour and personal attention galore. Amenities, room size and comfort levels vary widely, but in an effort to keep up with the big boys, many have recently been renovated and upgraded. Private bathrooms, wi-fi and other such mod-cons are increasingly the norm, while rooms featuring a washbasin and/or shower cubicle but no private toilet are, thankfully, a dying breed.

Berlin's hostel scene is as vibrant as ever and standards are exceptionally high. They're worth considering even if you're not a backpacker, as most now offer private rooms, often with en suite facilities, and even small apartments alongside traditional dorm accommodation.

Many properties set aside rooms or entire floors for nonsmokers; these are identified with the nonsmoking icon ⊠ in this book.

Check-in & Check-out Times

Normal check-in time at hotels is 4pm and you're expected to vacate your room by 11am or noon. Late check-in is possible in most cases but you should notify the reception staff so they don't give your room to someone else. Arranging an arrival time (and sticking to it) is especially important at smaller, private places, which are not staffed around the clock. Once you've checked in, you'll get a set of house keys to allow you to come and go as you please.

Price Ranges

Berlin's room rates are low compared to other European capitals. Recommendations in this book cover the entire price spectrum, with an emphasis on midrange places, which generally offer the best value. Hostels and simple lodgings are covered under Cheap Sleeps.

Prices listed in this book are the official rates supplied by the properties and do not – in fact cannot – take into account seasonal or promotional discounts. Higher rates may apply during major events, holidays and trade-show activity. Prices are quoted per room. Reviews below indicate whether breakfast is included in the rate or whether an extra (optional) per-person charge applies.

Reservations

It's always a good idea to make reservations, but especially so from May to September, around major holidays (see p296), during major events (see p8) and when big trade shows are in town.

Most properties accept reservations by phone, fax and, increasingly, the Internet. You can also book a room through **Berlin Tourismus Marketing** (☎ 250 025; www.btm .de; see Tourist Information, p301), the city's official tourist office. This is a free service and they even have a best-price guarantee. Note that agents can only make reservations at member hotels (which includes most listed in this book). Online booking services to try include www.hrs.de, www .ehotels.de, www.venere.com and, for hostels, www.gomio.com and www.hostelworld.com.

Long-Term Rentals

If you're planning to stay in Berlin for a month or longer, consider renting a room or an apartment through a *Mitwohnzentrale* (flat-sharing agency). These match people willing to let their digs to those needing a temporary home. Accommodation can be anything from rooms in shared student flats to furnished apartments. Agencies to try include the following:

Erste Mitwohnzentrale (Map p344; ☎ 324 3031; www.mitwohn.com; Sybelstrasse 53, Charlottenburg; Ⓞ Adenauerplatz, Ⓡ Charlottenburg)

HomeCompany (Map p344; ☎ 194 45; www.homecompany.de; Joachimstaler Strasse 17, Charlottenburg; Ⓞ Kurfürstendamm)

Room with a Loo (Map pp332–3; ☎ 4737 2964; www.roomwithaloo.com; Jablonskistrasse 3, Prenzlauer Berg; Ⓡ Greifswalder Strasse, Ⓡ M4) English-speaking accommodation-finding service affiliated with the expat-oriented *ExBerliner* magazine.

Euroflat (Map pp336–7; ☎ 786 2003; www.wohnung-berlin.de; Stresemannstrasse 72, Kreuzberg; Ⓡ Anhalter Bahnhof)

PRICE GUIDE

The following breakdown is a rough guide and refers to one night in a double with private bathroom, outside of major events, holidays or trade-show periods.

€€€	over €160
€€	€80 to €160
€	under €80

MITTE

Mitte puts you smack bang in the thick of things, from the blockbuster sights to happening nightlife and fabulous restaurants. No other district has seen as many new hotels in recent years, and there's more on the way. The high-end international chains cluster around Gendarmenmarkt, while their smaller artsy cousins prefer the real estate north of Unter den Linden, especially in or near the Scheunenviertel. Mitte also has the greatest concentration of top-notch hostels.

ADLON KEMPINSKI Map pp340-1   Hotel €€€
☎ 22 610; www.hotel-adlon.de; Unter den Linden 77; s €320-440, d €370-490, ste €650-8500, breakfast €32; P ⨯ ⌧ ⌨ ⌸ ⟐ ; Ⓡ Unter den Linden
Berlin's most high-profile defender of the grand tradition has been a celebrity magnet since first opening its portals in 1907. Faithfully rebuilt after the fall of the Berlin Wall, it again woos presidents, diplomats, stars and the merely rich, with front-row vistas of the Brandenburg Gate, top-notch rooms and off-the-charts service. The movie *Grand Hotel* was inspired by the Adlon.

ALEXANDER PLAZA Map pp340-1   Hotel €€
☎ 240 010; www.hotel-alexander-plaza.de; Rosenstrasse 1; s €110-170, d €120-180, breakfast €15; P ⨯ ⌧ ⌨ ⌸ ; Ⓡ Hackescher Markt
Late-19th-century glamour meets new-millennium comforts in this sophisticated hotel, on a quiet side street close to the fun Scheunenviertel quarter. Beautiful period details, such as a well-worn mosaic floor and stucco-adorned floating stairway,

blend smoothly with contemporary rooms accented by Vitra chairs and Tolomeo lamps. Most rooms are generously sized and sport desks, good closet space and extra-big showers.

ANDECHSER HOF Map pp332-3 Hotel €€
☎ 2809 7844; www.andechserhof.de; Ackerstrasse 155; s €50-70, d €70-90, all incl breakfast; ✗ ⓓ ; ⓔ Rosenthaler Platz

This little oasis of charm puts you within steps of good shopping, dining and partying. Rooms are spread over two buildings linked by a tiled courtyard that's great for summery breakfasts. Those in front are bigger and brighter, but staying at the back will give you sparkling new bathrooms and hand-painted armoires. There's an onsite restaurant and free wi-fi.

ARCOTEL VELVET Map pp340-1 Hotel €€
☎ 278 7530; www.arcotel.at; Oranienburger Strasse 52; s/d €110-220, ste €150-450, breakfast €15; Ⓟ ✗ ▨ 🖳 ⓖ ; ⓔ Oranienburger Tor

This sassy new kid in town wows you with edgy custom design, from the chilled street-level lounge to the swank penthouse suites. Rooms feature a plethora of mould-breaking perks, including hi-tech window vents and blackout blinds – perfect for sleeping off that hangover. Breakfast is a fancy spread served at the posh Lutter & Wegner restaurant, which otherwise specialises in Austrian fare.

ARTIST RIVERSIDE HOTEL & DAY SPA
Map pp340-1 Hotel €€
☎ 284 900; www.great-hotel.de; Friedrichstrasse 106; s €60-220, d €80-240, ste €290-340, breakfast €9; Ⓟ ✗ 🖳 ▨ ⓖ ; ⓔ ⓡ Friedrichstrasse

If you like a hotel with a flair for the dramatic, this plush place in the heart of the Theatre District is your stage. Behind a somewhat soulless façade overlooking the Spree River awaits an eccentric and colourful fantasy world with rooms matching all wallet sizes. At the in-house day spa you can unwind in a golden clamshell tub called a *Flotarium*.

ART'OTEL BERLIN MITTE
Map pp340-1 Hotel €€
☎ 240 620; www.artotels.de; Wallstrasse 70-73; s/d incl breakfast €130/260; Ⓟ ✗ ▨ 🖳 ⓖ ; ⓔ Märkisches Museum

This refined boutique hotel wears its 'art' moniker with a justified swagger: hundreds of works by renowned contemporary German artist Georg Baselitz decorate its striking lobby, hallways and rooms. Fans of cutting-edge Italian design will also be happy here, especially in the suites with their extra-cool bathrooms. It also caters particularly well for non-smokers and for people with disabilities.

BOARDING HOUSE MITTE
Map pp340-1 Serviced Apartments €€
☎ 2804 5306; www.boardinghouse-mitte.com; Mulackstrasse 1; 1-/2-room apartments from €120/135; Ⓟ ✗ ; ⓔ Weinmeisterstrasse, Rosa-Luxemburg-Platz

You won't miss many comforts of home in these breezy apartments, where a full kitchen and large closet are as much a part of the inventory as the direct-dial phone, VCR and CD player. The split-level units have terrific views over the rooftops of the Scheunenviertel. Rates drop for stays of more than four days.

Suite with a view at the Adlon Kempinski (p251)

DORINT SOFITEL AM GENDARMEN-
MARKT Map pp340-1   Hotel €€€

☎ 203 750; www.dorint.de/berlin-gendarmen markt; Charlottenstrasse 50-52; s €230-250, d €260-280, breakfast €23; P ⊠ ⊠ 🖳 🕭 ; ⊖ Französische Strasse

This cocoon of quiet sophistication, right on graceful Gendarmenmarkt, has the character of a small boutique hotel, yet the amenities of a grand 'hotel de luxe'. After a day of turf pounding, relax in the stress-melting spa before retiring to your stylish room, which, like the rest of the place, is a sensory interplay of marble, glass and light.

HONIGMOND GARDEN HOTEL
Map pp332-3   Hotel €€

☎ 2844 5577; www.honigmond-berlin.de; Invalidenstrasse 122; s €89-114, d €108-164, all incl breakfast; P 🖳 ; ⊖ Zinnowitzer Strasse

Never mind the busy thoroughfare, this 20-room guesthouse is an utterly enchanting retreat from the urban bustle. Before you even reach your comfortable, antique-filled room, you'll fall in love with the idyllic garden, complete with koi pond, fountain and old trees. The clubby lounge, with Internet access, an honour bar and magazines, is tailor-made for gathering with other guests.

HOTEL AUGUSTINENHOF
Map pp340-1   Hotel €€

☎ 308 860; www.hotel-augustinenhof.de; Auguststrasse 82; s €114-162, d €142-190, weekend discounts, breakfast €11; P ⊠ 🕭 ; ⊖ Oranienburger Tor, 🚊 Oranienburger Strasse

Owned by a Christian charity organisation, the Augustinenhof occupies a pretty mid-19th-century brick building and has

66 rooms wrapped around two peaceful courtyards. Staff will greet you warmly, then lead you to a fairly good-sized room with all major mod-cons. Soothing gold, green and brown shades dominate, while wooden floors add character and original art provides pleasing colour accents.

HOTEL GARNI GENDARM
Map pp340-1   Hotel Garni €€

☎ 206 0660; www.hotel-gendarm-berlin.de; Charlottenstrasse 61; s €125, d €150, all incl breakfast; P ⊠ 🕭 ; 🚊 Stadtmitte

This small hotel puts you smack dab into the poshest part of Mitte but keeps its price tag surprisingly modest. Tall and narrow, with a sleek white façade and flag-decorated entrance, the building perfectly blends with its historical surroundings but is, in fact, brand-new. The 27 rooms are decorated in English empire–style, with appealing vanilla, yellow and blue hues.

HOTEL HACKESCHER MARKT
Map pp340-1   Hotel €€

☎ 280 030; www.loock-hotels.com; Grosse Präsidentenstrasse 8; s €120-150, d €150-180, all incl breakfast; P ⊠ 🖳 ; 🚊 Hackescher Markt

The historic-looking façade of this elegant hotel, with its doesn't-get-more-central location, belies the fact that it's actually only a few years old. This translates into traditional rooms dressed in English country–style, paired with such hi-tech touches as heated bathroom floors. Get one facing the ivy-covered courtyard to cut down on the noise level from passing trams and revellers. Ask about their limo pick-up service.

HOTEL HONIGMOND Map pp340-1   Hotel €€

☎ 284 4550; www.honigmond-berlin.de; Tieckstrasse 12; s €60-115, d €110-155, d shared facilities €80-115, all incl breakfast; P ⊠ 🕭 ; ⊖ Oranienburger Tor

This delightful hotel scores a perfect 10 on our 'charm-meter,' not for being particularly lavish but for its familial yet elegant ambience. Rabbits frolic in the garden, the restaurant is a local favourite and rooms sparkle in restored glory. The nicest are in the new wing and flaunt their historic features – ornate stucco ceilings, frescoes, parquet floors – to maximum effect.

HOTEL KASTANIENHOF

Map pp332-3   Hotel €€

☎ 443 050; www.kastanienhof.biz; Kastanienallee 65; s €73-108, d €103-138, ste €123-138, all incl breakfast; P ✗ 🖥 ; 🖳 Rosenthaler Platz
This family-run hotel sits right on Kastanienallee, one of Berlin's most sizzling eat-drink-shop streets. Although the place itself scores low on the hipness scale, it has won a loyal clientele with its fair prices, family character and friendly staff. Rooms can be a bit of a squeeze, but they're comfortable with pine-type furniture and tasteful Berlin-themed art.

HOTEL PRINZALBERT

Map pp332-3   Hotel €€

☎ 590 029 420; www.prinzalbert-berlin.de; Veteranenstrasse 10; s €60-90, d €80-120, all incl breakfast; 🖳 Rosenthaler Platz
Although just a few rooms above a hip restaurant-bar, this place has a lot to recommend it. Rooms are about shoebox size but have modern, minimalist flair accented by platform beds, floor-to-ceiling windows and open closets. Some overlook the sweet, little Weinbergspark, a pretty spot for a picnic in the sun or a stroll with your sweetie. Being close to happening nightlife and restaurant scenes makes it attractive to a plugged-in crowd ready for a night on the razzle.

KÜNSTLERHEIM LUISE

Map pp340-1   Hotel €€

☎ 284 480; www.kuenstlerheim-luise.de; Luisenstrasse 19; s €80-95, d €120-140, shared bath s €48-56, d €69-88, breakfast €8; Ⓢ 🖳 Friedrichstrasse
At this 'gallery with rooms' you can you sleep in a bed built for giants (room 107), in the company of astronaut suits (310) or inside a 'painting' by Carl Spitzweg. Each room reflects the vision of different artists, who receive royalties whenever their room is rented. Art fans on a budget should ask about the smaller, bathless rooms. The website has pictures.

MARITIM PROARTE

Map pp340-1   Hotel €€€

☎ 203 35; www.maritim.de; Friedrichstrasse 151; s €150-260, d €170-280, ste from €300, breakfast €19; P ✗ 🖥 🖳 🖳 🖳 ; 🖳 Ⓢ Friedrichstrasse
It may seem like an oxymoron, but the Maritim is indeed an arty business hotel. Sculpture and canvases abound wherever you go, from the grand lobby to the hallways, restaurants, bar and lavish pool and spa area. Rooms are top-notch, even if the décor plays it fairly safe. The Carrara marble in the bathrooms, though, adds a nice luxury touch.

PARK INN BERLIN-ALEXANDERPLATZ

Map pp340-1   Hotel €€

☎ 23 890; www.parkinn.com; Alexanderplatz 8; s/d €90-120, breakfast €15; P ✗ 🖥 🖳 🖳 🖳 ; Ⓢ 🖳 Alexanderplatz
After an extreme make-over, this hulking GDR-era tower flaunts its rejuvenated look with pride. Rooms are snug but handsome, with soothing earth tones and such state-of-the-art touches as flat screen TVs, heated bathroom floors and noiseless air-con. You really get good value here, given the central location and full range of facilities, including a gym, sauna and top-floor casino.

RADISSON SAS HOTEL

Map pp340-1   Hotel €€€

☎ 238 280; www.radissonsas.com; Karl-Liebknecht-Strasse 3; s/d €140/380, ste €230-380, breakfast €21; P ✗ 🖥 🖳 🖳 🖳 ; 🚌 100, 200, TXL
At this swish and super-central contender, right next to Museum Island, you will quite literally 'sleep with the fishes', thanks to the AquaDom, a 25m-high aquarium that's the lobby's eye-popping centrepiece (p92). Elsewhere, the streamlined design scheme radiates an urban poshness rarely found in chain hotels. This also extends to the two restaurants, including the excellent pan-Asian Noodle Kitchen (p170), and the hipper-than-thou Aqua Lounge. There's free wi-fi for hotel guests throughout.

CHEAP SLEEPS

BAXPAX DOWNTOWN Map pp340-1   Hostel €

☎ 251 5202; www.baxpax-downtown.de; Ziegelstrasse 28; dm €13-22, linen €2.50, s €30-79, tw €48-93, apt €80-140, breakfast €4; Ⓢ Oranienburger Tor, 🖳 Oranienburger Strasse

This hostel hadn't opened at research time, but it promises to take budget hospitality to a whole new level, so we wanted at least to give it a mention. Party zones include a rooftop terrace with small pool, a good-sized garden, a sauna and an in-house club. Most rooms have en suite bathrooms as well as TV, telephone and Internet access.

CIRCUS HOSTEL WEINBERGSWEG

Map pp332-3   Hostel €

☎ 2839 1433; www.circus-berlin.de; Weinbergsweg 1a; 3-8-bed dm €17-21, s/d/tw shared bathroom €33/50/50, s/d/tw private bathroom €46/62/62, linen €2, 2-/4-person apt €77/134 with 2-night minimum; ✕ 💻 ♿ ; ⊖ Rosenthaler Platz

This hostel consistently fires on all cylinders. Clean, cheerfully painted rooms, excellent showers (and lots of them) and competent and helpful staff are just a few factors that catapult this place to the top of the hostel heap. Stay in dorms, private rooms (some with en suite baths) or a penthouse apartment with kitchen and terrace. The downstairs café serves inexpensive breakfasts, drinks and small meals, and the basement bar puts on different activities nightly. It's fully wheelchair accessible and there's free wi-fi available throughout.

Lamp in the lobby of the Artist Riverside Hotel (p252)

CIRCUS HOSTEL ROSA-LUXEMBURG-STRASSE Map pp340-1   Hostel €

☎ 2839 1433; www.circus-berlin.de; Rosa-Luxemburg-Strasse 39; dm €17-21, s/d/tw shared bathroom €33/50/50, linen €2, s/d private bathroom €45/60, 2-/4-person apt €77/134, incl linen, breakfast €2.50-5; ✕ 💻 ; ⊖ Rosa-Luxemburg-Platz

A big thumbs-up for this recently ex-panded entry whose central location and plethora of perks and features make it a favourite with pennywise nomads. Dorms and rooms are clean, cheerfully decorated and equipped with single pine beds (no bunks) with individual reading lamps. The new streetlevel café-bar-reception area with its grand, oval bar is the heart and soul of this place and conducive for meeting fellow travellers. Same goes for the 'backpacker lounge' with pool table on the mezzanine level. There's free wi-fi access.

CITYSTAY HOSTEL Map pp340-1   Hostel €

☎ 2362 4031; www.citystay.de; Rosenstrasse 16; dm €15-18, s/d €34/48, linen €2.50, breakfast €4; ✕ 💻 ; ⊖ 🚊 Alexanderplatz, 🚌 100, 200, TXL

Inside an immaculately restored 1896 de-partment store, this top-notch newcomer didn't take long to make its mark with trav-ellers, and for three good reasons: location, service and design. Modern and sophisti-cated, this place is loaded with more mod-cons than your average hotel, including top security, quality mattresses, a lift and a restaurant-bar with courtyard tables. Many blockbuster sights are just minutes' away. Busabout (p290) stops outside.

HEART OF GOLD HOSTEL

Map pp340-1   Hostel €

☎ 2900 3300; www.heartofgold-hostel.de; Johannisstrasse 11; dm €17-19, s/d with shower €40/56, breakfast €3; ✕ 💻 ; ⊖ Oranienburger Tor, 🚊 Oranienburger Strasse

Prepare for blast-off at this spacey hostel themed around Douglas Adams' 1979 science fiction spoof *The Hitchhiker's Guide to the Galaxy*. Dorms (called 'cabins') come equipped with individual lockers, steel-pipe bunks and comfortable mattresses. Down-stairs, the kool kids behind the reception-bar-lounge ('the bridge') can help you fill your caffeine or alcohol quota any time of day. There's free towels and sheets.

MITTE'S BACKPACKER HOSTEL

Map pp332-3   Hostel €

☎ 2839 0965; www.backpacker.de; Chausseestrasse 102; dm €15-21, s/d shared bathroom €30/48, d with bathroom €56, discounts Nov-Mar, except holidays; P ✗ ▯ ; ⊖ Zinnowitzer Strasse

Buckets full of imagination were mixed into the paint at this well-established 'art hostel' in a former hat factory near the Mitte fun zone. Each room has its own wacky theme created by travelling artists or artistic travellers. Choices include the Kafka-esque Beetle Room, the romantic Arabic Room and the elegant Marlene Dietrich Room. Self-caterers will appreciate the small communal kitchen.

TIERGARTEN

You'll be mixing it up with moguls, movie stars and power mongers when staying in Tiergarten, which offers easy access to the government and embassy quarters. The ritziest accommodation options are in the Potsdamer Platz area. The slim-wallet crowd, alas, will need to look elsewhere.

GRAND HYATT Map p346   Hotel €€€

☎ 2553 1234; www.berlin.grand.hyatt.com; Marlene-Dietrich-Platz 2; s €230-305, d €260-345, breakfast €24; P ✗ ▯ ▯ ▯ ▯ ; ⊖ ▯ Potsdamer Platz

Madonna, Gwyneth Paltrow and Marilyn Manson are among the celebs who've slept, dined and partied at this stomping ground of the rich and famous. The moment you step into the lavish, cedar-clad lobby, you sense that it's luxury all the way from here to the breathtaking rooftop pool. Each room is wired for connectivity and filled with pragmatic and artistic touches.

MANDALA HOTEL

Map p346   Suite Hotel €€€

☎ 590 050 000; www.themandala.de; Potsdamer Strasse 3; ste €140-450, breakfast €21; P ✗ ▯ ▯ ; ⊖ ▯ Potsdamer Platz

How 'suite' it is to be staying at this swank and ultra-discreet retreat, a place of casual sophistication and unfussy ambience. Six types of suites, ranging from 40 to 101 sq metres, are available, each outfitted for maximum comfort and ideal working conditions, in case you're here to ink that deal.

Bonuses include a Michelin-star restaurant and one Berlin's best hotel bars.

MÖVENPICK HOTEL BERLIN

Map pp336-7   Hotel €€€

☎ 230 060; www.moevenpick-berlin.com; Schöneberger Strasse 3; s €180-245, d €200-265, breakfast €17; P ✗ ▯ ▯ ▯ ▯ ; ▯ Anhalter Bahnhof

This snazzy new hotel cleverly marries bold contemporary design with the industrial aesthetic of the historic Siemenshöfe. It's one of those rare places that manage to appeal both to the suit brigade and to chic city-break types. Rooms vamp it up with Philippe Starck lamps and sinks, glass cube walls and furniture made from sensuous olive wood.

RITZ-CARLTON BERLIN

Map p346   Hotel €€€

☎ 337 777; www.ritzcarlton.com; Potsdamer Platz 3; s €250-330, d €280-410, ste €450-5000, rates usually include breakfast, otherwise €22; P ✗ ▯ ▯ ▯ ▯ ; ⊖ ▯ Potsdamer Platz

Only a discrete logo reveals that you've arrived at one of Berlin's newest temples of luxury. In an ambience of effortless sophistication, you'll find all the trappings of a big-league player. This includes a delightful French brasserie (Desbrosses, see p172), a luxurious spa, and a clubby bar with 400 types of schnapps.

HOTEL SPREE-BOGEN

Map pp330-1   Hotel €€€

☎ 399 200; www.hotel-spreebogen.de; Alt-Moabit 99; s €84-132, d €98-192, all incl breakfast; P ✗ ▯ ▯ ; ⊖ Turmstrasse

This classy hotel occupies a heritage-listed ex-dairy and fuses postmodern chic with early-20th-century industrial architecture. It's a full-service affair, hugging an idyllic stretch of the Spree, with the Federal Ministry of the Interior as an immediate neighbour. Sleek rooms brim with designer furniture and hi-tech gadgetry (including free wi-fi); the nicest enjoy river views.

CHARLOTTENBURG

Sure, it will never be close to the trophy sights or nightlife but, for now at least, Charlottenburg still offers great value for money and the city's greatest concentration of mid-priced abodes. This is where traditional Old Berlin pensions rub shoulders with posh designer temples favoured by urban hipsters. For many of the older properties here it's been a game of 'upgrade or die', which has resulted in higher standards overall. Excellent public transport puts you within easy reach of everything.

BLEIBTREU HOTEL BERLIN
Map p344   Hotel €€

☎ 884 740; www.bleibtreu.com; Bleibtreustrasse 31; s €120-220, d €130-230, breakfast €15; ✕ ▢ ♿ ; ⊖ Uhlandstrasse

The Bleibtreu flaunts an edgy urban feel, tempered by the warmth of Italian design and the ample use of natural, eco-friendly materials. Subtlety is king here. In fact, from the street it doesn't even look like a hotel, tucked away as it is behind a flower shop, a bar and a deli, all of which are often swarmed by clued-up neighbours.

CASA HOTEL Map p344   Hotel €€

☎ 280 3000; www.hotel-casa.de; Schlüterstrasse 40; s €80-120, d €100-140, all incl breakfast; ℗ ✕ ⬚ ; ⊖ Uhlandstrasse, Adenauerplatz

Take an aging hotel, gut it, apply vision and money and end up with a modern-design abode for fashion-forward travellers without a trust fund. Fresh colour accents – orange, lavender, minty green, sky blue – brighten the 29 comfortable rooms, which mix custom-designed furniture with pieces by Philippe Starck. The swivelling flat screen TV and cordless phones are handy tech touches.

HECKER'S HOTEL Map p344   Hotel €€

☎ 889 00; www.heckers-hotel.de; Grolmanstrasse 35; s €125-250, d €140-280, ste €310-550, breakfast €18; ℗ ✕ ⬚ ⬚ ; ⊖ Uhlandstrasse

Flaunting a subdued urban feel, this private boutique hotel prides itself on lavishing its guests with personal attention. The lobby, with its ice-blue backlit bar, gives way to

---

TOP FIVE HISTORIC CHARMERS

- Hotel Askanischer Hof (right)
- Hotel-Pension Dittberner (p258)
- Hotel-Pension Funk (p258)
- Hotel Bogota (right)
- Pension Kettler (p259)

---

over-sized, elegant rooms, some with walk-in closets and thoughtful touches such as complimentary mineral water. The hotel's ultimate trump card, though, is its three themed suites: cool Bauhaus, cosy Tuscany and exotic Colonial.

HOTEL ART NOUVEAU
Map p344   Hotel-Pension €€

☎ 327 7440; www.hotelartnouveau.de; Leibnizstrasse 59; s/d/ste incl breakfast €95/120/175; ℗ ✕ ⬚ ; ⊖ Adenauerplatz

A rickety birdcage lift drops you off with a belle époque flourish at one of Berlin's finest boutique pensions. Its rooms (all nonsmoking) skimp neither on space or charisma, and offer a unique blend of youthful flair and tradition. The honour bar is handy for feeding late-night cravings for Becks or grappa. Great freebies include wi-fi, tea and coffee.

HOTEL ASKANISCHER HOF
Map p344   Hotel €€

☎ 881 8033; www.askanischer-hof.de; Kurfürstendamm 53; s €95-120, d €107-165, all incl breakfast; ✕ ⬚ ; ⊖ Adenauerplatz

In a city that likes to teeter on the cutting edge, this charismatic 17-room hotel catapults you back to the Roaring Twenties. An ornate oak door leads to a quiet oasis of eclectic antiques, lacy window drapes, frilly chandeliers and fading oriental rugs. Its quaint Old Berlin charms have long been a magnet for celebs, including David Bowie and Helmut Newton.

HOTEL BOGOTA Map p344   Hotel €€

☎ 881 5001; www.hotelbogota.de; Schlüterstrasse 45; s/d €72/98, s/d shared facilities €44/69, all incl breakfast; ℗ ✕ ; ⊖ Uhlandstrasse

This Charlottenburg pearl feels like a cross between a friendly pension and a fading grand hotel, all at prices even the cash-strapped can afford. It's a rambling, slightly eccentric place, inside a landmark building that has weathered the ups-and-downs of Berlin's tumultuous 20th-century history like few others. Room sizes and amenities vary greatly, so inspect before deciding.

HOTEL GATES Map p344   Hotel €€

☎ 311 060; www.hotel-gates.com; Knesebeckstrasse 8-9; s €95-210, d €120-250, breakfast €5, buffet €12.50; ℗ ✕ ⬚ ; ⊖ Ernst-Reuter-Platz

Sleeping

CHARLOTTENBURG

If you're a serious surfer (of the Internet, that is), this is the place for you. Rates include unlimited, round-the-clock high-speed access on your in-room flat-screen PC. Room sizes vary, but all are comfortable, if a tad functional. In its earlier incarnation as the Hotel Windsor, stars such as Marlon Brando and Claudia Cardinale used to shack up here.

HOTEL MEINEKE ARTE Map p344   Hotel €€
☎ 889 2120; www.ahc-hotels.de; Meinekestrasse 10; s/d incl breakfast €100/150; P X ; ⊖ Kurfürstendamm, Uhlandstrasse

Close to the Ku'damm shopping mile, this 60-room hotel earns its 'arte' moniker with the works of Austrian artist Günter Edlinger, whose abstract oils add splashes of colour to the rooms and hallways. Alas, a lot less creativity has gone into the room furnishings, which are pleasant but in no danger of winning any design awards.

HOTEL Q! Map p344   Hotel €€
☎ 810 0660; www.loock-hotels.com; Knesebeckstrasse 67; s €150-170, d €170-190, studios €190-290, penthouse €190-290, all incl breakfast; P X ⊠ ⌨ ; ⊖ Uhlandstrasse

No fancy marquee here, only an innocuous grey façade signals your arrival at this new high-octane hot spot. Its cool, Zeitgeist-capturing look pulls in style-conscious hipsters and even such gossip mag royalty as Brad Pitt and Drew Barrymore. Corners are eschewed, from the tunnel-like crimson lobby to the sexy rooms where you could literally slide from the tub into the bed.

HOTEL-PENSION DITTBERNER
Map p344   Hotel-Pension €€
☎ 884 6950; www.hotel-dittberner.de; Wielandstrasse 26; s €67-87, d €95-120, all incl breakfast; ⚿ ; ⊖ Adenauerplatz

It's hard not to be charmed by this traditional 3rd-floor pension and its friendly owner, Frau Lange. The soaring ceilings, plush oriental rugs and armloads of paintings and lithographs ooze genuine Old Berlin flair. The location is great for city explorations, while direct-dial phones and free wi-fi and DSL make keeping in touch with the folks back home a snap.

HOTEL-PENSION FUNK
Map p344   Hotel-Pension €€
☎ 882 7193; www.hotel-pensionfunk.de; Fasanenstrasse 69; s €52-82, d €82-112, s shared bathroom €34-57, d shared bathroom €52-82, all incl breakfast; ⊖ Uhlandstrasse, Kurfürstendamm

If you're looking for quirkiness and true Berlin character, you'll find heaps of it at this charismatic pension just off the Ku'damm. Once the home of Danish silent-movie siren Asta Nielsen, it transports you back to the glamour and decadence of the 1920s. Filled with antiques and old-time accoutrements, it's also incredibly good value and often booked to bulging.

LOUISA'S PLACE Map p344   Hotel €€
☎ 631 030; www.louisas-place.de; Kurfürstendamm 160; ste €120-250, breakfast €18; P X ⌨ ⊠ ♨ ⚿ ; ⊖ Adenauerplatz

Louisa's is the kind of place that dazzles with class not glitz, a discrete deluxe hideaway, perfect for people tired of anonymous big-city hotels. We know of few properties that put more emphasis on customising guest services. They'll even send you a pre-arrival questionnaire asking for your likes and dislikes! Suites here are huge, the spa heavenly and the library regal.

SAVOY HOTEL Map p344   Hotel €€€
☎ 311 030; www.hotel-savoy.com; Fasanenstrasse 9-10; s €115-235, d €140-260, all incl breakfast; X ⊠ ⌨ ; ⊖ ⓡ Zoologischer Garten

Writer Thomas Mann called it 'charming and cosy' while Talking Head's David Byrne

Bauhaus suite at Hecker's Hotel (p257)

loved it for being 'friendly and helpful'. In business since 1929, there's something comfortably stuffy about this intimate grand hotel with its cosy cigar bar and jazzy restaurant. Rooms exude a pleasant lived-in feel while sporting all the mod-cons you'd expect from a hotel of this pedigree.

CHEAP SLEEPS

A&O HOSTEL AM ZOO Map p344   Hostel €
☎ 297 7810, toll-free 0800 222 5722; www.aohostel.com; Joachimstaler Strasse 1-3; dm from €10, linen €3, breakfast €5, s/tw with bathroom, linen & breakfast from €30/34; ⊠ ▯; ☺ ▣ Zoologischer Garten

Right opposite Zoo station, this is a con-vivial, international place with a big com-munal room and a fun bar right next to the train tracks. Dorms and rooms are bright, with neat laminate flooring, metal-frame beds and large lockable cabinets. There are also branches in **Friedrichshain** (Map pp336–7; ☎ 297 7810; Boxhagener Strasse 73; ▣ Ostkreuz) and southern **Mitte** (Map pp336–7; ☎ 809 470; Köpenicker Strasse 127-129; ▣ Ostbahnhof).

CORBUSIERHAUS   Apartments €
☎ 3020 9811; www.domizil-berlin.com; Flatowallee 16; apt €37-97; ▣ ⊠; ▣ Olympiastadion

Not only fans of French architect Le Corbusier will like the dozen or so fully furnished flats (with kitchens) available for rent in this modern architecture clas-sic (also see p117). Comfort levels, décor, amenities and facilities vary; the website has full details about each unit. The Olym-pic Stadium and the Grunewald forest are only a short walk away.

HOTEL-PENSION KORFU II
Map p344   Hotel-Pension €
☎ 212 4790; www.hp-korfu.de; Rankestrasse 35; s €53-79, d €67-99, s/d shared bathrooms from €33/47, breakfast €6; ▯; ☺ Kurfürstendamm

Opposite the Gedächtniskirche, this is a great bargain base for exploring Berlin. The pleasantly bright, carpeted rooms sport high ceilings, Scandinavian-style furniture and more amenities than one would expect for the price, including cable TV, telephone, hairdryer and in-room safe.

PENSION KETTLER Map p344   Pension €
☎ 883 4949; Bleibtreustrasse 19; s/d €75/80, all incl breakfast; ☺ Uhlandstrasse

Owner, Isolde Josipovici, presides over this six-room nostalgic retreat, which spills over with knick-knacks, framed photographs of former guests and original art. Our favour-ite room oozes sexy boudoir charm with its grand sleigh bed and pink wallpaper. The place's most memorable 'feature', though, is Frau Josipovici herself. A one-time model, she now works tirelessly to save Berlin's fountains and is well known as the city's *Brunnenfee* (Fountain Fairy).

WILMERSDORF

Wilmersdorf, just south of Charlottenburg, may be light on sights and have a rather sedate flair, but it's quiet, pretty and still reasonably close to where you truly want to be. Oddly, it's also home to the most 'out-there' of Berlin's art hotels, the Propeller Island City Lodge, and the sassy 'lifestyle' hotel Ku'Damm 101.

ART'OTEL CITY CENTER WEST
Map p344   Hotel €€€
☎ 887 7770; www.artotels.de; Lietzenburger Strasse 85; s €140-220, d €170-260, breakfast €14; ▣ ⊠ ♿; ☺ Adenauerplatz, Uhlandstrasse

This sleek and chic haven pays homage to the father of pop art, Andy Warhol. More than 200 originals turn the lobby, lounge and rooms into a veritable art gallery. The bar is great for a nightcap before retreat-ing to the comforts of the 91 cutting-edge rooms, with white leather beds, designer lamps and bold colour accents such as a purple chair.

BRANDENBURGER HOF
Map p344   Hotel €€€
☎ 214 050; www.brandenburger-hof.com; Eislebener Strasse 14; s €170-260, d €245-295, ste €345-515, all incl breakfast; ▣ ⊠ ▯; ☺ Augsburger Strasse

Opposites attract – the timeworn adage certainly rings true in this intimate grand hotel. In an amazing feat of stylistic al-chemy, it blends Prussian elegance with Italian *dolce vita*, Zen influences and edgy Bauhaus. Every detail speaks of refinement here, from the glass-tented indoor piazza, wrapped around a petite garden, to the Michelin-starred restaurant and the airy spacious rooms.

FRAUENHOTEL ARTEMISIA
Map p344   Hotel €€

☎ 873 8905; www.frauenhotel-berlin.de; Brandenburgische Strasse 18; s €70-80, d €100-115, all incl breakfast; ✗ ; ⊝ Konstanzer Strasse
Named after a 16th-century Italian female artist, this 12-room hotel was the first in Germany to cater exclusively for women. Owners Manuela and Renata have created a friendly and low-key hospitality zone, where rooms feature modern furniture and changing art exhibits brighten the walls. The rooftop terrace is great for breakfast, sunbathing and meeting fellow guests.

HOTEL-PENSION WITTELSBACH
Map p344   Hotel-Pension €€

☎ 864 9840; www.hotel-pension-wittelsbach.de; Wittelsbacherstrasse 22; s €51-92, d €87-128, ste €120-170, f €80-130, all incl breakfast; ✗ 👶 ♿ ; ⊝ Konstanzer Strasse
If you're travelling with the sticky-fingered set, you'll find plenty to like about this place with its special kids' floor. Little ones love the big rooms, where they can clamber around a western fort or castle and sleep in Porsche or Barbie beds. **Babysitters** (per hour €8) are available. The other floors have regular – and quieter – rooms.

KU'DAMM 101 Map p344   Hotel €€
☎ 520 0550; www.kudamm101.com; Kurfürstendamm 101; s €100-138, d €120-145, breakfast €13; Ⓟ ✗ 🖳 ♿ ; 🚆 Halensee

This sassy lifestyle hotel gets minimalism right. Design and décor are reduced to their purest forms but without sacrificing comfort. The lobby and rooms are dressed in cool colours and edgy furniture by young German designers. Breakfast is a highlight, not only for its liberal buffet spread, but for its views over the rooftops of Berlin.

CHEAP SLEEPS
HOTEL-PENSION MÜNCHEN
Map p344   Hotel-Pension €

☎ 857 9120; www.hotel-pension-muenchen-in-berlin.de; Güntzelstrasse 62; s €55-60, d €70-80, apt €75-105, all incl breakfast, apt €75, breakfast not incl; ✗ ; ⊝ Güntzelstrasse
This small and good-value pension is filled with lithographs of Berlin-based artists and the evocative sculptures of your gracious hostess, Renate Prasse. Furnishings are mostly of the IKEA persuasion, the pair of Marcel Breuer Bauhaus chairs in the lobby notwithstanding. For extra legroom, and pretty Mediterranean style, book the studio apartment with kitchen.

SCHÖNEBERG
Lodging options are thin on the ground in this delightful but overwhelmingly residential area. It's a shame, really, because it's close to fabulous nightlife and shopping, and well served by public transport.

ARCO HOTEL Map p344   Hotel €€
☎ 235 1480; www.arco-hotel.de; Geisbergstrasse 30; s €57-75, d €75-97, all incl breakfast; 🖳 ; ⊝ Wittenbergplatz

ASLEEP IN THE TWILIGHT ZONE
It is only fitting that Berlin's most original hotel takes its name from a novel by the master of imagination, Jules Verne. Each of its 32 rooms is a journey to a unique, surreal and slightly wicked world, spawned by the vision of artist-composer-owner Lars Stroschen. To be stranded on Propeller Island means waking up on the ceiling (in the Upside-Down Room), in a comfortable prison cell (Freedom Room) or inside a kaleidoscope (Mirror Room). The only aspect this place shares with other hotels is that each room has a bed or two. Except here it's a rotating round bed, a 'flying' bed, one that's suspended on ship's rope and others on a ziggurat platform, in a lion's cage or inside a coffin. It took Lars, who designed and crafted every piece of furniture and accessory, some six years to finish this creative tour de force, mostly using recycled materials. There are sinks wrought from metal beer barrels, faucets made from heater valves and table bases carved from tree trunks. Absent are any of the usual hotel trappings: no telephone, no room service, no pillow treats. Instead, each room has an audio-system playing 'sound sculptures' composed by – who else? – Lars himself. **Propeller Island City Lodge** (Map p344; ☎ 891 9016 8am-noon, 0163 256 5909 noon-8pm; www.propeller-island .de; Albrecht-Achilles-Strasse 58; r €59-180, breakfast €7; ✗ ; ⊝ Adenauerplatz).

In a quiet residential area, near the famous KaDeWe department store, this hotel occupies a recently overhauled turn-of-the-20th-century building. It rents 20 pleasant, if rather nondescript, rooms with all major mod-cons, at prices that won't dent your wallet too badly. On balmy days, breakfast is best enjoyed alfresco in the lovely back garden dotted with mature trees.

HOTEL ARTIM Map pp338-9   Hotel €€
☎ 210 0250; www.hotel-artim.de; Fuggerstrasse 20; s/d/tr/ste €110/134/159/184, all incl breakfast; Ⓟ ✗ ♿ ; ◉ Wittenbergplatz
Conveniently located between Charlottenburg shopping and Schöneberg nightlife, the Artim has large, appealing rooms, most sheathed in a subdued primary colour scheme. It's popular with tour groups and families, who find much to like about the good value, two-room suites sleeping up to five people. It has five rooms specially designed for the mobility-impaired.

CHEAP SLEEPS
ENJOY BED & BREAKFAST
Map pp338-9   B&B €
☎ 2362 3610; http://ger.ebab.com; Bülowstrasse 106; ☒ reservations 4.30-9.30pm; s from €15, d from €25; ◉ Nollendorfplatz
This private room-referral service caters specifically for gays and lesbians. It is affiliated with the central information centre Mann-O-Meter, although it's easiest to make reservations online. The website has all the details.

KREUZBERG
There's much to recommend Kreuzberg as a base of operation, especially the western half around Viktoriapark. For some reason, though, it has been almost completely bypassed by Berlin's growing new-hotel scene and offers only a few standbys, but they're reliable.

HOTEL AM ANHALTER BAHNHOF
Map pp336-7   Hotel €€
☎ 251 0342; www.hotel-anhalter-bahnhof.de; Stresemannstrasse 36; s €50-75, d €75-105, tr €90-125, q €104-140, all incl breakfast; ⓡ Anhalter Bahnhof, ◉ ⓡ Potsdamer Platz

A fairly recent makeover has catapulted this budget staple, close to Potsdamer Platz, into the 21st century. Sure, the furnishings are still not the latest, but rooms are mostly good-sized, clean and comfortable. Those with private bath generally face away from the busy street. A handy computerised system allows you to check in 24/7. Rooms with shared bath are about 30% cheaper.

HOTEL RIEHMERS HOFGARTEN
Map pp336-7   Hotel €€
☎ 7809 8800; www.riehmers-hofgarten.de; Yorckstrasse 83; s €98-108, d €125-140, all incl breakfast; ✗ 🖳 ; ◉ Mehringdamm
This artistic hotel near Viktoriapark is a delightful marriage of tradition and trendiness. It's part of an elegant late-19th-century housing estate, wrapped around an idyllic inner courtyard. Large double French doors lead to mostly spacious, high-ceilinged rooms, that are modern but not stark. Fun shopping, cafés and eateries on Bergmannstrasse are only a quick stroll away.

CHEAP SLEEPS
MEININGER CITY HOSTELS
Map pp336-7   Hostel €
☎ 6663 6100, toll-free 0800 634 6464; www.meininger-hostels.de; Hallesches Ufer 30 & Tempelhofer Ufer 10; 8-bed dm €13.50, 4- & 5-bed dm €25, s/d/tr €49/66/87, all incl linen & breakfast; Ⓟ ✗ 🖳 ; ◉ Möckernbrücke
Occupying two buildings separated by a busy road, the Landwehrkanal and the U-Bahn tracks (which run above-ground here), Meininger offers modern rooms with en suite bathrooms and a comfort level rivalling basic hotels. It has great frills and freebies (including linen, towels, lockers and breakfast) but gregarious types looking for a party vibe are probably better off elsewhere.

RIVERSIDE LODGE HOSTEL
Map pp336-7   Hostel €
☎ 6951 5510; www.riverside-lodge.de; Hobrechtstrasse 43; dm €17-22, d €52, linen €2.50, breakfast €3.50; ✗ 🖳 ; ◉ Schönleinstrasse
This sweet little 12-bed hostel is as warm and welcoming as an old friend's hug thanks to its wonderful owners, Jutta and Liane. Both avid travellers, they have created a cosy place where you can enjoy free

Propeller Island City Lodge (p260)

coffee, tea and fruit, surf the Web and burn CDs, and rent bikes or canoes. In the large dorm, beds can be curtained off for extra privacy.

FRIEDRICHSHAIN

With its gritty GDR aesthetic, Friedrichshain may not be as pretty as heavily gentrified Mitte and Prenzlauer Berg, but your euro will stretch a lot further here. All places mentioned below are within walking distance of the district's vibrant bar, café and club scene. Kreuzberg, with plenty more options, is just across the Spree River.

EAST-SIDE HOTEL Map pp336-7   Hotel €€
☎ 293 833; www.eastsidehotel.de; Mühlenstrasse 6; s €60-80, d €70-100, all incl breakfast; P ; ☉ ® Warschauer Strasse
The East-Side's white-and-butter-yellow classical façade is really a bit of a tease, for inside this protected building awaits an ultramodern hotel whose 36 rooms are a meditation in minimalism. It sits right next to the Spree River, opposite the East Side Gallery, the longest remaining stretch of the Berlin Wall. Breakfast is served any time of day or night.

HOTEL 26 Map pp336-7   Hotel €€
☎ 297 7780; www.hotel26-berlin.de; Grünberger Strasse 26; s €50-80, d €70-100, all incl breakfast; P ✕ 🖳 🛠 ; ☉ ® Warschauer Strasse, ® M10 Grünberger Strasse

If you've outgrown hostels but don't like dropping bundles of cash for shelter, this modern hotel decked out in cheery citrus colours may be a good fit. Although it seems sparse and no-nonsense, it has a lot going on that doesn't immediately meet the eye, including an eco-friendly approach to hospitality. Rooms are nonsmoking and the breakfast is entirely organic.

HOTEL & HOSTEL FRIEDRICHSHAIN
Map pp336-7   Hotel/Hostel €
☎ 9700 2030; www.home-from-home.com; Warschauer Strasse 57; dm €25, s €50, d €70-80, tr €105, breakfast €5; P ✕ 🛠 ; ☙ reception staffed 8am-6pm; ☉ ® Warschauer Strasse
This friendly, clean and efficient abode combines a simple hotel and an upmarket hostel under one roof. Modern furnishings and a young, good-natured crew give the place a fresh, upbeat ambiance. Guests enjoy kitchen access and rooms sheathed in warm Mediterranean colours with comfy twin-sized beds dressed in crisp, quality linen and decorated with a little pillow treat.

JUNCKER'S HOTEL Map pp336-7   Hotel €
☎ 293 3550; www.junckers-hotel.de; Grünberger Strasse 21; s/d/tr/q €59/73/93/112, breakfast €6; P ; ☉ ® Warschauer Strasse, ® M10 Grünberger Strasse
This is one of the best small, family-run hotels that money can buy in Berlin, given the quality of the rooms, caring staff that don't chintz with smiles and the good

location near public transport and nightlife. Rooms aren't particularly large, and are in no danger of appearing in *House Beautiful*, but everything is in immaculate shape and squeaky clean.

UPSTALSBOOM HOTEL
FRIEDRICHSHAIN Map pp336-7   Hotel €€

☎ 293 750; www.upstalsboom-berlin.de; Gubener Strasse 42; s €85-150, d €100-165, all incl breakfast; Ⓟ ✕ ; Ⓔ Ⓡ Warschauer Strasse, Ⓣ M10, M13 Revaler Strasse

If this modern and well-kept hotel feels like a breath of fresh air, it may be because it's the Berlin branch of a small chain of German seaside resorts. Rooms have a clean, uncluttered look and come in four sizes. An unexpected spot is the lavender-scented rooftop garden. Rates include bicycle rentals and access to a sauna, solarium and fitness area.

CHEAP SLEEPS
EASTERN COMFORT HOSTELBOAT
Map pp336-7   Hostel €

☎ 6676 3806; www.eastern-comfort.com; Mühlenstrasse 73-77; dm €17-19, s €32-58, d €50-72, breakfast €3; Ⓔ Ⓡ Warschauer Strasse

Berlin's first floating hostel is moored in the Spree River right by the East Side Gallery (p128) and in between the entertainment districts of Friedrichshain and Kreuzberg. Cabins are carpeted and trimmed in wood, but pretty snug. The '70s-inspired top deck lounge is great for chilling with a beer at sunset.

ODYSSEE GLOBETROTTER HOSTEL
Map pp336-7   Hostel €

☎ 2900 0081, toll-free reservations 0800 2665 2233-02; www.globetrotterhostel.de; Grünberger Strasse 23; dm €13-19; s/d shared bathroom €35/45, d with shower €52, all incl linen, breakfast €3; ✕ Ⓛ ; Ⓔ Ⓡ Warschauer Strasse, Ⓣ M10 Grünberger Strasse

This eastside hostel puts the 'fun' in funky and is a great base for making an in-depth study of Friedrichshain's nightlife. It's run by a young and energetic crew of friends, who constantly dream up new ways to keep their guests happy and entertained. Recent additions include a pub and a concert venue. Rooms are artily decorated, clean and have lockers.

PRENZLAUER BERG

www.lonelyplanet.com

Prenzlauer Berg is one of Berlin's prettiest neighbourhoods, still central, yet quieter than Mitte, with handsome architecture and a dynamic after-dark scene. It's hard to fathom why more hoteliers haven't yet capitalised on its considerable assets.

ACKSEL HAUS
Map pp332-3   Serviced Apartments €€

☎ 4433 7633; www.ackselhaus.de; Belforter Strasse 21; apt €66-160; Ⓔ Senefelderplatz

This charismatic place on a pretty residential street has 10 apartments (most sleeping two – some up to four – with full kitchen). Each light-filled unit has unique décor ranging from romantic (with four-poster bed) to exotic (with African sculptures) and nautical (lots of blue), all with voicemail and DSL. The nicest ones overlook the flowery garden. There's a nice café and wi-fi throughout.

EASTSIDE PENSION
Map pp332-3   Guesthouse €

☎ 4373 5484; www.eastside-pension.de; Schönhauser Allee 41; s €34-39, d €64-59, tr €79-84; ⏰ check-in noon-8pm Mon-Sat or by arrangement; Ⓔ Eberswalder Strasse

This gay-oriented guesthouse consists of just a few functional, but large, rooms. Check-in is in a shop stocked with all kinds of fun accoutrements. The scene is just steps away and host Ulli will quickly fill you in on the local hangouts. Discounts are available Monday to Thursday, and for stays over four nights.

HOTEL ADELE Map pp332-3   Hotel €€
☎ 4432 4350; www.adele-hotel.de; Greifswalder Strasse 227; s/d incl breakfast €80/120; Ⓛ ; Ⓣ M4 to Am Friedrichshain

Tucked between a chic coffee shop and bistro-lounge, this is a smart new designer

---

TOP FIVE DESIGNER ABODES

- Arcotel Velvet (p252)
- Brandenburger Hof (p259)
- Dorint Sofitel Am Gendarmenmarkt (p253)
- Hotel Adele (above)
- Ku'Damm 101 (p260)

hotel with street cred. Pick up a bottle of bubbly from the wine store around the corner, then retire to rooms brimming with exquisite details such as diaphanous curtains, leather headboards, sensuous faux fur blankets and lacquered furniture. Even the bathrooms, with their sleek Italian looks, are oh-so stylish.

HOTEL GREIFSWALD

Map pp332-3   Hotel €

☎ 442 7888; www.hotel-greifswald.de; Greifswalder Strasse 211; s €58-70, d €63-73, apt €63-100, breakfast €7.50; P ; 🚐 100, 🚃 M4 to Hufelandstrasse

This 30-room hotel, tucked into a back building away from tram and traffic noise, has a serious rock pedigree. The teensy lobby doubles as a veritable hall of fame featuring former guests, including Mitch Ryder and Steppenwolf. Rooms are handsome, if rather generic, but it's the awesome breakfast spread – served until 1pm – that gets our thumbs up.

MYER'S HOTEL Map pp332-3   Hotel €€

☎ 440 140; www.myershotel.de; Metzer Strasse 26; s €85-140, d €110-175, all incl breakfast; 🍴 🐾 🐦 ; 🚇 Senefelder Platz

This 41-room boutique hotel combines the elegance of your rich uncle's mansion, the cheerful warmth of your parents' home and the casual comforts of your best friend's pad. Rooms are classically furnished with rich woods and sheathed in soothing colours. Unwinding spots include the 24-hour lobby bar, a ruby-walled

tearoom, the light-filled gallery lounge and a bucolic garden.

CHEAP SLEEPS

EAST SEVEN HOSTEL Map pp332-3   Hostel €

☎ 9362 2240; www.eastseven.de; Schwedter Strasse 7; dm €12-19, s €28-30, d €40-44; 🍴 💻 🐦 ; 🚇 Senefelder Platz

This friendly, familial and fun hostel is well positioned for access to all kinds of bars, cafés, restaurants and even the U-Bahn station. Its fairly small size creates a low-key atmosphere where cultural and language barriers melt faster than snow in the Sahara. The homely kitchen (with dishwasher!), retro lounge and idyllic back garden are all fabulous conversation corners. Dorms and private rooms are bright with bold colours and pine beds.

LETTE 'M SLEEP Map pp332-3   Hostel €

☎ 4473 3623; www.backpackers.de; Lettestrasse 7; dm €15-19, d with shared bathroom €48, apt €66, discounts Oct–mid-May; 🍴 💻 ; 🚇 Eberswalder Strasse

This hostel is as hostels used to be: low-key, low-tech, welcoming and equipped with a kitchen-lounge for meeting fellow travellers. It's right on hip Helmholtzplatz, perfect for plunging into Berlin's swirling nightlife vortex. Dorms sleep three to six and have a sink, lockers and table. Bathrooms were recently redone. Twin rooms have a small fridge and four new apartments come with kitchens.

Excursions ■

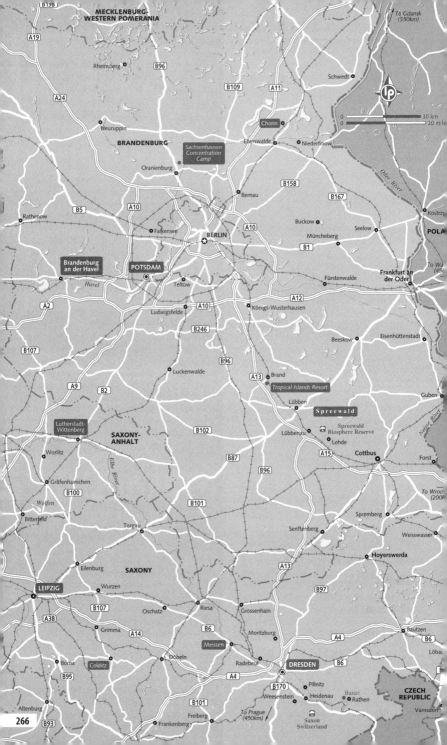

Excursions

It may not be the most popular part of the republic, but almost everything worth seeing around Berlin is in the surrounding state of Brandenburg, which boasts a wide range of undervisited attractions. Efficient rail links also mean that major cities such as Dresden and Leipzig are within easy reach and make for good overnight trips.

PARKS & PALACES

Few places in Germany can compete with the pomp and splendour of historic Potsdam (p268), a superbly civilised break from the bustle of cutting-edge Berlin. Easily reached on local transport, it's an essential day trip for anyone with a few hours to spare.

ARCHITECTURE

Despite the notoriously heavy bombing at the end of WWII, the centre of Dresden (p278) is still a treasure-trove of architectural gems, including the nationally renowned Semperoper. Just walking around the Altstadt (old town) for a day should be enough to satisfy most building buffs. Further classical treats can be found in Leipzig (p283).

WETLANDS, WATERWAYS & WATERWORKS

Brandenburg an der Havel (p273), once a major river-trade town, is set on three islands and has plenty to offer visitors. Further south, the Spreewald (p274) is a great place to get out onto the many miles of canals, rivers and marshes that litter the landscape around Berlin. Sun-starved visitors can also get a taste of the exotic at the unique Tropical Islands Resort (p276).

WINING & DINING

Why confine yourself to the Berlin scene? Doing the culinary rounds in Leipzig (p285) makes for equally lively nights, and few visitors fail to pop into the legendary Auerbachs Keller, Goethe's old local. For sheer density and variety, the Neustadt area of Dresden (p282) can also more than hold its own.

PILGRIMAGES

As the name would suggest, Lutherstadt-Wittenberg (p277) is a magnet for devotees of Great Reformer Martin Luther. Anyone interested in religion or this period of history should find plenty to see here.

ACOUSTICS

Berlin itself is a goldmine of classical-music venues, but for a special treat try the summer concerts at the ancient red-brick monastery (p276) in Chorin, known throughout Brandenburg for its exceptional atmosphere and acoustics.

Bach Memorial outside Thomaskirche, Leipzig (p283)

BRANDENBURG

POTSDAM

Potsdam, on the Havel River just south-west of Greater Berlin, is the capital of Brandenburg state and the largest single tourist attraction in the region after Berlin itself. Visitors flock here in their thousands to admire the stunning architecture of this former Prussian royal seat and soak up the elegant air of history that still characterises its parks and gardens.

In the 17th century, Elector Friedrich Wilhelm of Brandenburg made it his second residence. With the creation of the Kingdom of Prussia, Potsdam became a royal seat and garrison town. In the mid-18th century Friedrich II (Frederick the Great) built many of the marvellous palaces to which visitors flock today. In April 1945, Royal Air Force bombers devastated the historic centre of Potsdam, including the City Palace on Am Alten Markt, but fortunately most other palaces escaped undamaged.

Potsdam's focal point is **Sanssouci Park**, a sprawling beast with crisscrossing trails strewn throughout; take along the free map provided by the tourist office or you'll find yourself up the wrong path at almost every turn. The various palaces are spaced fairly far apart – it's about 15km to complete the entire circuit. Sadly, cycling is not allowed in the park.

Begin your park tour with Georg Wenzeslaus von Knobelsdorff's celebrated rococo **Schloss Sanssouci** (1747). Only 2000 visitors a day are allowed entry to the glorious interiors (a rule laid down by Unesco), so tickets are usually sold out by 2.30pm, even in the quiet seasons – arrive early and avoid weekends and holidays. Tours run by the tourist office guarantee entry.

Our favourite rooms include the frilly rococo **Konzertsaal** (Concert Hall) and the bed chambers of the **Damenflügel** (Ladies' Wing), including a boudoir reputedly occupied by French writer Voltaire on his frequent visits to the court. Just opposite the palace is the **Historische Mühle** (Historical Windmill), which was designed to give the palace grounds a rustic appeal.

The palace is flanked by the twin **Neue Kammern** (New Chambers), which served as a guesthouse and orangery. The chambers include the large **Ovidsaal**, with its gilded reliefs and green-and-white marble floor, and Meissen porcelain figurines in the last room to the west. Nearby, the **Bildergalerie** (Picture Gallery) was completed in 1764 as Germany's first purpose-built art museum. It contains a rich collection of 17th-century paintings by Rubens, Van Dyck, Caravaggio and others.

The Renaissance-style **Orangerie** (Orangery Palace), built in 1864 as a guesthouse for foreign royalty, is the largest of the Sanssouci palaces but hardly the most interesting. The six sumptuous rooms on display include the **Raphaelsaal**, featuring 19th-century copies of Italian Renaissance painter Raphael's work, and a **tower** that can be climbed for great views over the Neues Palais and the park. Part of the west wing is still used to keep sensitive plants alive in the cold, north-German winter.

Two interesting buildings west of the Orangerie are the pagoda-like **Drachenhaus** (Dragon House, 1770), which houses a café-restaurant, and the rococo **Belvedere**, the only building in the park to suffer serious damage during WWII (but fully restored in 1999).

The late-baroque **Neues Palais** (New Palace), built in 1769 as the royal family's summer residence, is one of the most imposing buildings in the park and the one to see if your time is limited. The tour takes in about a dozen of the palace's 200 rooms, including the **Grottensaal** (Grotto Hall), a rococo delight with shells, fossils and baubles set into the walls and ceilings; the **Marmorsaal** (Marble Room), a large banquet hall of white Carrara marble with a wonderful ceiling fresco; the **Jagdkammer** (Hunting Chamber), which has lots of dead

> ### GETTING INTO TOWN
> **Distance from Berlin** 24km.
> **Direction** Southwest.
> **Travel Time** 30 minutes.
> **Train** The S7 links central Berlin stations including Ostkreuz, Alexanderplatz, Friedrichstrasse, Zoo and Charlottenburg, with Potsdam Hauptbahnhof about every 10 minutes. Regional DB trains are faster but only operate twice hourly. You need a ticket covering zones A, B and C (€2.60) for either service.

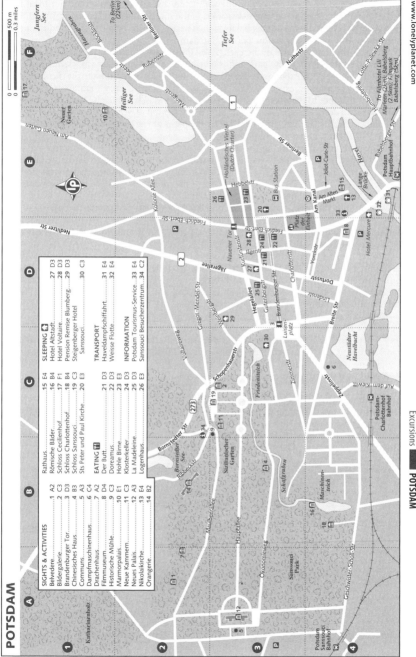

POTSDAM

SIGHTS & ACTIVITIES
Belvedere........................	1	A2
Bildergalerie....................	2	C3
Brandenburger Tor..........	3	D3
Chinesisches Haus...........	4	B3
Communs.........................	5	A3
Dampfmaschinenhaus.....	6	C4
Drachenhaus....................	7	A2
Filmmuseum....................	8	D4
Historische Mühle...........	9	C3
Marmorpalais..................	10	E1
Neue Kammern................	11	C3
Neues Palais...................	12	A3
Nikolaikirche...................	13	E4
Orangerie........................	14	B2
Rathaus...........................	15	E4
Römische Bäder..............	16	B4
Schloss Cecilienhof..........	17	F1
Schloss Charlottenhof.....	18	B4
Schloss Sanssouci...........	19	C3
Sts Peter und Paul Kirche.	20	E3

EATING 🍴
Der Butt..........................	21	D3
Doreamus........................	22	D3
Hohle Birne.....................	23	E3
Klosterkeller...................	24	D3
La Madeleine...................	25	D3
Logenhaus.......................	26	E3

SLEEPING 🛏
Hotel Altstadt.................	27	D3
Hotel Voltaire.................	28	D3
Pension Remise Blumberg.	29	D3
Steigenberger Hotel
Sanssouci.....................	30	C3

TRANSPORT
Haveldampfschiffahrt......	31	E4
Weisse Flotte..................	32	E4

INFORMATION
Potsdam Tourismus-Service.	33	E4
Sanssouci Besucherzentrum.	34	C2

www.lonelyplanet.com

furry things and fine gold tracery on the walls; and several chambers fitted out from floor to ceiling in rich red damask. The **Schlosstheater** in the south wing has classical-music concerts at weekends. Opposite the Neues Palais is the **Communs**, which originally housed the palace servants and kitchens but is now part of Potsdam University.

Towards the southern end of the park, **Schloss Charlottenhof** (1826) was Karl Friedrich Schinkel's main contribution to the park and is considered one of his finest works, but don't wait around if the queues are too long. The exterior (modelled after a Roman villa) is more interesting than the interior, especially the Doric portico and the bronze fountain to the east.

A short distance to the northeast, on the edge of the Maschinenteich (Machine Pond), the **Römische Bäder** (Roman Baths) were built in 1836 by a pupil of Schinkel but were never used. The floor mosaics and caryatids, inspired by the baths at Herculaneum, are impressive, and we also like the flounder spitting into a clamshell near the entrance.

Follow the path north along the west bank of the Schafgraben to Ökonomieweg, then head east, and you'll come to what many consider to be the pearl of the park: the **Chinesisches Haus** (Chinese Teahouse, 1757), a circular pavilion of gilded columns, palm trees and figures of Chinese musicians and animals. One of the monkeys is said to have the features of Voltaire, a dubious tribute to the great Frenchman!

Moving into the town itself, the baroque **Brandenburger Tor** (Brandenburg Gate, 1770), on Luisenplatz at the western end of the old town, is hardly on the scale of its namesake in Berlin, but is actually older. From this square, pedestrian Brandenburger Strasse runs east to the **Sts Peter & Paul Kirche** (Church of Sts Peter & Paul, 1868).

North of here, bounded by Friedrich-Ebert-Strasse, Hebbelstrasse, Kurfürstenstrasse and Gutenbergstrasse, the **Holländisches Viertel** (Dutch Quarter) has 134 gabled red-brick houses, built for Dutch workers who came to Potsdam in the 1730s at the invitation of Friedrich Wilhelm I. The homes have been prettily restored and now house all kinds of galleries, cafés and restaurants.

South of here, past the monumental Platz der Einheit, is the great neoclassical dome of Schinkel's **Nikolaikirche** (1850) on Am Alten Markt. Recently restored, the building almost looks new, and is complemented by an obelisk and a small pavilion in front on the old market square. On the eastern side of the square is Potsdam's old **Rathaus**, dating from 1753, which now contains several exhibition rooms.

A short distance beyond the 'bay' of the Havel is the wonderful **Dampfmaschinenhaus** (pump house), a Moorish-style structure often called the *Moschee* (mosque), which was built in 1842 to house the palace waterworks.

Northeast from the centre of Potsdam, you'll find the **Neuer Garten**, a winding lakeside park on the west bank of the Heiliger See – it's a fine place to relax after all the baroque-rococo and high art of Sanssouci. The **Marmorpalais** (Marble Palace) on the lake, built in 1792 by Carl Gotthard Langhans, has been carefully restored.

Surreal Caligari Hall, part of the Filmpark Babelsburg (opposite page), Potsdam

DETOUR: RIVER ROUTES

Potsdam's location on the Havel makes it a great starting point for a whole range of river trips, transporting budding boaters and keen cruisers all around this watery corner of Brandenburg. The principal operator is **Weisse Flotte** (☎ 0331-275 9210; www.schiffahrt-in-potsdam.de; Lange Brücke 6; ⏰ 8.45am-4.15pm Apr-Oct), whose services depart regularly from the dock near Lange Brücke, by the towering Hotel Mercure.

The core schedule includes a sightseeing tour passing the various waterside palaces (€9), a trip round the main Havel lakes (€12), a two-hour ride covering the seven lakes up to Wannsee (€11), and a full-day tour to the town of Brandenburg an der Havel (€20). As well as these daytime routes, regular evening and special events are offered, including weekend brunch (€28) and a variety of sunset, music and dinner cruises.

Weisse Flotte's sister company **Haveldampfschiffahrt** (☎ 0331-275 9233) has steamboat tours of the same areas, leaving from the opposite end of Lange Brücke.

Further north is **Schloss Cecilienhof**, a rustic, English-style country manor contrasting with the extravagant rococo palaces and pavilions of Sanssouci. Cecilienhof was the site of the 1945 Potsdam Conference, where captured German territory was reassigned to Poland, and large photos of the participants – Stalin, Truman and Churchill – are displayed inside. The conference room can be visited on a guided tour.

It's not just history buffs that Potsdam caters for: the town was the centre of Germany's influential film industry from the very early days of the medium, and the mighty UFA and DEFA studios were based here, in the southeastern district of Babelsberg. Today **Filmpark Babelsberg** occupies the site. Filming still goes on here, including for the hit TV soap *Gute Zeiten Schlechte Zeiten* (Good Times Bad Times), though the main reason to visit is the theme park that now takes up much of the grounds.

New attractions are added yearly to complement the various sets; current features include a 4-D cinema, a Panama boat ride and the spectacular volcano stunt show. You can also watch animal actors being trained and tour the warped, expressionistic Caligari Hall. The guided tram ride around the backlot is great if your German's good enough. To get to the park, take the S1 to Babelsberg and then bus No 690 to Ahornstrasse; bus 601 and 619 also run here directly from Potsdam Hauptbahnhof. Alternatively, get off the S-Bahn at Griebnitzsee and take bus 696 to the Drewitz stop.

For a slightly more studious take on Potsdam's cinematic history, the **Filmmuseum** on Breite Strasse is located in the Marstall (1746), the former royal stables designed by Knobelsdorff. It contains exhibits on the history of the Babelsberg studios, Marlene Dietrich costumes and rare footage from Nazi-era and German Democratic Republic (GDR) films.

Information

Potsdam Tourismus-Service (☎ 0331-275 580; www .potsdamtourismus.de; Am Neuen Markt 1; ⏰ 9.30am-6pm Mon-Fri, to 4pm Sat & Sun Apr-Oct, 10am-6pm Mon-Fri, 9.30am-2pm Sat & Sun Nov-Mar)

Sanssouci Besucherzentrum (☎ 0331-969 4200; www .spsg.de; An der Orangerie 1; ⏰ 8.30am-5pm Mar-Oct, 9am-4pm Nov-Feb)

Sights

Sights within **Sanssouci Park** (admission free; ⏰ dawn to dusk):

Belvedere (admission €1; ⏰ 10am-5pm Tue-Sun Apr-Oct)

Bildergalerie (☎ 0331-969 4181; adult/concession €2/1.50; ⏰ 10am-5pm Tue-Sun 14 May–16 Oct)

Chinesisches Haus (☎ 0331-969 4222; admission €1; ⏰ 10am-5pm Tue-Sun 14 May–16 Oct)

Damenflügel (Schloss Sanssouci; adult/concession €2/1.50; ⏰ 10am-5pm Sat & Sun 14 May–16 Oct)

Historische Mühle (☎ 0331-969 4284; adult/concession €2/1; ⏰ 10am-6pm)

Neue Kammern (☎ 0331-969 4206; adult/concession €2/1.50; ⏰ 10am-5pm Tue-Sun 15 May–Oct, 10am-5pm Sat & Sun Apr–14 May)

Neues Palais (☎ 0331-969 4255; adult/concession €5/4; ⏰ 9am-5pm Sat-Thu Apr-Oct, to 4pm Nov-Mar)

Orangerie (☎ 0331-969 4280; tours adult/concession €3/2.50, tower €1; ⏰ 10am-5pm Sat & Sun Apr-May, 10am-5pm Tue-Sun May-Oct)

Römische Bäder (☎ 0331-969 4225; adult/concession €3/2.50; ⏰ 10am-5pm Tue-Sun 14 May–16 Oct)

Schloss Charlottenhof (☎ 0331-969 4228; tours adult/concession €4/3; ☼ 10am-5pm Tue-Sun 14 May–16 Oct)

Schloss Sanssouci (☎ 0331-969 4190; tours adult/concession €8/5; ☼ 9am-5pm Tue-Sun Apr-Oct, to 4pm Tue-Sun Nov-Mar)

Other sights:

Dampfmaschinenhaus (☎ 0331-969 4248; cnr Breite Strasse & Zeppelinstrasse; tours adult/concession €2/1.50; ☼ 10am-5pm Sat & Sun 14 May-16 Oct)

Filmmuseum (☎ 0331-271 8112; Breite Strasse; admission adult/concession €3.50/2.50, films €4.50/3.50; ☼ 10am-6pm)

Filmpark Babelsberg (☎ 0331-212 755; www.filmpark.de; Grossbeerenstrasse; adult/concession/child €17/15.50/12.50; ☼ 10am-6pm Mar-Oct)

Marmorpalais (☎ 0331-969 4246; adult/concession €2/1.50; ☼ 10am-5pm Tue-Sun Apr-Oct, to 4pm Sat & Sun Nov-Mar)

Nikolaikirche (Alter Markt; ☼ 2-5pm Mon, 10am-5pm Tue-Sat, noon-5pm Sun)

Rathaus (Alter Markt; ☼ 2-7pm Tue-Sun)

Schloss Cecilienhof (☎ 0331-969 4244; tours adult/concession €5/4; ☼ 9am-5pm Tue-Sun Apr-Oct, to 4pm Nov-Mar)

Eating

Der Butt (☎ 0331-200 6066; Gutenburgstrasse 25; mains €12.60-17.70) Excellent fish restaurant serving scaly specimens fresh from the lakes.

Doreamus (☎ 0331-201 5860; Brandenburger Strasse 30/31; mains €7.80-13.50) Some of the finest views you'll get over the Altstadt, with decent food and Sunday jazz brunch.

Hohle Birne (☎ 0331-280 0715; Mitstrasse 19; mains €4-13) Earthy but tasty German cuisine, plus a huge beer and wine menu. The name (literally 'hollow pear') is a local insult.

Klosterkeller (☎ 0331-291 218; Friedrich-Ebert-Strasse 94; mains €7.80-13.90) Touristy but fun restaurant, wine bar, beer garden and cocktail bar serving traditional regional dishes.

La Madeleine (☎ 0331-270 5400; Lindenstrasse 9; mains €2.50-11) Very French café-restaurant, serving good-value daily set menus (€13).

Logenhaus (☎ 0331-2002 9945; Kurfürstenstrasse 51; mains €5.50-13.90) A majestic 1879 Freemasons lodge that houses a restaurant, summer garden and the Luz Lounge bar-club.

Sleeping

Filmhotel Lili Marleen (☎ 0331-743 200; Grossbeerenstrasse 75; s €49-75, d €55-134) Near Babelsberg, Lili boasts plenty of filmic decor, as befits the grand dame of German cinema.

Hotel Altstadt (☎ 0331-284 990; Dortusstrasse 9/10; s €50-65, d €68-95) The Altstadt offers a good range of rooms and has plenty of extra services, which makes it a decent bet.

Hotel Voltaire (☎ 0331-231 70; Friedrich-Ebert-Strasse 88; s €76-119, d €90-133) Posh address opposite the Dutch Quarter, with two restaurants, roof terrace and wellness area.

Pension Remise Blumberg (☎ 0331-280 3231; Weinbergstrasse 26; s/d €53/81) Big rooms with kitchenette conveniently opposite Sanssouci Park. Good for courtyard breakfasts in summer.

Steigenberger Hotel Sanssouci (☎ 0331-909 10; Allee nach Sanssouci 1; s €90-127, d €104-150) Another high-class option bordering right onto the park, nicely styled with copious facilities.

SACHSENHAUSEN CONCENTRATION CAMP

In 1936 the Nazis opened a 'model' concentration camp for men in a disused brewery in Sachsenhausen, near the town of Oranienburg. By 1945 about 220,000 men from 22 countries had passed through the gates – labelled, as at Auschwitz, *Arbeit Macht Frei* (Work Sets You Free). About 100,000 were murdered here, their remains consumed by the fires of the horribly efficient ovens.

After the war, the Soviets and the communist leaders of the new GDR set up Speziallager No 7 (Special Camp No 7). An estimated 60,000 people were interned here between 1945 and 1950, and up to 12,000 are believed to have died. There's a mass grave of victims at the camp and another one 1.5km to the north.

The **Sachsenhausen Memorial & Museum** consists of several parts. Even before you enter you'll see a **memorial** to the 6000 prisoners who died on the *Todesmarsch* (Death March) of April 1945, when the Nazis tried to drive the camp's 33,000 inmates to the Baltic in advance of the Red Army.

About 100m inside the camp is a mass grave of 300 prisoners who died in the infirmary after liberation in April 1945. Further on is the camp commandant's house and the so-called

'Green Monster' building, where SS troops were trained in camp maintenance and other, more brutal activities. At the end of the road is the **Neues Museum** (New Museum), which has excellent exhibits. East of the museum are **Barracks 38 & 39**, reconstructions of typical huts housing most of the 6000 Jewish prisoners brought to Sachsenhausen after *Kristallnacht* (November 1938). North of here is the **prison**, where particularly brutal punishment was meted out to prisoners. Inside the prison yard is a **memorial** to the homosexuals who died here, one of the few monuments you'll see anywhere to these 'forgotten victims' (there's another at Berlin's Nollendorfplatz U-Bahn station, p120).

To get to the **Lagermuseum** (Camp Museum), with moth-eaten and dusty exhibits on both the Nazi and GDR camps, walk north along the parade ground, past the site of the gallows. The museum is in the building on the right, which was once the camp kitchen. In the former laundry room opposite, a gruesome film of the camp after liberation is shown throughout the day.

Left of the tall and ugly **monument** (1961), erected by the GDR in memory of political prisoners interned here, is the **crematorium** and **Station Z extermination site**, a pit for shooting prisoners in the neck with a wooden 'catch' where bullets could be retrieved and recycled. A crumbling **memorial hall** now stands on the site of the gas chamber as a final reminder of the brutality.

Sights

Sachsenhausen Memorial and Museum (☎ 03301-200 200; www.gedenkstaette-sachsenhausen.de; admission free; ♥ 8.30am-6pm Tue-Sun Apr-Sep, to 4.30pm Oct-Mar)

GETTING THERE

Distance from Berlin 35km.
Direction North.
Travel Time One hour.
Train The easiest way to get here is the frequent S1 to Oranienburg (€6.45). There are also RB trains from Berlin-Lichtenberg (€6, 30 minutes). From Oranienburg it's an easy 20-minute walk.

BRANDENBURG AN DER HAVEL

Brandenburg is the oldest town in the March (duchy) of Brandenburg, with a history going back to at least the 6th century. It was an important bishopric from the early Middle Ages and the seat of the Brandenburg margraves until they moved to Berlin in the 15th century. Severe damage suffered during WWII as well as GDR neglect is gradually being repaired, and the baroque churches and waterside setting make for a refreshing day trip.

Brandenburg is split into three sections by the Havel river, the Beetzsee and their canals. The Neustadt occupies an island in the centre; the Dominsel is to the north; and the Altstadt, on the mainland, is to the west.

Begin a stroll at the Romanesque **Dom St Peter & Paul** (Cathedral of St Peter & Paul), on the northern edge of Dominsel. Begun in 1165 by Premonstratensian monks and completed in 1240, this red-brick edifice contains the wonderfully decorated **Bunte Kapelle** (Coloured Chapel), with a vaulted and painted ceiling; the carved 14th-century **Böhmischer Altar** (Bohemian Altar) in the south transept; a fantastic baroque **organ** (1723), which was restored in 1999; and the **Dommuseum**.

Heading back towards the centre, Molkenmarkt, the continuation of Mühlendamm, runs parallel to Neustädtischer Markt and leads to the **Pfarrkirche St Katharinen** (Parish Church of St Catherine). This Gothic brick church was originally two chapels, the first from 1395. See how many New Testament characters you can spot on the 'Meadow of Heaven' painted ceiling.

To reach the Altstadt, walk up the pedestrianised Hauptstrasse and then west over the Jahrtausendbrücke (Millennium Bridge). Passing the **glockenspiel** (Ritterstrasse 64; ♥ rung hourly 9am-7pm), you reach the **Stadtmuseum im Frey-Haus**. It's a local history museum with much emphasis on the EP Lehmann factory, which produced cute mechanical toys and pottery.

GETTING INTO TOWN

Distance from Berlin 60km.
Direction Southwest.
Travel Time 40 minutes.
Train Frequent regional trains link Brandenburg with Berlin-Zoo (€6) and Potsdam (€4.80).

Bearing right, you'll come to the **Altstädtisches Rathaus** (Old-Town Town Hall), a red-brick edifice built in 1450 in much the same style as the city's many churches. The interior can't be visited. Outside stands a lanky statue of the mythological figure **Roland**, a symbol of justice and integrity. The moss growing on his head slightly undermines the dignity of the statement!

The road past the Rathaus leads to Brandenburg's third major church, the **Gotthardtkirche** (Church of St Gotthardt, 1147). The west wing is one of the oldest surviving structures in the state; inside the greying brick walls you'll find a tall vaulted interior with a colourful crucifix above the aisle and lots of 16th-century ornamentation.

Information

Tourist Information (☎ 03381-585 858; www.stadt-brandenburg.de; Steinstrasse 66/67; ⊙ 9am-7pm Mon-Fri, 10am-3pm Sat & Sun May-Sep, 10am-7pm Mon-Fri, to 2pm Sat Oct-Apr)

Sights

Dom St Peter und Paul (☎ 03381-112 221; Burghof 9; admission free; ⊙ 10am-5pm Mon,Tue & Thu-Sat, to noon Wed, 11am-5pm Sun)

Dommuseum (☎ 03381-200 325; Dom St Peter & Paul; adult/concession €3/2)

Gotthardtkirche (Gotthardtkirchplatz; admission free; ⊙ 11am-5pm Mon-Sat, 11.30am-5pm Sun)

Pfarrkirche St Katharinen (Katharinenkirchplatz 2; admission free; ⊙ 10am-4pm Mon-Sat, 1-4pm Sun)

Stadtmuseum im Frey-Haus (☎ 03381-522 048; Ritterstrasse 96; adult/concession €3/1.50; ⊙ 9am-5pm Tue-Fri, 10am-5pm Sat & Sun)

Eating

Bismarck Terrassen (☎ 03381-300 939; Bergstrasse 2; mains €7.40-13.90) Dine on hearty French-German food or a 'surprise platter' (€17.90) amid Bismarck memorabilia.

Cafébar Kanu (☎ 03381-229 048; Ritterstrasse 76; breakfast €3.60) Right by the river, this little café-kiosk also rents out boats (from €10).

Marienberg (☎ 03381-794 960; Am Marienberg 1; mains €6.50-12.50) Huge beer garden and restaurant in the Stadtpark. Come here for Oktoberfest if you can't make Munich.

Sleeping

Pension Zum Birnbaum (☎ 03381-527 500; Mitstrasse 1; s/d/tr €31/48/60) Between the station and the Neustadt, with a modest assortment of good-value rooms.

Sorat Hotel Brandenburg (☎ 03381-5970; Altstädtischer Markt 1; s/d €65/81) Brandenburg's main upper-end choice and the only central place with wheelchair access. Champagne breakfast and sauna use are included.

SPREEWALD

The rivers, canals and streams of the 287-sq-km 'Spree Forest' are the closest thing Berlin has to a back garden. Visitors come here in droves to punt on more than 400km of waterways, hike countless nature trails and fish in the region that was declared a biosphere reserve by Unesco in 1990. The region is renowned throughout Germany for its gherkins – over 40,000 tons of cucumbers are harvested here every year!

The two main towns here are **Lübben**, in the drier Unterspreewald (Lower Spreewald), and **Lübbenau**, 13km away in the Oberspreewald (Upper Spreewald). There's a certain amount of friendly rivalry between the two, especially in the peak summer season.

Lübben, a tidy and attractive town at the centre of the Spreewald Biosphere Reserve, feels that bit more like a 'real' town and has a history going back at least two centuries further than its neighbour. The compact **Schloss** is worth a visit but the real highlight is a (free) wander through the gardens of the **Schlossinsel**, an artificial archipelago with gardens concealing cafés, jetties and all kinds of play areas.

Lübbenau is just as pretty but has more of a model-village air, despite being considerably bigger overall. The secluded Altstadt is almost invariably crammed with tourists

GETTING THERE

Distance from Berlin 80km.
Direction Southeast.
Travel Time Up to two hours.
Bus There are frequent buses between Lübben and Lübbenau on weekdays, but it's much quicker to catch a train.
Train Regional trains serve Lübben and Lübbenau every one to two hours from Berlin-Ostbahnhof (€8.40) en route to Cottbus.

SPREEWALD SORBS

The Spreewald region is part of the area inhabited by the Sorbian people, Germany's only indigenous minority. This intriguing group numbers just 60,000, descended from the Slavic Wends, who settled between the Elbe and Oder Rivers in the 5th century in an area called Lusatia (Luzia in Sorbian).

Lusatia was conquered by the Germans in the 10th century, subjected to brutal Germanisation throughout the Middle Ages and partitioned in 1815. Lower Sorbia, centred around the Spreewald, went to Prussia while Upper Sorbia, around Bautzen (Budyšin), went to Saxony. The Upper Sorbian dialect, closely related to Czech, enjoyed a certain prestige in Saxony, but the Kingdom of Prussia tried to suppress Lower Sorbian, which is similar to Polish. The Nazis, of course, tried to eradicate both.

The Sorbs were protected under the GDR, but their proud folk traditions didn't suit the bland 'proletarian' regime. Since reunification, interest in the culture has been revived through the media and colourful Sorbian festivals such as the *Vogelhochzeit* (Birds' Wedding) on January 25 and a symbolic *Hexenbrennen* (witch-burning) on April 30.

Sorbian heritage is also increasingly marketed locally as a tourist attraction, allowing the restoration and display of some fine old relics. From Lübbenau, walkers can follow a 30-minute trail west to Lehde, where the wonderful **Freilandmuseum** (☎ 03542-2944; admission adult/concession €3/2; ۞ 10am-6pm Apr–15 Sep, 10am-5pm 16 Sep–Oct) boasts traditional Sorbian thatched houses and farm buildings.

---

trying to get out onto the canals on *Kähne* (punt boats), which were once the only way to get around in these parts. If you want to join them, head for the **Grosser Hafen** (large harbour) or **Kleiner Hafen** (small harbour). You can take tours or rent boats from around €3.50 per hour.

Of course, you'll find a visit to either town has its merits, and the main point of coming here is to get straight back out into the countryside. The Spreewald has hiking and walking trails to suit everyone – local tourist offices sell a good range of useful maps.

Information

Spreewaldinformation/Tourismus Lübben (☎ 03546-3090; www.luebben.de; Hafen 1, Ernst-von-Houwald-Damm 15; ۞ 10am-6pm)

Touristinformation Lübbenau (☎ 03542-668; www.spreewald-online.de; Ehm-Welk-Strasse 15; ۞ 9am-6pm Mon-Fri, to 1pm Sat)

Sights

Grosser Hafen (☎ 03542-2225; Dammstrasse 77a, Lübbenau)

Kleiner Hafen (☎ 03542-403 710; Spreestrasse 10a, Lübbenau)

Schloss Lübben (☎ 03546-87 478; Ernst-von-Houwald-Damm 14, Lübben; adult/concession €4/2; ۞ 10am-5pm Tue-Sun)

Eating

Bubak (☎ 03546-186 144; Ernst-von-Houwald-Damm 9, Lübben; mains €6.80-15.30) A characterful roadside restaurant named after a local bogeyman, with weekly concerts and a singing proprietor.

Lübbenauer Hof (☎ 03542-83 162; Ehm-Welk-Strasse 20, Lübbenau; mains €9.40-12.90) Fish forms the basis of the menu here, often 'duetting' with game and other meats.

Zur Stadtmauer (☎ 03545-185 453; Badergasse 2, Lübben; mains €7.50-13.90) Part of the old city walls, right on the river. Huge mixed fish grills and ostrich dishes perk up the menu.

Sleeping

Hotel Spreeufer (☎ 03546-27 260; Hinter der Mauer 4, Lübben; per person €30-45) The Spreeufer is a smart, friendly hotel near the river.

Schloss Lübbenau (☎ 03542-8730; Schlossbezirk 6, Lübbenau; s €52-82, d €104-134) Check into your local castle for all the old-fashioned class you can handle.

Schlosskirche, Lutherstadt-Wittenberg (p277)

CHORIN

The tiny village of Chorin, part of the Schorfheide-Chorin Biosphere Reserve, is not exactly a tourist hub. However, plenty of people do make the day trip from Berlin to visit the renowned **Kloster Chorin** (Chorin Monastery), one of the finest red-brick Gothic structures in northern Germany, situated on a small, quiet lake.

Some 500 Cistercian monks laboured over six decades starting from 1273 to erect their monastery and church on a granite base (a practice copied by the Franciscans at the Nikolaikirche and Marienkirche in Berlin). The monastery was secularised in 1542 and fell into disrepair after the Thirty Years' War. Renovation has gone on in a somewhat haphazard fashion since the early 19th century, and changing exhibitions are now held in many of the various buildings, including the former storeroom and brewery.

The entrance to the monastery is through the ornate western façade and leads to the central cloister and ambulatory. To the north is the early-Gothic **Klosterkirche**, with its wonderful carved portals and long lancet windows.

The celebrated **Choriner Musiksommer** (Chorin Summer of Music; www.choriner-musik sommer.de, in German) concerts take place in the monastery cloister on Saturdays and Sundays from June to August; expect to hear some top talent. At 4pm some Sundays from late May to August there are chamber-music concerts in the church, which is said to have near-perfect acoustics.

If you want to walk from the station, you can reach the monastery in less than 30 minutes via a pretty, marked trail through the woods.

GETTING INTO TOWN

Distance from Berlin 50km.

Direction Northeast.

Travel Time 50 minutes.

Train Chorin is served by regional trains from Berlin-Ostbahnhof or Berlin-Lichtenberg (€7.20) roughly every hour. Kloster Chorin is 3km southeast of the train station by road.

Sights

Choriner Musiksommer (☎ 03334-657 310; Schickel-strasse 5, Eberswalde-Finow)

Kloster Chorin (☎ 033366-70 377; Amt Chorin 11a; admission adult/child €3/2; ☻ 9am-6pm Apr-Oct, 9am-4pm Nov-Mar)

Eating & Sleeping

Hotel Haus Chorin (☎ 033366-500; Neue Klosterallee 10; s €39-65, d €55-86) If you need to stay over or just fancy a bite to eat, this lakeside hotel has decent rooms and claims to have the world's only speciality honey restaurant (mains €8.90-13.10).

TROPICAL ISLANDS RESORT

If the Central European climate just isn't sultry enough for you, check into this stunning artificial oasis for all the steamy rest and relaxation you can handle. Covering nearly seven hectares, the massive heated dome is the largest freestanding structure of its kind in the world, one of those enterprises that seem utterly ludicrous in theory and utterly staggering in practice. Step inside and it really does resemble an entire multiethnic beach community built from scratch – think *The Truman Show* on Hawaii.

Luckily you don't have to be Jim Carrey to enjoy the range of facilities on offer. The **beaches**, bays and lagoons are obvious attractions, but the creators' ambitions didn't stop there: you can also explore a **village** of authentically built houses from cultures around the world, an 8000 sq m **rainforest** complete with mangrove swamp and walking trails, an exotic **market**, an exhibition space and an event centre. There are even hot-air balloon flights over it all for a bird's-eye view of the man-made expanses.

To complete the picture, four restaurants and six bars cater for the needs of the flesh, while evening performances and song-and-dance shows provide entertainment. From Thursday to Saturday DJs stir up the sand at some full-on beach parties.

Best of all, the place never closes, so if you don't want to venture back into the cold hard world you don't have to. The temperature is maintained at a constant 23° at night, and the water is heated to a luscious 31° all year round. You can even hire a tent and pick out a spot on the sand! Sadly the state-subsidised project, set up to reuse the hangar of a failed airship company, has not been the runaway success originally hoped for, and despite continued investment there's every chance the whole thing may fold if visitor numbers don't improve.

Information

Tropical Islands Resort (☎ 035477-605050; www.my -tropical-islands.com; Tropical-Islands-Allee 1, Krausnick; admission €15-25; ☺ 24hr)

GETTING THERE

Distance from Berlin 60km.
Direction South.
Travel Time One hour.
Car Head towards Dresden on the A13, then follow the signs from the Staakow exit (exit 6).
Train Take the RE from Berlin Ostbahnhof or RB from Schönefeld airport to Brand (€7.20), where you can catch a shuttle bus direct to the resort.

SAXONY-ANHALT

LUTHERSTADT-WITTENBERG

As the crucible of the Reformation, where Protestant Christians first split from the Roman Catholic Church, Wittenberg is Saxony-Anhalt's premier tourist attraction. Religious pilgrims, scholars, film fans and the merely curious all swarm here to follow in the footsteps of Martin Luther, whose campaigning zeal changed the face of Europe. Quaint and picturesque, Wittenberg can easily be seen in a day. The town is busiest in June, during the Luther's Wedding festival, and on 31 October, the anniversary of the publication of Luther's '95 Theses'.

If you only visit one of the various museums in Germany devoted to the father of the Reformation, make it the **Lutherhaus**. The exhibition here, in Luther's one-time home, was revamped in 2003 to the tune of €17.5 million, and even those with no previous interest in the subject will be drawn in by its combination of accessible narrative, personal artefacts, Cranach paintings and interactive multimedia displays. There's also an original room furnished by Luther in 1535, decorated with a bit of royal graffiti from Russian Tsar Peter the Great in 1702.

Legend has it that it was the door of the **Schlosskirche** (Castle Church) where Luther, on 31 October 1517, nailed his '95 Theses' confronting the Catholic Church. There's no hard evidence this happened, especially as the door in question was destroyed by fire in 1760. In its place stands an impressive bronze **memorial** (1858) inscribed with the theses in Latin. Inside the church is Luther's tombstone, opposite that of fellow reformer Philipp Melanchthon.

If the Schlosskirche was the billboard used to advertise the forthcoming Reformation, the **Stadtkirche St Marien** (City Church of St Marien) was where the real revolution began, hosting the world's first Protestant worship services in 1521. It was also here that Luther preached his famous Lectern sermons and married ex-nun Katharina von Bora. The centrepiece is the large **altar**, designed jointly by Lucas Cranach the Elder and his son. The side facing the nave shows Luther, Melanchthon and other Reformation figures, as well as Cranach himself, in biblical contexts. Behind it, on the lower rung, you'll see a seemingly defaced painting of heaven and hell. Medieval students etched their initials into the painting's divine half if they passed their final exams – or into purgatory if they failed.

Modern history, too, has found a place amid the Reformation nostalgia. The **Haus der Geschichte** (House of History) is a collection of everyday artefacts and furnished rooms from the GDR, showcasing the peculiarities of East German design.

Northeast of the centre, true modernity is embodied in Wittenberg's crazy Martin Luther Gymnasium, usually called the **Hundertwasser School**. Viennese artist and architect Freidenreichs Hundertwasser remodelled the old East German concrete blocks into one of his signature buildings, with ecological materials, brightly coloured elements, touches of gold, mosque-like cupolas and rooftop vegetation. It's possible to view the exterior any time, but tours wait for at least four participants before they start.

GETTING INTO TOWN

Distance from Berlin 100km.
Direction Southwest.
Travel Time 1½ hours.
Train Wittenberg is on the direct RE line from Berlin-Ostbahnhof (€16.70) and Schönefeld airport. Be sure to board for 'Lutherstadt-Wittenberg' – there's also a Wittenberge west of Berlin.

Information

Wittenberg-Information (☎ 03491-498 610; www
.wittenberg.de; Schlossplatz 2; ⏲ 9am-6pm Mon-Fri,
10am-3pm Sat, 11am-4pm Sun)

Sights

Haus der Geschichte (☎ 03491-409 004; Schlossstrasse
6; adult/concession €3/2; ⏲ 10am-5pm Mon-Fri,
11am-6pm Sat & Sun)

Hundertwasser School (☎ 03491-881 131; Strasse der
Völkerfreundschaft 130; tours €1; ⏲ 1.30-5pm Tue-Fri,
10am-5pm Sat & Sun)

Lutherhaus (☎ 03491-42 030; Collegienstrasse 54;
adult/concession €5/3; ⏲ 9am-6pm daily Apr-Oct,
10am-5pm Tue-Sun Nov-Mar)

Schlosskirche (admission free, tour adult/concession
€1.50/0.75; ⏲ 10am-5pm Mon-Sat, 11.30am-5pm Sun)

Stadtkirche St Marien (admission free; ⏲ 9am-5pm
Mon-Sat, 11.30am-5pm Sun)

Eating

Café Hundertwasserschule (☎ 03491-410 685; Markt
15; mains €5-13.80) Health-conscious modern café

complete with no-smoking policy, vegetarian options and
fresh juices.

Schlosskeller (☎ 03491-480 805; Schlossplatz; mains
€6.90-11.80) Old-school German food in the original
castle cellars. The outdoor Schlossschänke is popular in
summer.

Zur Schlossfreiheit (☎ 03491-402 980; Coswigerstrasse
24; mains €8.75-13.50) Cosy, dark-wood surrounds and
quirky themed dishes, including *Lutherschmaus* (duck in
peppery sultana sauce).

Sleeping

Alte Canzley (☎ 03491-429 190; Schlossplaz 3; r
€66-132) A new apartment hotel and restaurant right
opposite the Schlosskirche. Peter the Great once stayed in
the building.

Brauhaus Wittenberg (☎ 03491-433 130; Im
Beyerhof, Markt 6; s/d €50/70) For a room with
a brew, try this busy hotel/restaurant on the main
square.

Hotel Garni Am Schwanenteich (☎ 03491-402 807;
Töpferstrasse 1; s/d from €31/54) Neat, modern accom-
modation just north of the town centre, opposite the
'Swan Pond'.

SAXONY

DRESDEN

Sixty years after it began, the resurrection
of Dresden is finally complete. With the
rededication of the city's famous Frauenkirche, the final traces of the city's destruction in 1945 have been expunged from the
landscape, and Saxony's capital can look
forward to a glowing future rather than
back onto the tragic recent past. With Dresden's 800th jubilee in 2006, now is very
much the time to rediscover one of Germany's best-loved destinations.

In the 18th century the Saxon capital was

GETTING INTO TOWN

Distance from Berlin 200km.
Direction South.
Travel Time 2½ hours.
Car Take the A113 to the A13, which runs all the
way to Dresden.
Train Regular trains run from Berlin-Ostbahnhof
(€26).

famous throughout Europe as 'Florence on the Elbe', a centre of artistic activity presided
over by Augustus the Strong and his son Augustus III. Since February 1945, however, Dresden has been synonymous with the controversial Allied bombing campaign that devastated
the city, killing 35,000 people in attacks that had scant strategic justification. The resurgence
of Dresden as a cultural bastion is founded to some degree on this historical resonance,
giving the city's great baroque buildings a weighty gravitas all their own.

The city now attracts around 7 million visitors a year and has seen an 11.5% increase in
overnight stays recently, a veritable tourist boom richly justified by its wealth of attractions.
Trivia fans may like to know that it's twinned with Brazzaville, the capital of Congo.

Reminders of Dresden's golden age are a big draw. The **Altmarkt** area is Dresden's historic
centre and the starting point for most visitors, though it's still undergoing considerable renovations. Many restaurants have set up street-side tables, and when markets aren't operating it's

DRESDEN

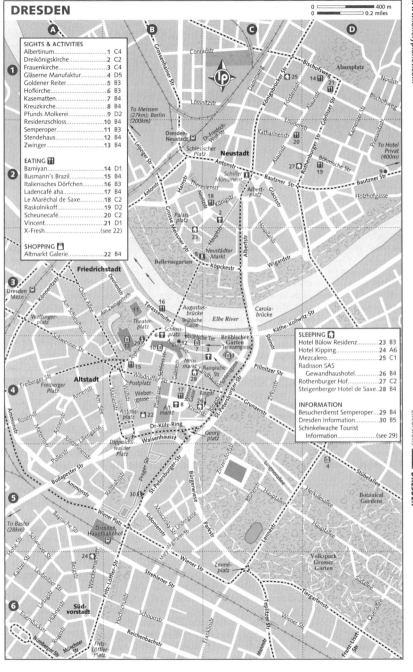

0 _____ 400 m
0 _____ 0.2 miles

SIGHTS & ACTIVITIES
Albertinum.................................1 C4
Dreikönigskirche.......................2 C2
Frauenkirche.............................3 C4
Gläserne Manufaktur................4 D5
Goldener Reiter.........................5 B3
Hofkirche..................................6 B3
Kasematten...............................7 B4
Kreuzkirche...............................8 B4
Pfunds Molkerei........................9 D2
Residenzschloss......................10 B3
Semperoper..............................11 B3
Stendehaus..............................12 B4
Zwinger....................................13 B4

EATING 🍴
Bamiyan....................................14 D1
Busmann's Brazil......................15 B4
Italienisches Dörfchen..............16 B3
Ladencafé aha..........................17 B4
Le Maréchal de Saxe.................18 C2
Raskolnikoff.............................19 D2
Scheunecafé............................20 C2
Vincent.....................................21 D1
X-Fresh..................................(see 22)

SHOPPING 🛍
Altmarkt Galerie.......................22 B4

SLEEPING 🛏
Hotel Bülow Residenz.............23 B3
Hotel Kipping..........................24 A6
Mezcalero...............................25 C1
Radisson SAS
  Gewandhaushotel...............26 B4
Rothenburger Hof...................27 C2
Steigenberger Hotel de Saxe...28 B4

INFORMATION
Besucherdienst Semperoper....29 B4
Dresden Information...............30 B5
Schinkelwache Tourist
  Information........................(see 29)

Theatherplatz and Semperopera, Dresden (this page)

nice to sit outside and gaze across the square. The modern glass **Altmarkt Galerie** (9.30am-8pm Mon-Sat) shopping centre is also excellent.

From the square, proceed east to the rebuilt **Kreuzkirche** (1792). Originally the Nikolaikirche, the church was renamed for a *Kreuz* (cross) found floating in the Elbe River by fishermen. The church is famous for its 400-strong boys' choir, the Kreuzchor.

Pass through Galeriestrasse, to the right, and you'll reach the **Neumarkt** – no longer a market these days – with the **Frauenkirche** (Church of Our Lady; 1726–43) at its eastern end. Built under the direction of baroque architect George Bähr, the Frauenkirche is one of Dresden's most beloved symbols. Until the end of WWII it was Germany's greatest Protestant church; the bombing raids of 13 February 1945 flattened it, and the communists decided to leave the rubble as a war memorial. After reunification, the movement to rebuild the church prevailed and a huge archaeological dig began in 1992. Donations were so generous that the reconstruction, originally scheduled for completion in 2006, actually finished early, and the church was officially reconsecrated in October 2005. Visitors can now climb to the viewing platform above the cupola or attend a wide range of concerts, events and services in the painted interior.

From the Frauenkirche, turn up Rampische Strasse and veer northeast to the **Brühlscher Garten**, the lovely green park east of the main terrace. In front stands the **Albertinum**, which houses many of Dresden's art treasures, including the **New Masters Gallery**, with renowned 19th- and 20th-century paintings from leading French and German Impressionists, and the **Skulpturensammlung**, which includes classical and Egyptian works.

West of the Albertinum is the **Brühlsche Terrasse**, a spectacular promenade that's been called the 'Balcony of Europe', with a pavement nearly 15m above the southern embankment of the Elbe. In summer it's a must for strolling, with expansive views of the river and the opposite bank. Beneath the promenade is the Renaissance brick bastion known as the **Kasematten**, which has a museum showing how the fortress was used.

Further west, off the Neumarkt, you'll find the fabulous **Augustusstrasse**, with its 102m-long *Procession of Princes* mural depicted on the outer wall of the former **Stendehaus** (Royal Stables). The scene, a long row of royalty on horses, was painted in 1876 by Wullhelm Walther and then transferred to some 24,000 Meissen porcelain tiles. Join the crowds standing and squinting across the street.

Augustusstrasse leads directly to **Schlossplatz** and the baroque Catholic **Hofkirche** (1755), which contains the heart of Augustus the Strong. Just south of the church is the neo-Renaissance **Residenzschloss** (palace), which contains several museums, including one of the world's finest collections of jewel-studded precious objects, the **Grünes Gewölbe** (Green Vault).

On the western side of the Hofkirche is **Theaterplatz**, with Dresden's dramatic and long-suffering **Semperoper**. The original opera house on the site opened in 1841 but burned down less than three decades later. Rebuilt in 1878, it was pummelled in WWII and reopened only in 1985 after the communists invested millions in restoring this neo-Renaissance jewel. The 2002 floods closed it down yet again, albeit only briefly. Thanks to a recent beer commercial, the Semperoper is probably one of the best-known buildings in Germany.

From the opera house, proceed south a few metres to reach the sprawling baroque **Zwinger** palace (1728). An open-air gallery and several charming portals frame its lovely, fountain-studded courtyard. Conceived by star architect Matthäus Daniel Pöppelmann for royal tournaments and festivals, the exterior has some fine examples of baroque sculpture, and the courtyard is a popular summer venue. Atop the western pavilion stands a tense-looking Atlas; opposite is a cutesy carillon of 40 Meissen porcelain bells, which chime on the hour.

The palace also houses four museums. The most important are the **Old Masters Gallery**, featuring masterpieces like Raphael's *Sistine Madonna,* and the **Rüstkammer** (armoury), a superb collection of armour, ordnance and ceremonial weapons. The dazzling **Porcelain Collection** is another highlight, with plenty of Meissen classics among its 20,000-odd items. Old instruments, globes and timepieces are displayed in the **Mathematics and Physics Salon**.

Crossing the Elbe, you enter the **Neustadt**, actually an old part of Dresden largely untouched by the wartime bombings. After reunification this became the centre of the city's alternative scene, but as entire street blocks are renovated it's losing some of its bohemian feel.

As you cross the river, the **Goldener Reiter statue** (1736) of Augustus the Strong stands at the northern end of the Augustusbrücke. This leads to the pleasant pedestrian mall of **Hauptstrasse**. Moving north you'll come to the newly renovated **Dreikönigskirche**, the parish church designed by Pöppelmann. It houses some lovely Renaissance artworks, including the *Dance of Death* frieze, which once hung in the Schloss. **Königstrasse**, which runs roughly parallel and to the west of Hauptstrasse, is developing into a swish shopping district. The district has one of the densest concentrations of nightlife in Germany, and Dresden's many students are never short of ideas for entertainment.

On **Albertplatz** two lovely fountains flank the walkway down the centre, representing turbulent and still waters. East of here is 'the world's most beautiful dairy shop', **Pfunds Molkerei**, a riot of handpainted tiles and enamelled sculpture. Founded in 1880, the dairy claims to have invented condensed milk. It was nationalised by the GDR in 1972 and fell into disrepair before restoration in 1995. The shop sells replica tiles, wines, cheeses and, of course, milk, and there's a café-restaurant upstairs.

Finally, back across the river, one more highly unusual attraction remains: the **Gläserne Manufaktur**, Volkswagen's stunning transparent car factory. This ambitious, impossibly stylish glass building was a huge prestige project for the long-running automobile company, and has become such a feature of the city scene that it even hosted operas and other performances when the Semperoper was out of commission.

DETOUR: MEISSEN

Ever heard of Dresden china? Some of the most distinctive blue-and-white pottery actually comes from the nearby town of **Meissen**, where the famous firm of the same name still has a factory.

Some 27km northwest of Dresden, Meissen is a compact, perfectly preserved old town dating back an amazing 1075 years. It's the centre of a rich wine-growing region and makes a great day trip if you have a bit of time to spare in Dresden.

The undisputed highlight here is the town's medieval fortress, the **Albrechtsburg**, which crowns a ridge high above the Elbe River. The walled site contains the former ducal **palace** (☎ 47 070; Domplatz 1; adult/concession €3.50/2.50; ⊗ 10am-6pm Mar-Oct, 10am-5pm Nov-Feb) and the towering medieval **cathedral** (☎ 452 490; Domplatz 7; adult/concession €2/1.50; ⊗ 10am-6pm Mar-Oct, to 4pm Nov-Feb), a magnificent Gothic structure. Even the views from here are spectacular.

Oh, and about that pottery: the Albrechtsburg palace was the original manufacturing base when the industry was introduced by Augustus the Strong in 1710, but the **Porzellan Manufaktur** (Porcelain Factory; ☎ 468 700; Talstrasse 9; collection adult/concession €4.50/4, workshop €3; ⊗ 9am-6pm May-Oct, to 5pm Nov-Apr) is now 1km southwest of the Altstadt, in an appropriately beautiful 1916 building.

To reach Meissen, simply hop on the S-Bahn from Dresden (€5.10, 40 minutes).

Information

Besucherdienst Semperoper (☎ 0351-49 110; Schinkelwache, Theaterplatz 2; ☼ 10am-6pm Mon-Fri, to 1pm Sat) Information, tickets and tours.

Dresden Information (☎ 0351-4919 2100; www.dresden -tourist.de; Prager Strasse 21; ☼ 9.30am-6.30pm Mon-Fri, to 6pm Sat)

Schinkelwache Tourist Information (☎ 0351-491 1705; Theaterplatz 2; ☼ 10am-6.30pm Mon-Thu, to 7pm Fri & Sat, to 5pm Sun)

Sights

Albertinum (☎ 0351-491 4619; Brühlsche Terrasse; adult/concession €5/2.50; ☼ 10am-6pm Fri-Wed)

Dreikönigskirche (☎ 0351-812 4102; An der Dreikönigskirche; admission free; ☼ 10am-6pm Mon-Sat & 11.30am-6pm Sun Mar-Oct, 10am-4.30pm Mon-Sat & 11.30am-4.30pm Sun Nov-Feb)

Frauenkirche (☎ 0351-439 3934; Neumarkt; cupola adult/concession €8/5; ☼ 10am-6pm)

Gläserne Manufaktur (☎ 01805 896 268; Grosser Garten; adult/concession €5/4; ☼ 8am-8pm)

Grünes Gewölbe (☎ 0351-4914 2000; Residenz Schloss; adult/concession €6/3.50; ☼ Wed-Mon 10am-6pm)

Hofkirche (☎ 0351-484 4712; Schlossplatz; admission free; ☼ 9am-5pm Mon-Thu, 1-5pm Fri, 10.30am-4pm Sat, noon-4pm Sun)

Kasematten (☎ 0351-491 4786; Brühlsche Terrasse; adult/child €3.10/2; ☼ 10am-5pm)

Kreuzkirche (Altmarkt; ☼ 10am-6pm Mon-Sat, 11am-6pm Sun Apr-Oct, to 4pm Nov-Mar, concerts 6pm Sat)

Mathematics & Physics Salon (☎ 0351-491 4622; Zwinger; adult/concession €3/2)

Old Masters Gallery (☎ 0351-491 4619; Zwinger; adult/concession €6/3.50)

Pfunds Molkerei (☎ 0351-816 20; Bautzner Strasse 79; ☼ 10am-6pm Mon-Sat, to 3pm Sun)

Porcelain Collection (☎ 0351-491 4622; Zwinger; admission adult/concession €5/3)

Rüstkammer (☎ 0351-491 4619; Zwinger; adult/ concession €3/2)

Semperoper (Theaterplatz; ☎ 0351-491 1496; tours adult/concession €6/3)

Zwinger (Theaterplatz 1; ☼ 10am-6pm Tue-Sun)

Eating

Bamiyan (☎ 0351 210 5774; cnr Alaunstrasse & Bischofsweg; mains €5.50-10) Ever eaten Afghan before? Well, now's your chance to try it.

Busmann's Brazil (☎ 0351-862 1200; Kleine Brüdergasse 5; mains €8.90-18.90) Brazilian food and drink culture beyond the *caipirinha*, with such strange delicacies as rattlesnake (€39.90).

Italienisches Dörfchen (☎ 0351-498 160; Theaterplatz 3; mains €7-21) Four stylish restaurants offering varied cuisine ranging from bargain barbecue to swish Italian and Saxon.

Ladencafé aha (☎ 0351-496 0673; Kreuzstrasse 7; mains €7.80-10.20) Free-trade shop and café by the busy Weisse Gasse restaurant strip.

Le Maréchal de Saxe (☎ 0351-810 5880; Königstrasse 5; mains €6.80-12.80) Upscale bistro in a smart area, offering good international cuisine.

Raskolnikoff (☎ 0351-804 5706; Böhmische Strasse 34; mains €5.85-7.45) Good-value light meals on a bohemian, eastern-European trip.

Scheunecafé (☎ 0351-802 6619; Alaunstrasse 36-40; mains €6.90-9.90) Indian food situated somewhat unusualy in an alternative-rock venue, with regular crowds in the beer garden.

Vincent (☎ 0351-563 5725; Sebnitzstrasse 11; mains €7-16) Excellent tapas (from €2.50) and more substantial dishes in cosy brick surrounds.

X-Fresh (☎ 0351-484 2791; Altmarkt Galerie; mains €5.50-11.50) Look after yourself with healthy salads and meals from this 'wellness bistro'.

Sleeping

Hotel Bülow Residenz (☎ 0351-800 30; Rähnitzstrasse 19; s/d €180/220) A real gem on a quiet street near Palaisplatz. The house restaurant is rated one of the best in Saxony.

Hotel Kipping (☎ 0351-478 500; Winckelmannstrasse 6; s €70-100, d €85-120) Family-run, family-friendly hotel just behind the Hauptbahnhof.

Hotel Privat (☎ 0351-811 770; Forststrasse 22; s €49-63, d €65-89) One of Germany's few entirely nonsmoking hotels.

Mezcalero (☎ 0351-810 770; Königsbrücker Strasse 64; s/d from 30/50) An off-the-wall Mexican-style B&B with tequila bar.

Radisson SAS Gewandhaushotel (☎ 0351-494 90; Ringstrasse 1; r €128-200) Top choice for class and personal service.

Rothenburger Hof (☎ 0351-812 60; Rothenburger Strasse 15-17; s €75-115, d €99-140) Clean, bright atmosphere and lots of beauty treatments.

Steigenberger Hotel de Saxe (☎ 0351-438 60; Neumarkt 9; r from €119) The latest luxury chain to hit Dresden, bang opposite the Frauenkirche.

LEIPZIG

Always an independent-minded entity, Leipzig became known as the Stadt der Helden (City of Heroes) for its leading role in the 1989 democratic revolution. Residents organised protests against the communist regime in May of that year; by October, hundreds of thousands were staging demonstrations, placing candles outside the Stasi headquarters and attending peace services. By the time the secret police started pulping their files, Leipzigers were partying in the streets, and they haven't stopped since!

GETTING INTO TOWN

Distance from Berlin 160km.
Direction Southwest.
Travel Time 2½ hours.
Car Leipzig lies just south of the A14 and east of the A9 Berlin-Nuremberg road. It's best to leave your vehicle in one of the parking lots outside the Altstadt.
Train Regular regional trains link Leipzig and Berlin-Ostbahnhof (€25.20).

Leipzig has some of the finest classical music and opera in the country, and its art and literary scenes are flourishing. It was once home to Bach, Wagner and Mendelssohn, and to Goethe, who studied here. Despite the failure of its bid for the 2012 Olympics, modern Leipzig is arguably the most dynamic city in eastern Germany; it was the only eastern city to host World Cup football games in 2006, and great things are expected here in the next few years.

Leipzig's centre lies within a ring road that outlines the town's medieval fortifications. To reach the centre from the railway station, cross Willy-Brandt-Platz and continue south along Nikolaistrasse until Grimmaische Strasse; the central **Markt** is a couple of blocks west, currently undergoing massive building works for the new City Tunnel railway project. On the east side of the Markt, the Renaissance **Altes Rathaus** (1556), one of Germany's most stunning town halls, houses the **City History Museum**. Tickets include entry to the Neubau (annexe) on Sachsenplatz.

Move south across Grimmaische Strasse to enter the orange, baroque **Apelshaus** (1606–07), with its lovely bay windows. It's now a contemporary shopping mall known as the Königshaus Passage, but in its heyday overnight guests included Peter the Great and Napoleon. The Passage leads directly into the **Mädlerpassage**, which must be one of the world's most beautiful shopping arcades. A mix of neo-Renaissance and Art Nouveau, it opened as a trade hall in 1914 and was renovated at great expense in the early 1990s. Today it's home to shops, restaurants, cafés and, most notably, **Auerbachs Keller** (see p285). There are statues of Faust, Mephistopheles and some students at the northern exit; according to tradition you should rub Faust's foot for good luck.

Next to this exit, the haunting yet uplifting **Forum of Contemporary History** depicts the history of the GDR, from division and dictatorship to resistance and demise.

North of the Mädlerpassage is the **Naschmarkt** (snack market), which is dominated by the **Alte Börse** (1687), an ornate former trading house. In front is a statue of **Goethe** (1903). Today, the Alte Börse is a private cultural centre, with concerts, plays and readings throughout the year.

North of the Naschmarkt is Sachsenplatz, a massive open square that now houses two newly built cultural outlets: the **Museum of Fine Arts**, one of Leipzig's most prestigious collections and the **City History Museum Annexe**, hosting temporary exhibitions on a range of Leipzig-related people and themes.

East of here is the chunky **Nikolaikirche** (1165). Begun in Romanesque style, it was enlarged and converted to late Gothic, and has an amazing classical interior. The church was the main meeting point for demonstrators from May 1989, shortly before the GDR imploded.

Carry on east through the Theaterpassage to reach **Augustusplatz**, Leipzig's cultural nerve centre. The glass structures (actually lifts to the underground car park) glow at night, lending the concrete slabs some much-needed warmth. Pivot left and you'll see the neoclassical **Royal Palace**, which is now a university building.

To the north is the functional **Opernhaus** (opera house, 1956–60), which has a **statue of Richard Wagner** out the back. To the west, the 11-storey **Kroch Haus** was Leipzig's first 'skyscraper' and now houses part of the university's art collection. At the southern end of the

Excursions

LEIPZIG

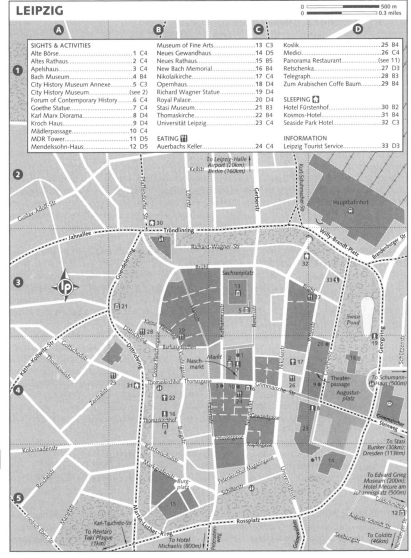

LEIPZIG

0 _____ 500 m
0 _____ 0.3 miles

SIGHTS & ACTIVITIES		Museum of Fine Arts.....................13 C3	Koslik......................................25 B4
Alte Börse.....................................1 C4		Neues Gewandhaus.....................14 D5	Medici.....................................26 C4
Altes Rathaus...............................2 C4		Neues Rathaus.............................15 B5	Panorama Restaurant............(see 11)
Apelshaus....................................3 C4		New Bach Memorial.....................16 B4	Retschenka...............................27 D3
Bach Museum..............................4 B4		Nikolaikirche................................17 C4	Telegraph.................................28 B3
City History Museum Annexe........5 C3		Opernhaus...................................18 D4	Zum Arabischen Coffe Baum....29 B4
City History Museum...............(see 2)		Richard Wagner Statue.................19 D4	
Forum of Contemporary History....6 C4		Royal Palace................................20 D4	SLEEPING
Goethe Statue.............................7 C4		Stasi Museum..............................21 B3	Hotel Fürstenhof.......................30 B2
Karl Marx Diorama.......................8 D4		Thomaskirche..............................22 B4	Kosmos-Hotel...........................31 B4
Kroch Haus..................................9 D4		Universität Leipzig........................23 C4	Seaside Park Hotel.....................32 C3
Mädlerpassage...........................10 C4			
MDR Tower.................................11 D5		EATING	INFORMATION
Mendelssohn-Haus.....................12 D5		Auerbachs Keller.........................24 C4	Leipzig Tourist Service................33 D3

square are the modern, heroic **Neues Gewandhaus** (1981), home to the city's classical and jazz concerts, and the **MDR tower** (1970), occupied by the Mitdeutscher Rundfunk broadcasting company.

On the west side of the square just south of Grimmaische Strasse, at the entrance to Universität Leipzig, is a revolting bronze **diorama** that depicts Karl Marx. The red steel A-frame around it is a **monument** to St Paul's Church (Paulinerkirche), which was destroyed during WWII.

Heading west around the ring road, you confront the impressive 108m-high tower of the baroque **Neues Rathaus**. Although the building's origins date back to the 16th century, its current manifestation was completed in 1905. Recently renovated, the interior makes it one of the finest municipal buildings in Germany.

MUSICAL FOOTNOTES

Besides Bach, three other renowned composers have museums dedicated to them in Leipzig: Felix Mendelssohn-Bartholdy, who lived (and died) in the **Mendelssohn-Haus** (☎ 0341-127 0294; Goldschmidtstrasse 12; admission €3; ☾ 10am-6pm, concerts 11pm Sun); and Robert Schumann, who spent the first four years of his marriage to Leipzig pianist Clara Wieck in the **Schumann-Haus** (☎ 0341-393 9620; Inselstrasse 18; admission €2; ☾ 2-5pm Wed-Sat).

On Ferdinand-Rhode-Strasse you'll also find a **plaque** dedicated to the little-known Japanese composer Rentaro Taki (1879–1903). Taki was the first Japanese artist to study music in Europe – where else but at the Leipzig Conservatory?

Norwegian composer Edvard Grieg was another frequent visitor to the city, and once renovation is complete, his old guest rooms at the former CF Peters music publishers will be fully open as a **museum** (☎ 993 9661; Talstrasse 10).

From Burgplatz, walk up Burgstrasse to the **Thomaskirche** (St Thomas Church; 1212), which contains the tomb of composer Johann Sebastian Bach. The church was extended and converted to Gothic style in 1496, and hosted the baptisms of Richard Wagner, Karl Liebknecht and all of Bach's offspring. Bach worked here as a cantor from 1723 until 1750. Outside the church is the **New Bach Memorial** (1908), showing the composer standing against an organ.

Opposite the church, in a baroque house, is the **Bach Museum**, which focuses on the composer's life in Leipzig. The *Matthäus Passion, Johannes Passion, Weihnachts Oratorium* and the *H-Moll Messe*, among others, were written here.

Back on the ring road, the chilling **Stasi Museum** is in the former headquarters of the East German secret police, a building known as the Runde Ecke (Round Corner). At the front are photographs of demonstrations in October and November 1989; inside are exhibits on propaganda, preposterous disguises, surveillance photos and, in the back, mounds of papier-mâché created when officers shredded and soaked secret documents before the fall of the GDR. On the last weekend of every month, you can also visit the **Stasi bunker** outside town.

Information

Leipzig Tourist Service (☎ 0341-710 4260; www.leipzig.de; Richard-Wagner-Strasse 1; ☾ 9am-6pm Mon-Fri, 9am-4pm Sat & Sun, 10am-6pm Mon-Fri Jan-Feb & Jul-Aug)

Sights

Alte Börse (☎ 0341-961 0368; ☾ tours by appointment 5pm Mon-Fri)

Bach Museum (☎ 0341-964 110; Thomaskirchhof 16; adult/concession €3/2; ☾ 10am-5pm)

City History Museum (☎ 0341-965 130; Markt 1; adult/child €3/2; ☾ 10am-6pm Tue-Sun); **Annexe** (Böttchergässchen 3)

Forum of Contemporary History (☎ 0341-222 20; Grimmaische Strasse 6; admission free; ☾ 9am-6pm Tue-Fri, 10am-6pm Sat & Sun)

Museum of Fine Arts (☎ 0341-216 990; Katharinenstrasse 10; adult/concession €2.50/1; ☾ 10am-6pm Tue & Thu-Sun, noon-8pm Wed)

Neues Gewandhaus (☎ 0341-127 00; Augustusplatz 8)

Neues Rathaus (☎ 0341-1230; admission free; ☾ 6.45am-4.30pm Mon-Fri)

Nikolaikirche (☎ 0341-960 5270; Nikolaiplatz; admission free; ☾ 10am-6pm)

Opernhaus (☎ 0341-126 1261; Augustusplatz)

Stasi Museum (☎ 0341-961 2443; Dittrichring 24; admission free; ☾ 10am-6pm)

Stasi Bunker (Flurstück 439, Machern; tour adult/concession €3/2; ☾ 1-4pm Sat & Sun monthly)

Thomaskirche (☎ 0341-960 2855; Thomaskirchhof; admission free; ☾ 9am-6pm)

Eating

Auerbachs Keller (☎ 0341-216 100; Mädlerpassage; mains €11.40-21.40) One of Germany's classic restaurants, founded in 1525 and featured in Goethe's *Faust – Part I*. Ludicrously popular with locals and tourists alike.

Koslik (☎ 0341-998 5993; cnr Gottschedstrasse & Zentralstrasse; mains €7.30-12.80) Stylish interior and excellent mixed cuisine, from Italian standards to Thai and Latin flavours.

Medici (☎ 0341-211 3878; Nikolaikirchhof 5; mains €18-25) Thoroughly classy Italian, widely regarded as one of the best restaurants in Leipzig.

Panorama Restaurant (☎ 0341-710 0590; MDR Tower, Augustusplatz 9; mains €8.20-15.60) Look down on all you survey from this posh 120m-high gastro rendezvous.

Retschenka (☎ 0341-149 2235; Steibs Hof, Brühl 64/66; mains €9.40-15.50) Russian and Eastern European specialities, recently graced by Mikhail Gorbachev himself.

Excursions

SAXONY

285

DETOUR: COLDITZ

In the secluded Zwickauer Mulde valley, 46km south of Leipzig, lies the sleepy town of Colditz and its impressive (though run-down) fortress. The Renaissance structure was used by Augustus the Strong as a hunting lodge in the 17th century and became a mental hospital in the 1800s. In WWII the Nazis converted it into a high-security prison, known as Oflag IVc (Officer's Camp IVc).

Its inmates, mostly Allied officers who had already escaped from other prisons, proved that putting hardened jail-breakers together was a mistake. Between 1939 and 1945 there were more than 300 escape attempts, earning Colditz the reputation as a 'bad boys' camp. In all, 31 men managed to flee, aided by ingenious self-made gadgetry, such as a glider made of wood and bed sheets. Most astounding, though, is the 44m-long tunnel that French officers dug between 1941 and 1942 before the Germans caught them.

Today the fortress houses a small but fascinating **Escape Museum** (☎ 034381-44 987; admission adult/concession €3/2; ☺ 10am-5pm).

Bus 931 and 690 run to Colditz from Leipzig. You can also take a train to Bad Lausick and catch bus 613. The town is at the junction of the B107 and B176 between Leipzig and Chemnitz.

Telegraph (☎ 0341-149 4990; Dittrichring 18-20; mains €6-13) This smart but relaxed lounge bistro also hosts occasional events.

Zum Arabischen Coffe Baum (☎ 0341-965 1321; Kleine Fleischergasse 4; mains €7.50-15) Leipzig's oldest café; excellent meals over three floors, plus a coffee museum.

Sleeping

Hotel Fürstenhof (☎ 0341-1400; Tröndlinring 8; s €230-300, d €265-325) Luxurious grand hotel that combines a 200-year tradition and more mod cons than you can imagine.

Hotel Mercure am Johannisplatz (☎ 0341-97 790; Stephanstrasse 6; s €60-108, d €64-138) The nicest of the multiple Mercures around town, just out to the east.

Hotel Michaelis (☎ 0341-26 780; Paul-Gruner-Strasse 44; s €70-95, d €85-125) Superior three-star townhouse south of the centre, offering neat well-equipped rooms.

Kosmos-Hotel (☎ 0341-233 4422; Gottschedstrasse 1; s/d €46/66) Creative theatre-inspired hotel with individually styled rooms – wake up next to Marilyn Monroe or in equally fantastical surrounds.

Seaside Park Hotel (☎ 0341-98 520; Richard-Wagner-Strasse 7; s €110-150, d €126-160) Art Nouveau style in a convenient central spot, plus a commendable restaurant.

Directory ■

Directory

TRANSPORT

Don't forget flights, tours and rail tickets can be booked online at www.lonelyplanet.com/travel_services.

AIR

Lufthansa, most major European airlines and several low-cost carriers operate direct flights to Berlin from most European cities. With few exceptions, travelling to the German capital from overseas will involve a change of planes in another European city such as Frankfurt or Amsterdam.

Your best friend in ferreting out deals is the Internet. Start by checking fares at online travel agencies such as Expedia, Opodo or Zuji (see Online Ticketing), then run the same flight request through metasearch engines such as **SideStep** (www.sidestep.com), **Kayak** (www.kayak.com), **Mobissimo** (www.mobissimo.com), **Qixo** (www.qixo.com) or **Farechase** (www.farechase.com). To get the skinny on which budget airlines currently serve Berlin, consult www.whichbudget.com or www.skyscanner.net. For bookings go to the airline websites directly or try www.openjet.com.

Airlines

Here's a sampling of airlines serving Berlin's three airports.

EUROPEAN CARRIERS

Air Berlin (AB; ☎ 01805-737 800; www.air-berlin.com)

Air France (AF; ☎ 01805-830 830; www.airfrance.com)

Alitalia (AZ; ☎ 01805-074 747; www.alitalia.com)

British Airways (BA; ☎ 01805-266 522; www.britishairways.com)

Deutsche BA (DI; ☎ 01805-359 3222; www.flydba.com)

easyJet (EZY; ☎ 01803-654 321; www.easyjet.com)

Germania Express (ST; ☎ 01805-737 100; www.gexx.com)

German Wings (4U; ☎ 0900-191 9100, billed per min €0.99; www.germanwings.com)

Iberia (IB; ☎ 01803-000 613; www.iberia.com)

KLM (KL; ☎ 01805 214 201; www.klm.com)

Lufthansa (LH; ☎ 01803-803 803; www.lufthansa.com)

Ryan Air (FR; ☎ 0190-170 100; www.ryanair.com)

SAS (SK; ☎ 01803-234 023; www.scandinavian.net)

Swiss (LX; ☎ 01803-000 337; www.swiss.com)

OVERSEAS CARRIERS

Air Canada (AC; ☎ 01805-024 7226; www.aircanada.ca)

Air New Zealand (NZ; ☎ 0800-5494 5494; www.airnz.co.nz)

American Airlines (AA; ☎ 0180-324 2324; www.aa.com)

Continental (CO; ☎ 0180-321 2610; www.continental.com)

Delta Airlines (DL; ☎ 01803-337 880; www.delta.com)

Qantas Airways (QF; ☎ 01805-250 620; www.quantas.com)

United Airlines (UA; ☎ 069-5007 0387; www.ual.com)

US Airways (☎ 01803-000 609; www.usairways.com)

ONLINE TICKETING

Recommended online ticketing agents:

Australia (www.travel.com.au; www.flightcentre.com.au; www.statravel.com.au; www.zuji.com)

Canada (www.expedia.ca; www.travelocity.ca; www.travelcuts.ca)

France (www.anyway.fr; www.fr.lastminute.com; www.nouvelles-frontieres.fr; www.opodo.fr; www.otu.fr)

Italy (www.cts.it; www.eviaggi.com)

New Zealand (www.travel.co.nz; www.flightcentre.co.nz; www.statravel.co.nz; www.zuji.com)

Spain (www.barceloviajes.com)

UK & Ireland (www.ebookers.com; www.flightcentre.co.uk; www.opodo.co.uk; www.questravel.com; www.statravel.co.uk; www.trailfinders.co.uk; www.travelbag.co.uk)

USA (www.cheapair.com; www.cheaptickets.com; www.expedia.com; www.lowestfare.com; www.orbitz.com; www.sta.com; www.travelocity.com; www.travelzoo.com)

Airports

Berlin has three airports, the busiest of which is Berlin International Airport in Tegel (TXL). About 8km northwest of the city centre, it primarily serves destinations within Germany and western Europe.

Berlin Brandenburg Airport in Schönefeld (SXF), 22km southeast of the city centre, handles flights to/from Europe, including eastern Europe, Africa and Asia. Direct flights on Delta and Continental from New

York also land here, as do such discount carriers as easyJet and Ryan Air. Both airports have **left-luggage offices** (⏱ 5.30am-10pm), ATMs, currency exchange desks, postal facilities and other infrastructure.

The third airport is the central but tiny Berlin Tempelhof Airport (THF), just south of Kreuzberg, which handles flights to and from European destinations only. Plans to close this airport may come to fruition as early as the summer of 2007.

For information about all three airports go to www.berlin-airport.de or call ☎ 0180-500 0186.

TEGEL

The airport in Tegel (Map pp328–9) is connected to Mitte by express bus TXL, which makes the trip to/from Alexanderplatz via Unter den Linden in about 30 minutes. If you're heading to the western city centre, you're better off hopping aboard express bus X9, which takes you to Bahnhof Zoo (Zoo station) in just under 20 minutes. Bus 109 is slower but better if you need to go somewhere along the Kurfürstendamm.

Tegel is not directly served by the U-Bahn. The nearest station is Jakob-Kaiser-Platz (U7) from where you can catch bus 109.

The fare for any of these rides is a standard AB zone ticket for €2.10 (see Tickets & Fares, p290).

The average taxi fare from Tegel is €15 to Bahnhof Zoo and €20 to Alexanderplatz.

SCHÖNEFELD

Schönefeld airport is served twice hourly by the AirportExpress train, with departures from Zoo station (30 minutes), Friedrichstrasse (23 minutes), Alexanderplatz (20 minutes) and Ostbahnhof (15 minutes). Note that these are regular regional RE or RB trains, although they are also designated as AirportExpress train in the timetable.

The much slower S9 makes the trip from Alexanderplatz in 40 minutes and from Bahnhof Zoo in 50 minutes. The S45 is another alternative if you're travelling to the airport from somewhere outside the central city.

The Schönefeld train station is about 500m from the terminal to which it is linked by a free shuttle bus every 10 minutes. Walking takes about five to 10 minutes.

Bus 171 links the terminal directly with the U-Bahn station Rudow (U7) with connections to central Berlin.

The fare for any of these trips is €2.10.

A taxi from Schönefeld to central Berlin costs between €25 and €35.

TEMPELHOF

Tempelhof airport (Map pp328–9) is served by the U6 (get off at Platz der Luftbrücke) for €2.10. A taxi to Bahnhof Zoo or Alexanderplatz costs between €10 and €15.

BICYCLE

The German bicycle club **ADFC** (Map pp332–3; ☎ 448 4724; www.adfc-berlin.de; Brunnenstrasse 28; ⏱ noon-8pm Mon-Fri, 10am-4pm Sat) publishes an excellent guide showing all the bike routes throughout Berlin. It's available at ADFC's office/shop and also in bookshops and bike stores.

Bicycles (Fahrräder) are allowed all day in designated areas on U-Bahn and S-Bahn trains and trams, but not on buses. The cost per trip is a reduced single ticket (see the table, p291) in addition to your regular fare.

Taking your bike on a Deutsche Bahn train costs €3 on regional trains such as those designated RE, RB and IRE and €8 on long-distance IC and EC trains. Bikes are not allowed on the superfast ICE trains.

Hire & Purchase

Several agencies rent bicycles with costs ranging from €9 to €25 per day and €35 to €85 per week, depending on the model. A minimum deposit of €30 (more for fancier bikes) and/or ID is required.

Fahrradstation (central reservations ☎ 0180-510 8000) Auguststrasse (Map pp340-1; ☎ 2859 9661; Auguststrasse 29a; ⏱ 10am-7pm Mon-Fri, to 3pm Sat; ◉ Weinmeisterstrasse); Bergmannstrasse (Map pp336-7; ☎ 215 1566; Bergmannstrasse 9; ⏱ 10am-7pm Mon-Fri, to 4pm Sat; ◉ Mehringdamm); Goethestrasse (Map p344; ☎ 9395 2757; Goethestrasse 46; ⏱ 10am-7pm Mon-Fri, to 4pm Sat; ◉ Wilmersdorfer Strasse); Friedrichstrasse (Map pp340-1; ☎ 2045 4500; Friedrichstrasse 95, enter at Dorotheenstrasse 30; ⏱ 10am-7pm Mon-Fri, to 3pm Sat Nov-Feb, to 7pm daily Mar-Oct; ◉ 🚊 Friedrichstrasse) The largest outfit.

Fat Tire Bike Tours (Map pp340-1; ☎ 2404 7991; Panoramastrasse 1a, below TV Tower; ⏱ 9.30am-7.30pm; ◉ 🚊 Alexanderplatz)

Pedal Power (Map pp336-7; ☎ 7899 1339; Grossbeerenstrasse 53; ⏱ 10am-6.30pm Mon-Fri, 11am-2pm Sat; ◉ Mehringdamm)

Prenzlberger Orange Bikes (Map pp332-3; ☎ 442 8122; Kollwitzstrasse 35; ⏱ 2.30pm-7pm Mon-Fri, 10pm-7pm Sat; ◉ Senefelderplatz) Bikes hired on Saturday can be returned on Sunday. Run by a youth group; rentals are just €5 per day.

If you'd like to purchase a used bicycle, try the flea markets (see the Shopping chapter, p232) or www.zweitehand.de.

BUS

Berlin's central bus station, ZOB (Masuren-allee 4-6), is actually not particularly central. In fact, it's about 4km west of Zoo station, right by the Funkturm radio tower in western Charlottenburg. Taking the U2 to Kaiserdamm or the S41, S42, S45, S46 or S47 to Messe Nord/ICC will get you there.

Tickets are available from the ZOB Reisebüro (☎ 301 0380; ☽ 6am-9pm Mon-Fri, 6am-3pm Sat & Sun), which is right at the bus station, although many travel agencies in town also sell them. The main operator is Berlin-LinienBus (☎ 861 9331; www.berlinlinienbus.de) with departures for destinations throughout Europe. Gulliver's (☎ 311 0211; www.gullivers.de) also has an extensive route system. Both companies offer discounts to students and people under 26 and over 60.

Backpacker-oriented hop-on hop-off service Busabout (☎ 020 7950 1661 in the UK; www.busabout.com) also passes through Berlin, currently stopping at the Citystay Hostel in Mitte (p255).

See opposite for details about Berlin's local bus network.

CAR & MOTORCYCLE
Driving

Berlin is less congested than other capitals, making getting around by car compara-tively easy, but we still don't recommend it. The public transport system is wonderfully efficient, easy to comprehend and generally a much faster, comfortable and environ-mentally friendly way of getting around. If you're driving, keep in mind that finding parking in the central city can be difficult or at least expensive, with public garages charging a cool €1 to €2 per hour.

Rental

All the major international chains main-tain branches at the airports, major train stations and throughout town. Contact the following central reservation numbers for the one nearest you:

Avis (☎ 01805-217 702; www.avis.com)

Budget (☎ 01805-244 388; www.budget.com)

Europcar (☎ 01805-8000; www.europcar.com)

Hertz (☎ 01805-938 814; www.hertz.com)

You can book right there with the reserva-tion agent, although it may be worth check-ing directly with the local branch for special promotions.

You may also do better by renting from a local outfit. One of the most popular and reliable is Robben & Wientjes (www.robben-wientjes.de, in German; Kreuzberg, Map pp336–7; ☎ 616 770; Prinzenstrasse 90-91; ☻ Moritzplatz; Prenzlauer Berg, Map pp332–3; ☎ 421 036; Prenzlauer Allee 96; ☗ Prenzlauer Allee). Prices may be even lower at Das Hässliche Entlein (Map p344; ☎ 0180-343 3683; www.die-ente.de, in German; Budapester Strasse 6; ☻ ☗ Zoo-logischer Garten, ☻ Kurfürstendamm) in Charlottenburg, where daily rentals start at €14, including tax and unlimited kilo-metres.

If you get 'Harley hunger', try Classic Bike Harley-Davidson (Map pp330–1; ☎ 616 7930; Salzufer 6; ☗ Tiergarten) or Rent-a-Harley (Map p344; ☎ 882 4915; Lietzenburger Strasse 90; ☻ Uhlandstrasse). Daily rates start at €55 for the Sportster 883 and €115 for the Fat Boy.

LOCAL TRANSPORT

Berlin's public transport system is composed of buses, trams, the U-Bahn (subway), the S-Bahn (light rail), Regionalbahn (RB) and Regionalexpress (RE) trains, and ferries.

The main operator, BVG, operates an in-formation kiosk (Map p344; Hardenbergplatz; ☽ 6am-10pm) outside Zoo station. Staff members hand out free route network maps and also sell tickets. For general and trip planning information, call the 24-hour hot-line at ☎ 19 449 or use the online function at www.bvg.de.

For information on S-Bahn, RE and RB connections, you can also visit the Reise-zentrum (Travel Centre) inside any train station, call ☎ 11 861 or ☎ 0800-150 7090 or check www.bahn.de.

Tickets & Fares

Berlin's metropolitan area is divided into three tariff zones – A, B and C. Tickets are available for zones AB, BC or ABC. Unless you're venturing to Potsdam or the very outer suburbs, you'll only need the AB ticket. For short trips, buy the *Kurzstreck-*

enticket for €1.20. It's good for three stops on the U-/S-Bahn or six on any bus or tram; no changes allowed. The Group Day Pass is valid for up to five people travelling together. Kids below age six travel for free. Children aged six to 14 qualify for reduced (*ermässigt*) rates.

Ticket type	AB	BC	ABC
Single	€12.10	€12.30	€12.60
Reduced single	€11.40	€11.60	€11.90
Day Pass	€15.80	€15.70	€16
Group Day Pass (up to 5 people)	€114.80	€114.30	€115
7-Day Pass	€125.40	€126.20	€131.30

Buying & Using Tickets

Bus drivers sell single tickets and day passes (*Tageskarten*), but tickets for U-/S-Bahn trains and other multiple, weekly or monthly tickets must be purchased before boarding from orange vending machines (with instructions in English) at any U-/S-Bahn station. Tickets must be stamped (validated) at station platform entrances or at bus stops before boarding. The on-the-spot fine for getting caught without a valid ticket is €40. Once the domain of retired gentlemen, inspectors now come in all ages, races and genders. To stop potential impostors, all inspectors carry a BVG identity card with their photograph.

Buses & Trams

Berlin's buses are rather slow, but being ensconced on the upper level of a double-decker is an inexpensive way to do some easy sightseeing (see the boxed text on below).

Bus stops are marked with a large 'H' (for *Haltestelle*) and the name of the stop. The next stop is usually announced via loudspeaker or digitally displayed. Push the button on the handrails if you want to get off.

Night buses take over from about 12.30am to 4.30am, running at roughly 30-minute intervals. Normal fares apply. Night bus route maps are available at the BVG information kiosk (opposite). On nights when there is no U-Bahn service, buses N2, N5, N6, N8 and N9 follow more or less the routes of the U2, U5, U6, U8 and U9.

Trams only operate in the eastern districts. The M10, N54, N55, N92 and N93 offer continuous service throughout every night.

S-Bahn & Regional Trains

S-Bahn trains make fewer stops than U-Bahns and are therefore handy for longer distances, but they don't run as frequently. They operate from around 4am to 12.30am and throughout the night on Friday, Saturday and public holidays.

Destinations further afield are served by RB and RE trains. You'll need an ABC or Deutsche Bahn ticket to use these trains.

See Train (p292) for information on long-distance travel within Germany and Europe.

U-Bahn

The most efficient way to travel around Berlin is by U-Bahn, which operates from 4am until just after midnight, except at weekends and public holidays when it continues through the night on all lines but the U4. The next station is usually announced and also digitally displayed in newer carriages.

ALL ABOARD! BERLIN FROM BUS 100 & 200

One of the best bargains in Berlin is a self-guided city tour aboard a public double-decker bus. Both bus 100 and 200 follow routes that take in nearly every major sight in the central city for the modest price of €2.10, a standard single AB ticket. You can even get off as often as you wish within the two hours of its validity as long as you continue in the same direction. If you plan on exploring all day, the *Tageskarte* (Day Pass) for €5.80 is your best bet.

Bus 100 travels from Zoo station to Alexanderplatz passing by such landmarks as the Gedächtniskirche, Tiergarten with the Victory Column, the Reichstag, the Brandenburg Gate and Unter den Linden.

Bus 200 also starts at Zoo station but takes a more southerly route past the Kulturforum and Potsdamer Platz, before travelling on to the Holocaust Memorial and Unter den Linden. From here the route travels via Alexanderplatz to the Volkspark Friedrichshain, culminating at the Jewish Cemetery Weissensee.

If you don't interrupt your trip, the entire one-way journey takes about 30 minutes on bus 100 and 45 minutes on bus 200 in ideal traffic conditions. There's no commentary but you can pick up a map and information leaflet from the BVG information kiosk (opposite). Note that both bus lines are targeted by pickpockets, so keep a close eye on your belongings.

Starting in 2007 a new U-Bahn line, the U55, is scheduled to begin service between the new Hauptbahnhof (main train station) and Unter den Linden station via the Reichstag. Eventually this line will continue below Unter den Linden to Alexanderplatz.

TAXI

You'll find taxi ranks at the airports, major train stations and throughout the city. Flag fall is €2.50, then it's €1.50 per kilometre up to 7km and €1 for each kilometre after that. Taxis can also be ordered on ☎ 19 410, 0800-8001 1554 or 0800-222 2255. There should be no surcharges for night trips; bulky luggage costs an extra €1 per piece. A ride from Alexanderplatz to Bahnhof Zoo costs about €15 to €18.

For short trips, you can use the €3 *Kurzstreckentarif* (short-trip rate), which entitles you to ride for up to 2km. It is *only* available if you flag down a moving taxi and request this special rate before the driver has activated the regular meter. If you continue past 2km, regular rates apply.

Velotaxis

A nonpolluting alternative for short hops is a **velotaxi** (☎ 0800-8356 8294; www.velotaxi .com), a comfortable two-seater pedicab, aided by an electric engine. They can be ordered or simply flagged down. They operate from late March to October from noon to 8pm along four routes: Kurfürstendamm, Unter den Linden, Potsdamer Platz and Tiergarten. The cost is €2.50 per person for the first kilometre, then €1 per person for each additional kilometre. Half-hour tours are €7.50 per person.

TRAIN

Berlin is well connected by train to other German cities, as well as destinations like Prague, Warsaw and Amsterdam. German trains are operated by the **Deutsche Bahn** (DB; reservations & information ☎ 118 61, toll-free automated timetable ☎ 0800-150 7090; www.bahn.de).

At the time of writing, construction crews were working feverishly to complete Berlin's new Hauptbahnhof (Map pp330–1) by May 2006, in time for the soccer World Cup. The futuristic glass hall hemmed in by two office buildings replaces the Lehrter Stadtbahnhof and is poised to be Europe's most modern and efficient railway hub. National and in-

ternational long-distance trains departing in all directions are joined by S-Bahn trains. Perhaps as early as 2007, a new U-Bahn line, the U55, will begin operating between here and Unter den Linden station.

The U-Bahn and north- and southbound trains depart below ground, while east- and westbound trains, as well as the S-Bahn, run from platforms above street level.

While all long-distance trains converge at the Hauptbahnhof, some may also stop at other Berlin stations such as Spandau, Ostbahnhof and Lichtenberg. Bahnhof Zoo, meanwhile, has been demoted to a regional train station.

Hauptbahnhof predictably has the best infrastructure with left-luggage offices, coin lockers, car-rental agencies, currency exchange offices and various shops and fast-food restaurants. The other stations, though smaller, have many of the same facilities.

Tickets can be bought from agents inside the *Reisezentrum* (Travel Centre) and, for shorter distances, from vending machines. Buying tickets on board (cash only) incurs a surcharge of €2 to €7.50. For trips over 51km, you can also buy tickets online (www.bahn.de) up to one hour before departure at no surcharge; you'll need a major credit card and a print-out of your ticket to present to the conductor.

Seat reservations for long-distance travel are highly recommended, especially if you're travelling on a Friday or Sunday afternoon, during holiday periods or in summer. The fee is €3 per person or €6 for groups of up to five people. If you reserve seats at the time of ticket purchase, the price drops to €1.50 and €3, respectively. Reservations can be made as late as a few minutes before departure.

PRACTICALITIES

ACCOMMODATION

Accommodation listings in the Sleeping chapter (p250) are organised by district, and then in alphabetical order. Most of our recommendations are midrange options, because these generally offer the best value for money. Expect clean, comfortable and decent-sized rooms with at least a modicum of style, a private bathroom, TV and telephone. Our selection also includes a few top-end hotels, which have an international standard of amenities and perhaps a scenic location, special décor or historical ambience. Budget places (listed under Cheap Sleeps) are generally hostels and other simple establishments where bathrooms may be shared.

Berlin is busiest between May and September, with the thinnest flow of visitors arriving between November and March, when rates may drop and special deals abound. Prices generally soar during busy trade shows like the ITB (International Tourism Fair) in early March, mega-events like Christopher Street Day in June, and major holidays, especially New Year's Eve.

For additional details refer to the introduction of the Sleeping chapter (p250).

BUSINESS

Berlin hotels generally cater well for the needs of business travellers. The top-end international chains often have full business centres with meeting rooms and secretarial services. But even many midrange establishments now offer wireless and/or high-speed Internet access in addition to such general business services as photocopying and PC and fax-machine rentals. English is widely spoken.

All major international courier services operate in Berlin. To schedule a pick-up, call **FedEx** (☎ 0800-123 0800), **UPS** (☎ 0800-882 6630) or **DHL** (☎ 0800-5345 2255).

If you need your own office to ink that deal, you can rent one through such companies as **Regus Berlin** (☎ 206 590; www.regus.com) or **Worldwide Business Centres** (☎ 243 1020; www.wwbcnetwork.com). Both provide furnished offices and conference rooms, secretarial services, video conferencing and other telecom needs. Offices are usually in prestigious locations.

Business Hours

Shops in malls and along major shopping streets, such as the Kurfürstendamm, are usually open from 9.30am to 8pm Monday to Saturday. Small boutiques and suburban stores, however, tend not to open until midmorning or noon and often close at 6pm or 7pm weekdays and at 4pm on Saturday. Train stations, petrol stations and the supermarkets listed in the Eating chapter (p167) are good places for stocking up on basic supplies after hours.

Banking hours are from 8.30am to 4pm Monday to Friday with most staying open until 5.30pm or 6pm on Thursday. Post office hours vary widely, but core hours are 9am to 6pm Monday to Friday and 9am to 1pm on Saturday (also see Post, p299).

Travel agencies and other service-oriented businesses are usually open from 9am to 6pm weekdays and till 1pm or 2pm on Saturday. Government offices, on the other hand, close for the weekend as early as 1pm on Friday. Many of the major museums are closed on Monday but stay open late one evening a week.

For restaurant hours, see the Eating chapter (p166). Bar and club hours are discussed in the Entertainment chapter (p192 and p199).

CHILDREN

Travelling to Berlin with tots can be child's play, especially if you keep a light schedule and involve the kids in the day-to-day planning. Lonely Planet's *Travel with Children*, by Cathy Lanigan, offers a wealth of tips and tricks on the subject.

There's certainly no shortage of things to see and do around Berlin, from zoos to kid-oriented museums to magic and puppet shows. Parks and imaginative playgrounds abound in all neighbourhoods, but especially in Prenzlauer Berg, the district most popular with young families. On hot summer days, a few hours spent at a public outdoor pool or on a lakeside beach will go a long away towards keeping toddlers' tempers cool. For more ideas, see the boxed text on p116.

Baby food, infant formulas, soy and cow's milk, disposable nappies (diapers) and the like are widely available in chemists (drugstores) and supermarkets. Breastfeeding in public is practised, although most women are discreet about it.

Children enjoy a wide range of discounts for everything from museum admissions to bus fares and hotel stays, although the cut-off age can be anything from six to 18. At hotels, ask for family rooms with three or four beds; practically all hotels can provide rollaway beds or cots.

Baby-Sitting

Ask staff at your hotel for a referral, or try one of the following agencies:

Aufgepasst (☎ 851 3723; www.aufgepasst.de) English-speaking baby-sitters, nannies and daycare.

Asterix (☎ 8459 1604) A 24-hour baby-sitting service

Kinder-Hotel (Map pp332-3; ☎ 4171 6928; www.kinderinsel.de; Eichendorffstrasse 17, Mitte; ⊙ Zinnowitzer Strasse) For 24-hour day-care in 12 languages. Fees per hour are €10, overnight (14 hours) €60 and for 24 hours €100.

CLIMATE

Berlin has a moderately cool and humid climate and is generally comfortable to visit any time of year. The weather is most pleasant in summer, which is rarely suffocatingly hot (usually around 25°C), the occasional heat wave notwithstanding. Spring is beautiful but can be slow to arrive, even if jackets are sometimes stripped off as early as April. Early autumn brings the added bonus of bright foliage and sunshine, which can keep outdoor cafés open through to October. Predictably, December to February is the coldest period. When fierce winds blow in from Russia, it gets mighty chilly, often with sub-zero temperatures but clear, cloudless skies. Rain is a possibility any time of year.

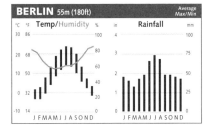

CUSTOMS

Most articles that you take to Germany for your personal use may be imported free of duty and tax. The following allowances apply to duty-free goods purchased in a non-EU country. In addition, you can bring in other products up to a value of €175.

Alcohol 1L of strong liquor *or* 2L of less than 22% alcohol by volume *and* 2L of wine (if over age 17)

Coffee & Tea 500g of coffee or 200g of extracts and 100g of tea or 40g of tea extracts (if over age 15)

Perfume 50g of perfume or scent and 0.25L of eau de toilette

Tobacco 200 cigarettes or 100 cigarillos or 50 cigars or 250g of loose tobacco (if over age 17)

DISABLED TRAVELLERS

Overall, Berlin caters fairly well for the needs of the *Behinderte* (disabled), especially the wheelchair-bound. You'll find access ramps and/or lifts in many public buildings, including train stations, museums, theatres and cinemas. For specifics, check **Mobidat** (www .mobidat.net in German), a databank evaluating 18,000 public places – hotels, restaurants, department stores, museums etc – on

accessibility for the mobility-impaired. Hotels offering at least one wheelchair-friendly room are identified with the 🐾 icon in the Sleeping chapter.

If your wheelchair breaks down, call ☎ 0180-111 4747 for 24-hour assistance. Free wheelchair rentals are available at ☎ 341 1797.

Getting around Berlin in chairs using public transport is possible – with some planning. Four out of five buses and just over half of all trams have special ramps or lifts that enable the wheelchair-bound to get on and off without help. Look for the blue wheelchair symbol on the vehicles.

Getting into U-Bahn and S-Bahn trains isn't as difficult as getting onto the platform itself. The BVG route map available at the information kiosk (p290) identifies which stations have lifts or ramps. The same information is found at www.bvg .de (currently under Timetable/Routes & Maps/BVG Transit Network Map). For additional information, call BVG at ☎ 194 19. To assist blind passengers, stations are being equipped with grooved platform borders for better orientation. Upcoming station and stop names are announced via loudspeakers on nearly all public transport vehicles.

If you need a private transport service, contact **Gebus GmbH** (☎ 319 8010; www.ge bus-gmbh.de), which can also organise city sightseeing tours.

DISCOUNT CARDS

Cutting costs while exploring Berlin is as easy as locating the TV Tower in the city skyline. If you're a full-time student, the **International Student Identity Card** (ISIC; www.isic .org) is your ticket to savings on airline fares, travel insurance and many local attractions. For nonstudents under 26, the International Youth Travel Card (IYTC) or the **Euro<26 youth card** (www.euro26.org) grant similar savings and benefits. All these cards are issued by student unions, hostelling organisations and youth-oriented travel agencies.

The following Berlin-specific discount cards will help you stretch your travel euros even further, regardless of age:

Berlin WelcomeCard (for 48/72 hr €16/22) Entitles one adult and up to three children under 14 to unlimited public transport within the Berlin-Potsdam area and free or discounted admission to museums, shows, attractions, sightseeing tours and boat cruises. It's available at the BTM tourist offices (p301), at the airports, the ticket-vending machines in U-Bahn and S-Bahn stations and many hotels.

SchauLust Museen Berlin (adult/child €15/7.50) An unbeatable deal for museum-lovers, this pass is valid for three consecutive days and gives unlimited admission to about 70 Berlin museums, including blockbusters such as the Pergamon and the Egyptian. Sold at the BTM tourist offices (p301) and any participating museum.

CityTourCard (for 48/72 hr €14.50/18.90) Includes transport and small discounts for attractions and tours. Available at some hotels and through U-Bahn and S-Bahn vending machines.

ELECTRICITY

Standard voltage throughout Germany is 220V, 50 Hz AC. Plugs are the Continental type with two round pins. Your 220V appliances may be plugged into a German outlet (if necessary with an adaptor), but their 110V cousins (eg from North America) require a transformer. Most shavers and laptops are designed to work on both 110V and 220V. For more information on electricity and adaptors, see www.kropla.com.

EMBASSIES & CONSULATES

Most embassies and their consular divisions can be reached by telephone from 8am or 9am until 5pm or 5.30pm Monday to Friday. Walk-in office hours are usually limited to the morning, but afternoon appointments are possible. Call for details.

Australia (Map pp340-1; ☎ 880 0880; www.Australian-embassy.de; Wallstrasse 76-79, Mite; ◉ Märkisches Museum)

Canada (Map p346; ☎ 203 120; www.kanada-info.de; Leipziger Platz 17, Tiergarten; ◉ ◉ Potsdamer Platz)

Czech Republic (Map pp340-1; ☎ 226 380; www.mzv.cz/berlin; Wilhelmstrasse 44, Mitte; ◉ Mohrenstrasse)

France (Map pp340-1; ☎ 590 039 000; www.botschaft-frankreich.de; Pariser Platz 5, Mitte; ◉ Unter den Linden, ◉ 100, 200, TXL)

Ireland (Map pp336-7; ☎ 220 720; www.botschaft-irland.de; Friedrichstrasse 200, Mitte; ◉ Kochstrasse)

Italy (Map p346; ☎ 254 400; www.botschaft-italien.de; Hiroshimastrasse 1, Tiergarten; ◉ 200)

Japan (Map p346; ☎ 210 940; www.botschaft-japan.de; Hiroshimastrasse 6, Tiergarten; ◉ 200)

The Netherlands (Map pp340-1; ☎ 209 560; www.dutch embassy.de; Klosterstrasse 50, Mitte; ◉ Klosterstrasse)

New Zealand (Map pp340-1; ☎ 206 210; www.nzembassy.com; Friedrichstrasse 60, Mitte; ◉ Stadtmitte)

Poland (☎ 223 130; www.botschaft-polen.de; Lassenstrasse 19-21, Charlottenburg; ◉ Grunewald)

Russia (Map pp340-1; ☎ 229 1110; www.russische-botschaft.de; Unter den Linden 63-65, Mitte; ◉ Unter den Linden, ◉ 100, 200, TXL)

South Africa (Map p346; ☎ 220 730; www.suedafrika.org; Tiergartenstrasse 18, Tiergarten; ◉ 200)

Spain (Map pp338-9; ☎ 254 0070; www.spanischebotschaft.de; Lichtensteinallee 1, Tiergarten; ◉ 100, 200)

Switzerland (Map pp330-1; ☎ 390 4000; www.botschaft-schweiz.de; Otto-von-Bismarck-Allee 4a, Mitte; ◉ 100)

UK (Map pp340-1; ☎ 204 570; www.britischebotschaft.de; Wilhelmstrasse 70, Mitte; ◉ Unter den Linden, ◉ 100, 200, TXL)

USA (Map pp340-1; ☎ 238 5174; www.us-botschaft.de; Neustädtische Kirchstrasse 4-5, Mitte; ◉ ◉ Friedrichstrasse)

USA Consulate (☎ 832 9233; Clayallee 170, Zehlendorf; ◉ 8.30am-noon Mon-Fri; ◉ Oskar-Helene-Heim)

EMERGENCY

For emergency assistance call the **police** (☎ 110) or **fire department/ambulance** (☎ 112). Other useful phone numbers and addresses include:

ADAC Car Breakdown Service (☎ 0180-222 2222)

American Hotline (☎ 0177-814 1510) Crisis hotline and referral service for English speakers.

BVG Public Transport Lost & Found (Map pp338-9; ☎ 194 49; Potsdamer Strasse 180/182; ◉ 9am-6pm Mon-Thu, to 2pm Fri; ◉ Kleistpark)

Deutsche Bahn Lost & Found (☎ 01805-990 599) For items lost on RE, RB or other DB trains.

Drug Hotline (☎ 19 237)

Emergency Dental Referrals (☎ 8900 4333; ◉ after 8pm Mon-Fri, 24hr Sat & Sun)

International Helpline (☎ 4401 0607 in English; ◉ 6pm-midnight) Volunteer-run, anonymous help for people in any crisis situation.

Medical Emergencies for Berlin Visitors (☎ 01804-2255 2362)

Municipal Lost & Found (Map pp336-7; ☎ 7560 3101; Platz der Lufbrücke 6, Tempelhof airport; ◉ 8am-3pm Mon & Tue, 1-6pm Thu, 8am-noon Fri; ◉ Platz der Luftbrücke)

Police Headquarters (Map pp336-7; ☎ 466 40; Platz der Lufbrücke 6, Tempelhof airport; ◉ Platz der Luftbrücke)

Rape Crisis Hotline (☎ 251 2828, 615 4243 or 216 8888)

GAY & LESBIAN TRAVELLERS

Berlin's legendary liberalism has spawned one of the world's biggest gay and lesbian scenes. Anything goes in 'Homopolis' – and we mean *anything*, from the highbrow to the hands-on, the bourgeois to the bizarre, the mainstream to the flamboyant.

Berlin's emergence as a gay mecca was kick-started by sexual scientist Magnus Hirschfeld who, in 1897, founded the Scientific Humanitarian Committee in the city, which paved the way for gay liberation. The 1920s were especially wild and wacky, a demi-monde that drew and inspired writers like Christopher Isherwood until the Nazis put an end to the fun in 1933. Postwar recovery came slowly, but by the 1970s the scene was firmly reestablished, at least in the western city. Since 2001, Berlin has been governed by an openly gay mayor, Klaus Wowereit, who outed himself by saying 'I'm gay, and that's a good thing'.

Consistent with Berlin's decentralised nature, the city has no dedicated gay ghetto, although established bar and club scenes exist along Motzstrasse and Fuggerstrasse in Schöneberg; Schönhauser Allee, Greifenhagener Strasse and Gleimstrasse in Prenzlauer Berg; Oranienstrasse in Kreuzberg and around Samariterplatz in Friedrichshain. In early June, huge crowds turn out in Schöneberg for the Schwul-Lesbisches Strassenfest (Gay-Lesbian Street Fair), which basically serves as a warm-up for Christopher Street Day later that month.

The best listings and news source is the free **Siegessäule** (www.siegessaeule.de), which also publishes the English/German booklet **Out in Berlin** (www.out-in-berlin.de). *Sergej* is another magazine, although it only caters for men. *Zitty* and *030* also have listings.

For advice and information, gay men can turn to **Mann-O-Meter** (Map pp338–9; ☎ 216 8008; Bülowstrasse 106; ◉ Nollendorfplatz) or the **Schwulenberatung** (Gay Advice Hotline; ☎ 19 446). For lesbians there is the **Lesbenberatung** (Lesbian Advice Hotline; ☎ 215 2000).

Also see the boxed texts Zero Intolerance (p14) and Best of Gay Berlin (p191) for further insight into Berlin's lesbigay landscape.

HOLIDAYS

Berlin has eight religious and three secular holidays. Shops, banks, government offices and post offices are closed on these days.

Germans are big fans of mini-vacations built around public holidays – especially those in spring – meaning that the city is likely to be more crowded and lodging can be at a premium.

For a list of the major festivals and special events in Berlin, see the City Calendar on p8.

The following are *gesetzliche Feiertage* (public holidays) observed in Berlin.

Neujahrstag (New Year's Day) 1 January

Ostern (Easter) March/April – Good Friday, Easter Sunday & Easter Monday

Christ Himmelfahrt (Ascension Day) 40 days after Easter

Maifeiertag (Labour Day) 1 May

Pfingsten (Whitsun/Pentecost Sunday & Monday) May/June

Tag der Deutschen Einheit (Day of German Unity) 3 October

Weihnachtstag (Christmas Day) 25 December

2. Weihnachtstag (Boxing Day) 26 December

INTERNET ACCESS

Internet cafés abound (see the list below) and all hostels and many hotels offer Internet terminals for their guests (identified in the Sleeping chapter with the Internet icon ▢). High-speed access is increasingly common as is wireless service, and not only in hotels courting a business clientele. Many cafés and restaurants also offer wi-fi, sometimes at no charge with purchase. The entire Sony Center on Potsdamer Platz is a free public hotspot zone. To locate access points, check the directories at www.jiwire .com or www.hotspot-locations.com.

If you're travelling with your own laptop or PDA, beware of digital phones without built-in data ports, which may fry your modem unless you're using a digital-to-analogue converter. You may also need adapters for German electrical outlets and telephone sockets, which are widely available in larger electronics stores such as Saturn (p236).

For a full run-down on connectivity issues see www.kropla.com.

Internet Cafés

Almost all places listed here offer high-speed access and let you surf, email, chat and download, print and scan files, burn CDs and fax documents. Some also have wi-fi access.

Al Hamra (Map pp332-3; ☎ 4285 0095; Raumerstrasse 16, Prenzlauer Berg; per 15 min €1, wi-fi per hr €1; ☼ 10-3am; ◉ Prenzlauer Allee) Surfing goes exotic with water pipes and cocktails.

easyInternetcafé (per hr from €2) Hardenbergplatz (Map 342; Hardenbergplatz 2, Charlottenburg; ☼ 6am-11pm;

⊖ ⓦ Bahnhof Zoo); Kurfürstendamm (Map p344; Kurfürstendamm 224, Charlottenburg; ⊙ 6.30am-2am; ⊖ Kurfürstendamm); Mitte (Map pp340-1; Rathausstrasse 5, Mitte; ⊙ 6.30am-midnight Sun-Thu, to 1am Fri & Sat; ⊖ ⓡ Alexanderplatz); Tiergarten (Map p346; Potsdamer Strasse 2, Sony Center, Tiergarten; ⊙ 6am-midnight Sun-Thu, to 1.30am Fri & Sat; ⊖ ⓡ Potsdamer Platz) The Kurfürstendamm place is huge, with over 300 terminals. Other branches are above Dunkin' Donuts.

Fat Tire Bike Tours Office (Map pp340-1; ☎ 2404 7991; Panoramastrasse 1a; all-you-can-surf €1.99; ⊙ 9.30am-7.30pm; ⊖ ⓡ Alexanderplatz) Below TV Tower.

Internet(t) Cafe (Map pp332-3; Kastanienallee 94; per hr €2, all-day wi-fi €5; ⊙ 9am-midnight Mon-Fri, 10am-11pm Sat, 11am-noon Sun; ⊖ Eberswalder Strasse)

Surf & Sushi (Map pp340-1; ☎ 2838 4898; Oranienburger Strasse 17, Mitte; per 30 min €1; ⊙ noon-late Mon-Sat, 1pm-late Sun; ⓡ Hackescher Markt, Oranienburger Strasse)

LEGAL MATTERS

German police are well trained, fairly 'enlightened' and usually treat tourists with respect. Most can speak some English. By German law you must carry some form of photographic identification, such as your passport, national identity card or driving licence.

Reporting theft to the police is usually a simple, if occasionally time-consuming, matter. Remember that the first thing to do is show some form of identification.

The legal drinking age is 16, and the legal driving age is 18. The permissible blood-alcohol limit is 0.05%; drivers caught exceeding this amount are subject to big fines, a confiscated licence and even jail time.

The sensible thing is to avoid illegal drugs entirely, as penalties can be harsh. Although treated as a minor offence, the possession of even small quantities of cannabis for personal use remains illegal, and getting caught may result in a court appearance. In practice, the courts often waive prosecution if it's a first offence involving only a small amount of cannabis. The definition of 'small', however, is up to the judge, so there are no guarantees. Most other drugs are treated more seriously.

If you are arrested, you have the right to make a phone call and are presumed innocent until proven guilty. If you don't know a lawyer, contact your embassy.

MAPS

The maps in this book should suffice in most cases, although the foldout map available for €1 from the BTM tourist offices (p301) might be a useful supplement.

For detailed explorations of outlying suburbs, you might need a larger city map such as those by ADAC, the RV Verlag Euro City or Falkplan. These are widely available at petrol stations, bookshops, newsagents and tourist offices and cost between €4.50 and €7.50.

MEDICAL SERVICES

The standard of healthcare is excellent in Germany, and with nearly 9000 doctors and dentists in Berlin alone you're never far from medical help. The US and UK consulates are among those who can provide you with lists of English-speaking doctors. Also see Emergency, p295.

If you are a citizen of the EU, the European Health Insurance Card (EHIC) entitles you to reduced-cost or free medical treatment due to illness or injury, though not for emergency repatriation home. Check with your local health authorities for information on how to obtain an EHIC. Non-EU citizens should check if a similar reciprocal agreement exists between their country and Germany, or if their policy at home provides worldwide healthcare coverage.

If you need to buy travel health insurance, be sure to get a policy that also covers emergency flights back home. While some plans pay doctors or hospitals directly, note that many healthcare providers may still demand immediate payment – usually in cash – from nonlocals. Most do not accept credit cards. Except in emergencies, call around for a doctor willing to accept your insurance.

There are no vaccinations required to visit Germany.

Emergency Rooms

Hospitals are plentiful throughout Berlin. The following are university-affiliated and have large 24-hour emergency rooms:

Charité Campus Benjamin Franklin (☎ 84 450; Hindenburgdamm 30; ⓡ Botanischer Garten) In the Steglitz district in southern Berlin.

Charité Campus Mitte (Map pp330-1; ☎ 450 50; Schumannstrasse 20-21; ⊖ Oranienburger Tor, ⓡ Hauptbahnhof-Lehrter Bahnhof) The most central of the big hospitals.

Directory

PRACTICALITIES

Charité Campus Virchow-Klinikum (Map pp330-1; ☎ 450 50; Augustenburger Platz 1; 🔵 Amrumer Strasse) In the Wedding district in northern Berlin.

Zahnklinik Medeco (Dental Clinic) (Map p346; ☎ 2309 5960; Stresemannstrasse 121; ⏰ 7am-9pm; 🔵 🚇 Potsdamer Platz) Call or check the *Yellow Pages* for other branches.

METRIC SYSTEM

Germany uses the metric system; there's a conversion table on the inside front cover of this book. Germans indicate decimals with commas and thousands with points (ie 10,000.00 is 10.000,00).

Clothing sizes – especially for women's clothing – are quite different from those in North America (NA) and Great Britain (UK). For details, see the clothing conversion table on p235 in the Shopping chapter.

MONEY

The euro has been Germany's official currency since 2002. Euros come in seven notes (five, 10, 20, 50, 100, 200 and 500 euros) and eight coins (one- and two-euro coins and one-, two-, five-, 10-, 20- and 50-cent coins). Cash is still king in Germany, so you can't really avoid having at least some notes and coins, say €100 or so, on you at all times. At the time of writing, the euro was a strong and stable currency, although some minor fluctuations are common. See the exchange-rate table on the inside front cover for some guidelines. For an overview of costs in Berlin, see p20.

Atms

Usually the easiest and quickest way to obtain cash is by making a withdrawal from your home bank account via an ATM. These are ubiquitous in Berlin and most are linked to international networks such as Cirrus, Plus, Star and Maestro.

Many ATMs also spit out cash if you use a credit card. This method, however, tends to be costlier because, in addition to a service fee, you'll be charged interest immediately (ie there's no grace period as with purchases).

For exact fees, check with your bank or credit-card company.

Changing Money

The exchange services listed here usually offer among the best rates available, but you can also change money at most banks, post offices and airports. Remember that banks only exchange foreign notes and not coins.

American Express (Map pp340-1; ☎ 2045 5721; Friedrichstrasse 172; ⏰ 9am-7pm Mon-Fri, 10am-1pm Sat; 🔵 Französische Strasse)

Cash Express (Map pp338-9; ☎ 2045 5096; Bahnhof Friedrichstrasse; ⏰ 7am-8pm Mon-Fri, 8am-8pm Sat & Sun; 🔵 🚇 Friedrichstrasse)

Reisebank (Map p344; ☎ 881 7117; Hardenbergplatz, Bahnhof Zoo; ⏰ 7am-10pm; 🔵 🚇 Zoologischer Garten, 🚌 100)

Reisebank (Map pp336-7; ☎ 296 4393; Ostbahnhof; ⏰ 7am-10pm Mon-Fri, 8am-8pm Sat & Sun; 🚇 Ostbahnhof)

Thomas Cook/Travelex (Map pp336-7; ☎ 2016 5916; Friedrichstrasse 56; ⏰ 9am-6.30pm Mon-Fri, 9.30am-1pm Sat; 🔵 🚇 Friedrichstrasse)

Credit Cards

Germany is still a largely cash-based society. Although major credit cards are becoming more widely accepted in central Berlin, it's best not to assume that you'll be able to use one – enquire first. Even so, a piece of plastic is vital in emergencies and also useful for phone or Internet bookings. Report lost or stolen cards to the following:

American Express (☎ 01805-840 840)

MasterCard (☎ 0800-819 1040)

Visa (☎ 0800-811 8440)

Travellers Cheques

Travellers cheques, which can be replaced if lost or stolen, are hardly accepted anywhere in Berlin, even if denominated in euros. Usually they must be cashed at a bank or exchange outlet (bring a passport). Cheques issued by American Express can be cashed free of charge at American Express offices. Always keep a record of the cheque numbers separate from the cheques themselves.

NEWSPAPERS & MAGAZINES

Berliners are news junkies who support five daily local newspapers, including the mainstream *Der Tagesspiegel* and *Berliner Morgenpost*, the left-leaning *Berliner Zeitung* and *taz*, and the sensationalist *BZ*. *Zitty*, *Tip* and *Prinz*, in that order, are the dominant entertainment-listings magazines, although the freebie *030* is popular as well. The free *Sieggesäule* is required reading for Berlin's

Directory

PRACTICALITIES

large gay and lesbian community. *ExBerliner* (www.exberliner.de) is an English-language magazine geared towards travellers and expats. It usually has some interesting articles and essays as well as a listings section. For the complete low-down on all these publications, see Media (p18) and Listings (p191).

Most neighbourhoods have newsstands selling not only all of these German titles but also a healthy selection of international ones, including the major European dailies, *USA Today* and the *International Herald Tribune*. The Friday edition of the latter comes with a handy supplement of translated articles from the *Frankfurter Allgemeine Zeitung,* one of Germany's most respected dailies. Most places also stock *Newsweek,* the international edition of *Time* and the *Economist.* For the best selection, swing by any major train station, which will have large newsstands with everything from *Cosmo* to *National Geographic.*

Most of Berlin's cafés have piles of publications for their patrons to enjoy while nursing their coffee or beer.

PHARMACIES

German chemists (drugstores) do not sell any kind of medication, not even aspirin. Even for over-the-counter *(rezeptfrei)* medications for minor health concerns, such as a cold or upset stomach, you need to go to a pharmacy *(Apotheke).* For more serious conditions, you will need to produce a prescription *(Rezept)* from a licensed physician. For medication after hours, call ☎ 310 031. The names and addresses of pharmacies open after hours (these rotate) are posted in every pharmacy window. Alternatively call ☎ 01 141.

POST

The German postal service (www.deutsche post.com) is efficient and post offices ubiquitous in Berlin. The branch at **Joachimstaler Strasse 7** (Map p344; ☉ ⓡ Zoologischer Garten) is open from 9am to 8pm Monday to Saturday. Stamp machines can be found outside many offices as well. For standard post office hours, see Business Hours p293.

Mail can be sent poste restante (general delivery) to any branch – select one, then ask for the exact address. Items must be marked *postlagernd.* There's no charge, but you must show your passport or other photo ID when picking up mail. Post offices will hold mail for two weeks.

Within Germany, postal rates are €0.45 for standard-sized postcards and €0.55 for letters up to 20g. Mail sent to other European destinations costs €0.65 and €0.70, respectively, while rates to the rest of the world are €1 for postcards and €1.70 for 20g letters. A surcharge applies to oversized items.

Letters sent within Germany take one to two days for delivery; those addressed to destinations within Europe or to North America take four to six days, and to Australasia five to seven days.

RADIO

Berlin's radio dial is crowded with stations. Some of the most popular ones mix chart music with inane talk and ads, such as the youth-oriented Fritz at 102.6 (www.fritz .de), the rhythm n' blues channel Kiss at 98.8 (www.kissfm.de) or the Top 40-oriented Radio Energy at 103.4 (www.energy.de). The BBC World Service broadcasts at 90.2. Among the more sophisticated stations is Radio Eins (95.8; www.radioeins.de), which alternates pop music with cultural and political reports and interviews. Radio Multikulti (106.8; www.multikulti.de) is a feast for world-music fans and also has regular programming in various foreign languages. All radio stations mentioned above offer live web streaming via the Internet. Also see Media (p18) for additional station information.

SAFETY

By all accounts, Berlin is among the safest and most tolerant of European cities. Walking alone at night is not usually dangerous, although there's always safety in numbers as in any urban environment.

Despite some bad press, racial attacks are quite rare in Berlin. Having said that, although people of any skin colour are usually safe in the central districts, prejudice towards foreigners and gays is more likely to rear its ugly head in the outlying eastern districts such as Marzahn, Lichtenberg and Hohenschönhausen, which are scarred by high unemployment and post-reunification depression. No matter the colour of your skin, if you see any 'white skins' (skinheads wearing jackboots with white boot laces) heading your way, run the other way – fast.

Drugs should be avoided for obvious reasons, but particularly because a lot of the stuff is distributed by mob-like organisations and the exact contents are unknown.

Most U-/S-Bahn stations are equipped with electronic information and emergency devices labelled 'SOS/Notruf/Information' and are indicated by a large red bell. If you require emergency assistance, simply push the 'SOS' button. The information button allows you to speak directly with the stationmaster. When riding alone at night, enter the car right behind the driver or, on a bus, sit in a seat where the driver can see you.

TAX & REFUNDS

Most German goods and services include a value-added tax (VAT), called *Mehrwertsteuer* (or MwSt), and currently set at 16%. If your permanent residence is outside the EU, you can have up to 12.7% refunded if you take goods home with you within three months of purchase. The only hitch is that this scheme is only good for items bought at stores displaying the 'tax free shopping' sign.

At the time of purchase (€25 minimum), you must request a global refund cheque from the sales staff. When you get to the airport, show your unused goods, receipts and passport to customs officials *before* checking in for your flight (with the exception of Frankfurt, where you check in yourself but not your luggage, then go to customs, then check in your luggage). The customs official will stamp your global refund cheques, which you can then take straight to the cash refund office and walk away with a wad of money. Alternatively, you can mail your cheques to the address provided in the envelope for a refund via credit card or bank cheque. For full details, see www.globalrefund.com.

TELEPHONE
Fax

Faxes can be sent from and received at most hotels, photocopy shops and Internet cafés (p296).

Phone Codes

German phone numbers consist of an area code (030 for Berlin) followed by the local number, which can be between three and nine digits long. From landlines, numbers dialled within Berlin don't require the area code.

If calling Berlin from abroad, first dial your country's international access code, then 49

(Germany's country code), then 30 (dropping the initial 0) and the local number. Germany's international access code is 00. For directory assistance in English, dial ☎ 11 837 (charged at €0.20 connection fee plus €1 per minute, ☺ 6am-11pm).

Numbers starting with 0800 are toll free, 01801 numbers are charged at 4.6 cents per minute, 01803 at 9 cents and 01805 at €0.12. Calls to numbers starting with 01802 cost a flat 6.2 cents, while those to 01804 numbers cost a flat €0.24. Most 0190 numbers cost €0.62 per minute; 900 numbers are €0.99 or more. Direct-dialled calls made from hotel rooms are usually charged at a premium.

If you have access to a private phone, you can benefit from cheaper rates by using a call-by-call access code offered by a bewildering number of providers. Rates are published in the daily newspapers or online at www.billigertelefonieren.de.

Mobile Phones

Mobile phones are called *handys* and work on the GSM 900/1800 standard, which is compatible with those used in the rest of Europe, Australia and parts of Asia, but not in North America or Japan. Multiband GSM phones that work worldwide are becoming increasingly common.

If you have an unlocked GSM or multiband phone, buying a prepaid, rechargeable SIM chip (or card) might work out cheaper than using your own network. Chips are available at any telecommunications store (eg T-Online, Vodafone, E-Plus or O2) and give you a local number without signing any contract. All include voice mail, text messaging and free incoming calls. You can easily recharge your airtime by buying scratch-off cards at any news kiosk or even the ticket vending machine at U-Bahn and S-Bahn stations.

If your phone doesn't work in Germany, you can buy a GSM prepaid phone, including some airtime, starting at €30 at any telecommunications store.

Note: calls made to a mobile phone are more expensive than those to a stationary number, but incoming calls are free.

Phonecards

Most public pay phones only work with Deutsche Telecom (DT) phonecards, available in denominations of €5, €10 and €20 from post offices, newsagents and tourist offices.

For long-distance or international calls, prepaid calling cards issued by other companies tend to offer better rates than DT's phonecards. Look for them at newsagents and discount telephone call shops. Most of these cards also work with payphones but usually at a surcharge – read the fine print on the card itself. Those sold at Reisebank outlets (see Changing Money, p298) have some of the most competitive prices.

TELEVISION

Many budget and all midrange and top-end hotel rooms have a TV set, and most will be hooked up to a cable connection or a satellite dish, providing access to at least 15 channels. English-language channels broadcasting within Germany include CNN, BBC World, CNBC and MSNBC.

Germany has two national public television channels, the ARD (Allgemeiner Rundfunk Deutschland, commonly known as Erstes Deutsches Fernsehen) and the ZDF (Zweites Deutsches Fernsehen). The main regional channel is RBB (Rundfunk Berlin Brandenburg). Generally, public TV programming is a fairly highbrow cocktail of political coverage, discussion forums and foreign films. Advertising is limited to the two hours between 6pm and 8pm.

Private cable TV offers the familiar array of sitcoms and soap operas (including many dubbed US shows), chat and game shows and, of course, feature films of all genres. DSF and EuroSport are dedicated sports channels, and MTV and its German equivalent VIVA can also be viewed. Commercial breaks are frequent on these stations.

For additional information, see Media on p18.

TIME

Clocks in Germany are set to central European time (GMT/UTC plus one hour). Daylight-saving time comes into effect at 2am on the last Sunday in March and ends on the last Sunday in October. Without taking daylight-saving times into account, when it's noon in Berlin, it's 11am in London, 6am in New York, 3am in San Francisco, 8pm in Tokyo, 9pm in Sydney and 11pm in Auckland. The use of the 24-hour clock (eg 6.30pm is 18.30) is common.

TIPPING

Restaurant bills always include a service charge (Bedienung), but most people add 5% or 10% unless the service was abhorrent (also see p167). At hotels, bellhops are given about €1 per bag and it's also nice to leave a few euros for the room cleaners. Tip bartenders about 5% and taxi drivers around 10%.

TOURIST INFORMATION

Berlin Tourismus Marketing (BTM; www.berlin -tourist-information.de) operates three tourist offices, and a **call centre** (☎ 250 025; 🕑 8am-7pm Mon-Fri, 9am-6pm Sat & Sun) whose multilingual staff can answer general questions and make hotel and event bookings. When not staffed, you can listen to recorded information or order brochures. BTM also maintains the three branches listed below. From April to October, hours may be extended depending on demand.

BTM Tourist Office Brandenburger Tor (Map pp340-1; south wing; 🕑 10am-6pm; 🚇 Unter den Linden, 🚌 100)

BTM Tourist Office Europa-Center (Map p344; Europa-Center, enter at Budapester Strasse 45; 🕑 10am-7pm Mon-Sat, to 6pm Sun; Ⓢ 🚇 Zoologischer Garten, 🚌 100)

BTM Tourist Office TV Tower (Map pp340-1; ground level TV Tower; 🕑 10am-6pm; Ⓢ 🚇 Alexanderplatz)

Euraide (Map p344; www.euraide.de; Bahnhof Zoo; 🕑 8am-noon & 1-6pm daily Jun-Oct, 8am-noon & 1-4.45pm Mon-Fri Nov-May; Ⓢ 🚇 Zoologischer Garten) Inside Zoo station, behind the Reisezentrum, this helpful office sells and validates rail passes and provides advice and information on trains, lodging, tours and other travel-related subjects in English.

VISAS

Most EU nationals only need their national identity card or passport to enter, stay and work in Germany. Citizens of Australia, Canada, Israel, Japan, New Zealand, Poland, Switzerland and the US are among those countries that need only a valid passport but no visa if entering Germany as tourists for up to three months within a six-month period. Passports must be valid for at least another four months from the planned date of departure from Germany.

Nationals from most other countries need a so-called Schengen Visa, named after the 1995 Schengen Agreement that abolished

www.lonelyplanet.com

Directory

PRACTICALITIES

301

passport controls between Austria, Belgium, Denmark, Finland, France, Germany, Iceland, Italy, Greece, Luxembourg, Netherlands, Norway, Portugal, Spain and Sweden. You must apply for the Schengen Visa with the embassy or consulate of the country that is your primary destination. It is valid for stays up to 90 days. Legal residency in any Schengen country makes a visa unnecessary, regardless of your nationality. For full details, see www.auswaertiges-amt.de and check with a German consulate in your country.

Visa applications are usually processed within two to 10 days, but it's always best to start the process as early as possible.

WOMEN TRAVELLERS

Berlin is generally a safe place to travel for women, but naturally this doesn't mean you can let your guard down and entrust your life to every stranger. Simply use the same common sense as you would at home. Getting hassled in the streets does happen but is usually limited to wolf-whistles and unwanted stares.

Meeting Germans is actually not so easily done as they tend to be a rather reserved and cliquish bunch. This shouldn't stop you from approaching them, though, since most will quite happily respond and even be extra-helpful once they find out you're a traveller. Women don't need to be afraid of taking the first step, even with men. Unless you're overtly coquettish, it most likely won't be interpreted as a sexual advance.

It's perfectly acceptable to go alone to cafés, restaurants and bars and clubs, although how comfortable you feel doing so depends entirely on you. If you don't want company, most men will respect a firm but polite 'no thank you'. If you feel threatened, protesting loudly will often make the offender slink away with embarrassment – or will at least spur other people to come to your defence.

Women's cultural centres are great for meeting other women in a pleasant and low-key setting. Try Kreuzberg's **Schokofabrik** (p205) or **Begine** (p204) in Schöneberg.

Physical attack is unlikely but, of course, it does happen. If you are assaulted, you could call the **police** (☎ 110) immediately, although you do not need to do so in order to get help. Many women prefer to first

contact a women's or rape crisis centre whose staff members are trained to help you deal with emotional and physical issues surrounding an assault. They can also make referrals to medical, legal and or social-service providers. Try the following hotlines: ☎ 251 2828, ☎ 615 4243 and ☎ 216 8888. Note that none are staffed around the clock. Don't get discouraged, and try again later.

WORK

Non-EU citizens cannot work legally in Germany without a residence permit *(Aufenthaltserlaubnis)* and a work permit *(Arbeitserlaubnis)*. EU citizens don't need a work permit but they must have a residence permit, although obtaining one is a mere formality. Since regulations change from time to time, it's best to contact the German embassy in your country for the latest information.

Because of its high unemployment, finding skilled work in Berlin can be a full-time job in itself. A good place to start is at the local employment offices *(Arbeitsamt)*, which maintain job banks of vacancies. The classified sections of the daily papers are another source, as are private placement and temp agencies. Obviously, the better your German, the greater your chances.

If you're not in the market for a full-time job but simply need some casual work to pad your travel budget, options might include baby-sitting, cleaning, English tutoring, tour guiding, bar tending, yoga teaching, donating sperm (www.berliner-samenbank.de), nude modelling for art classes, or working as an extra in film or TV (www.berlincast .de). None of these pay big money, of course, but neither do they require a high skill level, much training, or fluent German. Start by placing a classified ad in a local newspaper, listings guide or the English-language magazine *ExBerliner*. Other places to advertise include notice boards at universities, photocopy shops and local supermarkets.

Citizens of Australia, New Zealand and Canada between the ages of 18 and 30 may apply for a Working Holiday Visa, which entitles them to work in Germany for up to 90 days in a 12-month period. Contact the German embassies in those countries for details (p295).

Directory

PRACTICALITIES

Language

Language

It's true – anyone can speak another language. Don't worry if you haven't studied languages before or that you studied a language at school for years and can't remember any of it. It doesn't even matter if you failed English grammar. After all, that's never affected your ability to speak English! And this is the key to picking up a language in another country. You just need to start speaking.

Learn a few key phrases before you go. Write them on pieces of paper and stick them on the fridge, by the bed or even on the computer – anywhere that you'll see them often.

You'll find that locals appreciate travellers trying their language, no matter how muddled you may think you sound. So don't just stand there, say something! If you want to learn more German than we've included here, pick up a copy of Lonely Planet's user-friendly *German Phrasebook*.

SOCIAL
Meeting People
Hello.
Guten Tag.
Goodbye.
Auf Wiedersehen.
Please.
Bitte.
Thank you (very much).
Danke (schön).
Yes/No.
Ja/Nein.
Do you speak English?
Sprechen Sie Englisch?
Do you understand (me)?
Verstehen Sie (mich)?
Yes, I understand (you).
Ja, ich verstehe (Sie).
No, I don't understand (you).
Nein, ich verstehe (Sie) nicht.

Could you please ...?
Könnten Sie ...?
  repeat that
  das bitte wiederholen
  speak more slowly
  bitte langsamer sprechen
  write it down
  das bitte aufschreiben

Going Out
What's on ...?
Was ist ... los?
  locally
  hier

this weekend
dieses Wochenende
today
heute
tonight
heute Abend

Where are the ...?
Wo sind die ...?
  clubs
  Klubs
  gay venues
  Schwulen- und Lesbenkneipen
  restaurants
  Restaurants
  pubs
  Kneipen

Is there a local entertainment guide?
Gibt es einen Veranstaltungskalender?

PRACTICAL
Numbers & Amounts
1	eins
2	zwei
3	drei
4	vier
5	fünf
6	sechs
7	sieben
8	acht
9	neun
10	zehn
11	elf

12	zwölf
13	dreizehn
14	vierzehn
15	fünfzehn
16	sechzehn
17	siebzehn
18	achtzehn
19	neunzehn
20	zwanzig
21	einundzwanzig
22	zweiundzwanzig
30	dreizig
40	vierzig
50	fünfzig
60	sechzig
70	siebzig
80	achtzig
90	neunzig
100	hundert
1000	tausend

Days

Monday	Montag
Tuesday	Dienstag
Wednesday	Mittwoch
Thursday	Donnerstag
Friday	Freitag
Saturday	Samstag
Sunday	Sonntag

Banking

I'd like to ...
Ich möchte ...
  cash a cheque
  einen Scheck einlösen
  change money
  Geld umtauschen
  change some travellers cheques
  Reiseschecks einlösen

Where's the nearest ...?
Wo ist der/die nächste ...? m/f
  automatic teller machine
  Geldautomat
  foreign exchange office
  Geldwechselstube

Post

I want to send a ...
Ich möchte ... senden.

fax	ein Fax
parcel	ein Paket
postcard	eine Postkarte

I want to buy a/an...
Ich möchte ... kaufen.

aerogram	ein Aerogramm
envelope	einen Umschlag
stamp	eine Briefmarke

Phones & Mobiles

I want to make a ...
Ich möchte ...
  call (to Singapore)
  (nach Singapur) telefonieren
  reverse-charge/collect call (to Singapore)
  ein R-Gespräch (nach Singapur) führen

I want to buy a phonecard.
Ich möchte eine Telefonkarte kaufen.

Where can I find a/an ...?
Wo kann ich ... kaufen?
I'd like a/an ...
Ich hätte gern ...
  adaptor plug
  einen Adapter für die steckdose
  charger for my phone
  ein Ladegerät für mein Handy
  mobile/cell phone for hire
  ein Miethandy
  prepaid mobile/cell phone
  ein Handy mit Prepaidkarte
  SIM card for your network
  eine SIM-Karte für Ihr Netz

Internet

Where's the local Internet café?
Wo ist hier ein Internet-Café?

I'd like to ...
Ich möchte ...
  check my email
  meine E-Mails checken
  get Internet access
  Internetzugang haben

Transport

What time does the ... leave?
Wann fährt ... ab?

boat	das Boot
bus	der Bus
train	der Zug

What time's the ... bus?
Wann fährt der ... Bus?

first	erste
last	letzte
next	nächste

What time does the plane leave?
Wann fliegt das Flugzeug ab?
Where's the nearest metro station?
Wo ist der nächste U-Bahnhof?
Are you free? (taxi)
Sind Sie frei?
Please put the meter on.
Schalten Sie bitte den Taxameter ein.
How much is it to ...?
Was kostet es bis ...?
Please take me to (this address).
Bitte bringen Sie mich zu (dieser Adresse).

FOOD

For more detailed information on food and dining out, see the Eating chapter, p165.

breakfast	Frühstück
lunch	Mittagessen
dinner	Abendessen
snack	Snack

Can you recommend a ...?
Können Sie ... empfehlen?

bar/pub	eine Kneipe
café	ein Café
coffee bar	eine Espressobar
restaurant	ein Restaurant
local speciality	eine örtliche Spezialität

What's that called?
Wie heisst das?

Is service included in the bill?
Ist die Bedienung inbegriffen?

EMERGENCIES

It's an emergency!
Es ist ein Notfall!
Call the police!
Rufen Sie die Polizei!
Call a doctor/an ambulance!
Rufen Sie einen Artzt/Krankenwagen!
Could you please help me/us?
Könnten Sie mir/uns bitte helfen?
Where's the police station?
Wo ist das Polizeirevier?

HEALTH

Where's the nearest ...?
Wo ist der/die/das nächste ...?

(night) chemist	(Nacht) Apotheke
dentist	Zahnarzt
doctor	Arzt
hospital	Krankenhaus

Symptoms

I have (a) ...
Ich habe ...

diarrhoea	Durchfall
fever	Fieber
headache	Kopfschmerzen
pain	Schmerzen

GLOSSARY

You may encounter the following terms and abbreviations while in Berlin.

Abfahrt – departure (trains and buses)
Ankunft – arrival (trains and buses)
Ärztlicher Notdienst – emergency medical service
Ausgang, Ausfahrt – exit

Bahnhof (Bf) – train station
Bahnpolizei – train station police
Bahnsteig – train station platform
Bedienung – service, service charge
Behinderte – disabled persons
Berg – mountain
Bezirk – district
Bibliothek – library
BRD – Bundesrepublik Deutschland (abbreviated in English as FRG – Federal Republic of Germany); see also *DDR*
Brücke – bridge
Brunnen – fountain or well
Bundestag – German Parliament

CDU – Christliche Demokratische Union (Christian Democratic Union), centre-right party

DB – Deutsche Bahn (German railway)
DDR – Deutsche Demokratische Republik (abbreviated in English as GDR – German Democratic Republic); the name for the former East Germany; see also *BRD*
Denkmal – memorial, monument
Deutsches Reich – German Empire 1871-1918
Dom – cathedral
Drittes Reich – Third Reich; Nazi Germany 1933-45

Eingang – entrance
Eintritt – admission
ermässigt – reduced (as in admission fee)

Fahrplan – timetable
Fahrrad – bicycle
FDP – Freie Demokratische Partei (Free Democratic Party), liberal-centrist party
Feuerwehr – fire brigade
Flohmarkt – flea market
Flughafen – airport

FRG – Federal Republic of Germany; see also *BRD*

Gasse – lane or alley

Gästehaus, Gasthaus – guesthouse

Gaststätte – informal restaurant

GDR – German Democratic Republic (the former East Germany); see also *DDR*

Gedenkstätte – memorial site

Gepäckaufbewahrung – left-luggage office

Gestapo – Geheime Staatspolizei (Nazi secret police)

Gründerzeit – literally 'foundation time'; early years of German Empire, roughly 1871-90

Hafen – harbour, port

Haltestelle – bus stop

Hanseatic League – an alliance that created a trade monopoly over northern Europe between the 13th and 17th centuries

Hauptbahnhof (Hbf) – main train station

Heilige Römische Reich – Holy Roman Empire; 8th century to 1806

Hochdeutsch – literally 'High German'; standard spoken and written German, developed from a regional Saxon dialect

Hof (Höfe) – courtyard(s)

Hotel garni – a hotel without a restaurant where you are only served breakfast

Imbiss – snack bar, takeaway stand

Insel – island

Jugendstil – Art Nouveau

Kabarett – satirical stand-up, sketch or musical comedy

Kaffee und Kuchen – literally 'coffee and cake'; traditional afternoon coffee break

Kaiser – emperor; derived from 'Caesar'

Kapelle – chapel

Karte – ticket

Kartenvorverkauf – ticket booking office

Kino – cinema

König – king

Konzentrationslager (KZ) – concentration camp

Kristallnacht – literally 'Night of Broken Glass'; Nazi program against Jewish businesses and institutions on 9 November 1938

Kunst – art

Kunsthotels – hotels either designed by artists or liberally furnished with art

Kurfürst – elector (ie rulers who had a vote in the election of the emperor)

Land (Länder) – state(s)

lesbisch – lesbian (adj)

Lesbe(n) – lesbian(s)

Mehrwertsteuer (MWST) – value-added tax

Mietskaserne(n) – tenement(s) built around successive courtyards

Notdienst – emergency service

Ossis – literally 'Easties'; nickname for East Germans

Ostalgie – word fusion of Ost and Nostalgie, meaning nostalgia for East Germany

Palais – small palace

Palast – palace

Parkhaus – car park

Passage – shopping arcade

PDS – Partei des Demokratischen Sozialismus (Party of Democratic Socialism)

Pfand – deposit levied on most beverage containers

Platz – square

Rathaus – town hall

Reich – empire

Reisezentrum – travel centre in train or bus stations

Rezept – prescription

rezeptfrei – describes over-the-counter medications

SA – Sturmabteilung; the Nazi Party militia

Saal (Säle) – hall(s), large room(s)

Sammlung – collection

Schiff – ship

Schifffahrt – literally 'boat way'; shipping, navigation

Schloss – palace

schwul – gay (adj)

Schwuler, Schwule (pl) – gay (n)

SED – Sozialistische Einheitspartei Deutschland (Socialist Unity Party of Germany); only existing party in the GDR

See – lake

SPD – Sozialdemokratische Partei Deutschlands (Social Democratic Party of Germany)

SS – Schutzstaffel; organisation within the Nazi party that supplied Hitler's bodyguards, as well as concentration camp guards and the Waffen-SS troops in WWII

Stasi – GDR secret police (from Ministerium für Staatssicherheit, or Ministry of State Security)

Strasse (often abbreviated to Str) – street

Szene – scene (ie where the action is)

Tageskarte – daily menu; also day ticket on public transport

Telefonkarte – phonecard

Tor – gate

Trabant – GDR-era car boasting a two-stroke engine

Trödel – junk, bric-a-brac

Turm – tower

Übergang – transit point

Ufer – bank

verboten – forbidden

Viertel – quarter, neighbourhood

Wald – forest

Weg – way, path

Weihnachtsmarkt – Christmas market

Wende – 'change' or 'turning point' of 1989, ie the collapse of the GDR and the resulting German reunification

Wessis – literally 'Westies'; nickname for West Germans

Zeitung – newspaper

Language

Behind the Scenes

THE LONELY PLANET STORY

The story begins with a classic travel adventure: Tony and Maureen Wheeler's 1972 journey across Europe and Asia to Australia. There was no useful information about the overland trail then, so Tony and Maureen published the first Lonely Planet guidebook to meet a growing need.

From a kitchen table, Lonely Planet has grown to become the largest independent travel publisher in the world, with offices in Melbourne (Australia), Oakland (USA) and London (UK). Today Lonely Planet guidebooks cover the globe. There is an ever-growing list of books and information in a variety of media. Some things haven't changed. The main aim is still to make it possible for adventurous travellers to get out there – to explore and better understand the world.

At Lonely Planet we believe travellers can make a positive contribution to the countries they visit – if they respect their host communities and spend their money wisely. Every year 5% of company profit is donated to charities around the world.

THIS BOOK

This 5th edition of *Berlin* was researched and written by Andrea Schulte-Peevers and Tom Parkinson. Andrea has worked on all five editions of this book – co-authoring the 1st edition with David Peevers, acting as sole author on the 2nd and 3rd editions and then co-authoring this and the 4th edition with Tom Parkinson. This guidebook was commissioned in Lonely Planet's London office, and produced by the following:

Commissioning Editors Judith Bamber, Janine Eberle

Coordinating Editor Craig Kilburn

Coordinating Cartographer Malisa Plesa

Coordinating Layout Designer Yvonne Bischofberger

Layout Designers Laura Jane, Pablo Gastar, Jim Hsu, Christine Wieser, Wibowo Rusli

Managing Cartographer Mark Griffiths

Assisting Editors Pat Kinsella, Jackey Coyle, Gina Tsarouhas

Cover Designer Annika van Roojun

Project Manager Glenn van der Knijff

Language Content Coordinator Quentin Frayne

Thanks to Tashi Wheeler for helping develop the author brief and to Meagan Williams from Talk2Us. Thanks also to Celia Wood and Sally Darmody.

Cover photographs: Interior of the New Jewish Museum in Berlin, Guy Moberly/Lonely Planet Images (top); Café, Berlin, Photolibrary (bottom); DJ at Reingold Bar, Mitte, Richard Nebesky/Lonely Planet Images (back).

Internal photographs by Lonely Planet Images and Richard Nebesky except for the following: p84 (#3), 86 (#3) Ion Davison; p2 (#5) Krzysztof Dydynski; p225 (#1) Lee Foster; p10, p90 (#2) Rick Gerharter; p223 (#3) Izzet Keribar; p16, p90 (#3), p220 (#1), p181 Guy Moberly; p83 (#1 & 3), p85 (#1 & 2), p87 (#3), p110, p150, p219 (#2 & 3), p220 (#2), p267, p280 Martin Moos; p83 (#4) Nicholas Pavloff; p219 (#4), p223 (#2), p275 David Peevers; p133, p270 Andrea Schulte-Peevers; p89 (#2), p156 Tony Wheeler; p90 (#1), p246 Thomas Winz.

All images are the copyright of the photographers unless otherwise indicated. Many of the images in this guide are available for licensing from Lonely Planet Images: www.lonelyplanetimages.com.

THANKS

ANDREA SCHULTE-PEEVERS

A small army of folks deserves heartfelt thank yous, no-one more so than David, my husband, soul mate and companion in life and travel. My dear friends Kerstin, Marco, Holger, Alexandra, Joerg, Chris, Jeremy and Petra all get big hugs for being such constants in my life. You're among the reasons I feel 'at home' in Berlin. Two more constants are Natasha Kompatzki and Dr Heinz Buri of Berlin Tourismus Marketing, who again kept me clued in about the latest changes in the city – big thanks to you both. Special nods go to Henrik for the good company, introductions and spot-on insights; to Dieter for the spontaneous invite and great meal; and to dozens of people at hotels, restaurants, museums and other places who fed me tips, advice and even some bullshit. Last but not least, big thanks to my commissioning editor, Judith Bamber, for again entrusting me with this gig; to my fellow author Tom Parkinson, especially for his awesome dedication to Berlin's nightlife; and to the fleet of diligent editorial and production wizards that gets these books into your hands.

TOM PARKINSON

Herzlichen Dank once again to Anne Becker and Marko for giving up their living room in the name of research – apologies for those few days when I got in before you got up! Thanks to everyone I met, talked to and played Kicker with on my way round the *Szene*: Rosie & Rachel; Karsten, Nicole et al; Nils & friends; Jillian, Blair, Jason 'Chubbs' & Tim 'fat boy'; Rob et al; Annika & Andreas (thanks for the party); and to the many, many others, especially bar staff, whose names I forgot instantly due to mild inebriation… Also slightly queasy thanks to reader Bastian Zuberbühler for pointing out the delights of monkey puke. On the LP side, cheers to Andrea for coming exploring in Prenzl'berg and to Tashi & Judith for keeping up the editorial end. Finally, *tack* Cecilia, you'll get here one day!

OUR READERS

Many thanks to the travellers who used the last edition and wrote to us with helpful hints, useful advice and interesting anecdotes:

Lisa Adams, Carlos Alvarez Leyla Bagloul, Carolina Barreira, Emily Berquist, Ivana Bezecna, Sven Birkemeier, Anne Brasier, Caryl Burgess, Christian Byhahn Dave Carter, Amy Cavagna, George Chatziargyris, Florence Choo, Bev Crawford, Chris Crowther Alan Dangerfield, Annemie Deruytter, Andrew Dier, Anke Dijkstra, Anne Dilbjerg-Jensen Rosalee Firth, Ole Fosse Fardal, Lynette Filips, Catarina Frazão, Adrian Fry, Anne Fullwood Bernadette Gabris, Diana Gill, Malby Goodman, Ira Goosen-Clarenbach, Lewis Goulding, Martijn Grimmius, Susil Gupta, Anna Guttman Eveline Hagenbeek, Kerstin Hagenhoff, Ronald Hakenberg, Erja Hänninen Paul Jackson, Ann Jarjoura, Alex Julyan, Ann Jurewicz Russell Kallen, Kosta Karapas, Roni & Ayala Klaus, Floris Kortie, Nicolas Kucera Colin Lamont, Sarah Lawson, Ame Latine, Tony Lees, Mauro Leoni, Ken Levy Dawn MacDonald, David Marchant, Fergus Mitchell, Gabi McNicol, Simon McSorley, Heather Monell, Ana Montenegro Gretchen Newberry, Boonsin Ng Keith O'Brien, Anthony Oldfield, Reinhard Oliver Christopher Prusaski Scott Quellhorst Thomas Reydon, Frank Reynolds, Cari van Rood, Sue Royal Seumas Sargent, Peter van Schijndel, Alice Seet, Merron Selenitsch, Amy Shoffner-Fritschka, Cindy Shurtleff, Clare Staines, Ivan Stockley, Karin Sturzenegger Lynette Taylor, Fab Tomlin Reg Urquhart Mário Vilar Eva-Lena Weinstock, B Weston, Ian Williams, Edwin Avenel Wolff Jan van der Zaan, Bastian Zuberbühler,

SEND US YOUR FEEDBACK

We love to hear from travellers – your comments keep us on our toes and help make our books better. Our well-travelled team reads every word on what you loved or loathed about this book. Although we cannot reply individually to postal submissions, we always guarantee that your feedback goes straight to the appropriate authors, in time for the next edition. Each person who sends us information is thanked in the next edition – and the most useful submissions are rewarded with a free book.

To send us your updates – and find out about Lonely Planet events, newsletters and travel news – visit our award-winning website: www.lonelyplanet.com /feedback.

Note: We may edit, reproduce and incorporate your comments in Lonely Planet products such as guidebooks, websites and digital products, so let us know if you don't want your comments reproduced or your name acknowledged. For a copy of our privacy policy visit www.lonelyplanet.com/privacy.

ACKNOWLEDGMENTS

Many thanks for the use of the following content: Berlin S+U-Bahn Map © 2006 Berliner Verkehrbetriebe (BVG)

Notes

Notes

Notes

Notes

Index

See also separate indexes for Eating (p320), Entertainment (p321), Shopping (p322) and Sleeping (p322).

Index

ENTERTAINMENT

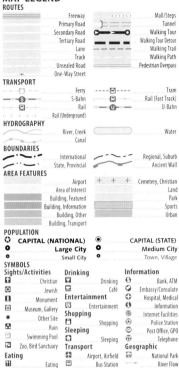

MAP LEGEND

ROUTES

Freeway	Mall/Steps
Primary Road	Tunnel
Secondary Road	Walking Tour
Tertiary Road	Walking Tour Detour
Lane	Walking Trail
Track	Walking Path
Unsealed Road	Pedestrian Overpass
One-Way Street	

TRANSPORT

Ferry	Tram
S-Bahn	Rail (Fast Track)
Rail	U-Bahn
Rail (Underground)	

HYDROGRAPHY

River, Creek	Water
Canal	

BOUNDARIES

International	Regional, Suburb
State, Provincial	Ancient Wall

AREA FEATURES

Airport	Cemetery, Christian
Area of Interest	Land
Building, Featured	Park
Building, Information	Sports
Building, Other	Urban
Building, Transport	

POPULATION

✪ **CAPITAL (NATIONAL)**	◉ **CAPITAL (STATE)**
● **Large City**	● **Medium City**
● Small City	° Town, Village

SYMBOLS

Sights/Activities	Drinking	Information
⛪ Christian	🍺 Drinking	🏧 Bank, ATM
✡ Jewish	☕ Café	🏛 Embassy/Consulate
🗿 Monument	**Entertainment**	✚ Hospital, Medical
🏛 Museum, Gallery	🎭 Entertainment	❶ Information
● Other Site	**Shopping**	@ Internet Facilities
⛲ Ruin	🛍 Shopping	👮 Police Station
⬚ Swimming Pool	**Sleeping**	✉ Post Office, GPO
🦜 Zoo, Bird Sanctuary	🛏 Sleeping	☎ Telephone
Eating	**Transport**	**Geographic**
🍴 Eating	✈ Airport, Airfield	🏞 National Park
	🚍 Bus Station	River Flow

Maps ◗

BERLIN TRANSIT MAP

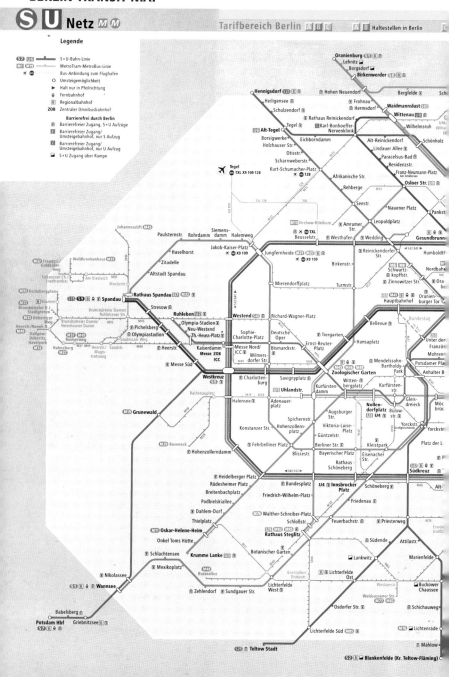

BERLIN TRANSIT MAP

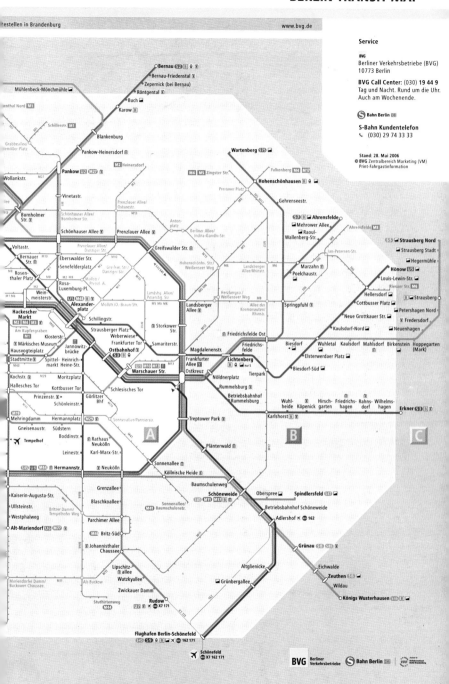

Service

BVG
Berliner Verkehrsbetriebe (BVG)
10773 Berlin

BVG Call Center: (030) 19 44 9
Tag und Nacht. Rund um die Uhr.
Auch am Wochenende.

S Bahn Berlin

S-Bahn Kundentelefon
(030) 29 74 33 33

Stand: 28. Mai 2006
© BVG Zentralbereich Marketing (VM)
Print-Fahrgastinformation

BVG Berliner Verkehrsbetriebe   S Bahn Berlin

Tegel Airport

Osloer S

U Rehberge   Barfusstr   Schillerpark   Städtischer Urnen-friedhof   B96

Möwensee

Volkspark Rehberge

A111

WEDDING   Naue Pla

See Northern Charlottenburg & Northern Tiergarten Map (pp330–1)

Saatwinkler Damm

U Seestr   Schultr   Reinickendorfer Str

Hohenzollernkanal

Goethepark   Seestr   U Luxemburger Str   Leopoldplatz   Müllerstr   Weddi

Volkspark Jungfernheide

Heckerdamm

Friedrich-Olbricht-Damm   Amruner Str   U Amrumer Str   Reinickendorfer Str   Fennstr   Sellerst   Weddi

Berlin-Spandauer Schiffahrtskanal   Föhrer Str   U

Halemweg   U

Jakob-Kaiser-Platz U   Goerdeler Damm   Westhafen   Westhafen   Nordhafen

Westhafenkanal   Quitzowstr

Siemensdamm   Stadtring   A100   U Beusselstr

A100   Birkenstr   Stromstr   Perleberger Str   Rathenower Str   Heidest

U Jungfernheide   Sickingenstr   Beusselstr   U

Gaussstr   Huttenstr   Turmstr   TIERGARTEN   Hauptbahnhof (Main Train Station)   S

Mierendorffplatz U   Turmstr   Turmstr   U   Hauptb Lehrter Ba

Kaiserin-Augusta-Allee   Turmstrasse   Invalidenstr   S

Tegeler Weg   Osnabrücker Str U   Alt-Moabit   Alt-Moabit   Paulstr   Willy-Brand-Str

Schlossgarten Charlottenburg   Helmholtzstr   Levetzowstr   Bellevue S

To Spandau (6km)   Spree River   Franklinstr   Bachstr   Hansaplatz U   Spree River

Spandauer Damm   Wiltenstr   Lessingstr   Altonaer Str   Spreeweg

Westend   Schlossstr   Otto-Suhr-Allee   Cauerstr   Marchstr   Tiergarten S   Str des 17 Juni   Tiergarten   B8

To Georg-Kolbe-Museum (1.7km); Corbusierhaus (2.5km); Olympia-Stadion & Teufelsberg (3km); Waldbühne (3.5km); Grunewaldturm (8km)   Richard-Wagner-Platz   Deutsche Oper U   Bismarckstr   Str des 17 Juni   See Potsdamer Platz Map (p346)

Sophie-Charlotte-Platz   Kaiserdamm   U Bismarckstr   U Ernst-Reuter-Platz   Hofjägerallee   Klingelhöfer   Tiergartenstr

Kaiserdamm   Windscheidstr   See Charlottenburg & Northern Wilmersdorf Map (p344)   Zoologischer Garten   TIERGARTEN

S Witzleben   Suarezstr   Kaiser-Friedrich-Str   Bahnhof Zoo   Zoologischer Garten   V-d-Heydt-Str   Tiergartenstr

Neue Kantstr   CHARLOTTENBURG   Handelstr   Uhlandstr   Budapester Str   Lützowufer   Reichpietschufer   Schöneberger Ufer

To ICC Messe (500m); Funkturm & ZOB (400m); Die Wühlmäuse (800m)   U Wilmersdorfer Str   Kantstr   Schillstr   Lützowstr

Charlottenburg   Savignyplatz   Joachimstaler Str   Kurfürstendamm   An der Urania   Einemstr   Potsdamer Str

Westkreuz   Leibnizstr   Uhlandstr U   Kurfürsten-damm   Nürnberger Str   Wittenbergplatz U   Kleiststr   U Kurfürstenst

Lewishamstr   Brandenburgische Str   Kurfürstendamm   Bundesallee   Spichernstr   Augsburger Str   Nollendorfplatz U   Bülowstr

Halensee S   Adenauerplatz U   Lietzenburger Str   Viktoria-Luise-Platz   SCHÖNEBERG

Joachim-Friedrich-Str   Droysenstr   Konstanzer Str   Uhlandstr   Spichernstr U   Pallasstr   Potsdamer Str   Goltzstr   Yorc

Deutscher Fussball-Bund   Paulsborner Str   Westfälische Str   Hohenzollernplatz   Nachodstr   Hohenstaufenstr   Goebenstr   Yorckstr S

U Konstanzer Str   Hohenzollerndamm   U Güntzelstr   Goltzstr   Grunewaldstr   Kleistpark   Yorck

WILMERSDORF   Seesener Str   Rudolstädter Str   Fehrbelliner Platz U   Uhlandstr   Bayerischer Platz   Eisenacher Str

Hohenzollerndamm   Stadtring   A104   Berliner Str   Berliner Str U   Berliner Str   Martin-Luther-Str   Hauptstr   Leberstr

Hubertus-Sportplatz   Berliner Str   Blissestr   Badensche Str   Naumannstr

To Polish Embassy (500m)   Heidelberger Platz   WILMERSDORF   Blissestr   Rathaus Schöneberg   Dominicusstr   Schöneberg   Tempelhofer Weg

To Brücke Museum (2km); Jagdschloss Grunewald (3km); Alliierten Museum (3.5km); USA Consulate (3.5km); Freie Universität (4km); Museumsdorf Düppel (8km); Grave of Heinrich Kleist (12km); Liebermann-Villa am Wannsee & Haus der Wannsee-Konferenz (14km); Jagdschloss Glienicke, Schloss Glienicke & Pfaueninsel (19km); Glienicker Brücke (20km)   A100   Bundesallee   Detmolder Str   U Wexstr   SCHÖNEBERG   Innsbrucker Platz   Schöneberg   S Sachsendamm

Breite Str   Bundesplatz   Innsbrucker Platz   To KitKat Club (800m)   S S Papest

To Charité Campus Benjamin Franklin, Botanischer Garten & Museum (2km); Domäne Dahlem (2.75km); Museen Dahlem (3km)   See Wilmersdorf & Schöneberg Map (pp338–9)

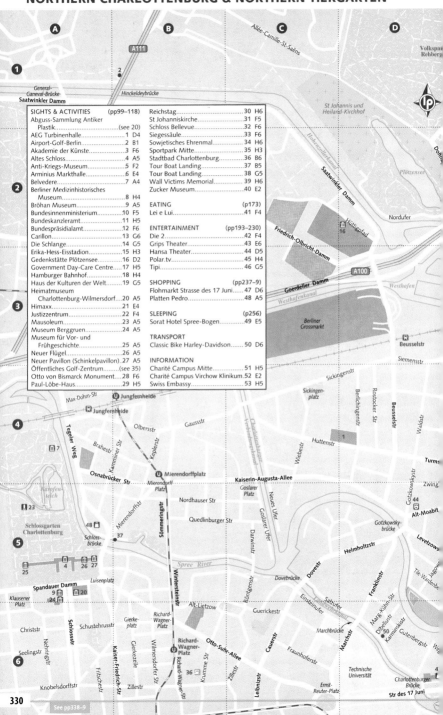

SIGHTS & ACTIVITIES	(pp99–118)
Abguss-Sammlung Antiker Plastik	(see 20)
AEG Turbinenhalle	1 D4
Airport-Golf-Berlin	2 B1
Akademie der Künste	3 F6
Altes Schloss	4 A5
Anti-Kriegs-Museum	5 F2
Arminius Markthalle	6 E4
Belvedere	7 A4
Berliner Medizinhistorisches Museum	8 H4
Bröhan Museum	9 A5
Bundesinnenministerium	10 F5
Bundeskanzleramt	11 H5
Bundespräsidialamt	12 F6
Carillon	13 G6
Die Schlange	14 G5
Erika-Hess-Eisstadion	15 H3
Gedenkstätte Plötzensee	16 D2
Government Day-Care Centre	17 H5
Hamburger Bahnhof	18 H4
Haus der Kulturen der Welt	19 G5
Heimatmuseum Charlottenburg-Wilmersdorf	20 A5
Himaxx	21 E4
Justizzentrum	22 F4
Mausoleum	23 A5
Museum Berggruen	24 A5
Museum für Vor- und Frühgeschichte	25 A5
Neuer Flügel	26 A5
Neuer Pavillon (Schinkelpavillon)	27 A5
Öffentliches Golf-Zentrum	(see 35)
Otto von Bismarck Monument	28 F6
Paul-Löbe-Haus	29 H5

Reichstag	30 H6
St Johanniskirche	31 F5
Schloss Bellevue	32 F6
Siegessäule	33 F6
Sowjetisches Ehrenmal	34 H6
Sportpark Mitte	35 H3
Stadtbad Charlottenburg	36 B6
Tour Boat Landing	37 B5
Tour Boat Landing	38 G5
Wall Victims Memorial	39 H6
Zucker Museum	40 E2

EATING	(p173)
Lei e Lui	41 F4

ENTERTAINMENT	(pp193–230)
Die 2	42 F4
Grips Theater	43 E6
Hansa Theater	44 D5
Polar.tv	45 H4
Tipi	46 G5

SHOPPING	(pp237–9)
Flohmarkt Strasse des 17 Juni	47 D6
Platten Pedro	48 A5

SLEEPING	(p256)
Sorat Hotel Spree-Bogen	49 E5

TRANSPORT	
Classic Bike Harley-Davidson	50 D6

INFORMATION	
Charité Campus Mitte	51 H5
Charité Campus Virchow Klinikum	52 E2
Swiss Embassy	53 H5

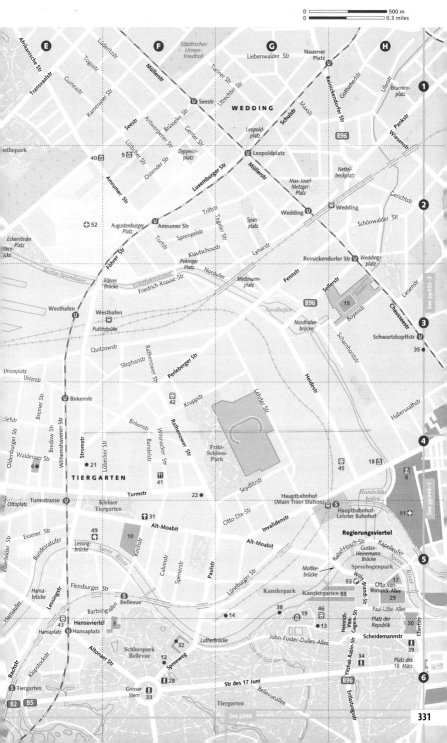

A B C D

1 2 3 4 5 6

See pp330–1

See pp340–1

Pankstr
Pankstr
Badstr
Brunnen-platz
Grüntaler Str
Bellermannstr
Böttgerstr
13
Gesundbrunnen
2
Ramlerstr
Behmstr
Malmöer Str
Schivelbeiner Str
Paul-Robeson-Str
Arnim-platz
91
86
Schönhauser Allee
Schönhauser Allee
83
8
Kopenhagener Str
Dänenstr
Greifenhagener Str
Stargarder Str
Gleimstr
Falkplatz
55
Gaudystr
6544
Milastr
21
94
48
107
Helmholtz-platz
92
Eberswalder Str
34
Eberswalder Str
82
30
Danziger Str
37
96
39
Lychener Str
Raumer Str
Dunckerstr

Volkspark Humboldthain
Hochstr
Humboldthain
Gustav-Meyer-Allee
Rügener Str
Graunstr
Friedrich-Ludwig-Jahn Sportpark
Maurerpark
68

Grenzstr
Scheringstr
Hussitenstr
Voltastr
Voltastr
Voltastr
Demminer Str
Swinemünder Str
Wolliner Str
Lortzingstr
Putbusser Str
Pulbusser Str
Vinetaplatz

Usedomer Str
Straßburger Str
Bernauer Str
Rheinsberger Str
Schwedter Str
Kastanienallee
Schönhauser Allee
53
80
36
87
101
17
12
42
115
78
@
69
Kulturbrauerei
1
74
93
95
89
64
Friedhof St Hedwig
Gartenplatz
Ackerstr
Cartenstr
Bergstr
Bernauer Str
Strelitzer Str
70
7
22
Bernauer Str
Arkona-platz
81
Anklamer Str
57
111
Zionskirch-platz
46
105
Choriner Str
Schwedter Str
51
10
77
11
Wörther Str
Kollwitz-platz
20
27
31
47
24
112
Senefelder-platz
Senefelderplatz
109
Teutoburger Platz
71
23
Metzer Str
Saarbrücker Str
76

Schwartzkopffstr
Chausseestr
Nordbahnhof
Bergstr
Invalidenstr
Habersaathstr
108
15
72
73
102
Zinnowitzer Str
116
Tieckstr
Gartenstr
Pappel-platz
38
98
Rosenthaler Platz
41
99
45
Weinbergsweg
Volkspark Weinberg
60
106

Platz vor dem Neuen Tor
Hannoversche Str
Dorotheen-städtischer Friedhof
Novalistr
Torstr
Tucholskystr
Oranienburger Tor
Linienstr
Koppenplatz
Rosenthaler Platz
Rosenthaler Str
Gormannstr
Linienstr
Schönhauser Tor
Mulackstr
Steinstr
Weinmeisterstr
Alte Schönhauser Str
Max-Beer-Str
Rosa-Luxemburg-Str
Rosa-Luxemburg-Platz
B109
Prenzl
Torstr
Weydingerstr
Hirtenstr
Waldeck Str

Oranienburger Tor
Oranienburger Str
Oranienburger Str
Johannisstr
Ziegelstr
Augustr
Gipsstr
Grosse Hamburger Str
Sophienstr
Münzstr
Dircksenstr
Keibelstr
Alexanderplatz
Alexander-platz
Alexanderplatz

Luisenstr
Schumannstr
Reinhardtstr
Albrechtstr
Bertolt-Brecht-Platz
Karl-platz
Marienstr
Am Weidendamm
Am Kupfergraben
Monbijoustr
Tucholskystr
MITTE
Monbijou-platz
Monbijou Park
Neue Promenade
Hackescher Markt
Rochstr
Burgstr
Bode-Str
Rochstr
Alexanderplatz
Alexandenstr

Schiffbauerdamm
Friedrichstr
Spree River
Reichstagufer
Georgenstr
Planckstr
Universitätsstr
Bauhofstr
Hegel-platz
Lust-garten
Marx-Engels-Forum
Karl-Liebknecht-Str
Spandauer Str
Rathausstr
Grunerstr
Klosterstr
Molkenmarkt
Stralauer Str
Littenstr
Dircksenstr

Dorotheenstr
Mittelstr
Unter den Linden
Charlottenstr
Bebelplatz
Schloss-platz
Breite Str
Postr
Jannowitzbrücke
Jannowitzbrücke

Pariser Platz
B2 B5
Unter den Linden
Behrenstr
Französische Str
Französische Str
Wilhelmstr
Mauerstr
Glinkastr
Jägerstr
Werderscher Markt
Werderstr
Oberwallstr
Am Zeughaus Niederlagstr
Petri-Platz
Fischerinsel
Kölnischer Park
Wallstr
Märkisches Museum
B1

Holocaust Memorial
Hannah Arendt-Str
Cora-Berliner-Str
Jägerstr
Taubenstr
Hausvogtei-platz
Spreekanal
Mühlendamm
Brüderstr

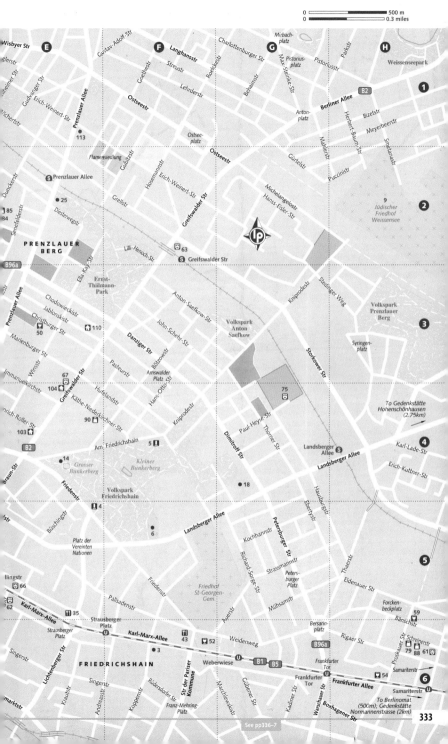

A
Jägerstr
Mauerstr
Gertrud-Kolmar-Str
Thälmann-platz
Taubenstr
Glinkastr
Stadtmitte
U Mohrenstr
Mohrenstr

B
Hausvogtei-platz **U**
Hausvogtei-platz
Markgrafenstr
Kronenstr

Oberwasserstr
Kurstr
B1
Spittel-markt
U Spittel-markt
Seydelstr

Fischerinsel
Märkisches Ufer
Wallstr

C

Neue Rossstr
Neue Jakobstr

Märkisches Museum
Köllnischer Park
Schultze-Delitzsch-Platz

D
Brückenstr
See pp340-1

1
Ebertstr
Vossstr
S
Leipziger Platz
U Potsdamer Platz
8
30
1

Leipziger Str
25 **m**
Mauerstr
159
S 163

Krausenstr
Schützenstr
Zimmerstr
Friedrichstr

Axel-Springer-Str
Kommandantenstr

Annenstr
Köpenicker Str
Heinrich-Heine-Str
Heinrich-Heine-Str **U**
331
Schmidtstr

Niederkirchner Str
m 32
● 5
10
14
Kochstr
U Kochstr
Charlottenstr

Lindenstr
Alte Jakobstr
Waldeck-park
Oranienstr

Sebastianstr
Michaelkirchpl

Heinrich-Heine-Platz

2
See p346
Schöneberger Str
Askanischer Platz
152
144
Anhalter Str
Wilhelmstr
Stresemannstr
Anhalter Bahnhof
2
13
117
147

K R E U Z B E R G
Am Berlin Museum
17
6
118
Franz-Künstler-Str
Neuenburger Str

Rittterstr
Lobeckstr
158
Prinzenstr
Wassertorstr

Moritz-platz **U** Moritzplatz
104
Oranien-platz
90
92
Dresdner Str
51
54
49
Oranienstr
19
82

B96
Möckernbrücke
105
151
U
Halllesches Ufer
Mehring-platz
37
Prinzenstr
Wassertor-platz
Kottb Tor
U

B96
Tempelhofer Ufer
35
150
U Halllesches Tor
America Memorial Library
Gitschiner Str
34
41
Carl-Herz-Ufer
Böckler Park
Urbanhafen
Admiralstr

3
Möckernstr
Hornstr
Grossbeerenstr
Obentrautstr
Blücherstr
Blücher Platz
11
Friedhöfe vor dem Halleschen Tor
Mehringdamm
46
Baruther Str
Bergvogel
Baerwaldstr
Urbanstr
Krankenhaus am Urban
Planufer
38
53
Böckhstr
Marianne
Dieffenbachstr
Hohenstaplatz
Urbanstr

4
Kreuzbergstr
43
148
47
Hagelberger Str
157
45
64
127
31
U Gneisenaustr
Gneisenaustr
107
65
138
130
137
27
134
U
131
Schleiermacher Str
Baerwaldstr
Blücherstr
48
55
Körtestr
U Südstern
Südstern
Fichtestr
Graefestr

Viktoriapark
18
26
124
133
156
132
123
42
9
78
101
24
103
Chamisso-platz
Fidicinstr
Zossener Str
Mittenwalder Str
Marheinekeplatz
Bergmannstr
Cemeteries
Hasenheide
Standort-Friedhof

5
Bayernring
Dudenstr
Mehringdamm
71
94
84
Jüterboger Str
Friesenstr
Schwiebusser Str
21
100
Columbiadamm
161
● 160
Platz der Luftbrücke
Platz der Luftbrücke
U

Zülllichauer Str
Lilienthalstr
Volkspark Hasenheide
Columbiadamm

6
Adolf-Scheidt-Platz
Bundesring
Leonhardtweg
Paradestr
Kleineweg
Manfred-von-Richthofen-Str
Wolffring
Kaiserkorso
Tempelhofer Damm
Paradestr **U**
Tempelhof Airport
TEMPELHOF **B96**
Thuyring

Garnison-Friedhof
Hertfu
Oderstr

WILMERSDORF & SCHÖNEBERG

Map labels: See pp330-1 · Danckelmannstr · Sophie-Charlotte-Platz · Bismarckstr · Str des 17 Juni · Charlottenbr Brücke · Kaiserdamm · Bismarckstr · Deutsche Oper · Ernst-Reuter-Platz · Ernst-Reuter-Platz · Technische Universität · Fasanenstr · Witzleben platz · Suarezstr · Windscheidstr · Kaiser-Friedrich-Str · Wilmersdorfer Str · Krumme Str · Wernarer Str · Karl-August-Platz · Leibnizstr · Goethestr · Schillerstr · Steinplatz · Hardenbergstr · Bahnhof Zoo · Zoologischer Garten · Hertziallee · Neue Kantstr · Lietzensee · Pestalozzistr · CHARLOTTENBURG · Kantstr · Knesebeckstr · Uhlandstr · Zoologischer Garten · Hardenbergstr · Charlottenburg · Wilmersdorfer Str · Stuttgarter Platz · Gervinusstr · Niebuhrstr · Savignyplatz · Savignyplatz · Grolmanstr · Kurfürstendamm · Suarezstr · Rönnestr · Gervinusstr · Lewishamstr · Droysenstr · Sybelstr · Dahlmannstr · Mommsenstr · Meyerinckplatz · Leibnizstr · Wielandstr · Schlüterstr · Bleibtreustr · Knesebeckstr · Grolmanstr · Uhlandstr · Kurfürstendamm · Fasanenstr · Meinekestr · Joachimstaler Str · Rankestr · Holtzendorff-platz · Damaschkestr · Adenauerplatz · Walter-Benjamin-Platz · George-Grosz-Platz · Kurfürstendamm · Eisler Str · Adenauerplatz · Xantener Str · Olivaer Platz · Pariser Str · Lietzenburger Str · Rankeplatz · Lehniner Platz · Eisenzahnstr · Brandenburgische Str · Düsseldorfer Str · Württembergische Str · Sächsische Str · Emser Str · Pfalzburger Str · Pariser Str · Fasanenplatz · Ludwigkirch-platz · Ludwigkirchstr · Bundesallee · Spichernstr · Henrietten-platz · Joachim-Friedrich-Str · Nestorstr · Cicerostr · Hochmeisterplatz · Albrecht-Achilles-Str · Paulsborner Str · Zähringerstr · Bayerische Str · Wittelsbacherstr · Hohenzollerndamm · Hohenzollernplatz · Spichernstr · Nachods · Halensee · See p344 · Westfälische Str · Konstanzer Str · Pommersche Str · Hohenzollernplatz · Prager Platz · Grieser Platz · Seesener Str · Nestorstr · Cicerostr · WILMERSDORF · Mansfelder Str · Preussen-park · Fehrbelliner Platz · Emser Platz · Siegmundshof · Holsteinische Str · Nassauische Str · Traudenstr · Günzelstr · Günzelstr · Friedrichsruher Str · Charlottenbrunner Str · Kudowastr · Hohenzollerndamm · Rudolstädter Str · Hohenzollerndamm · H-v-Fallersleben-Platz · Barstr · Fehrbelliner Platz · Fehrbelliner Platz · Brandenburgische Str · Fechnerstr · Habermann-platz · Blissestr · Uhlandstr · Berliner Str · Berliner Str · Berliner St · Sälzbrunner Str · A100 · Stadtring · Berliner Str · Mannheimer Str · Wilhelmsaue · Wilhelmsaue · Badensche Str · Flinsberger platz · Friedhof Wilmersdorf · Prinzregentenstr · Fennsee · Volkspark · Am Volkspark · Hildegardstr · Birger-Forell-Platz · WILMERSDORF · Blissestr · Bundesplatz · Bundesallee · Bundesplatz · Wexstr · Bundesplatz · Detmolder Str · A100 · Varziner Str · Varziner Str · Handjerystr · Hanauer Str · Fehlerstr · Laubacher Str · Homburger Str · Südwestkorso · Südwestkorso · Götzstr · Cosimaplatz · Perels · Friedrich-Wilhelm-Platz · Durlacher Str

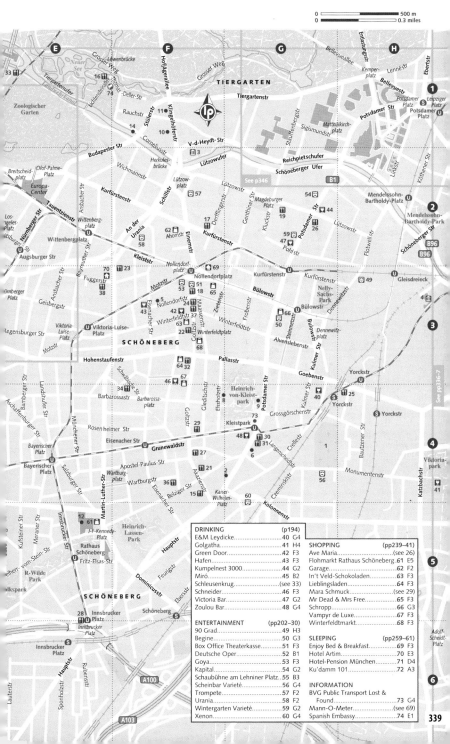

339

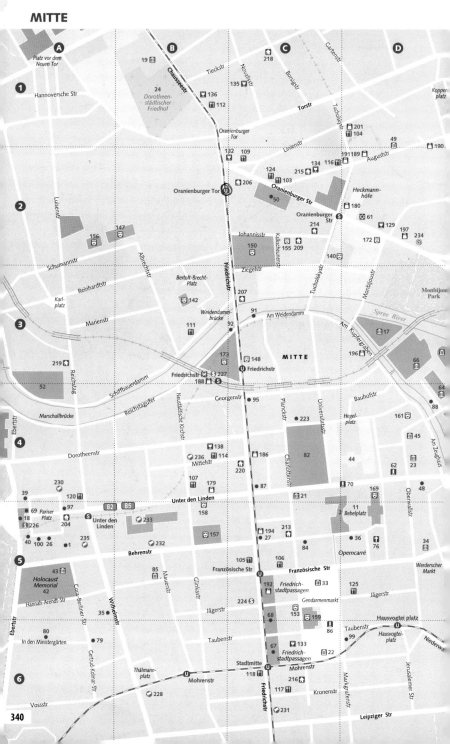

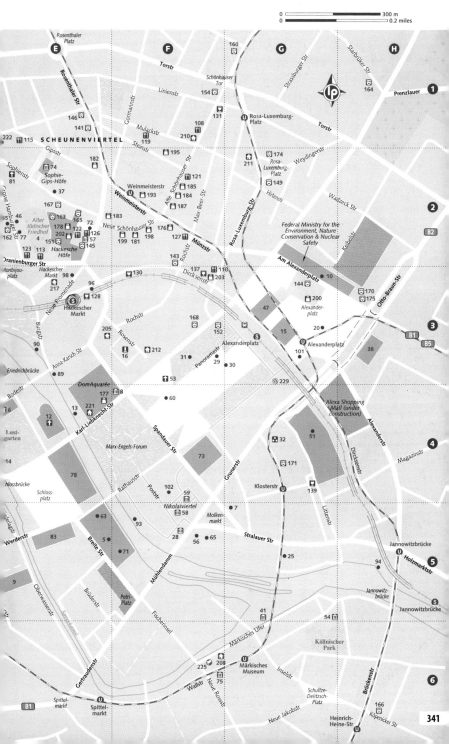

MITTE (pp340–1)

SPANDAU

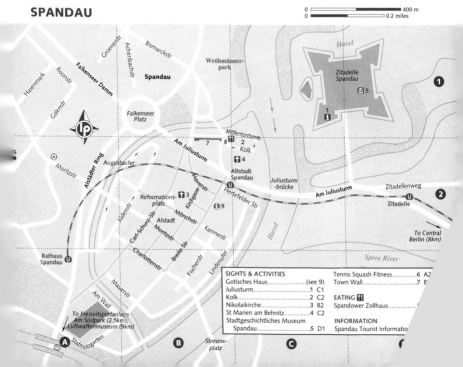

SIGHTS & ACTIVITIES			
Gotisches Haus..................(see 9)		Tennis Squash Fitness...........6 A2	
Juliusturm...........................1 C1		Town Wall............................7 B	
Kolk..................................2 C2			
Nikolaikirche........................3 B2		EATING 🍴	
St Marien am Behnitz..............4 C2		Spandower Zollhaus................	
Stadtgeschichtliches Museum			
Spandau...........................5 D1		INFORMATION	
		Spandau Tourist Informatio	

CHARLOTTENBURG & NORTHERN WILMERSDORF

CHARLOTTENBURG & NORTHERN WILMERSDORF

POTSDAMER PLATZ

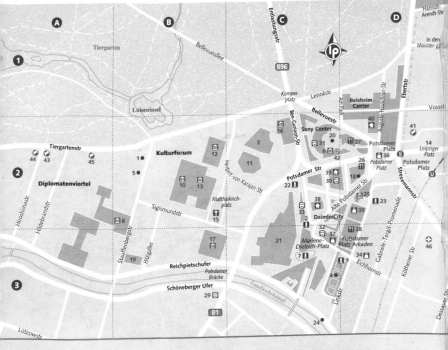